THE LOYALISTS IN ONTARIO

The Sons and Daughters of
The American Loyalists
Of Upper Canada

WILLIAM D. REID

GENEALOGICAL PUBLISHING Co., Inc.

1001 N. Calvert Street
Baltimore, Maryland 21202
Library of Congress Catalogue Card Number 94-76083
International Standard Book Number 0-8063-1440-0

PREFACE

The late Mr. William D. Reid, who died in 1969, performed a valuable service for genealogists by bringing together a vast number of records into the single compilation contained in the pages of this book. He must have known in the beginning the magnitude of the task he had set himself, but his work came to fruition by means of a carefully laid out plan joined with diligence and patience. His compilation was made during his years of employment at the Ontario Archives. It is with pleasure, mingled with a feeling of awed respect for Mr. Reid, that the publisher presents this work to the public.

Sincere thanks are hereby tendered to Mrs. William D. Reid and to her son Mr. Roger Reid for permission to publish this work and to Dr. James J. Talman of the University of Western Ontario whose encouragement and assistance made publication possible. Mr Edward Phelps, also of the University of Western Ontario, gave valuable assistance by aiding in the mechanics of getting the data ready for publication.

INTRODUCTION

In the years following the close of the American Revolutionary War, the Loyalists who settled in Ontario were given land grants in partial recognition of their losses and services during that conflict. In addition, a provision was made that each of their children in turn were eligible for land grants free of fees as they came of age or married. As these sons and daughters of Loyalists petitioned for the lands they were entitled to, a notation was made of the authorization for each grant in the records of the Council of Upper Canada. Essentially what Mr. Reid did was to extract from the Orders-In-Council thousands of references to the land grants made to the sons and daughters of the Loyalists and arrange them systematically under the name of the Loyalist parent. What evolved, then, is a great collection of family group records. While not all the family groups are complete, most are.

The references in the Orders - In - Council (O. C.) generally provide, in the case of sons, only the name of the petitioner, his place of residence, and the name of his father - the Loyalist through whom he claimed the land grant. In the case of daughters, the reference states the name of her husband, their place of residence and the name of her father.

ALL OTHER INFORMATION IS EXTRANEOUS to this basic record and consists of data found by Mr. Reid in other sources. It should be clearly grasped that not all the information provided in this compilation comes from the basic source, the Orders in Council. Only the data as outlined in the preceding paragraph come from that source. As an example, marriage dates do not come from the Orders-in-Council but were added to the basic record by Mr. Reid from other sources.

Mr. Reid often names wives of the sons of Loyalists. This information seldom comes from the Orders - In - Council. The same would apply to birth years, baptismal records, death dates and similar information. But almost all, if not all, sources used by Mr. Reid are to be found in the Ontario Archives. It becomes apparent that he certainly used the records of the Heir & Devisee Commission and also that he probably used some records in the "Township Papers." He perhaps used to some extent the Fiat File, Fiat Books and the Warrant Books.

When a year and place of birth are stated for a Loyalist, the source is often a character certificate given to the Loyalist by a local justice of the peace. These certificates turn up in many different places (see, for example, a small group presently located in the Canadian Archives, published in v. 2 of The Ontario Register). By far the largest number are at the Ontario Archives in different record groups. Some are in the "Township Papers" while a few additional certificates are in the Heir and Devisee File. As the certificates generally stated the age of the applicant rather than the year of birth, the latter data when given by Mr Reid in connection with a birthplace or occupation will be treated by the genealogist as only an approximate birth year.

The lot and concession numbers given by Mr. Reid for the land grants of the Loyalists perhaps come from the "Township Papers." These papers are arranged by lot and concession number within the various townships.

Baptismal and marriage records were extracted by Mr. Reid from church registers published in the earlier volumes of the Ontario Historical Society's "Papers & Records" while others are from manuscript sources at the Ontario Archives. Death notices appear largely to have come from newspapers which the genealogist should easily be able to track down.

Those notes made in parenthesis marks, ( ), are as written by Mr. Reid, as are all queries indicated by question marks. A few added notes made by the publisher are all indicated by square brackets, [ ].

The index cards on which Mr. Reid entered all his data came with the passage of time to be housed in the Regional History Collection of Lawson Library at the University of Western Ontario, London. A typescript was subsequently made from the data on the cards, and a copy of it was placed in the Ontario Archives in Toronto where it is now nearly worn out after years of use. After the typescripts were made, it was discovered that some cards had been removed from Mr. Reid's file and the data had been omitted from the typescripts. The present publication is based on the original cards supplemented by a comparison with the typescript to try to ensure that none of the cards were missing for publication. Actually, Mr. Edward Phelps of the Lawson Library found some additional cards, and these form the basis of the Addenda of this publication. (See the prefatory note at the beginning of the Index to Stray Names).

Thomas B. Wilson
Lambertville, NJ

A

ABRAHAMS, Christian of Ernestown, m. Eva Amey Feb 12, 1788.
    John of Ernestown, m. Rachel Snyder 23 Dec 1814. O.C. 26 March 1817.
    Rachel, m. Henry Cole of Ernestown 18 Sept 1810. O.C. 25 Feb 1812.
    Catherine, m. John Perry of Ernestown, 1810. O.C. 11 March 1811.
    Eve, m. Peter Lockwood of Thurlow. O.C. 4 Jan 1840.
    Jonas of Ernestown. O.C. 5 Sept 1833.
    Hannah. O.C. 3 Oct 1833.
    Henry of Ernestown. O.C. 7 Aug 1834.

ACRE, Lambert of Grantham, m. Mary dau Jonas Larraway, UE of Louth.
    Peter of Grantham. O.C. 20 May 1817.
    Hannah, m. Mathias Oswald of Stamford. O.C. 12 June 1822.
    Amelia, m. John Jones of Thorold. O.C. 8 July 1806.
    Mary, md. David Trowbridge of Grantham. O.C. 9 July 1806.
    Elizabeth, m. Luther Brown of Caistor. O.C. 17 June 1806.
    Jacob of Grantham. O.C. 26 Aug 1834.
    Eve, m. Nicholas De Peel of Grantham. O.C. 8 Jan 1835.
    Sarah, O.C. 20 Feb 1840.

ADAIR, John of Clinton.
    Hannah, m. Wm Kennedy of Clinton. O.C. 9 March 1816.
    John of Clinton, carpenter. O.C. 6 Oct 1819.
    William of Clinton. O.C. 17 Apr 1822.
    Joseph of Clinton. O.C. 7 Aug 1822.
    David of Saltfleet. O.C. 7 Aug 1822.
    Mary, m. John Crawley of Clinton. O.C. 20 Nov 1810.
    Abigail, m. Ashel Ward of Grimsby. O.C. 17 June 1806.
    Daniel of Saltfleet. O.C. 18 Feb 1824.
    Abraham of Trafalgar. O.C. 7 March 1833.
    Hiram of Trafalgar. O.C. 7 March 1833.
    Phoebe. O.C. 8 Nov 1832. Trafalgar.
    Sarah, m. John Springsteen of Saltfleet. O.C. 23 June 1828.
    James of Saltfleet. O.C. 23 Nov 1825.

ADAMS, Andrew of Edwardsburgh, m. Rachel Froom. From the "Weekly
Globe" March 21, 1856: Died at the residence of her son, Abel H. Adams,
of Edwardsburgh, on 29th ult., Rachel, relict of the late Capt. Andrew
Adams, in her 86th year.
   Thomas of Edwardsburgh. O.C. 23 May 1839.
   Mary, m. Theophilus Blake of Oxford Twp. O.C. 15 May 1835.
   James of Oxford. O.C. 1 May 1834.
   Charlotte. O.C. 27 Oct 1832.
   Bethiah. O.C. 20 Oct 1832.
   Abel H. of Edwardsburgh. O.C. 13 Sept 1832.
   Margaret, bapt. 28 May 1793; m. David Snyder of Edwardsburgh. O.C.
      11 May 1825.
   Andrew of Edwardsburgh. O.C. 4 July 1827.

ADAMS, Ezra of Edwardsburgh.
   Lydia. O.C. 2 March 1816.
   Samuel T. of Edwardsburgh. O.C. 6 Oct 1819.
   Ezra of Edwardsburgh. O.C. 28 Sept 1820.
   Elias of Edwardsburgh. O.C. 17 Dec 1840.
   Rocksy (dau.) O.C. 28 Oct 1835.
   Lemuel of Edwardsburgh. O.C. 20 Oct 1832.
   Sarah, m. Chester Forrester of Edwardsburgh. O.C. 20 Oct 1832.
   Charles of Edwardsburgh. O.C. 27 March 1846.

ADAMS, Gideon of South Gower. Lt., Loyal Rangers. m. Mary Snyder.
   William of South Gower, bapt. 11 March 1792. O.C. 2 March 1816.
   Gideon of South Gower. O.C. 19 April 1816.
   Samuel of South Gower. O.C. 19 April 1816.
   Ruth, m. Erastus Fenton of Hope. O.C. 6 Dec 1808.
   Mary, bapt. 12 Feb 1789. O.C. 5 Feb 1835. Edwardsburgh.
   John of South Gower, bapt. 3 June 1796. O.C. 18 July 1834.
   Joseph of South Gower. O.C. 2 March 1837.
   Abel of Oxford-on-Rideau. O.C. 28 Oct 1835.

ADAMS, Elijah Curtis of Edwardsburgh.
   Hannah, m. John Anderson of Edwardsburgh. O.C. 13 Feb 1816.
   Curtis of Edwardsburgh. O.C. 18 Oct 1820.
   Martha, m. Peter Coons of Matilda. O.C. 14 May 1823.
   Beldin of Edwardsburgh. O.C. 6 Dec 1832.
   Clarissa. O.C. 6 Sept 1832.
   Elizabeth, m. Reuben Hill of Edwardsburgh. O.C. 2 Feb 1832.

ADAMS, James of Kingston. m. Elizabeth.
   Maria, bapt. 21 April 1811. O.C. 11 Jan 1834. Monaghan.
   Elizabeth, m. Thomas Clifford of Hope. O.C. 16 March 1830.
   Eleanor, bapt. 19 Feb 1809; m. James Sage of Peterborough.
      O.C. 5 Aug 1830.
   Mary Ann, bapt. 9 Dec 1804; m. John Bateson of Hamilton. O.C. 3 May

1832.
William of Hope. O. C. 14 Nov 1831.
Henry of Monaghan, bapt. 15 March 1807. O. C. 22 April 1831.

ADAMS, Joel of Edwardsburgh. m. Margaret Snyder.
Joel of Edwardsburgh. O. C. 13 Feb 1816.
Peter of Edwardsburgh, bapt. 12 Feb 1789; m. Catharine Anderson dau of Henry Anderson, U. E. O. C. 13 Feb 1816.
Margaret, m. Henry Lewis of Edwardsburgh. O. C. 13 Feb 1816.
Mary Esther, bapt. 12 Feb 1789; m. William Guernsey of Edwardsburgh O. C. 16 June 1807.
John of Edwardsburgh. O. C. 28 Oct 1835.
Levi of Edwardsburgh. O. C. 7 Feb 1833.
Catherine, m. Ebenezer Willson of Elizabethtown. O. C. 2 Feb 1832.
Ruth. O. C. 5 Aug 1830.

ADAMS, William Samuel of Edwardsburgh. m. Catharine Snyder.
Morenda, m. Charles Peters of Edwardsburgh. O. C. 21 March 1821.
Hiram of Edwardsburgh. O. C. 27 Nov 1822.
Elijah of Augusta. O. C. 2 Dec 1806.
Esther, bapt. 12 Feb 1789; m. Ezra Graves of Elizabethtown. O. C. 17 February 1807.
Edmund Burritt of Edwardsburgh. O. C. 2 Oct 1834.
Philena, m. John Froom of Edwardsburgh. O. C. 6 Aug 1829.
George of Oxford. O. C. 7 March 1833.

AGLER (ACKLER), William of Stamford.
Hannah, md. William Aglor of Stamford. O. C. 29 May 1822.
Catherine, m. Henry Warren of Bertie, 23 Aug 1792. O. C. 23 Feb 1808.

ALBRANT, Francis of Osnabruck.
Mary. O. C. 25 Feb 1806.

ALBRANT, Henry of Matilda.
Catherine, m. Samuel Stoddard of Matilda. O. C. 4 July 1815.
Elizabeth, m. William Baxter of Matilda. O. C. 18 June 1799.
John of Williamsburgh. O. C. 3 March 1809.
Henry of Kingston. O. C. 10 May 1838.
Francis of Matilda. O. C. 17 Feb 1825.

ALGIRE, Jacob.
Hannah, m. ---- Jacocks of Osnabruck. O. C. 20 Oct 1801.
Sophia, m. John Doren of Matilda. O. C. 13 March 1807.
Jacob of Cornwall. O. C. 5 Jan 1798.

ALGUIRE, John of Cornwall. See O. C. 9 Apr 1831, and 15 Dec 1832.
Sarah. O. C. 25 June 1840.
William of Cornwall. O. C. 27 Aug 1840.   [Cont'd]

Jacob of Williamsburgh. O.C. 8 Sept 1840.
Catharine, m. ---- Loucks of Sidney. O.C. 17 Nov 1836.
David of Cornwall. O.C. 28 Oct 1835.
Elizabeth, m. John Armstrong of Cornwall. O.C. 28 Oct 1835.
Mary. O.C. 3 Dec 1835.
Daniel of Cornwall. O.C. 3 Dec 1835.
Catharine, m. Michael Billow of Cornwall. O.C. 3 Dec 1835.
Nancy, m. John P. Loucks of Thurlow. O.C. 3 March 1836.
Rosanna, m. Felix Mulligan. O.C. 14 April 1836.
Daniel of Town of Cornwall. O.C. 25 July 1833.
Margaret, m. Henry Burton of Charlottenburgh. O.C. 2 Jan 1834.
Margaret, m. Nicholas Wallison of Cornwall. O.C. 24 March 1835.
Sarah, m. George Stallmayer of Town of Cornwall. O.C. 28 Feb 1833.
Philip of Cornwall. O.C. 22 Dec 1832.
Martin of Town of Cornwall. O.C. 22 Dec 1832.
Henry of Osnabruck. O.C. 22 Dec 1832.
John of Matilda. O.C. 22 Dec 1832.

ALGUIRE, Martin of Osnabruck, m. Eve Hone.
Hannah, bapt. 11 Sept 1791. O.C. 19 April 1816.
Catherine, m. John Helmer of Osnabruck. O.C. 19 Apr 1816.
Henry of Osnabruck. O.C. Nov 5, 1818.
Martin of Osnabruck. O.C. 5 March 1823.
Daniel. O.C. 10 June 1800.
John of Osnabruck. O.C. 26 Jan 1808.
Margaret, bapt. 17 Nov 1793.
Philip of Osnabruck. O.C. 12 Nov 1840.
Solomon of Osnabruck. O.C. 26 March 1836.
Harmonius of Osnabruck. O.C. 11 Jan 1834.
Peter of Osnabruck. O.C. 11 Jan 1834.
Nancy. O.C. 16 March 1825.

ALLEN, Joseph of Adolphustown. Capt. Associated Loyalists. See O.C.
25 November 1800.
Jonathan.
John.
Ursula, m. Alexander Van Alstine of Adolphustown, 26 June 1798.
Rachel, m. John Watson of Adolphustown. O.C. 6 Oct 1836.
Elizabeth, m. John Cumming of Marysburgh, 21 June 1789. O.C. 13
December 1810.
Ursula m. (2) David McWhirter of Marysburgh, 13 Jan 1810.

ALLEN, Weston of Augusta.
Phoebe. O.C. 23 Sept 1800.
Sarah, m. Nicholas Mosher of Augusta. O.C. 24 Sept 1799.
Anne. O.C. 22 June 1799.
Ebenezer of Augusta. O.C. 22 June 1799.
Ruth, m. Rice Honeywell of Augusta. O.C. 9 June 1798.

ALTHOUSE, Nicholas of Ernestown.
   Mary, m. Marshall Loveless of Ernestown. O.C. 14 May 1823.
   Andrew of Ernestown. O.C. 1 April 1840.
   Rachel, m. Peter Babcock of Ernestown. O.C. 2 June 1831.
   Jacob of Ernestown. O.C. 12 March 1827.
   John of Ernestown. O.C. 17 Aug 1842.
   Simon of Camden East. O.C. 17 Aug 1842.
   Peter of Camden East. O.C. 17 Aug 1842.
   Elizabeth, m. Peter Van Buren of Camden East. O.C. 17 Aug 1842.

AMEY, Jonas of Ernestown.
   Joseph of Ernestown, m. Elizabeth Shibley, 13 Feb 1810. O.C. 7 Feb 1809.
   Israel of Ernestown, m. Elizabeth Thomas. O.C. 30 Jan 1808.
   Sarah, m. Theophilus Lockwood of Ernestown 14 Nov 1811. OC 26 Jan 1808
   John of Ernestown. OC 25 Feb 1812.
   Hannah, m. David Boyce of Ernestown. OC 25 Feb 1812, 1 Sept 1834. (Pen-
      cilled note: David Amey md. Hannah Boyce ?)
   Rachel, m. Abraham Snyder of Ernestown, 18 Nov 1788. Land Board
      Certificate. 29/5 Ernestown.
   Evah, m. Christian Abrahams of Ernestown, 12 Feb 1788. Land Board
      Certificate. 8/9 Thurlow.

AMEY, Nicholas of Ernestown.
   Mary, m. John Asselstine of Ernestown, son of Peter Asseltine, U.E.,
      20 Feb 1812. O.C. 23 Nov 1816.
   Nicholas of Ernestown, m. Mary Snider 10 March 1812. O.C. 16 June 1819.
   Abraham of Ernestown, m. Charity Sager. O.C. 7 June 1800.
   David of Ernestown, m. Catharine Snider. O.C. 26 Jan 1808.
   Joseph of Ernestown, m. Phebe Combes 29 Aug 1811. O.C. 26 Jan 1808.
   Peter of Ernestown, m. Mary Baker 28 Nov 1811. O.C. 16 Feb 1811.
   Elizabeth, m. John Snyder of Ernestown. L.B. Cert. 27/5 Ernestown.
   John of Ernestown. Land Board Certificate. 13/3 Camden.

ANDERSON, Benjamin of Cornwall, m. Anna Bird.
   Catharine, m. Philip R. Empey of Cornwall. O.C. 18 Mar 1818, and
      17 June 1819.
   Richard, bapt. 13 Feb 1791.
   John of Cornwall, bapt. 13 Feb 1791. O.C. 5 Jan 1798.
   Benjamin of Cornwall. O.C. 22 July 1836.
   Samuel of Town of Cornwall. O.C. 9 March 1837.
   Charlotte, m. ---- Lyon of Cornwall. O.C. 23 June 1837.

ANDERSON, Elias of Clinton and York. Corp'l, Butler's Rangers. O.C. 8
   July 1806.
   Susannah, m. Joseph LaCompte of York, 29 Jan 1812. O.C. 3 Feb 1816.
   Elias of York. O.C. 23 Nov 1816.
   Sarah, m. Thomas Bray of Town of York. O.C. 20 May 1817.
   Robert of York. O.C. 19 April 1820.   [Cont'd]

ANDERSON, Elias - Cont'd
  Jacob of York, m. Elizabeth Clock 10 Dec 1810. O.C. 3 Nov 1807.
  George of York. O.C. 11 Nov 1806.
  Stephen of York. O.C. 5 Nov 1835.
  Benjamin of Grimsby. O.C. 6 July 1825.

ANDERSON, George of Cornwall.
  Samuel I. B. of Cornwall, m. Amelia Maria Johnson. O.C. 21 Sept 1837.
  Louisa H., m. Alexander McDonell of Cornwall. O.C. 27 Aug 1840.
  Michael George of Cornwall. O.C. 13 July 1841.
  Thomas G. of Cornwall. O.C. 22 Dec 1842.

ANDERSON, Henry of Edwardsburgh.
  John of Edwardsburgh. O.C. 2 March 1816.
  Catherine, m. Peter Adams of Edwardsburgh, son of Joel Adams, U.E.
    O.C. 13 Feb 1816.
  Elizabeth. O.C. 13 Feb 1816.
  Mary, m. Mathew Main of Edwardsburgh. O.C. 23 Feb 1809.
  William of Edwardsburgh. O.C. 2 May 1833.
  Henry of Edwardsburgh. O.C. 6 Sept 1832.

ANDERSON, James of Cornwall.
  Delia H. O.C. 24 Oct 1839.
  James Alexander of Cornwall. O.C. 16 Feb 1837.
  Eliza, m. ---- Drew of Cornwall. O.C. 16 Feb 1837.
  Lucy Ann, m. William McCuen of North Gower. O.C. 16 Feb 1837.
  Mary Ann, m. James Cryderman of Osnabruck. O.C. 18 May 1837.
  John J. of Cornwall. O.C. 12 Oct 1841.
  Margaret. O.C. 12 Oct 1841.

ANDERSON, John of Fredericksburgh. See O.C. 2 July 1799.
  Margaret, m. Jeremiah Chapman of Fredericksburgh 14 Sept 1801;
    O.C. 20 Nov 1798.
  Susannah, m. Jacob Finkle of Fredericksburgh 3 Jan 1804. O.C. 17
    March 1804.
  John of Fredericksburgh. O.C. 8 Feb 1808.
  Alexander of Fredericksburgh. O.C. 16 February 1811.

ANDERSON, Joseph of Cornwall, m. Joanna Farrand.
  Robert G. of York. O.C. 23 Dec 1815.
  Anne, bapt. 1 May 1796; m. James Pringle (81st Regt.) of Cornwall; d.
    26 Aug 1870. O.C. 23 Dec 1815.
  Delia E., m. James Clowes of Cornwall 26 Feb 1827. O.C. 19 Feb 1823.
  Mary Catharine, bapt. 27 Sept 1790.
  Jacob Farrand, b. 29 May 1804.

ANDERSON, Peter of Markham, later of Stamford. Ensign, King's Rangers
  formerly of N.J. Vols. O.C. 27 May 1800; O.C. 2 Dec 1806; O.C. 17 Jan

1807. Married Abigail Fortner.
William of Markham, m. Rebecca Osburn. O.C. 20 Aug 1811.
Martin of Stamford. O.C. 29 Feb 1812.
Elizabeth, m. Joseph Defield of Willoughby. O.C. 17 Mar 1812.
Charles of Stamford, m. Sallie Brooks. O.C. 20 Nov 1809.
Mary, b. Nova Scotia 22 Nov 1784; m. James Lundy of Stamford; d. Stamford 18 Dec 1848. O.C. 17 Oct 1809; O.C. 20 Oct 1836.
Andrew of Bayham. O.C. 4 May 1836.

ANDERSON, Samuel of Cornwall. Capt. K.R.R.N.Y., m. Deliverance. He died in 1836 aged 98.
Ann, m. Lawrence McKay of Charlottenburgh. O.C. 22 July 1797.
Mary, m. ---- Donovan of Cornwall. O.C. 5 Jan 1798.
Cyrus of Cornwall. O.C. 22 July 1797.
James of Cornwall. b. 1781. O.C. 29 July 1797; O.C. 11 Oct 1838.
Joseph of Cornwall, U.E.
Ebenezer.
Elisha.
John.
Thomas Gummersall of Cornwall, b. 12 Nov 1779. O.C. 26 Oct 1802.
George of Cornwall, b. 1783. O.C. 25 July 1809.

ANDERSON, Walter of Charlotteville.
Walter of Charlotteville. O.C. 25 Feb 1820.
Joseph of Charlotteville. O.C. 13 May 1824.
John of Charlotteville. O.C. 6 Feb 1828.

ANDREWS, Benjamin of Elizabethtown.
Nancy, m. B.C. Wright of Elizabethtown. O.C. 11 June 1823.
Paulina, m. Samuel Mott of Elizabethtown. O.C. 8 Feb 1808.
Polly. O.C. 26 January 1808.
Lydia, m. William Botsford of Elizabethtown. O.C. 26 January 1808.
Margaret, m. Simeon Morrill of Elizabethtown. O.C. 17 Sept 1823; O.C. 21 March 1844.
Michael J. of Elizabethtown.
Lydia, m. (2) Neil Palmer.

ANGER, August of Moulton.
Margaret, m. Oliver Burnham of Dunn. O.C. 12 Oct 1837.
Charles of Moulton. O.C. 20 Oct 1836.
Michael of Dunn. O.C. 27 July 1837.
Eliza, m. Avery Burnham. O.C. 27 July 1837.
Frederick of Bertie. O.C. 11 May 1825.
Mary. O.C. 11 May 1825.

ANGER, Charles of Bertie. [Also known as John Charles. An abstract of his will appears in v.4 of TOR] Soldier, Butler's Rangers. m. Abigail.
Frederick of Trafalgar. O.C. 19 May 1819.   [Cont'd]

ANGER, Charles - Cont'd.
 Anna Christeen, bapt. 26 Feb 1794; m. Robert McClintock of Malahide.
  O.C. 12 Jan 1820.
 Catharine. OC. 11 April 1833.
 Philip of Bertie. O.C. 11 April 1833.
 George Near of Bertie, bapt. 18 Jan 1811. O.C. 3 Oct 1833.
 Abigail, m. Jacob Near of Bertie. O.C. 3 Oct 1833.
 Jacob of Brantford. O.C. 27 Nov 1834.
 William of Bertie. O.C. 31 Jan 1826.
 Charles of Bertie. O.C. 11 May 1825.
 Henry of Bertie. O.C. 11 May 1825.

ANGER, Frederick Sr. of Bertie. [Butler's Rangers. He and his family
 were at Niagara in 1783, The Ontario Register v. 1, p. 206]
 Frederick of Bertie, U.E.
 Charles of Bertie, U.E.
 Augustus of Bertie, U.E.
 Christiana, m. John House of Bertie. O.C. 23 May 1796; O.C. 4 Aug 1806

ANGER, Frederick Jr. of Bertie.
 Frederick of Bertie, bapt. 14 Feb 1795. O.C. 1 Nov 1820.
 Augustus of Bertie. O.C. 4 Apr 1821.
 Henry of Bertie. O.C. 9 May 1821.
 John of Bertie. O.C. 9 May 1821.
 Peter of Bertie. O.C. 5 Oct 1837.
 Magdalen, m. Charles Ellsworth of Bertie. O.C. 4 April 1833.
 Catharine. O.C. 7 August 1834.
 Margaret. O.C. 5 July 1826.
 William of Bertie. O.C. 8 March 1826.
 Mary, m. Thomas Ashley of Bertie. O.C. 11 May 1825.
 Christina, m. William Carter of Bertie. O.C. 28 Nov 1821.
 David of Bertie. O.C. 11 July 1833.

ANGUISH, Henry of Bertie, m. Elizabeth.
 Lewis of Trafalgar. O.C. 4 April 1839.
 Mary, m. Conrad House of Trafalgar. O.C. 19 March 1840.
 Jane Ann. O.C. 28 Oct 1833. Willoughby.
 Elizabeth, bapt. 12 April 1793.
 Jacob of Willoughby. O.C. 3 May 1832.

ANGUISH, Jacob. Served in Butler's Rangers. m. Elizabeth. [He and his
 family were at Niagara in 1783, TOR 1:207] 1 & 3/9 Rainham.
 Hannah, m. Henry Putman of Bertie. O.C. 8 Oct 1796.
 Henry of Bertie, m. Elizabeth. O.C. 12 May 1796.
 Jacob.
 Elizabeth, m. Peter Lawr of Pickering. O.C. 5 March 1829.
 Barbara, m. Peter Hoyerbrecht. [In 1800 she apparently was married to
  Frederick Garrison. See a note on the Anguish family in v. 4 of TOR]

ANNABLE, John of Cornwall.

    George of Cornwall. O. C. 17 Feb 1816.

    Elizabeth, m. Alexander McNairn of Cornwall son of John McNairn, U. E. O. C. 17 Feb 1816.

    Joshua of Cornwall. O. C. 19 Feb 1817.

    John of Cornwall, m. Ann Dixon. O. C. 23 Feb 1808.

    Catherine. O. C. 25 Feb 1809.

    Mary, m. Erastus Rowley of Cornwall. O. C. 3 Dec 1835.

    Vinson of Cornwall. O. C. 4 April 1833.

    Alva of Cornwall. O. C. 2 May 1833.

    Hiram of Cornwall. O. C. 18 May 1833.

    Hannah, m. Jacob Waggoner of Cornwall. O. C. 27 June 1833.

ANSLEY, Amos of Kingston, m. Christina McMichael 20 March 1780. See O. C. 27 Jan 1807.

    Samuel of Kingston, bapt. 16 Aug 1795. O. C. 6 Aug 1816.

    Daniel of Kingston, bapt. 3 March 1793; m. Hannah Burnett. O. C. 6 Aug 1816.

    Elizabeth, bapt. 3 Feb 1799; m. Charles Merrill of Kingston. O. C. 6 Aug 1816.

    Henry Hamilton of Kingston. O. C. 22 Feb 1810.

    Mary, m. Samuel Knapp of Kingston. O. C. 16 June 1807.

    Catherine, m. Ebenezer Boss of Kingston, OC 3 June 1800; of Woodhouse, OC 7 May 1840.

    Amos of Kingston, bapt. 25 Jan 1801. O. C. 18 Aug 1824.

    Ann, m. Rev(?) Abraham Fuller Atkinson of Town of Bath. O. C. 3 Nov 1836.

ARMSTRONG, Edward of Augusta. O. C. 12 May 1808.

    Edward of Grantham. O. C. 16 June 1819.

    James of Grantham. O. C. 30 June 1819.

    Margaret, m. John Fletcher of Grantham. O. C. 25 Aug 1819.

    Adolphus of Elizabethtown, m. Charity Dopp. O. C. 2 March 1811.

    John of Elizabethtown. O. C. 2 March 1811.

ARMSTRONG, Thomas of Edwardsburgh (Sr.)

    John of Mountain. O. C. 18 July 1816.

    Henry of Edwardsburgh. O. C. 13 Oct 1807.

    Sarah, m. Richard Boulton of Edwardsburgh. O. C. 16 June 1807.

    Elizabeth, m. Thomas Marlett of Edwardsburgh. O. C. 26 Feb 1805.

    Jane, m. Andrew O'Neil of Edwardsburgh. O. C. 26 June 1799.

ARNER, Jacob of Gosfield.

    Susan, m. John Whittle of Raleigh. O. C. 13 Aug 1840.

    Jacob of Gosfield. O. C. 4 Feb 1836.

    Mary Ann, m. Henry Huffman of Colchester. O. C. 4 Feb 1836.

ARNOLD, Oliver of Darlington, m. Elizabeth, dau of Sam Brownson, Jr.,

U. E. [An Oliver Arnold served in Butler's Rangers. He and his wife Mary
were at Niagara in 1783. The Ontario Register 1: 202]
   Isaac of Darlington. O. C. 24 Sept 1840.
   Amos of Darlington, bapt. 9 July 1809. O. C. 3 April 1834.
   Benjamin of Darlington. O. C. 3 April 1834.
   Elizabeth, bapt. 8 Jan 1800. O. C. 1 May 1834. Haldimand.
   Susannah, bapt. 10 March 1807; m. ---- Dent of Darlington. O. C. 1 May
    1834.
   Samuel Brownson of Darlington, bapt. 16 Feb 1803. O. C. 17 Aug 1842.
   Mary, m. William Munson of Darlington. O. C. 18 April 1843.

ARNOLD, Richard of Augusta, son of General Benedict Arnold; married
  Margaret Weatherhead who died 10 May 1835.
   Margaret. O. C. 18 Apr 1839.
   George Weatherhead of Elizabethtown. O. C. 4 Jan 1840.
   Sophia M., m. Rev. Vincent B. Howard 16 Feb 1841. O. C. 4 Jan 1840.
   Lydia M., m. Joseph Clowes of Augusta 14 Oct 1835. O. C. 4 Jan 1840.
   Eliza, m. William F. Wallace 5 Jan 1831; d. Brantford 13 March 1835.
   Edward William Benedict of Leeds (Port Sarnia, 1848); m. Ellen Louisa
    Cornish 17 Oct 1848. O. C. 29 June 1843.
   H. J., of Hungerford.
   Charlotte Montague, m. Stephen Boyce Shipman of Brockville. O. C. 18
    Feb 1843. Stephen Boyce Shipman died at Oliver's Ferry 30 July 1852
    See Report Book #29, p. 514.
   Ellen Amelia, m. James Porter of Port Sarnia 9 Nov 1848. OC 18 Feb 1843.

ASHFORD, Nathaniel of Hope, m. Nancy. His widow married Abraham
  Hagerman of Hamilton. Heir & Devisee Com., June 1806. 1/1 Hope.
   Nathaniel of Hope. O. C. 6 Feb 1822.
   Mary, m. Christopher Cross of Percy. O. C. 10 Aug 1837.
   John of Hamilton. O. C. 19 Jan 1837.
   Sarah, m. Thomas Mallory of Hamilton. O. C. 30 March 1837.

ASSELSTINE, John of Ernestown.
   Andrew of Ernestown. O. C. 27 Feb 1818; O. C. 17 Nov 1830.
   Catharine, m. Regis Lessard of Ernestown 15 Sept 1818. OC 26 Feb 1819.
   Mary, m. Cyrenius Corban of Ernestown. O. C. 14 July 1819.
   Peter of Ernestown. O. C. 16 Feb 1810.
   Elizabeth. O. C. 23 Feb 1808.
   Abraham of Markham. O. C. 9 March 1803.
   Isaac of Ernestown. O. C. 9 March 1803.
   Michael of Ernestown. O. C. 25 Feb 1812.
   Jane, m. John Watson of Ernestown, January 1810. O. C. 2 Dec 1810;
    O. C. 7 April 1812.

ASSELSTINE, Peter of Ernestown, m. Christina (Davy, of Bath).
   John of Ernestown, m. Mary Amey dau Nicholas Amey, U. E. O. C. 23
    November 1816.   [Cont'd]

ASSELSTINE, Peter - Cont'd
    George of Ernestown, b. 29 March 1794, d. 16 Aug 1861. O. C. 23 Nov 1816.
    Peter of Ernestown. O. C. 8 Feb 1808.
    Michael of Ernestown. O. C. 25 Feb 1812.
    Elizabeth, m. John Hadley of Fredericksburgh. O. C. 13 Jan 1831.
    Margaret. O. C. 22 June 1825.

AULT, Everhart of Matilda.
    John of Matilda. O. C. 25 Feb 1812.
    Nancy, m. Jacob Barkley of Williamsburgh. O. C. 1 Aug 1833.
    Sophia, m. James Thomb of Williamsburgh. O. C. 5 Feb 1835.
    Parmelia, m. Moses Bradstead [i. e., Bedstead] of Matilda. O. C. 28
        June 1832.
    Rachel. O. C. 26 Nov 1831.
    Elizabeth, m. Mark Redmond of Matilda. O. C. 26 Nov 1831.

AULT, John of Cornwall, m. Rebecca Boug.
    Sophia, m. Conrad Snyder of Williamsburgh. O. C. 26 Feb 1806.
    Catharine, bapt. 27 March 1791.

AULT, Michael of Matilda, m. Ann Brouse at Montreal, July 1784. He died
    13 February 1829.
    John of Matilda. O. C. 20 May 1817.
    George of Matilda. O. C. 20 May 1817.
    Margaret. O. C. 26 Jan 1808.
    Maria, m. ---- Kellogg of Matilda. O. C. 8 Nov 1832.
    Jacob of Matilda. O. C. 2 June 1829.
    Michael of Matilda. O. C. 2 June 1829.
    Nancy, m. ---- Bowen of Matilda. O. C. 2 June 1829.
    Simon of Matilda. O. C. 6 August 1829.

AULT, Nicholas of Osnabruck.
    Nicholas of Osnabruck, m. Margaret Ross; d. 1871 aged 77. O. C. 19
        April 1816.
    Peter of Osnabruck. O. C. 19 April 1816.
    Catherine, m. John Weart of Osnabruck. O. C. 19 April 1816.
    John of Osnabruck. O. C. 5 March 1810.
    Richard of Osnabruck. O. C. 17 Feb 1825.

AUSTIN, Solomon of Woodhouse.
    Anne, m. David Marr of Woodhouse. O. C. 26 Mar 1817; O. C. 25 July 1821.
    Philip of Woodhouse, b. 1790; m. Mary Slaght; d. 1876. O. C. 28 Apr 1812
    Solomon of Woodhouse. O. C. 15 May 1805.
    Jonathan of Woodhouse. O. C. 29 March 1808.
    Elizabeth, m. John Pegg of Woodhouse. O. C. 12 Oct 1810.
    Esther, m. Reynard Potts of Woodhouse. O. C. 12 Oct 1810.
    Moses of Woodhouse. O. C. 3 March 1831.

AVERY, Joseph of Augusta.
  Benoni of Bathurst. O.C. 3 May 1826.

BABCOCK, Benjamin of Kingston.
  John of Camden East. O.C. 3 Apr 1834. O.C. 28 Feb 1835.
  William of Camden East. O.C. 28 Feb 1835.
  Sarah, m. Thomas Shannon of Camden East. O.C. 28 Feb 1835.
  Samuel of Camden East. O.C. 28 Feb 1835. O.C. 26 May 1836.
  Jacob of Camden East. O.C. 24 Apr 1835.
  Rachel, m. George Dies of Tyendinaga. O.C. 15 May 1835.
  Meriam, m. Benjamin Cloveland of Fredericksburgh. O.C. 11 Feb 1836.
  Elizabeth. O.C. 29 Dec 1836. Lunatic.
  Johnston of Kingston. O.C. 1 June 1837.
  Catharine, m. William Kelly of Elizabethtown. O.C. 18 July 1839.
  David of Camden East. O.C. 7 May 1840.
  Hannah, m. John Case of Kingston. O.C. 27 Aug 1840.

BABCOCK, Benjamin of Ernestown.
  Rachel, m. James Powley of Kingston. O.C. 23 Nov 1816.
  Sarah, m. Isaac Smith Jr. of Kingston 21 March 1819. O.C. 26 July 1820.
  Peter of Ernestown. O.C. 17 March 1824.
  James of Ernestown. O.C. 2 June 1831.
  Panina, m. Cornelius Hogaboom of Ernestown. O.C. 2 June 1831.
  Benjamin of Ernestown. O.C. 19 Aug 1833.

BABCOCK, David of Kingston.
  Margaret, m. Samuel Smith of Kingston. O.C. 17 March 1812.
  Benjamin of Kingston. O.C. 1 Sept 1824; O.C. 19 March 1840.
  John of Kingston. O.C. 26 May 1840.
  Darius of Kingston. O.C. 27 June 1833.
  Mary, m. William Scott of Ameliasburgh. O.C. 18 July 1834.
  Belknap of Sidney. O.C. 27 Nov 1834.
  Daniel of Kingston. O.C. 28 April 1832.
  Elizabeth, m. Stephen Middaugh of Pickering. O.C. 2 Feb 1825.

BABCOCK, John of Ameliasburgh.
  John of Ameliasburgh. O.C. 15 March 1838.
  Margaret, m. ---- Wees of Ameliasburgh. O.C. 15 March 1838.
  Mary, m. ---- Wannamaker of Ameliasburgh. O.C. 15 March 1838.
  Phoebe, m. ---- Wees of Ameliasburgh. O.C. 15 March 1838.

BABCOCK, Rachel of Camden East, widow of Samuel Babcock.
  Mary, m. David Kelly of Camden East. O.C. 25 Feb 1809.
  Elizabeth, m. William Lewis of Camden East. O.C. 25 Feb 1809.
  Keziah, m. William Cook of Camden East 17 Dec 1792. O.C. 28 Feb 1809.
  Sarah, m. Thaddeus Scott of Camden East. O.C. 25 Feb 1812.
  Benjamin of Camden East. O.C. 2 April 1835.

BAILEY, Levi of Cornwall.
 Chloe, m. Joseph Sawyers of Cornwall. O.C. 7 Feb 1804.
 John of Cornwall. O.C. 25 Feb 1812.

BAKER, Adam.
 Hannah, m. Richard Empey of Osnabruck. O.C. 25 Feb 1806.
 Catharine, m. Charles Curtis Farrand of Osnabruck. O.C. 26 Jan 1808.
 Elizabeth, m. William Campbell of Osnabruck. O.C. 25 Feb 1806.
 Adam. O.C. 11 June 1798.
 William.
 John.

BAKER, Benjamin of Cornwall, m. Abigail Wade.
 Clarissa, bapt. 11 May 1790 aged 3 yrs. O.C. 17 Aug 1808.
 James of Cornwall, bapt. 11 May 1790 aged 5 yrs. O.C. 4 Feb 1807.
 Lucy, bapt. 11 May 1790 aged 7 yrs. O.C. 19 May 1807.
 Sarah, bapt. 11 May 1790 aged 1 year 5 mos.; m. Abner Young of Corn-
  wall. O.C. 23 Feb 1808.
 Edward of Cornwall. O.C. 1 Dec 1819.
 Benjamin, b. about 1781, bapt. 11 May 1790.
 Anna, bapt. 29 Nov 1792; m. ---- Wade of Cornwall. O.C. 10 Mar 1834.

BAKER, Conrad of Williamsburgh.
 Frederick of Williamsburgh. O.C. 19 April 1816.
 Michael of Williamsburgh. O.C. 16 April 1818.
 Catharine, m. John Helmer Jr. of Williamsburgh. O.C. 1 Aug 1833.
 Juliann. O.C. 1 Aug 1833.
 Peter of Caledon. O.C. 24 Nov 1832.

BAKER, Frederick of Ernestown.
 Peter of Ernestown. O.C. 16 Feb 1811.
 Mary, m. Peter Amey of Ernestown. O.C. 25 Feb 1812.
 Henry of Ernestown. O.C. 23 Nov 1816.
 John of Ernestown. O.C. 17 Dec 1836.
 Elizabeth, m. Joseph Amey of Ernestown. O.C. 12 Jan 1837.
 William of Ernestown. O.C. 30 May 1834.
 Thomas of Ernestown. O.C. 30 May 1834.
 George of Ernestown. O.C. 7 Aug 1834.
 Margaret, m. ---- Miller of Camden. O.C. 14 May 1830.

BAKER, John of Osnabruck.
 Jacob of Osnabruck. O.C. 15 May 1835.
 John of Osnabruck. O.C. 15 May 1835.
 Catharine, m. Adam Snyder of Osnabruck. O.C. 15 May 1835.
 Nancy, m. John Waldroff of Osnabruck. O.C. 15 May 1835.
 Marian. O.C. 11 Jan 1834.
 Margaret Harriett, m. Peter Smith of Osnabruck. O.C. 18 Jan 1834.

BAKER, William of Camden.
    Ann, m. Joseph Eberts of Chatham. O.C. 10 March 1834.
    Catharine, m. ---- Knight of Camden. O.C. 10 March 1834.

BAKER, William of Kingston.
    Elizabeth, m. Charles J. Peters of St. John, N.B. O.C. 6 June 1798.

BALL, Jacob Sr. of Niagara. Lieut., Butler's Rangers.
    Peter Mann of Niagara, b. 24 Feb 1755, d. May 1836. O.C. 17 Mar 1797.
    Jacob of Thorold, b. 15 Dec 1756. O.C. 17 Aug 1795.
    John of Niagara, b. 1760, d. 13 March 1822.
    George of Louth, b. 25 July 1765, d. 10 Feb 1854.
    Dorothy, b. 20 Nov 1762, m. Adam Hutt of Niagara.
    Mary, b. 31 May 1769, d. 20 May 1858, m. John Clement of Niagara.
    Margaret Sophia, b. 13 Nov 1771, d. 18 Nov 1853; m. William Nelles of
        Grimsby (Grand River) 16 July 1799. O.C. 9 May 1797.
    Catharine, b. 16 Dec 1777, d. 23 Dec 1829; m. Abraham Nelles of
        Grimsby 2 May 1797. O.C. 9 May 1797.

BALL, Jacob Jr. of Thorold.
    Elizabeth, m. Thomas Ker of Grantham. O.C. 21 Feb 1807.
    Jacob J. of Thorold, m. Catharine Chrysler. O.C. 13 March 1810.
    Margaret, m. ---- Ward. O.C. 2 March 1816.
    Henry of Thorold. O.C. 20 May 1817.
    Mary, m. Robert Wilkinson of Thorold. O.C. 20 May 1817.
    Ann Dorothy, m. Rev. Thomas Creen of Niagara 25 Dec 1823. O.C. 5
        May 1826.
    Catharine. O.C. 5 May 1826.

BALL, Peter Mann of Niagara; his wife Elizabeth died at Niagara in
    December 1844 aged 81.
    George Augustus of Niagara, m. Ann Pawling 1 Nov 1807. O.C. 17 Feb
        1807.
    Gertrude. O.C. 27 Jan 1816.
    Hannah, m. Ralph M. Long of Niagara. O.C. 27 Jan 1816.
    Peter Mann of Niagara, m. Jane Wilson 15 Aug 1822; d. Nassageweya in
        1883 in 93rd year. O.C. 27 Jan 1816.
    John Clement of Niagara, m. Margaret Frey 15 March 1814. O.C. 27
        January 1816.
    Jacob. O.C. 7 Feb 1797.
    Elizabeth, m. D. Servos of Niagara. O.C. 30 June 1819.
    William M. of Niagara, m. Margaret Notman 26 Feb 1822. OC 20 Oct 1819.

BALL, Shadrack of Ernestown.
    Timothy T. of Loughborough. O.C. 4 Sept 1834.
    Angel of Pittsburgh. O.C. 4 Sept 1834.
    Cyrenus of Loughborough. O.C. 4 Sept 1834.
    Sanford of Pittsburgh. O.C. 4 Sept 1834.   [Cont'd]

BALL, Shadrack - Cont'd
Belknap of Pittsburgh. O.C. 29 September 1834.

BALL, Solomon of Ernestown.
Mercy, m. Philip Stafford of Ernestown. O.C. 19 Dec 1806.
Mary, m. John Hough of Ernestown. O.C. 30 June 1819.
Sarah, m. Asa Elmer of Ernestown. O.C. 25 June 1823.
Susan, m. Hudson Walker of Ernestown 17 Dec 1820. O.C. 1 July 1830;
    O.C. 16 April 1840.
Rachel, m. ---- Peters of Ernestown. O.C. 27 Feb 1834.
Lucinda, m. John Sweep of Ernestown. O.C. 6 Dec 1832.
Philip of Ernestown. O.C. 3 Oct 1827.
Solomon of Portland. O.C. 18 Aug 1824.

BANTA, Weart.   Lieut.
Sarah, m. ---- Van Wyck of Stamford. O.C. 10 Nov 1801.
Elizabeth, m. Isaac Davis. O.C. 13 May 1797.
John. O.C. 13 May 1797.

BARGER, Walter.
Margaret, m. ---- Ferro. O.C. 28 Feb 1798.

BARKLEY, Anolvas of Williamsburgh.
Casper of Williamsburgh. O.C. 19 April 1816.

BARKLEY, Christian of Williamsburgh.
Elizabeth, m. George Marseles of Williamsburgh. O.C. 4 Apr 1816.
Catharine, m. Peter Outerkirk of Williamsburgh. O.C. 4 Apr 1816.
Henry of Williamsburgh. O.C. 4 Apr 1816.
Margaret, m. Henry Markle of Williamsburgh. O.C. 4 Apr 1816.

BARKLEY, Everhart of Williamsburgh. [Evort Berckly, of Butler's Rangers,
and his family were at Niagara in 1783. The Ontario Register 1:206]
Everhart of Williamsburgh. O.C. 4 July 1815.
Margaret, m. Peter Witticker of Williamsburgh. O.C. 13 March 1807.
Barbara, m. Daniel Shell of Williamsburgh. O.C. 23 June 1801.

BARKLEY, Peter of Williamsburgh.
Martin of Williamsburgh. O.C. 19 April 1816.
Peter of Williamsburgh. O.C. 2 May 1833.
Everett P. of Williamsburgh. O.C. 2 May 1833.
Andrew of Williamsburgh. O.C. 18 May 1833.
Margaret, m. Henry Armstrong of Williamsburgh. O.C. 27 June 1833.
Jacob P. of Williamsburgh. O.C. 1 Aug 1833.
Catharine, m. Charles Loughrin of Williamsburgh. O.C. 19 Dec 1833.
Henry of Williamsburgh. O.C. 19 Dec 1833.
Elizabeth, m. Michael Kenny of Williamsburgh. O.C. 2 Jan 1834.

BARKLEY, Philip.
    Mary, m. Henry Stata of Williamsburgh. O.C. 28 Feb 1798.

BARNHART, Charles of Fredericksburgh, m. Catharine ---- 16 Feb 1789.
    John of Fredericksburgh, m. Sarah Clark 26 Dec 1816. O.C. 19 Apr 1816.
    Peter of Fredericksburgh, bapt. 8 July 1792. O.C. 19 Apr 1816.
    Samuel of Fredericksburgh, bapt. 3 Oct 1790; m. Maryann Sills, 28 Sept
        1819; born August 1789. O.C. 19 Apr 1816.
    Sarah, m. Nicholas Rambough of Camden East 29 Jan 1822. O.C. 19 Aug
        1833.
    Mary, m. Peter Sills of Fredericksburgh. O.C. 4 Oct 1826.

BARNHART, George of Town of Cornwall, Sgt. R.R.N.Y. Married Catharine Sharpston.
    William George of Cornwall. O.C. 11 July 1799; O.C. 13 June 1809.
    Catharine, m. Peter House of Cornwall. O.C. 25 Feb 1806.
    Mary, m. John Phillips of Osnabruck. O.C. 25 Feb 1806.
    Mary, m. John McDonell of Osnabruck. O.C. 5 Jan 1798.
    [Inserted in the margin near the two listings for Mary was: Same?]
    John of Cornwall, bapt. 26 Sept 1790. O.C. 7 Aug 1811.
    Charles of City of Toronto. O.C. 28 Feb 1835.

BARNHART, Jacob of Cornwall, m. Catharine Bedford.
    Benjamin of Cornwall. O.C. 24 Dec 1823.
    Charlotte, bapt. 27 Aug 1797; m. Joseph Tilton of Cornwall. O.C. 8th
        March 1826.
    Jacob of Cornwall. O.C. 4 Dec 1834.
    Sarah. O.C. 5 Jan 1835.
    Catharine. O.C. 5 Jan 1835.
    John of Cornwall. O.C. 5 Jan 1835.
    Margaret. O.C. 8 March 1826.
    Mary Ann. O.C. 8 March 1826.

BARNHART, John
    Mary, m. ---- Steinhoff of Woodhouse. O.C. 17 March 1801.
    Catharine, m. Peter Pelkie of Bertie. O.C. 15 May 1805.
    Frederick of Woodhouse. O.C. 7 May 1811.

BARNHART, John of Williamsburgh and Markham. Pvt., K.R.R.N.Y.
    Charity. O.C. 19 Apr 1816.
    Margaret, m. Jacob Waldenbarger of Markham. O.C. 17 Sept 1823.
    Anne, m. John Waldenbarger of Markham. O.C. 4 Feb 1824.
    Elizabeth, m. John Prior of Markham. O.C. 4 Feb 1830.
    Jacob of Markham. O.C. 6 May 1830.
    Peter of Town of Cornwall. O.C. 8 March 1826.
    George of Markham. O.C. 23 June 1824.

BARNHART, Nicholas of Cornwall, m. Anne Prentice.
   William of Cornwall. O.C. 13 June 1818.
   Rebecca, bapt. 29 Oct 1797; m. John Marks of Cornwall. OC 5 Nov 1818.
   George of Cornwall. O.C. 21 Feb 1821.
   James of Cornwall. O.C. 10 July 1822.
   William N. of Town of Cornwall. O.C. 3 Nov 1836.
   Hiram E. of Cornwall. O.C. 19 May 1836.
   David of Cornwall. O.C. 13 June 1836.
   Juliann. O.C. 25 July 1833.
   Catharine, m. Michael H. Gallinger of Cornwall. OC 6 Dec 1832.
   Charles of Cornwall. O.C. 22 May 1832.
   Mercy. O.C. 22 July 1824.

BARNUM, Nathaniel Bunnell of Charlotteville.
   David Wheeler of Charlotteville. O.C. 4 Dec 1834.
   Charles D. of Charlotteville. O.C. 17 Oct 1839.
   Thomas Arnold of Charlotteville. O.C. 28 Jan 1841.
   Lois Green, m. William Kimber of Charlotteville. O.C. 3 Oct 1833.
   Henry V. of Charlotteville. O.C. 10 March 1834.
   James Russell of Charlotteville. O.C. 10 March 1834.
   Christina, m. Henry Liger of Woodhouse. O.C. 7 Feb 1833.
   Andrew Willson of Bayham. O.C. 22 Dec 1832.
   Samantha M., m. James Clark of Walsingham. O.C. 6 Feb 1828.

BARTLEY, Isaiah of Fredericksburgh. Pvt., 2nd Batt., R.R.N.Y.
   John of Adolphustown. O.C. 28 Feb 1799.
   Eleanor, m. Micaheh Jaynes of Richmond. O.C. 28 Feb 1799.
   Cornelia. O.C. 26 Jan 1808.
   Elizabeth, m. Andrew Loyst of Fredericksburgh 7 Aug 1791. Land Board
      Certificate. 21/6 Richmond.
   Janet, m. ---- Harns. Land Board Certificate. 17/6 Sidney.

BARTLEY, Michael of Fredericksburgh, m. Mary Peters of Fredericks-
burgh on 12 February 1788.
   Magdalene, bapt. 2 Oct 1792; m. Robert Nicholson of Fredericksburgh.
      O.C. 27 Feb 1812.
   Henry of Fredericksburgh, bapt. 7 March 1790. O.C. 25 Feb 1812.
   John, bapt. 27 Feb 1805.
   Jenny, bapt. 14 Sept 1802; m. Samuel Green of Sidney. O.C. 19 July 1826.
   Mary, bapt. 31 Oct 1798; m. Ebenezer Green of Sidney. OC 8 Oct 1830.
   Elizabeth, bapt. 21 June 1796.
   Joseph, bapt. 1 January 1794.

BARTON, Thomas of Augusta.
   Eunice, m. Moses Shatford of Augusta (Wolford). O.C. 24 Sept 1799.
   Helche, m. ---- Hazelton of Wolford. O.C. 10 June 1800.
   John of Augusta. O.C. 10 June 1800.
   Rosannah, m. ---- Thompson of Augusta. O.C. 23 June 1801.

BARTON, William of Augusta.
    Rachel, m. ---- Wiley of Kitley. O.C. 10 June 1800.
    Eleanor, m. Joel Smades of Hope. O.C. 17 Feb 1816.
    John of Elizabethtown. O.C. 10 June 1800.

BASTEDO, Jacob of Kingston and Stamford, m. Clarissa Jean Van Slyke.
    Joseph of Niagara. O.C. 2 Jan 1811.
    Gilbert Tice of Stamford, m. Marian Thompson. O.C. 27 May 1806.
    Abraham of Stamford. O.C. 30 June 1819.
    John of Stamford, m. Mary Flewelling. O.C. 30 June 1819.
    Louis of Nelson. O.C. 9 March 1837.
    David, m. Elizabeth McMicking.
    Cornelius.

BATES, William of Trafalgar.
    John of Saltfleet. O.C. 11 Dec 1806.
    Walter of Saltfleet. O.C. 11 April 1809.
    Philo D. of Nelson. O.C. 17 May 1820.
    David of York. O.C. 23 July 1823.
    Henry W. of Saltfleet. O.C. 3 Dec 1829.

BATTER, Philip of Hope. [Philip Bater, of Butler's Rangers, and his family
  were at Niagara in 1783. The Ontario Register 1: 206]
    George of Hope. O.C. 23 June 1808.
    Catherine, m. Christopher Merkley of Hope. O.C. 12 July 1808.
    Susan, m. Daniel Wright of Hope. O.C. 16 Feb 1816.
    Elias of Hope, m. Betsy Bedford (?). O.C. 13 Feb 1816.
    Elizabeth. O.C. 13 Feb 1816.
    Philip of Hope. O.C. 25 Feb 1819.
    Barbara, m. William Preston of Hope. O.C. 6 March 1821.
    David of Hope. O.C. 3 May 1826.

BAXTER, William.
    Margaret, m. ---- Buchanan of Cornwall. O.C. 11 July 1799.
    Daniel of Cornwall. O.C. 11 July 1799.

BAYEUX, Thomas.
    Abigail, m. Elijah Vincent of Willoughby. O.C. 4 May 1804.

BEACH, John. Sgt.
    Stephen Todd of Elizabethtown, Sgt., R.C.V.; m. Catherine Spicer.
      O.C. 1 March 1805.
    John.
    Mary, m. Daniel McEathron of Elizabethtown.

BEACH, Samuel of Ernestown.
    Cynthia, m. Haskell Dyer of Yonge. O.C. 8 Sept 1836.

BEASLEY, Richard of Barton, b. August 1761; m. Henrietta dau David and
Margaret (Oliver) Springer. She d. at Hamilton 29 July 1845. He died at
Hamilton 10 Feb 1842 in his 81st year, aged 80 yrs 7 mos.
   Henry of Barton, bapt. 27 Apr 1793; d. at Hamilton 5 August 1859 aged
      66. O.C. 25 Feb 1818.
   David of Barton, bapt. 6 March 1794. O.C. 25 Feb 1818.
   Margaret, m. David Stegman of Barton. O.C. 26 July 1820.
   Hannah, m. William B. Van Every of Barton. O.C. 30 Apr 1823.
   Keziah, m. Nehemiah Ford of Town of Hamilton. O.C. 27 Aug 1840.
   Richard George of Town of Hamilton, bapt. 2 Mar 1811. OC 4 July 1833.
   Mary Sarah, bapt. 2 Mar 1811; m. Patrick Hammell of Ancaster. O.C.
      19 December 1833.
   Catharine, m. Colin Campbell Ferrie of Town of Hamilton, 1830; died at
      Hamilton 11 March 1866, aged 54.

BEDFORD, Jonathan of Hope.
   Jonathan of Hope. O.C. 5 March 1808.
   Stephen of Hope. O.C. 5 March 1808.
   David of Hope. O.C. 13 Feb 1816.
   Hannah. O.C. 13 Feb 1816.
   Nancy. O.C. 13 Feb 1816.
   Betsey, m. Elias Batter of Hope. O.C. 13 Feb 1816.
   John of Hope. O.C. 18 March 1818.
   Luke of Hope. O.C. 1 May 1822.
   Charlotte, m. Nathan Choate of Hope. O.C. 19 Nov 1831.

BEEBE, Edin of Louth.
   Drusilla, m. Daniel McIntyre of Grimsby. O.C. 9 Oct 1810.
   Lucretia, m. Adam Smith of Saltfleet. O.C. 27 March 1813, 8 Sept 1819.
   Joshua of Louth. O.C. 19 May 1819.
   Amassa of Louth. O.C. 8 Sept 1819.
   Solomon of Louth, b. 19 May 1798; m. Temantha Beach, 1835; d. 27 Jan
      1847. O.C. 22 May 1820.
   Asa of Louth. O.C. 3 April 1822.

BELL, Duncan of Fredericksburgh, m. Anna.
   John of Fredericksburgh. O.C. Feb 25, 1809.
   Ruth, bapt. 1 Jan 1789; m. Gilbert Sharp of Fredericksburgh, 29 October
      1807. O.C. 25 Feb 1809.
   Abigail, bapt. 27 Apr 1794; m. Abraham Taylor of Fredericksburgh.
      O.C. 16 Feb 1811.
   Isaac of Fredericksburgh. O.C. 18 March 1818.
   Eleanor, bapt. 26 March 1799; m. Jonathan Phillips of Sidney. O.C. 18
      March 1818.
   William of Thurlow, bapt. 11 Aug 1805. O.C. 1 May 1834.
   Jehiel of Fredericksburgh, bapt. 10 Oct 1802; O.C. 5 May 1831.
   Flora, buried 3 Feb 1802.
   Flora Ann, m. Daniel Chapman of Fredericksburgh. O.C. 3 March 1831.

BELL, Thomas of Fredericksburgh and Pittsburgh.
 Elizabeth. O.C. 8 July 1801.
 Frederick of Fredericksburgh, bapt. 19 Feb 1788. O.C. 23 Feb 1809.
 Catherine, m. ---- Hesse of Richmond. O.C. 27 Oct 1801.
 Hannah, bapt. 13 Jan 1789; m. Abel Scott of Camden East. OC 25 Feb 1809.
 John B. of Sidney. O.C. 14 Nov 1839.
 George of Camden East. O.C. 3 April 1834.
 Thomas, bapt. 25 Jan 1792.
 Sylvester of Pittsburgh. O.C. 2 Oct 1834.
 Agnes. O.C. 27 Nov 1834.
 Magdalen. O.C. 4 Dec 1834.

BELL, William of Fredericksburgh. William Bell Sr. died in January 1805.
 William of Fredericksburgh. O.C. 25 July 1809.
 Jane, m. Andrew Embury of Fredericksburgh. O.C. 12 July 1797.
 Eleanor, m. Asa Hough of Fredericksburgh 11 May 1790. OC 8 July 1797.
 Ann, m. Lambert Van Alstine of Fredericksburgh 22 July 1788. O.C. 8
    July 1797.
 James of Camden East. O.C. 14 June 1839.
 Catharine. O.C. 14 June 1839.
 Margaret, m. ---- Sills of Fredericksburgh. O.C. 3 Sept 1840.
 Edward C. of Camden East. O.C. 3 March 1836.
 Elizabeth, m. ---- Embury of Camden East. O.C. 19 May 1836.
 David S. of Camden East. O.C. 6 November 1834.

BELL, William of Fredericksburgh and Camden.
 David Fraser of Camden East. O.C. 27 Nov 1834.
 Helen, m. Mathias Switzer of Camden East. O.C. 19 June 1832.
 Isabella, m. (1) John Sills of Fredericksburgh 23 Feb 1794; m. (2) Martin
    Hough of Fredericksburgh 12 Oct 1801. O.C. 8 July 1797, 5 July 1826.
 John of Camden East. O.C. 14 Sept 1825.

BENDER, George.
 Mary, m. Barnabas Hart of Cornwall. O.C. 5 Jan 1798.

BENDER, Philip of Stamford.
 Eleanor, m. John Burch of Stamford. O.C. 15 May 1805.
 Elizabeth. O.C. 15 May 1805.
 Barbara, m. John Murray of Crowland. O.C. 26 March 1811.
 Mary, m. Peter Buckner of Crowland. O.C. 5 July 1796.

BENDER, Tunis of Cornwall.
 Richard D. of Cornwall. O.C. 15 March 1838.
 Mary, m. ---- Eamer of Cornwall. O.C. 15 March 1838.
 Catharine, m. Alexander Stelmagor of Town of Cornwall. OC 26 Mar 1840
 George of Cornwall. O.C. 22 July 1836.
 James of Cornwall. O.C. 12 Jan 1837.
 Margaret, m. ---- Baxter of Cornwall. O.C. 12 Jan 1837.   [Cont'd]

BENDER, Tunis - Cont'd
William of Cornwall. O.C. 17 March 1836.
Elizabeth, m. John Sheets of Cornwall. O.C. 17 March 1836.

BENEDICT, Joseph of Bastard, b. 1 Aug 1749 son of Jonathan and Lucy
(Castle) Benedict of New Milford, Conn. and Manchester, Vt., m. Esther
Ketchum; d. 1 Sept 1844 in 96th year. See Benedict Book published 1870.
Mary, m. ---- Losee. O.C. 18 June 1799.
Parthena, m. Samuel Olds of Elizabethtown. O.C. 22 Feb 1810.
Nancy, m. Ira Gilbert of Lansdowne. O.C. 22 Feb 1810.
John of Bastard, b. 22 May 1792; m. Phoebe Brown; d. 10 May 1830.
O.C. 14 July 1819.
Esther, m. David Bogart of Elizabethtown 7 June 1815. O.C. 26 July 1820
Rachel, m. Benjamin Kilborn of Kitley; d. Sept 1855. O.C. 17 Sept 1823.

BENN, John of Fredericksburgh.
George of Fredericksburgh, m. Susannah dau John Mitts. OC 16 Feb 1811.
Peter of Fredericksburgh. O.C. 16 Feb 1811.
John of Fredericksburgh. O.C. 26 March 1817.
Hugh of Fredericksburgh. O.C. 3 May 1820.
Elizabeth, m. ---- Jewell. Not. Rec. 7 July 1836.
Valentine of Fredericksburgh. O.C. 13 June 1833.
Florence of Fredericksburgh, b. there 1805; m. Catherine Asselstine in
1828; d. 17 Aug 1880. O.C. 19 Aug 1833.
James of Fredericksburgh. O.C. 12 June 1834.
Hannah, m. Jacob Asselstine of Fredericksburgh. O.C. 5 Feb 1835.
Elizabeth, m. Richard Lloyd of Fredericksburgh. O.C. 7 Feb 1833.
Conrad of Fredericksburgh. O.C. 22 June 1825.
Lucetta, m. Philip Simmons of Camden East. O.C. 9 March 1843.
Sarah Ann, m. Abner Soles of Camden East. O.C. 9 March 1843.
Adam of Camden East. O.C. 9 March 1843.

BENSON, Albert of Adolphustown.
David of Ameliasburgh. O.C. 18 March 1818.
Peter of Adolphustown. O.C. 28 March 1833.
Mathew of Adolphustown. O.C. 11 July 1833.
Margaret, m. James J. Terrill of Murray. O.C. 1 Aug 1833.
Garrett of Adolphustown. O.C. 12 June 1832.
Sophia, m. Charles Alger of Hallowell. O.C. 28 Apr 1832.
John of Adolphustown. O.C. 14 March 1826.

BENSON, Mathew of Sophiasburgh.
John of Sophiasburgh, b. 1779; m. Mary Valleau 17 Nov 1801; d. in May
1864. O.C. 18 Nov 1797.
Richard of Sophiasburgh. O.C. 18 Nov 1797.
Elizabeth, m. Matthew Steel of Adolphustown. Land Board Certificate
22 January 1793.

BERDAN, Albert of Woodhouse.
    Albert of Woodhouse. O.C. 9 Oct 1810.
    Samuel of Woodhouse. O.C. 19 April 1816; O.C. 6 Aug 1829.
    Jacob of Woodhouse. O.C. 19 Apr 1816. O.C. 6 Aug 1829.
    Margaret, m. David Ellis of Woodhouse. O.C. 19 April 1816.
    Susannah, m. Samuel Thompson of Charlotteville. O.C. 20 May 1817.
    Daniel of Woodhouse. O.C. 6 Oct 1819.
    Margaret, m. Elijah Clark of Southwold. O.C. 26 Nov 1823.
    Henry of Woodhouse. O.C. 21 Jan 1824.
    David of Woodhouse. O.C. 8 March 1830.
    Jonathan Williams of Southwold. O.C. 25 Jan 1831.

BERNARD, Alexander of Augusta.
    Jerusha, m. John Gordon of Ernestown. O.C. 7 Aug 1810.
    Hannah, m. Isaac Nichols of Augusta. O.C. 3 Apr 1810.
    John of Augusta. O.C. 2 April 1816.
    Eleanor, m. Summers Walker of Augusta. O.C. 16 June 1818.
    Sally, m. William L. Hamblin of Augusta 27 Oct 1816. O.C. 28 Oct 1835.
    Samuel of Ernestown. O.C. 2 Oct 1834. O.C. 5 Feb 1829.
    Elizabeth, m. Elwick Randall of Augusta. O.C. 23 July 1830.
    Ann, m. Peter Thomas of Ernestown 16 Aug 1818. O.C. 2 Sept 1830.

BESSEY, Jacob of Grantham.
    David of Grantham. O.C. 18 May 1819.
    Mary Catharine, m. Frederick Smith of Thorald. O.C. 8 Sept 1819.
    John of Grantham. O.C. 17 Oct 1821.
    George of Grantham. O.C. 22 July 1824.

BESSEY, Robert of Grantham.   Sr. or Jr. ?
    David of Grantham. O.C. 23 June 1802.
    Elizabeth, m. James Newkirk of Thorald. O.C. 24 March 1797.
    Rebecca. O.C. 17 July 1817.
    Priscilla, bapt. 12 May 1793. O.C. 17 July 1817.
    Jane. O.C. 17 July 1817.
    Mary. O.C. 18 May 1819.
    James of Grantham. O.C. 18 May 1819.
    John of Grantham. O.C. 19 May 1819.   ? son of Jacob
    John R. of Grantham. O.C. 23 July 1823.
    Catharine, m. William Reid of Grantham. O.C. 24 March 1797.

BESSEY, Robert of Grantham.
    Margaret, m. ---- Applebee of Grantham. O.C. 15 May 1835.
    Elizabeth. O.C. 15 May 1835.
    Robert of Grantham. O.C. 6 Aug 1828.

BETHUNE, Angus of Charlottenburgh.
    Mary. O.C. 9 July 1802.
    Ann, m. Peter Ferguson Jr. of Charlottenburgh. O.C. 15 March 1806.

BETHUNE, Angus - Cont'd
  Elizabeth. O.C. 22 Feb 1810.
  Donald of Charlottenburgh. O.C. 23 Nov 1816.
  Duncan of Charlottenburgh, d. 22 July 1871 ae 79. O.C. 23 Nov 1816.

BETHUNE, Rev. John of Charlottenburgh.
  Cecelia, m. (1) Walter Butler Wilkinson of Cornwall Town 8 March 1803;
    m. (2) Hon. John Kirby of Kingston; d. Kingston 20 January 1842. O.C.
    31 May 1803.
  Christy, b. 24 Feb 1787; m. John Low Farrand of Cornwall 6 Feb 1807;
    d. 16 May 1865. O.C. 23 Feb 1808.
  Rev. John of Augusta, b. 5 Jan 1791; m. Eliza Hallowell 27 Aug 1816.
    O.C. 11 Nov 1815.
  Angus of Hamilton, b. 9 Sept 1783; m. Louisa Mackenzie; d. 13 Nov 1858
    at Toronto. O.C. 26 Jan 1837.
  James Gray of Hamilton, b. 1 Apr 1793; m. Martha Covert. O.C. 26 Jan
    1837.
  Rev. Alexander Neil of Cobourg, b. 20 Aug 1800; m. Jane Eliza Crooks
    17 Apr 1827; d. Toronto 3 Feb 1879. O.C. 29 Apr 1835.
  Donald of Cobourg, b. 11 July 1802; m. Janet Smith 5 Nov 1828. O.C. 29
    April 1835.
  Ann, b. 22 May 1798; m. Henry Mackenzie of Montreal 23 May 1815; d.
    Cobourg 3 May 1835 aged 37. O.C. 29 April 1835.
  Norman, b. 10 March 1789; m. Margaret Kitson 25 Aug 1822; d. 27 July
    1848 at Montreal.
  Christy m. (2) Robert Henry of Montreal, 2 Nov 1817.

BETRON, David
  Lucretia, m. Enoch Stuart of Niagara. O.C. 22 Dec 1801.

BIRDSALL, Samuel of Stamford, wife Elizabeth. She m. (2) John Darling.
  See O.C. 18 April 1797.
  Jacob of Thorold. O.C. 4 May 1802.
  Benjamin of Crowland. O.C. 17 Oct 1809.
  Martha, m. Elijah Shotwell of Thorold. O.C. 17 Oct 1809.
  Samuel of Canborough. O.C. 27 Aug 1840.

BISSELL, David of Augusta.
  Catherine, b. 1786 in Connecticut; m. Abraham Clark of Elizabethtown in
    1800. O.C. 26 May 1801.
  Edward of Augusta. O.C. 24 Feb 1801.
  John of Augusta. O.C. 28 Oct 1835.
  Zenos of Augusta. O.C. 28 Oct 1835.

BLACK, Jonathan of Augusta.
  Jonathan of Augusta. O.C. 15 March 1803.
  Elizabeth, m. Jesse Sparks of Augusta. O.C. 20 Feb 1809.
  Mary, m. Jason Cross of Augusta. O.C. 20 Feb 1809.   [Cont'd]

BLACK, Jonathan - Cont'd
   Joseph of Augusta. O.C. 13 June 1818.
   Esther, m. Alexander Umphrey of Augusta. O.C. 7 Jan 1830.

BLACKBURN, John of Chatham.
   Isaac of Chatham. O.C. 24 Nov 1836.
   Leonard of Chatham. O.C. 24 Nov 1836.
   Robert of Chatham. O.C. 24 Nov 1836.
   Rachel, m. Peter French of Chatham. O.C. 28 Oct 1835.
   Joseph of Chatham. O.C. 3 March 1836.

BLAKELY, James of Hallowell. Commissary. Married (1) Ann Keogh; (2)
   Mrs. Mary Smith, 29 April 1805.
   Ann, m. Isaac Murrison (Mowerson) of Hallowell. O.C. 23 June 1801.
   William of Hallowell, m. Hannah Mowerson. O.C. 21 Dec 1802.
   Samuel of Hallowell, m. Anna C. Smith 15 Apr 1805. OC. 8 March 1804.
   Susannah, m. Charles Bennett of Hallowell. O.C. 16 April 1818.
   James of Hallowell, m. Elizabeth Mowerson. O.C. 30 Aug 1797.
   John. See O.C. 30 May 1834.
   Isabella.

BLAKELY, John. See Land Book "O" p. 169
   Mary, m. ---- Tappin of Charlottenburgh. O.C. 15 Jan 1803.

BOGART, Abraham of Adolphustown, m. 18 March 1792, Mary Lazier who
   was b. at Tappan, N.J., 10 Aug 1772. She d. 30 Jan 1874.
   Abraham L. of Hallowell. O.C. 3 April 1834.
   Charity C., m. James Hubbard Meacham of Ameliasburgh. O.C. 4 Sept
      1834.
   David D. of Adolphustown. O.C. 15 Dec 1832.
   Gilbert Curtis of Adolphustown. O.C. 15 Dec 1832.
   Cornelius V. of Adolphustown. O.C. 11 Oct 1832.
   James of Adolphustown. O.C. 23 June 1828.
   Nicholas of Adolphustown. O.C. 28 Feb 1829.
   John of Adolphustown. O.C. 28 Feb 1829.
   Lewis of Adolphustown. O.C. 2 April 1829.

BOGERT, Christopher.
   Frances, m. Caleb Mattison of Edwardsburgh. O.C. 18 June 1807.
   Mary, m. Henry Jackson of Mountain. O.C. 29 March 1808.

BOICE, John Sr. of Niagara, m. Elizabeth. See O.C. 24 Jan 1797. [He
   served in Butler's Rangers. He and his family were at Niagara in 1783.
   See The Ontario Register 1: 205]
   Elizabeth, m. Peter Coghill of Niagara, 13 Aug 1799. O.C. 9 July 1802.
   Mary, m. James Cushman of Niagara, 19 Jan 1802. O.C. 10 March 1804.
   Jacob of Niagara. O.C. 29 Sept 1819.
   Sarah, m. Richard Springer of Town of Hamilton. O.C. 3 Dec 1840.

BOICE, John
    Mary, m. ---- Fether. O.C. 18 June 1799.

BOND, George of York. Capt., King's South Carolina Regt.
    George of York, m. Hannah Hill, 13 Feb 1814. O.C. 17 Feb 1816. From
        the "Weekly Globe" 18 June 1875: Died June 9th, at the residence of
        Geo. Ward, Eglinton, Hannah, relict of the late Geo. Bond, aet. 86 ys.
    Sarah, m. Robert Bright of York 21 April 1814. O.C. 17 Feb 1816.
    Richard of Thorold. O.C. 23 Nov 1816.

BONESTEEL, Jacob of Edwardsburgh and South Gower, m. Christian Welch.
    Margaret. O.C. 18 March 1818. Osnabruck.
    Catharine, m. Joshua Willcox of Elizabethtown. O.C. 13 June 1818.
    Jacob of Elizabethtown. O.C. 7 July 1818.
    Barbara, bapt. 28 May 1793.
    Merila, m. ---- Laushway of Mountain. O.C. 23 Nov 1837.
    John of Mountain. O.C. 8 Nov 1838.
    Nancy, m. ---- Bilrose of Mountain. O.C. 15 Nov 1838.
    Elizabeth, m. ---- Alport of Mountain. O.C. 15 Nov 1838.
    Susannah, m. ---- Conway of Mountain. O.C. 15 Nov 1838.
    Mary, m. Elijah Smith of South Gower. O.C. 4 Jan 1840.

BONESTEEL, Jacob of South Gower.
    David of St. Vincent. O.C. 16 April 1840.

BOOTH, John of Elizabethtown.
    Berthier, m. ---- Terry. O.C. 29 Oct 1800.
    Charles of Elizabethtown. O.C. 23 Feb 1808.
    Isaac of Elizabethtown, m. Thirza Wing. O.C. 23 Feb 1808.
    Abner of Elizabethtown. O.C. 23 Feb 1808.
    Samuel of Elizabethtown. O.C. 23 Feb 1808.
    Phebe, m. James Campbell of Elizabethtown. O.C. 23 Feb 1808.
    Ann, m. ---- Lee of Elizabethtown. O.C. 23 Feb 1808.
    Vincent of Elizabethtown. O.C. 23 Feb 1808.
    John G. of Elizabethtown. O.C. 6 Aug 1829.

BOOTH, Joshua of Ernestown, m. Margaret dau Daniel Fraser, U.E.; died
at Ernestown on October 30, 1813 aged 55.
    Abraham of Ernestown. O.C. 23 Feb 1808.
    Sarah, m. Daniel Bedell Dorland of Marysburgh 5 Sept 1808. O.C. 23
        February 1809.
    Benjamin of Ernestown, m. Catharine Dorland 9 Nov 1809. OC 23 Feb 1808.
    Joshua of Ernestown. O.C. 2 March 1816.
    Mary, m. Philip Daly of Ernestown. O.C. 6 Aug 1816.
    Hester Taylor, m. James Stalker of E.town 15 Nov 1812. OC 20 May 1817.
    Harriet. O.C. 4 July 1833.
    Charles Andrew of Ernestown. O.C. 4 July 1833.
    Eleanor. O.C. 7 Aug 1829.

BOTTUM, Elijah of Augusta, m. Molly dau of Phineas Hurd, U. E.
   William Henry of Augusta. O. C. 20 Feb 1810.
   Polly. O. C. 16 Feb 1811.
   Lucy, m. Duncan Campbell of Augusta. O. C. 5 April 1820.
   Ruth. O. C. 28 Oct 1835.
   Elisha of Augusta, m. Almira Burritt. O. C. 28 Oct 1835.
   Elijah of Augusta. O. C. 18 July 1833.
   Isaac of Oxford. O. C. 1 Aug 1833.
   Harriet Theresa, m. Alonzo Hurd of Augusta. O. C. 5 Sept 1833.
   Louisa. O. C. 15 May 1832.

BOUCK, Adam.
   Christian. O. C. 18 June 1799.
   Catharine, m. George Reed of Williamsburgh. O. C. 25 Feb 1806.
   Mary, m. ---- Barkley of Williamsburgh. O. C. 17 March 1804.
   David of Williamsburgh. O. C. 5 March 1810.

BOUCK, Frederick of Williamsburgh, m. Elizabeth McCaffrey.
   Helena. O. C. 18 June 1799.
   Margaret, m. ---- Ault of Williamsburgh. O. C. 17 March 1804.
   John of Williamsburgh. O. C. 17 March 1807.
   Mary, bapt. 9 March 1795; m. David Doren of Williamsburgh. O. C. 2
      September 1818.
   Susannah, m. John J. Loucks of Williamsburgh. O. C. 2 Sept 1818.
   David of Madoc. O. C. 3 Sept 1840.

BOUCK, Frederick of Matilda.
   John C. of Matilda. O. C. 26 Jan 1837.
   Frederick of Matilda. O. C. 4 July 1833.
   Christian. O. C. 22 Feb 1834.
   Jacob of Matilda. O. C. 5 June 1834.

BOUCK, Frederick (Jr. ?) of Cornwall. See Heir & Devisee Commission,
   July 1837.
   Mary, m. Peter Brouse of Williamsburgh 3 July 1815. O. C. 14 Nov 1818.
   Elizabeth, m. Samuel P. Buell of Kitley. O. C. 1 Feb 1826.
   Margaret, m. John D. Doran of Mountain. O. C. 2 June 1829.
   Eleanor, m. James P. Kidder of Lisbon Twp., N. Y. O. C. 27 Oct 1832.
   Rachel. Kitley.

BOULTON, Abraham of Elizabethtown, m. Leah Sax.
   Ann. O. C. 20 May 1817. O. C. 5 Feb 1823. Brock.
   Hannah, bapt. 12 Feb 1789. O. C. 22 Oct 1817.
   Margaret. O. C. 22 Oct 1817.
   Isabella, m. John Rose of Edwardsburgh. O. C. 22 Oct 1817.
   Rachel, bapt. 11 March 1792; m. Nicholas Horton of Elizabethtown.
      O. C. 11 June 1823.
   Henry, bapt. 12 Feb 1789.   [Cont'd]

BOULTON, Abraham - Cont'd
Abraham of Elizabethtown, bapt. 11 March 1792. O.C. 6 Sept 1832.
James of Edwardsburgh, bapt. 27 May 1793. O.C. 2 April 1828.
Jane. O.C. 29 Sept 1835.
Mary, m. Hiram Bellamy of Augusta. O.C. 2 Apr 1828, 4 Feb 1836.
Thomas of Edwardsburgh. O.C. 4 July 1833.
Susannah, m. Daniel Hoover of Elizabethtown 20 Sept 1820. OC 6 Sept 1832.
Lydia, m. Martin Hoover of Elizabethtown 30 July 1822. OC 6 Sept 1832.
Hugh of Edwardsburgh. O.C. 23 July 1832.
Almira, m. Alva Rowley of Elizabethtown 10 Dec 1827. O.C. 27 Apr 1832.

BOULTON, George of Elizabethtown.
Thomas of Elizabethtown. O.C. 16 Feb 1811.
Elsea, m. ---- Curry. O.C. 30 July 1799.
Benjamin of Elizabethtown. O.C. 9 May 1812.
Hugh of Elizabethtown. O.C. 26 March 1817.

BOURDETT, John of Sophiasburgh (or Kingston)
Stephen of Sophiasburgh. O.C. 16 Feb 1811.
John of Sophiasburgh. O.C. 25 Feb 1812.
David of Sophiasburgh. O.C. 16 April 1818.
James of Sophiasburgh. O.C. 13 Nov 1818.
Benjamin F. of Sophiasburgh. O.C. 25 Feb 1819.
Margaret, m. Samuel H. Barton of Sophiasburgh. O.C. 25 Feb 1819.
Mary Ann, m. Ira Butler of Sophiasburgh. O.C. 25 Feb 1819.
Hannah, m. Guilliame Demorest of Sophiasburgh. O.C. 25 Feb 1819.
Oliver of Sophiasburgh. O.C. 16 Oct 1822.

BOWEN, Cornelius of Bertie, m. Rebecca. Mrs Rebecca Bowen m. Daniel
Baxter. [Cornelius Bowen served in Butler's Rangers, and he and his
family were at Niagara in 1783. See The Ontario Register 1: 208]
Gertrude, m. Peter Plato of Bertie. O.C. 23 May 1798.
Christiana, m. William Davis of Bertie. O.C. 28 Oct 1835.
Cornelius of Bertie. O.C. 28 Oct 1835.
Daniel, bapt. 12 April 1793.

BOWEN, Luke
Luke of Richmond. O.C. 11 Feb 1806.
Uriah of Matilda. O.C. 17 March 1807.
Peggy, m. ---- Fralick. O.C. 23 June 1801.
Elizabeth, m. Christopher Gague of Matilda. O.C. 26 Jan 1808.
Nancy, m. ---- Sager of Richmond. O.C. 28 Feb 1804.
Catharine, m. James More of Augusta. O.C. 26 Feb 1805.
William L. of Richmond. O.C. 23 Feb 1809.
Mary, m. Adam Shaver. O.C. 22 June 1797.

BOWEN, Victor of Fredericksburgh, m. Maria.
Margaret, m. Gilbert Sager of Richmond. O.C. 22 Dec 1842.   [Cont'd]

BOWEN, Victor - Cont'd
   Anne, b. 17 Sept 1800; m. Jonas Dulyea of Richmond. O. C. 22 Dec 1842.
   Catharine, bapt. 8 June 1796; m. John W. Mackle of Tyendinaga. O. C.
      22 Dec 1842.
   Sarah, bapt. 13 June 1798; m. ---- Culbertson of Tyendinaga. O. C. 22
      December 1842.
   John of Richmond. O. C. 22 Dec 1842.

BOWEN, William. Pvt., 2nd Batt., K.R.R.N.Y.
   Angelica, m. James Demorest of Fredericksburgh. O. C. 24 July 1797.
   Victor of Richmond. Land Board Certificate. 3/3 Richmond.

BOWER, Adam of Camden East, m. Elizabeth.
   Nicholas of Camden East. O. C. 16 Feb 1810.
   Gasper A. of Camden East. O. C. 30 Jan 1808.
   Elizabeth, m. Jonathan Knowlton of Portland. O. C. 26 Jan 1808.
   Peter of Camden East, bapt. 25 Jan 1792. O. C. 20 May 1817.
   Charity, m. Jacob Kimmerly of Richmond 26 June 1816. O. C. 20 May 1817.
   Hannah, m. Samuel Scott of Camden East 11 July 1813. O. C. 27 Feb 1818.

BOWER, Peter of Fredericksburgh, m. Catharine. [He and his wife were at
   Niagara in 1783. See TOR 1: 205]
   Henry of Camden East, bapt. 15 Jan 1788. O. C. 16 Feb 1810.
   Catherine, m. Charles Green of Amherst Island. O. C. 16 Feb 1810.
   Dorothy, bapt. 12 Oct 1790; m. Asa Worden of Amherst Is. OC 16 Feb 1811.
   Elizabeth, m. Adam Foster of Niagara. O. C. 5 March 1811.
   Gasper, bapt. 13 Jan 1789.
   Adam, bapt. 25 Jan 1792.
   Margaret, bapt. 4 March 1794.

BOWERMAN, Richard of Sophiasburgh.
   Mary Ann, m. Judah Bowerman of Hallowell. O. C. 13 Feb 1816.

BOWLBY, Thomas of Woodhouse, m. Sarah Axford.
   Axford of Woodhouse, m. Hannah Beemer. O. C. 20 May 1817.
   Martha Anne, m. Andrew Dobbie of Bayham. O. C. 8 Nov 1832.
   John A. of Woodhouse, m. Rachel Ann Birdsall. O. C. 8 Nov 1832.
   Thomas W. of Woodhouse, m. Harriet Lymburner. O. C. 12 Aug 1850.
   Richard. died young
   Woolster. died young
   Abraham. died young.

BOWMAN, Abraham of Stamford. Widow, Dorothy (?)
   Christeen, m. William Hendershot of Stamford. O. C. 26 March 1817,
      O. C. 18 Aug 1810.
   Mary, m. James Schram of Louth. O. C. 25 June 1805.
   Elizabeth, m. David Kemp of Stamford. O. C. 6 Aug 1816.
   Adam of Stamford. O. C. 20 May 1817.   [Cont'd]

BOWMAN, Abraham - Cont'd
 Peter of Stamford. O.C. 22 May 1820.
 David of Stamford. O.C. 4 Sept 1822.
 Anna Maria, m. Hiel Bingham of Ancaster. O.C. 28 Oct 1835.
 Isaac of Stamford. O.C. 17 Nov 1830.

BOWMAN, Adam Sr.
 Eve, m. Adam Beemer of Louth. O.C. 10 March 1804.
 Susannah, m. Christian McDonell of Gainsborough. O.C. 17 Oct 1809.
 Margaret, m. Geo. Darby of Grantham. O.C. 11 Oct 1796, 21 Feb 1807.
 Hannah, m. Valentine Schram. O.C. 25 Feb 1797.
 John of Pelham. O.C. 20 May 1817. (son of George A. Bowman)
 Adam. O.C. 26 Jan 1797. (son of Geo. Adam Bowman)
 Peter of Louth. O.C. 27 July 1837. (son of Geo. Adam Bowman of Thorold)
 Catherine, m. George Woodley of Grantham, 12 Feb 1797.

BOWMAN, Henry of Pelham.
 Magdalene, m. Christian Brown of Pelham. O.C. 23 Nov 1816.
 John of Pelham. O.C. 27 June 1821.
 Henry of Pelham. O.C. 12 Jan 1837.
 Jacob of Pelham. O.C. 8 Dec 1835.
 Phillip of Pelham. O.C. 8 Dec 1835.
 George Adam of Caistor. O.C. 8 Dec 1835.
 Mary, m. Abraham Clark of Pelham. O.C. 27 June 1833.
 Elizabeth, m. Henry Snure of Pelham. O.C. 25 July 1833.
 Margaret, m. Joel Berringer of Pelham. O.C. 30 May 1834.
 Eve, m. Stephen Beckett of Pelham. O.C. 8 March 1830.

BOWMAN, Jacob of Thorold. Butler's Rangers. [Jacob Bowman of Butler's
 Rangers and his family were at Niagara in 1783. Ontario Register 1: 206]
 Mary, m. Charles Gisso of Niagara Town. O.C. 22 Oct 1811.
 Eve, m. John Morden of Ameliasburgh. O.C. 12 May 1797.
 Elizabeth, m. Abraham Deforest of Stamford. O.C. 26 March 1817.
 Margaret, m. Peter Hare of Clinton. O.C. 20 May 1817.
 Ann (dau of Geo. Jacob) m. Holley Ervine of Thorold. O.C. 18 July 1834.
 John of Thorold. O.C. 25 April 1797.
 Hannah, m. ---- Riven of Niagara. O.C. 21 March 1797.

BOWMAN, Peter of Ancaster.
 Elizabeth, m. Philip Spawn of Ancaster. O.C. 2 Feb 1825.

BOYCE, Andrew of Ernestown, m. Elizabeth Hartman.
 David of Ernestown, m. Hannah Amey. O.C. 25 Feb 1812.
 Mary, m. Adam Van Wicklin of Ernestown 29 Aug 1811. O.C. 25 Feb 1812.
 Benjamin of Ernestown. O.C. 27 June 1833.
 Nicholas of Marysburgh. O.C. 4 Sept 1834.
 Cyrenus of Hungerford. O.C. 4 Sept 1834.
 Zachariah of Hungerford. O.C. 4 Sept 1834.   [Cont'd]

BOYCE, Andrew - Cont'd
   Cornelius of Rawdon. O.C. 4 Sept 1834.

BOYCE, John of Matilda.
   Jenny, m. Siah Pedge of Matilda. O.C. 25 Feb 1806.
   Mary, m. ---- Feather. (Feader?) O.C. 18 June 1799.
   Sarah, m. Robert B. Dick of Hamilton. O.C. 13 Nov 1818.
   Nancy, m. William Hanes of Ernestown. O.C. 18 June 1840.
   John of Matilda. Not. Rec. 7 Sept 1840.
   Mary, m. John Shaver of Matilda. O.C. 1 Oct 1840.
   Elizer (son) of Matilda. O.C. 2 May 1836.
   William of Matilda. O.C. 2 May 1836.
   Jane, m. Thomas Langhorn of Matilda. O.C. 2 May 1836.
   Margaret, m. Mac Putney of Matilda. O.C. 2 May 1836.
   Elizabeth, m. Richard J. Empey of Williamsburgh. O.C. 11 Jan 1834.
   Phoebe, m. Paul Comer of Ernestown. O.C. 4 Sept 1834.
   Lemuel of Pittsburgh. O.C. 2 Oct 1834.
   Theophilus of Pittsburgh. O.C. 2 Oct 1834.
   William of Darlington. O.C. 5 July 1826.

BOYCE, Stephen of Ernestown and Kingston, m. Elizabeth Conklin.
   Mary. O.C. 3 March 1809.
   Abraham of Ernestown. O.C. 16 Feb 1811.
   Joseph of Kingston. O.C. 4 April 1839.
   Clara, b. 22 Apr 1799; m. Tobias McGuire of Kingston. O.C. 26 May 1840.
   Jane. O.C. 18 May 1833. Kingston.
   Harriet, m. William Leonard of Kingston. O.C. 27 Nov 1834.
   Mishel, m. William Caldwell of Sidney. O.C. 24 March 1835.
   Experience, m. William Reed of Loughborough. O.C. 3 Jan 1827.
   Andrew of Kingston. O.C. 7 May 1828.
   Sarah, m. Charles Abrams of Loughborough. O.C. 7 May 1828.
   Almira, m. Michael Quin of Town of Kingston. O.C. 7 May 1828.

BOYD, Thomas Sr. of Edwardsburgh, m. Barbara Marriott.
   Margaret, m. Daniel Shipman of Elizabethtown. O.C. 7 July 1802.
   Rose. O.C. 26 Feb 1805.
   Mary, m. Dayle Selleck of Edwardsburgh. O.C. 16 June 1807.
   Augustus of Edwardsburgh. O.C. 22 Feb 1808.
   James. O.C. 15 July 1797.
   Andrew of Edwardsburgh, bapt. 28 May 1793. O.C. 13 Feb 1816.

BRADSHAW, Asahel of Fredericksburgh, m. Azubah Hawley (?) See O.C.
   12 July 1797.
      Esther, bapt. 9 Sept 1792; m. John Ham of Fredericksburgh 10 Apr 1808;
         O.C. 23 Feb 1809.
      Jeptha of Fredericksburgh, bapt. 3 Sept 1795. O.C. 4 Nov 1818.
      Charles of Fredericksburgh, bapt. 3 Sept 1800. O.C. 6 Feb 1822.
      Leslie of Darlington, bapt. 2 Sept 1810. O.C. 19 Apr 1838.   [Cont'd]

BRADSHAW, Asahel - Cont'd
  Sheldon H. of Sidney, bapt. 24 Feb 1808. O. C. 23 Nov 1840.
  Martin of Thurlow, bapt. 8 June 1803. O. C. 21 Dec 1840.
  David of Sophiasburgh, bapt. 30 May 1798. O. C. 25 July 1833.
  George of Portland, bapt. 28 Aug 1805; d. 17 Aug 1867. O. C. 1 May 1834.
  Isabel, bapt. 20 Feb 1799.
  James of Fredericksburgh. O. C. 19 Feb 1828.

BRADSHAW, David of Fredericksburgh, m. Isabella McKay, 25 Nov 1784 by
  Rev. John Bethune.
  Elizabeth. O. C. 26 Jan 1808.
  Lydia, bapt. 13 Nov 1787; m. George Smith of Fredericksburgh. O. C. 25
      February 1812.
  John of Fredericksburgh, bapt. 18 Dec 1792. O. C. 2 March 1816.
  William of Haldimand, bapt. 1 Jan 1790. O. C. 6 Aug 1816. See Commis-
      sion. July 1831.
  Isabella, m. George Fraser of Fredericksburgh. O. C. 27 Aug 1840.
  Margaret, bapt. 14 Sept 1803.

BRADSHAW, James Sr. Lieut. See O. C. 12 July 1797.
  James. O. C. 16 Nov 1797.
  Asahel. O. C. 16 Nov 1797.
  David.

BRADSHAW, James Jr. of Fredericksburgh and Thurlow, m. Peggy Bowen
  of Fredericksburgh on 15 January 1788.
  Lois, bapt. 3 July 1789; m. Daniel Palmer of Thurlow. O. C. 5 March 1811.
  William of Thurlow, bapt. 7 June 1791. O. C. 4 July 1815, 18 Feb 1843.
  Asahel of Fredericksburgh, bapt. 8 June 1796. O. C. 24 Nov 1836.
  Victor. O. C. 1 Dec 1836.
  Anna, bapt. 14 Oct 1801; m. Mathew Jones of Thurlow. O. C. 30 May 1835.
  Azubah, bapt. 15 Jan 1806; m. John Grant of Richmond. O. C. 5 June 1834.
  Thomas of Thurlow, bapt. 5 Feb 1794. O. C. 9 July 1827.
  Catharine, bapt. 5 Sept. 1798.
  John of Thurlow, bapt. 18 Jan 1804. O. C. 28 Feb 1833.

BRADSHAW, John of Osnabruck.
  Nancy, m. David McWilliams of Osnabruck. O. C. 25 Feb 1809.
  Mary, m. Jacob Papst of Osnabruck. O. C. 17 Apr 1812.
  William of Osnabruck. O. C. 17 Feb 1816.
  James of Osnabruck. O. C. 17 Feb 1816.
  Jane. O. C. 13 Nov 1818.
  Margaret, m. Jacob Rambough of Osnabruck. O. C. 13 Nov 1818.
  Elizabeth, m. John Collins of Osnabruck. O. C. 17 Feb 1825.

BRADT, Capt. Andrew of Louth (Barton?). [He and his wife Rachel were at
  Niagara in 1783. The Ontario Register 1: 199]
  John of Louth. O. C. 29 July 1806.   [Cont'd]

BRADT, Andrew - Cont'd
   Thomas of Louth. O.C. 29 July 1806.
   Eunice, m. Thomas Kelly of Louth. O.C. 25 July 1809.
   Arent Butler of Louth. O.C. 25 July 1809. O.C. 22 May 1820.
   Andrew of Barton. O.C. 22 Jan 1823.
   Eve, m. William Schram of Ancaster. O.C. 2 May 1821.
   Simon of Barton. O.C. 1 Feb 1826.
   Walter of Saltfleet. O.C. 5 July 1826.

BRADT, Arent.
   Roger of Niagara. O.C. 7 March 1797.
   Peter of Niagara. O.C. 8 Oct 1796.

BRADT, Arent of Nelson.
   Mary. O.C. 3 Nov 1819.
   Albert of Nelson. O.C. 3 Nov 1819.
   Walter of Nelson. O.C. 3 Nov 1819.
   Isaac of Nelson. O.C. 3 Nov 1819.
   Storm of Nelson. O.C. 1 Dec 1819.
   Peter of Nelson. O.C. 5 Oct 1820.
   Leona, m. Francis Powers of Malahide. O.C. 27 Aug 1840.
   Christian, m. Elisha R. Smith of Malahide. O.C. 28 Oct 1835.
   William of Nelson. O.C. 5 Aug 1830.
   Christopher of Nelson. O.C. 2 June 1831.

BRADT, John of Niagara.
   Susannah, m. ---- Ferguson. O.C. 3 March 1801.
   Nancy, m. Levi Burtch of Louth. O.C. 13 Jan 1819.

BRADT, Minor of Niagara. Soldier, Butler's Rangers.
   John of Niagara Town. A Sgt. Can. Fencibles. O.C. 22 Jan 1811.
   Catharine, m. John Bender of Niagara, 2 May 1813. O.C. 20 May 1817.
   Susannah, m. Harmonus House of Willoughby 2 Jan 1808. OC 2 June 1819.
   Emanuel of Grantham, bapt. 14 Sept 1800. O.C. 24 Dec 1831.
   William of Grantham, bapt. 24 Apr 1803. O.C. 24 Dec 1831.
   George of Niagara. O.C. 6 Sept 1826.
   Margaret, bapt. 20 Dec 1807.

BRADY, Luke of Cornwall.
   Elizabeth. O.C. 10 June 1800.
   Margaret, m. Lewis Bright of York. O.C. 15 Jan 1803.
   Catharine, m. Horatio Brownson of Cornwall. O.C. 23 Feb 1808.
   Sarah, m. Peter Tosdwine of Town of Kingston. O.C. 17 Feb 1816.
   Michael of Cornwall. O.C. 29 Aug 1839.

BRANT, Capt. Joseph
   Jacob of Flamboro East. O.C. 21 Oct 1806.
   Christiana, m. Aaron Hill of Grand River. O.C. 21 Oct 1806.   [Cont'd]

BRANT, Capt. Joseph - Cont'd
Joseph of Flamborough East, m. Margaret Deseronti. O. C. 11 Nov 1806.
Margaret, m. Powlis, a Mohawk of Nelson. O. C. 3 Apr 1810.
Mary, m. Seth, a Mohawk, of Nelson. O. C. 3 Apr 1810.
Catharine, m. Peter John of Nelson. O. C. 11 Nov 1815.
John of Trafalgar. O. C. 16 Jan 1816.
Elizabeth, m. William J. Kerr of Wellington Square; d. 25 Apr 1845.
O. C. 2 May 1827.
Isaac. O. C. 6 July 1798. O. C. 21 Oct 1806.

BRANT, Mrs. Mary (Johnston) of Kingston, wife of Sir William Johnson, Bt.
She died at Kingston in April 1796.
Mary, d. unm. 10 May 1813 aged 44. O. C. 1 Sept 1801.
Magdalene, m. John Ferguson of Kingston, 1791; d. 19 Jan 1818. No
issue. O. C. 20 July 1797.
Margaret, m. Capt. George Farley of Kingston. O. C. 13 June 1836.
Anne, m. Capt. Hugh Earl of Kingston; d. 17 Feb 1818. O. C. 20 July 1797
George of Kingston and Haldimand Co. O. C. 14 Oct 1818.
Peter Warren, d. prior to 1788.
Elizabeth, m. Dr. Robert Kerr of Niagara; d. 24 Jan 1794, aged 32.
Susan, m. Ensign Henry LeMoine of Kingston (24th Regt.) 5 June 1793;
d. in December 1795. Lt. Henry Lemoine, 60th Regt., committed
suicide at Kingston, 24 June 1796.

BRANTS, Henry of Fredericksburgh.
Jane, m. William McLaughlin of Camden East. O. C. 1 Apr 1840.
Anne, m. Anthony De Rushe of Camden East. O. C. 8 Sept 1836.
Mary, m. John Lindsay of Thurlow. O. C. 8 Sept 1836.
Lany. O. C. 8 Sept 1836.
Nancy, m. Alanson Howard of Thurlow. O. C. 8 Sept 1836.
Catharine, m. William Van Alstine of Fredericksburgh. O. C. 8 Sept 1836.

BRASS, David of Kingston. Lieut., Butler's Rangers. m. Mary Magdalen.
He d. at Kingston 14 Oct 1834 aged 84. [He and his family were at Niagara
in 1783. The Ontario Register 1: 209]
Henry of Kingston, m. Bathsheba Ryder 21 March 1809. O. C. 31 May 1803.
John of Kingston. O. C. 16 Nov 1807. Bastard Township ?
David of Kingston. O. C. 16 Nov 1807.
Peter of Kingston. O. C. 26 March 1817.
William of Kingston, bapt. 8 May 1796. O. C. 22 Oct 1817.

BREAKENRIDGE, David of Augusta.
John of Augusta, b. 11 May 1789; m. Mary W. Baldwin 25 Aug 1816; died
Niagara 3 Apr 1828. O. C. 28 Aug 1810.
David of Wolford. O. C. 7 March 1807.
Mary, m. Thomas Madden of Augusta. O. C. 16 Feb 1811, 16 July 1816.
Jennet, m. John L. Read of Augusta; d. 1832 in 37th yr. O. C. 26 Mar 1817
Sarah, m. Paul Glasford of Augusta. O. C. 9 July 1823.   [Cont'd]

BREAKENRIDGE, David - Cont'd
  George McKendry of Augusta. O. C. 16 May 1839.
  Solomon of Augusta. O. C. 6 Aug 1840.
  Betsey, m. John Dougall of Hallowell. O. C. 17 Sept 1823.
  Charlotte. O. C. 18 May 1833.
  Eliza, m. Samuel Thomas of Augusta; d. 21 June 1836 aged 30. O. C.
      8 November 1833.
  Francis A. of Augusta. O. C. 7 March 1833.
  Electa. O. C. 10 Jan 1833.
  Harriet, m. John Morey of Elizabethtown. O. C. 2 March 1825.

BREAKENRIDGE, James of Elizabethtown.
  Eliza A. M. , m. James A. Chambers of Elizabethtown. O. C. 2 Jan 1834.
  Robert of Elizabethtown. O. C. 8 Nov 1832.
  James of Elizabethtown. O. C. 23 July 1830.

BREWER, Aaron of Kingston.
  Margaret, m. Jarvis Worden of Kingston 1 June 1804. O. C. 27 May 1806.
  John of Kingston, m. Ann Warner 20 Sept 1807. O. C. 2 March 1816.
  Sarah, m. William Spafford of Hallowell 7 Aug 1808. O. C. 25 Feb 1818.
  Aaron of Kingston. O. C. 5 Nov 1818.
  Philip of Kingston. O. C. 4 Jan 1840.
  Elizabeth, m. William Jackson of Kingston. O. C. 4 Jan 1840.

BRISBIN, William
  Margaret, m. Daniel Patterson of Yonge. Land Board Certif. 10/1 Yonge

BRISCO, Isaac of Ernestown, m. Ruth Hawley (Archives Report 1904 p. 436)
  Anne, m. ---- Bell. O. C. 8 July 1797.
  Nathan of Ernestown, U. E.
  Norris of Ernestown, U. E.

BRISCO, Nathan of Ernestown, m. Mary dau Joseph Hoffman Sr. , U. E.
  Isaac Norris of Ernestown. O. C. 19 Sept 1839.
  Jane Maria, m. Nelson Shorey of Camden East. O. C. 28 Nov 1839.
  Mary Ann. O. C. 22 Sept 1836.
  Adam Jehiel of Fredericksburgh. O. C. 28 Oct 1833.
  Sarah Amanda, m. ---- Empey of Ernestown. O. C. 28 Oct 1833.
  Eve, m. ---- Empey of Ernestown. O. C. 28 Oct 1833.
  Hannah Maria, m. John Aylsworth of Ernestown; d. 12 Nov 1841 in 31st
      year. O. C. 4 Sept 1834.

BRISCO, Norris of Ernestown, m. Elizabeth Aylesworth 19 Jan 1795.
  Ruth. O. C. 11 Feb 1836.
  Catharine Eliza. O. C. 3 April 1834.
  Sarah Ann. O. C. 3 April 1834.
  Benjamin of Ernestown. O. C. 3 April 1834.
  Esther, m. Peter Miller of Ernestown. O. C. 3 April 1834.   [Cont'd]

BRISCO, Norris - Cont'd
   Nathan A. of Ernestown. O.C. 3 April 1834.
   Isaac of Ernestown. O.C. 3 April 1834.

BROOKS, John of Sophiasburgh.
   Margaret. O.C. 21 Sept 1837.
   Nancy. O.C. 15 March 1838.
   Mary, m. Stephen Weeks of Hillier. O.C. 15 March 1838.
   Adam of Hillier. O.C. 18 July 1839.
   Laura L. O.C. 1 April 1840.
   Julia Ann. O.C. 8 September 1836.
   John of Hillier. O.C. 28 Feb 1835.
   James of Hamilton. O.C. 28 Feb 1835.

BROUSE, George of Matilda.
   Nicholas of Matilda. O.C. 27 June 1833.
   Jacob of Matilda. O.C. 1 Aug 1833.
   Margaret, m. ---- Shaver of Matilda. O.C. 1 Aug 1833.

BROUSE, Joseph of Matilda and Oxford.
   Martha, m. Charles Prosser of Mountain. O.C. 14 Nov 1839.
   Elijah of Oxford. O.C. 28 March 1833.
   Clarissa. O.C. 2 May 1833.
   Samuel of Oxford. O.C. 8 May 1833.
   Martha, m. Charles Prosser of Matilda. O.C. 18 May 1833.
   Fanny. O.C. 27 June 1833.
   George of Oxford. O.C. 18 July 1833.
   Rachel. O.C. 1 Aug 1833.
   Mary. O.C. 1 Aug 1833.
   Sophia. O.C. 3 Oct 1833.
   Nancy. O.C. 19 Dec 1833. South Gower.
   Elizabeth, m. John Adams of South Gower. O.C. 11 Jan 1834.

BROUSE, Peter of Matilda, m. Catherine, dau Michael Carman Sr., U.E.
  Peter Brouse died in 1809, and his widow m. (2) in 1815 John Van Camp of
  Matilda.
   George of Matilda. O.C. 25 Feb 1812.
   Peter of Matilda. O.C. 19 Apr 1816.
   Mary, m.(1) ---- Henderson. O.C. 14 May 1799. m. (2) Nicholas
     Shaver of Matilda. O.C. 19 Apr 1816.
   Betsy, m. ---- Burnside of Matilda; d. 13 May 1843. O.C. 3 Feb 1834.
   Michael of Matilda. O.C. 3 July 1834.
   Frederick of Matilda. O.C. 6 Dec 1832.
   William of Matilda. O.C. 1 July 1830.
   Catharine, m. Elijah Van Camp. O.C. 1 July 1830.
   Rachel. O.C. 2 Dec 1830.

BROWN, Abraham of Elizabethtown. O.C. 2 Jan 1811.
  Edward of Elizabethtown. O.C. 23 Sept 1800.
  Benjamin of Elizabethtown. O.C. 9 March 1803.
  Henry of Elizabethtown. O.C. 23 Feb 1809.

BROWN, Henry
  Sarah, m. Harris Outwater of Adolphustown. O.C. 3 Apr 1830.

BROWN, Hezekiah of Yonge.
  William B. of Kitley. O.C. 16 April 1818.
  Jonah. O.C. 6 Aug 1798.

BROWN, Jesse Sr.
  Dorothy, m. Heman Landon of Augusta. O.C. 22 July 1797.
  Phoebe, m. John Chester of Montague. O.C. 3 July 1798.

BROWN, John of Kingston.
  Susan, m. John Jenkins of Ernestown 3 March 1812. O.C. 9 March 1843.
  Margaret, m. George Storms of Ernestown. O.C. 9 March 1843.
  David of Ernestown. O.C. 9 March 1843.
  Henry of Ernestown. O.C. 9 March 1843.
  Samuel of Ernestown. O.C. 9 March 1843.
  Jane. O.C. 9 March 1843.
  Polly, m. William Tryan of Ernestown. O.C. 9 March 1843.

BROWN, John of Thorold, soldier, Butler's Rangers. See Archives Report
  1904, p.997. Not to be confused with John Brown of Thorold, soldier, 62nd
  & 60th Regts. [John of B.R. and his family were at Niagara in 1783. See
  The Ontario Register v.1, p. 203]
  Magdalene, m. Conrad Miller of Clinton 6 Jan 1802. O.C. 10 March 1804.
  Catharine, m. Aaron Dennis of Thorold. O.C. 10 March 1804.
  Christian of Pelham, m. Magdalene Bowman. O.C. 23 Nov 1816.
  Adam of Thorold. O.C. 30 June 1819.
  John of Thorold. O.C. 22 May 1820.
  Abraham of Thorold. O.C. 2 Oct 1829.
  Eve, m. John Bowman. O.C. 11 March 1797.
  Sophia, m. Zachariah Hainer of Grantham 19 March 1797. OC 12 May 1797

BROWN, Joseph of Niagara, m. Rebecca.
  Mary, m. Solomon Vrooman of Niagara 19 March 1807. O.C. 6 Dec 1808.
  John J. of Niagara. O.C. 20 May 1817.
  Henry of Niagara. O.C. 20 May 1817.
  Adam of Niagara, m. Mary Mattice. O.C. 25 Feb 1818.
  Joseph of Niagara. O.C. 25 Feb 1818.
  Andrew of Niagara, d. in August 1828 aged 27 (?). O.C. 2 Oct 1818.
  Catharine. O.C. 23 June 1824.

BROWN, Nathaniel of Elizabethtown
   James of Elizabethtown. O.C. 30 July 1799.
   Nathaniel of Elizabethtown. O.C. 25 Feb 1809.
   Nancy, m. Jonathan Fulford of Elizabethtown. O.C. 30 July 1799.
   Jean, m. Adoniram Young of Wolford. O.C. 17 June 1806.
   Mary, m. Edward McCrea of Montague. O.C. 16 June 1807.
   Hannah, m. Isaac Coon of Elizabethtown. O.C. 1 Sept 1812.
   Margaret, m. Stephen Merrick of Montague. O.C. 14 Nov 1818.
   Amy, m. Archibald Fletcher of Elizabethtown. O.C. 9 Nov 1837.
   Michael of Elizabethtown. O.C. 25 Aug 1838.
   Levi of Elizabethtown. O.C. 4 Jan 1840.
   Samuel of City of Toronto. O.C. 17 Sept 1840.
   Phoebe, b. 3 Feb 1797; m. Stephen Sheldon of Kitley; d. 12 Feb 1872.
      O.C. 1850 or 1851. m. (1) John Benedict of Bastard.

BROWN, Thomas of Augusta, m. Desire Hulbert.
   Thomas of Augusta. O.C. 31 Jan 1809.
   Deborah, m. Daniel Mixter of Edwardsburgh. O.C. 17 June 1806.
   Desire, b. 22 Dec 1796; m. Samuel Gray of Niagara. O.C. 19 June 1817.
   Heman of Augusta. O.C. 20 May 1817.
   Rebecca, m. Alexander Campbell of Augusta. O.C. 6 Sept 1820.
   Lyman of Augusta. O.C. 6 March 1821.

BROWN, William of Stamford
   Margaret, m. ---- Jennings of Stamford. O.C. 3 Nov 1836.
   Martha Elizabeth, m. ---- Leech of Stamford. O.C. 13 June 1836.

BROWNSON, Samuel Sr.
   Annah, m. Thomas Sherwood of Elizabethtown. O.C. 30 June 1797.

BROWNSON, Samuel Jr.
   Elizabeth, m. Oliver Arnold of Richmond. O.C. 8 July 1801.
   Samuel of Fredericksburgh. O.C. 23 Feb 1809.
   Peter of Thurlow. O.C. 3 July 1834.
   Thomas of Thurlow. O.C. 3 July 1834.

BRUCE, Alexander. His wife Margaret d. at Cornwall 21 July 1819 in her
   75th year.
   David.
   Margaret, m. Donald McAuley.
   Sarah, m. ---- Van Koughnet of Town of Cornwall. O.C. 5 Jan 1798.

BRUNDAGE, James of Grantham.
   Theophilus of Grantham. O.C. 11 June 1840.

BRUNDAGE, John of Yonge, soldier, Delancey's Corps of Refugees.
   Mary, m. ---- Boice. O.C. 18 June 1799.
   Elizabeth, m. William Purdy of Yonge. O.C. 18 June 1799.   [Cont'd]

BRUNDAGE, John - Cont'd
    Nancy, m. Peter Bice of Hope. O. C. 17 Feb 1816.
    Joseph of Augusta. O. C. 11 June 1821.
    Nehemiah of Augusta. O. C. 21 Sept 1837.
    Elizabeth, m. Peter Street of Wolford. O. C. 8 Dec 1826.

BRYAN, John of Cornwall.
    Mary, m. Richard Bristol of Cornwall. O. C. 16 Feb 1811.
    William. O. C. 30 June 1801.
    Catharine. O. C. 18 March 1808.
    Thomas of Town of Cornwall. O. C. 11 Nov 1815.
    William of Elizabethtown. O. C. 1 April 1830.

BUCHNER, John Sr.
    Margaret, m. Jacob Willson of Windham. O. C. 18 Nov 1806.
    Jacob of Woodhouse. Land Board Certificate. 3/1 Woodhouse.

BUCK, George of Kingston.
    Margaret, m. William Ashley of Town of Kingston 6 July 1788. O. C. 16
        June 1807.
    Mary, m. Samuel Smith of Kingston. O. C. 23 Feb 1808.
    George of Kingston, m. Hannah Snook.
    Hannah, m. Moses Smith of Kingston. O. C. 23 Feb 1808.
    Catharine, m. John Horning of Kingston. O. C. 23 Feb 1808.
    Eve, m. Daniel Howe of Kingston. O. C. 23 Feb 1808.
    Adam of Kingston, m. Rachel Emons. O. C. 16 Feb 1810.
    Frederick of Kingston, m. Dorothy Snook. O. C. 25 March 1809.
    Susannah, m. John Leoney of Kingston. O. C. 17 Nov 1797.

BUCK, George Jr. of Kingston, m. Hannah Snook. See 31/8 Darlington.
    Elizabeth, bapt. 1 Feb 1795; m. Oliver Lyons of Loughborough. O. C. 18
        Feb 1843.
    Susannah, m. Henry Christopher of Kingston. O. C. 19 Sept 1839.
    Catharine, m. David Hughston of Loughborough 31 July 1814. O. C. 18
        Feb 1843.
    Martin of Loughborough, bapt. 17 Dec 1809. O. C. 18 Feb 1843.
    George of Kingston. O. C. 18 Feb 1843.
    Philip of Kingston. O. C. 18 Feb 1843.

BUCK, George of Elizabethtown.
    Joseph of Lansdowne. O. C. 7 Aug 1834.
    Katherine, m. ---- Pattison. O. C. 31 May 1830.

BUCK, Mehitable of Augusta.
    Mary, m. Andrew Liddel of Elizabethtown. O. C. 8 Feb 1808.
    Samuel M. of Edwardsburgh. O. C. 13 June 1818.
    Asenath, m. John Baldwin of Matilda. O. C. 30 Oct 1822.

BUCK, Philip of Bertie. [He served in Butler's Rangers. He and his family were at Niagara in 1783. See The Ontario Register 1: 208]
Elizabeth, m. Charles Hibbard of Bertie. O.C. 15 May 1805.
George of Niagara. O.C. 25 June 1805.
Philip of Bertie. O.C. 25 June 1805.
William of Bertie. O.C. 12 July 1808.
Catharine, m. Morris Neagle of York. O.C. 24 Jan 1821.
Abraham of Trafalgar, tanner. O.C. 24 Jan 1821.
Peter of Ancaster. O.C. 6 Dec 1832.
Margaret, m. Silas Carter of Bertie. O.C. 4 Jan 1840.
Margaret, m. Joseph Walterhouse of Louth. O.C. 12 Nov 1827.
Rosanna, m. Augustus Anger of Bertie. O.C. 11 May 1825.

BUCKNER, Henry of Crowland, m. Joannah Ainsley, dau Ozias Ansley, Ensign, 1st Batt., N.J. Vols., of New Brunswick. O.C. 19 Feb 1807. [The Ansley's, or Ainsley's, were originally of Sussex County, N.J. as were the Buchner's, or Boughner's]
Martin of Willoughby. O.C. 23 May 1809.
John of Willoughby. O.C. 8 Sept 1801.
Catharine, m. John Pettit of Willoughby. O.C. 15 Apr 1806.
Elsie, m. Henry Buck of Crowland. O.C. 19 Aug 1806.
Margaret, m. Robert Stringer of Crowland. O.C. 19 Aug 1806.
Anna, m. Daniel Howey of Crowland. O.C. 19 Aug 1806.
Elizabeth, m. Abner Owen of Woodhouse. O.C. 25 June 1807.
Mary, m. Joseph Wilson Jr. of Windham. O.C. 26 Mar 1811, 20 May 1817.
Ozias of Crowland. OC. 14 Dec 1816.
Daniel of Crowland. O.C. 1 July 1818.

BUCKNER, Henry of Crowland.
Joana, m. John Byam of Crowland. O.C. 22 July 1818.
Frederick of Crowland. O.C. 17 Oct 1828.

BUCKNER, Mathias.
John of Willoughby, m. Rachel Smith. O.C. 30 Sept 1800.
Mathias of Willoughby, m. Sarah Misener; d. 1855 in 78th yr. O.C. 30 September 1800.
Anna. d. unmd. O.C. 23 June 1803.
Alexander of Windham, m. Gertrude Glover. O.C. 25 June 1807.
Martin of Windham, m. (1) Elizabeth Wade; d. 1861 in 77th yr. O.C. 7th April 1812.
Mary, m. Jacob Beam of Clinton. O.C. 29 Aug 1797.
Joseph of Malahide, m. Nancy Merritt. O.C. 8 May 1818.
Elsa, m. Noah Millard of Charlotteville. O.C. 12 May 1797.
Peter, m. Sarah Robbins.
Christine, m. Nathaniel White.

BUELL, Bemslee of Elizabethtown, m. Lois Sherwood.
Timothy of Elizabethtown. O.C. 2 March 1811. [Cont'd]

BUELL, Bemslee - Cont'd
   Annah, m. Guy Carlton Read of Augusta. O. C. 30 June 1812.
   William of Elizabethtown. O. C. 11 Nov 1815.
   Nancy, m. William Moore of Elizabethtown. O. C. 18 March 1818.
   Lois, m. James Murdock of Elizabethtown. O. C. 14 Nov 1818.
   Mercy, m. Richard Boulton of Augusta. O. C. 21 Feb 1821.
   James of Elizabethtown. O. C. 5 Sept 1833.
   Samuel P. of Elizabethtown, m. Elizabeth Bouck(?), 18 March 1824.
      O. C. 5 September 1833.
   Thomas Sherwood of Leeds, m. Julia Prevost, 23 Oct 1831. OC 2 Apr 1828.
   Caroline. O. C. 26 May 1843. Drummond.

BUELL, Jonathan.
   Samuel P. of Escott. O. C. 11 Apr 1851.
   Alexander A. of Escott. O. C. 11 Apr 1851.
   Rinaldo of Kitley. O. C. 11 April 1851.
   Sabina, m. ---- Maggs of Elizabethtown. O. C. 11 April 1851.
   Almira, m. ---- Rutledge of Bastard. O. C. 11 April 1851.
   Olive, m. ---- Rowland of Elizabethtown. OC 29 April 1851.

BUELL, William of Elizabethtown, born in Hebron, Conn., 5 Oct 1751 son
   of Timothy and Mercy (Peters) Buell. He m. 10 March 1782 at St. John's,
   L. C., Martha Naughton, dau of Andrew Naughton, U. E. She was born at
   Farmington, Conn., 27 Feb 1762 and died at Brockville 7 Dec 1823. He m.
   2ndly Margaret Barnard 31 March 1827. He d. at Brockville 8 Aug 1832. A
   sister of Wm Buell Sr., Sabina, m. Daniel Flynn of the Cedars, L. C.
   Sabina, d. unmd. at Brockville, 3 Nov 1859 in 73rd yr. O. C. 24 Apr 1810.
   Anna, m. Andrew (Andre) Prevost of Elizabethtown. O. C. 11 Dec 1806.
   Phoebe, m. Stephen Richards of Elizabethtown; d. 27 Feb 1858. O. C. 22
      September 1812.
   William of Elizabethtown, b. 28 Feb 1792. O. C. 12 June 1812.
   Andrew Norton of Elizabethtown, b. 20 Apr 1798; m. (1) Calcina Richards,
      6 March 1827; m. (2) Mrs. Ann Eliza Van Doren at Brooklyn, N. Y., 5
      Jan 1859; d. at Toronto, 9 Nov 1880. O. C. 8 June 1825.
   Joseph Peters of Elizabethtown, m. Eliza.   O. C. 15 May 1835.
   Martha Jane (Ann), m. Robert Findlay of Belleville. O. C. 2 Aug 1849.

BULL, Margaret, wife of Aaron Bull, Loyal Rangers.
   Margery, m. John Rowshorn of Kingston. O. C. 26 Jan 1808.

BUNKER, Bethuel of Augusta, m. Anna Dicher.
   Margaret, m. David Carter of Augusta. O. C. 31 May 1803.
   Gideon, bapt. 27 May 1793.
   Jane, bapt. 27 May 1793.
   Rachel, bapt. 27 May 1793.

BUNKER, John of Augusta
   Drusilla, m. John McNeil of Augusta. O. C. 23 Feb 1809.

BUNKER, John - Cont'd
Rosannah, m. Thomas Taylor of Niagara. O.C. 23 Nov 1837.
Ezekiel of Niagara. O.C. 27 July 1837.
Elizabeth, m. Andrew Perrin of Augusta. O.C. 5 Apr 1832.
John of Augusta. O.C. 6 Aug 1828.

BURCH, John, m. Martha who died 28 Nov 1823 aged 77 years. He died 7
March 1797 in his 55th year.
John of Stamford, m. Eleanor Bender; d. 15 August 1822, aged 38 years
5 mos. O.C. 19 Aug 1806.

BURGESS, Dennis.
Polly, m. William Titus of Bastard. O.C. 29 Oct 1800.
Betsy, m. ---- Huntley of Bastard. O.C. 1 Sept 1801.
Josiah Dennis of Bastard. O.C. 1 Sept 1801.
Noah of Bastard. O.C. 29 Oct 1800.

BURK, John of Edwardsburgh.
Peter of Edwardsburgh. O.C. 18 Feb 1816.
Elizabeth, m. John Peoples of Edwardsburgh. O.C. 29 April 1835.

BURLEY, Freeman of Ernestown.
Cornelius of Ernestown. O.C. 12 Nov 1811.
Elizabeth, m. Peter Kane of Ernestown 28 May 1811. O.C. 12 Nov 1811.
Jemima, m. Jonas Kemble of Ernestown. O.C. 13 Nov 1818.
Henry of Ernestown. O.C. 25 Feb 1819.
David of Ernestown. O.C. 1 April 1840.
Jane, m. David Baldwin of Ernestown. O.C. 29 June 1837.
Hannah, m. --- Knox of Hallowell. O.C. 1 May 1834.
Deborah. O.C. 30 May 1834.
Lydia, m. Anthony Lapp of Hamilton. O.C. 29 Sept 1824.
Jane, m. ---- Steel of Haldimand. O.C. 22 July 1824.

BURLEY, John of Ernestown.
Ira of Ernestown. O.C. 31 May 1838.
Arthur of Thurlow. O.C. 14 June 1838.
Freeman J. of Ernestown. O.C. 17 Jan 1839.
Cyrus of Portland. O.C. 18 July 1839.
Sylvester of Ernestown. O.C. 7 Nov 1839.
Ezekiel of Clarke. O.C. 28 Nov 1839.
Joseph of Clarke. O.C. 4 Jan 1840.
Lydia Jane, m. ---- Devel of Clarke. O.C. 4 Jan 1840.
Dorcas, m. ---- Hicks of Clarke. O.C. 4 Jan 1840.

BURNETT, John of Pittsburgh, Kingston, m. Elizabeth dau Matthew Van
Order, U.E.
Margaret, m. William Baker of Pittsburgh. O.C. 26 March 1817.
Mathew of Kingston, bapt. 9 March 1794. O.C. 28 July 1819.   [Cont'd]

BURNETT, John – Cont'd
  Catharine, bapt. 31 Dec 1797; m. John Howey of Kingston. OC 18 Mar 1818.
  Hannah, bapt. 11 Oct 1795; m. Daniel Ansley of Kingston. OC 16 May 1818.
  Elizabeth, bapt. 7 Feb 1802; m. John Ashley of Kingston. O. C. 26 July
      1820.
  Mary, bapt. 5 Feb 1804. O. C. 20 July 1825.
  Martha, bapt. 5 Feb 1804. O. C. 20 July 1825.
  John Nelson of Kingston, bapt. 20 March 1808. OC. 5 Sept 1833.
  William Collingwood of Kingston. O. C. 5 Sept 1833.
  Thomas of Kingston. O. C. 8 June 1825.

BURNETT, Thomas of Kingston, m. Margaret; died 20 Feb 1813 aged 84.
  Catherine, m. Harvey Rood of Kingston; d. at Kingston, 1857, in 98th
      year. O. C. 11 Feb 1806.
  Mary, m. George Krun of Kingston Town. O. C. 11 Feb 1806.
  John of Kingston, U. E., m. Elizabeth Van Order.
  Matthew, drowned 1792. See O. C. 21 July 1807.

BURRITT, Adoniram of Augusta, m. Sally.
  Tamer. O. C. 28 Sept 1820.
  Melissa, m. Wellington Landon of Yonge 30 Sept 1835. OC 26 Mar 1836.
  William of Augusta. O. C. 5 Sept 1833.
  Almira, m. Elisha Bottum of Augusta. O. C. 5 Sept 1833.
  Sally, m. James Howard of Augusta 13 October 1824; d. 23 July 1846.
      O. C. 19 December 1833.
  Eliza, m. Charles Lemon of Augusta. O. C. 4 Oct 1826, 15 May 1832.
  Charles of Augusta, m. Martha Dulmage. O. C. 3 Nov 1831.
  Read of Augusta. O. C. 24 Dec 1831.

BURRITT, Daniel of Augusta.
  Urania, m. ---- Phillips of Augusta. O. C. 30 Sept 1800.
  Nancy, m. Thomas McIlmoyle of Edwardsburgh. O. C. 3 March 1809.
  Tamer, m. David Wright of Cornwall. O. C. 17 May 1799.
  Lois, m. Jehiel Hurd of Augusta. O. C. 16 Feb 1837.

BURRITT, Stephen of Marlborough.
  Henry of Marlborough, b. 26 Aug 1791. O. C. 11 Nov 1815.
  Edmund of Marlborough, b. 8 Dec 1793; d. Thornbury, Grey Co., 28 Apr
      1880 aged 86 yrs 5 mos. O. C. 11 Nov 1815.
  Sally, b. 20 Feb 1801. O. C. 5 April 1832.
  Stephen of Marlborough, b. 5 Nov 1805. O. C. 17 Nov 1830.
  William Augustus of Marlborough, b. 18 May 1803. O. C. 8 Dec 1826.
  Hamilton, b. 29 June 1809.

BURTCH, Charles of Burford.
  Charles of Burford. O. C. 8 Dec 1801.
  Mary, m. Henry Gates of Burford. O. C. 26 Jan 1802.
  Martha, m. John Baker of Burford. O. C. 16 Jan 1816.   [Cont'd]

BURTCH, Charles - Cont'd
   Masa, m. Daniel Millard of Burford. O.C. 15 Nov 1820.
   Sarah, m. ---- Green. O.C. 11 May 1797.
   Morilla, m. ---- Matthews of Aldborough. O.C. 28 March 1797.
   Jane, m. (1) Moses Mount; m. (2) Swain Passel Corlis of Burford. O.C.
      26 January 1802.

BURTCH, Edse of Mount Pleasant.
   Olive, m. Stratton Rowell of Mount Pleasant. O.C. 17 May 1820.
   Absalom of Grand River. O.C. 6 March 1822.
   David of Brantford. O.C. 25 Oct 1828.

BURTCH, Nathan of Blenheim, b. 1752, N.Y. State; m. Lucy dau Thomas
   and Elizabeth (DeCost) Hinckley of Plymouth, Mass.; d. 13 October 1829
   aged 77 years.
   Ann, m. Stephen Chase of Haldimand Co. O.C. 13 Feb 1806.
   Nathan of Blenheim. O.C. 13 Feb 1806.
   Polly, m. Silas Dean of Blenheim. O.C. 24 Feb 1807.
   Abigail, m. Murdock McAuley of Haldimand Co. O.C. 2 March 1807.
   Margaret. O.C. 16 Jan 1816.
   Charlotte, m. John Doyle of Blenheim. O.C. 16 Jan 1816.
   Archibald of Blenheim. O.C. 16 Jan 1816.
   Ethan of Blenheim. O.C. 18 June 1817.
   Calvin of Westminster, m. Elizabeth Schram; d. 1865 ae 65. OC. 7th
      February 1821.

BURWELL, James of Bertie and Talbot Road, b. at Rockaway, N.J., on
   18 January 1754; came to U.C. 1796; died at Southwold, 18 June 1853 ae
   99 years, 5 mos.
   John of Southwold. O.C. 7 Jan 1824.
   Robert of Southwold. O.C. 8 June 1825.
   Samuel of Southwold. O.C. 5 April 1831. O.C. 8 March 1831.
   Lewis of Southwold. O.C. 4 September 1834.
   Susannah. O.C. 4 Sept 1834.
   Anne, m. Stewart Bissell of Southwold. O.C. 4 Sept 1834.
   Mary, m. Charles Benedict of Southwold. O.C. 4 Sept 1834.
   Adam of Southwold. O.C. 28 Feb 1833.
   William of Southwold. O.C. 28 Feb 1833.
   James of Southwold. O.C. 3 March 1831.

BUSH, Henry of Ernestown and Osnabruck.
   Mary Ann m. James Wilson of Richmond. O.C. 16 Feb 1837.
   Margaret, m. Jesse Prosser of Osnabruck. O.C. 28 Oct 1835.
   Divina, m. Barney Tinkes of Osnabruck. O.C. 28 Oct 1835.
   John of Osnabruck. OC. 3 Dec 1835.
   Simon of Osnabruck. O.C. 3 Dec 1835.
   Philip of Osnabruck. O.C. 11 Feb 1836.
   William of Camden East. O.C. 18 July 1834.   [Cont'd]

BUSH, Henry - Cont'd
    Garret of Ernestown. O.C. 18 July 1834.
    Christopher of Ernestown. O.C. 18 July 1834.
    Julia Ann, m. Benjamin Clark of Ernestown. O.C. 18 July 1834.

BUTLER, Andrew of Niagara, m. Ann who died 21 May 1804.
    Joseph Walter of Niagara, bapt. 24 Dec 1797. O.C. 30 June 1819.
    Margaret Thompson, bapt. 17 Aug 1800; m. Mathew Crooks of Ancaster.
        O.C. 24 January 1821.
    Thomas of Ancaster, bapt. 27 May 1804. O.C. 8 Nov 1831.
    Catelina, bapt. 11 Feb 1794; buried 9 July 1809.
    John Andrew, bapt. 31 Dec 1802; buried 2 Jan 1803.

BUTLER, James of Elizabethtown.
    Roby, m. Sheldon Warren. O.C. 11 Aug 1836.
    Ira of Augusta. O.C. 16 June 1834.
    Dorcas, m. Amasa Harrington of Augusta. O.C. 16 June 1834.
    Phoebe, m. Elijah Rockwood of Bastard. O.C. 7 Aug 1834.

BUTLER, Johnson of Niagara, m. Eve, who was buried 6 Nov 1800; m. (2)
    Susan Hatt, 15 July 1802; he was buried 14 Dec 1812. O.C. 28 June 1832.
    Helen Eliza, bapt. 13 July 1806; m. Robert Berrie of Hamilton.
    Mary, m. Edward Haycock of Oxford West.
    Richard Hatt, bapt. 11 Sept 1808; buried 30 Sept 1809.
    Christopher Yates, bapt. 11 Nov 1798.

BUTLER, Col. John of Niagara, b. in New London, Conn.; bapt. 28 April
    1728; he was buried 15 May 1796. He m. Catherine, who d. 29 May 1793
    and was buried 31 May 1793, aged 58 years. [An article in The American
    Genealogist, v.36 (1960) pp. 201-203, indicates that Catherine was a dau
    of Capt.Andries Bratt by his first wife Ariaantje, dau of Johannes Wemple]
    Johnson of Niagara, Lt.Col. 4th Lincoln, died December 1812.
    Thomas of Niagara, U.E., d. in December 1812.
    Andrew of Niagara, U.E.
    Deborah, m. James Muirhead of Niagara, 19 May 1795.

BUTLER, Thomas of Niagara, m. Ann. He was buried 17 Dec 1812.
    Catherine, m. Alexander Cameron 16 Dec 1811. O.C. 11 Apr 1809.
    Thomas of Niagara, m. Ann Ten Broeck 4 Nov 1804. O.C. 13 Aug 1799.
    Mary, m. William Crooks of Grimsby 1 Dec 1808. O.C. 11 Apr 1809.
    Deborah, bapt. 16 July 1792. O.C. 16 July 1816.
    Walter of Niagara. O.C. 30 June 1819.
    James of Niagara. O.C. 10 July 1822.
    Andrew of Niagara, bapt. 2 March 1802. O.C. 5 Feb 1823.
    William of Grantham, bapt. 1 December 1808. O.C. 7 August 1834. Ni-
        agara. O.C. 2 Sept 1830.
    Johnson of Grimsby, bapt. 24 June 1804. O.C. 6 Sept 1826.
    John, buried 9 January 1794.

BUTLER, Truelove of Elizabethtown, m. Mary McEachron.
Jenny, m. ---- Manhart. OC 30 July 1799.
Anna, m. John Wilson. OC 8 Nov 1797.
Mary, m. Linus Field of Elizabethtown. Land Board Certif. 18/4 Yonge.
Truelove of Elizabethtown. OC 25 Feb 1818. OC 6 March 1821.
Margaret.
Jemima.

BYCROFT, Benjamin, or Bigcraft, was born about 1762 in New York Prov-
ince, a farmer; settled on Lot 11 Con 2 of Ancaster; married Elizabeth
Westbrook, sister of Andrew Westbrook; d. prior to 1801. OC 24 Feb 1801.
Anne, m. Benjamin Hunt of Ancaster. OC 23 Nov 1816.
James of Grand River. OC 23 Nov 1816.
Sarah. OC 25 Feb 1819.
Anthony of Fairchild's Creek. OC 2 Oct 1822.

CADMAN, John Jr. of Osnabruck, son of John Cadman Sr., U.E. Married
Mary, who m.(2) Jacob Eaman.
Mary, m. Cornelius Bodine of Osnabruck. O.C. 30 June 1812.
Elizabeth, m. Leonard Stoneburner of Osnabruck. O.C. 15 Dec 1818.
George of Osnabruck. O.C. 11 July 1833.
Margaret, m. James O'Connor of Osnabruck. O.C. 9 July 1827, 28 Feb
1833.
Catharine, m. James Conner of Town of Niagara. O.C. 7 Aug 1834.

CADMAN, John Sr. of Osnabruck.
John of Osnabruck, U.E.
Peggy, m. John Reddick of Osnabruck. O.C. 5 Jan 1798.

CADMAN, William of Fredericksburgh. Pvt., 2nd Batt., K.R.R.N.Y.
Asa of Fredericksburgh. O.C. 8 July 1797.
Deborah, m. James Hogle of Ernestown. O.C. 8 July 1797.
Elizabeth, m. George Miller of Ernestown. O.C. 8 July 1797.
Joshua of Fredericksburgh. O.C. 8 July 1797
Sylvia, m. John Green of Marysburgh. O.C. 8 July 1797.
William of Fredericksburgh. O.C. 10 March 1834.
Alpheus of Fredericksburgh, m. Sarah Taylor 4 Oct 1802. Land Board
Certificate. 28/6 Sidney.
Anna, m. Robert Sills of Fredericksburgh. O.C. 2 Sept 1830.
Amy, m. Sebastian Hogle of Fredericksburgh, 14 Dec 1789. Land Board
Certificate. 29/6 Sidney.

CAFFREY, John
Mary, m. ---- De Grote of Charlottenburgh. O.C. 11 July 1799.

CAIN, John of Niagara.
Margaret, d. unmd. O.C. 8 Sept 1819.
Peter of Niagara. O.C. 22 May 1820.   [Cont'd]

CAIN, John - Cont'd
  Catherine, m. William Garner of Thorold. O.C. 31 May 1820.
  John of Niagara. O.C. 12 Dec 1826.
  George of Niagara. O.C. 2 July 1829.

CAIN, John of Charlottenburgh. m. Elizabeth Prentice.
  Barnabas of Cornwall. O.C. 14 June 1811.
  Lenah, m. George Crites of Cornwall. O.C. 17 Feb 1816.
  Daniel of Charlottenburgh. O.C. 23 Nov 1816.
  Stephen of Charlottenburgh, bapt. 4 Jan 1795. O.C. 26 March 1817.
  Eleanor, m. ---- Barry. O.C. 28 July 1819.
  Mary, m. William Hall of Charlottenburgh. O.C. 18 Jan 1834.

CAIN, Josiah of Yonge.
  Barnabas. O.C. 1 July 1799.
  David of Yonge. O.C. 13 June 1818.
  Rebecca, m. Elijah Lines of Yonge; d. July 1825. O.C. 14 Nov 1821.
  Mary, m. John Hogeboom of Yonge. O.C. 5 Nov 1835.
  Rebecca, m. (1) John Wood of Yonge. O.C. Wm Wood, 1848.

CALDER, William. He was born in Scotland, came to America in 1773 and
  died in spring of 1782. Married Janet.
  John. O.C. 10 March 1801.

CALDWELL, John of Charlottenburgh and Ernestown, m. Julianna Miller on
  11 March 1788.
  Elizabeth, m. James Caverly of Sidney. O.C. 4 Jan 1840.
  Catharine, m. Jacob Hartman Sr. of Ernestown. O.C. 18 Feb 1836.
  William of Sidney, m. Mishel Boyce. O.C. 27 Nov 1834.
  Dorothy, m. Edward Lloyd of Thurlow. O.C. 28 Feb 1835.
  Joseph of Thurlow. O.C. 28 March 1835.
  George of Sidney. O.C. 28 March 1835.
  Jacob of Thurlow. O.C. 28 March 1835.

CALDWELL, William of Malden.
  Thomas of Malden. O.C. 7 April 1812.
  Susanne. O.C. 7 April 1812.
  William of Malden. O.C. 6 Nov 1834, 8 Sept 1836.
  Theresa. O.C. 26 Jan 1837.
  Francis of Malden. O.C. 10 March 1834.
  Elizabeth, m. James Kevill of Amherstburgh. O.C. 9 Feb 1832.
  John. O.C. 2 Feb 1832.

CAMERON, Alexander. Lot 25/Front, Lancaster.
  Isabella, m. William McIntosh of Charlottenburgh. O.C. 9 March 1803.
  Marjory, m. Ralph Westley of Lancaster. O.C. 16 Feb 1811. m. (2)
      Philip (or Finlay) Munro of Charlottenburgh, 29 March 1814.
  James of Lancaster. O.C. 20 November 1809. (?)

CAMERON, Alexander Jr., of 6/4, E half, Cornwall.
    John of Cornwall. O.C. 4 July 1815.
    Mary. O.C. 4 July 1815.
    Janet, m. David Ramage of Cornwall. O.C. 16 June 1819.
    Robert of Cornwall. O.C. 28 July 1819.

CAMERON, Alexander of Cornwall and Nissouri.
    Sophia, m. William Withers of Nissouri. O.C. 21 Feb 1832.
    Allan of Burford. O.C. 21 Feb 1832.

CAMERON, Alexander. /4 Cornwall.
    Alexander of Cornwall. O.C. 22 Sept 1812. O.C. 16 July 1816.
    Sarah. O.C. 23 June 1819.

CAMERON, Allan of Cornwall.
    Ann, m. John Cumming of Cornwall. O.C. 11 Nov 1815.
    Mary. O.C. 13 Feb 1816.
    Janet, m. George Gallinger Jr., of Cornwall. O.C. 15 Dec 1821.
    Alexander of South Gower. O.C. 19 March 1840.
    Susannah, m. William Cumming of South Gower. O.C. 19 March 1840.
    Harriet, m. Christjohn Selumser of Osnabruck. O.C. 20 Oct 1832.
    Allan of Cornwall. O.C. 14 Nov 1831.
    Hugh of Cornwall. O.C. 19 Jan 1825.

CAMERON, Archibald, of E. half 50/1 Charlottenburgh.
    Angus of Charlottenburgh. O.C. 11 Nov 1815.
    Eleanor, m. John McNaughton of Lancaster. O.C. 6 Aug 1816.
    William of Charlottenburgh. O.C. 20 May 1817.
    John of Charlottenburgh. O.C. 28 July 1819.
    Archibald of Charlottenburgh. O.C. 12 Nov 1840.
    Duncan of Charlottenburgh. O.C. 27 June 1833.
    Elizabeth. O.C. 12 June 1834.
    Allan of Charlottenburgh. O.C. 12 June 1834.
    Ann. O.C. 12 June 1834.
    Alexander of Charlottenburgh. O.C. 26 Nov 1831.

CAMERON, Daniel of 6/1 Roxborough.
    John of Roxborough. O.C. 15 Dec 1821.

CAMERON, Donald, sometimes called Daniel, of Lot 16, south side River
aux Raisins, Cornwall. Middle Branch.
    Marjory, m. John McLeod of Roxborough. O.C. 26 March 1817.
    Donald of Roxborough. O.C. 26 March 1817.
    Charles of Roxboroguh. O.C. 20 May 1817.
    William of Roxborough. O.C. 20 May 1817.
    Ann, m. John McMillan of Finch. O.C. 3 June 1817.
    Angus of Cornwall. O.C. 9 Dec 1815.

CAMERON, Duncan of Edwardsburgh, m. Mary dau Wm Grant; b. ca. 1766.
Elizabeth, bapt. 12 Feb 1789; m. Robert Thompson of Edwardsburgh.
  O. C. 13 Oct 1807.
Margaret, bapt. 7 March 1792; m. John Parker of Elizabethtown. O. C.
  15 October 1819.
Mary, bapt. 2 June 1796. O. C. 26 July 1820. dau Daniel?
Duncan, bapt. 2 June 1796.
Catharine, m. William Landon of Augusta. O. C. 17 Sept 1823.
Isabella. O. C. 8 Nov 1832.
William of Edwardsburgh. O. C. 20 Oct 1832.
John of Edwardsburgh. O. C. 20 Oct 1832.
Penelope, m. John Saunders of Vaughan. O. C. 1 March 1832.

CAMERON, Hugh of Charlottenburgh and Cornwall. Soldier, K. R. R. N. Y.
Elizabeth, m. Alexander Murchison of Charlottenburgh. O. C. 8 Sept 1819
Archibald of Lancaster. O. C. 8 March 1820.
Minnie, m. George Glasford of Augusta. Cornwall. O. C. 28 July 1836.
Mary, m. John Scott Jr. of Augusta. Cornwall. O. C. 28 July 1836.
Maria, Charlottenburgh. O. C. 29 Sept 1836.
Donald of Wolfe Island. O. C. 12 June 1832.
Alexander of Charlottenburgh. O. C. 22 May 1832.
Elizabeth. Charlottenburgh. O. C. 22 May 1832.
John of Charlottenburgh. O. C. 6 Feb 1828.
Samuel of Charlottenburgh. O. C. 6 Feb 1828.

CAMERON, John. East half 30/1 Lancaster.
Elizabeth. O. C. 9 March 1803.
Ann. O. C. 28 April 1815.
Daniel of Lancaster. O. C. 20 Nov 1809.

CAMERON, John of Kingston. Son of Ensign Duncan Cameron, K. R. R. N. Y. ?
Abraham of Kingston. O. C. 3 July 1834.
Nancy, m. Russell Howard of Kingston. O. C. 15 May 1832.

CAMERON, John of West half 17/1 Charlottenburgh.
Alexander of Charlottenburgh. O. C. 25 Feb 1818.

CAMERON, John. Lot 23/1, south side River aux Raisins.
Peter of Charlottenburgh. O. C. 9 July 1802.

CAMERON, John of Charlottenburgh.
John of Lancaster, b. 1766. Land Board Certif. 32/5 Lancaster.
Christie, m. Donald Cameron of Lancaster. L. B. Certif. 35/9 Lochiel.
Donald of Charlottenburgh. O. C. 17 March 1804.

CAMERON, John
Peggy, m. Alexander McLeod of Lancaster. O. C. 5 Jan 1798.

CAMERON, John, West half 6/4 Cornwall.
  John of Cornwall. O.C. 9 July 1802.
  Susannah, m. John Cameron of Cornwall. O.C. 17 March 1804.
  Janet, m. Alexander McDonell of Cornwall. O.C. 12 Dec 1821.
  Allan of Cornwall. O.C. 10 May 1803.

CAMERON, William of Charlottenburgh. K.R.R.N.Y.
  Mary. O.C. 3 March 1801.
  Daniel of Charlottenburgh. Land Board Certif. 18/8 Lancaster.
  Katherine, m. ---- McDonell. Land Board Certif. 33/9 Lochiel.

CAMPBELL, Alexander of Edwardsburgh, New Johnstown.
  Margaret, m. Isaac(?) Russell of New Johnstown. O.C. 23 Dec 1800.
  Alexander of New Johnstown. O.C. 23 Dec 1800. OC. 20 May 1817?
  James Ellice of New Johnstown, Montreal. O.C. 23 Dec 1800.
  Anne, m. Jonathan Scott of Augusta. O.C. 27 Feb 1806.

CAMPBELL, Alexander of Adolphustown.
  Ann, m. Thomas Radenhurst of Montreal in Aug. 1786. O.C. 27 Aug 1829.
  Archibald of Adolphustown, U.E.
  Mary, m. Thomas Ridout of Town of York.
  Jennet, m. ---- Miller of Hallowell. Lots 14 & 15, Con 10, Cramahe.

CAMPBELL, Alexander of Augusta. Lt., Loyal Rangers, m. Abigail Brown.
See Heir and Devisee Commission, July 1841.
  Duncan of Augusta, bapt. 11 March 1792; m. Lucy Bottum. O.C. 30 June
    1812. O.C. 5 November 1835.
  Archibald of Augusta, bapt. 11 March 1792. O.C. 30 June 1812.
  Rebecca, bapt. 11 March 1792.
  John, bapt. 26 May 1793.
  Anna, bapt. 6 June 1796; m. Joseph K. Hartwell of Bastard, 18 Nov 1818.
  Alexander, b. 22 May 1798.
  Abigail, m. Lewis Dunham of Elizabethtown 11 Nov 1818. OC. 31 Mar 1824.
  Daniel B. of Augusta. Not. Rec. 5 March 1840.

CAMPBELL, Allan of Edwardsburgh and Lancaster, m. Magdalen Chenay.
  John of Cornwall, bapt. 15 Aug 1789. O.C. 19 Apr 1816.
  James of Cornwall. O.C. 20 May 1817.

CAMPBELL, Archibald of Adolphustown.
  Phoebe. O.C. 21 Jan 1824.
  Sarah, b. 14 Aug 1800; m. Henry Davis Jr. of Adolphustown, 1820; died
    1873(?). O.C. 21 Jan 1824.
  Archibald of Adolphustown. O.C. 7 Oct 1826. O.C. 11 Feb 1836.
  Eleanor. OC. 2 Oct 1834.
  John of Adolphustown. O.C. 2 Oct 1834.
  Catharine. O.C. 6 Sept 1832.
  Lanor (dau.) OC 6 Sept 1832.   [Cont'd]

CAMPBELL, Archibald - Cont'd
  Alexander of Adolphustown. O.C. 8 June 1825.

CAMPBELL, Daniel of Cornwall, merchant.
  Eleanor, m. Hector Manson of Cornwall. O.C. 28 Nov 1809.

CAMPBELL, Daniel. Capt., Stormont Militia.
  Margaret. O.C. 2 Jan 1829.
  Elizabeth, m. James Millroy of Cornwall. O.C. 2 Jan 1829.

CAMPBELL, Daniel of Cornwall. Sgt., R.R.N.Y.
  William of Cornwall. O.C. 4 July 1815.

CAMPBELL, Daniel
  Isabella, m. ---- McLaughlin of Cornwall. O.C. 21 Sept 1800.

CAMPBELL, Daniel Jr., of Charlottenburgh, m. Isabel McKay.
  Arthur of Charlottenburgh, bapt. 12 June 1791. O.C. 26 March 1811.
  Donald of Charlottenburgh. O.C. 16 July 1816.
  William of Charlottenburgh, bapt. 15 May 1791. O.C. 23 Nov 1816.
  Lawrence of Charlottenburgh. O.C. 10 Dec 1823.

CAMPBELL, Elizabeth of Lancaster, widow of Moses Campbell, who died
  1781. She m.(2) John Finlayson, bookbinder, formerly Sgt., 1st Batt.,
  84th Regt., on 6 September 1783.
  James of Lancaster. O.C. 17 Aug 1808.
  Elizabeth, m. William Bland of Lancaster. O.C. 17 Aug 1808.
  Allan of Lancaster. O.C. 30 June 1798. See O.C. 5 Feb 1810.
  Alexander of Lancaster, m. Mary Crone.
  Anne, m. Walter Sutherland of Lancaster.
  Catherine.
  Isabel.
  John.

CAMPBELL, George of Niagara.
  Rebecca, m. Silas Thomas of Niagara. O.C. 9 Oct 1810.
  Nelly, m. Nathaniel McCormick of Niagara. O.C. 9 Oct 1810.
  John of Ancaster. O.C. 23 Nov 1816.
  Mary, m. ---- Lyons of Ogdensburg, N.Y. O.C. 22 July 1836.

CAMPBELL, James of Augusta. Ensign, Loyal Rangers. Son of Duncan
  Campbell, 7 & West half 8/4 Oxford. Married (1) Elizabeth Clark. m.(2)
  Phoebe, dau John Booth, U.E.
  Catharine, b. 7 June 1798.
  James of Augusta, bapt. 6 June 1796. O.C. 6 Aug 1829.
  Elizabeth, bapt. 27 May 1793.
  Anna, bapt. 11 March 1792. O.C. 23 June 1801.
  Thomas Duncan of Augusta, bapt. 11 Mar 1792. O.C. 19 Mar 1804. [Cont'd]

CAMPBELL, James - Cont'd
   Maria, m. James L. Schofield of Elmsley 23 Oct 1833. O. C. 22 Oct 1840.
   Phoebe, m. John McDonell of Matilda. O. C. 9 March 1843.

CAMPBELL, James of Osnabruck.
   Catharine, m. Allan Barber of Osnabruck. O. C. 26 Feb 1806.
   Eleanor, m. Daniel Rickerson of Osnabruck. O. C. 26 Feb 1806.
   Abby, m. Godfrey Myers of Osnabruck. O. C. 25 Feb 1806.
   Margaret, m. John Ruport of Osnabruck. O. C. 17 March 1807.

CAMPBELL, Robert of Grantham. Sgt. Major, Butler's Rangers, m. Mary
   dau Frederick Smith, U. E. He died prior to 1831. Most of this family
   later lived in Chinguacousy.
   James of Gainsborough. O. C. 30 July 1806.
   Deborah, m. Daniel Reilly of Stamford. O. C. 17 June 1806.
   Margaret, m. Joel Smith of Thorold. O. C. 19 July 1806.
   Mary, m. Peter McCollum of Grimsby. O. C. 7 Nov 1809.
   Martha, m. William McCoy of Nelson. O. C. 13 Feb 1816.
   Peter Smith of Grantham. O. C. 13 Feb 1816.
   Alexander of Grantham, m. Rachel McCollum. O. C. 10 March 1819.
   John of Grantham. O. C. 5 May 1819.
   Robert of Grantham, m. Elizabeth Rowe. O. C. 5 May 1819.
   Henry of Chinguacousy. O. C. 24 Nov 1832.
   Francis (son) of Grantham. OC 5 May 1819.
CAMPBELL, William of Adolphustown.
   Archibald of Kingston. O. C. 28 Oct 1835.

CAMPBELL, William.
   Margaret, m. ---- Patterson of Cornwall. O. C. 23 Sept 1800.

CANNIFF, James of Adolphustown.
   Jonas of Adolphustown; m. Letty Flagler, 1 June 1813; d. 15 Jan 1882 ae
      92. O. C. 16 Feb 1811.
   John of Thurlow. O. C. 20 May 1817.
   Mary, m. Rykerson R. Haight of Fredericksburgh. O. C. 6 Feb 1823.
   Sarah, m. Thomas Casey of Marysburgh. O. C. 19 Feb 1823.
   Margaret, m. John Singleton of Murray, 3 Feb 1810. O. C. 23 July 1823.
   Allida, m. ---- Clapp of Adolphustown. O. C. 7 Oct 1830, 9 March 1837.
   Cleo. O. C. 7 Feb 1833.
   Elizabeth, m. ---- Hawley of Adolphustown. O. C. 7 Feb 1833.
   Nancy, m. Cornelius Van Horn of Hillier. O. C. 22 June 1825.

CANNIFF, John of Thurlow, b. 23 Jan 1757; d. 22 Feb 1843.
   Mary, m. Samuel Miller of Adolphustown. O. C. 7 Apr 1807.
   Alley, m. Joseph Rattan of Adolphustown. O. C. 26 Jan 1808.
   Elizabeth, m. Peter Carley of Sidney. O. C. 26 March 1811.
   Phoebe, b. 7 Jan 1797; m. Shubel Foster of Sidney 19 May 1812; died at
      Belleville 9 Feb 1877. O. C. 20 May 1817.   [Cont'd]

CANNIFF, John - Cont'd
    Joseph of Thurlow. O.C. 13 June 1821.
    David (Daniel ?) of Thurlow. O.C. 5 Feb 1823.

CANNON, John of Kingston, m. Sarah.
    James of Kingston, m. Sarah. O.C. 25 Nov 1802.
    Martha, m. Daniel Walker Jr. of Ernestown. O.C. 17 Feb 1807.
    John of Kingston. O.C. 20 Sept 1810.
    Sarah, m. George Barns of Kingston. O.C. 29 Aug 1797.
    David of Kingston. O.C. 16 Feb 1811.
    Abraham of Kingston, bapt. 8 Sept 1793. O.C. 14 Nov 1818.
    Mary, m. Daniel Williams of Kingston. O.C. 7 May 1828.

CAREY, Bernard of York. O.C. 14 Feb 1798. O.C. 19 Dec 1806. Lot 5 on
the west side of Yonge Street.
    Margaret, m. Jonathan Hale of York 7 April 1803. O.C. 28 Apr 1807.
    Thomas Benjamin of York. O.C. 6 Jan 1816.
    George of York. O.C. 1 Sept 1801. O.C. 24 Nov 1807.

CARL, John of Thorold and Pelham.
    Sarah. O.C. 20 May 1817.
    James of Thorold. O.C. 20 May 1817.
    John of Thorold. O.C. 20 May 1817.
    Jacob of Thorold. O.C. 20 May 1817.
    Philip of Crowland. O.C. 1 May 1834.
    Elizabeth. O.C. 1 May 1834.
    Mary. O.C. 1 May 1834.

CARLEY, Abraham of Elizabethtown, m. Miriam Stockwell.
    Miriam, bapt. 26 May 1793; m. Dougald McLean of Murray. OC 26 Jan 1808
    Joseph, bapt. 26 May 1793.
    Mary Ann Elizabeth, m. Daniel D. Coon of Alnwick. O.C. 3 Feb 1834.

CARLEY, Bartholomew of Elizabethtown, b. Nobletown (or Hillsdale) Albany
County, N.Y.; m. Anne Thomson; appointed Colonel 18 June 1823; d. 3 Oct
1844 in his 87th year.
    Catharine. O.C. 24 April 1810.
    James of Elizabethtown. O.C. 2 March 1811.
    Duncan of Elizabethtown. O.C. 4 July 1815.
    Bartholomew of Elizabethtown, bapt. 5 June 1796. O.C. 17 July 1817.
    Richard of Elizabethtown, b. 16 Oct 1797. O.C. 20 Oct 1819.
    Alexander C. of Elizabethtown. O.C. 11 June 1823.

CARMAN, George of Matilda.
    Magdalen, m. John White of Mountain. O.C. 22 Feb 1834.
    Nicholas of Matilda. O.C. 2 Dec 1830.
    George of Matilda. O.C. 2 Dec 1830.

CARMAN, Michael Sr. of Matilda.
John George of Matilda, U. E. , b. 23 Nov 1766.
Magdalina, b. 24 Oct 1767; m. Martin Walter of Matilda. OC 22 June 1797.
Michael of Matilda, b. 15 Feb 1769.
Anna Katharina, b. 19 Nov 1771; m. Peter Brouse of Matilda, 1788; died
15 June 1843. O. C. 31 May 1803.
Jacob of Matilda, b. 9 June 1774. O. C. 18 June 1799.
Rebecca, b. 19 Jan 1776.
Catherine, m. 2. John Van Camp of Matilda, 1815.
Mary, m. Martin Walter of Matilda. O. C. 22 June 1797.
Elizabeth, m. David Seely of Elizabethtown. O. C. 8 Dec 1836.

CARN, Mathias of Stamford.
Elizabeth, m. George Cutting of Stamford. O. C. 30 June 1819.
Jane, m. Alvin D. Marvin of Stamford. O. C. 14 March 1839.

CARNAHAN, Joseph of Adolphustown.
Aaron of Hallowell. O. C. 17 March 1804.
Moses of Adolphustown, m. Ann Wilkins dau Robert Wilkins. O. C. 8 Oct
1796; O. C. 8 June 1798.
Elizabeth, m. Robert Pealing of Ernestown. O. C. 17 Feb 1807.
Sarah, m. Bishop Hannah of Adolphustown 29 May 1810; O. C. 26 Mar 1811.
Sarah, m. Chris. Schultz of Cramahe. O. C. 18 March 1818.

CARPENTER, Peter of Cornwall, m. Mary Farlinger.
Margaret, m. Donald McDonell of Cornwall. O. C. 15 Aug 1809.
John of Cornwall. O. C. 7 Aug 1811.
Peter of Cornwall. O. C. 19 April 1816.
Mary, bapt. 29 Oct 1797; m. Edward Baker of Cornwall. OC 3 Nov 1819.
Elizabeth. O. C. 5 Feb 1823.
Lewis of Town of Cornwall, bapt. 4 June 1797; m. Catharine Grant. O. C.
25 July 1833.
Sophia, m. John Ross of Williamsburgh. O. C. 28 March 1833.
James of Cornwall. O. C. 27 May 1833.
Martha, m. Philip Selimser of Cornwall. O. C. 11 Jan 1834.
David of Cornwall. O. C. 20 Oct 1832.
Jacob of Cornwall. O. C. 4 Feb 1830.

CARR, Daniel Jr. of Ernestown.
Catharine, m. Joseph McGown of Kingston. O. C. 25 July 1833.
Esther, m. Henry Atkinson of Kingston. O. C. 25 July 1833.
Elizabeth, m. Peter Luck of Ameliasburgh. O. C. 8 Jan 1835.

CARR, Daniel Sr. of Ernestown.
Margaret, m. Jacob Cline of Fredericksburgh 2 Oct 1808. OC 15 Dec 1807
Barbara, m. Peter Asselstine of Ernestown 27 Aug 1809. OC 16 Feb 1810.
Daniel of Camden East. O. C. 25 Feb 1812.
Elizabeth, m. Samuel Hibbard of Hope. O. C. 13 June 1818.   [Cont'd]

CARR, Daniel Sr. - Cont'd
  Margaret M. O. C. 11 June 1840. Daniel Jr.?
  Jacob of Rawdon. O. C. 13 Oct 1836. Daniel Jr.?

CARR, William of Cornwall.
  Sarah, m. ---- McCuin. O. C. 10 June 1800.
  John of Tyendinaga. O. C. 27 July 1837.
  Jemima, m. John Houk of Whitby. O. C. 7 Aug 1834.
  Mary, m. Newman Turtle of Whitby. O. C. 7 Aug 1834.
  William of Whitby. O. C. 7 Aug 1834.
  Catharine, m. John Taylor of Whitby. O. C. 7 Aug 1834.

CARSCALLEN, Edward of Fredericksburgh.
  Luke of Fredericksbrugh. O. C. 5 Nov 1828.

CARSCALLEN, George of Fredericksburgh.
  Edward R. of Portland. O. C. 9 March 1837.
  Ann. O. C. 19 Dec 1833.
  Elizabeth. O. C. 2 Jan 1834.
  Catharine, m. ---- Wilde of Fredericksburgh. O. C. 2 Jan 1834.

CARSCALLEN, James.
  Martha, m. John Wilson Ferguson of Adolphustown. O. C. 2 Jan 1829.

CARSCALLEN, John of Fredericksburgh, m. Esther Fraser.
  Elizabeth, m. John Neely of Fredericksburgh 17 Mar 1802. OC 29 Mar 1803
  Catherine, bapt. 17 Sept 1791; m. Henry Dillenbeck of Camden East on
      1 April 1810. O. C. 16 Feb 1811.
  Sarah, bapt. 29 June 1788; m. John Spafford of Camden East on 8 March
      1810. O. C. 16 Feb 1811.
  Archibald of Fredericksburgh, m. Dorothy Thomas 18 January 1810.
      O. C. 29 March 1803.
  Mary, m. William Burtel (Bartles) of Ernestown 14 September 1817.
      O. C. 22 March 1820.
  George of Camden East. O. C. 11 June 1840.
  John Edward of Camden East. O. C. 23 Nov 1825; O. C. 18 May 1833.
  Luke of Camden East. O. C. 5 Sept 1833.
  James Edward of Camden East. O. C. 23 Nov 1825.
  James, bapt. 17 March 1790; buried 21 March 1790.

CARSCALLEN, Luke of Fredericksburgh.
  Edward of Fredericksburgh. O. C. 15 Dec 1807.
  John of Fredericksburgh, bapt. 15 June 1789. O. C. 5 June 1810.
  Isaac of Fredericksburgh, m. Sarah. O. C. 20 May 1817.
  Elizabeth. O. C. 20 May 1817.
  James of Fredericksburgh. O. C. 18 March 1818.
  George of Fredericksburgh. O. C. 4 July 1833.
  Thomas B. of Fredericksburgh. O. C. 1 Aug 1833.   [Cont'd]

CARSCALLEN, Luke - Cont'd
  Archibald H. of Fredericksburgh. O.C. 8 Oct 1833.
  Luke C. of Fredericksburgh. O.C. 1 Aug 1833.
  Benjamin M. of Camden East. O.C. 2 Jan 1834.

CARSON, William
  Eleanor, m. John Nugent of Marysburgh, 14 July 1800. O.C. 27 Oct 1801.

CARTER, Thaddeus
  Matilda, m. ---- Miller of Augusta. O.C. 24 Feb 1801.

CARTWRIGHT, Hon. Richard of Town of Kingston. His wife died at Kingston
24 January 1827.
  Robert David, b. 17 Sept 1804, of Town of Kingston; m. Harriet Dobbs;
    d. 1843. O.C. 25 Jan 1834.
  John S. of Town of Kingston, b. 17 Sept 1804; m. Sarah Hayter Macaulay
    on 11 Jan 1830; d. 15 Jan 1845. O.C. 25 Jan 1834.
  Thomas Robison of Town of Kingston, b. 13 Jan 1799; m. Anne Fisher on
    29 Jan 1821; d. 2 June 1826.
  Mary Magdalen, b. 26 Feb 1796; m. Alexander Thomas Dobbs, Comman-
    der, R.N., 17 Feb 1814; d. 4 Jan 1839 in 43rd yr.
  Hannah, b. 25 Dec 1792; d. unmd. 21 Dec 1812. O.C. 2 Aug 1803.
  Stephen H., b. 24 Jan 1801; d. unmd. 20 June 1814 aged 13 yrs 6 mos.
  James. O.C. 2 Aug 1803.
  Richard. O.C. 2 Aug 1803.

CASEY, William of Fredericksburgh and Adolphustown.
  Elizabeth, m. William Thorn of Adolphustown. O.C. 17 March 1807.
  Samuel Robison of Fredericksburgh, m. Cynthia Sharp 21 November 1808
    O.C. 19 April 1816.
  Phoebe, m. Henry A. Johnson of Adolphustown. O.C. 26 March 1817.
  Waty, m. John West of Ameliasburgh. O.C. 18 March 1818.
  Mary, m. John Way of Ameliasburgh. O.C. 18 March 1818.
  Jane, m. Philip Roblin of Adolphustown. O.C. 3 April 1819.
  William of Adolphustown. O.C. 5 Feb 1823.
  Willet W. of Adolphustown. O.C. 11 Oct 1832.
  Martha, m. Allan Wells of Ernestown. O.C. 14 March 1826.

CASS, Elihu of Co. of Prescott.
  Mary F., m. James Murray of Longueuil. O.C. 7 Nov 1839. See O.C.
    14 February 1828.
  Charlotte. O.C. 3 March 1836.
  Sarah, m. John Bangs of Longueuil. O.C. 28 Oct 1833.
  Nancy, m. Angus McDonald of Longueuil. O.C. 28 Oct 1833.
  Stephen of Hawkesbury. O.C. 26 Dec 1834.
  Josiah of Longueuil. O.C. 19 Feb 1828.
  Margaret, m. Oliver St. Julian of Longueuil. O.C. 19 Feb 1828.
  Elizabeth, m. Donald McDonald of Longueuil. O.C. 25 May 1825.

CASS, Joseph Pomeroy of Hawkesbury. O. C. 14 Feb 1798.
   Olive, m. Godfrey Valley of Caledonia. O. C. 17 Oct 1839.
   Anna, m. Josiah Jackson of Longueuil. O. C. 28 Oct 1835.
   Jehiel of Longueuil. O. C. 7 Dec 1830. O. C. 13 June 1836.
   Simeon of Hawkesbury. O. C. 5 Feb 1835.
   Rachel, m. John C. S. McCann of Hawkesbury. O. C. 5 Feb 1835.
   Maria. O. C. 7 Feb 1833. Longueuil.
   Mercy, m. Peter Van Kleek of Longueuil. O. C. 7 Feb 1833.
   Joseph of Hawkesbury. O. C. 7 Dec 1830.
   Hannah, m. Abel Waters Wells of Longueuil. OC 7 Dec 1830.

CASS, Josiah of Hawkesbury. (b. Hebron, Conn. 2 Feb 1730)
   Mary, m. Jacob Marston of Longueuil. O. C. 17 March 1807.
   Daniel of Hawkesbury. O. C. 24 March 1807.
   Elizabeth, m. David Willcox of Longueuil. O. C. 12 Dec 1821.
   Moses of Hawkesbury. O. C. 16 Feb 1837.
   Janet, m. David McKay of Hawkesbury. O. C. 16 Feb 1837.

CASSADA, Daniel of Niagara.
   Jane, m. Hiram Swayze of Clinton. O. C. 10 Feb 1819.
   Abner of Ancaster. O. C. 2 June 1819.
   Ann, m. John Smith of Grimsby. O. C. 5 Feb 1823.
   Daniel of Ancaster. O. C. 12 Nov 1823.
   Rosy, m. Charles Field. O. C. 1794(?)

CASSELMAN, Conrad of Williamsburgh.
   Catharine, m. John V. Bedstead of Williamsburgh. O. C. 11 Apr 1833.
   Mary, m. John Casselman of Williamsburgh. O. C. 11 Apr 1833.
   Margaret, m. Peter Hawes of Williamsburgh. O. C. 28 Feb 1833.

CASSELMAN, Henry of Williamsburgh.
   George H. of Williamsburgh. O. C. 8 Dec 1835.
   Margaret, m. John Weaver of Williamsburgh. O. C. 27 June 1833.
   Warner of Williamsburgh. O. C. 4 Sept 1834.
   Henry of Williamsburgh. O. C. 28 Feb 1833.
   Elizabeth. O. C. 28 Feb 1833.
   John of Williamsburgh. O. C. 28 Feb 1833.
   Eve. O. C. 28 Feb 1833.
   Marilla, m. Francis Vincent of Osnabruck. O. C. 18 Feb 1843.
   Edward of Williamsburgh. O. C. 27 Sept 1844.

CASSELLMAN, John of Niagara. [He served in Butler's Rangers. He and
his family were at Niagara in 1783. The Ontario Register; 1: 207]
   Maria, m. Castle Corus [or Carston Chorus] of Niagara 30 May 1809.
      [OHSP 3: 58] O. C. 20 November 1809.
   William of Niagara. O. C. 20 May 1817.
   Eve, m. David (Daniel) McPherson of Westminster. O. C. 1 October 1823;
      Land Board Certificate. 10/2 Ancaster.

CASSELLMAN, Richard
  Margaret, m. Caleb R. Whiting of Williamsburgh. O.C. 26 Jan 1806.

CASSELMAN, Sufrenus of Williamsburgh.
  Martin S. of Williamsburgh. O.C. 24 Nov 1842.
  Conrad of Williamsburgh. O.C. 24 Nov 1842.
  William of Williamsburgh. O.C. 24 Nov 1842.
  Peter of Williamsburgh. O.C. 24 Nov 1842.
  Sally, m. George Cook of Williamsburgh. O.C. 24 Nov 1832.
  Mary, m. George Doren of Matilda. O.C. 27 Oct 1832.

CASSELLMAN, Suffrenius of Williamsburgh.
  Charity, m. Henry Cassellman of Williamsburgh. O.C. 25 Feb 1806.
  Margaret, m. John Hickey of Williamsburgh. O.C. 25 Feb 1806.
  Hannah, m. Philip Stata of Williamsburgh. O.C. 19 April 1816.
  Suffrenus of Williamsburgh. O.C. 18 March 1818.
  Elizabeth, m. Jacob J. Merkley of Williamsburgh. O.C. 28 Oct 1835.
  Henry S. of Matilda. O.C. 18 Feb 1836.
  William of Matilda. O.C. 27 Nov 1834.

CASSELMAN, Suffrenus Jr. of Williamsburgh.
  Margaret, m. Stephen Peters of Johnstown. O.C. 8 Jan 1835.

CASSELMAN, Thomas of Williamsburgh.
  John of Williamsburgh. O.C. 19 April 1816.
  Eleanor, m. Cephrenus Casselman of Williamsburgh. O.C. 23 June 1821.
  Rosanna M. O.C. 19 Sept 1839.
  Warner of Williamsburgh. O.C. 8 Sept 1836.
  Thomas of Matilda. O.C. 1 Aug 1833.
  Catharine. O.C. 5 Feb 1835.
  Jacob of Williamsburgh. O.C. 6 Sept 1832.

CASSELMAN, Warner.
  Rachel, m. ---- Bush of Williamsburgh. O.C. 18 June 1800.
  Warner of Williamsburgh. O.C. 17 March 1807.

CASSELLMAN, William
  William of Matilda. O.C. 1850 or 51.
  Catherine.
  John W. of Matilda.
  Michael of Matilda.
  Sophrenus of Matilda.
  Sally, m. ---- Cook of Matilda.
  Nancy, m. ---- Merkley of Matilda.
  Deborah, m. ---- Garlough of Matilda.
  Laney, m. ---- Hanson of Matilda.

CASSELLMAN, William of Williamsburgh.
  Mary, m. Abraham Scott of Williamsburgh. O.C. 20 March 1807.
  Elizabeth, m. George Brown of Montreal. Not. Rec. 26 January 1808.

CASWELL, Lemuel of Elizabethtown.
  Phoebe, m. Peter Clow Jr. of Elizabethtown. O.C. 2 March 1811.
  Welthy. O.C. 26 March 1817.
  Stephen of Elizabethtown. O.C. 13 June 1818.
  Mary. O.C. 4 Aug 1831.

CAUGHELL, George of Niagara. [See also Cockle]
  Alexander of Yarmouth. O.C. 16 May 1839.
  Jacob of Yarmouth. O.C. 16 May 1839.

CAUGHEL, John of Niagara and Yarmouth. [See also Cockell]
  David of Yarmouth. O.C. 18 Feb 1824.
  Mary, m. John Lee of Westminster. O.C. 19 Feb 1825.
  Peter of Yarmouth, m. Mary Culver 1 Nov 1827. O.C. 6 Feb 1828.
  Benjamin of Yarmouth. O.C. 21 May 1840.
  Jemima, m. Peter Charlton of Yarmouth. O.C. 4 May 1837.
  James of Yarmouth. O.C. 10 March 1834.
  George A. of Yarmouth. O.C. 10 March 1834.
  Elizabeth, m. Joseph Marlatt of Yarmouth, 4 Sept 1827. OC 10 Mar 1834.
  John of Yarmouth, m. Abigail Hughes 4 May 1829. O.C. 3 Apr 1834.

CAVERLEY, Joseph of Thurlow.
  James of Sidney, m. Elizabeth Caldwell. O.C. 2 Jan 1834.
  Nathaniel of Kingston. O.C. 16 June 1834.
  Sarah, m. Eli Benedict of Sidney. O.C. 24 March 1835.
  Joseph R. of Kingston, m. Mary Purdy. O.C. 29 Sept 1824.
  Jacob of Rawdon. O.C. 7 March 1833.

CHAMBERS, Abijah of Saltfleet.
  John of Dumfries. O.C. 27 Aug 1840.
  Abijah of Clinton. O.C. 17 Sept 1823.
  Amos of Saltfleet. O.C. 4 Feb 1836.
  Robert of Saltfleet. O.C. 4 Feb 1836.
  Daniel of Puslinch. O.C. 21 May 1834.
  Henry of Saltfleet. O.C. 12 June 1832.

CHAMBERS, James of Augusta.
  Jane, m. ---- O'Docherty of Augusta. O.C. 24 Sept 1840.
  Joseph T. of Brockville. O.C. 8 Sept 1836.
  James A. of Elizabethtown. O.C. 11 April 1833.
  John McGill of Elmsley, b. 1803. O.C. 11 April 1833.
  Sophia, m. Richard Honeywell of Augusta. O.C. 5 Feb 1835.

CHAMBERLAIN, Jacob B. of Fredericksburgh, m. Ann Embury of Fredericksburgh 20 March 1796. See O. C. 7 March 1829.
  James of Fredericksburgh. O. C. 27 Aug 1833.
  Mary, m. ---- Fraser of Fredericksburgh. O. C. 5 Sept 1833.
  George of Fredericksburgh. O. C. 12 Sept 1833.
  Thomas of Ernestown. O. C. 19 Dec 1833.
  Anna. O. C. 25 Jan 1834.
  Ann, m. ---- Dunham of Fredericksburgh. O. C. 22 Dec 1832.
  Charles of Richmond. O. C. 10 Dec 1832.
  John of Fredericksburgh. O. C. 8 March 1830.

CHARTERS, George of Ernestown. Sgt., Loyal Rangers.
  Mary, m. ---- Johnson of Bertie. O. C. 30 March 1837.
  George of Ernestown. O. C. 18 Nov 1797.
  Sarah, m. ---- Hoffman. O. C. 8 July 1797.

CHASE, Walter.
  Isabella, m. Lemuel Lincoln of Hawkesbury. O. C. 17 March 1807.
  Walter of Hawkesbury. O. C. 24 March 1807.
  John of Hawkesbury. O. C. 24 March 1807.

CHATTERTON, John of Elizabethtown.
  Stephen of Yonge. O. C. 21 Sept 1837.
  Hiram of Elizabethtown. O. C. 26 Sept 1839.
  James of Elizabethtown. O. C. 6 Aug 1840.
  Merriam, m. Michael Flanagan of Elizabethtown. O. C. 18 May 1837.
  John C. of Elizabethtown, m. Charlotte Fraser. O. C. 14 Apr 1836.
  Samuel D. of Elizabethtown, m. Julian Lenox. O. C. 11 Jan 1834.
  Jacob of Elizabethtown. O. C. 3 April 1834.
  Ann, m. Jeremiah Pearsall of Elizabethtown. O. C. 4 Sept 1834.

CHESTER, John of Montague.
  Mary, m. Peter Minor of Montague. O. C. 11 Nov 1815.
  Elizabeth, m. Stephen Willcox of Montague. O. C. 5 April 1820.
  Thomas of Oxford-on-Rideau. O. C. 1 June 1837.
  Ursula, m. Sidney S. Powers of Montague. O. C. 10 April 1834.
  Michael. O. C. 3 April 1828.
  John. O. C. 3 April 1828.

CHISHOLM, Allan of Charlottenburgh, K. R. R. N. Y. East half of 16/2 on the south side of River aux Raisins.
  Christy, m. William Smith Jr. of Charlottenburgh (Sidney). O. C. 5 June 1817. O. C. 24 Sept 1840.
  Eleanor, m. Malcolm McGillivray of Charlottenburgh. O. C. 2 February 1819. O. C. 19 February 1831.
  Alexander of Sidney. O. C. 5 Sept 1833.

CHISHOLM, Alexander. Of west half G/Front, Charlottenburgh. Of Kenyon
   in 1816.
   Eleanor. O.C. 23 Nov 1816.
   Margaret. O.C. 23 Nov 1816.
   Mary. O.C. 23 Nov 1816.
   Anne. O.C. 23 Nov 1816.
   Christy. O.C. 23 Nov 1816.

CHISHOLM, Alexander of 15/1 Kenyon.
   Hugh of Kenyon. O.C. 9 Dec 1815.
   Colin of Kenyon. O.C. 9 Dec 1815.

CHISHOLM, Alexander Sr.
   Catherine. O.C. 9 March 1803.

CHISHOLM, Duncan of Lancaster and Charlottenburgh, west half 17/7.
   Nelly, m. ---- Ferguson of Charlottenburgh. O.C. 16 March 1802.
   Hugh of Charlottenburgh. O.C. 20 Nov 1809.
   Mary. O.C. 9 Dec 1815.
   Donald of Charlottenburgh. O.C. 9 Dec 1815.
   Jennet. O.C. 25 Feb 1818.
   Catharine. O.C. 28 July 1819.
   Elizabeth. O.C. 14 Nov 1821.
   William of Charlottenburgh. O.C. 10 Apr 1834.
   Alexander of Charlottenburgh. O.C. 26 Nov 1834.

CHISHOLM, George of Flamborough East.
   Mary, m. Ephraim Land of Flamborough E. O.C. 17 June 1806.
   John of Flamborough E., b. 24 May 1791; d. 4 March 1861; OC 18 June 1806.
   William of Flamborough E., b. 15 Oct 1788; m. Rebecca Silverthorne;
      O.C. 13 March 1810.
   Barbara, m. George King of Nelson. O.C. 26 March 1811.
   George of Flamborough E. O.C. 17 Feb 1816.
   Christy, m. Alexander McKenzie of Sandwich. O.C. 17 Feb 1816.

CHISHOLM, Hugh.
   Catherine, m. William Murchison of Lancaster. O.C. 11 July 1799.
   Ann, m. ---- Christie of Cornwall. O.C. 21 Sept 1800.
   Archibald. O.C. 3 March 1801.
   Flora. O.C. 23 Feb 1808. Charlottenburgh.

CHISHOLM, John of Lot 1/7 Cornwall.
   David of Cornwall. O.C. 20 May 1817.
   John of Cornwall. O.C. 20 May 1817.
   Hugh of Cornwall. O.C. 20 May 1817.
   Ann. O.C. 20 May 1817.
   William of Grantham. O.C. 22 May 1820.
   Donald of Niagara. O.C. 20 March 1822.   [Cont'd]

CHISHOLM, John - Cont'd
Ranald of Cornwall. O.C. 19 Feb 1823.

CHISHOLM, John of Queenston, Stamford(?), Niagara(?)
William of Nelson. O.C. 16 Apr 1811.
Jennet, m. John Miller of Niagara (Chinguacousy). O.C. 20 Aug 1817.
Jane, m. Joseph Silverthorne of Toronto. O.C. 7 Apr 1819.
George of Niagara. O.C. 12 June 1822.

CHISHOLM, Lewis of Charlottenburgh.
Eleanor, m. Francis Logan of Toronto. O.C. 10 March 1834.
Allan of Charlottenburgh. O.C. 10 Apr 1834.
Donald of Charlottenburgh. O.C. 10 Apr 1834.
Flora. O.C. 10 Apr 1834.
John of Charlottenburgh. O.C. 10 Apr 1834.
Anne, m. John Grant of Charlottenburgh. O.C. 10 Apr 1834.
Mary, m. Alexander McLeod of Charlottenburgh. O.C. 10 Apr 1834.
Catharine. O.C. 25 Nov 1842.
Jannet. O.C. 27 March 1850.

CHISHOLM, William of Charlottenburgh.
Mary, m. Archibald Cameron of Charlottenburgh. O.C. 19 Aug 1819.

CHRISTIE, Abijah of Cornwall, m. Elizabeth Millross.
Sarah, bapt. 27 March 1791. O.C. 4 July 1815.
Andrew of Cornwall, bapt. 29 Apr 1792. O.C. 4 July 1815.
Mary Anne, bapt. 13 Oct 1793; m. Alexander McLean of Charlottenburgh,
    27 September 1814. O.C. 28 April 1815.
Thomas, bapt. 11 Oct 1795.
Elizabeth, bapt. 4 June 1797.
Abijah of Cornwall. O.C. 10 Oct 1834.
Eunice, bapt. 12 Apr 1801. O.C. 10 Oct 1834.

CHRISTIE, John.
John of Cornwall. O.C. 7 Oct 1800.
Mary, m. ---- Cameron. O.C. 10 June 1800.

CHRYSDALE, John of Thurlow and Sidney.
Isabel, m. Daniel Ostrum of Sidney. O.C. 29 May 1804.
Rebecca. O.C. 11 Feb 1806.
Elsie, m. William Sherrard of Sidney. O.C. 11 Feb 1806.
Nancy, m. John Barnum of Sidney. O.C. 13 July 1802.
Catharine, m. Josiah White of Sidney (Tnp. of Hamilton). O.C. 27 Feb
    1812; O.C. 20 May 1817.
Joshua of Sidney. O.C. 17 Feb 1816.

CHRYSLER, Adam. Lt., Indian Dept. [He and his family were at Niagara in
1783. See The Ontario Register 1: 211]
   Maria, m. Aaron Stevens of Niagara. O.C. 4 Feb 1797.
   Catherine, m. James Clement of Niagara. O.C. 12 May 1796.
   John of Niagara, U.E., m. Elizabeth Morden, 3 March 1795.
   Margaret, m. John Clement.

CHRYSLER, John of Niagara. He was son of Adam Chrysler, and married on
3 March 1795 Elizabeth Morden.
   Margaret, m. Lewis Clement of Niagara. O.C. 9 March 1809.
   Ann Mary, bapt. 28 July 1799; m. Elias Durham of Grantham. O.C. 19
      April 1820.
   Catharine, bapt. 28 July 1799; m. Jacob J. Ball of Grantham. O.C. 22
      May 1820.
   Ralph Morden of Niagara, b. 22 Dec 1795; m. (1) Sarah Overfield; m. (2)
      Elsie Gansevoort of Albany, 21 July 1830. O.C. 31 May 1820.
   Jane, m. George Stull of Grantham. O.C. 6 Aug 1828.
   Hannah. O.C. 6 Aug 1828.
   James of Niagara. O.C. 9 Nov 1825.

CHRYSLER. see also Crysler.

CHURCH, Jonathan Mills of Elizabethtown, b. 26 Oct 1760; m. (1) Jerusha
Johns, 22 May 1786. She died 1 July 1795; m. (2) Mary, dau of Moses Mun-
sall, U.E., 11 May 1797. She died 3 Dec 1812; m. (3) Ursula Rowe on 14
January 1814. He died 31 May 1846.
   Susannah, b. 25 Feb 1787; m. Samuel Brooker of Elizabethtown. O.C. 25
      March 1806.
   Hannah, b. 14 Jan 1790; m. Abel Newman of Elizabethtown. OC 2 Dec 1806.
   Jonathan Mills of Elizabethtown, b. 19 May 1794. O.C. 5 Apr 1820.
   Peter Howard of Wolford, b. 12 Aug 1805; m. Sylvia Comstock Coller;
      died 20 April 1875. O.C. 4 Apr 1839.
   Basil R. of Wolford, b. 8 Oct 1801; m. Emily Lawrence 26 February 1822;
      O.C. 28 November 1839.
   Sarah, b. 18 Oct 1799; m. William Booth of Elizabethtown 31 December
      1823; O.C. 23 June 1824. O.C. 17 Dec 1840.
   Daniel John of Elizabethtown, b. 17 Sept 1791. O.C. 5 Nov 1835.
   Horatio Nelson of Wolford, b. 14 Dec 1810. O.C. 19 Dec 1833.
   Jerusha, b. 4 May 1798; m. Selah Hawks of Yonge. O.C. 2 March 1825.
   Hiram Turner Munsell, b. 15 Jan 1804; d. 14 Sept 1804.
   Benjamin Ruggles Munsell, b. 15 Nov 1807.
   Hiram Turner, b. 24 Nov 1815; d. 24 March 1816.
   Emily, b. 12 Sept 1820.

CHURCH, Oliver of Fredericksburgh, m. Jemima dau Lt. John Richards UE.
   Elizabeth. O.C. 10 May 1803.
   Mary, m. William T. Pruyn of Fredericksburgh 3 Apr 1807. O.C. 26
      January 1808.   [Cont'd]

CHURCH, Oliver - Cont'd
   John of Fredericksburgh. O.C. 7 Feb 1809.
   Eleanor, bapt. 26 Dec 1789. O.C. 16 Feb 1811.
   William of Fredericksburgh, bapt. 5 Feb 1791. O.C. 9 July 1817.
   Malachi, bapt. 9 July 1788; buried 16 Feb 1789.

CLARK, Alexander of Fredericksburgh, b. 1760; son of Hugh Clark, U.E.
   m. Elizabeth McCleve at Montreal, February 1781; d. 4 August 1825.
   Elizabeth, m. Benjamin Seymour of Fredericksburgh, 13 April 1801.
      O.C. 8 July 1801.
   Margaret. O.C. 3 Nov 1807. Fredericksburgh.
   John of Fredericksburgh, bapt. 22 Aug 1791. O.C. 13 June 1818.
   Nancy, m. Joseph Gunsolus of Fredericksburgh. O.C. 13 June 1818.
   Jane, bapt. 16 Feb 1794; m. Daniel Young of Fredericksburgh. O.C. 13
      June 1818.
   Harriet, b. 27 Feb 1807; m. Capt. James McNabb. O.C. 25 Aug 1838.
   Isabella, b. 17 July 1802; m. Adam Lloyd of Thurlow. O.C. 16 Feb 1837.
   George Alexander of Town of Brantford, bapt. 5 March 1797. OC 2 May 1833
   Hugh, bapt. 12 Dec 1787; buried 13 Dec 1787.
   Mary, bapt. 31 May 1789.
   Benjamin of Hamilton. O.C. 7 Feb 1833.
   Charles of Fredericksburgh. O.C. 5 March 1829.

CLARK, Francis of Cornwall, m. Margaret Callachan.
   William of Cornwall. O.C. 11 July 1799. O.C. 7 Aug 1811.
   Charles of Cornwall. O.C. 15 March 1803.
   Francis of Cornwall. O.C. 17 March 1807.
   Eleanor, bapt. 12 June 1791; m. Alpheus Elsworth of Cornwall. O.C. 23
      May 1809.
   Margaret, twin, bapt. 9 Feb 1790; m. Jacob Vandewarker of Cornwall.
      O.C. 31 October 1809.
   Martha, twin, bapt. 9 Feb 1790; m. Amos Eldridge of Cornwall. O.C. 16
      August 1810.
   Anthony, bapt. 11 Feb 1786.
   Elizabeth, bapt. 28 Aug 1791.
   Catharine, bapt. 17 Nov 1793; m. Joseph Briggs of Cornwall. O.C. 5
      November 1828.
   Sarah, bapt. 4 June 1797; m. Josiah Butterfield of Cornwall. O.C. 28
      July 1836.
   Ann. O.C. 5 Nov 1828.
   Barbara, m. William Moseley of Cornwall. O.C. 1 Sept 1824.

CLARK, Hugh of Fredericksburgh.
   Jannett, m. ---- Anderson of Fredericksburgh. O.C. 20 Nov 1798.
   Nancy, m. ---- Harlowe of Fredericksburgh. O.C. 20 Nov 1798.
   Hugh of Burford. O.C. 17 Nov 1836.
   Hannah. O.C. 24 Nov 1836.
   Elizabeth, m. Henry Hanmer of Burford. O.C. 24 Nov 1836.   [Cont'd]

CLARK, Hugh - Cont'd
  Jennett, m. James N. Oakley of Burford. O.C. 24 Nov 1836.
  Almira, m. William Lewis of Burford. O.C. 24 Nov 1836.

CLARK, James of Charlottenburgh. Sgt., K.R.R.N.Y.
  John of Charlottenburgh. O.C. 19 Dec 1806.
  Alexander of Charlottenburgh. O.C. 19 Dec 1806.
  Daniel of Charlottenburgh. O.C. 13 Oct 1807.

CLARK, John of Grantham. See OC 27 May 1808. m. Jane. His widow md.
  ---- Hartsell.
  Abigail, m. John Bessey of Grantham. O.C. 28 March 1797.
  Sarah, m. Thaddeus Davis of Grantham. O.C. 28 March 1797.

CLARK, Robert of Ernestown, b. at Quaker Hill, Dutchess Co., N.Y., on
  16 March 1744; m. Isobel Ketchum who was born on Long Island, N.Y., in
  1751; he died in Ernestown on 17 December 1823.
  Robert of Ernestown and Hope; d. at Hope 11 Sept 1813; O.C. 7 June 1800.
  Reuben of Ernestown. O.C. 27 Oct 1801.
  Phoebe, m. Henry Galloway of Ernestown 9 March 1808. OC 19 Dec 1806.
  John Collins of Ernestown. O.C. 3 March 1809.
  William of Ernestown, d. there 7 July 1815 ae 25. O.C. 25 Feb 1812.
  Matthew of Ernestown, m. Anna McKay, 28 Feb 1792. Land Board Cer-
    tificate, 12/9 Thurlow.

CLARK, William of Adolphustown.
  Joseph of Adolphustown. O.C. 17 March 1807.
  Mary, m. Belyatter Outwater of Adolphustown 1 Nov 1808. OC 23 Feb 1809.
  James of Adolphustown. O.C. 19 Apr 1816.
  John of Sophiasburgh. O.C. 19 Nov 1831.

CLAUS, John of Clinton.
  John of Clinton. O.C. 2 June 1831.
  Nicholas of Clinton. O.C. 14 May 1840.
  Rosena. O.C. 28 Dec 1835.
  Phillip of Clinton. O.C. 28 Dec 1835.

CLAUS, Hon. William of Niagara, m. Catherine, dau of Jacob Jordan,
  Seigneur of Terrebonne, L.C. She d. 4 Oct 1840 aged 72.
  Catharine, m. Lt. Benjamin Geale of Niagara (41st Regt) 30 March 1812.
    O.C. 16 March 1814. She m. (2) John Lyons, barrister, 15 June 1833.
  William of Town of Niagara. O.C. 25 Feb 1818.
  John of Town of Niagara, bapt. 18 May 1800; m. Mary Stewart. O.C. 3
    November 1836.
  Warren of Town of Niagara, bapt. 31 March 1805. O.C. 8 Nov 1832.
  Augusta, bapt. 7 March 1798.
  Annabella, bapt. 9 June 1807; buried 23 August 1812.
  Julia Caroline, bapt. 25 Nov 1802; d. 11 Feb 1827, aged 25. Unmarried.

CLEMENT, James of Niagara, m. Catherine dau of Adam Chrysler, U.E.
  Mary, m. Alexander Stevens of Niagara. O.C. 9 Oct 1810.
  Joseph of Niagara. O.C. 25 Feb 1812.
  John P. of Niagara, bapt. 30 Jan 1793. O.C. 20 May 1817.
  Samuel Thompson of Niagara. O.C. 20 May 1817.
  Lewis James of Niagara. O.C. 4 March 1819.
  Adam C. of Niagara. O.C. 17 March 1822.
  Robert Addison of Niagara, bapt. 22 May 1811. O.C. 3 Nov 1836.
  George Miller of Niagara. O.C. 14 May 1830.
  William C. of Niagara. O.C. 5 Dec 1827.

CLEMENT, John P. of Niagara, m. Mary.
  Catharine, m. Jacob Ball of Thorold 4 May 1809. O.C. 20 May 1817.
  Jemima. O.C. 20 May 1817.
  Mary Elizabeth. O.C. 30 June 1819.
  Margaret Sophia, bapt. 18 April 1793; m. William Nelles of Haldimand
    County. O.C. 6 Sept 1826.
  Peter Ball of Niagara, bapt. 4 Oct 1807. O.C. 2 Feb 1832.
  Caroline. O.C. 2 Feb 1832.

CLEMENT, John.
  Lewis of Niagara. O.C. 25 Feb 1809.
  George A. of Niagara. O.C. 27 Nov 1834(?)

CLEMENT, John of Ernestown.
  Catharine, m. ---- Van Luvan of Kingston. O.C. 14 Oct 1834.
  Elizabeth, m. Peter Davy of Ernestown. O.C. 14 Oct 1834.
  Ruth, m. Lewis Comer of Ernestown. O.C. 14 Oct 1834.
  Lewis of Loughborough. O.C. 14 Oct 1834.
  John Martin of Camden East. O.C. 6 Nov 1834.

CLEMENT, Joseph of Niagara.
  Catherine, m. Francis Lowell of Niagara. O.C. 14 June 1811.
  Ann, m. Richard Woodruff of Niagara. O.C. 14 June 1811.
  Margaret, m. William Woodruff. O.C. 20 May 1817.
  John B. of Niagara, bapt. 9 Aug 1792. O.C. 1 Dec 1819.
  Mary Ann. O.C. 12 June 1822.
  James Augustine of Niagara. O.C. 4 Jan 1840.
  Richard of Niagara, m. Deborah Meddaugh. O.C. 24 Nov 1836.
  Joseph D. of Niagara, bapt. 22 Apr 1802. O.C. 4 May 1836.

CLEMENT, Lewis. Lieut. md. Catherine. [See The Ont. Register 1: 211]
  Anne, m. ---- Butler. O.C. 8 Oct 1796.
  Jemima, m. ---- Thompson. O.C. 8 Oct 1796.
  James of Niagara, U.E.

CLENCH, Ralfe of Niagara, m. Elizabeth dau Lt. Brant Johnson; she died
  15 Aug 1850 ae 77. He died 19 Jan 1828 ae 66.   [Cont'd]

CLENCH, Ralfe - Cont'd
   Joseph Brant of Niagara. O.C. 20 Feb 1811.
   Margaret, m. Capt. Richard Bullock (88th Regt) 13 March 1828. O.C.
      23 Nov 1816.
   Hannah Catherine, bapt. 29 Jan 1795. O.C. 23 Nov 1816.
   Ann Kerr, bapt. 30 July 1797. O.C. 7 Jan 1824.
   Euretta Johnson, bapt. 30 July 1797; buried 27 Sept 1797.
   Priscilla Stuart, bapt. 27 Apr 1800. O.C. 28 Apr 1825.
   Robert Addison of Niagara, bapt. 25 Jan 1805; d. in Brantford Tnp. on 30
      August 1848 in his 47th year. O.C. 23 June 1824.
   Eliza Euretta, bapt. 25 Jan 1805; m. Charles Richardson of Niagara on
      2 April 1827; d. 28 Sept 1833. O.C. 6 May 1830.
   Benjamin of the Town of Niagara, bapt. 25 Jan 1805. O.C. 19 Feb 1828.
   Francis Andrew Bernard of Town of Niagara. O.C. 15 May 1835.
   Johnson of Town of Niagara, m. Eliza Whistler 5 Oct 1831. OC 4 Dec 1834.
   Ralfe of Niagara, d. 18 Nov 1880 aet. 74 yrs. O.C. 6 Jan 1831.

CLENDENNING, Abraham of Grantham, m. a dau of John Hainer, U.E.
   John of Grantham. O.C. 27 Nov 1815.
   Margaret. O.C. 5 May 1819.
   Eve, m. Lewis Haines of Louth, 1 July 1807. O.C. 29 Nov 1820.
   George of Louth. O.C. 29 Nov 1820.
   Thomas of Grantham. O.C. 25 June 1823.
   Daniel of Niagara, b. 3 May 1793. O.C. 7 Jan 1824.
   Catharine. O.C. 17 March 1836.

CLENDENNING, James. Butler's Rangers.
   John of Grantham. O.C. 26 Jan 1797.
   Walter of Gainsborough. O.C. 26 Jan 1797.
   Abraham of Grantham, m. ---- Hainer 2 Jan 1788. O.C. 26 Jan 1797.
   James. O.C. 26 Jan 1797.
   Ann, m. Jonathan Matthews of Darlington. O.C. 25 Feb 1797.
   Eve, m. Peter May of Caistor.
   [pencilled note by Mr. Reid: Rebecca Clendenning, 3/7 Caistor?]

CLENDENNING, John of Grantham.
   James of Grantham. O.C. 26 Jan 1808.
   Rachel, m. Philip Bellinger of Bertie. O.C. 19 April 1816.
   Walter of Grantham. O.C. 27 Feb 1818.
   Margaret, m. James Carr of Bertie. O.C. 27 Feb 1818.
   John F. of Grantham. O.C. 13 June 1821.
   Martha, m. John Shearer of Grantham. O.C. 17 March 1836.
   Rachel, m. Philip Bellinger of Port Talbot. O.C. 27 June 1833.

CLENDENNING, Walter of Gainsborough, m. a dau of Jacob Walker, U.E.
   James of Gainsborough. O.C. 16 Dec 1815.
   Daniel of Gainsborough. O.C. 20 May 1817.
   John of Gainsborough. O.C. 20 May 1817.   [Cont'd]

CLENDENNING, Walter - Cont'd
Rebecca, m. ---- Shingler. O.C. 27 Jan 1819.
Jeremiah of Gainsborough. O.C. 17 Apr 1822.
Robert of Gainsborough. O.C. 19 Feb 1823.
William of Gainsborough. O.C. 27 June 1833.

CLINE, Adam.
Margaret, m. Conrad Ruport of Osnabruck. O.C. 20 March 1807.
Polly. O.C. 20 March 1807.
Philip of Osnabruck. O.C. 20 March 1807.

CLINE, Michael of Cornwall, m. Catharine Vick.
Dorothy, m. John Dewitt of Cornwall. O.C. 5 Jan 1806.
Hannah, m. Stephen Brownell of Cornwall. O.C. 25 Feb 1806.
Catharine, m. Joseph Cryderman of Cornwall. OC 5 Jan 1798, 19 Apr 1808
Michael of Cornwall, bapt. 16 May 1790. O.C. 16 Feb 1811.
Catherine, m. Peter Eamer Jr. of Cornwall 22 Oct 1805. OC 27 Mar 1813
Margaret, bapt. 12 Oct 1794. O.C. 13 Feb 1816.

CLOSSON, Caleb of Augusta.
Nancy, m. ---- Gilchrist of Augusta. O.C. 23 Sept 1800.
Sarah, m. William Davies Jr. of Wolford. O.C. 27 Feb 1806. See O.C.
    5 June 1810. Johnstown Com. 1803.
Asa of Augusta. O.C. 20 May 1817.
Thirza, m. Charles Burnham of Augusta. O.C. 15 May 1834.
Polly, m. Thomas Hill of Brockville. O.C. 3 Jan 1834.

CLOW, Henry of Elizabethtown.
Mary, m. David McCrady of Elizabethtown. O.C. 10 Apr 1805.
Peter of Elizabethtown. O.C. 2 Dec 1806.
Simon of Elizabethtown. O.C. 2 March 1811.
Henry D. of Elizabethtown. O.C. 8 Sept 1836.

CLOW, William of Elizabethtown, m. Sophia Strader dau of Simon Strader,
U.E. She died 25 Nov 1851 aged 85.
Sophia, b. 1 Oct 1786. O.C. 8 Feb 1808.
Rebecca, b. 12 May 1785. O.C. 8 Feb 1808.
Peter of Elizabethtown, b. 12 Feb 1788. O.C. 2 March 1811.
John of Elizabethtown, b. 25 May 1794. O.C. 18 March 1818.
Henry of Elizabethtown, b. 1 March 1796. O.C. 18 March 1818.
William of Elizabethtown, b. 24 July 1790. O.C. 18 March 1818.
James of Elizabethtown, b. 21 July 1792; bapt. 26 May 1793. OC 18 March
    1818.
Ann, b. 11 Jan 1798. O.C. 2 June 1819.
Susannah, b. 5 July 1806; m. ---- Selby of Richmond. O.C. 7 May 1840.
Duncan of Elizabethtown, b. 17 Dec 1801. O.C. 17 Sept 1823.
Daniel of Elizabethtown, b. 12 Nov 1808. O.C. 1 May 1834.
Jane, b. 6 Aug 1799. O.C. 1 May 1834.   [Cont'd]

CLOW, William - Cont'd
   Robert of Elizabethtown, b. 5 Dec 1803. O.C. 27 April 1832.

COCKLE, George of Niagara. [A George Cockel, of Butler's Rangers, and
   his family were at Niagara in 1783. His son Peter was granted a lot in
   Gainsborough. The Ontario Register, v. 1, pp. 16, 208]
   Abraham of Haldimand County. O.C. 6 April 1839.
   Ann, bapt. 3 Oct 1800, m. Joseph Clement of Niagara. O.C. 6 Apr 1839.
   Elizabeth, m. John Upper of Stamford. O.C. 6 April 1839.
   Catherine, m. Robert A. Clement of Windham. O.C. 26 Nov 1840.
   John of Niagara. O.C. 27 July 1837.

COCKELL, John of Niagara. Butler's Rangers.
   Margaret, m. (1) Jacob Sporbeck of Niagara. Land Board Certificate
      30/1 Beverly; m. (2) Alexander Allen.

COLE, Adam of Elizabethtown, m. Thankful dau of Jonathan Fulford, U.E.
   She died 1840 aged 74. He died at Elizabethtown 3 Aug 1832 aged 72.
   Sarah, b. 16 Jan 1785; m. George Allen of Elizabethtown. OC 31 May 1803.
   Rachel, b. 30 Sept 1786; m. Edward Brown of Elizabethtn. OC 5 Mar 1808.
   Peter of Elizabethtown, b. 8 March 1788; m. Jane Elliott. OC 9 July 1811.
   Titus of Elizabethtown, b. 11 Aug 1790; m. Anna Brown. OC 25 Feb 1812.
   George of Elizabethtown, b. 11 Feb 1795; m. (1) Julia Hunter; m. (2) Lydia
      (Myers) Randolph. O.C. 29 Dec 1819.
   Isaac of Elizabethtown, b. 10 March 1796; m. Electa Brondy. O.C. 28
      September 1820.
   Irene, b. 3 Apr 1801; m. David Connell (Cornell?) of Yonge 22 Jan 1822.
      O.C. 8 November 1838.
   Adam of Brockville, b. 26 Sept 1802; m. Mehitable Connell. O.C. 28
      October 1835.
   Eleanor, b. 26 Nov 1799; m. Morris Hartwick of Cobourg 13 January 1824;
      O.C. 27 Feb 1834.
   Abel of Elizabethtown, b. 14 Dec 1805; m. Catherine Seaman. O.C. 19
      January 1833.
   Lois, b. 8 June 1789.
   John, b. 30 Nov 1791.
   Jonathan, b. 28 Oct 1793; m. ---- McLean.
   Jacob, b. 10 April 1798.
   Nancy, b. 29 Dec 1803; m. George Wilcox.
   Thankful, b. 2 March 1808.

COLE, Bernard of Adolphustown.
   Margaret, m. Aaron Carnaham of Marysburgh. O.C. 15 March 1838.
   James of Cramahe. O.C. 11 July 1833.
   Alley, m. Abraham Brooks of Cramahe. O.C. 1 August 1833.
   Elizabeth, m. Nelson Hudgin of Hallowell. O.C. 12 June 1832.
   Conrad B. of Adolphustown. O.C. 1 March 1832.
   Jemima, m. Noxon Williams of Adolphustown. O.C. 14 March 1826.

COLE, Daniel of Adolphustown, m. Mary. [See also The Ontario Register,
v. 1, p. 212, and v. 4, p. 50]
Jacob of Adolphustown. O. C. 25 Nov 1800.
John of Adolphustown. O. C. 25 Nov 1800.
Catherine. O. C. 8 Aug 1798. Fredericksburgh.
Sarah. O. C. 17 Feb 1807.
Abraham of Adolphustown, bapt. 23 March 1789. O. C. 16 Feb 1810.
Henry of Adolphustown, bapt. 16 May 1791. O. C. 25 Feb 1812. O. C. 25
February 1818.
Mary, m. William Huff of Marysburgh. O. C. 5 Jan 1827.
Conrad of Hallowell. O. C. 5 July 1798.
Elizabeth, m. ---- Ferguson. Land Board Certificate. 27/8 Thurlow.

COLE, John of Elizabethtown.
Peter of Elizabethtown. O. C. 3 Oct 1839.
Rachel, m. Cyrus Bigelow of Elizabethtown. O. C. 5 May 1831.
Sarah, m. Alfred Steel of Elizabethtown. O. C. 27 March 1829.

COLE, Peter of Adolphustown, m. Jane dau George Parliament 5 Jan 1794.
Samuel of Sophiasburgh. O. C. 6 Aug 1840.
Peter of Sophiasburgh. O. C. 6 Aug 1840.
Margaret, m. Smith Benedict of Sophiasburgh. O. C. 6 Aug 1840.
Elizabeth, m. Hiram Thompson of Sophiasburgh. O. C. 4 July 1836.
Jane. O. C. 4 February 1836.
Mary, m. Peter Barriger of Sophiasburgh. O. C. 3 May 1826.
Paul of Sophiasburgh. O. C. 22 June 1825.
Hannah, m. Eleazer Williams of Sophiasburgh. OC 22 June 1825.

COLE, Simon J. of Sophiasburgh.
Christina, m. Richard Davenport of Sophiasburgh. O. C. 20 June 1797.

COLERICK, Peter of Willoughby.
Mary, m. William Hathaway of Willoughby. O. C. 16 Feb 1811.
Amelia. O. C. 12 Nov 1817.

COLLARD, Abraham of Loughborough, m. Hannah (born about 1760) dau of
Peter Cramer, U. E. of Williamsburgh.
Elizabeth, m. James Hannah of Kingston. O. C. 20 Nov 1810.
Mary. O. C. 16 Feb 1811.
Rebecca, m. John Greeizen of Kingston. O. C. 20 May 1817.
Isaac of Loughborough. O. C. 4 Aug 1836.
Abraham of Loughborough. O. C. 27 June 1833.

COLLARD, John of Niagara, m. Anna, dau of Moses Pingray of Delancey's
Corps, on 13 Sept 1781 in N. Y. State. O. C. 28 March 1797.
Hannah, b. 1785; m. Edward Taylor of Niagara 27 Aug 1801; OC 9 July 1802.
Margaret, b. 1784. O. C. 23 April 1805.
Elijah of Niagara, b. 1782. O. C. 24 May 1805.   [Cont'd]

COLLARD, John - Cont'd
  Sarah, b. 1789; m. Isaiah Millard of Stamford. O.C. 8 July 1806.
  Susannah, b. 1787. O.C. 25 Feb 1812.
  Rachel, b. 1791; m. David Millard of Niagara. O.C. 25 Feb 1812.
  Isabella, b. 1794. O.C. 20 May 1817. O.C. 21 March 1844.
  Stephen of Niagara. O.C. 3 Nov 1819.
  Richard, b. 1796.

COLLINS, Alexander of Wainfleet.
  Patrick of Wainfleet. O.C. 28 Nov 1839.
  Thomas of Gainsborough. O.C. 19 Dec 1833.
  John McGaw of Gainsborough, schoolmaster. O.C. 7 Aug 1834.
  Margaret, m. Benjamin Aikens of Gainsborough. O.C. 6 Nov 1829.
  James of Grimsby. O.C. 27 March 1829.

COLLISON, John of Matilda, died in October 1832.
  Nancy, m. John Albrant of Matilda. O.C. 5 March 1810.
  Hannah, m. Faxton Rathbone of Matilda. O.C. 4 July 1815.
  James of Matilda. O.C. 19 April 1816.
  Hugh of Matilda. O.C. 19 April 1816.
  John of Matilda. O.C. 20 May 1817. O.C. 24 March 1835.
  Peter of Matilda. O.C. 2 June 1829.
  Nelly, m. Michael McErlain of Matilda. O.C. 2 June 1829.

COLLVER, Timothy.
  Elizabeth, m. Aaron Collver. O.C. 15 Oct 1799.
  Anna, m. Jabez Collver. O.C. 15 Oct 1799.
  Martha. O.C. 15 Oct 1799.
  Marian, m. John Collver. O.C. 15 Oct 1799.
  Unice, m. Abraham Beemer of Townsend. O.C. 7 April 1807.
  Ebenezer of Townsend. O.C. 12 Oct 1810.

COLTMAN, John of Middleton, born about 1759 in England.
  George of Middleton. O.C. 5 Feb 1823.
  Camilla, m. Charles Biggar of Ameliasburgh. O.C. 25 June 1840.
  Elizabeth, m. William Butler of Ameliasburgh. O.C. 25 June 1840.
  James of Middleton. O.C. 2 May 1833.
  Benjamin of Middleton. O.C. 1 Aug 1833.
  Charlotte. O.C. 5 Sept 1833.
  Maria, m. James Tisdale of Charlotteville. O.C. 25 Jan 1834.

COMER, Jacob of Ernestown.
  Henry of Ernestown. O.C. 15 May 1835.
  Lewis of Ernestown. O.C. 15 May 1835.
  Hannah, m. ---- Hogle of Ernestown. O.C. 15 May 1835.
  Elizabeth, m. ---- Parks of Camden East. O.C. 15 May 1835.

COMER, Paul of Ernestown, m. Phoebe Boyce of Ernestown 28 Apr 1789.
Mary. O.C. 27 Feb 1818. O.C. 29 June 1843.
Margaret, m. Levi Lee of Ernestown. O.C. 27 Feb 1818.
Sarah, m. (1) ---- Van Ness of Loughborough. O.C. 27 Feb 1818. m. (2) ---- Blake.
Jacob of Ernestown. O.C. 6 March 1821.
John of Darlington. O.C. 31 Oct 1821.
Elizabeth, m. Archibald Cary of Ernestown. O.C. 19 Dec 1833.
William of Camden East, b. 10 Dec 1800. O.C. 10 March 1834.

COMER, Thomas
Margaret, m. William Boice of Ernestown, 29 May 1804. OC 17 Feb 1807.

CONGER, David. His name struck off U.E. List: O.C. 28 Feb 1805.
Dorcas, m. Daniel Young of Sophiasburgh 2 March 1790. OC 20 June 1797.
Peter Designea of Hallowell.

CONKLIN, John of Ernestown, m. Phoebe Hough or Huff.
Abraham of Reach. O.C. 23 June 1836.
Hannah. O.C. 28 Oct 1835. Ameliasburgh.
Joseph of Ernestown, b. 3 Aug 1800. O.C. 4 Apr 1833.
Sarah, m. George Moore of Ameliasburgh. O.C. 30 May 1834.
Olivia. O.C. 12 June 1834. Town of Kingston.
Elijah of Town of Kingston. O.C. 18 July 1834.
Eleanor, m. Chester Hatch of Town of Kingston. O.C. 5 Feb 1829.

CONKLIN, Joseph
John of Ernestown, U.E.

CONNER, John of Kingston, m. Sarah; drowned about 1795; his widow m. (2)
David Hogan of Town of Kingston.
Sarah, m. Thomas Stickney of Marysburgh. O.C. 17 March 1807.
Aaron of Marysburgh. O.C. 16 Feb 1810.
Catherine, m. Peter Howe of Kingston. O.C. 20 Nov 1810.
Bridget, m. John Waggoner of Kingston. O.C. 21 July 1812, 7 Aug 1834.
John of Marysburgh. O.C. 4 Nov 1818.
David of Marysburgh. O.C. 4 Nov 1818. O.C. 26 May 1836.
Sarah, m. Wm Lighthall of Town of Kingston. O.C. 20 May 1817.

COOK, John of Camden East.
Ann, m. Artemus Williams Cushman of Camden East. O.C. 8 Feb 1808.
John of Camden East. O.C. 8 Feb 1808.
Richard of Thurlow, b. Kinderhook, 1772. 3/9 Thurlow.
William of Camden East. Land Board Certificate. 9/2 Camden.

COOK, John of Osnabruck.
Jacob of Osnabruck. O.C. 20 March 1807.
Michael of Williamsburgh. O.C. 20 March 1807.   [Cont'd]

COOK, John - Cont'd
  Elizabeth, m. John Fike of Osnabruck. O.C. 25 Feb 1809.
  Susannah, m. Conrad Snyder of Williamsburgh. O.C. 5 March 1810.
  Hannah, m. Joshua White of Williamsburgh. O.C. 7 Aug 1811.
  Catharine, m. Robert Fields of Osnabruck. O.C. 21 July 1812.
  John of Osnabruck. O.C. 19 April 1816.
  William of Osnabruck. O.C. 17 March 1824.
  Polly. O.C. 17 March 1824.

COOK, Michael of Edwardsburgh and Kingston. O.C. 15 Aug 1821. Gaoler.
  Elizabeth. O.C. 7 July 1802.

COOK, Michael of Williamsburgh.
  Charity, m. Gasper Salisbury of Williamsburgh. O.C. 5 June 1810, and
    O.C. 13 Nov 1818.
  Michael of Williamsburgh. O.C. 13 Nov 1818.
  Elizabeth, m. ---- Pillar of Williamsburgh. O.C. 13 Nov 1818.
  Ann, m. Simon Baker of Williamsburgh. O.C. 9 March 1837.
  Catharine, m. Samuel Weagent of Williamsburgh. O.C. 19 Dec 1833.
  George P. of Osnabruck. O.C. 28 Feb 1833.
  Elias of Williamsburgh. O.C. 28 Feb 1833.
  Abraham of Williamsburgh. O.C. 28 Feb 1833.
  Abigail, m. Adam Snyder of Osnabruck. O.C. 28 Sept 1832.
  David of Williamsburgh. O.C. 17 Feb 1825.

COOK, William of Ernestown.
  Thaddeus of Whitby. O.C. 27 Aug 1840.
  Sarah, m. John White of Alnwick. O.C. 22 Oct 1840.
  Benjamin J. of Cramahe. O.C. 18 May 1837.
  John C. of Tyendinaga. O.C. 3 March 1836.

COON, John of Niagara. Sgt., Butler's Rangers. [A Sgt. John Coon of B.R.
  and his family were at Niagara in 1783. The Ontario Register 1: 201]
  Margaret, m. Peter Murray of Niagara. O.C. 21 March 1809.
  Christiana, m. John McKinney of Niagara. O.C. 20 Nov 1809.
  Mary, m. John Austin of Niagara. O.C. 26 March 1811.
  Jane. O.C. 7 May 1811. Flamborough West.
  Catharine. O.C. 16 Jan 1816. Flamborough West.
  Hannah, m. Samuel Van Every of Flamborough West. O.C. 12 July 1796.
  Nancy, m. John Elliott Jr. of Oxford West. O.C. 17 March 1836.
  Walter of Glanford. O.C. 7 May 1829.

COONS, Gasper of Matilda.
  George of Matilda. O.C. 17 March 1807.
  Elizabeth, m. Giles Stamp of Matilda. O.C. 13 March 1807.
  Jacob of Matilda, b. 1787, m. Rebecca Brady; d. Prescott, 1882. O.C.
    25 Feb 1812.
  Joseph of Matilda. O.C. 19 April 1816.   [Cont'd]

COONS, Gasper - Cont'd
Elizabeth, m. George Kintner of Matilda. O.C. 30 June 1819.
Peter of Matilda. O.C. 15 Dec 1821.
Sarah, m. David Hitzman of Matilda. O.C. 1 April 1840.
Nancy, m. John Hitzman of Matilda. O.C. 1 April 1840.
Margaret, m. Alexander Fraser of Town of Cornwall. O.C. 2 Jan 1834.
Polly, m. ---- Johnson of Matilda. O.C. 4 Feb 1830.
William of Matilda. O.C. 17 Nov 1847.

COONS, Jacob of Matilda.
Margaret. O.C. 25 Feb 1806.
Hannah. O.C. 22 Feb 1810.
Elizabeth, m. Henry Albrant of Matilda. O.C. 22 Feb 1810.
Catharine, m. Elam Hitchcock of Matilda. O.C. 25 Feb 1806.
Mary. O.C. 4 July 1815.
David of Matilda. O.C. 23 June 1821.
Abigail, m. John Van Camp of Matilda. O.C. 23 June 1821.
Mathew of Matilda. O.C. 23 June 1821.
Lavinia. O.C. 1 July 1830.
James of Matilda. O.C. 23 June 1828.
Rachel. O.C. 23 June 1828.

COONS, John
John G. of Sidney. O.C. 9 March 1843.

CORBIN, Nathaniel of Augusta and Ernestown.
Nathaniel W. of Camden East. O.C. 7 May 1835.
Elizabeth, m. Frederick Dodge of Ernestown. O.C. 28 Oct 1835.
Polly, m. Asahel Cross of Montague. O.C. 18 Nov 1835.

CORBMAN, Jacob of Ameliasburgh.
Daniel of Ameliasburgh. O.C. 13 Feb 1816.
Jane, m. James Brooks of Hamilton. O.C. 14 March 1839.
Margaret, m. ---- Chase of Ameliasburgh. O.C. 18 July 1833.
Catharine, m. ---- Masters of Ameliasburgh. O.C. 18 July 1833.
Lydia, m. ---- Clark of Hillier. O.C. 19 Aug 1833.
Sarah, m. John McLean of Murray. O.C. 30 May 1834.
Mary, m. Stephen Blythe of Murray. O.C. 5 June 1834.
Ann, m. Henry Brooks of Hillier. O.C. 5 June 1834.
William of Ameliasburgh. O.C. 26 Dec 1834.

CORNELIUS, John of Fredericksburgh, m. Cornelia.
Catherine, m. Henry Sinclair of Fredericksburgh. O.C. 8 July 1801.
Isaac of Fredericksburgh. O.C. 8 February 1808.
Peter of Fredericksburgh, bapt. 12 Jan 1789; m. Peggy Dingman, 30 Nov 1808. O.C. 25 Feb 1812.
John of Fredericksburgh, bapt. 24 Jan 1791; m. Levina Woodcock, 8 Jan 1818 (widow?). O.C. 18 March 1818.   [Cont'd]

CORNELIUS, John - Cont'd
    Nicholas of Fredericksburgh, bapt. 11 June 1793. O. C. 12 June 1834.

CORNELL, Albert of Adolphustown.
    John of Adolphustown. O. C. 16 Nov 1807.
    Elias of Adolphustown. O. C. 14 March 1809.
    Margaret, m. John Johnston of Adolphustown. O. C. 25 Feb 1812.
    Mary, bapt. 31 Dec 1787; m. Ashel Rohley of Fredericksburgh. O. C. 25
        February 1812.
    Daniel of Adolphustown. O. C. 29 December 1819.
    Jane. O. C. 7 Feb 1821. (Lunatic)
    Margaret, m. ---- Davis of Tyendinaga. O. C. 1 April 1840.

CORNWALL, John, m. Mary.
    Mary, b. 1792; m. William McCormick of Colchester (Pelee Island). O.C.
        5 March 1810.
    Joshua.
    Wheeler.
    John.

COSBEY, George of Pelham.
    George of Pelham. O. C. 31 May 1808.
    Elet of Grimsby. O. C. 26 March 1817.
    Arthur of Gainsborough. O. C. 8 Jan 1823.
    Nancy. O. C. 7 March 1833. Wainfleet.
    Mary, m. Jesse Henry of Wainfleet.
    Charlotte, m. Daniel Vaughan of Wainfleet. O. C. 7 March 1833.
    John of Gainsborough. O. C. 23 Dec 1825.

COTTER, James Jr. of Fredericksburgh, m. Magdalena Hoffman 4 Nov 1794;
    died in Sophiasburgh 18 Jan 1849 aged 78 years.
    James B. F. of Hamilton. O. C. 23 Nov 1840.
    Richard C. H. of Ameliasburgh. O. C. 4 Feb 1837.
    Samuel P. M. of Sophiasburgh. O. C. 17 Aug 1842.
    Elizabeth, bapt. 11 March 1804; m. Allen Munro of Sophiasburgh. O. C.
        17 August 1842.
    William H. of Sophiasburgh. O. C. 17 August 1842.
    Eleanor, bapt. 10 Dec 1797; m. Samuel Solmes of Sophiasburgh, 22 May
        1817. O. C. 17 Aug 1842.
    Lucretia, m. Samuel Munro of Sophiasburgh. See ret. 1850.

COTTER, James Sr. of Fredericksburgh. Pvt., 1st Batt., K. R. R. N. Y.
    Eleanor, m. John Duzenberry of Ernestown. Land Board Certificate,
        66/2 Ameliasburgh.
    James of Fredericksburgh, U. E.
    Richard of Fredericksburgh, U. E.

COTTER, Richard of Fredericksburgh, m. Experience dau of Mathias Rose
Sr., U.E., 23 Oct 1788; she m.(2) John Fraser of Ernestown, 4 March
1792. He was buried 13 Feb 1791.
   David of Thurlow, bapt. 28 June 1789. O.C. 16 Feb 1811.

COUGH, John.
   Catherine, m. ---- Shaver of Matilda. O.C. 18 June 1800. Com. 1840,
   Samuel Shaver.

COUNTRYMAN, Jacob.
   Margaret, m. ---- Aman. O.C. 10 June 1800.
   Coonrad of Osnabruck. O.C. 5 Jan 1798.
   Christian, m. Jacob Stoneburner of Cornwall. O.C. 5 Jan 1798.
   Catherine, m. Thomas Johnson of Osnabruck. O.C. 17 March 1807.
   John of Osnabruck. O.C. 7 August 1811.
   Margaret, m. John Hardy of Williamsburgh. O.C. 21 Sept 1837.
   Nancy, m. John Prunner of Williamsburgh. O.C. 21 Sept 1837.
   Hannah, m. Stephen Brownell of Osnabruck. O.C. 22 Sept 1836.
   Mary, m. Stephen Woodman of Williamsburgh. O.C. 3 Dec 1835.

COVELL, Simon.
   Susannah, m. Edward Jessup Jr. of Augusta. O.C. 29 June 1799.
   James of Montague. O.C. 4 Feb 1836.

COX, Samuel of Niagara, cabinet maker, born about 1755 in New York; m.
Barbara.
   Deborah, m. William Parker of Niagara. O.C. 30 Oct 1810.
   Elizabeth, m. John Smith of Niagara 18 June 1809. O.C. 30 Oct 1810.
   John of Niagara, bapt. 22 March 1793; m. Salome Hughston 23 May 1816.
      O.C. 20 May 1817.
   Susannah, m. Bryan Condon of Binbrook 5 Sept 1816. O.C. 31 May 1820.
   Ann. O.C. 31 May 1820.
   Mary Ann, bapt. 4 Sept 1805.

COZENS, Joshua Young of Town of Cornwall, m. Susannah Page at York
(Toronto) 20 Nov 1801; died at Cornwall 24 June 1852 aged 86.
   Helen W. O.C. 7 Feb 1839.
   Christy Ann. O.C. 18 Feb 1836.
   Alexander F. of Town of Cornwall. O.C. 3 March 1836.
   Emily. O.C. 4 Sept 1834.
   William Zane. O.C. 4 Sept 1834.
   Benjamin Small of Town of Cornwall. O.C. 4 Sept 1834.
   Diana. O.C. 4 Sept 1834.
   Isaac Brock of Town of Cornwall. O.C. 4 Sept 1834.
   Julia Ann. O.C. 4 Sept 1834.
   Margaret. O.C. 4 Sept 1834.
   Matilda. O.C. 4 Sept 1834.
   Nelson of Town of Cornwall. O.C. 26 Dec 1834.

CRAWFORD, David of Pickering.
Caleb of Pickering. O.C. 7 April 1807.
Henry of Pickering. O.C. 7 April 1807.
Jacob of Pickering. O.C. 5 Aug 1807.
Joseph of Pickering. O.C. 3 April 1810.

CRAWFORD (Crafford), James of Thorold.
John of Thorold. O.C. 24 April 1833.
Phoebe. O.C. 24 April 1833.
Ruth, m. James Burger of Thorold, 22 June 1834. O.C. 24 Apr 1833.
Deborah, m. Cornelius Losee of Pelham. O.C. 19 Dec 1833.
Amy, m. Edmond Woodrow of Pelham. O.C. 19 Dec 1833.

CRAWFORD, William Redford. Capt., K.R.R.N.Y.
Redford of Kingston. O.C. 17 Nov 1797.
Mary, m. William Robbins of Adolphustown. O.C. 2 Sept 1797.
Catherine, m. Archibald Grant of Chippawa. O.C. 2 Sept 1797. And O.C.
    13 March 1810.
Lewis.
Bryan.

CRIPPEN, Darius.
Samuel. O.C. 5 January 1799.

CRITES, George of Cornwall. 18/2
George of Cornwall, m. Lenah Cain. O.C. 21 July 1812.
John of Cornwall. O.C. 20 May 1817.
Catharine, m. David Wood of Cornwall. O.C. 4 Nov 1818.
Christian of Cornwall. O.C. 17 Sept 1823.
Jacob of Cornwall. O.C. 17 Sept 1823.
Michael of Cornwall. O.C. 3 March 1831.
Christeen. O.C. 7 May 1829.

CRON, James of Augusta. See O.C. 8 Nov 1797 and 13 June 1836.
Mary, m. John Galbraith of Blenheim. O.C. 24 Dec 1811.
John of Augusta. O.C. 28 April 1812.

CRONKITE, Hercules of Ernestown.
Anthony of Madoc. O.C. 4 Sept 1834.
Darius of Madoc. O.C. 4 Sept 1834.
Alfred of Marysburgh. O.C. 29 Sept 1834.
Paul C. of Marysburgh. O.C. 2 Oct 1834.

CRONKITE, John of Ernestown.
Simon of Ernestown. O.C. 1 April 1840.
Norton of Rawdon. O.C. 4 Sept 1834.
Augustus of Rawdon. O.C. 4 Sept 1834.

CROSS, Henry of Lansdowne.
    Lois, m. Anthony Lenz of Augusta. O.C. 11 Dec 1810.
    Esther, m. Abraham Talman of Augusta. O.C. 2 Jan 1811.
    Patty, m. William Talman of Augusta. O.C. 2 Jan 1811.
    Polly, m. Alpheus Reynolds of Augusta. O.C. 30 June 1797.
    John of Lansdowne. O.C. 26 Nov 1840.
    Lavinia, m. Lewis Jones of Lansdowne. O.C. 16 Feb 1837.
    Moses of Lansdowne. O.C. 27 March 1830.

CROWDER, Anthony of Osnabruck.
    Lydia, m. Francis Smith of Mountain. O.C. 27 Aug 1840.
    Hannah Eve, m. John Cook of Osnabruck. O.C. 27 May 1833.
    Mary. O.C. 19 Dec 1833.
    John of Matilda. O.C. 8 Nov 1832.

CROWDER, Isaac, m. Lydia.
    Hannah, bapt. 15 Oct 1787; m. Henry Utman of Williamsburgh. O.C. 16
        February 1811.

CROWDER, James of Osnabruck.
    Nelly, of Town of New Johnstown. O.C. 15 March 1803.
    Hannah, m. ---- Swart of Osnabruck. O.C. 14 June 1798.
    Sarah. O.C. 17 March 1807. Osnabruck.
    Catharine, m. Philip Cline of Osnabruck. O.C. 25 Feb 1809.
    Martha, m. Henry Putman of Town of Hammond, N.Y. Not. Rec. 12 Oct
        1837.
    James of Osnabruck. O.C. 25 July 1833.
    Paul of Osnabruck. O.C. 30 May 1834.
    Grace, m. Eliakim Norton of Osnabruck. O.C. 5 Feb 1831.

CROWDER, William of Osnabruck.
    Charles of Osnabruck. O.C. 16 April 1818.
    Elizabeth, m. Abraham Hopper of Osnabruck. Land Board Certificate,
        31/8 Williamsburgh.

CROWDER, William of Matilda.
    Mary, m. Peter Hopper of Matilda. O.C. 24 April 1835.
    Elizabeth, m. Richard Lewis of Matilda. O.C. 15 May 1835.
    Catharine, m. John Foy of Cornwall. O.C. 11 Feb 1836.
    Andrus of Matilda. O.C. 6 Dec 1832.
    Sally, m. Christian Knight of Matilda. O.C. 6 Dec 1832.
    William of Matilda. O.C. 5 March 1828.

CROWDER, William III of Osnabruck.
    Margaret, m. Charles Lasart of Williamsburgh. O.C. 2 Sept 1818.

CRUMB, Benoni of Louth, widow, Sarah.
    Mary. O.C. 27 March 1813.   [Cont'd]

CRUMB, Benoni - Cont'd
  Cornelius of Louth. O.C. 20 May 1817.
  Jane, m. John Lake of Trafalgar. O.C. 28 March 1833.
  Albert of Louth. O.C. 28 March 1833.
  Margaret, m. Jacob Weaver of Grantham. O.C. 15 Aug 1833.
  Isaac, bapt. 13 July 1792.
  Benjamin of Carradoc. O.C. 6 Sept 1832.

CRUMB, William of Haldimand County. Indian Dept. [See TOR 1: 212]
  Sarah, m. John File of Haldimand County. O.C. 13 October 1796.

CRYDERMAN, Hermanus of Cornwall, m. Olive Bennett.
  Lydia, m. Daniel Algire of Cornwall. O.C. 7 Nov 1809.
  Mary, m. Philip Eamer of Cornwall, 10 March 1807. O.C. 7 Aug 1811.
  Elizabeth. O.C. 19 April 1816.
  Harmonus of Cornwall. O.C. 19 April 1816.
  Olive, bapt. 23 Aug 1795; m. John C. Horton of Cornwall 12 October 1812
    O.C. 18 March 1818.
  John H. of Cornwall. O.C. 21 Feb 1821.

CRYDERMAN, John of Cornwall, m. Catharine Hartle.
  James of Osnabruck. O.C. 25 July 1833.
  Ann, m. Henry Gallinger of Osnabruck. O.C. 25 July 1833.
  Jacob of Cornwall. O.C. 5 Sept 1833.
  Hannah, m. Jacob Alguire of Cornwall. O.C. 19 Dec 1833.
  Mary, m. John McKay of Cornwall. O.C. 19 Dec 1833.
  Margaret, b. 27 Oct 1798; m. Michael Gallinger of Osnabruck. O.C. 19
    December 1833.
  William of Cornwall. O.C. 19 December 1833.
  John of Osnabruck. O.C. 19 December 1833.
  Elizabeth, bapt. 30 July 1797; m. Oliver Raymond of Cornwall. O.C. 11
    January 1834.
  Catharine, m. Henry Gallinger of Osnabruck. O.C. 7 Feb 1833.
  Benjamin, b. 6 May 1810.
  Simon, b. 18 July 1813.

CRYDERMAN, Joseph of Cornwall, m. Catharine dau of Michael Cline, U.E.
  Hannah, bapt. 15 Nov 1795. O.C. 13 Feb 1816.
  Margaret. O.C. 13 Feb 1816.
  Catharine. O.C. 21 Feb 1821.
  John of Cornwall. O.C. 2 Oct 1822.
  Valentine of East Gwillimbury, bapt. 12 July 1791; m. Sarah Gallinger.
    O.C. 5 December 1827.
  Joseph of Cornwall. O.C. 7 May 1829.

CRYDERMAN, Valentine, m. Catherine.
  Michael of Marysburgh, U.E., m. Mary
  Joseph of Cornwall, U.E., m. Catharine Cline.

CRYDERMAN, Valentine - Cont'd
   Hermanus of Cornwall, U.E., m. Olive Bennett.
   John of Cornwall, U.E., m. Catharine Hartle.
   Catherine, m. Michael Gallinger Jr. of Cornwall. O.C. 5 June 1798.

CRYSLER, Geronimus of Williamsburgh (eldest son of Philip Crysler ?). He
   was granted 32/5 and 37/6, Williamsburgh.
   Margaret, m. John McDonell of Finch. O.C. 26 March 1840.
   Elizabeth, m. James Riddell of Montague. O.C. 3 March 1836.
   Mary, m. Albert Hollister of Osnabruck. O.C. 11 July 1833.
   Peter of Williamsburgh. O.C. 3 April 1834.
   Margaret G. O.C. 24 Nov 1832.
   John G. of Williamsburgh, m. Elizabeth Merkley. O.C. 26 Oct 1825.

CRYSLER, John of Williamsburgh and Finch, m. Nancy dau Richard Loucks,
   U.E.
   Eliza, m. Seneca Deuel of Williamsburgh. O.C. 4 July 1815.
   Caroline, m. ---- Carter of Town of Cornwall. O.C. 15 Feb 1838.
   Ann, m. John Sedley of City of Quebec. O.C. 18 July 1839. Jno. Sedley,
      see Q211-1, p. 501-508.
   Margaret, m. William Loucks of Finch. O.C. 26 March 1840.
   Gordon H. of Williamsburgh. O.C. 26 Nov 1840.
   Lucretia Valentine, m. John C. Munro of Town of Hamilton, 1 June 1850;
      O.C. 26 Nov 1840.
   George M. of Cornwall, m. Sophia Ann McArthur 19 March 1835. O.C.
      16 February 1837.
   James of Williamsburgh. O.C. 3 April 1834.
   Charles Baker of Williamsburgh, b. 15 Dec 1810; d. in Kingston, 6 Feb
      1886. O.C. 3 April 1834.
   Samuel Ira of Williamsburgh, m. Sally Hickey. O.C. 3 Apr 1834.
   John Martin of Cramahe. O.C. 14 Sept 1825.
   Pembroke Guy of Finch. O.C. 16 Dec 1843.
   John Pliny of Williamsburgh, b. 26 Feb 1801; d. Morrisburg 7 Apr 1881.
      O.C. 2 February 1825.
   Mary Ellen, b. 9 July 1825; m. William Oliver Buchanan of Stamford on
      22 Oct 1845; d. 3 Sept 1905. O.C. 6 Sept 1847.
   William Ira of Cornwall, d. 8 July 1836.
   Adealaide A. O.C. 12 August 1850.

CRYSLER, Philip of Williamsburgh. [Philip Crysler, of Butler's Rangers,
   and his family were at Niagara in 1783. The Ontario Register 1: 206]
   Catherine. O.C. 18 June 1799.
   Dorothy. O.C. 18 June 1799.
   Leany, m. ---- Piller. O.C. 18 June 1799.
   Mary, m. Aaron Brink of Williamsburgh. O.C. 17 March 1804.
   John of Williamsburgh. O.C. 12 Jan 1837. double grant.

CRYSLER, William. Inserted on U.E. List. O.C. 17 March 1807.

CUMMING, John of Marysburgh.
> James of Marysburgh. O. C. 14 March 1839. O. C. 29 June 1837.
> William of Adolphustown, m. Mary McIntosh, 21 April 1807. O. C. 27 April 1837.
> Gitty, m. James Todman of Marysburgh. O. C. 29 June 1837.
> Joseph of Marysburgh. O. C. 27 July 1837.

CUMMING, Thomas of Chippawa. Butler's Rangers. Married Jane Christie 13 March 1788. She died 13 February 1821. He died at Chippawa 3 March 1823, aged about 65 years.
> Jane, b. 24 July 1791; m. James Crooks of Town of Niagara 8 Dec 1808. O. C. 3 March 1809.
> James of Willoughby, b. 12 Apr 1789; m. (1) Priscilla Nelles 22 Jan 1818; m. (2) Sophia Macklem, 4 Feb 1828; d. 27 Feb 1875. From Weekly Mail Aug 9, 1878: Died at Goderich, 1 August, in her 78th year, Sophia, widow of the late James Cummings of Chippawa.

CUMMING, William of Cornwall.
> Peter of South Gower. O. C. 16 June 1807.
> Marjory. O. C. 21 July 1812. Cornwall.
> Christy, m. John Hartle, Jr. of Cornwall. O. C. 11 Nov 1815.
> Mary, m. John Carpenter of Cornwall. O. C. 11 Nov 1815.
> John of Cornwall, bapt. 15 Dec 1793. O. C. 11 Nov 1815.
> William of Cornwall. O. C. 18 March 1818.
> Donald, bapt. 29 Aug 1790.

CURLAND, John of Grantham. See O. C. 7 June 1826.
> Ann, m. Ezekiel Cudney of Grantham. O. C. 27 April 1837.
> John of Niagara. O. C. 5 Sept 1833.
> Susannah, m. Daniel Cudney of Grantham. O. C. 1 May 1834.
> Sophia, m. Joseph Chatterton of Ancaster. O. C. 24 March 1835.

CURRY, Ephraim of Edwardsburgh, m. Alice Boulton.
> Nancy, m. Gideon Adams Jr. of Edwardsburgh. O. C. 2 March 1816.
> Rachel, bapt. 11 March 1792; m. Lemuel Hough of Edwardsburgh. O. C. 2 March 1816.
> John of Edwardsburgh. O. C. 22 Oct 1817.
> Mary, b. 30 Oct 1797; m. Samuel Hunter of South Gower. OC 22 Oct 1817.
> Ephraim of Edwardsburgh, m. Nancy Helmer. Grand River, Haldimand. 95th Claim Heir & Devisee Commission, 1842.
> Abraham of Pembroke. O. C. 4 April 1839.
> Elizabeth, m. Philomon Thrasher of South Gower.
> George of Edwardsburgh. O. C. 2 April 1828.

CURRY, James of Lancaster.
> Catherine, m. Enos Pettingal of Lancaster. O. C. 7 August 1811.

CURRY, John of Lancaster, m. Elizabeth Snyder.
    John of Lancaster, bapt. 17 Oct 1790; m. Mary McKie 23 March 1813.
        O. C. 23 Nov 1816.
    James of Lancaster. O. C. 20 May 1817.
    Elizabeth, m. James Penn Campbell of Lancaster 18 Oct 1809. O.C. 20
        May 1817.
    William of Lancaster. O. C. 2 Oct 1822.
    George of Lancaster, Jr., bapt. 13 Aug 1797. O. C. 2 October 1822.
    Seraphina, b. 26 Sept 1813. O.C. 10 Aug 1837.
    Margaret, m. Alexander McBain of Lancaster. O. C. 12 Nov 1827.
    Solomon of Lancaster. O. C. 17 Jan 1829.
    Morella, m. Peter McKey of Lancaster. O. C. 17 Jan 1829.
    Robert of Lancaster. O. C. 19 Jan 1825.

CUTHBERT, Donald of Charlottenburgh, m. Mary (Flora) Cameron.
    Donald of Charlottenburgh. O. C. 9 March 1803.
    Mary, bapt. 14 Nov 1790; m. George Ross of Eldon. O. C. 18 July 1839.
    Janet, bapt. 12 June 1791.

D

DAFOE, Abraham, m. Catharine. See O. C. 7 Jan 1830, John Diamond.
    Jacob of Fredericksburgh. O. C. 26 Jan 1808.
    Elizabeth. O. C. 23 Feb 1809.
    George of Fredericksburgh, bapt. 9 March 1788. O. C. 16 Feb 1810.
    Lucy, bapt. 11 December 1791.

DAFOE, Conrad of Osnabruck.
    John of Osnabruck. O. C. 25 Feb 1812.
    Mary. O. C. 19 April 1816.
    William of Osnabruck, m. Nancy Loucks. O. C. 19 April 1816.
    Daniel of Osnabruck. O. C. 18 March 1818.
    Richard of Osnabruck. O. C. 2 Feb 1825.
    Catharine, m. John P. Shaver of Osnabruck. O. C. 28 Sept 1825.

DAFOE, Daniel of Fredericksburgh, m. Elizabeth.
    Mary, bapt. 21 Sept 1791; m. John Phillips of Fredericksburgh in Decem-
        ber 1810. O. C. 25 Feb 1812.
    William G. of Fredericksburgh. O. C. 18 October 1838.
    Caleb of Fredericksburgh. O. C. 2 March 1840.
    Hannah. O. C. 10 March 1834.
    Catharine, m. ---- Benedict of Sheffield. O. C. 10 March 1834.
    Andrew of Sheffield. O. C. 1 May 1834.
    Samuel of Sheffield. O. C. 1 May 1834.
    David of Huntingdon. O. C. 30 May 1834.
    John of Fredericksburgh. O. C. 4 February 1830.
    Michael of Adolphustown. O. C. 25 January 1831.
    Conrad of Fredericksburgh. O. C. 5 April 1825.

DAFOE, John Sr.
  Mary, m. Andrew Rickley of Fredericksburgh. O.C. 18 Nov 1797.

DAFOE, John of Richmond, formerly of Fredericksburgh, m. Lois, dau of
Joel and Deborah Prindle.
  Nancy, bapt. 31 Dec 1787; m. Simeon Prindle of Adolphustown. O.C. 23
    March 1802.
  Deborah, bapt. 29 March 1792; m. Joseph Prindle of Richmond. O.C. 25
    February 1812.
  Mary, bapt. 18 Nov 1794; m. James Phillips of Fredericksburgh. O.C. 26
    March 1817.
  Abraham of Richmond. O.C. 20 May 1817.
  Conrad of Richmond, bapt. 8 Feb 1797. O.C. 26 Feb 1818.
  Lucy, m. Jacob Shaw of Fredericksburgh. O.C. 6 Sept 1820.
  Calvin of Sidney. O.C. 10 March 1834.

DAFOE, Michael of Fredericksburgh, b. 1766; m.(1) Rachel, dau of John
and Rachel Holcomb; m.(2) Rachel, dau Zenas and Rachel Ross; living in
1859, aged 93. See O.C. 31 July 1834.
  John of Fredericksburgh, bapt. 9 Feb 1789. O.C. 3 April 1810.
  Daniel of Richmond. O.C. 15 Feb 1838.
  Abraham of Richmond. O.C. 15 Feb 1838.
  Caleb of Richmond. O.C. 16 May 1839.
  Jacob of Markham. O.C. 1 Aug 1839.
  Michael of Richmond, bapt. 21 Sept 1791. O.C. 1 April 1840.
  William of Pickering, bapt. 25 Jan 1796. O.C. 16 April 1840.
  Zenas of Belleville. O.C. 28 Feb 1842.
  Elizabeth, m. Joshua Miller of Pickering 30 Aug 1831. OC 28 Nov 1839.
  Mary, bapt. 19 Sept 1809; m. Manuel Northrup of Belleville. O.C. 26
    May 1845.
  Rachel, m. Jacob Van Norman of Ameliasburgh in April 1821. O.C. 14
    October 1842.

DALY, Peter of Ernestown, m. Mary, dau of David Hartman, U.E., of
Ernestown.
  Catherine, m. Jacob Shibley of Ernestown, 9 Feb 1806. OC 17 Feb 1807.
  Susannah, m. Joseph Aikens of Sidney. O.C. 20 Jan 1816.
  Mary, m. Joshua Booth Jr. of Ernestown. O.C. 2 March 1816.
  Lewis of Ernestown. O.C. 27 Feb 1818.
  Phillip of Ernestown, m. Mary Booth; d. 1861. O.C. 27 Feb 1818.
  David of Ernestown, m. Hannah Thomas, 11 March 1819. OC 27 Feb 1818.
  Charles of Ernestown, b. 7 Oct 1809. OC 1 Aug 1833.
  Thomas of Ernestown, b. 29 Apr 1807. OC 1 Aug 1833.
  Rachel. O.C. 19 Dec 1833.
  Ann, m. Asahel Rockwell of Ernestown. OC 19 July 1826.

DAVEY, Henry of Ernestown.
  George of Ernestown. OC 31 Oct 1809.   [Cont'd]

DAVEY, Henry - Cont'd
  Elisabeth, m. James Laughlin of Ernestown. O.C. 5 June 1810.
  Mary. O.C. 3 June 1817.
  Eliza, m. Joseph Lee (See ?) of Sheffield. OC 10 March 1834.
  Richard of Sidney. O.C. 16 June 1834.
  Jacob of Sidney. O.C. 16 June 1834.
  Joseph of Sidney. O.C. 16 June 1834.

DAVEY, John of Ernestown.
  Catharine, m. Solomon Smith of Ernestown 9 Feb 1804. OC 25 Feb 1806.
  Eve, m. Peter Lard of Ernestown. OC 28 Feb 1806.
  Peter of Ernestown. O.C. 20 Nov 1810. O.C. 26 March 1817.
  John of Ernestown. O.C. 26 March 1817.
  Margaret, m. Seba Murphy of Town of Bath. O.C. 3 March 1836.
  George Huffnail of Ernestown. O.C. 11 April 1833.
  Benjamin Fairfield of Ernestown. O.C. 11 April 1833.
  Sophia, m. Ira Billings of Sidney 20 Jan 1816. O.C. 11 Jan 1834.

DAVEY, Michael of Ernestown. [See also Davy, Michael]
  Peter of Ernestown. O.C. 26 March 1840.
  Benjamin D. of Ernestown. O.C. 16 April 1840.
  Sally. O.C. 16 Feb 1837.
  Adam of Ernestown. O.C. 18 May 1837.
  John M. of Fredericksburgh. O.C. 4 Feb 1836.
  Salome. O.C. 26 May 1836.
  Elizabeth, m. William Bruce of Ernestown. O.C. 4 Sept 1834.
  Mary, m. James McLaughlin of Ernestown. O.C. 4 Sept 1834.
  George M. of Ernestown. O.C. 4 Sept 1834.
  Thomas M. of Ernestown. O.C. 4 Sept 1834.

DAVEY, Peter
  Mary, m. ---- Amey of Ernestown. O.C. 16 Nov 1797.
  Hannah, m. ---- Asselstine of Ernestown. O.C. 27 Oct 1801.

DAVIE, Peter of Williamsburgh.
  William of Williamsburgh. O.C. 2 Nov 1816.

DAVIE, Peter.
  Catherine, m. John Rock of Crowland. O.C. 2 March 1811.

DAVIES, Walter of Elizabethtown and Wolford.
  Anna, m. ---- Bissell. O.C. 23 Sept 1800.
  Mary. O.C. 8 July 1806.
  John H. of Wolford. O.C. 13 June 1818.
  Walter of South Crosby. O.C. 17 March 1812.
  Jemima, m.(1) ---- Hall. Land Board Certificate, 8/4 S. Crosby.
    O.C. 10 July 1806. m.(2) ---- Merrick of S. Crosby.

DAVIS, Peter
    Charles. O.C. 18 June 1799.
    John. O.C. 18 June 1799.

DAVIS, Richard of Wolfe Island, m. Susan.
    Peter C. of Wolfe Island. O.C. 2 March 1816.
    Thomas of Wolfe Island. O.C. 2 March 1816. O.C. 18 Feb 1843.
    John of Wolfe Island. O.C. 2 March 1816. O.C. 28 Oct 1835.
    Susannah. O.C. 2 March 1816.
    Hannah. O.C. 2 March 1816.
    David Frederick of Wolfe Island, bapt. 11 June 1808. OC 28 Oct 1835.
    James Samuel of Wolfe Island, bapt. 21 July 1805. OC 28 Oct 1835.
    William of Wolfe Island, bapt. 6 July 1800. OC 28 Oct 1835.
    Eleanor, m. William Allen of Drummond. OC 9 March 1843.

DAVIS, Thaddeus of Willoughby and Thorold.
    Phoebe, m. William H. Lee of Thorold. OC 25 Feb 1809.
    Jane, m. Andrew Ostrander of Stamford. OC 5 Feb 1810.
    Lydia, m. Peter Ostrander of Thorold. OC 5 Feb 1810.
    Loyal of Thorold. OC 3 April 1810.
    Thaddeus of Thorold, d. August, 1830, aged 56. OC 3 April 1810.
    Hall of Thorold. O.C. 3 April 1810.
    Wright of Thorold. O.C. 3 April 1810.
    Richard of Thorold. O.C. 28 Aug 1810.
    William of Thorold. O.C. 18 June 1811.
    Deborah, m. Simeon Relyea of Thorold. O.C. 19 May 1812.
    Lois, m. Cornelius Van Volkenburgh of Thorold. O.C. 27 March 1813.

DAVIS, Thomas of Barton and Woodhouse.
    Jane, m. William Potts of Woodhouse. OC 12 Oct 1810.
    Mary, bapt. 28 Apr 1793; m. William Vail of Windham. OC 26 March 1817
    Fanny, m. Usual Willson of Charlotteville. O.C. 20 May 1817.
    Thomas of Barton. O.C. 4 April 1821.
    Anne, m. James Stewart of London. O.C. 15 March 1838.
    Elizabeth, m. Caleb Wood of Windham. O.C. 11 Feb 1836.
    Margaret, m. Joseph B. Rousseaux of Barton. O.C. 8 May 1833.
    Robert of Walpole. OC 27 Feb 1834.
    William Alexander of Barton. O.C. 7 Feb 1833.
    John of Barton. O.C. 6 Dec 1832.
    Susan, m. Michael Burkholder of Barton. O.C. 6 December 1832.
    James of Saltfleet. OC 25 Nov 1842.
    David of Saltfleet. OC 14 Oct 1842.

DAVIS, William of Saltfleet, b. 23 Dec 1741 son of Thomas and Mary Davis
  on a plantation near Baltimore, Md. He came to Upper Canada in August
  1792. Married Hannah Phillips.
    Kezia, b. 1785; m. John Kline of Saltfleet. OC 17 June 1806.
    Jonathan of Saltfleet, b. 25 Jan 1783; m. Jane Long. OC 19 Aug 1806 [Cont'd

DAVIS, William - Cont'd
  Sarah, b. 2 Nov 1787; m. John Chisholm of Flamborough East. O.C. ⁄16
    April 1811.
  Mary, b. in North Carolina 22 Oct 1777; m. James Gage of Saltfleet; died
    Hamilton, 18 Oct 1853. O.C. 22 July 1797.
  Asahel of Nelson, b. Orange Co., N.C., 1774; m. Ann Morden; d. 24
    March 1850, aged 76. O.C. 22 July 1797.
  William of Niagara, b. 1776; m. Mary Long. O.C. 23 April 1797(?);
    O.C. 23 April 1798.
  Elizabeth, b. 29 Oct 1772; m. Thomas Ghent of Saltfleet; moved to Nelson
    1805. O.C. 22 July 1797.

DAVY, Michael of Ernestown. [See also Davey, Michael]
  Michael of Ernestown. O.C. 27 Nov 1834.
  Henry of Ernestown. O.C. 27 Nov 1834.

DAWSON, James of Kingston, m. Leah.
  John of Town of Kingston, tailor. O.C. 12 Nov 1817.
  William of Kingston, bapt. 1 June 1794. O.C. 22 Oct 1817.
  Elizabeth, bapt. 7 Apr 1793; m. Henry Ansley of Camden East. O.C. 27
    November 1834.
  Rachel, bapt. 1 Feb 1795; m. John Spence of Kingston. OC 11 May 1830.
  Jane, bapt. 18 March 1798; m. James Moody of Town of Kingston.
    O.C. 13 June 1836.
  James of Kingston. O.C. 13 June 1836.

DAY, Barnabas of Kingston.
  Barnabas of Kingston. O.C. 17 Nov 1797.
  Lewis of Kingston, m. Mary Hill. O.C. 17 Nov 1797.
  David. Land Board Certificate, 2/5 Portland.

DAYTON, Nathan of Elizabethtown.
  Abraham of Elizabethtown, m. Olive. His will is dated 13 August 1836.
    O.C. 14 August 1804.
  Abigail, m. Truelove Butler of Elizabethtown. O.C. 30 June 1812, and
    17 July 1817.
  Anna, m. Stephen Cromwell of Elizabethtown. O.C. 17 July 1817.
  Hannah, m. John Robinson of Elizabethtown. O.C. 25 Jan 1834.

DECKER, Thomas of Pelham. Butler's Rangers. His widow m.(2) Jacob
  Servos of Pelham. See O.C. 14 July 1797.
  Nancy, m. John Rogers of Louth. O.C. 25 Feb 1812.
  Laney, m. Daniel Kennedy of Clinton. O.C. 9 March 1816.
  Isaac of Gainesborough. O.C. 22 Sept 1819.

DECOW, Jacob of Thorold and Burford.
  Jane, m. John Losee of Stamford. O.C. 25 Oct 1798.
  Edmund of Thorold. O.C. 17 June 1806.   [Cont'd]

DECOW, Jacob - Cont'd
  Abner of Burford. O.C. 19 Aug 1806.
  Abraham of Burford. O.C. 19 Aug 1806.
  Sarah, m. John Vollick of Burford. O.C. 20 Oct 1798.
  John of Thorold, m. Catherine Docksteder, 9 Aug 1798.

DEDERICK, Jacob of Grantham, m. Margaret dau of William Pickard, Sr.,
  U.E.
  Catherine, m. George Hainer of Grantham. O.C. 6 Apr 1803, 7 July 1831.
  Robert of Grantham, m. Ann. O.C. 17 Feb 1807.
  James of Grantham. O.C. 8 Feb 1808.
  Margaret, m. John Clendenning of Grantham 18 Jan 1816. OC 25 Feb 1818.
  Jemima. O.C. 31 May 1820.
  William of Grantham. O.C. 31 May 1820.
  Caroline, m. Horatio Nelson Camp of Dunnville 28 Feb 1832. O.C. 7
    August 1834.
  Jacob of Grantham. O.C. 9 November 1825.
  Walter of Grantham. O.C. 9 November 1825.

DEDRICK, Lucas of Walsingham.
  John of Walsingham. O.C. 27 March 1813. O.C. 11 Aug 1847.
  Hannah, m. John Backhouse Jr. of Walsingham. O.C. 9 Dec 1815.
  Lucas of Walsingham. O.C. 27 Aug 1840.
  Cornelius of Walsingham. O.C. 16 Feb 1837.

DE FOREST, Abraham of Stamford and Toronto, 2nd Batt., K.R.R.N.Y.,
  married Elizabeth dau of Jacob Bowman, U.E.
  John of Stamford, bapt. 22 July 1792. O.C. 26 March 1817.
  Mary, m. Adam Bowman of Stamford. O.C. 26 March 1817.
  James of Stamford. O.C. 20 May 1817.
  Simon of Toronto. O.C. 16 June 1819.
  Abraham of Nelson. O.C. 28 Feb 1833.
  Hannah, m. William Weir of Nelson. O.C. 4 Feb 1830.

DE FOREST, Simon, m. Mary. O.C. 9 July 1801.
  Rebecca, m. Robert McLean of Elizabethtown. O.C. 18 Nov 1797.
  Ann, m. Stephen Secord of Niagara in February 1784. O.C. 7 July 1796.
  Mary, m. Mathew Pruyn of Ernestown, 5 Apr 1790. O.C. 30 Aug 1797,
    O.C. 21 Dec 1840.
  Abraham of Stamford, U.E., m. Elizabeth Bowman.
  Dorothy, m. Samuel Marther of Town of York 10 July 1794. OC 11 July
    1795.
  Sarah, m. Ebenezer Washburn of Hallowell.

DELL, Basnett.
  Rebecca, m. Charles Green Jr. of Stamford. O.C. 3 Nov 1801.

DELL, Henry of Wainfleet.
  Elizabeth, m. Robert Frank of Stamford and Westminster; d. June, 1874.
    O.C. 5 June 1810.
  Nathaniel of Willoughby. O.C. 1 July 1834.
  Basnett of Louth. O.C. 3 July 1834.
  Anna, m. John Read of Westminster. O.C. 28 June 1832.
  Henry of Wainfleet. O.C. 28 June 1832.
  Samuel of Willoughby. O.C. 28 June 1832.
  Hannah, m. John Nunnamaker of Thorold. O.C. 24 Oct 1831.
  Adoram of Louth. O.C. 13 April 1825.

DEMILL, Anthony of Kingston; died there 17 Jan 1813, aged 62.
  Margaret, b. 1783; m. Alexander Douglas of Bertie 22 Feb 1800; d. 28
    Sept 1838. O.C. 26 March 1817.
  Susannah, m. Charles Launier of Sophiasburgh. O.C. 16 June 1819.

DEMILL, Isaac of Sophiasburgh.
  Elizabeth, m. Henry William Fox of Sophiasburgh. O.C. 17 Feb 1807.
  Catharine, m. Jacob Bellue of Ameliasburgh. O.C. 26 Jan 1808.
  Susannah, m. Israel Tripp of Sophiasburgh. O.C. 5 July 1798.
  Mary, m. Richard Tripp of Sophiasburgh. OC 30 June 1812; 20 May 1817.
  John of Sophiasburgh. O.C. 25 Feb 1818.
  Jane, m. Samuel Cooley. OC 25 Feb 1818. Not. Rec. 17 Dec 1840.
  Barbara, m. Daniel Lambert of Sophiasburgh. O.C. 25 Feb 1818.
  Sarah, m. Reuben Way of Ameliasburgh. O.C. 19 March 1840.
  Isaac of Sophiasburgh. O.C. 28 Sept 1832.
  Peter of Sophiasburgh. O.C. 11 Sept 1832.

DEMOREST, James of Fredericksburgh.
  James of Richmond. O.C. 19 Feb 1817.
  Catharine, m. William Bowen of Richmond 29 March 1818. OC 7 May 1828.
  Margaret, m. Abraham Prindle of Fredericksburgh. O.C. 7 May 1828.

DEMPSEY, Thomas of Ameliasburgh.
  Sarah, m. Cornelius Benson of Ameliasburgh. O.C. 17 July 1817.
  Margaret, m. John Bonter of Ameliasburgh. O.C. 18 March 1818.
  Isaac of Ameliasburgh. O.C. 18 March 1818.
  Peter of Ameliasburgh. O.C. 18 March 1818.
  Ann, m. William Wannamaker of Ameliasburgh. O.C. 18 March 1818.
  William of Ameliasburgh. O.C. 22 June 1825.
  Catherine, m. Simon Delong of Ameliasburgh. O.C. 22 June 1825.

DENNIS, John of York. (John McLaney is stated on the U.E. List to be a
  step-son of John Dennis).
  Hannah, m. Thomas Johnson of York 24 June 1802. O.C. 10 May 1803.
  Joseph of Town of Kingston, m. (1) Mary Stoughton who d. 25 June 1841 ae
    43 yrs 5 mos; m. (2) Margaret Deacon widow of Robert Richardson of
    Town of Kingston; d. 17 June 1867. O.C. 2 March 1816.   [Cont'd]

DENNIS, John - Cont'd
  Rebecca, m. James Richardson Jr. of Town of Kingston 31 Jan 1813.
    O.C. 2 March 1816.
  Elizabeth. O.C. 14 Feb 1798.

DENNISTON, Robert of Stamford.
  Sarah, m. Thomas Millard Jr. of Stamford. OC 26 Feb 1799.

DENYKE, Andrew of Kingston Town. Pvt., New Jersey Vols., m. Cather-
  ine Burn. A dau (4th) Polly died at Town of Kingston, Sunday morning 20
  March 1814 aged 17 years 4 mos and 5 days. She was b. November 1796.
  Jane, m. Samuel Howe of Kingston 30 Aug 1808. OC 3 March 1809.
  Elizabeth, m. Elijah Tonny in June 1811. O.C. 22 Feb 1810.
  Catharine, bapt. 14 Apr 1793; m. John Ward of Town of Kingston on 30
    March 1815. O.C. 23 Nov 1816.
  Mary, bapt. 1 Feb 1795; buried 27 Sept 1795.
  Mary (Maria?) bapt. 22 Jan 1797; m. James Lane of Hillier. O.C. 25
    November 1842.
  Sarah, bapt. 6 Sept 1800.
  William of Fredericksburgh, b. 22 Nov 1810. OC 5 Sept 1833.
  Ann Robinson. O.C. 9 May 1834. Fredericksburgh.
  Anthony of Kingston. O.C. 4 Feb 1830.
  Isaac of Fredericksburgh. O.C. 2 Apr 1828.
  Andrew of Hallowell. O.C. 17 March 1824.

DEPUE, Charles of Barton.
  Elizabeth, m. Josiah Bennett of Barton. O.C. 17 June 1806.
  Susannah. O.C. 13 Feb 1816.
  Mary, m. Peter Jones of Barton. O.C. 18 Aug 1819.
  Charles of Barton. O.C. 19 Apr 1820.
  William of Barton. O.C. 22 May 1820.
  Catharine. O.C. 2 May 1821.
  John of Barton, m. Elizabeth Springer. O.C. 2 May 1821.
  Timothy of Saltfleet. O.C. 2 May 1833.
  Rachel, m. Abner Rosebrugh of Flamborough West. O.C. 18 July 1833.
  George of Barton. O.C. 24 Dec 1831.
  Nancy, m. Henry Hannon of Glanford. O.C. 11 May 1825.
  Sarah. O.C. 11 May 1825.

DEPUE, John Jr. of Barton.
  John of Barton. O.C. 8 May 1833.
  Elizabeth, m. Pierres Curtis of Barton. O.C. 19 Jan 1833.
  Deborah, m. Thomas Reynolds of Barton, 8 Apr 1819. OC 1 Nov 1832.
  James of Barton, m. Catherine Meddaugh. O.C. 27 April 1832.
  Abraham of Barton. O.C. 5 April 1832.
  Conrad of Ancaster. O.C. 5 April 1832.

DEPUE, John Sr., m. Mary. [He and his family were at Niagara in 1783; see The Ontario Register, v.1, p. 213]
    Marianne, m. Frederick Williams of Ancaster. O.C. 24 Feb 1801.
    Mary, m. Charles Stewart of Barton. O.C. 9 Jan 1797.
    William. (See O.C. 17 May 1797).
    Charles of Barton, U.E.
    John of Barton, U.E.

DERBY, John of Grantham.
    Ann, m. John Schram of Grantham. O.C. 18 March 1818.

Detlor, John of Fredericksburgh, Kingston and York. K.R.R.N.Y. Married Jerusha, dau of Titus Simons, U.E.
    Catharine Hill, m. William M. Roblin of Adolphustown, 21 March 1844. O.C. 19 April 1820.
    George Hill of Fredericksburgh, m. Maria Roblin; d. Napanee 31 Dec 1883 aet. 89 yrs 5 mos. O.C. 6 March 1822.
    Elizabeth, m. Joseph Lockwood of Brighton. O.C. 2 February 1837.
    John McGill of Richmond, m. Hetty Lazier. O.C. 10 March 1834.
    Ann, m. John Chamberlain of Fredericksburgh. OC 5 March 1829.

DETLOR, Peter of Fredericksburgh.
    George of Fredericksburgh. O.C. 27 August 1833.
    Stephen L. of Fredericksburgh. O.C. 27 August 1833.

DETLOR, Samuel of Fredericksburgh, son of Valentine Detlor.
    Catherine Hill. O.C. 27 Aug 1840.
    Elizabeth. O.C. 3 April 1834.
    John Valentine of Richmond. O.C. 3 April 1834.
    Samuel of Fredericksburgh. O.C. 3 April 1834.
    Thomas Empey of Fredericksburgh. O.C. 29 June 1843.
    George.
    Ann.

DETLOR, Valentine of Fredericksburgh. See Haldimand Papers B214:47.
    Ann. O.C. 8 July 1797.
    Elizabeth, m. Darius Dunham of Fredericksburgh. O.C. 8 July 1797.
    Hannah, m. Elias Dulmage of Edwardsburgh. O.C. 8 July 1797.
    Samuel of Fredericksburgh. Land Board Certificate, 13/1 Camden.
    George of Fredericksburgh.
    John of Kingston and York, U.E.

DEWITT, Garton of Cornwall, m. Phoebe Waterman.
    Mary, m. Adam Hartle of Cornwall. O.C. 5 Jan 1798.
    Abigail, m. John Jackson of Cornwall. O.C. 8 March 1803.
    Zephaniah of Fort George, Pvt., 41st Regt. O.C. 19 May 1807.
    Elizabeth. O.C. 22 Feb 1810.
    Rachel, bapt. 26 July 1789.

DIAMOND, Jacob of Fredericksburgh.
   Mary, m. Peter Bowen of Fredericksburgh. OC 2 July 1799, 31 Oct 1821.
   Catherine, m. Staats Sager of Richmond 1 Jan 1799. OC 28 Feb 1804.
   Elizabeth, m. Peter Barton of Richmond. OC 23 Feb 1809.
   Laney, m. Asa Schermerhorn of Richmond. OC 2 May 1833.
   William of Richmond. OC 7 March 1827.

DIAMOND, Jacob Jr. of Fredericksburgh.
   Catharine, m. Daniel Gould of Richmond. O. C. 18 May 1833.

DIAMOND, John of Fredericksburgh and Kingston.
   Elizabeth, m. Thomas Moon of Kingston. O. C. 2 April 1828.
   Robert of Kingston. O. C. 1 July 1830.
   Baltus of Fredericksburgh. O. C. 8 Feb 1827.

DIAMOND, John of Fredericksburgh.
   Jane, m. Daniel Carr of Camden East. OC 26 Jan 1808.
   Catharine, m. Orin Dibble of Fredericksburgh. OC 9 July 1817.
   William of Fredericksburgh. O. C. 26 July 1820.
   Abraham of Fredericksburgh. O. C. 21 Feb 1821.
   John of Fredericksburgh. OC 21 Feb 1821. Of Kingston, OC 6 Oct 1831;
      OC 5 Jan 1832.
   Mary, m. Hezekiah Loree of Richmond. O. C. 10 March 1834.
   Clara. O. C. 15 May 1832. Kingston.
   Sarah, m. Simon Redding of Loughborough. O. C. 15 May 1832.
   Anne, m. Adam Vanvalkenburg of Kingston. O. C. 6 Oct 1831.
   Henry of Kingston. O. C. 1 July 1830.
   Andrew of Fredericksburgh. O. C. 22 June 1825.

DIES, Mathew of Fredericksburgh. Qr. Mr. K. R. R. N. Y. See OC 2 Jan 1817.
   John of Ernestown. O. C. 6 Aug 1840(?)
   Mathew of Ameliasburgh. O. C. 12 Oct 1841(?)
   Lydia. Land Board Certificate. 16/6 Richmond.
   Rebecca, m. David Fraser of Ernestown. Land Board Certificate, 17/6
      of Richmond.
   Catharine, m. Abraham Larraway of Fredericksburgh 6 July 1790. Land
      Board Certificate, 13/3 of Richmond.

DINGMAN, John of Westminster. Corp'l, Butler's Rangers.
   Elizabeth, m. George Minard of Westminster. O. C. 26 Oct 1825.
   Lawrence of Westminster. O. C. 23 June 1824.
   David of Westminster. O. C. 6 Dec 1832.
   William of Lobo. O. C. 19 Dec 1833.
   Mary, m. Frederick Lown of Westminster 17 Aug 1829. OC 7 Feb 1839.
   Henry of Westminster. O. C. 11 Jan 1834.
   George of Westminster. O. C. 28 Feb 1835.
   Nancy, m. John Young of London. O. C. 24 March 1835.
   Catharine, m. Arganus Bertlett of Carradoc. OC 6 Dec 1832.   [Cont'd]

DINGMAN, John - Cont'd
  Anna, m. Thomas Cunningham of Adelaide. O. C. 23 July 1832.
  Margaret, m. Benjamin Schram of Westminster. O. C. 28 June 1832.

DINGMAN, Richard (Derrick) of Matilda, soldier, Capt. Angus McDonell's
  Compnay, R. R. N. Y. He was drowned, with his wife and one small child,
  in the St. Lawrence River in May 1790, a little above Weager's Mill, in
  Williamsburgh Township.
  Eve, b. 9 Jan 1786; m. Archibald Hill of Montague. O. C. 31 May 1803.
  Mary, b. 22 March 1774, m. Roswell Everts of Augusta. OC 15 Mar 1803.
  Rachel, b. 30 May 1783; m. David Aldridge of Augusta. OC 15 Mar 1803.
  Leah, b. 14 March 1778; m. (1) Charles Bursett; m. (2) Abial Walton.
  Sarah, b. 9 April 1776; m. Richard Smith. O. C. 5 Jan 1798.

DINGWALL, James of Charlottenburgh, m. Katharine Ferguson.
  Ann. O. C. 27 Jan 1807.
  Mary, bapt. 8 May 1791; m. John McNaughton Jr. of Charlottenburgh on
      27 Oct 1808. O. C. 7 Feb 1807.
  Alexander of Charlottenburgh, b. 8 Jan 1787. O. C. 16 Aug 1810.
  Donald of Charlottenburgh, b. 8 Feb 1789. O. C. 16 Aug 1810.
  John of Charlottenburgh, bapt. 27 July 1794. O. C. 23 Nov 1816.
  Isabel, bapt. 12 Feb 1797.
  Margaret, m. ---- McIntosh of Cornwall. O. C. 4 Apr 1839.
  Catharine. O. C. 3 Jan 1831.
  James of Charlottenburgh. O. C. 8 Dec 1826.

DINGWALL, John of Charlottenburgh. He was born in 1745 in the Parish of
  Duthill, Speyside, Morayshire, Scotland, son of Alexander Dingwall of
  Knockel-Granish. He died in December, 1819.
  Sophia. O. C. 3 March 1801.
  Isabella. O. C. 9 March 1803.
  Elizabeth. O. C. 8 Dec 1826.

DIXON, Francis of Ernestown.
  Eliza, m. George Barton of Camden East. O. C. 3 Oct 1839.
  Andrew of Thurlow. O. C. 19 March 1840.
  Elizabeth, m. William Reid of Thurlow. O. C. 1 April 1840.
  Dorcus, m. ---- Applebee of Thurlow. O. C. 3 Sept 1840.

DIXON, John Sr. of Cornwall.
  Elizabeth, m. ---- Snyder. O. C. 3 March 1801.
  Sarah, m. William Wood of Cornwall. O. C. 5 Jan 1798.
  Andrew of Cornwall. O. C. 19 Dec 1806.
  Mary, m. William Anderson of Osnabruck. O. C. 23 Feb 1809.
  Ann, m. John Annable Jr. of Cornwall. O. C. 20 Feb 1809.
  George of Cornwall. O. C. 7 Aug 1810.
  Thomas of Cornwall. O. C. 19 Feb 1817.

DIXON, Robert. See 31/3 Lancaster.
  Jennett, m. Malcolm McKillop of Charlottenburgh. O.C. 17 Aug 1808.
  Robert of Cornwall. O.C. 31 Oct 1809.
  William of Lancaster. O.C. 7 Aug 1811.
  Julia, m. William Dixon of Osnabruck. O.C. 9 March 1837.
  Sarah, m. ---- McLelland of Cornwall.

DOAN, Aaron of Humberstone.
  Levi of Humberstone. O.C. 3 June 1817.
  Martha, m. Manuel Winters of Humberstone. O.C. 22 Aug 1839.
  Ruth, m. William Pawling of Humberstone. O.C. 19 Aug 1833.
  Huldah. O.C. 1 May 1834.
  Sarah. O.C. 5 Feb 1835.
  Mary, m. Jacob Wade of Humberstone. O.C. 5 Feb 1835.
  Robert of Humberstone. O.C. 3 Dec 1828.
  Timothy of Humberstone. O.C. 3 Nov 1831.
  Joshua. O.C. 10 Dec 1831.

DOAN, Joseph of Humberstone and Walpole, born in Bucks County, Pa.
  Moses of Humberstone, cooper, m. Mary Wintermute. OC 23 May 1809.
  Mahlon of Humberstone. O.C. 9 Oct 1810.
  Leah, m. Adam Dennis of Walpole. O.C. 21 Feb 1821.
  Joseph of Walpole. O.C. 25 June 1823.
  Mary, m. George Waggoner of Walpole. O.C. 25 June 1823.
  Abraham of Walpole. O.C. 1 April 1840.
  Esther, m. Frederick Gibbs of Walpole. O.C. 26 Dec 1834.

DOCKSTEDER, Frederick.
  Catherine, m. John Decew of Thorold. O.C. 4 May 1804.

DOCKSTADER, George Adam. Sgt., K.R.R.N.Y.
  George H. See O.C. 29 July 1795.
  John. O.C. 2 Oct 1829.

DOCKSTEDER, John. Sgt., R.R.N.Y.
  Nicholas of Haldimand County. O.C. 28 April 1812.
  Catharine, m. Lyman Burham of Haldimand. O.C. 25 Feb 1819.

DOLSON, Isaac of Raleigh. Butler's Rangers. Married Mary, dau of George
  Fields, U.E. [Isaac Dolsen and his family, including John Dolsen aged 81,
  were at Niagara in 1783. See The Ontario Register, v.1, p. 213]
  Mathew of Raleigh. O.C. 19 Dec 1806.
  Isaac of Dover. O.C. 25 Sept 1804.
  Gilbert of Raleigh. O.C. 20 Feb 1810.
  Elizabeth, m. ---- Forsyth of Raleigh. O.C. 14 Aug 1804.
  Mary, m. John H. Dawsey of Raleigh. O.C. 20 Feb 1810.
  Jacob of Raleigh. O.C. 20 Feb 1810.
  Hannah, m. Michael Traxler of Chatham. O.C. 18 Feb 1834.

DOLSON, Mathew of Dover. Butler's Rangers. Married Hannah, daughter of George Fields, U. E.
John of Dover. O. C. 20 Aug 1817.
Isaac of Dover. O. C. 10 Sept 1817.

DOPP, Peter of Montague and Augusta, m. Deborah, dau of Stephen and Charity Farrington.
David of Augusta, bapt. 9 March 1788. O. C. 25 Feb 1812.
Charity, m. Adolphus Armstrong of Augusta. O. C. 25 Feb 1812.
Henry of Oxford. O. C. 22 May 1820.
Phoebe, m. Ebenezer Simons of Yarmouth. O. C. 8 Oct 1840.

DOREN, David of Matilda.
Peter of Matilda. O. C. 15 Nov 1838.
Catharine, m. ---- Serviss of Matilda. O. C. 27 June 1833.
Rachel, m. Hugh Bailey of Matilda. O. C. 25 Jan 1834.
Ephraim of Matilda. O. C. 6 Dec 1832.
Martin of Matilda. O. C. 27 Oct 1832.
Mary. O. C. 27 Oct 1832.
John D. of Matilda. O. C. 4 Feb 1830.

DORIN, Jacob of Matilda. K. R. R. N. Y.
John of Matilda, called Jr. O. C. 7 Nov 1797.

DORIN, John of Matilda.
Margaret, m. James Jackson of Matilda. O. C. 6 Dec 1803.
Hannah, m. John McIntosh of Matilda. O. C. 6 Dec 1803.
Catherine. O. C. 17 Dec 1840.
Elizabeth, m. James Jackson of Edwardsburgh. O. C. 17 Dec 1840.

DORLAND, Philip of Adolphustown.
Philip of Ameliasburgh. O. C. 30 Jan 1808.
Daniel Bedell of Adolphustown, m. Sarah Booth, 5 Sept 1808. O. C. 8
    February 1808.
Anna, m. Philip D. Haight of Adolphustown 6 June 1808. OC 23 Feb 1809.
Caty, m. Benjamin Booth of Ernestown 9 Nov 1809. OC 16 Feb 1811.
Arnoldi of Ameliasburgh. O. C. 25 Feb 1818.
Elizabeth. O. C. 8 March 1820.

DORLAND, Thomas of Adolphustown.
Deborah, m. James Fairlie of Sidney 2 March 1806. OC 17 Feb 1807.
Samuel of Adolphustown, m. Jane Huyck, 12 Apr 1806. OC 22 Feb 1808.
Peter V. of Adolphustown. O. C. 20 May 1817.

DOUGALL, William of Hallowell.
James of Hallowell. O. C. 23 June 1801.
Ann, m. Jonathan Allen of Adolphustown. O. C. 12 July 1797.
Eleanor, m. Benjamin B. Raney of Hallowell. OC 5 July 1798.   [Cont'd]

DOUGALL, William - Cont'd
  Catharine, m. Samuel Wright of Hallowell 20 Sept 1803. OC 12 July 1797.

DOUGHERTY, Anthony. He was born in Pennsylvania about 1748; he was a
  shoemaker.
  Mary, m. ---- Davis of Windham. O.C. 10 March 1801.
  Margaret, m. Nathaniel Root of Townsend. O.C. 14 March 1811.
  Elizabeth, m. Alexander Taggart of Townsend. O.C. 14 March 1811.
  Martha, m. Samuel Millard of Malahide. O.C. 23 June 1824.

DOUGHERTY, James of Osnabruck.
  James of Osnabruck. O.C. 17 March 1807.
  Mary, m. John Fike of Osnabruck. O.C. 13 March 1807.
  Margaret. O.C. 17 March 1812. Cornwall.
  Nancy, m. John Munro of Charlottenburgh, 6 Sept 1814. O.C. 13 Nov
    1818; O.C. 1 Feb 1826; O.C. 28 Oct 1835.
  Peggy. O.C. 16 June 1819. Cornwall.
  Alexander of Charlottenburgh. O.C. 21 June 1819.
  John of Charlottenburgh. O.C. 21 June 1819.
  Jeremiah of Osnabruck. O.C. 30 June 1819.
  Matilda. O.C. 2 Dec 1830.

DOYLE, Benjamin of Burford. [Benjamin Doyle, of Butler's Rangers, and
  his family were at Niagara in 1783. The Ontario Register, 1:198]
  Elizabeth, m. Henry Slawson of Townsend. O.C. 5 Jan 1808.
  John of Blenheim. O.C. 16 Jan 1816.
  Henry of Westminster. O.C. 25 Feb 1818.
  David of Blenheim. O.C. 31 May 1820.
  Mary, m. Elial Martin of Blenheim. O.C. 31 May 1820.
  Samuel of Burford. O.C. 25 Aug 1836.
  Ann, m. James Pelton of Blenheim. O.C. 2 Jan 1834.
  Sarah, m. Jacob Beemer of Burford. O.C. 15 Dec 1832.
  Eleanor. O.C. 15 Dec 1832.
  Rebecca, m. George Beemer of Burford. O.C. 2 Feb 1825.

DOYLE, Sarah.
  Margaret, m. Frederick Lewis of Edwardsburgh. O.C. 26 Feb 1805.
  Jane, m. William McNeal of Edwardsburgh. O.C. 25 Feb 1805.

DRUMMOND, Peter of Edwardsburgh.
  Catherine, m. John Fraser of Edwardsburgh. O.C. 2 March 1816. See
    O.C. 13 March 1810, and 3 April 1810.
  George of Edwardsburgh. O.C. 13 June 1818.
  Anne, m. James S. Johnston of Edwardsburgh. O.C. 3 Sept 1829.
  Betsey, m. Thomas Reilly of Edwardsburgh. O.C. 13 June 1831.

DUCULON, Stephen.
  Claudius of Elizabethtown. O.C. 14 Feb 1798.   [Cont'd]

DUCULON, Stephen - Cont'd
  Peter of Elizabethtown. O.C. 31 Oct 1809.
  Stephen of Elizabethtown. O.C. 11 Dec 1810.
  Adam of Elizabethtown. O.C. 3 Feb 1834.

DUGGAN, Cornelius.
  James of Townsend. O.C. 28 Oct 1835.
  Margaret, m. George Lester of Townsend. O.C. 28 Oct 1835.
  William of Woodhouse. O.C. 28 June 1832.
  Mary, m. Charles Green of Townsend. O.C. 4 Dec 1828.

DULMAGE, David of Marysburgh.
  David of Hallowell. O.C. 17 March 1804.
  Mary, b. Oswegatchie 19 July 1781; m. Owen P. Roblin of Ameliasburgh;
    died 13 Sept 1868. O.C. 26 Feb 1806.
  John of Marysburgh. O.C. 8 Feb 1808.
  James of Marysburgh. O.C. 20 Feb 1810.
  Edward of Marysburgh. O.C. 25 Feb 1818.
  Philip of Marysburgh. O.C. 25 Feb 1818.

DULMAGE, John of Edwardsburgh, m. Sophia Hick.
  Samuel of Edwardsburgh, bapt. 11 March 1792. O.C. 28 May 1811.
  Jacob of Matilda. O.C. 19 April 1816. O.C. 19 Apr 1816; 22 Feb 1834.
  Margaret, bapt. 11 March 1792; m. John Lawrence Jr. of Edwardsburgh.
    O.C. 13 June 1818.
  Elizabeth, m. Dr. Truman Raymond of Augusta. O.C. 28 June 1820.
  Elias of Edwardsburgh. O.C. 7 Nov 1797.
  Philip of Edwardsburgh. O.C. 7 Nov 1797.
  Ann. O.C. 7 Nov 1797.

DULMAGE, Philip of Augusta.
  James of Augusta. O.C. 16 Feb 1837.
  Sarah. O.C. 16 Feb 1837.
  Sophia, b. 21 May 1817; m. Amos Knapp Jr. of Augusta 7 September 1836;
    died 17 Nov 1886. O.C. 16 Feb 1837.
  Elizabeth. O.C. 25 Jan 1834.
  Margaret, b. 30 Aug 1803; m. Rev. Sylvester Hurlbut of Augusta, 1826;
    died 13 June 1873. O.C. 3 Nov 1831.
  Ann, m. Rev. Thomas Bevett. O.C. 3 Nov 1831.
  Mary, m. Heman Hurlbut of Augusta. O.C. 27 Oct 1832.
  Samuel. O.C. 3 Nov 1831.
  John. O.C. 3 Nov 1831.
  Martha, m. Charles Burritt of Augusta. O.C. 3 Nov 1831.
  Eliza Jane, m. Lawrence Dulmage of Ramsay. O.C. 15 Feb 1847.

DULYEA, Peter Jr. of Richmond.
  Isaac of Richmond. O.C. 18 March 1818.
  Maria. O.C. 14 April 1836.   [Cont'd]

DULYEA, Peter Jr. - Cont'd
    Jonas of Richmond, m. Ann Bowen 1 May 1820. O.C. 19 May 1836.
    Margaret. O.C. 4 Sept 1834.
    Elizabeth, m. David Palmer of Richmond. O.C. 28 Feb 1835.
    Jane, m. Staats W. Sager of Richmond. O.C. 28 Feb 1835.
    Samuel.
    Peter.

DULYEA, Peter (Dullier, Pierre) of Adolphustown.
    Samuel. O.C. 23 June 1801.
    Joseph, b. 1770. Land Board Certificate, 22/5 Camden.
    Mary, m. Arthur Orser of Kingston. O.C. 17 Nov 1797.
    Peter of Richmond, b. 1766.

DUNHAM, Daniel of Augusta, m. Isabel.
    James of Augusta. O.C. 22 Sept 1812. O.C. 14 Apr 1825.
    Catharine, m. James Moor of Elizabethtown. O.C. 22 Sept 1812.
    Anna, b. 17 Jan 1793.
    Ann. O.C. 1 July 1797.

DUNN, John Lancaster. Served in the Indian Department.
    John of Lancaster, m. Mary Williams. O.C. 7 Aug 1811.
    Mary, m. George Ross of Lancaster 10 March 1796. O.C. 5 Jan 1798.

DUSLER, William of Cornwall and Osnabruck.
    Catharine. O.C. 24 Feb 1820.
    Nancy. O.C. 24 Feb 1820.
    Elizabeth, m. Peter Chesley of Cornwall. O.C. 24 Oct 1839.
    Andrew of Town of Cornwall. O.C. 28 March 1833.
    William of Town of Cornwall. O.C. 28 March 1833.
    Christiana, m. John Peckman of Cornwall. O.C. 19 Dec 1833.
    Mary. O.C. 1 Nov 1826.

DUZENBERRY, John of Ernestown.
    Lucretia, m. ---- Althouse of Ernestown. O.C. 31 May 1803.
    Eleanor, m. AEneas McMullen of Ernestown, 10 Aug 1809. O.C. 20 Feb
        1810. O.C. 1 May 1834.
    John of Ernestown, m. Wilhelmina Hess. O.C. 25 Feb 1818.
    James of Ernestown. O.C. 25 Feb 1818.
    Benjamin of Sophiasburgh. O.C. 4 Feb 1836.
    Ann, m. James Hart of Sophiasburgh 7 May 1817. O.C. 1 May 1834.
    Margaret, m. Hezekiah Morse of Kingston. O.C. 25 Nov 1842.

DYRE, Barrett of Sophiasburgh. Capt.
    Nancy, m. Henry Young of Hallowell, 30 Aug 1791. OC 20 June 1797.
    William of Sophiasburgh. O.C. 20 June 1797.
    Katharine. O.C. 20 June 1797.
    Silas of Hallowell. O.C. 30 Aug 1797.

DYRE, William of Sophiasburgh and Hallowell.
  Mahalla M. O.C. 18 April 1839.
  Daniel Y. of Hallowell. O.C. 3 Dec 1835.
  Barrett of Hallowell. O.C. 18 July 1834.
  William of Hallowell. O.C. 18 July 1834.
  Mary, m. ---- Huycke of Hallowell. O.C. 6 Sept 1832.
  Sarah, m. Daniel Ryckman of Hillier. O.C. 7 Dec 1830.
  Henry of Hallowell. O.C. 6 June 1827.
  Silas of Hallowell. O.C. 7 May 1828.
  Waity, m. Samuel Ryckman of Hallowell. O.C. 28 Sept 1825.

E

EAMAN, Jacob of Osnabruck.
  John of Osnabruck. O.C. 17 March 1808.
  Mary, m. James Grant of Osnabruck. O.C. 23 Feb 1809.
  George of Osnabruck. O.C. 9 July 1817.
  Jacob of Osnabruck. O.C. 18 March 1818.
  Rachel, m. James Bradshaw of Osnabruck. O.C. 17 March 1824.
  Lawrence of Osnabruck. O.C. 28 Oct 1835.
  Margaret, m. Francis J. O'Connor of Hamilton. O.C. 18 Feb 1836.
  Joseph of Osnabruck. O.C. 2 May 1833.
  Nicholas of Osnabruck. O.C. 2 May 1833.
  Charles of Osnabruck. O.C. 19 Dec 1833.
  Frances, m. Michael Gaffney of Osnabruck. O.C. 5 May 1826.

EAMER, Peter of Cornwall, m. Catharine dau Michael Gallinger Sr., U.E.
  Philip of Cornwall, bapt. 11 Feb 1786; m. Mary Cryderman 10 March
    1807. O.C. 20 Nov 1809.
  Olive, m. Philip Empey of Cornwall. O.C. 16 Feb 1811.
  Mary. O.C. 16 Feb 1811.
  Barbara, bapt. 23 June 1793. O.C. 16 Feb 1811.
  Catherine, m. William Nokes of Cornwall. O.C. 16 Feb 1811.
  Peter of Cornwall, m. Catharine Cline 22 Oct 1805. OC 19 Apr 1816.
  Jacob of Montague, bapt. 7 May 1797. O.C. 12 Jan 1837.
  Daniel of Cornwall. O.C. 11 Apr 1833.

EAMER, Philip
  Dorothy, m. Henry Gallinger of Cornwall. O.C. 10 June 1800.

EARHART, Adam of Fredericksburgh, m. Eunice. 2/8 Darlington, D.U.E.
  Samuel of Fredericksburgh, bapt. 12 Oct 1790. O.C. 25 Feb 1812.
  Ashael of Fredericksburgh. O.C. 25 Feb 1812.
  William of Richmond, bapt. 11 Sept 1793. O.C. 20 May 1817.
  Christeen, bapt. 5 Feb 1798; m. Philip Smith. O.C. 26 July 1820.
  Margaret. O.C. 6 Aug 1840.
  John Collins, bapt. 10 Feb 1788.   [Cont'd]

EARHART, Adam - Cont'd
   Anna, bapt. 3 Feb 1811; m. David Wager of Fredericksburgh. O. C. 27
     September 1833.
   Tamar, bapt. 15 July 1795; m. John Mercer of Fredericksburgh. O. C.
     7 August 1834.
   Henry of Fredericksburgh, bapt. 9 July 1800. O. C. 23 June 1828.
   James, bapt. 9 July 1800.
   Elizabeth, bapt. 17 March 1803.
   Adam of Fredericksburgh, bapt. 17 June 1807. O. C. 13 June 1831.

EARHART, Simon of Ernestown.
   William of Markham. O. C. 24 Nov 1812.
   Catharine, m. Robert Lord Williams of Vaughan 30 March 1810. OC 17
     July 1816.
   John of Ernestown. O. C. 24 Nov 1812.
   Christeen, m. (1) James Costilo of Camden East. O. C. 30 June 1819.
     m. (2) ---- Morris. See O. C. 15 December 1832.
   Mary, m. Samuel Babcock of Richmond. O. C. 10 March 1834.

EASTMAN, Benjamin of Cornwall, m. Hannah Sherman.
   Mary, m. Henry Waggoner of Cornwall. O. C. 8 March 1803.
   Samuel of Cornwall, m. Ann Waterbury. O. C. 31 Oct 1809.
   John of Charlottenburgh, m. Elizabeth Cryderman. O. C. 31 Oct 1809.
   Benjamin of Cornwall, bapt. 16 Jan 1791; m. Margaret McEwen. OC 25
     February 1812.
   Rachel, bapt. 13 Oct 1793; m. Nicholas Mattice of Cornwall. OC 4 July 1815
   Simon Sherman of Hawkesbury, bapt. 17 Jan 1796. O. C. 5 Feb 1823.
   Elizabeth. O. C. 16 April 1840.
   Solomon of Cornwall. O. C. 1 Dec 1836.
   James of Cornwall. O. C. 29 June 1837.
   Sarah, m. Levi Groves of Cornwall. O. C. 27 June 1833.
   Isaac of Osnabruck. O. C. 7 Feb 1833.
   Hannah, m. John Jardine of Cornwall. O. C. 7 Feb 1833.
   Joel of Cornwall. O. C. 5 March 1828.

EASTMAN, Nadab of Cornwall, m. Elizabeth dau of John Phillips, U. E.
   Anna. O. C. 7 Aug 1811.
   Mehitable, m. Andrew Christie of Cornwall. O. C. 4 July 1815.
   Elizabeth. O. C. 4 July 1815.
   Nadab of Cornwall, bapt. 18 Nov 1796. O. C. 18 March 1818.
   Diadema, b. 2 Oct 1798. O. C. 24 Feb 1820.
   Ziba of Cornwall. O. C. 26 Nov 1823.
   Robert P. of Cornwall. O. C. 15 March 1838.
   Mary, m. David McEwen Jr. of North Gower. O. C. 28 March 1833.

ELIGH, Jacob of Osnabruck.
   Peter of Osnabruck. O. C. 4 Sept 1834.
   Catharine, m. Adam Baker of Osnabruck. O. C. 6 Nov 1834.

ELIGH, Jacob - Cont'd
  David of Osnabruck. O. C. 6 Nov 1834.
  George of Matilda. O. C. 6 Nov 1834.
  Elizabeth, m. John Link of Finch. O. C. 6 Nov 1834.
  Andrew of Osnabruck. O. C. 24 March 1835.

ELLERBECK, Emanuel of Kingston, m. Sarah. He was buried 26 Sept 1809.
  Richard of Kingston, m. Hannah Pearsons of Ameliasburgh in 1813. O. C.
    16 November 1807.
  Mary. O. C. 30 October 1810.
  Jane, m. Thomas Smith of Kingston, hatter, 9 June 1813. OC 20 May 1817
  William of Kingston. O. C. 25 Feb 1818.
  John of Kingston, shoemaker, m. Eliza Andrews 9 March 1814. O. C. 25
    February 1818.
  James of Elizabethtown. O. C. 27 April 1837.

ELLIOTT, David of Elizabethtown.
  Mary, m. ---- Boulton. O. C. 26 May 1801.
  Aaron. O. C. 26 May 1801.
  Moses of Elizabethtown. O. C. 26 March 1817.
  Martha, m. William Boulton of Elizabethtown. O. C. 20 May 1817.
  Benjamin of Elizabethtown. O. C. 13 June 1818.
  Lucy, m. David Mattice of Elizabethtown. O. C. 13 June 1818.

ELLIOTT, Jacob of Elizabethtown and Pickering.
  Jane, m. Peter Cole of Elizabethtown. O. C. 9 July 1811.
  Luther of Pickering. O. C. 12 July 1820.
  Olive, m. Thomas Russell of Pickering 23 Aug 1817. OC 12 July 1820.
  Catharine, m. Asa Storey of Elizabethtown. O. C. 28 Oct 1835.
  Calvin of Elizabethtown. O. C. 28 Oct 1835.
  Luther of Elizabethtown. O. C. 28 Oct 1835.
  George of Elizabethtown. O. C. 28 Oct 1835.
  Nelson of Elizabethtown. O. C. 28 Oct 1835.

ELLIOTT, John of Elizabethtown.
  Henry of Elizabethtown. O. C. 14 June 1839.
  Hannah, m. Nathan Dayton of Elizabethtown. Married Abel Coleman(?)
    O. C. 14 June 1839.
  Elizabeth, m. John Hall of Elizabethtown. O. C. 14 June 1839.
  Susanna, m. Samuel Griffin of Yonge. O. C. 14 June 1839.
  Margaret, m. John McIntosh of Edwardsburgh. O. C. 14 June 1839.
  Jacob of Elizabethtown. O. C. 28 June 1799. O. C. 25 June 1840.
  Catherine, b. February, 1769; m. Samuel Shipman of Yonge; d. 1811.
  Judah, m. John Ferris.
  Samuel.
  Polly, m. Abel Fulford of Yonge.
  Phebe, m. Aaron Comstock.

ELLIOTT, Mathew of Malden; d. at Burlington Heights May 7, 1814.
   Mathew of Malden. O.C. 1 April 1840.
   R.H. Barclay of Malden. O.C. 18 April 1848.
   Rev. Francis Gore of Malden. O.C. 18 April 1843.

ELLIOTT, Thomas of Elizabethtown, died March, 1801.
   Abraham of Elizabethtown. O.C. 23 September 1800.
   Mary, m. Barney Emery of Elizabethtown. O.C. 12 June 1798.
   Catherine, m. ---- McCue of Lansdowne. O.C. 18 August 1801.
   Dorcas, m. Thomas Wood of Elizabethtown. O.C. 12 June 1798.

ELSWORTH, Francis of Bertie. [He and his wife were at Niagara in 1783.
   See The Ontario Register 1: 213]
   George of Wainfleet. O.C. 3 Nov 1819.
   Rachel, m. ---- Edsall of Bertie. O.C. 4 Apr 1833.
   Clarissa Ann, m. Thomas Adkinson of Humberstone. OC 6 Sept 1832.
   David of Bertie. O.C. 6 Sept 1832.
   Catharine, m. John Davis of Bertie. O.C. 23 June 1828.
   Charles of Bertie. O.C. 6 Sept 1826.
   Elizabeth, m. George Foster of Bertie. O.C. 5 July 1826.
   Sarah, m. Henry Anger of Bertie. O.C. 5 July 1826.
   Margaret, m. William Anger of Bertie. O.C. 25 May 1825.

EMBURY, Andrew of Fredericksburgh, m. Jane, dau William Bell, Sr.
   Philip of Fredericksburgh. O.C. 15 Nov 1808.
   William Bell of Fredericksburgh. O.C. 28 May 1811.
   Isabel, m. Cornelius Gunsoles of Fredericksburgh, March, 1810.
      O.C. 28 May 1811.
   Peter, bapt. 2 June 1791. O.C. 4 July 1815. Fredericksburgh.
   Anne. O.C. 20 May 1817.
   Samuel of Fredericksburgh. O.C. 6 Feb 1822.
   Andrew of Fredericksburgh. O.C. 6 Feb 1822.
   Margaret, m. John G. Hough of Fredericksburgh. O.C. 5 Nov 1835.
   Flora, m. Gilbert Griffiths of Fredericksburgh. O.C. 26 May 1836.
   David S. of Fredericksburgh. O.C. 27 June 1833.
   Elizabeth, m. ---- Dafoe of Richmond. O.C. 10 March 1834.

EMBURY, David.
   Margaret, m. Jacob Huffman of Fredericksburgh. O.C. 14 Oct 1842.

EMBURY, John of Fredericksburgh, m. Mary.
   George of Fredericksburgh. O.C. 17 March 1804.
   David of Fredericksburgh. O.C. 15 Dec 1807.
   Mary, bapt. 25 Jan 1789; m. Micajah Purdy of Kingston. OC 5 June 1810.
   Anna, m. Jacob Empey of Ernestown. O.C. 18 March 1818.
   Valentine of Town of Kingston. O.C. 16 June 1819.

EMMETT, Stephen of Grantham.
John of Grantham, m. Elizabeth Lawrence. O.C. 21 April 1819.
Lydia, m. Hugh Craig of Grantham. O.C. 5 May 1819.
Sarah, m. Martin Salsbury of Grantham. O.C. 2 June 1819.
Mary, m. James Armstrong of Niagara. O.C. 1 May 1822.
David of Grantham. O.C. 1 May 1822.
James of Grantham. O.C. 20 Feb 1840.
Stephen of Grantham. O.C. 20 Feb 1840.
Elizabeth, m. Daniel Nighton of Bertie. O.C. 18 May 1837.
Eliza Ann, m. John Wright Jr. of Grantham 14 Nov 1830. OC 28 Dec 1835
Abigail, m. Lewis J. Clement of Niagara. O.C. 7 May 1829.

EMONS, John of Kingston.
Sarah, m. Henry Staker of Kingston. O.C. 24 Nov 1807.
Rachel, m. Adam Buck of Kingston. O.C. 24 Nov 1807.
Eli of Kingston. O.C. 23 Feb 1808.
Catharine, m. Jacob Moore of Kingston. O.C. 17 Sept 1823.

EMPEY, Adam of Osnabruck.
Margaret, m. William Hutchins of Osnabruck. O.C. 16 March 1825.
Levi of Osnabruck. O.C. 5 Nov 1835.
William A. of Osnabruck. OC 2 May 1833.

EMPEY, Adam of Cornwall. Sgt., K.R.R.N.Y. His wife Allada married (2)
a Vrooman. See O.C. 2 July 1808.
Elizabeth. O.C. 13 March 1807.
Allada.

EMPEY, Christopher of Cornwall, m. Christeen Summers, dau of Andrew
Summers, U.E. She died at Osnabruck 13 Aug 1836 in her 74th year.
Catharine, m. John Fulton of Town of Cornwall. O.C. 17 March 1807.
Elizabeth, bapt. 11 Feb 1786. O.C. 17 March 1807.
Mary, m. John Campbell of Cornwall and St. Regis. O.C. 7 Apr 1812.
Philip C. of Cornwall, bapt. 27 March 1791. O.C. 11 Nov 1815.
Ann Eve. O.C. 17 March 1836.
Christiana, m. John Karston of Osnabruck. O.C. 24 Jan 1828; 2 May 1833.
Peter of Town of Cornwall. O.C. 25 Jan 1831.
Eve, b. 5 Dec 1801.

EMPEY, Henry of Cornwall.
Philip H. of Lancaster. O.C. 11 May 1837.
Fanny, b. 28 Apr 1807; m. William D. Munger of Belleville. O.C. 28
October 1835.
Sarah Eve, m. Thomas Raymore of Belleville. O.C. 28 October 1835.
Purlina, m. Conrad Hawn of Osnabruck. O.C. 28 October 1835.
Margaret, m. Geo. Wereley Jr. of Osnabruck. O.C. 28 October 1835.
Elizabeth, m. Peter P. Loucks of Wolford. O.C. 26 March 1836.
Jacob H. of Williamsburgh. O.C. 27 June 1833.   [Cont'd]

EMPEY, Henry - Cont'd
    Mary, m. Andrew Eligh of Osnabruck. O.C. 2 Oct 1834.
    Barbara, m. John Dixon of Osnabruck. O.C. 27 Nov 1834.
    William H. of Osnabruck. O.C. 7 Feb 1835.

EMPEY, Jacob of Cornwall, m. Elizabeth dau of Jacob Rambough, U.E.
    Mary, m. Michael Loucks of Cornwall. O.C. 13 March 1807.
    Elizabeth. O.C. 5 January 1798.

EMPEY, John Sr.
    John of Osnabruck. O.C. 17 March 1807.
    Mary. O.C. 13 March 1807.

EMPEY, John Jr. of Osnabruck and Cornwall.
    Philip J. of Cornwall. O.C. 23 June 1819.

EMPEY, John W. of Osnabruck.
    Richard of Osnabruck. O.C. 2 March 1811.
    David of Osnabruck. O.C. 19 April 1816.
    Margaret, m. Joshua Wait of Osnabruck. O.C. 30 Oct 1822.
    Nancy, m. Hiram Southworth of Williamsburgh. O.C. 19 Dec 1833.

EMPEY, Peter of Osnabruck, soldier R.R.N.Y. Born in Province of New
    York, 21 Aug 1759, son of Philip Sr. and Laney (Moreland) Empey. He
    married Eve Merkley, 21 September 1785.
    Margaret, m. George Land of Osnabruck. O.C. 13 March 1807.
    Philip of Osnabruck. O.C. 23 Feb 1808.
    Michael of Osnabruck. O.C. 25 Feb 1812.
    John P. of Osnabruck, bapt. 22 Jan 1792. O.C. 4 July 1815.
    Jacob P. of Osnabruck. O.C. 19 April 1816.

EMPEY, Philip Jr. of Cornwall, m. Elizabeth Dillibough.
    Christopher of Cornwall, bapt. 26 Aug 1792. O.C. 19 April 1816.
    William of Cornwall, bapt. 23 Aug 1795. O.C. 19 April 1816.
    Philip of Cornwall. O.C. 7 April 1812.

EMPEY, Philip Sr. of Cornwall.
    Mary, m. John Link of Cornwall. O.C. 22 Dec 1797. O.C. 5 Jan 1798.
    Barbara, m. Michael Venice of Cornwall. O.C. 5 March 1808.

EMPEY, William of Cornwall, died prior to 1809.
    Jacob of Osnabruck. O.C. 13 June 1809.
    Philip W. of Osnabruck. O.C. 13 June 1809.
    Adam of Cornwall. O.C. 16 Feb 1811.

EMPEY, William of Osnabruck. Died between 1813 and 1816 ?
    Abraham of Osnabruck. O.C. 2 Feb 1825.
    Margaret, m. Jacob Stata of Osnabruck. OC 7 Aug 1811.   [Cont'd]

EMPEY, William - Cont'd
   Elizabeth, m. David Zeron of Osnabruck. O. C. 27 March 1813.

EMPEY, William Sr. of Cornwall.
   Richard of Osnabruck. O. C. 5 Jan 1798.
   Catharine, m. Christian Hanes of Williamsburgh. O. C. 25 Feb 1806.
   William of St. Regis, Lower Canada. Heir & Devisee Commission, 1830.

ENGLAND, William, Sgt., Loyal Rangers. His wife married (2) ---- Wollet
   of Lancaster. See O. C. 17 November 1807.
   Conradt of Lancaster. O. C. 24 Nov 1807.
   Margaret. O. C. 20 May 1817.
   Robert of Cornwall. O. C. 1 April 1840.
   John of Cornwall. O. C. 12 Oct 1841.
   Mary Ann, m. ---- Gagnon of Yamachich. O. C. 25 Jan 1850.
   Hannah, m. ---- St. Pierre of Yamachich. O. C. 25 Jan 1850.

EVERINGHAM, James
   William of Thorold. O. C. 10 Apr 1805.
   James of Stamford. O. C. 30 Sept 1806.
   Adoram of Crowland. O. C. 17 March 1807.
   Anna, m. Henry Hoshall of Stamford. O. C. 17 July 1817.
   Jacob of Willoughby. O. C. 15 Nov 1838.

EVERITT, John of Kingston, m. Mercy dau Gilbert Purdy Sr., U. E. He
   died 28 June 1825, aged 82 years.
   Esther, m. Peter Grass of Kingston 9 Feb 1808. O. C. 17 Feb 1807.
   Charles of Kingston, m. Sarah Hawley 19 May 1807. O. C. 16 Nov 1807.
   Mary, bapt. 12 Feb 1797; m. William H. Walbridge of Ameliasburgh.
      O. C. 14 March 1809.
   Daniel of Kingston, m. Mary Ann Hawley. O. C. 16 Feb 1811.
   John of Thurlow, m. Margaret Walbridge 30 Jan 1812. O. C. 19 Apr 1816.
   Jane, bapt. 12 Feb 1797. O. C. 14 May 1816.
   Sarah Ann, bapt. 12 Feb 1797; m. Thomas Coleman of Thurlow. O. C. 14
      May 1816.
   Charlotte, bapt. 23 May 1802; m. John Turnbull of Belleville. O. C. 22
      December 1842.
   Mercy, bapt. 9 Feb 1800; m. Lewis Daly of Kingston. O. C. 19 July 1826.

EVERSON, John
   Elizabeth, m. ---- Cheffe of Yonge Street. O. C. 22 Sept 1801.
   Mary, m. Thomas Gray of York. O. C. 12 May 1801.
   Samuel of York. O. C. 5 May 1801.

EVERSON, John
   Hannah, m. Benjamin Runions of Osnabruck. O. C. 3 March 1807.

EVERTS, Oliver of Augusta, m. Honoria Fleming at Montreal in May 1786.

EVERTS, Oliver - Cont'd
    George of Augusta. O. C. 25 Feb 1809.
    William of Augusta. O. C. 22 Sept 1812.
    David of Augusta. O. C. 16 June 1818.
    Johannah, m. Duncan McLennan of Augusta. OC 26 Oct 1825; 18 Apr 1843.

EVERTS, Roswell of Augusta. Married 14 July 1796, by Jeremiah French,
    J. P., Mary dau of Richard Dingman, U. E.
    Samuel of Augusta. O. C. 13 June 1818.
    Sarah. O. C. 4 April 1821.
    Elisha of Augusta. O. C. 17 Sept 1823.
    Linus Richard of Augusta. O. C. 28 Oct 1835.
    Maria, m. Martin Kelly of Montague. O. C. 6 Sept 1832.
    Silvanus Roswell of Augusta. O. C. 6 Sept 1832.
    Reuben. O. C. 3 Nov 1831.
    Mary Ann, m. Ebenezer Avery of Augusta. O. C. 3 Nov 1831.

EYRES, Ephraim of Yonge. He died in June 1803.
    Phoebe, m. Israel Mallory of Yonge. O. C. 23 Feb 1808.
    Closson of Yonge. O. C. 17 March 1812.

F

FAIRCHILD, Benjamin Jr. of Niagara, m. Mary.
    Elizabeth, m. (1) ---- Willson of Niagara; m. (2) John Bessey of Gran-
        tham. O. C. 27 March 1813.
    Margaret, bapt. 6 March 1794; m. Henry Hoover of Townsend. O. C. 27
        March 1813.
    John Hare of Thorold, bapt. 18 Aug 1805. O. C. 22 May 1820.

FAIRCHILD, Benjamin Sr.
    Peter of Townsend. O. C. 24 July 1793. O. C. 18 April 1797.
    Mary, m. John Myers of King. O. C. 25 Feb 1797. O. C. 18 April 1797.
    Ruth, m. Daniel Springer of Delaware. O. C. 18 April 1797.
    Benjamin of Niagara, m. Mary. O. C. 18 April 1797.
    Joshua of Townsend, m. Elizabeth. O. C. 18 April 1797.
    Isaac of Townsend. O. C. 18 April 1797. O. C. 3 July 1797.
    Deborah, m. Mordecai Sayles of Oxford. O. C. 18 April 1797.

FAIRCHILD, Eleazer of Yonge. Ensign, King's American Regt.
    Ann, m. ---- Tryon of Elizabethtown. O. C. 23 Sept 1800.
    Phoebe, m. (1) Robert Boice of Yonge. O. C. 9 July 1811. m. (2) Solomon
        D. Colby of Bathurst and Woolwich.

FAIRCHILD, Peter of Townsend.
    Rebecca, m. Joseph Merrill of Charlotteville. O. C. 28 May 1811.
    Elizabeth, m. Jesse Smith of Charlotteville. O. C. 28 May 1811. [Cont'd]

FAIRCHILD, Peter - Cont'd
  Benjamin of Townsend. O.C. 16 July 1816.
  Sarah, m. ---- Post. O.C. 16 July 1816.
  Esther, m. John Haviland Jr. of Townsend. O.C. 16 July 1816.
  Mary, m. Abraham Nelles of Townsend. O.C. 17 May 1820.
  Abial of Townsend. O.C. 31 Oct 1839.
  Peter of Townsend. O.C. 28 Nov 1839.
  Cornelius of Brantford. O.C. 27 May 1848.

FAIRFIELD, Archibald of Kingston, m. Mary.
  Amelia, m. Henry L. Holcomb of Ernestown. O.C. 12 Nov 1827.
  Sabra Ann, bapt. 7 June 1795; m. William Garbutt of Ernestown, 1820.
    O.C. 12 November 1827.
  Mary, m. ---- Fraser of Ernestown. O.C. 10 June 1846.

FAIRFIELD, William Sr. of Ernestown.
  Jonathan of Ernestown, m. Charity Ryder, 22 Apr 1795. OC 13 Nov 1797.
  Stephen of Ernestown, m. Mary Pruyn, 11 March 1799. OC 17 Ov 1797.
  William of Ernestown, m. ---- Billings. O.C. 17 Nov 1797.
  Benjamin of Ernestown, b. 1772(?); m. Nabby Hawley, 11 April 1797; d.
    9 May 1842. O.C. 17 Nov 1797.
  Abigail, m. Heinrich Ripsome of Ernestown, 13 June 1799. OC. 25 Nov
    1800.
  Sarah, m. Manuel Overfield of Flamborough West, 7 August 1805. O.C.
    8 July 1806.
  Mary, m. Ichabod Hawley of Ernestown. O.C. 19 Nov 1798, 27 Feb 1818.
  Clara, m. Benjamin Brown of Ernestown 19 May 1802. OC 1 May 1834.
  Archibald of Kingston, U.E., m. Mary Howland.
  Sabra, m. William Willcox, 28 Aug 1797. O.C. 18 Nov 1797.
  John of Ernestown, m. Elizabeth Clapp. O.C. 19 April 1816.
  Janet, m. Daniel Sheldon of Ernestown 10 Jan 1811. O.C. 13 Nov 1822.

FAIRFIELD, William Jr. of Ernestown.
  Caroline E. O.C. 3 Nov 1836.
  Charles of Ernestown. OC 28 July 1836.

FAIRMAN, John of Thurlow, m. Elizabeth.
  Hugh of Thurlow. O.C. 29 March 1803.
  Henry R. of Yonge, bapt. 16 Aug 1788. O.C. 7 Aug 1811, 19 March 1840.
  Thomas of Sophiasburgh, m. Anna Huffman, 21 Apr 1815. OC 20 May 1817.
  David of Thurlow. O.C. 8 Aug 1821.
  George of Thurlow. O.C. 4 April 1833.

FALCONER, James of Adolphustown, Hamilton and Toronto. (Faukiner). He
  was born in Cumberland, England; died in Toronto Tnp., 20 March 1835,
  ae 82 ys 5 ms. His wife Catharine died 14 Nov 1855 aged 85 years, 7 mos.
  Both are buried at St. Peter's Church, Erindale.
  Isaac of Toronto. O.C. 21 April 1819.   [Cont'd]

FALCONER, James - Cont'd
  John of Toronto. O.C. 21 April 1819.
  William Henry of Yonge. O.C. 6 Feb 1841.
  James of Toronto. O.C. 3 Dec 1829.
  George of Toronto. O.C. 3 Dec 1829.
  Jane Anne, m. H. Row of Toronto.

FARLINGER, John of Cornwall.
  James of Penetanguishene, blacksmith. O.C. 17 Nov 1830.
  John of Cornwall. Land Board Certificate, 31/4 Matilda.

FARRINGTON, Samuel of Marysburgh, m. Katharine Brown of Marysburgh,
  15 April 1792.
  Edward of Marysburgh. O.C. 28 Oct 1835.
  Samuel of Marysburgh. O.C. 11 Feb 1836.
  James of Marysburgh. O.C. 3 March 1836.
  Joseph of Marysburgh. O.C. 3 March 1836.

FAULKINER, Ralph of Lancaster, m. Mary H.
  Catherine. O.C. 3 March 1801.
  James. O.C. 30 June 1801.
  Francis Johnson of Lancaster, bapt. 27 Jan 1790. O.C. 18 June 1811.

FAULKINER, William of Lancaster, m. Mary Edge at Montreal, Feb, 1781.
  Samuel of Lancaster. O.C. 9 March 1803.
  Ann, bapt. 25 July 1790; m. Arthur Campbell of Charlottenburgh, 7 March
    1810. O.C. 28 Aug 1810.
  Eleanor. O.C. 2 March 1811.
  Margaret, bapt. 5 June 1791; m. Gershom French of Lancaster. O.C. 5
    March 1811.
  Ralph of Edwardsburgh, bapt. 20 May 1792; O.C. 16 July 1816.
  Henry of Lancaster, bapt. 27 July 1794. O.C. 16 July 1816.
  William of Lancaster. O.C. 23 Nov 1816.
  James of Lancaster. O.C. 21 June 1819.
  John of Lancaster. O.C. 29 Sept 1824.

FEADER, Lucas.
  Philip. O.C. 18 June 1799.
  Elizabeth, m. ---- Adams of Augusta. O.C. 1 July 1797.
  John of Matilda. O.C. 31 May 1803.
  Hannah, m. ---- Dorin of Matilda. O.C. 17 March 1804.
  Christiana. O.C. 17 March 1804.
  Hannah, m. Isaac Keck of Matilda. O.C. 26 January 1808.
  Jacob of Matilda. O.C. 25 Feb 1812.

FELL, Frederick.
  Christiana, m. ---- Wallaser of Matilda. O.C. 16 June 1800.
  Daniel of Augusta. O.C. 23 Sept 1800.   [Cont'd]

FELL, Frederick - Cont'd
  David of Augusta. O.C. 23 Sept 1800.
  Mary, m. William Rood of Augusta. O.C. 23 Sept 1800.
  Charity, m. ---- Nettleton. O.C. 10 June 1800.

FENNELL, John of Osnabruck.
  James of Matilda. O.C. 5 Jan 1798.
  Jane. O.C. 27 Aug 1805. Osnabruck.
  Abel of Haldimand Tnp. O.C. 14 Dec 1816.

FENNELL, Peter.
  Margaret, m. James McIlmoyle. Land Board Certif., 17/4 Lansdowne.

FERGUSON, Alexander of Edwardsburgh.
  Benjamin of Ameliasburgh. O.C. 3 Sept 1840.

FERGUSON, Arra of Hallowell ard Adolphustown, m. Catharine dau of John
  Shorts of Butler's Rangers. O.C. 8 July 1797; 6 Feb 1828.
  Patience. O.C. 4 July 1815.
  Richard of Hallowell. O.C. 2 April 1835.
  Frederica, m. John Hare of Haldimand. O.C. 18 Feb 1836.
  Amelia. O.C. 1 Aug 1833.
  Mary, m. John Coleman of Hallowell. O.C. 2 July 1829.

FERGUSON, Farrington of Hallowell.
  Patience, m. John Cole of Hallowell 4 March 1812. O.C. 20 May 1817.
  Rachel, m. Henry Garetsee of Hallowell 4 March 1812. OC 20 May 1817.
  Mary, m. Rowland Jackson of Hallowell. O.C. 20 May 1817.
  Israel of Hallowell. O.C. 25 Feb 1816.
  Farrington of Hallowell. O.C. 22 Jan 1823.
  Barney of Hallowell. O.C. 21 Sept 1837.
  Daniel of Sophiasburgh. O.C. 11 Feb 1836.
  Hester. O.C. 6 April 1836.
  Huldah, m. Ira Brown of Hallowell. O.C. 3 April 1834.
  Charlotte, m. Peter Daynard of Marysburgh. O.C. 28 Sept 1832.
  Elizabeth, m. Andrew Daynard of Marysburgh. O.C. 19 July 1826.
  Eleanor, m. John Daynard of Marysburgh. O.C. 7 July 1831.

FERGUSON, John Sr.
  Elizabeth, m. (1) William Fraser, Adjt., K.R.R.N.Y. m. (2) Timothy
    Thompson of Fredericksburgh.
  John of Kingston, m. Magdelene Johnson.

FERGUSON, Peter of West half 50/1 Charlottenburgh, m. Jane Cameron.
  (A Peter Ferguson of Charlottenburgh, and wife Mary McKay, had a dau
  Margaret bapt. 14 July 1793).
    Alexander of Charlottenburgh. O.C. 25 June 1807.
    William of Charlottenburgh. O.C. 25 June 1807.   [Cont'd]

FERGUSON, Peter - Cont'd
  Catherine, m. Alexander McNaughton of Charlottenburgh. OC 3 Mar 1809.
  Ann, m. Alexander McNaughton of Lancaster. O.C. 16 Feb 1811.
  Mary, m. Gregor McGregor of Charlottenburgh; bapt. 27 Jan 1793; m. 12
    May 1812. O.C. 6 Aug 1816.
  Margaret, bapt. 25 July 1790; m. James McGregor of Charlottenburgh.
    O.C. 6 August 1816.
  James of Charlottenburgh. O.C. 20 May 1817.

FERGUSON, Richard Sr.
  Millicent, b. 4 May 1766; m. (1) Jacob Hoover of Adolphustown 19 May
    1789; m. (2) Conrad Van Duzen of Adolphustown 31 July 1791; died 7
    April 1829. Land Board Certificate.
  Rachel, m. ---- Hare of Sophiasburgh. O.C. 20 June 1797.

FERGUSON, Rozel of Fredericksburgh.
  Miles of Ameliasburgh. O.C. 18 July 1839.
  John H. of Hallowell. O.C. 28 Oct 1835.
  Jane, m. Orange O. Ogden of Hallowell. O.C. 28 Oct 1835.
  Jacob of Hallowell. O.C. 3 Dec 1835.
  Maria. O.C. 11 Feb 1836.
  Rachel, m. John Brooks Sr. of Hillier. O.C. 5 June 1834.
  Elizabeth. O.C. 6 June 1827.

FERRIS, John of Kingston.
  Mary, bapt. 15 Feb 1795; m. Albert McMichael (Meikle) of Kingston, 31
    July 1814. O.C. 2 March 1816.
  Daniel of Kingston. O.C. 2 March 1816.
  Elizabeth, m. David Henderson of Kingston. O.C. 22 March 1820.
  Jane, bapt. 24 Dec 1797; m. John Dunlap of Kingston. O.C. 2 Sept 1830.
  Ann, m. David Dick of Kingston. O.C. 7 Aug 1834.
  Neil of Kingston. O.C. 2 Sept 1830.

FERRIS, Peter. Soldier, McAlpin's Corps.
  Elizabeth, m. Silvester Moore of Edwardsburgh. O.C. 22 June 1797.

FERRO, Peter of Humberstone.
  Catherine, m. Hill Carney of London. O.C. 16 April 1840.
  Mary, m. John Beach of Westminster. O.C. 27 June 1833.
  Sarah, m. Amassa Grant of Bertie. O.C. 17 June 1806.
  Henry of Humberstone. O.C. 17 June 1806.
  Valentine of Humberstone. O.C. 9 July 1823.
  Elizabeth, m. John Harp of Bertie. O.C. 5 Feb 1823.

FETTERLY, John.
  Philip of Williamsburgh. O.C. 26 Jan 1808.

FETTERLY, Peter
  Hannah, m. David Bouck of Williamsburgh. O.C. 5 March 1810.
  George of Williamsburgh. O.C. 20 May 1817.
  Peter of Williamsburgh.

FIELDS, Alexander.
  Hannah, m. James Burns of Howard. O.C. 14 June 1811.

FIELDS, Daniel of Harwich.
  Alexander of Harwich. O.C. 20 Feb 1810.
  George of Niagara. O.C. 5 March 1810.
  Rebecca, m. James Boyle of Chatham. O.C. 12 Nov 1811.

FIELDS, George. Butler's Rangers. Married Rebecca. Died 1785. [He and
  and his wife were at Niagara in 1783. The Ontario Register, v. 1, p. 213]
  Mary, m. Isaac Dolson Sr. of Raleigh. O.C. 20 Feb 1810.
  Hannah, m. Mathew Dolson of Dover. O.C. 20 Feb 1810.
  Ann, m. Allan McDonald of Gainsborough. O.C. 19 Jan 1801.
  Daniel of Harwich, U.E.
  Gilbert of Niagara, U.E.
  Nathan of Harwich, U.E.

FIELDS, Gilbert of Niagara, m. Eleanor Morden. Buried 23 Dec 1814.
  George of Niagara. O.C. 9 March 1811.
  David McFall of Niagara, bapt. 26 June 1796. O.C. 27 Nov 1815.
  Daniel of Niagara. O.C. 27 Nov 1815.
  George of Niagara. O.C. 27 Nov 1815.
  John Morden of Niagara; bapt. 30 June 1794. O.C. 27 Nov 1815.
  Ralfe of Niagara, bapt. 1 Oct 1801. O.C. 17 July 1817.
  James of Ancaster, bapt. 21 June 1804. O.C. 15 May 1835.
  Nathan of Niagara, bapt. 19 March 1807. O.C. 12 March 1833.
  Gilbert C. of Niagara. OC 12 March 1833.
  Hiram of Niagara. O.C. 12 March 1833.
  Rebecca, m. John Meddaugh of Niagara. O.C. 8 Nov 1832.

FIELDS, Nathan of Harwich, m. Amy dau of James Slack (Slaght) of New
  Jersey.
  Rebecca, m. Peter Traxler of Harwich. O.C. 22 Feb 1810.
  James of Harwich. O.C. 28 Nov 1821.
  Gilbert of Howard. O.C. 12 June 1822.
  George of Harwich. O.C. 12 June 1822.
  Catharine, m. Edward Charles Scarlett of Howard. O.C. 18 Feb 1824.
  Daniel of Harwich. O.C. 24 April 1835.
  Hannah, m. Henry Fleming of Mosa. O.C. 27 Aug 1840.
  Peter of Mosa. O.C. 4 Sept 1834.
  Nathan of Harwich. O.C. 18 Feb 1843.

FIKE, Daniel of Osnabruck.
  Elizabeth, m. John Wart of Osnabruck. O. C. 20 March 1807.
  Jacob of Hamilton. O. C. 29 Dec 1819.
  Mary, m. Henry Snyder of Osnabruck. O. C. 19 Feb 1823.
  Francis of Hamilton. See O. C. 7 Aug 1828.

FIKE, Henry.
  John. O. C. 10 June 1800.

FIKE, John of Osnabruck.
  Francis of Osnabruck. O. C. 3 Dec 1840.
  Elizabeth. O. C. 28 Oct 1835.
  Daniel of Osnabruck. O. C. 25 Jan 1834.
  John of Osnabruck. O. C. 25 Jan 1834.

FILE, John of Ancaster. Corp'l, K. R. R. N. Y.
  Malachi of Ancaster, m. Elizabeth. O. C. 23 Nov 1816.
  Elizabeth, m. James Powers of Ancaster. O. C. 26 March 1817.
  Benjamin of Grand River. O. C. 8 March 1820.
  Mary, m. Robert Vanderlip of Haldimand County 17 December 1818.
    O. C. 26 June 1822.
  John Johnson of Haldimand County. O. C. 26 June 1822.
  Charlotte, m. Henry Hawley. O. C. 3 Oct 1833.
  Catharine, m. William Johnson of Beverly. O. C. 5 June 1834.
  Lavinia, m. Allan Sage of Haldimand County. O. C. 13 Sept 1832.

FINCH, James.
  Humphrey of Gwillimbury East. O. C. 8 April 1801.

FINKLE, George of Fredericksburgh.
  John of Fredericksburgh. O. C. 8 July 1797.
  Hannah, m. Solomon Rosebush of Sidney. O. C. 23 Feb 1809.
  Catharine, m. James Sharp of Sidney. O. C. 17 Nov 1836.
  Margaret, m. John Bell of Fredericksburgh. O. C. 10 March 1834.

FINKLE, Henry of Ernestown, m. Lucretia Blacker. See 26/6 Sidney.
  Nancy, m. John Crysler of Williamsburgh. O. C. 3 March 1809.
  George of Hamilton. O. C. 12 Nov 1817.
  Maria, m. Solomon Johns of Town of Kingston. O. C. 13 June 1818.
  Sarah, m. Henry Gildersleeve of Town of Kingston. O. C. 16 Feb 1837.
  Minerva, m. James McCutcheon of Kingston. O. C. 11 Feb 1836.
  William of Fredericksburgh. O. C. 8 Nov 1832.

FINNEY, Peter of Osnabruck.
  Jane, m. Conrad Wart of Osnabruck. O. C. 9 July 1801, 9 July 1802.
  Mary. O. C. 19 May 1812. Charlottenburgh.

FISHER, Alexander of Adolphustown, m. Henrietta dau of Allan McDonell,
U.E. of Kingston, 15 March 1802.
  Mary. O.C. 28 Apr 1815.
  Anne, m. (1) Thomas R. Cartwright of Kingston. O.C. 18 Aug 1824. m. (2)
    Dr. John M. Bartley of 15th Regt., in 1828.
  Henrietta, b. 27 March 1811; m. Stafford F. Kirkpatrick. OC 4 Sept 1834.
  Helen, b. 31 March 1807; m. Thomas Kirkpatrick of Kingston. O.C. 4
    September 1834.
  Janet, m. James Wallis of Fenelon Falls, 23 April 1840. OC 24 Nov 1836.

FISHER, George.
  Margaret, m. Philip Beamer of Woodhouse. O.C. 28 June 1799.

FISHER, John.
  Margaret, m. ---- Stalker. Land Board Certificate, 26/6 Thurlow.

FITCHETT, James of Fredericksburgh. Soldier, K.R.R.N.Y. He had 12
children, see "Church", Feb 24, 1843.
  Joseph of Fredericksburgh. O.C. 6 March 1822.
  Sarah, m. Henry Jarvies of Fredericksburgh. O.C. 3 April 1822.
  Aaron of Fredericksburgh. O.C. 15 Oct 1840.
  David of Fredericksburgh. O.C. 27 Oct 1836.
  Eleanor, m. George Smith of Fredericksburgh. O.C. 12 Jan 1837.
  James of Fredericksbrugh. O.C. 10 March 1834.
  Catharine, m. James Houlbert of Fredericksburgh. O.C. 28 Feb 1833.
  Elizabeth, m. Peter Benn of Fredericksburgh. O.C. 14 March 1826.
  Mary Ann. O.C. 14 March 1826.

FITCHETT, Richard of Fredericksburgh and Richmond.
  Mary, m. John Thomson of Richmond. O.C. 7 March 1812, 11 Nov 1815.
  Abraham of Camden East. O.C. 26 Feb 1819, 21 March 1844.
  Sarah, m. Samuel Crippen of Trafalgar. O.C. 26 Nov 1823.
  Henry of Matilda. O.C. 19 Dec 1833.
  Peter of Pickering. O.C. 25 Jan 1831. O.C. 15 May 1832.
  Isaac of Pickering. O.C. 15 May 1832.

FITZPATRICK, Peter of Cornwall.
  Elizabeth, m. ---- Presley. O.C. 10 June 1800.
  William. O.C. 10 June 1800.
  Hugh of Cornwall. O.C. 16 Feb 1811.
  Richard of Charlottenburgh. O.C. 20 May 1817.

FLACK, Archibald of Louth. He was born about 1761 in Ireland.
  Agnes. O.C. 20 May 1817.
  Jane. O.C. 20 May 1817.
  Elizabeth, m. John Gregory of Louth. O.C. 15 June 1820.
  Eleanor. O.C. 6 Sept 1820.
  Mary, m. Thomas Orchard of Southwold. O.C. 5 Apr 1832.   [Cont'd]

FLACK, Archibald - Cont'd
   Margaret, m. Jeremiah Moore of Malahide. O.C. 2 Feb 1832.

FORSYTH, James of Cornwall, m. Margaret Milligan. O.C. 5 Jan 1798.
   John of Cornwall, m. Agnes McNairn 5 Apr 1802. O.C. 5 Jan 1798.
   James of Cornwall. O.C. 19 Dec 1806.
   William of Cornwall. O.C. 29 March 1808.
   Margaret. O.C. 16 Feb 1811.
   Marion, bapt. 14 Aug 1791. O.C. 11 Nov 1815.

FORSYTH, James. [He and his family were at Niagara in 1783. TOR 1: 212]
   Caleb of Barton. O.C. 16 April 1811.
   Sarah, m. Christopher Buckner of Stamford. O.C. 10 May 1797.
   William of Stamford. O.C. 8 Oct 1796.

FORTUNE, William.
   Jane Elizabeth. O.C. 23 Feb 1808. Hawkesbury.

FOSTER, Edward.
   Mary, m. ---- Shaver. Land Board Certif. 20/3 Tp. 10, Eastern Dist.

FOSTER, John of Matilda.
   William of Matilda. O.C. 9 Nov 1837.
   George of Nottawasaga. O.C. 21 Dec 1840.
   James of Matilda. O.C. 24 Nov 1836.
   John of Matilda. O.C. 27 June 1833.
   Edward of Matilda. O.C. 11 Jan 1834.
   Nancy, m. ---- Locke of Matilda. O.C. 17 March 1834.
   Mary, m. Josiah Payne of Matilda. O.C. 7 Aug 1834.
   Margaret, m. Jacob Barger of Matilda. O.C. 5 Feb 1835.

FOSTER, Moses of Fredericksburgh, m. Jenny McPhee.
   Samuel of Fredericksburgh, m. Mary Clark. O.C. 10 May 1803.
   Jane, m. Simon Van Muyre of Fredericksburgh, 9 Aug 1803. O.C. 3
      November 1807.
   Mary, bapt. 19 Apr 1789; m. Samuel McTaggart of Sophiasburgh. O.C.
      26 January 1808.
   John of Fredericksburgh, bapt. 20 Jan 1793. O.C. 25 Feb 1812.
   Sarah, bapt. 18 Sept 1791. O.C. 25 Feb 1812.
   Elizabeth, bapt. 6 Sept 1795; m. Aaron Mott of Fredericksburgh. O.C.
      25 Feb 1812.
   Rhoda. O.C. 18 Aug 1836.
   Moses of Marysburgh, b. 11 March 1800. O.C. 4 Oct 1826.

FOSTER, William cf Louth.
   Anne, m. Robert Dederick of Grantham. O.C. 19 May 1819.
   Alvah of Louth. O.C. 8 Sept 1819.
   Rachel, m. Jacob Haines of Grantham. O.C. 22 May 1820.   [Cont'd]

FOSTER, William - Cont'd
  Clarinda, m. Barnabas Gregory of Louth. O.C. 19 Sept 1821.
  Elizabeth, m. Peter Haines of Louth. O.C. 19 Sept 1821.

FOWLER, John of Burford.
  Selene of Burford. O.C. 23 Feb 1808.
  John of Burford. O.C. 4 July 1809.
  Thomas of Burford. O.C. 16 Jan 1816.
  William of Burford. O.C. 16 Jan 1816.
  Delia. O.C. 16 Jan 1816.
  Horatio of Burford. O.C. 22 May 1820.

FOX, Frederick of Richmond.
  Susannah, m. John Young Sr. of Ameliasburgh. O.C. 5 July 1798.
  Jean, m. Jacob Corbman of Ameliasburgh, 17 Feb 1793. Land Board
    Certificate, 89/3 Ameliasburgh.
  Margaret, m. Angus McDonald of Ameliasburgh. O.C. 13 Nov 1797.
    O.C. 4 Dec 1806.

FOX, William of Sophiasburgh.
  Henry W. of Sophiasburgh, m. Elizabeth DeMille. O.C. 28 Apr 1807.
  John of Sophiasburgh. O.C. 25 Feb 1809.
  Jacob of Sidney. O.C. 27 Feb 1834.

FRALICK, Adam of Matilda, m. Ann dau Barnet Snell of South Carolina.
  Susannah, m. John P. Shaver of Matilda. O.C. 26 Jan 1808.
  John of Williamsburgh. O.C. 23 Feb 1808.
  Margaret. O.C. 23 Feb 1809. Edwardsburgh.
  Catharine, m. Philip Servos of Matilda. O.C. 5 March 1810.
  David of Matilda. O.C. 20 May 1817.

FRALICK, Benjamin of Thorold. [Cpl. Benjamin Frelick of Butler's Rang-
  ers and his family were at Niagara in 1783. The Ontario Register 1:206]
  Magdalen, m. Ettiene Allair of Louth. O.C. 27 Feb 1806.
  Elizabeth, m. Samuel Durragh of Wainfleet. O.C. 27 Aug 1840.

FRALICK, Christopher of Ernestown, m. Catharine Smith, 22 Jan 1788.
  Benjamin of Ernestown. O.C. 28 Oct 1835.
  John Lewis of Sidney. O.C. 19 Dec 1835.
  Catharine, m. John Shibley of Portland. O.C. 18 Apr 1834.
  Jacob of Ernestown. O.C. 7 Oct 1831.
  John C. of Ernestown. O.C. 29 Sept 1824.

FRALICK, John of Stamford, m. Abigail dau Robert Spencer, U.E. She died
  30 Oct 1844 aged 83 yrs & 7 ms. He died 12 May 1839 aged 84 yrs & 3 ms.
  John of Stamford. O.C. 28 Nov 1809.
    Lydia, m. Hugh Wilson of Thorold. O.C. 16 Aug 1810, 13 Apr 1819.
    Mary, m. James Secord of Queenston. O.C. 19 Feb 1817.   [Cont'd]

FRALICK, John - Cont'd
  Catharine, m. Aaron Crane of Stamford. O.C. 16 Apr 1818.
  Elizabeth, m. William Lewis Smith. O.C. 18 March 1818.
  Robert of Stamford, m. Abigail Van Wyck; d. 9 Dec 1838, aged 43. O.C.
    2 June 1819.
  Barnabas of Stamford. O.C. 2 June 1819. O.C. 21 March 1844.
  Adam of Stamford. O.C. 11 Feb 1836.
  Robert of Stamford. O.C. 19 Dec 1833.

FRALIGH, Martin of Ernestown.
  Lewis of Ernestown. O.C. 23 Feb 1808.

FRALICK, Peter of Ernestown.
  Martin of Ernestown. O.C. 25 Feb 1809.
  John of Ernestown. O.C. 26 March 1817.
  Sarah, m. ---- Bell of Sidney. O.C. 3 Apr 1834.

FRANCIS, William of Walpole.
  Thomas of Walpole. O.C. 9 Feb 1820.

FRANKS, William of Williamsburgh and Caledon, m. Margaret Miller.
  Catharine, m. Michael Baker of Williamsburgh. O.C. 16 Apr 1818.
  William of Williamsburgh. O.C. 18 March 1818.
  Nancy, m. Frederick Baker of Williamsburgh. O.C. 2 Sept 1818.
  Simcoe of Augusta. O.C. 18 Aug 1836 (?)
  Sally, m. Jabez Lake of Caledon. O.C. 19 Dec 1833.
  Susannah, m. Isaac Nelson Hughson of Amaranth. O.C. 28 Feb 1835.
  Adam Nelson of Caledon. O.C. 28 Feb 1835.
  John of Caledon. O.C. 21 July 1831.
  Frederick of Caledon. O.C. 24 Nov 1824.
  Andrew of Williamsburgh. O.C. 22 July 1824.
  Dorothy, m. Peleg Lake of Williamsburgh. O.C. 12 May 1824.
  Mary, b. 14 Oct 1800; m. Jonathan McCurdy of Williamsburgh (Belleville)
    on 23 Dec 1822. O.C. 12 May 1824.

FRASER, Daniel Sr. of Ernestown. Artificer, Col. Bam's Artillery. He
  married Sarah Conklin 2 Apr 1760. Died 1812 (?)
  Margaret, m. Joshua Booth of Ernestown. Land Board Certificate,
    7/7 Thurlow.
  Esther, m. John Carscallen of Fredericksburgh. Land Board Certificate,
    8/6 Storrington.
  Hannah, m. David Lockwood of Ernestown, 1 July 1792. OC 13 Nov 1797.
  Daniel of Ernestown, m. Sarah Schouten, 19 Dec 1798. Land Board Cer-
    tificate, 21/7 Ernestown.
  Isaac of Ernestown, m. Hannah Storing, 12 Jan 1802. OC 24 Feb 1801.
  Abraham. O.C. 8 July 1801.
  Jacob of Ernestown, m. ---- Jones. O.C. 16 Nov 1807.
  John of Ernestown.   [Cont'd]

FRASER, Daniel Sr. - Cont'd
George of Sophiasburgh, m. Mary Vandusen, 2 Dec 1817. OC 25 Feb 1818.

FRASER, Daniel Jr. of Ernestown, m. Sarah Schouten, 19 Dec 1798. She
died in 1813 aged about 30.
John, b. 8 Aug 1800.
Richard of Ernestown, b. 6 Sept 1802; m. Jane Hogle, 13 July 1830. O. C.
15 May 1835.
Andrew of Fredericksburgh, b. 13 July 1804; m. Katharine Forshee, 4
May 1831. O. C. 15 May 1835.
William, b. 9 May 1806.
Mary, b. 20 Feb 1808; m. James Lee of Ernestown. O. C. 25 Feb 1836.
Margaret, b. 10 Apr 1810; m. Daniel Parrott Lake of Ernestown. O. C.
25 Feb 1836.

FRASER, David of Ernestown.
Mathew of Madoc. O. C. 17 May 1838.
Thomas of Ernestown. O. C. 18 May 1833.
Elizabeth, m. ---- Wormouth of Ernestown. O. C. 30 May 1834.
Catharine, m. Robinson Walker of Ernestown. O. C. 24 Oct 1831.

FRASER, Donald of Cornwall. 84th Regt.
Elizabeth, m. ---- Stephens of Cornwall. O. C. 14 July 1801.
Margery, m. Archibald McPhale of Cornwall. O. C. 5 Jan 1798.

FRASER, Hugh of Edwardsburgh.
Elizabeth, m. James Warren of Edwardsburgh. O. C. 18 June 1800.
Lucretia. O. C. 16 Sept 1809.
Charlotte, m. Horace Ward of Edwardsburgh. OC 25 Feb 1812; 18 May 1837
Sally, m. Simon Walter of Elizabethtown. O. C. 1 Oct 1840.

FRASER, Hugh of Matilda.
Catharine, m. Alexander McLeod of Matilda. O. C. 21 March 1821.

FRAZER, Hugh of Fredericksburgh.
Simon of York. O. C. 22 October 1817.

FRASER, Isabella of Cornwall, widow of Simon Fraser.
Nancy. O. C. 17 March 1797.
Peggy. O. C. 17 March 1797.
Belle. O. C. 17 March 1797.
Jenny. O. C. 17 March 1797.
Simon of Cornwall, discoverer of Fraser River. O. C. 17 March 1797.
Peter of Cornwall. O. C. 17 March 1797.
William of Coteau du Lac, U. E. Lieut. , K. R. R. N. Y.
Angus of Cornwall.

FRASER, Jeremiah of Bastard, soldier, Loyal Rangers.
  Jeremiah of Bastard. O.C. 29 Dec 1819.
  Collins of Bastard. O.C. 15 June 1820.
  William of Bastard. O.C. 15 Dec 1821.
  Daniel of Bastard. O.C. 20 March 1822.
  Joseph of Bastard. O.C. 25 May 1837.
  Charlotte, m. John C. Chatterton of Elizabethtown. O.C. 14 Apr 1836.
  Jerusha. O.C. 14 April 1836.
  Mary, m. Nathan Stevens of Bastard. O.C. 14 Apr 1836.

FRASER, John. Soldier, R.R.N.Y.
  Catherine, m. Thomas McLeod of Cornwall. O.C. 17 June 1806.
  Thomas of Lancaster. O.C. 5 Feb 1835 (?)

FRASER, Thomas of Ernestown. (Capt. ?)
  Elizabeth A. O.C. 8 Oct 1840.
  Katharine, m. John Perry of Loughborough. O.C. 16 Feb 1837.
  Susannah, m. Lansing Smith of Ernestown. O.C. 27 June 1833.
  Alexander of Thurlow. O.C. 4 Sept 1834.
  Angus of Sidney. O.C. 4 Sept 1834.
  Donald of Sidney. O.C. 4 Sept 1834.
  Arnold of Pittsburgh. O.C. 4 Sept 1834.

FRASER, Thomas of Edwardsburgh. Captain, Loyal Rangers. Born in Scot-
land, 1748; md. Mary McBean of Glenlochy;   m. Mary Macdonell of
St. Regis, 7 Feb 1795. She was the dau of John McDonell; he died at Matil-
da, 18 Oct 1821. O.C. 14 Aug 1797. Appt. Capt., 10th Co. Loyal Rangers
on 22 June 1782.
  Mary, b. 1785; m. Edward P. Kingsbury, Capt. 81st Regt.; d. 27 April
    1855. O.C. 16 June 1807.
  Richard Duncan of Edwardsburgh, b. 1792; m. Mary McDonell. O.C. 25
    May 1808.
  William of Edwardsburgh, b. 1772; O.C. 30 June 1798.
  John of Edwardsburgh, b. 1790; d. prior to 1826. O.C. 2 March 1816.
    Lieut. Glengarry Fencibles.
  Simon of Edwardsburgh. O.C. 26 March 1817.
  Grace T., b. 1777; m. Alexander McQueen of Edwardsburgh. O.C. 30
    June 1798.
  Margaret, bapt. 7 March 1792.
  Daniel of Edwardsburgh. O.C. 28 Oct 1835.
  Hugh of Matilda.

FRASER, Thomas of Edwardsburgh. Soldier, Loyal Rangers. Married Ann.
  Grace, b. 1 April 1798. O.C. 9 Jan 1822.
  Henry of Edwardsburgh. O.C. 9 Jan 1822.
  Jane, b. 1 July 1795.
  Thomas of Edwardsburgh. O.C. 1 July 1830.

FRASER, William. Adjt., R.R.N.Y. Married Elizabeth dau of John Ferguson, a Commissary in 1759 and in American Revolution until his death
in 1780. She later married Timothy Thompson, M.P., on 6 Feb 1791. OC
18 Nov 1797 and 14 July 1797. She died 1 Jan 1847.
  Mary Ann, m. James McNabb of Thurlow, 24 March 1801. OC 6 Dec 1808.
  Jane, m. John G. Clute of Fredericksburgh 2 Aug 1807. O.C. 25 Feb
    1809. From Whitby Chronicle, Feb 24, 1859: Died at Fredericksburgh
    near Bath, C.W. on 7th inst., Jane, wife of Jno. G. Clute Esq, ae 69.
  Margaret, m. John K. Simons of Thurlow. O.C. 16 Feb 1810.

FRASER, William of Edwardsburgh and Matilda. Capt., Loyal Rangers. See
  O.C. 2 July 1828. Married Lilly, dau of James Grant.
  James of Matilda, bapt. 8 March 1792. 34/1 Osgoode. OC 16 Feb 1811.
  Peter of Matilda. O.C. 3 Feb 1816.
  John of Matilda, bapt. 11 March 1792. O.C. 3 Feb 1816.
  Donald of Matilda, bapt. 12 Feb 1789. O.C. 3 Feb 1816, 10 Aug 1843.
  Thomas of Edwardsburgh. O.C. 30 June 1798.
  Grace W., O.C. 30 June 1798. m. Hugh(?) Munro of Edwardsburgh. [But
    see below]
  William Grant of Edwardsburgh. See O.C. 6 Dec 1803.

FRASER, William of Edwardsburgh, surveyor.
  Daniel of Town of Niagara. O.C. 13 Sept 1832.

FRASER, William Sr. of Edwardsburgh. From Straherrick, Argyleshire,
  Scotland - See P. Campbell, "Travels in North America", p.135. He drew
  lots 6/7, West half 32/1, West half 9/3, Edwardsburgh, (Pensioner).
  Nancy, m. John Fraser of Edwardsburgh. O.C. 15 June 1797.
  Thomas of Edwardsburgh, U.E.
  William of Edwardsburgh, U.E.
  Maria, m. Richard Duncan of Matilda.

FRASER, William of Edwardsburgh.
  Thomas of Edwardsburgh. O.C. 11 July 1833.
  Grace, m. Hugh Munro. O.C. 27 Sept 1833.
  Catharine. O.C. 3 Feb 1834.
  Susanna, m. William Tucker of Edwardsburgh. O.C. 10 Jan 1833.
  Alexander of Edwardsburgh. O.C. 6 Dec 1832.
  Edward of Edwardsburgh. O.C. 6 Dec 1832.
  William H. of Edwardsburgh. O.C. 7 May 1828.

FRASER, William of Cornwall. Corp'l, 84th Regt.
  Flora. O.C. 25 Feb 1818.

FRASER, William of Coteau du Lac. Lt., K.R.R.N.Y.
  Maria Grace. O.C. 12 April 1832.
  Malcolm William. O.C. 12 April 1832.
  Simon. O.C. 12 April 1832.

FRASER, William of Ernestown. Soldier, Loyal Rangers. O. C. 17 August 1810. East half 5/2.

FRASER, William of Lot 15/5 south side M. B. River aux Raisins, Cornwall.
    Duncan of Cornwall. O. C. 3 June 1817.
    Donald of Cornwall. O. C. 7 Feb 1821.

FRASER, William, /5 south side River aux Raisins, Cornwall.
    Ann, m. Donald McBean of Roxborough. O. C. 10 Sept 1817.
    Mary. O. C. 5 Feb 1823.

FRATTS, Henry of Williamsburgh, Soldier, 1st Batt., K. R. R. N. Y.
    Mary. O. C. 22 Feb 1810.
    Henry of Williamsburgh. O. C. 16 Feb 1811.
    John of Williamsburgh. O. C. 19 April 1816.
    Lenah, m. Henry Outerkirk of Williamsburgh. O. C. 20 May 1817.
    George of Williamsburgh. O. C. 15 May 1835.
    Francis of Williamsburgh. O. C. 11 April 1833.
    Philip of Williamsburgh. O. C. 11 April 1833.
    Peter of Williamsburgh. O. C. 11 April 1833.
    Jacob of Williamsburgh. O. C. 4 Sept 1834.
    Catharine, m. Francis Ulman of Williamsburgh. O. C. 28 Feb 1835.
    David of Williamsburgh, m. Elizabeth Prunner. O. C. 17 Feb 1825.
    Elizabeth, m. George Taylor of Williamsburgh. O. C. 30 Dec 1844.

FREDERICK, Conrad.
    Charity, m. James Gilbert. O. C. 21 May 1799.
    Catharine, m. George Reddock of Ameliasburgh. O. C. 12 March 1805.
    Polly, m. Daniel Silver of Thurlow. O. C. 12 March 1805.
    Elizabeth, m. Samuel Taylor of Ameliasburgh. O. C. 15 Nov 1808.
    Margaret, m. Robert Cunningham of Thurlow. O. C. 14 June 1811.
    John C. of Thurlow. O. C. 8 Aug 1821.
    Abigail, m. Jeremiah Wood of Cramahe. O. C. 23 July 1839.
    Martin of Ameliasburgh. O. C. 13 Nov 1797.

FREDERICK, Lodowick.
    Leany, m. Philip Shaver of Matilda. Land Board Certificate, 3/6 Yonge.

FREDERICK, Peter of Fredericksburgh.
    Peter of Fredericksburgh. O. C. 25 May 1808.
    John of Fredericksburgh. O. C. 17 Feb 1817.

FREEL, John [Served in the Indian Dept. He and his family were at Niagara in 1783. The Ontario Register, 1: 211]
    Hugh of Niagara. O. C. 22 July 1806. See also O. C. 10 Aug 1843.
    Barbara, m. ---- Cox. OC. 28 June 1832.
    James. O. C. 23 May 1818.

FREEL, Peter
Thomas of Yonge. O. C. 22 Dec 1801.
Rose, m. Abraham Dayton of Elizabethtown. O. C. 14 Aug 1804.
Harriet, m. Stephen Duculon Jr. of Elizabethtown. O. C. 14 Aug 1804.

FREEMAN, Thomas of Ernestown.
Clarenda, m. Peter Brown of Ernestown 26 July 1807. OC 3 March 1809.
John of Ernestown. O. C. 12 Nov 1811.
Evelina. O. C. 12 Nov 1811.
Edward of Loughborough. O. C. 11 Feb 1819.
Simeon of Loughborough. O. C. 19 May 1819.
Elizabeth, m. John Van Luvan of Loughborough. O. C. 24 Feb 1820.
Mathew of Loughborough. O. C. 15 Dec 1832.
Hannah, m. John Edgeworth of Loughborough. O. C. 8 Nov 1832.
Mary, m. George Williams of Loughborough. O. C. 2 July 1829.

FREES, John of Matilda. He died 1797. See O. C. 29 Jan 1808.
Mary, m. John Van Camp of Matilda. O. C. 8 Feb 1808.
Hannah, m. Charles Pettys of Elizabethtown. O. C. 9 March 1809.
Nicholas of Matilda. O. C. 17 Oct 1809.
Peter of Matilda. O. C. 7 Aug 1811.
John of Flamborough East. O. C. 9 June 1812.
David of Matilda. O. C. 20 May 1817.
Elizabeth, m. ---- Froom of Edwarsburgh. OC 15 June 1797, 11 Feb 1834.
Michael of Matilda. O. C. 1 Nov 1832.

FRENCH, Gershom of Cornwall.
Eleanor, m. Alexander Perry of Cornwall. O. C. 3 Dec 1835.
Margaret, m. Joseph Wilson of Cornwall. O. C. 3 Dec 1835.
William of Cornwall. O. C. 12 Oct 1841.

FRENCH, Henry of Augusta. Corp'l, Loyal Rangers. Apparently left Augus-
ta about 1815.
Charles of Augusta (Bastard Tp.) O. C. 2 Dec 1806.
Mary, m. Melvin Buker [i. e., Bunker ?] of Augusta. OC 8 Oct 1808.
Lucy, m. John McLean of Augusta. O. C. 24 April 1810.
Abigail. O. C. 22 Sept 1812.
David of Kingston. O. C. 26 Feb 1819.
Francis of Kingston. O. C. 26 Feb 1819.
Eunice, m. Ira Patterson of Yonge. O. C. 6 March 1821.
John of Raleigh. O. C. 5 March 1824.

FRENCH, Jeremiah of Cornwall.
Hannah, m. Stephen Miller of Cornwall. O. C. 5 Jan 1798.
Mary, m. Jacob Vanduzen of Cornwall. O. C. 5 Jan 1798.
Elizabeth. O. C. 27 Feb 1806.
Marilla, m. Alexander Hoover of Cornwall. O. C. 25 Feb 1812.
Benjamin of Cornwall, m. Mary Wood. OC 5 July 1796.   [Cont'd]

FRENCH, Jeremiah - Cont'd
Albert of Cornwall, m. Catharine McIntyre; d. 4 Feb 1836. OC 5 July 1796
Catherine, m. Abraham Marsh of Cornwall. O. C. 5 Jan 1798.
Mercy, m. David Sheek of Cornwall. O. C. 5 Jan 1798.

FREY, Bernard of Niagara. [Capt., Butler's Rangers. He and his family
were at Niagara in 1783. The Ontario Register, 1: 201]
Margaret, m. John Clement Ball of Niagara; d. at Merritton 2 Nov 1886,
aged 97. O. C. 27 Jan 1816.

FREY, Philip R. of Niagara.
Sarah, O. C. 24 Nov 1836. Brockville.
John W. of Brockville. O. C. 23 June 1837.
Adelia. O. C. 11 Feb 1836.
Samuel C. of Brockville. O. C. 12 Sept 1833.

FRIERMOUTH, John Adam of Ernestown, m. Esther. Buried 22 Aug 1808.
Elisabeth, m. Michael Davy of Sophiasburgh. OC 12 July 1798; 26 Oct 1802
Mary. O. C. 20 May 1816.
Susannah, m. Nicholas Snider of Ernestown. O. C. 27 Feb 1818.
John Adam of Lansdowne, bapt. 9 Feb 1800; m. Lavina Losee. O. C. 23
June 1836.
Esther, bapt. 17 Jan 1808; m. Ephraim Keys of Lansdowne. OC 1 Apr 1840
Fanny, m. John Nuttall of Leeds. O. C. 26 Nov 1840.

FROOM, James Jr. of Edwardsburgh.
Hester. O. C. 13 Oct 1836.
Elizabeth, m. Hiram Adams of Edwardsburgh. O. C. 17 Sept 1823.
James of Edwardsburgh. O. C. 3 Oct 1833.
David of Edwardsburgh. O. C. 11 Jan 1833.
Catharine. O. C. 11 Jan 1834.
Margaret, m. George Adams of Edwardsburgh. O. C. 3 Feb 1834.
John of Edwardsburgh. O. C. 6 Aug 1829.
Mary, m. Curtis Adams Jr. of Edwardsburgh. O. C. 2 May 1827.
Elijah of Edwardsburgh. O. C. 6 Sept 1832.

FROOM, James Sr.
David of Edwardsburgh, m. Chloe Rose. O. C. 7 July 1802.
Rachel, m. Andrew Adams of Edwardsburgh (?) O. C. 21 May 1834.

FROST, Edward of Middleton.
Perlina. O. C. 11 June 1840.
Margaret. O. C. 11 June 1840.
Hannah, m. James Crane of Windham. O. C. 5 Nov 1835.
Mary, m. Elias Horton of Windham. O. C. 5 Nov 1835.
Sarah, m. James Conklin of Windham. O. C. 10 March 1834; 5 Nov 1835.
Zephaniah of Windham. O. C. 2 May 1833.
Joseph of Windham. O. C. 24 March 1835.

FRYMIRE, Nicholas of Williamsburgh. Soldier, 1st Batt., K. R. R. N. Y.
Nancy. O. C. 25 Feb 1806. Williamsburgh.
Philip of Williamsburgh. O. C. 17 March 1807.
Catharine, m. Jacob Algire of Williamsburgh. O. C. 13 March 1810.
Peter of Williamsburgh. O. C. 2 Sept 1818.
Mary. O. C. 2 Sept 1818.
Conrad of Williamsburgh. O. C. 5 Nov 1818.
Elizabeth. O. C. 4 Sept 1834.

FRYMIRE, Philip.
Nicholas of Williamsburgh.
Sarah, m. ---- Bedstead of Williamsburgh. Both OC's 1850 or 1851.

FULFORD, Jonathan of Elizabethtown, m. Thankful, dau Phineas Doolittle
of Conn. She d. at Belleville, 2 Feb 1836, aged 94.
Abel of Yonge, m. Polly Elliott(?). O. C. 18 Aug 1801.
Jonathan of Elizabethtown, m. Nancy Brown. O. C. 12 May 1808.
Thankful, m. Adam Cole of Elizabethtown. O. C. 21 Aug 1797.

FULTON, James of Hallowell and Markham. Capt., King's American Dra-
goons. From New Brunswick. See O. C. 6 Aug 1796.
Caroline, m. John Munshaw of Markham. O. C. 26 March 1811.
James of Markham, m. Elizabeth Munshaw 2 Feb 1809. OC 16 Apr 1811.
Elizabeth, m. Richard Vanderburgh, 17 Oct 1816. OC 16 Dec 1815.
Clarissa, m. William Fairfield of Ernestown (Bath); d. 20 Apr 1845, in
60th yr. O. C. 3 Nov 1836.

FYKES, Peter of Fredericksburgh.
Mary, m. William Anderson of Fredericksburgh 6 May 1804. O. C. 28
February 1799.
Catherine, m. John Lansing of Fredericksburgh 6 March 1804. O. C. 28
February 1799.
Elizabeth, m. William Keller of Fredericksburgh. O. C. 26 Jan 1808.
William of Fredericksburgh. O. C. 16 Feb 1811.
Catharine, m. John Lansing of Fredericksburgh. OC 13 June, 2 Sep, 1818.
Mary, m. ---- Young of Fredericksburgh. O. C. 2 May 1833.

G

GALBREATH, John of Edwardsburgh, m. Eleanor Johnson.
Nancy, m. Aaron Rose of Edwardsburgh. OC 14 June 1797; 18 June 1799.
Mary, m. John Galer of Augusta, blacksmith. O. C. 15 March 1803.
Margaret, m. Levi Bigelow of Edwardsburgh. O. C. 16 June 1807.
Jane, (twin) bapt. 22 May 1793; m. Hezekiah Price (Pierce?) of Edwards
burgh. O. C. 20 Feb 1810.
Eleanor, m. John Anderson of Edwardsburgh. O. C. 22 Oct 1817.
James of Edwardsburgh, bapt. 7 March 1792. O. C. 23 June 1819.
Catharine, bapt. 7 March 1792.   [Cont'd]

GALBREATH, John - Cont'd
  Alice, (twin), bapt. 22 May 1793.
  Martha, m. ---- Fraser of Ernestown. O. C. 5 Sept 1833.
  Hannah. O. C. 6 Dec 1832.

GALLINGER, Christian of Cornwall. Pvt. , K. R. R. N. Y.   Married Sarah
  Runnions at Montreal in January 1784. See Bethune, p. 38 of typewritten
  copy.
  Michael of Cornwall. O. C. 31 Oct 1809.
  George of Cornwall. O. C. 16 Feb 1811.
  Henry of Cornwall. O. C. 16 Feb 1811.
  Mary, m. Michael Cline of Cornwall. O. C. 24 Feb 1820.
  Olive, bapt. 21 June 1795; m. George Hart of Osnabruck. OC 10 Mar 1834
  Christian of East Gwillimbury, b. 17 Feb 1801. O. C. 6 May 1830.
  Sarah, bapt. 7 May 1797; m. Valentine Cryderman of East Gwillimbury.
      O. C. 5 December 1827.
  Lene, bapt. 16 June 1791.
  Elizabeth, bapt. 21 Oct 1792.

GALLINGER, George of Cornwall. Pvt. , K. R. R. N. Y.   Married Margaret
  Warner, dau of Michael Warner, U. E.
  Michael of Cornwall. O. C. 23 Nov 1816.
  George of Cornwall, m. Janet Cameron, 7 April 1818; d. 14 Dec 1879.
      O. C. 23 Nov 1816.
  Catharine, bapt. 15 Dec 1793. O. C. 23 Nov 1816.
  Mary, bapt. 11 Dec 1791; m. George Snetsinger of Cornwall. O. C. 23
      November 1816.
  Benjamin of Cornwall. O. C. 15 March 1838.
  Elizabeth. O. C. 27 May 1833.
  Jacob of Cornwall. O. C. 4 July 1833.
  Henry G. of Osnabruck. O. C. 5 Sept 1833.

GALLINGER, Henry of Cornwall, m. Dorothy, dau Philip Eamer, U. E.
  Margaret, m. James Baker of Cornwall. O. C. 28 April 1807.
  Michael of Cornwall. O. C. 3 April 1810.
  Catharine, m. John Farlinger of Charlottenburgh. O. C. 7 Aug 1811.
  Philip of Cornwall. O. C. 19 April 1816.
  Henry of Cornwall. O. C. 18 March 1818.
  Olive, bapt. 25 Nov 1792. O. C. 5 Oct 1820.
  Christian of Cornwall. O. C. 21 Feb 1821.
  Dorothy, m. ---- Ross of Cornwall. O. C. 17 Nov 1836.
  Jacob of Lanark. O. C. 6 Sept 1832.
  John of Lanark. O. C. 6 Sept 1832.
  Frances, m. William Bender of Cornwall. O. C. 15 May 1832.
  William of Cornwall. O. C. 5 July 1826.
  Elizabeth, bapt. 4 June 1797.
  Mary, m. William Millroy of Cornwall. O. C. 1850 or 1851.

GALLINGER, Michael Jr. of Cornwall, m. Catherine dau Valentine Cryder-
man, U. E.
Catharine, m. Nathan Case of East Gwillimbury. O. C. 6 May 1830.
Simon of Cornwall. O. C. 5 July 1832.
Harmonus of Cornwall. O. C. 3 April 1834.
Hannah. O. C. 19 Dec 1833.
George of Cornwall. O. C. 19 Dec 1833.
Elizabeth, bapt. 11 Feb 1786. O. C. 19 Dec 1833.
Joseph of Cornwall. O. C. 25 July 1833.
Christian, bapt. 11 Dec 1791.
John of Cornwall, m. Hannah Hartell. O. C. 13 July 1841.
Henry of St. Martin, Isle of Jesus. O. C. 4 Aug 1847.

GALLINGER, Michael Sr. of Cornwall. Pvt., K. R. R. N. Y, 2nd Batt.
Michael of Cornwall, U. E., m. Catharine Cryderman.
Henry of Cornwall, U. E., m. Dorothy Eamer.
Christian of Cornwall, U. E., m. Sarah Runnions, January, 1784.
George of Cornwall, U. E., m. Margaret Warner.
Catherine, m. Peter Eamer of Cornwall. O. C. 11 July 1799.
Dolly, m. Solomon Tuttle of Cornwall. O. C. 5 Jan 1798.

GALLOWAY, George of Ernestown, m. Catharine.
Henry of Ernestown, m. Phoebe Clark, 9 March 1808. OC 16 Nov 1807.
Margaret, m. Mathew Howe of Kingston. O. C. 26 Jan 1808.
Hannah, m. Charles Hagedorn of Ernestown, 24 May 1808. OC 3 Apr 1810
Elizabeth, m. Elisha Rice 23 Apr 1810. O. C. 24 Dec 1811.
Catherine, m. Chester Nicholson of Ernestown 23 July 1811. O. C. 24
December 1811; 18 March 1818.
Jane, m. Benjamin Van Luvan of Loughborough. O. C. 5 May 1819.
John of Oxford. O. C. 7 Jan 1824.
Rachel, bapt. 16 March 1794, buried 14 December 1794.
Clarissa, bapt. 9 May 1802; m. Josiah Lamkins of Ernestown. O. C. 7
May 1828.
James, bapt. 5 Feb 1804.

GARDINER, George of Yonge.
Ann, m. ---- Trusdell of Yonge. O. C. 21 Aug 1797.
Jean, m. Alexander McLean of Yonge. O. C. 8 Nov 1797.
George of Yonge. O. C. 18 Nov 1806.
Martha, m. Alexander Kincaid of Yonge. O. C. 17 Feb 1807, 18 Aug 1819.
Nancy, m. Henry Clow of Elizabethtown 1 Jan 1818. OC 2 June 1819.
Catherine, m. Peter Purvis of Yonge. Land Board Certificate.
Emily, m. Isaiah Griffin of Yonge. O. C. 11 Feb 1836.

GARLOUGH, Henry of Williamsburgh.
Catharine, m. John Barkley of Williamsburgh. O. C. 20 May 1817.
Peter of Williamsburgh. O. C. 20 May 1817.
Jacob of Williamsburgh. O. C. 18 March 1818.

GARLOUGH, Jacob
   Elizabeth, m. Frederick Bouck of Williamsburgh. O. C. 13 March 1807.

GARLOUGH, Peter Sr.
   Leny, m. Edward Sullivan of Williamsburgh. O. C. 25 Feb 1809.

GARNER, John of Ancaster and Crowland.
   Rachel, m. William Shaver of Beverly. O. C. 26 March 1811.
   Deborah, m. Isaac Van Sickle of Ancaster. O. C. 16 Jan 1816.
   Rebecca, m. John Wilkins of Crowland. O. C. 19 Aug 1806.
   Elizabeth, m. Barnett Shaver of Ancaster. O. C. 16 July 1816.
   James of Ancaster. O. C. 6 Aug 1816.
   Mary, m. Abraham Zavitz of Yarmouth. O. C. 19 March 1840.

GEORGE, John of Ernestown.
   William of Ernestown. O. C. 19 March 1840.
   Ann, m. Nathan Johnston of Fredericksburgh. O. C. 27 Nov 1834.
   Janet, m. Cornelius Milligan of Camden East. O. C. 27 Nov 1834.
   Rachel, m. David Shibley of Ernestown. O. C. 27 Nov 1834.
   Amelia, m. ---- Van Dresser of Ernestown. O. C. 27 Nov 1834.
   Eleanor, m. Michael Wemp of Amherst Island. O. C. 27 Nov 1834.
   John of Ernestown. O. C. 5 Feb 1835.

GERMAN, Christopher of Adolphustown.
   William of Adolphustown. O. C. 19 April 1816.
   Mathew of Adolphustown, m. Margaret Smith 13 Sept 1813. OC 19 Apr 1816.
   Peter of Adolphustown. O. C. 18 March 1818.
   Elizabeth, m. Edward Huyck of Adolphustown; d. 1840 ae 44 years. O. C.
      7 February 1821.
   Lewis of Adolphustown. O. C. 16 Nov 1797.
   George of Adolphustown, m. Sarah N. Lewis. O. C. 22 Feb 1834.
   Catharine, m. William Valleau of Adolphustown. O. C. 6 Nov 1829.
   Maria. O. C. 28 Feb 1835.

GERMAN, Jacob of Adolphustown.
   Christopher of Adolphustown. O. C. 18 March 1818.
   John of Ameliasburgh. O. C. 25 June 1823.
   George of Hillier. O. C. 18 April 1839.
   Lucinda, m. Charles Bennet Clark of Hillier. O. C. 6 April 1836.
   William R. of Hillier. O. C. 4 April 1833.
   James W. of Hillier. O. C. 8 May 1833.
   Jane, m. Chester Potter of Hillier, 7 Feb 1832. O. C. 25 July 1833.
   Abraham of Hillier. O. C. 7 Aug 1834.
   Jacob of Ameliasburgh. O. C. 5 Dec 1827.

GERMAN, John of Adolphustown and Richmond. His wife, Mary Ryckman,
   O. C. 16 Nov 1797. His wife, Elizabeth Vanderburgh, O. C. 10 March 1834.
   Rebecca, m. Jacob Elliott of Elizabethtown. OC 22 Dec 1801.   [Cont'd]

GERMAN, John - Cont'd
Jane, m. Carr Draper of Cramahe. O.C. 7 Feb 1821.
Jacob of Adolphustown. O.C. 16 Nov 1797.
Henry of Ancaster. O.C. 7 June 1826.
George P. of Tyendinaga. O.C. 26 Jan 1837.
Garret of Tyendinaga. O.C. 10 March 1834.
Elizabeth. O.C. 10 March 1834. Tyendinaga.
Margaret, m. James Deans of Tyendinaga. O.C. 1 May 1834.
John of Richmond. O.C. 28 Feb 1833.
Eve, m. William Greggs of Richmond. O.C. 19 July 1826.

GERNON, James of Vaughan.
William of Markham. O.C. 5 May 1819.

GEROLAMY, James of Marysburgh.
Margaret, m. George McGuire of Marysburgh. OC 3 June 1817; 28 April
1815.
Ann, m. William Ashley of Kingston. O.C. 2 March 1816.
James of Adolphustown. O.C. 25 Feb 1818.
John of Marysburgh. O.C. 7 March 1822.
Augustus. See O.C. 10 Dec 1832.

GILBERT, Josiah of Norwich.
John of Norwich. O.C. 3 Oct 1839.
Abraham of Norwich. O.C. 15 May 1835.
Selina, m. Michael Maloney of Norwich. O.C. 1 Aug 1833.
Sarah, m. Michael Cain of Norwich. O.C. 19 Aug 1833.
Peter of Norwich. O.C. 23 Aug 1831.
Benjamin of Norwich. O.C. 23 Aug 1831.

GILCHRIST, Peter.
Duncan of Ernestown. O.C. 27 Oct 1801.
Neal of Ernestown. O.C. 27 Oct 1801.
William of Ernestown. O.C. 27 Oct 1801.
Archibald of Ernestown. O.C. 23 Feb 1809.
Catherine. O.C. 25 Feb 1809.

GILMORE, Benjamin of Grantham.
Moses of Grantham, m. Clarinda Markle. O.C. 20 May 1817.
Charity, m. John Smith of Thorold. O.C. 20 May 1817.
Phyly, m. William May Jr. of Caistor. O.C. 3 June 1817.
Henry of Gainsborough. O.C. 8 Dec 1835.
Catharine, m. Nicholas Patterson of Louth. O.C. 25 Oct 1828.
William of Thorold. O.C. 28 Feb 1829.

GIRTY, James of Malden and Gosfield. Died 15 April 1817.
James B. of Gosfield. O.C. 27 June 1833.

GIRTY, Simon of Malden.
  Sarah, m. Joseph Munger of Colchester. O. C. 30 Jan 1808.
  Anne, m. Peter Gauvreau of Malden. O. C. 19 May 1812.
  Prideaux of Malden. O. C. 15 Nov 1820.

GLASSFORD, John of Matilda.
  Jane, m. Henry Coons of Matilda. O. C. 18 June 1799; 5 Oct 1818.
  Martha. O. C. 9 July 1802.
  John of Matilda. Soldier, 41st Regt. O. C. 3 June 1810.
  Paul of Williamsburgh. O. C. 30 June 1798.

GLASSFORD, Lytle of Augusta, m. Sarah Wragg.
  Mary, bapt. 10 May 1785. O. C. 2 Dec 1806.
  Thomas of Augusta. O. C. 2 Dec 1806.
  John of Augusta, bapt. 26 Jan 1791. O. C. 12 Nov 1811.
  Sidney, m. Timothy Hodges of Augusta. O. C. 13 June 1818.
  Jane, bapt. 13 Feb 1789.
  William S. of Augusta. O. C. 13 Aug 1840.

GLASFORD, Paul of Augusta and Charlottenburgh, m. Manuel Christy.
  Benjamin of Charlottenburgh, bapt. 13 Feb 1789. O. C. 15 Nov 1808.
  Ann, bapt. 8 Feb 1795; m. Donald Grant of Charlottenburgh. O. C. 20
    May 1817.
  Jane, bapt. 27 Jan 1793. O. C. 25 Feb 1818.
  Lytle of Charlottenburgh, bapt. 16 Apr 1797. O. C. 23 July 1823.
  Eunice, bapt. 29 Jan 1791.
  William of Charlottenburgh. O. C. 4 July 1833.
  Paul of Charlottenburgh. O. C. 3 March 1831.

GLOVER, Jacob of Windham.
  Sarah. O. C. 16 Feb 1811.
  Getta (Gertrude), m. Alex. Boughner of Windham. O. C. 16 Feb 1811.
  John of Windham. O. C. 16 Dec 1815.
  Charles of Windham. O. C. 9 May 1821.
  Francis of Windham. O. C. 15 June 1820.
  William of Ancaster. O. C. 21 March 1821. O. C. 18 Feb 1843.
  Jonathan of Flamborough. O. C. 5 Nov 1823.
  Elizabeth, m. Michael Dody of Ancaster. O. C. 10 Aug 1837.
  Jacob of Townsend. O. C. 1 Aug 1839.
  Elizabeth, m. Lawrence Daniels of Burford. O. C. 17 Dec 1840.
  Mary, m. John Bowman of Burford. O. C. 27 June 1836.
  Pearce M. of Townsend. O. C. 4 Feb 1836.

GOES, Lawrence
  Jozina, m. Arent Van Dyck of Fredericksburgh. O. C. 25 Feb 1812.

GOLDSMITH, Thomas of Hallowell, m. Asenath Conger.
  Asenath, m. Gilbert Purdy of Hallowell 1 May 1816. OC 19 Apr 1820 [Cont]

GOLDSMITH, Thomas - Cont'd
   Stephen of Hallowell, m. Elizabeth Hagerman 10 Oct 1803. OC 6 Dec 1803.
   Rachel, m. David Gardiner of Hallowell 28 Apr 1800. O. C. 6 Dec 1803.
   Phoebe, bapt. 5 Sept 1791, m. David Cornwell of Hallowell. O. C. 26
      February 1806.
   Mary, m. Dr. William Oudendyke of Sidney 9 Feb 1807. OC 11 Nov 1815.
   Sabia Ann Gardiner, bapt. 18 Feb 1795; m. Richard G. Clute of Hallowell
      10 March 1810. O. C. 16 Jan 1816.
   David of Hallowell, bapt. 5 Sept 1791, m. ---- Johnson. OC 20 May 1817.
   John of Hallowell, bapt. 17 Feb 1796; m. Phoebe Orser, 19 June 1819.
      O. C. 20 May 1817.

GOOS, Frederick.
   Sarah, m. ---- Gallinger. O. C. 10 June 1800.
   Mary, m. ---- Moore of Osnabruck. O. C. 10 June 1800.
   Dorothy, m. William Sheets of Cornwall. O. C. 10 June 1800.

GORDON, John of Howard.
   Ephraim of Howard. O. C. 11 Feb 1834.
   Michael of Howard. O. C. 11 Feb 1834.
   Sarah, m. John Shippey of Howard. O. C. 3 April 1834.
   Elizabeth, m. George Hewitt of Howard. O. C. 3 April 1834.
   John. See O. C. 28 Feb 1835.
   Aaron. See O. C. 28 Feb 1835.

GORDON, Peter of Ancaster, m. Mary dau of Nathaniel Pettit, U. E.
   Elizabeth, m. James Mustard of Markham. O. C. 7 Aug 1810.
   Margaret, m. Samuel Green of Flamborough West. O. C. 16 Apr 1811.
   Anna, m. Benjamin Smith of Ancaster 10 Dec 1794. O. C. 16 Apr 1811.
   John of Ancaster. O. C. 24 Dec 1811.
   Nathaniel of Ancaster. O. C. 27 Nov 1815.
   Rachel, m. John Smith of Westminster. O. C. 18 July 1839.

GORDON, Robert of Charlottenburgh, m. Elizabeth Emery.
   Thomas of Yonge. O. C. 15 March 1803.
   Susannah, bapt. 20 July 1791. m. Thomas F. Howland of Leeds. O. C. 3
      April 1810.
   Catherine, m. William Sturdivant of Lansdowne. O. C. 3 April 1810.
   Robert, bapt. 20 July 1791.
   Elizabeth, bapt. 20 July 1791.
   Jane, bapt. 16 Dec 1793.

GORDONIER, Henry of Ernestown.
   Jacob of Ernestown. O. C. 10 Aug 1802.
   Elizabeth, m. John J. Frets of Fredericksburgh. O. C. 17 Feb 1807.
   Jane, m. John Simons of Sidney. O. C. 21 Feb 1807.
   Daniel of Ernestown. O. C. 8 Feb 1808.
   Lewis of Ernestown. O. C. 4 Oct 1826.   [Cont'd]

GORDONIER, Henry - Cont'd
  Mary, m. George Simmons of Fredericksburgh 24 May 1808. O.C. 23
    February 1809.
  Hannah, m. David Sole of Ernestown (Belleville). O.C. 20 May 1817;
    O.C. 1 April 1840.
  John of Ernestown. O.C. 27 Feb 1818.
  Henry of Ernestown. O.C. 27 Feb 1818.

GORDONIER, Jacob.
  Allany, m. John Shibley of Ernestown. O.C. 17 Feb 1807.
  Hannah, m. Peter Mattis of Ernestown. O.C. 30 May 1835.

GOULD, John of Cornwall, m. Ruth Ketchum.
  Joseph of Murray. O.C. 25 May 1837.
  James of Charlottenburgh. O.C. 25 May 1837.
  Lydia, bapt. 29 September 1812, aged 8 yrs; m. Abraham Stoneburgh of
    Murray. O.C. 25 May 1837.
  Betsy (Elizabeth), m. James Campbell of Murray (Charlottenburgh, on
    31 March 1812. O.C. 28 July 1836.
  Eunice, bapt. 29 Sept 1812, aged 10 yrs; m. John Turney of Murray.
    O.C. 28 July 1836.
  Sarah, m. Stoddard Coonstack of Murray. O.C. 26 Nov 1840.
  Benjamin, bapt. 29 Sept 1812, aged 5 yrs.

GOULD, John of Grantham.
  Catharine, bapt. 24 Sept 1792. O.C. 20 May 1817.
  Elizabeth, m. Henry Yocum of Grantham. O.C. 20 May 1817.
  Hannah. O.C. 4 March 1819.
  Jacob of Grantham. O.C. 4 March 1819.
  John of Grantham. O.C. 4 March 1819.
  Margaret, m. Adam Robins of Grantham. O.C. 28 March 1833.
  Lewis of Grantham. O.C. 2 May 1833.
  Hamilton of Grantham. O.C. 27 June 1833.
  Jane. O.C. 19 Aug 1833.
  Mary. O.C. 19 Aug 1833.
  Caroline. O.C. 3 Feb 1834.
  Adam of Grantham. O.C. 27 April 1832.
  Benjamin of Louth. O.C. 27 April 1832.

GRAHAM, Oliver of Elizabethtown.
  Hannah, m. Reuben Mott of Elizabethtown. O.C. 11 Dec 1810.
  Martin of Elizabethtown. O.C. 19 May 1812.
  Mary. O.C. 1 Sept 1812.
  Sarah, m. Joseph D. Brower of Elizabethtown. O.C. 13 June 1818.
  John of Elizabethtown. O.C. 15 May 1822.
  William T. of Fredericksburgh. O.C. 2 May 1833.
  Ann. O.C. 31 May 1830.
  Lydia, m. Arctus P. Billings. O.C. 23 August 1831.

GRAHAM, Robert of Kingston
   William of Kingston, m. Mary Wightman. O. C. 16 Nov 1807.
   Thomas of Kingston, m. Catherine Grass, 22 June 1809. OC 16 Feb 1811.
   Robert of Kingston. O. C. 16 Nov 1797.

GRAHAM, Thomas of Lancaster, m. Margaret.
   Isabella, m. ---- McDonell. O. C. 10 March 1801.
   Betsey. O. C. 15 March 1806. Lancaster.
   Alexander of Lancaster, bapt. 3 July 1791. O. C. 26 March 1817. See
      O. C. 9 February 1828.

GRAHAM, William of Whitchurch, m. ---- Taylor. He d. 1814. She d. 1815.
   William of Whitchurch, d. unmd. O. C. 10 July 1817.
   Jane, m. Thomas Coates of York. O. C. 21 April 1819.
   Margaret, m. James Edminson of Markham 28 July 1817. OC 12 Jan 1820.
   Peter of Whitchurch. O. C. 12 July 1820.
   Adam of Whitchurch, b. 10 July 1799; m. Elizabeth Edminson in 1832;
      d. 1 July 1874. O. C. 12 July 1820.

GRANT, Alexander of Lancaster. K. R. R. N. Y. Capt. Watts' Co.
   Isabella, m. John Martin of Lancaster. O. C. 14 Nov 1821.

GRANT, Alexander of Charlottenburgh.
   Alexander of Charlottenburgh. O. C. 10 Dec 1823.
   William of Charlottenburgh. O. C. 10 Dec 1823.

GRANT, Alexander of Lot 40, N.B. River aux Raisins, Charlottenburgh. Sgt.
   Catharine, m. Qr. Mr. Alex. Fraser, Canadian Fencibles. O. C. 28
      April 1815.
   Peter of Charlottenburgh. O. C. 20 May 1817.

GRANT, Alexander of West half D/ south side River aux Raisins, Char-
   lottenburgh.
   Peter of Charlottenburgh. O. C. 23 Nov 1816.
   Alexander of Cornwall. O. C. 13 June 1831.

GRANT, Allan of Elizabethtown.
   Allan of Elizabethtown. O. C. 17 Feb 1816.
   John of Elizabethtown. O. C. 11 June 1823.
   Anne, m. John McCready of Elizabethtown. O. C. 3 July 1798.

GRANT, Angus of Charlottenburgh.
   John of Charlottenburgh. O. C. 10 March 1801. O. C. 17 Nov 1801.
   Duncan. O. C. 14 April 1801.
   Christy, m. ---- Campbell of Charlottenburgh. O. C. 17 Nov 1801.
   Angus of Charlottenburgh. O. C. 16 March 1802.
   Margaret. O. C. 15 March 1806.
   Alexander of Charlottenburgh. O. C. 19 Dec 1806.   [Cont'd]

GRANT, Angus - Cont'd
  Janet. O. C. 16 Feb 1837.
  Allan of Charlottenburgh. O. C. 17 March 1836.

GRANT, Archibald of Charlottenburgh. Soldier, 84th Regt.
  Margaret. O. C. 15 March 1806. Charlottenburgh.
  John of Charlottenburgh. O. C. 19 Dec 1806.
  Archibald of Charlottenburgh. O. C. 4 Sept 1834.

GRANT, Archibald of East half 11/1 Charlottenburgh.
  Donald of Charlottenburgh. O. C. 28 April 1815.
  Angus of Charlottenburgh. O. C. 23 Nov 1816.
  Peter of Charlottenburgh. O. C. 23 Nov 1816.
  Duncan of Charlottenburgh. O. C. 25 Feb 1818.

GRANT, Donald Sr. (Caskey). Lot 13/2 south side River aux Raisins, S. B.,
  Charlottenburgh.
  Mary, m. ---- McDonell of Charlottenburgh. O. C. 27 July 1802.
  Donald of Charlottenburgh. O. C. 10 March 1801; O. C. 25 Jan 1831.
  Catharine, m. Angus McDonell of Charlottenburgh. O. C. 23 Nov 1816.
  Archibald of Charlottenburgh. O. C. 25 Jan 1831.
  Nancy, m. ---- McDonell of Lancaster. Land Board Certif. 27/8 Lochiel

GRANT, Donald Jr. of Charlottenburgh.
  John of Charlottenburgh. O. C. 6 Aug 1816. O. C. 23 June 1837?
  Catharine, m. Alexander McDonell of Charlottenburgh. O. C. 6 Aug 1816.
  Mary. O. C. 14 Dec 1816.
  Elizabeth. O. C. 5 Feb 1823.
  Nancy. O. C. 5 Feb 1823.
  Christy. O. C. 14 May 1823.

GRANT, Donald of west half 16/2 south side River aux Raisins, Charlottenburgh.
  Alexander of Charlottenburgh. O. C. 12 Nov 1817.

GRANT, Duncan of Augusta.
  Rachel, m. Isaac McCartney of Elizabethtown. O. C. 2 Dec 1806.
  Elizabeth, m. Thomas Moor of Marlborough. O. C. 5 March 1810.
  John of Marlborough. O. C. 30 May 1821.
  Robert of Oxford-on-Rideau. O. C. 28 Oct 1835.
  Duncan of Montague. O. C. 4 Feb 1836.

GRANT, Duncan of Charlottenburgh. West half 20 & East half 21/1.
  Catharine. O. C. 28 Feb 1835.

GRANT, James.
  Jenny, m. Alexander Mill of Edwardsburgh. O. C. 31 May 1803.

GRANT, John of Pittsburgh. Soldier, King's Rangers. O.C. 12 May 1808.
   Ann, m. Edward Jones of Pittsburgh 10 Feb 1806. O.C. 13 Oct 1807.
   James of Pittsburgh, bapt. 14 Feb 1796. O.C. 28 July 1819.
   Sarah Isabella, m. Christopher Miller of Camden East. OC 8 Dec 1835.
   Frances, bapt. 22 May 1803. O.C. 28 Nov 1826.
   Hannah, bapt. 12 Jan 1800. O.C. 28 Nov 1826.
   Jane, bapt. 14 Jan 1798.
   Peter, bapt. 11 Aug 1805.
   William Edward, bapt. 3 July 1808.

GRANT, John of East half 42, River aux Raisins, Charlottenburgh.
   Catharine. O.C. 28 April 1815.

GRANT, John of West half 17/2 Charlottenburgh.
   Ann. O.C. 23 Nov 1816.
   Alexander of Charlottenburgh. O.C. 19 Feb 1823.

GRANT, Lewis of Charlottenburgh, /2 River aux Raisins.
   Ranald of 7th Concession, Lancaster. O.C. 4 Sept 1834.
   Alexander of Charlottenburgh. O.C. 4 Sept 1834.
   John of Charlottenburgh. O.C. 4 Sept 1834.
   James of Charlottenburgh. O.C. 4 Sept 1834.
   Angus of Charlottenburgh. O.C. 4 Sept 1834.
   Mary. O.C. 4 Sept 1834.
   Flora. O.C. 4 Sept 1834.
   Margaret. O.C. 4 Sept 1834.
   Janet. O.C. 4 Sept 1834.

GRANT, Lewis of Charlottenburgh, 13/ N.B. S.B. River aux Raisins.
   Angus of Charlottenburgh. O.C. 7 Feb 1821.
   Peter of Charlottenburgh. O.C. 23 July 1839.
   Elizabeth. O.C. 15 Oct 1840. Fredericksburgh.

GRANT, Peter. E. half 10/ Front, Charlottenburgh. Soldier, R.R.N.Y.
   John of Charlottenburgh. O.C. 9 March 1803.
   Duncan of Charlottenburgh. Land Board Certificate. 22/8 Lochiel.

GRANT, Peter.
   Catharine. O.C. 28 Sept 1825.
   Archibald of Charlottenburgh. O.C. 28 Sept 1825.
   Alexander of Charlottenburgh. O.C. 28 Sept 1825.
   Duncan of Charlottenburgh. O.C. 28 Sept 1825.

GRANT, Peter of 12/5 Charlottenburgh. Sgt., K.R.R.N.Y.
   John of Charlottenburgh. O.C. 25 Feb 1818.

GRASS, Michael of Kingston, m. Margery or Margaret, dau Henry Swartz;
   he d. 25 April 1813 at Kingston.   [Cont'd]

GRASS, Michael - Cont'd
  Catharine, m. Thomas Graham of Kingston 22 June 1809. OC 19 Nov 1798.
  Daniel of North Gwillimbury. O. C. 17 March 1804.
  Eve, b. December, 1765; m. Peter Wartman of Kingston; d. 16 May 1858.
    O. C. 16 Nov 1797.
  John of Kingston, b. about 1774; m. Catherine Snook 19 March 1799.
    O. C. 17 Nov 1797.
  Peter of Kingston, m. Esther Everett, 9 Feb 1808. Land Board Certifi-
    cate, 14/4 Sidney.
  Mary, b. about 1776; m. Capt. Theophilus Samson of Kingston. O. C. 17
    November 1797.

GRAY, Alexander of York.
  Alexander of York, m. Hannah Boyer, 22 Dec 1811. O. C. 17 Nov 1807.
  William of York. O. C. 17 Nov 1807.
  Rebecca, m. Jonathan Willcut of York 2 Apr 1805. O. C. 5 Jan 1808.

GRAY, James of Yonge.
  Nancy, m. James Brown of Yonge. O. C. 11 Dec 1806.
  Catharine, m. Nehemiah Avery of Yonge. O. C. 11 Dec 1806.
  Esther, m. Benjamin Green of Yonge. O. C. 26 Jan 1808.
  Charlotte, m. Alexander McDonell of Cramahe. O. C. 2 Sept 1830.

GRAY, John.
  Ann, m. George Purvis of York . O. C. 3 Nov 1801.

GRAY, John of Kingston.
  Jane, m. James Bayman of Pittsburgh 25 Oct 1791. Land Board Certifi-
    cate, 28/4 Pittsburgh.

GRAY, John of Leeds. Sgt., 84th Regt.
  Sarah, m. Timothy Munro of Yonge. O. C. 17 July 1805.
  Jane, m. William Bogart of Elizabethtown. O. C. 8 Feb 1808.
  Hugh of Yonge. O. C. 24 Dec 1811.
  Margaret, m. Peter Rosebeck of Leeds. O. C. 4 March 1796.

GRAY, John of Elizabethtown.
  Samuel of Elizabethtown. O. C. 26 May 1801.

GREEN, Adam of Saltfleet.
  Ann, m. Andrew Muir of Grimsby. O. C. 11 Dec 1810.
  John of Saltfleet. O. C. 2 Jan 1811.
  Mary, m. John Yeager of Saltfleet. O. C. 14 June 1811.
  Samuel of Saltfleet. O. C. 28 May 1811.
  Sarah, m. Nicholas Witzell of Saltfleet. O. C. 25 Feb 1812.
  Decier, m. Isaac Corman of Saltfleet. O. C. 23 Nov 1816.
  Levi of Saltfleet. O. C. 27 April 1837.
  William of Saltfleet. O. C. 27 April 1837.   [Cont'd]

GREEN, Adam - Cont'd
  Freeman of Howard. O. C. 5 Nov 1835.
  Rebecca, m. William Lacey of Saltfleet. O. C. 12 Sept 1833.

GREEN, Benjamin of Townsend.
  Charles of Townsend. O. C. 6 Oct 1819.
  Jeremiah of Townsend. O. C. 19 March 1840.
  Priscilla. O. C. 19 March 1840.
  Fanny, m. Robert Stuart of Townsend. O. C. 7 May 1840.
  Rescom of Townsend. O. C. 31 Dec 1840.
  Archibald of Townsend. O. C. 27 Nov 1834.
  Braman of Townsend. O. C. 27 Nov 1834. [Notes on his descendnats
    appear in The Ontario Register, 2: 101-105; 3: 114-116]
  Benjamin of Townsend. O. C. 6 Sept 1839.

GREEN, John of Marysburgh & Louth, m. Sylvia dau Wm. Cadman, U. E.
  Mary, m. Abraham Sloot of Louth. O. C. 19 May 1812.
  Alexander of Louth. O. C. 19 May 1812.

GREEN, John of Flamborough West, m. Mary.
  Ann, m. John Belcher of Grantham. O. C. 11 July 1806.
  Daniel of Flamborough West. O. C. 15 Nov 1808.
  Susannah, m. John Main of Flamborough West. O. C. 6 April 1811.
  Hannah, bapt. 2 Feb 1793; m. Caleb Hopkins of Nelson. OC 2 March 1816.
  John Simcoe of Flamborough West. OC 7 Aug 1822. m. Susannah Ryckman.
  Sarah, m. William Markle Jr. of Flamborough West. OC 28 Oct 1835.
  Nancy, bapt. 2 Feb 1793.
  William of Flamborough West. O. C. 1 March 1832.

GREEN, Reuben of Townsend. Sgt., 1st Batt., N. J. Vols.
  Hannah, m. Isaac Pettit of Townsend. O. C. 23 Jan 1811.
  Jeremiah of Townsend. O. C. 23 Jan 1811.
  John of Townsend. O. C. 23 Jan 1811.
  Elizabeth, m. John Dickson of Townsend. O. C. 23 Dec 1815.
  Phoebe, m. Jonathan Silverthorne of Townsend. O. C. 23 Dec 1815.
  Charles of Townsend. O. C. 10 March 1834.

GREEN, William of Marysburgh.
  Jacob of Marysburgh. O. C. 2 Sept 1830.

GREENLAIR, Jonathan.
  Elizabeth, m. ---- Lymburner of Caistor. O. C. 2 May 1797.

GRIFFIN, Charles of Yonge.
  John of Yonge. O. C. 18 March 1818.

GRIFFIN, Joseph of Elizabethtown.
  Hannah, m. ---- Hagerman of Elizabethtown. OC 26 May 1801.   [Cont'd]

GRIFFIN, Joseph - Cont'd
 Orpah, m. John Watson of Kingston. O.C. 6 Dec 1808.
 Phoebe, m. Peter Degrote of Elizabethtown. O.C. 23 Feb 1809.
 Hannah, m. Joseph Wooley of Elizabethtown. O.C. 22 Feb 1810.
 Joseph of Flamborough East. O.C. 2 June 1819.
 Rhoda, m. John McKay of Bathurst. O.C. 26 Nov 1823.
 Hannah, m. Peet Seeley of Elizabethtown. O.C. 20 July 1837.

GRIFFIS, William of Fredericksburgh and Adolphustown.
 Philip of Fredericksburgh. O.C. 4 Nov 1818.
 William of Fredericksburgh. O.C. 26 July 1820.
 Gilbert of Fredericksburgh. O.C. 18 Feb 1824.
 Stephen of Fredericksburgh. O.C. 18 Aug 1824.

GROOMES, Elijah of Kingston. Soldier, 2nd Batt., N.J. Vols. Md. Rebecca.
 A daughter of Elijah Groomes was buried 20 July 1794.
 James of Kingston, m. Elizabeth. O.C. 9 Sept 1806.
 Hannah, bapt. 11 Jan 1795; m. Thomas Smith of Kingston. OC 15 Mar 1803.
 Richard of Belleville, bapt. 11 Jan 1795. Shoemaker. O.C. 20 May 1817.
 Mary, bapt. 21 Dec 1800; m. James C. Beebe of Kingston. OC 22 July 1818
 Anthony, bapt. 21 Dec 1800; buried 27 Aug 1802.
 Zeppaniah of Richmond, bapt. 11 Jan 1795. O.C. 3 Jan 1833.
 Margaret, bapt. 11 Jan 1795; buried 12 Sept 1802.

GROOMS, Joseph of Marysburgh.
 Ann, m. John McCrimmon of Hallowell. O.C. 18 March 1818.
 Joseph of Marysburgh. O.C. 5 Oct 1820.
 Thomas of Marysburgh. O.C. 3 Nov 1836.
 Ezekiel of Marysburgh. O.C. 21 March 1833.
 William of Barton. O.C. 27 June 1833.
 John of Barton. O.C. 27 June 1833.
 Catharine, m. Henry Smith of Loughborough. O.C. 3 Jan 1827.
 Rebecca, m. Francis McGuin of Barton. O.C. 4 Oct 1826.

GROUT, Ferdinand of Zorra.
 John C. of Oxford. O.C. 25 Aug 1836.
 Lyrena, m. Jeremiah Rounds of Zorra. O.C. 8 Sept 1836.
 George Chauncey of Zorra. O.C. 5 March 1835.
 Willard of Zorra. O.C. 5 March 1835.
 Anson H. of Zorra. O.C. 5 March 1835.

GUNN, David.
 Jennett. O.C. 3 March 1801.
 Ranald of Lancaster. O.C. 17 Nov 1801. (2 March 1813. Ronald, son of
   David & Janet (McDonell) Gunn, m. Magdaline, daughter of Alex. &
   Harriet (McD.) McDonell.)

HAGERMAN, James of Ernestown.
  Eleanor, m. William Coulter of Huntingdon. O. C. 16 Feb 1837.

HAGERMAN, John.
  Abigail, m. William LaRue of Yonge. O. C. 26 May 1801.
  Margaret, m. ---- Whitley. O. C. 26 May 1801.

HAGERMAN, Nicholas of Adolphustown, m. Anne Fisher of Montreal, 28
  October 1785. She d. 4 Jan 1847, aged 88. He d. at his residence in Adol-
  phustown, 19 Feb 1819, in 58th year.
  Eliza. O. C. 15 Nov 1808. Adolphustown.
  Maria, bapt. 16 Feb 1790; m. Rev. John Stoughton of Kingston 13 June
    1821. O. C. 6 March 1813.
  Daniel of Adolphustown. O. C. 23 Nov 1816.
  Christopher A. of Kingston, b. 28 March 1792; bapt. 2 Oct 1792; m. (1)
    Elizabeth Macaulay, 26 March 1817; m. (2) Elizabeth Emily Merry,
    17 Apr 1834; d. 14 May 1847. O. C. 19 May 1819.
  John, bapt. 23 March 1789.
  Joseph N. of Town of Kingston, d. 2 Aug 1833 ae 28 ys. OC 7 June 1827.
  Jane, m. (1) ---- [blank]   26 Oct 1822; m. (2) George Baker, 30
    May 1830; d. 25 Oct 1830.

HAGERMAN, Tunis of Ernestown.
  John of Ernestown. O. C. 5 Nov 1818.
  Cynthia. O. C. 18 Oct 1838.
  Abraham of Ernestown. O. C. 18 May 1837.
  Edward of Thurlow. O. C. 7 May 1835.
  Jane, m. Truman Potter of Pittsburgh. O. C. 7 May 1835.
  Elizabeth. O. C. 7 May 1828.
  Mehitable, m. Hugh Milligan of Ernestown. O. C. 7 May 1828.

HAGGART, John Sr. of Charlottenburgh.
  Donald of Charlottenburgh. O. C. 19 Dec 1806.
  John of Charlottenburgh. O. C. 19 Dec 1806.
  Duncan of Charlottenburgh. O. C. 25 Feb 1818.
  Anne, m. Hiram Burk of Ancaster. O. C. 5 Nov 1818.

HAGGERTY, Hugh of Stamford.
  Jane, m. Benjamin Sutton of Stamford. O. C. 19 Dec 1809.
  Mary. O. C. 8 Sept 1819.
  Tryphena, m. Peter Dell of Willoughby. O. C. 28 Sept 1820.
  Stephen of Stamford. O. C. 6 March 1822.

HAINER, Albert of Grantham.
  Dorothy, m. David Putman of Lough, 24 May 1807. O. C. 16 Aug 1810;
    O. C. 20 May 1817.
  Isaac of Grantham. O. C. 20 May 1817.
  Henry of Grantham. O. C. 20 May 1817.   [Cont'd]

HAINER, Albert - Cont'd
Mary. O. C. 20 May 1817.
John of Grantham. O. C. 26 Jan 1820.
Deborah, m. Mathias Fisher of Erin. O. C. 31 Jan 1839.
Catharine, m. Jonas Larraway of Grantham. O. C. 3 Nov 1836.
James of Grantham. O. C. 27 June 1833.
Hannah, m. John Swackhammer of Esquesing. O. C. 3 Feb 1834.
Sarah, m. John Bradt of Grantham. O. C. 2 Feb 1832.
Elizabeth. O. C. 11 Aug 1831. Grantham.

HAINER, John of Grantham. [A John Hanor served in Butler's Rangers and
was at Niagara in 1783. The Ontario Register, 1: 202]
Jacobus of Grantham. O. C. 27 Jan 1801.
David of Grantham. O. C. 26 Jan 1808.
Catherine, m. Simcoe Stephenson of Louth 19 May 1808. OC 6 Dec 1808.
George of Grantham. O. C. 4 April 1797.
dau. , m. Abraham Clendenning of Grantham. O. C. 29 July 1795.

HAINER, Richard of Grantham, m. a dau of Isaac Vollock, U. F. [Derrick
Hainer and his wife were at Niagara in 1783. The Ontario Register 1: 202]
Dorothy, m. John May of Grantham 5 Aug 1802. O. C. 15 May 1805.
Mary, m. George Ghasky of Grantham. O. C. 5 March 1810.
Elizabeth. O. C. 20 May 1817.
Clarinda, m. John Patterson of Louth. O. C. 19 May 1819.
Cornelia, m. Frederick A. Schram of Louth. O. C. 22 May 1820.
Eve, m. George Yocom of Louth. O. C. 12 July 1820.
Sarah, m. John Tinline of Louth. O. C. 23 May 1833.
Margaret, m. John Frederick Schram of Pelham. O. C. 19 Feb 1831.

HAINES, Adam of Grantham.
John of Grantham. O. C. 27 June 1821.
Barnabas of Clinton. O. C. 27 June 1821.
Adam of Grantham. O. C. 27 June 1821.
Jacob of Grantham. O. C. 27 June 1821.
Louis of Louth. O. C. 27 June 1821.
Mary, m. Phillip Shaddock of Clinton. O. C. 27 June 1821.
Elizabeth, m. Joseph Wheatton of Grantham. O. C. 27 June 1821.
Peter of Louth, m. Elizabeth Foster. O. C. 19 Sept 1821.

HAINES, Joseph Sr.
Philip of York. O. C. 10 July 1806.
Sarah m. (1) Roger Bland, 6 March 1797; m. (2) Thomas Otway Page.
O. C. 26 Feb 1797.
Mary, m. Philip Shaver of Grantham. O. C. 28 March 1797.

HAINES, Nathaniel of Grantham.
Catharine, m. John Risenburg of Niagara. O. C. 17 Nov 1808.
Benjamin of Niagara. O. C. 3 Nov 1836.   [Cont'd]

HAINES, Nathaniel - Cont'd
 Mary, bapt. 20 Feb 1801; m. Richard Ryan of Thorold. O. C. 21 June 1819
 Andrew, bapt. 15 July 1792.
 Elizabeth, bapt. 9 Sept 1804. O. C. 2 Sept 1830.
 Lany. O. C. 6 Aug 1828.
 Margaret, bapt. 12 May 1805.

HALL, Samuel of Sandwich. See O. C. 7 May 1828, Wm. Hall.
 Margaret, m. John Collins of Town of Sandwich. O. C. 28 Feb 1835.
 Mary, m. Morning Sykes of Town of Sandwich. O. C. 28 Feb 1835.
 Samuel of Town of Sandwich. O. C. 6 Nov 1829.
 William of Sandwich. O. C. 19 Feb 1828.

HAM, John of Ernestown. His wife, Elizabeth Densbaugh, died at Ernestown
 on 4 May 1845 in her 82nd yr.
 John of Fredericksburgh, m. Esther Bradshaw 10 Apr 1808; died 1843.
   O. C. 13 March 1810.
 George of Ernestown, m. Elizabeth Hanley; d. at Cobourg, 7 Feb 1843
   aet. 48 yrs. O. C. 18 March 1818.
 Mary, m. Peter Perry of Ernestown 19 June 1814. O. C. 3 Apr 1819.
 Henry of Ernestown, m. (1) ---- Perry; m. (2) Mrs. Frances Farnsworth.
   O. C. 24 December 1823.
 Elizabeth, b. 7 Aug 1808; m. Wm Fairfield of Ernestown. OC 7 Mar 1827.
 Benjamin of Ernestown, b. 4 Apr 1802; m. Rhoda Losee. OC 9 Feb 1830.
 Richard of Fredericksburgh, b. 23 Sept 1804; m. Sarah Blanchard. O. C.
   28 March 1833.
 Philip of Brantford, b. 29 March 1800; m. Frances E. Butler; d. 1847.
   O. C. 2 May 1833.
 Peter of Bath, m. Rebecca Lockwood; d. October, 1828.

HAMBLIN, Silas of Augusta.
 Francis of Augusta. O. C. 10 June 1800.
 Silas of Augusta. O. C. 9 July 1802.
 Nancy, m. William Knapp of Augusta. O. C. 9 July 1802.
 Elizabeth, m. Ebenezer Eaton of Augusta. O. C. 8 Oct 1808.
 Benjamin of Augusta. O. C. 24 April 1810.
 William of Elizabethtown. O. C. 2 March 1816.

HAMILTON, Andrew of Dover.
 John of Dover. O. C. 19 Nov 1831. See also O. C. 15 Aug 1821.

HAMILTON, Thomas of Town of York. Died there 28 Nov 1831 aged 62.
 Alexander Howe of Town of York. O. C. 10 Jan 1821.
 Horatio Nelson of York Town; d. 12 Feb 1832 ae 26. O. C. 23 June 1828.
 Sidney Smith of York, bapt. 7 June 1812; m. Anne Coulthard, 22 June
   1837. O. C. 17 March 1836.
 Robert Wilson of Town of York. O. C. 5 Feb 1829.
 William Archibald of Town of York. O. C. 23 Nov 1825.   [Cont'd]

HAMILTON, Thomas - Cont'd
   Thomas Gilbert of Town of York. O. C. 24 Dec 1830.
   Caroline Maria, m. Charles McIntosh of Town of York. OC 23 Nov 1825.

HANES, Christopher of Williamsburgh.
   Catharine. O. C. 19 April 1816.
   John of Williamsburgh. O. C. 19 April 1816.
   Joseph of Williamsburgh. O. C. 19 April 1816.
   William of Williamsburgh. O. C. 19 April 1816.
   Christopher of Williamsburgh. O. C. 5 Sept 1833.
   Adam of Williamsburgh. O. C. 5 Sept 1833.
   Jacob C. of Osnabruck. O. C. 3 April 1834.
   George of Williamsburgh. O. C. 2 March 1825.

HANES, John of Williamsburgh.
   Nancy, m. John P. Fetterley of Winchester. O. C. 1 Aug 1851.
   Margaret, m. Henry Bedstead of Winchester. O. C. 1 Aug 1851.
   James of Winchester. O. C. 1 Aug 1851.
   John of Winchester. O. C. 1 Aug 1851.
   Jeremiah of Winchester. O. C. 1 Aug 1851.

HANES, Michael.
   Elizabeth, m. Mathias Monk of Williamsburgh. O. C. 26 Jan 1808.

HANSON, Richard of Town of Niagara. Butler's Rangers. [He and his family
   were at Niagara in 1783. The Ontario Register, 1: 201]
   Nicholas of Town of Niagara. O. C. 22 July 1836.
   John B. of Town of Niagara. O. C. 27 Oct 1836.
   Peter of Town of Niagara. O. C. 27 Oct 1836.
   Mary, m. Henry Vosburgh. O. C. 17 Nov 1836.
   Angelica, m. ---- Dockstader of Town of Niagara. O. C. 19 May 1836.

HARDY, John of Stamford.
   Thomas of Gainsboro. O. C. 8 Sept 1836.
   Jane. O. C. 8 Sept 1836. Crowland.
   Margaret, m. Samuel Hatch of Crowland, 18 June 1829. OC 8 Sept 1836.
   Lavinia, m. Rev. James Ferguson of Stamford 11 Feb 1819. O. C. 8
      September 1836.
   Nancy, m. James Hardy of Stamford. O. C. 17 Nov 1836.
   John of Stamford. O. C. 24 Nov 1836.
   Eleanor, m. Thomas Helmer of Town of York, Grand River [i. e. , Haldi-
      mand County]. O. C. 23 June 1837.

HARE, Henry of Soulanges, Lower Canada. Lieut. His wife Allada. See OC
   7 March 1807. He was hanged at Mohawk River.
   Mary, m. Jacob Weagar of Williamsburgh. O. C. 30 June 1798.
   Barney.
   John. and Catharine.

HARE, James of Lancaster. See O. C. 28 July 1801.
    Mary. O. C. 17 March 1807. Cornwall.
    William of Osnabruck. O. C. 3 Dec 1835.
    Christeen, m. ---- Rambough of Osnabruck. O. C. 5 Jan 1798.

HARE, John of Cornwall, m. Ann Vrooman.
    Henry of Williamsburgh. O. C. 23 June 1836.
    Nancy. O. C. 1850 or 1851.
    Kadelia. O. C. 1850 or 1851.
    William of Matilda. O. C. 1850 or 1851.

HARE, Peter of Louth. Capt. Peter Hare Sr., b. May 11, 1748; Col. 4th
    Regt. Lincoln Militia; d. at Clinton, 6 April 1834 aged 85. His wife Mary
    (Margaret ?) d. 19 Dec 1851 in her 87th year. Wife Catharine. [He and his
    family were at Niagara in 1783. The Ontario Register, v. 1, p. 204]
    Catherine, m. Isaac Walker of Ancaster. O. C. 19 Aug 1800.
    Mary, m. Robert Brown of Grantham; d. March, 1849. OC 12 Mar 1805.
    Elizabeth, m. Thomas Bradt of Louth. O. C. 29 June 1806.
    Ann, m. John Bradt of Pelham. O. C. 12 Nov 1811.
    Peter of Clinton. O. C. 9 March 1816.
    Deborah, m. Joshua Beebe of Louth. O. C. 22 Oct 1817.
    William of Clinton. O. C. 19 May 1819.
    Margaret. OC 18 Feb 1836. m. R. Henry ?
    John, bapt. 2 Feb 1793.
    James of Niagara. O. C. 29 April 1824.

HARE, William of Flamborough West.
    John of Flamborough West. O. C. 20 May 1817.
    James D. of Flamborough West. O. C. 3 May 1820.
    Susannah. O. C. 16 May 1821.
    Walter of Flamborough West. O. C. 3 Nov 1836.
    Mary Ann, m. Charles Bruce; d. Nov., 1832. Not. Rec. 21 Mar., 1833.
    William of Flamborough West. O. C. 2 Feb 1832.
    Samuel H. of Flamborough West. O. C. 2 Dec 1830.
    Elizabeth. O. C. 11 Aug 1831.

HARNS, Gilbert of Fredericksburgh. His wife, Catharine, buried 9 Aug 1788
    Esther, m. Abraham Stoneburg of Fredericksburgh. OC 21 Feb 1821.
    Margaret, m. William Bell Jr. of Fredericksburgh. OC 25 May 1825.
    Thomas F. of Fredericksburgh. O. C. 7 March 1822.
    Deborah, m. Richard Simmons of Fredericksburgh. OC 6 Feb 1823.
    Gilbert, bapt. 25 Aug 1788; buried 7 Sept 1788.
    Phoebe, m. Nathan Durkee. O. C. 13 Nov 1797.

HARNS, Josiah of Fredericksburgh.
    Sarah, m. Peter Koughnet of Sophiasburgh. O. C. 7 Aug 1810.
    George C. of Fredericksburgh, bapt. 18 Jan 1796. OC 20 Feb 1840.
    Thomas of Fredericksburgh, bapt. 1 Jan 1794. OC 22 June 1825. [Cont'd]

HARNS, Josiah - Cont'd
  Deborah, bapt. 29 June 1791; m. William Bradshaw of Haldimand. O.C.
    14 Dec 1816.
  Elizabeth, bapt. 30 May 1798; m. Elias Hoffman of Fredericksburgh.
    O.C. 7 Aug 1822.
  Eleanor, bapt. 27 Jan 1789; buried 13 Feb 1793.
  Jenny, bapt. 8 June 1803.

HARNS, Thomas.
  Sarah, m. ---- Howard. O.C. 21 June 1799.

HARPEL, George of Kingston, m. Margaret dau Nathan & Elizabeth Stalker.
  Elizabeth, m. George Ashley of Kingston. O.C. 16 June 1819.
  John of Kingston. O.C. 22 March 1820.
  Eve, m. Samuel Babcock of Kingston. O.C. 22 March 1820.
  Margaret, m. Lorenzo Ruttan of Kingston. O.C. 28 Oct 1835.
  Esther, b. 17 Apr 1808; m. Abraham Collard Jr. of Loughborough. O.C.
    27 June 1833.
  Catharine, m. John Abrahams of Kingston. O.C. 19 Dec 1833.
  George of Kingston. O.C. 19 Dec 1833.
  Henry of Kingston. O.C. 19 Dec 1833.
  Jacob of Kingston. O.C. 18 Feb 1843.

HARPER, William.
  Thomas of Raleigh. O.C. 31 Oct 1809.

HARRIS, David of Fredericksburgh, m. Catharine Palmer, 30 Dec 1788.
  John of Tyendinaga. O.C. 29 Nov 1848.
  Bryan of Sidney. O.C. 29 Nov 1848.
  David of Sidney. O.C. 29 Nov 1848.
  Elizabeth, m. Gilbert P. Sharp of Sidney. O.C. 29 Nov 1848.
  Phoebe, m. William Fairman of Thurlow. O.C. 10 Jan 1849.

HARRIS, Myndert of Hope.
  Joseph of Hamilton, m. Rachel. See O.C. 30 Aug 1797, and 14 July 1797.
  Peter of Hamilton. O.C. 14 July 1797.
  Catherine, m. Asa Callender. O.C. 28 Feb 1799.
  Elizabeth, m. Elias Smith Jr. of Hope. O.C. 28 Feb 1799.
  Peggy, m. Elias Jones of Hamilton; d. Cobourg, 26 Sept 1834, aged 54.
    O.C. 12 July 1803.
  Hannah, m. Seth Soper of Hope. O.C. 2 March 1805. m.(2) John Burn-
    ham of Hamilton. O.C. 3 Nov 1807.
  Sally, m. Elisha Jones of Hamilton. O.C. 23 Feb 1808.
  Myndert of Hope, m. Phoebe Hawkins. O.C. 19 Apr 1808.
  Rebecca, m. Gilbert Livingston of Hope. O.C. 5 June 1810.
  Thomas of Hope. O.C. 19 Feb 1817.

HARRIS, Thomas of Grimsby.
John of Grimsby. O.C. 10 March 1804.
Sarah, m. Joseph Halstead of Grimsby. O.C. 4 July 1833.

HARSON, Felix of Fredericksburgh.
William of Queenstown. O.C. 29 March 1803.
Rosannah, m. Elijah Ferris of Queenstown. O.C. 31 May 1803.
John of Queenstown. O.C. 31 May 1803.
Margaret, m. Levi De Shea of Bertie. O.C. 16 Aug 1810.
Timothy of Vaughan. O.C. 19 April 1816.

HART, Barney (Barnabas) of Cornwall. Soldier, R.R.N.Y., Capt. Daly's
Company. Married Mary Bender.
George of Cornwall. O.C. 7 Aug 1811.
Henry of Cornwall, bapt. 17 Nov 1793. O.C. 5 April 1820.
Barnabas, bapt. 14 Aug 1791.
John of Cornwall. O.C. 18 May 1833.
Catharine, m. Winslow Wood of Osnabruck. O.C. 19 Dec 1833.
Mary, m. ---- O'Bryan of Osnabruck. O.C. 2 Jan 1834.
Nancy, m. Donald MacMillan of Osnabruck. O.C. 27 Feb 1834.
Jacob of Cornwall. O.C. 14 Nov 1831.
Tunis of Cornwall. O.C. 6 Feb 1828.

HARTLE, Adam of Cornwall, m. Mary De Witt.
Catharine, m. George Gallinger of Cornwall. O.C. 18 March 1818.
Elizabeth, bapt. 13 Nov 1791. O.C. 13 June 1818.
John of Cornwall. O.C. 21 Feb 1821.
Adam of Cornwall. O.C. 5 Feb 1823.
Michael of Cornwall. O.C. 15 March 1838.
Christopher of Osnabruck. O.C. 28 Feb 1833.
David of Cornwall. O.C. December 1832.
Rachel. O.C. 8 Nov 1832. Bathurst.
Hannah, m. John Gallinger of Cornwall. O.C. 13 July 1841.
Jane, O.C. 1850 or 1851.
Eleanor, m. ---- Lard of Cornwall. O.C. 1850 or 1851.

HARTLE, Christian of Cornwall, m. Elizabeth Cryderman.
Lucas of Cornwall. O.C. 4 Nov 1818.
Catharine, m. John Miltimore of Cornwall. O.C. 26 Nov 1823.
Elizabeth, bapt. 13 Sept 1795; m. James Cross of Cornwall. O.C. 23
June 1836.
John of Cornwall. O.C. 2 May 1836.
Margaret, m. Munson W. Cook of Fredericksburgh. O.C. 30 May 1834.
Ann. O.C. 8 Nov 1832.
Matthew of Matilda. O.C. 1 July 1830.

HARTLE, John Jr. of Cornwall, m. Sarah De Witt.
Phoebe, bapt. 13 Sept 1795. O.C. 24 Feb 1820.

HARTLE, John Sr. of Cornwall.
    Elizabeth, m. ---- Feader of Matilda. O. C. 18 June 1800.
    Catherine, m. John Cryderman of Cornwall. O. C. 5 Jan 1798.
    John of Cornwall. O. C. 11 Nov 1815.

HARTMAN, Abraham of Kingston.
    Christine, m. Thomas Comer of Loughborough. O. C. 6 May 1830.

HARTMAN, David of Ernestown.
    Margaret, m. Francis Hogle of Ernestown 3 March 1795. OC 2 June 1808.
    Mary, m. Peter Daly of Ernestown. Land Board Certif. 31/5 Camden.

HARTMAN, Jacob of Ernestown.
    Diana. O. C. 26 May 1840.
    Catharine, m. Sebastian Hogle of Ernestown. O. C. 11 Feb 1836.
    Sarah, m. Benjamin Hogle of Ernestown. O. C. 11 Feb 1836.

HARTMAN, Lewis of Ernestown.
    Lewis Daly of Ernestown. O. C. 1 Nov 1838.

HARTMAN, Ludowick of Ernestown.
    Dennis of Ernestown. O. C. 18 May 1837.
    Catharine, m. Nicholas Lake of Ernestown. O. C. 28 Feb 1835.
    Mary, m. David Snider of Ernestown. O. C. 28 Feb 1835.
    Christian, m. Simon Snider of Ernestown 16 March 1819. OC 24 Mar 1835.
    David of Camden East. O. C. 24 March 1835.
    Valentine of Ernestown. O. C. 24 March 1835.
    George of Camden East. O. C. 28 March 1835.
    Lawrence of Ernestown. O. C. 28 March 1835.

HARTMAN, Philip of Ernestown, m. Allada or Huldah Hough, daughter of
Barnabas Hough, U. E., 16 August 1792.
    Mary, m. Joshua B. Lockwood of Camden East. O. C. 21 Sept 1837.
    Hannah, b. 8 Aug 1800; m. ---- Van Luvan of Kingston, 17 July 1816.
        O. C. 4 April 1839.
    Jacob of Ernestown. O. C. 27 Nov 1834.
    Margaret, m. Jacob H. Stover of Ernestown. O. C. 27 Nov 1834.
    Eunice, m. Benjamin Van Winckle of Ernestown, 30 August 1811. O. C.
        27 November 1834.

HASKINS, Abial of Augusta. See O. C. 4 July 1827, 20/9 Ernestown.
    Tabitha, m. John Livingston of Clayton Twp, N. Y. O. C. 26 May 1801.
    Magdalene, m. Samuel Weatherhead of Augusta. O. C. 22 Dec 1801.
    David of Augusta. O. C. 22 Sept 1812.
    Lemuel of South Crosby. O. C. 18 March 1818.
    Samuel W. of Leeds. O. C. 27 Aug 1833.

HATTER, Thomas.
   Daniel of Cornwall. O. C. 13 Oct 1807.
   John of Cornwall. O. C. 13 Oct 1807.

HAVENS, George of Ernestown.
   Titus of Huntingdon. O. C. 4 Sept 1834.
   Obadiah S. of Huntingdon. O. C. 4 Sept 1834.

HAVENS, John of Ernestown.
   Ann. O. C. 7 Aug 1834. Sidney.
   Deborah. O. C. 7 Aug 1834. Sidney.
   Catharine. O. C. 7 Aug 1834. Camden.
   Thomas of Pittsburgh. O. C. 2 Oct 1834.
   Jacob G. of Pittsburgh. O. C. 14 Oct 1834.

HAVILAND, John of Hallowell and Townsend.
   Phoebe, m. John Smith of Hallowell. O. C. 17 March 1812.
   Elizabeth, m. Benjamin Fairchild of Townsend. O. C. 16 July 1816.
   Benjamin of Townsend. O. C. 16 July 1816.
   John of Townsend, m. Esther Fairchild. O. C. 16 July 1816.
   Sarah. O. C. 18 July 1816.
   Fanny. O. C. 18 July 1816.
   Annette, m. Hugh McCall of Charlotteville. O. C. 18 July 1816.
   Nancy, m. Roswell Adsit of Hillier. O. C. 8 Sept 1836.
   Jane, m. Henry Benham of Hillier. O. C. 8 Sept 1836.

HAWLEY, Davis of Ernestown.
   Jehiel of Ernestown. O. C. 14 March 1809.
   Rachel, m. John Miller of Ernestown. O. C. 16 Feb 1810.
   Sarah, m. Charles Everitt of Kingston, 19 May 1807. OC 22 Feb 1810.
   Josiah of Ernestown. O. C. 19 April 1816.
   Sheldon of Ernestown. O. C. 19 April 1816.
   Mary Ann, m. Daniel Everitt of Kingston. O. C. 4 March 1824.
   Amanda, m. Samuel Miller of Ernestown. O. C. 11 April 1833.
   Joseph C. of Fredericksburgh. O. C. 11 April 1833.
   Abijah of Ernestown. O. C. 11 July 1833.

HAWLEY, Ichabod of Ernestown, m. Mary, dau William Fairfield Sr, U. E.,
of Ernestown.
   Anna. O. C. 23 Feb 1809.
   William of Ernestown. O. C. 19 April 1816.
   Reuben of Ernestown. O. C. 19 April. O. C. 29 June 1843.
   Clarissa Eliza, m. ---- Robinson of Hillier. O. C. 7 Feb 1843.
   Benjamin of Ernestown. O. C. 12 Nov 1827.
   Peter of Ernestown. O. C. 12 Nov 1827.
   Mary, m. David Lillie of Ernestown. OC 12 Nov 1827.

HAWLEY, Jeptha.
    Nabby, m. Benjamin Fairfield of Ernestown 11 Apr 1797. OC 25 Nov 1800.
    Amarilla, m. Samuel McKay of Ernestown 27 Dec 1791. OC 8 July 1801.
    Esther, m. Rufus Shorey of Ernestown 5 Sept 1797. O. C. 28 Apr 1807.
    Davis of Ernestown. O. C. 17 Nov 1797.
    Martin of Ernestown. O. C. 17 Nov 1797.
    Russell of Ernestown. O. C. 17 Nov 1797.
    Sheldon of Ernestown. O. C. 17 Nov 1797.

HAWLEY, Martin of Fredericksburgh.
    William of Fredericksburgh. O. C. 16 Feb 1811.
    Anna, m. Thomas D. Sanford of Fredericksburgh 3 July 1810. O. C. 16
        February 1811.
    Azubah, m. Jesse Wells of Fredericksburgh. O. C. 25 May 1825.
    John of Fredericksburgh. O. C. 8 Feb 1827.
    Asahel of Town of York. O. C. 2 Oct 1829.
    Amarilla, m. William Scott of Fredericksburgh 23 Nov 1818. O. C. 28
        February 1833.
    James C. of Richmond. O. C. 28 Feb 1833.
    Jeptha of Cramahe. O. C. 21 March 1833.
    Mary, m. ---- Lasher. O. C. 6 Oct 1836.

HAWLEY, Sheldon of Ernestown, m. Hannah Johnson 16 Feb 1789.
    Hester, m. George Ham of Ernestown. O. C. 19 April 1816.
    Andrew of Ernestown. O. C. 19 April 1816.
    Johnston of Ernestown. O. C. 19 April 1816.
    Davis of Ernestown. O. C. 7 Feb 1821. Called Jr.
    William C. of Ernestown. O. C. 13 June 1833.
    James E. of Ernestown. O. C. 12 Sept 1833.
    Isabel. O. C. 7 Feb 1833.
    Mary Ann, m. ---- Simmons of Sidney. O. C. 7 Feb 1833.

HAWLEY, Zadock of Fredericksburgh.
    Murchison of Bastard. O. C. 4 Jan 1840.

HAWN, Hendrick.
    Hannah, m. Jacob Waggoner of Osnabruck. O. C. 13 March 1807.

HAWN, Henry.
    Mary, m. John Drus of Matilda. O. C. 25 Feb 1806.
    Rebecca, m. George Johnson of Matilda. O. C. 28 Feb 1809.
    Hannah, m. John Collison of Matilda. OC 3 March 1809.
    Eunice, m. Henry Woolery of Matilda. O. C. 5 March 1810.
    Mary, m. Martin Meddaugh of Augusta. O. C. 24 April 1810.

HAWN, Hermanus of Cornwall, m. Eleanor Putman.
    Eleanor, m. William Brown of Cornwall. O. C. 16 Dec 1818.
    Henry of Cornwall. O. C. 24 Feb 1820.

HAWN, John of Ernestown.
   Jacob of Ernestown. O. C. 28 Feb 1835.

HAWN, John of Cornwall & Town of York & Town of Niagara.
   Hannah, m. John Stevenson of Town of Niagara 28 June 1812. OC 8 Mar 1813
   John of York (Niagara), m. Mary Ann McGrutt, 15 Feb 1820. O. C. 13
      April 1819. O. C. 24 Sept 1840.
   Elizabeth, m. Peter Fisette of York, 1 Aug 1819. O. C. 19 Apr 1820.
   Sophia, m. George Thurston of Town of Niagara. O. C. 20 July 1837.
   Joseph of Town of Niagara. O. C. 1 Aug 1833.
   Philip of Town of Niagara. O. C. 11 Aug 1829.
   Mary Magdalen, m. John R. Shute of Town of Niagara. O. C. 17 Nov 1830.
   Margaret, m. Mathew Whiting Rosa of Niagara. O. C. 17 Nov 1830.
   Jacob of Niagara. O. C. 5 Sept 1827.
   William of Niagara. O. C. 24 Sept 1840.
   (Note: Margaret Hawn & Joseph Quseneus md. York, 19 September 1819.
      See "Church" 9 January 1841)

HAYE, Philip of Clinton.
   Angelica, m. John Morris of Clinton. O. C. 1 March 1832.

HAZELL, Edward of Mersea.
   Anne, m. Alexander Wilkinson of Mersea. O. C. 15 Nov 1820.
   Elizabeth, m. William Tofflemire of Gosfield. O. C. 12 Dec 1821.
   Agnes. O. C. 28 April 1840.
   Mary, m. Thomas Wilkinson of Mersea. O. C. 22 Sept 1836.
   Judy, m. John Deloriez of Mersea. O. C. 6 Nov 1834.

HAZEN, Daniel of Walsingham.
   Lydia. O. C. 29 July 1806.
   Daniel of Woodhouse, m. Anna Mathews. O. C. 19 Dec 1806.
   William of Walsingham. O. C. 5 Aug 1807.
   John of Walsingham. O. C. 13 Oct 1812.
   Rachel. O. C. 13 Oct 1812.
   Caleb of Walsingham. O. C. 14 May 1816.
   Elisha of Walsingham. O. C. 12 August 1818.
   Jacob of Walsingham. O. C. 11 December 1822.

HECK, Paul of Augusta.
   Samuel of Augusta, m. Lois Wright. O. C. 21 Aug 1797.
   Jacob of Augusta. O. C. 4 Feb 1836.

HECK, Samuel
   Catherine, m. William Schermerhorn of Ameliasburgh. OC 14 Jan 1812.

HELMER, John of Roxborough.
   Andrew of Tuckersmith. O. C. 8 Aug 1833.
   John of Nepean. O. C. 5 Feb 1835.   [Cont'd]

HELMER, John - Cont'd
  James of Roxborough. O.C. 5 Feb 1835.

HELMER, John.
  Elizabeth, m. Elijah Levans of Cornwall. O.C. 25 Feb 1806.
  Mary. O.C. 20 Feb 1808.
  Margaret, m. Peter Warley of Osnabruck. O.C. 25 Feb 1809.
  Philip of Cornwall. O.C. 23 May 1809.
  Isabel, m. Lawrence Markle of Williamsburgh. O.C. 16 Feb 1811.
  Mary Ann. O.C. 2 March 1811. Williamsburgh.
  Aaron of Roxborough. OC 20 May 1817. Son of John for Corn. now Rox.
  Gertrude. O.C. 12 Feb 1831. Williamsburgh.

HELMER, John P. of Cornwall and Roxborough.
  Thomas of Niagara, innkeeper. O.C. 10 Sept 1817.
  Alley (dau). O.C. 18 Oct 1820.
  William of Cornwall. O.C. 18 Oct 1820.
  Amelia Lucretia, m. Dougald Campbell of Charlottenburgh. OC 5 Mar 1828
  Benjamin of Roxborough. O.C. 16 March 1825.

HENDERSHOT, Peter of Pelham. Barton's Corps.
  Sarah, m. Michael Henn of Pelham. O.C. 11 March 1797.
  John of Pelham. O.C. 27 June 1833.
  Mary, m. Henry Johnson of Pelham. O.C. 1 May 1834.
  Elizabeth, m. David Moore of Pelham. O.C. 30 May 1834.
  William of Pelham. O.C. 30 May 1834.
  Henry Miles of Pelham. O.C. 30 May 1834.
  Peter of Pelham. O.C. 30 May 1834.
  Sarah, m. Benjamin Owens of Pelham. O.C. 5 June 1834.
  Anne, m. Jesse Thomas of Pelham. O.C. 5 June 1834.
  Abraham of Pelham. O.C. 3 Nov 1831.
  David of Pelham. O.C. 3 Nov 1831.

HENDERSON, Caleb of Gloucester and Elizabethtown.
  William of Gloucester. O.C. 5 Nov 1799.
  Margaret. O.C. 25 July 1798.
  Caleb of Elizabethtown. O.C. 5 April 1820.
  John of Elizabethtown. O.C. 11 June 1823.
  Mandana, m. Ichabod Wing of Elizabethtown. O.C. 25 July 1798. Later
    of Chautauqua, N.Y. O.C. 26 Jan 1837.

HENDERSON, David of Bastard.
  Jonathan of Bastard. O.C. 13 Jan 1807.
  Mary. O.C. 26 Jan 1808.
  James of Bastard. O.C. 17 Aug 1808.
  Hannah, m. John Kincaid of Kitley. O.C. 12 June 1798.
  Euterpie, m. Edward Soper of Kitley. O.C. 12 June 1798.
  Melinda. O.C. 28 June 1820.   [Cont'd]

HENDERSON, David - Cont'd
David of Yonge. O.C. 28 Oct 1835.

HENDERSON, Henry of Edwardsburgh (Anderson?)
Mary, m. Jonathan Main of Edwardsburgh. O.C. 26 Sept 1809.

HENN, Michael.
Ann, m. Henry Thomas of Pelham. O.C. 9 March 1803.
Elizabeth, m. John Disher of Pelham. O.C. 10 March 1804.
Sarah, m. John Overholt of Pelham. O.C. 12 March 1805.

HENRY, James of Clinton. Butler's Rangers. Died at Clinton 19 Jan 1827,
aged about 70 years.
Margaret, m. Jonathan Pettit of Saltfleet. O.C. 17 Oct 1809.
John of Clinton. O.C. 17 Oct 1809.
James Ralfe of Clinton. O.C. 26 March 1817.
Joseph of Grimsby. O.C. 6 Oct 1819.
Harman of Clinton. O.C. 7 Aug 1822.

HENRY, Philip of Gainsborough.
George of Gainsborough. O.C. 31 Oct 1821.
Jesse of Gainsborough. O.C. 28 Nov 1826.
Susannah, m. (1) Benoni Hill of Gainsborough; m. (2) Henry Heron of Thor-
old. O.C. 26 Nov 1826.
Philip of Dunwich, tanner. O.C. 27 Nov 1834.
Emily. O.C. 7 March 1833. Wainfleet.
Nancy, m. Hiram Cronkhite of Wainfleet. O.C. 7 March 1833.

HERCHMER, Capt. Hanyost of Kingston, m. Mary, who died in August 1805.
He died at Kingston in August, 1795.
George, Lt. Butler's Rangers, killed at Detroit.
Jean, m. Joseph Anderson of Town of Kingston; d. there 18 April 1850,
aged 87. O.C. 29 July 1797.
Lawrence of Town of Kingston, m. Elizabeth Kirby. O.C. 17 Nov 1797.
Jacob of Town of York, m. Margaret England(?); drowned on "Speedy."
O.C. 7 June 1797.
Nicholas of Kingston, m. Charlotte Purdy; d. 1809. OC 17 Nov 1797.
Mary, m. (1) Neil McLean of Kingston; m. (2) Hon. Robert Hamilton of
Queenston; d. 1808. O.C. 10 July 1793. O.C. 9 Nov 1798.
Catharine, m. Thomas Markland of Kingston. O.C. 7 June 1797.

HESS, Jacob of Ernestown.
John of Ernestown. O.C. 22 Feb 1810.
Catharine, m. Samuel Vandevoort of Sidney 8 Jan 1812. OC 20 Jan 1816.
Elizabeth. O.C. 2 March 1816.
Margaret. O.C. 2 March 1816.
Wilhelmina, m. John Dusenberry of Ernestown. O.C. 25 Feb 1818.
Henry of Ernestown. O.C. 1 Aug 1833.   [Cont'd]

HESS, Jacob - Cont'd
   Francis of Ernestown. O. C. 1 Aug 1833.
   Peter of Ernestown. O. C. 1 Aug 1833.
   Susannah. O. C. 1 Aug 1833.

HEWITT, Jacob of Yonge.
   Margaret, m. ---- Steel of Yonge. O. C. 18 Aug 1801.
   Esther, m. ---- Frisbee of Scarborough. O. C. 3 July 1798.

HICKEY, John of Williamsburgh. K. R. R. N. Y. m. Margaret dau Supphrenius
Cassellman, U. E.
   Catharine, m. Nicholas Ault of Williamsburgh. O. C. 19 April 1816.
   John of Williamsburgh, m. Dinah Van Allan. O. C. 19 April 1816.
   Sophrenus of Williamsburgh. O. C. 2 Sept 1818.
   Mary, m. Gabriel Forrester of Williamsburgh. O. C. 23 June 1821.
   Michael W. of Williamsburgh. O. C. 26 Jan 1837.
   Sally, m. Samuel I. Crysler of Williamsburgh. O. C. 3 April 1834.
   Margaret, m. Zenas H. Gurley of Williamsburgh. O. C. 5 Feb 1835.
   Martin of Williamsburgh. O. C. 2 Feb 1825.
   Nancy, m. Jacob Moore of Osnabruck. O. C. 16 March 1825.

HICKS, Benjamin of Sophiasburgh.
   Benjamin of Sophiasburgh. O. C. 6 March 1821.
   Ally. O. C. 21 June 1838.
   George of Marysburgh. O. C. 11 June 1840.
   David of Marysburgh. O. C. 5 June 1834.
   Joseph of Sophiasburgh. O. C. 27 Nov 1834.
   Sarah, m. James McNutt of Hallowell. O. C. 5 Feb 1831.
   Mary. O. C. 17 Oct 1828.

HICKS, Edward Sr. Soldier, Butler's Rangers. See O. C. 9 April 1831. His
widow Elvina m. (2) Joseph Wright on 5 Sept 1779.
   Daniel.
   David.
   Joseph of Marysburgh, U. E.
   Edward of Marysburgh, U. E.
   Elizabeth, m. (1) Peter Collier of Ameliasburgh; m. (2) Amos Knapp of
      Ameliasburgh. O. C. 30 Aug 1797.
   Benjamin of Sophiasburgh.
   Mary, m. Michael Cryderman of Marysburgh. 14/4 Alnwick.

HICKS, Edward Jr. of Marysburgh. O. C. 22 March 1830.
   Edward of Marysburgh. O. C. 5 Nov 1818.
   Solomon P. of Marysburgh. O. C. 11 June 1840.
   Peter of Marysburgh. O. C. 11 June 1840.
   Mary, m. Benjamin Hughes of Marysburgh. O. C. 25 July 1833.
   John of Marysburgh. O. C. 8 March 1826.

HICKS, Joseph of Marysburgh, m. Elizabeth Harrison.
  David of Marysburgh, m. Hannah Minaker. O.C. 11 Aug 1836.
  Nathan of Marysburgh, m. Mary McDonell. O.C. 11 Aug 1836.
  John Edward of Clarke. O.C. 28 Oct 1835.
  Joseph of Marysburgh, m. Mary Minaker. O.C. 8 May 1833.
  William of Marysburgh, m. Nancy Minaker. O.C. 8 May 1833.
  Alice, bapt. 23 Jan 1791; m. Peter Collier of Marysburgh. OC 27 Nov 1834
  Nelly, bapt. 25 Feb 1789.
  Mathew P. of Marysburgh, m. Elizabeth Dulmage. OC 4 Sept 1834.
  Ann, m. Cornelius Flumerfelt of Chatham. O.C. 22 Dec 1842.

HICKS, Lewis of Ernestown.
  Benjamin of Ernestown. O.C. 30 Jan 1808.
  James of Ernestown. O.C. 16 Feb 1810.
  Rachel, m. Richard Perry of Ernestown. O.C. 16 Feb 1810.
  John of Ernestown. O.C. 12 Nov 1811.

HILL, John Sr. of Short Hills, Thorold.
  Hannah of Pelham. Died unm. 17 June 1843. O.C. 6 June 1799.
  Joseph of Thorold. O.C. 29 June 1802.
  Deborah. Thorold. Died unm. 11 Nov 1852. O.C. 28 Feb 1804.
  Charles of Bertie. O.C. 27 May 1806.
  Elizabeth, b. about 1772; m. Nathan Havens of Bertie. OC 12 May 1797.
  John.

HILL, Nazareth of Marysburgh.
  Jane, m. Walter Cronston of Marysburgh. O.C. 31 May 1803.
  Catherine, m. AEneas McMullen of Kingston. O.C. 17 June 1806.
  Elizabeth, m. Samuel Hayes of Adolphustown. O.C. 23 Feb 1809.
  Robert of Marysburgh. O.C. 16 Feb 1811.
  Rebecca, m. Benonia Bowerman of Ameliasburgh 3 Nov 1808. O.C. 16
    February 1811.
  Ann, m. Charles Minaker of Marysburgh 15 Jan 1816. OC 3 June 1817.
  David of Marysburgh. O.C. 16 Feb 1811.
  Eleanor, m. John Lamb of Marysburgh. O.C. 21 March 1831.
  Mary, m. Lewis Day of Kingston. O.C. 17 Nov 1797.

HILL, Solomon of Grimsby, b. 30 Aug 1756 at Red Mills, Dutchess (now
  Mahopac Falls, Putnam) Co., N.Y., s. of Wm and Bethia (Smith) Hill; m.
  Dec., 1783, Bethiah, dau Richard & Mary (Smith) Griffin; d. at Smithville,
  30 Aug 1807. (Genealogy of Hill &c. by Franklin Couch, 1907)
    William of Clinton, b. 21 Oct 1784; m. Mary Tafford, 2 Apr 1804; d. at
      Smithville 22 Apr 1853. O.C. 17 Feb 1807.
    Abraham of Grimsby, b. 2 Feb 1787; m. Margaret Culp; d. Gainsborough
      March, 1867. O.C. 8 Feb 1808.
    Richard of Grimsby, b. 11 Jan 1789; m. Eleanor Mudge; d. 11 Aug 1826.
      O.C. 28 April 1812.
    Smith, b. 13 September 1799. Died young.   [Cont'd]

HILL, Solomon - Cont'd
  Smith, b. 21 Aug 1806. Died young.
  Solomon of Grimsby, b. 4 April 1793; m. Abigail Taylor, 11 Jan 1818; d.
    St. Catharines 20 Jan 1878. O.C. 16 Dec 1815.
  Mary, b. 26 Sept 1791; m. Robert Waddell of Grimsby, d. Smithville on
    3 Jan 1858. O.C. 9 March 1816.
  Jonathan of Grimsby, b. 31 July 1795; d. unmd. Grimsby about 1834.
    O.C. 5 November 1818.
  Cornelius of Grimsby, b. 22 Jan 1800; m. Catherine Kennedy; d. Smith-
    ville, 4 Aug 1854. O.C. 11 Dec 1822.
  Jane, b. 28 March 1790; m. John Robinson of Grimsby; d. Queenstown
    about 1868. O.C. 9 July 1823.
  Nathaniel of Grimsby, b. 5 May 1802; m. (1) Maria Hamilton Adams;
    m. (2) Eleanor Field; d. Smithville 13 March 1872. OC 27 Aug 1833.
  Bethiah, b. 19 Jan 1798; m. Ralph Field; d. 8 Apr 1884. OC 22 June 1825.

HILL, Thomas of York.
  Anne, m. William Hollingshed of Vaughan. O.C. 5 July 1798.
  Mary, m. Isaac Hollingshead of King. O.C. 23 March 1799.
  William of York, m. Abigail Montgomery(?). O.C. 21 Sept 1802.
  Harriet, m. Richard Heron of York, 14 Feb 1804. OC 4 September 1804.
    Richard Heron m. (2) Mrs. Helen Henry of York Twp. 20 March 1821.
  Hannah, m. George Bond of York, 13 Feb 1814. O.C. 7 April 1812.

HITCHCOCK, Miles
  Mary, m. Thomas Bell of Mersea. O.C. 22 Feb 1810.
  Miles of Niagara. O.C. 14 June 1811.

HODGES, Timothy.
  Cloe, m. ---- Van Volkenburgh of Augusta. O.C. 18 June 1800.
  Rachel, m. ---- Mosher.

HODGKINSON, John of Grantham.
  Samuel of Grantham. O.C. 16 June 1808.
  Francis of Grantham. O.C. 27 Nov 1815.
  Robert of Grantham. O.C. 27 Nov 1815.

HODGKINSON, William of Grantham, m. Mary.
  Eleanor, m. Abraham Phenix of Grantham 14 Sept 1806. OC 16 Feb 1810.
  William of Grantham. O.C. 4 July 1815.
  Thomas of Grantham. O.C. 21 Feb 1821.
  Roxanna, m. Mathew McMullen of Grantham 12 Jan 1820. OC 11 June 1821
  John of Grantham. O.C. 6 Feb 1822.
  George of Yarmouth, printer (St. Thomas village). O.C. 27 Nov 1834.
  Eleazer Alexander of Grantham. O.C. 1 Oct 1840.
  Benjamin of Grantham. O.C. 13 June 1836.
  Mary, bapt. 15 July 1792.
  Philip of Grantham. O.C. 29 Sept 1824.   [Cont'd]

HODGKINSON, William - Cont'd
Martha, m. Edward McMullen of Grantham. O.C. 29 Sept 1824.

HOFFMAN, David of Ernestown, m. Elizabeth Moore, 28 Aug 1792.
Catharine, m. Francois Lefebre of Kingston. O.C. 22 July 1818.
Nancy, m. Samuel Maby. O.C. 1 Dec 1836.
John of Ernestown. O.C. 30 May 1834.
Cyrus of Portland. O.C. 7 Aug 1834.
Frederick of Sheffield. O.C. 7 Aug 1834.
Elizabeth, m. Robert Parker of Rawdon. O.C. 4 Sept 1834.
Mary, m. Jacob Van Kleek of Town of Bath. O.C. 7 Feb 1833.

HOFFMAN, Jacob of Ernestown, m. Margaret.
Mary, bapt. 26 June 1792; m. Thomas Wager Jr. of Fredericksburgh.
O.C. 13 June 1818.
James of Fredericksburgh, bapt. 9 June 1801. O.C. 2 April 1823.
Rebecca, m. Peter Windover of Fredericksburgh. OC 2 April 1823.
Sarah, bapt. 25 Jan 1790; m. Isaac Post of Fredericksburgh. OC 3 Apr 1834
Lucy, bapt. 6 Sept 1796.
John of Fredericksburgh, bapt. 12 Sept 1803. O.C. 1 March 1832.
Margaret, bapt. 16 Nov 1807.
Margaret Anne, bapt. 25 June 1810.
Elias, bapt. 30 Dec 1787; buried 29 Oct 1788.

HOFFMAN, Joseph Sr. of Ernestown.
Joseph of Ernestown, m. Hannah Hough. O.C. 31 May 1803.
Hannah, m. Samuel Hough of Ernestown. O.C. 6 Dec 1803.
Mary, m. Nathan Brisco of Ernestown 10 Feb 1799. O.C. 10 May 1803.
Samuel of Ernestown. O.C. 17 March 1812.
Margaret Ann, m. George Brownson of Fredericksburgh. OC 5 Sept 1833.
Mathew of Hungerford. O.C. 29 Sept 1834.
Christopher of Thurlow. O.C. 29 Sept 1834.
Moses of Ameliasburgh. O.C. 2 Oct 1834.

HOFFMAN, Philip of Fredericksburgh.
Elias of Fredericksburgh. O.C. 7 Aug 1822.
Mary, m. Isaac Dulyea of Richmond. O.C. 2 Jan 1834.
Rebecca, m. ---- Grant of Camden East. O.C. 12 June 1834.
Peter of Camden East. O.C. 2 Oct 1834.
Michael of Fredericksburgh. O.C. 1 April 1834.

HOGLE, Lt. John, m. Elizabeth; killed at Bennington, August 1777.
Sebastian of Ernestown, m. Amy Cadman, 14 Dec 1789. OC 24 Nov 1807.
Francis of Sidney, m. Margaret Hartman, 3 March 1795. OC 20 June 1797

HOLLINGSHEAD, Anthony.
William of Vaughan, m. Anne Hill. O.C. 11 July 1798.
George of East Gwillimbury. O.C. 9 March 1837.   [Cont'd]

HOLLINGSHEAD, Anthony - Cont'd
  Elizabeth, m. Peter McMullen of Mount Pleasant. O.C. 11 April 1833.
  Anthony of Yonge Street, m. Eleanor Crossley, 31 October 1805. O.C.
      24 February 1801.
  Aschsah, m. Daniel Soules of Markham. O.C. 11 June 1798.

HOLLISTER, Elisha of Osnabruck, m. Mary Waggoner.
  Freeman of Osnabruck. O.C. 12 Nov 1840.
  Caroline. O.C. 28 July 1836.
  Jeremiah E. of Osnabruck. O.C. 9 March 1837.
  Mary, m. ---- Baker. See O.C. 3 Sept 1835.
  Charles of Osnabruck, bapt. 2 Aug 1795. O.C. 17 March 1836.
  Hiram of Osnabruck. O.C. 28 Oct 1835.
  Jacob of Osnabruck, m. Catherine Ross. O.C. 3 Dec 1835.
  Nancy, m. George Waggoner of Osnabruck. O.C. 17 March 1836.
  Albert of Osnabruck. O.C. 10 March 1834.
  Barnabas of Osnabruck. O.C. 10 March 1834.
  Catharine. O.C. 10 March 1834.
  William of Osnabruck, bapt. 7 May 1797. O.C. 9 May 1834.

HOLMES, Asa.
  Mehetable, m. John McDonell of Crowland. O.C. 21 March 1809.
  Mary, m. John Bowen of Bertie. O.C. 30 June 1819.
  Sarah, m. (1) Peter McDonell of Gainsborough. O.C. 17 March 1797.
      m. (2) ---- Dease of Charlotteville.
  Elizabeth, m. ----

HOLMES, John of Kingston.
  Deborah. O.C. 17 March 1812.
  Peter of Kingston. O.C. 17 March 1812.

HOOPLE, Henry of Osnabruck.
  John of Cornwall. O.C. 19 April 1816.
  Jacob of Osnabruck. O.C. 18 March 1818.
  George of Osnabruck. O.C. 15 Dec 1821.
  Norris of Richmond. O.C. 11 Aug 1836.
  Peter of Osnabruck. O.C. 5 Sept 1833.
  Joseph of Osnabruck. O.C. 5 Sept 1833.
  Philip of Wolford. O.C. 19 Dec 1833.
  Sarah. O.C. 27 Feb 1834.
  Daniel of Osnabruck. O.C. 3 April 1834.
  Michael of Osnabruck. O.C. 19 Jan 1825.
  Elizabeth, m. John J. Wart of Osnabruck. O.C. 14 April 1824.

HOOPLE, John of Osnabruck.
  Sarah, m. Septimus Tracy of Osnabruck. O.C. 26 Jan 1808.
  Elizabeth, m. Henry Deming of Osnabruck. O.C. 25 Feb 1809.
  John of Cornwall. O.C. 17 March 1812.   [Cont'd]

HOOPLE, John - Cont'd
Frances, m. Henry Capell of Osnabruck. O. C. 25 Feb 1812.
Susannah, m. ---- Bassett of Belleville. O. C. 10 March 1834.
William of Osnabruck. O. C. 1 July 1830.

HOOVER, Henry of Adolphustown.
Mary, m. Joseph B. Allison of Adolphustown. O. C. 21 Jan 1823.
Millicent. O. C. 31 Jan 1839.
Eve, m. Cyrus R. Allison of Adolphustown. O. C. 28 Oct 1835.
Samuel C. of Adolphustown. O. C. 1 May 1834.
Jane Anne. O. C. 1 May 1834.
Elizabeth, m. David Wright of Cramahe, 9 Nov 1816. O. C. 12 July 1830.
Margaret, m. Edward Squires of Huntingdon. O. C. 5 Feb 1831.
Henry of Adolphustown. O. C. 5 Feb 1831.

HOOVER, Jacob of Sophiasburgh, m. Millicent Ferguson, 19 May 1789.
Jacob of Sophiasburgh, bapt. 11 July 1790. O. C. 22 Feb 1834.

HOPKINS, Silas of Flamborough East.
Lydia, m. ---- McMurtrie. O. C. 24 Feb 1801.
Ephraim of Flamborough East. O. C. 10 July 1806.
Joseph of Flamborough West. O. C. 29 June 1806.
Mary, m. Jonas Seeley of Flamborough East. O. C. 19 June 1806.
Asubah, m. Jonathan Hagar of Thorold. O. C. 30 Sept 1806.
Elizabeth, m. Rev. Daniel Eastman of Thorold. O. C. 30 Sept 1806.
Caleb of Nelson, b. New Jersey, 1787; m. Hannah Green; died at Toronto
    8 October 1880. O. C. 10 Feb 1819.
Gabriel of Flamborough East. O. C. 10 Feb 1819.

HOPPER, Abraham of Osnabruck. Soldier, 1st Batt., K. R. R. N. Y. Married
Elizabeth, dau William Crowder, U. E.
Dorothy, m. Robert Carr of Osnabruck. O. C. 17 March 1807.
William of Osnabruck. O. C. 7 Aug 1811.
Elizabeth, m. John Cook Jr. of Osnabruck. O. C. 30 June 1812.
Mary (lunatic). O. C. 9 Sept 1818.
Henry of Osnabruck. O. C. 5 March 1823.
James of Williamsburgh. O. C. 4 Feb 1836.
Sarah. O. C. 7 Feb 1833.
Jemimah. O. C. 28 Sept 1832.
Michael of Osnabruck. O. C. 7 Dec 1825.
Abraham of Osnabruck. O. C. 7 Dec 1825.
Peter of Osnabruck. O. C. 7 Dec 1825.

HORTON, Edmund of Niagara. [Butler's Rangers. He and his wife were at
Niagara in 1783. The Ontario Register, 1:198]
Elizabeth, m. Samuel White of Niagara. O. C. 1 Dec 1819.
Emanuel of Niagara O. C. 12 June 1822.

HORTON, Isaac of Pelham, b. 1750 in Westchester Co., N.Y., s. of Caleb
Horton of White Plains. 1/5 Gainsborough.
   Isaac of Flamborough West. O.C. 13 April 1802.
   Ann, m. Joel Dennis of Clinton. O.C. 29 July 1806.
   Elizabeth, m. John Dennis of Clinton. O.C. 29 July 1806.
   Mary, m. Asa Brough of Clinton. O.C. 29 July 1806.
   Rebecca, m. George Acor of Clinton. O.C. 16 Nov 1807.
   David of Gainsborough. O.C. 10 July 1822.
   William of Clinton. O.C. 16 Feb 1837.
   Daniel of Gainsborough. O.C. 2 Feb 1832.

HOSTEDER, Herman of Grantham, m. Ann who died 23 Jan 1851 aged 92 ys.
He died 10 Dec 1812, aged 59 yrs, 4 months.
   Ann, m. Frederick Augustus Goring of Niagara 5 Nov 1805. OC 27 Feb 1806
   Catharine, m. William Westover of Grantham 2 July 1805. OC 27 Feb 1806
   Abraham of Grantham, m. Mary Donaldson, 11 Nov 1817. OC 22 Jan 1811.
   Mary, m. William Miller of Grantham 7 Sept 1817. OC 27 February 1818
    Niagara.
   Jacob of Grantham. O.C. 18 March 1818.
   Elizabeth, m. Jacob A. Ball, 7 Nov 1816. O.C. 18 March 1818.
   Abraham of Grantham. O.C. 18 March 1818.
   Sarah, m. John Gilleland of Grantham 9 March 1825. O.C. 4 March 1819.
   Rebecca. O.C. 7 Aug 1822.
   Herman of Erin, m. Catherine Carroll, 30 May 1827. O.C. 6 Aug 1828.
   Deborah, bapt. 22 Nov 1807; m. Thomas Gilleland of Grantham. O.C. 6
    May 1830.
   Charlotte, m. Lewis Traver of Grantham. O.C. 6 Sept 1826.

HOUGH, Asa of Fredericksburgh, m. Eleanor Bell dau of William Bell Sr.,
U.E., of Fredericksburgh, 11 May 1790.
   William Bell of Fredericksburgh, bapt. 20 March 1791; m. Nancy Mc-
    Mullen. O.C. 26 March 1817.
   James, bapt. 24 June 1792; buried 23 July 1795.
   Asa Bell of Kingston, bapt. 5 Jan 1794. O.C. 22 July 1818; 24 Nov 1832.
   Isaac of Camden East, bapt. 19 Apr 1795. O.C. 30 May 1834.
   Flora, bapt. 16 Apr 1797; m. Micajah Purdy of Kingston. OC 3 Feb 1834.
   Barnabas of Fredericksburgh, bapt. 27 Oct 1796. OC 27 June 1833.
   Eunice, bapt. 10 May 1801; m. Baltus Diamond of Fredericksburgh. OC
    13 June 1833.
   John of Fredericksburgh, bapt. 30 Dec 1804. OC 13 June 1833.

HOUGH, Barnabas of Ernestown.
   Elijah of Ernestown, m. Mary Wees. OC 18 June 1800.
   Jotham of Ernestown. OC 31 May 1803.
   Samuel of Ernestown, m. Hannah Hoffman. OC 6 Dec 1803.
   Hannah, m. Joseph Hoffman of Ernestown. OC 26 Sept 1809.
   Sarah, m. Alexander Nicholson of Fredericksburgh. Land Board Certifi-
    cate, 23/6 Sidney.   [Cont'd]

HOUGH, Barnabas - Cont'd
  Isaac of Ernestown, m. Elizabeth Hicks. OC 23 April 1798.
  Allida, m. Philip Hartman of Ernestown. OC 17 Nov 1797.
  Abigail, m. Robert Havens of Ernestown 24 Oct 1793. Land Board Certif-
    icate, 10/8 Thurlow.

HOUGH, Bruin of Ernestown, m. Mary Walker dau of Daniel Walker, U. E.,
  of Ernestown, 16 Dec 1790.
  Susannah, m. William Oxham of Kingston. O. C. 11 May 1818.
  Mary Elizabeth, bapt. 13 June 1797. O. C. 16 May 1818.
  John of Ernestown. O. C. 1 July 1819.
  Esther, m. William Sickles of Ernestown. OC 30 June 1819.
  James of Hallowell. OC 22 Aug 1821.
  Hannah Penelope. OC 11 April 1833.
  Philip Hartman of Ernestown. OC 27 June 1833.
  Peter of Ernestown. OC 5 Feb 1829.
  Sarah Ann, m. Samuel Genner of Ernestown. OC 5 Feb 1829.

HOUGH, John of Fredericksburgh. 2nd Batt., K. R. R. N. Y.
  Jacob of Fredericksburgh. OC 28 Feb 1799.

HOUSE, Daniel of Clinton.
  Mary, m. Samuel Stafford of Ancaster. OC 17 June 1806.
  Herman of Clinton. OC 9 July 1806.
  Margaret, m. ---- Hunsberrier of Grimsby. OC 9 Aug 1820.
  Elizabeth, m. Erastus Darby of Grimsby. OC 6 June 1827.
  Daniel of Dumfries. O. C. 5 May 1826.
  Patrick of Clinton. OC 12 June 1822.

HOUSE, George of Willoughby. Butler's Rangers. [He and his family were at
  Niagara in 1783. The Ontario Register, 1: 208]
  Hermanus of Willoughby. OC 2 Dec 1806.
  Lewis of Willoughby. OC 2 Dec 1806.
  Catherine, m. George Forbes of Willoughby. OC 26 Feb 1819.
  Nicholas of Clinton. OC 6 Sept 1832.
  Hannah, m. Charles Carpenter of Clinton. OC 7 May 1828.
  Mary, m. Philip House of Clinton. OC 17 March 1797.
  George of Bertie. OC 28 March 1797.

HOUSE, Hermanus.
  John of Clinton. OC 9 July 1802.
  Daniel of Clinton. OC 11 April 1797.
  James of Crowland. OC 29 Aug 1839.
  Mary, m. Conrad Lutz of Thorold. OC 29 Aug 1839.
  Julia Ann. OC 29 Aug 1839.
  Hulda, m. ---- Terryberry of Wainfleet. OC 28 Nov 1839.
  Catherine, m. ---- McMahon of Humberstone. OC 28 Nov 1839.
  Robert of Humberstone. OC 7 May 1840.   [Cont'd]

HOUSE, Hermanus - Cont'd
Margaret, m. Joseph Smith of Louth. O. C. 7 July 1796.

HOUSE, James of Bertie.
Daniel of Bertie. OC 18 June 1806.
Isaac of Clinton. OC 3 Jan 1842.
Lewis of Clinton. OC 3 Jan 1842.
James of Clinton. OC 3 Jan 1842.
Nancy, m. Andrew House of Clinton. OC 3 Jan 1842.

HOUSE, John of Bertie, m. Christina, dau of Frederick Anger Sr., U. E.
Augustus of Bertie. OC 25 June 1805.
Conrad of Bertie. O. C. 8 July 1806.
Frederick of Willoughby. OC 2 June 1819.
Dorothy, m. John Benner of Bertie. O. C. 21 March 1821.
Catharine, m. Amos Kindree of Trafalgar. OC 11 June 1823.
Mary, m. Barna Barnum of Willoughby. OC 4 Sept 1834.

HOUSE, Philip of Clinton.
Margaret, m. David Culp of Clinton. OC 17 June 1806.
Mary, m. Abraham Nelles of Clinton. OC 20 May 1817.
John of Clinton. OC 9 Feb 1820.
Catharine, m. Russell Green of Grimsby. OC 5 May 1819.
Sarah, m. Orange Lawrence of Trafalgar. OC 21 Jan 1824.
Huldah, m. George Morris of Clinton. OC 18 June 1840.
Frances E. OC 2 July 1840.
Daniel of Clinton. OC 6 July 1825.

HOWARD, Dyer of Elizabethtown.
Tillton of Elizabethtown, m. Jane Stephens, 3 Feb 1823. OC 24 Oct 1831.

HOWARD, Edward of Amherst Island.
Elizabeth Ann. OC 13 June 1833.
Catharine. OC 3 March 1831.
Mary. OC 3 March 1831.

HOWARD, John Jr. of Amherst Island, Pvt. 63rd Regt., m. Nancy, dau of
James Jackson, U. E., of Ernestown.
Jane. OC 7 May 1835.
John of Ernestown. OC 27 Nov 1834.
Thomas of Ernestown. OC 27 Nov 1834.
Mary Ann, m. John Anderson of Huntingdon. OC 15 May 1835.
Margaret, m. William McGinnis of Amherst Island. OC 26 Dec 1834.
George of Amherst Island. OC 5 March 1835.
William of Amherst Island. OC 5 March 1835.

HOWARD, John of Leeds.
Ann, m. George Cook of Lansdowne. OC 1 Apr 1840.   [Cont'd]

HOWARD, John - Cont'd
    James B. of Leeds. OC 19 Aug 1833.
    Charlotte. OC 5 Aug 1830. Ernestown.
    Pamelia, m. John B. Hewitt of Leeds. OC 7 May 1828.

HOWARD, John of Ernestown. Lt., K. R. R. N. Y.
    Jane, m. John Richards of Amherst Island, 26 Jan 1795. Land Board Certificate, 1/1 Hillier.
    Sarah, m. William McKenzie of Amherst Island 19 Sept 1803. OC 25 Feb 1809.
    Mary, m. Colin McKenzie Jr. of Ernestown. OC 17 Nov 1797. Died 1835.
    Edward of Ernestown, U. E.
    John of Amherst Island, U. E.
    Thomas of Ernestown, U. E.

HOWARD, Matthew.
    William of Elizabethtown. OC 9 July 1802.
    Sarah, m. ---- Adams of Augusta(?). OC 2 Dec 1806.
    Edward of Elizabethtown, died there 20 April 1866 ae 83. OC 8 Feb 1808.
    Stephen of Elizabethtown. OC 7 Nov 1797.
    John of Elizabethtown. OC 7 Nov 1797.
    Dyer of Elizabethtown. OC 7 Nov 1797.
    Peter. OC 7 Nov 1797. d. Etn 24 Nov 1843 ae 72; m (1) Sarah Munsall; m (2) 17 Oct 1833 Margaret Seaman who d. Owen Sound 7 Oct 1853 ae 69.

HOWARD, Stephen of Elizabethtown, b. 1762; d. 1828.
    Phoebe S., m. ---- Hallock of Elizabethtown. OC 20 March 1822.
    Mary, m. James Cromwell of Elizabethtown. OC 21 Feb 1839.
    Dyer of Elizabethtown. OC 29 Aug 1839.

HOWARD, Thomas of Ernestown and Adolphustown (Amherst Island).
    Susannah, m. Gilibs Ranney of Adolphustown. OC 6 Feb 1823.
    Edward of Adolphustown. OC 11 Dec 1822.
    John of Ameliasburgh. OC 28 Oct 1835.
    Thomas R. of Ameliasburgh. OC 28 Oct 1835.
    Jane. OC 12 June 1834.
    Mary, m. James Peterson of Ameliasburgh. OC 4 Feb 1830.

HOWE, William of Kingston.
    Peter of Kingston, m. Catharine Connor. OC 20 Nov 1810.
    George of Kingston. OC 23 Jan 1811.
    Mathew of Kingston, m. Margaret Galloway. OC 17 Nov 1797.
    William of Kingston. OC 5 March 1840.
    Elizabeth, m. David Babcock of Kingston. OC 17 Nov 1797.

HOWELL, John of Sophiasburgh.
    Mary Ann, m. Robert Vaughan of Sophiasburgh. OC 28 Apr 1807.
    Charles of Sophiasburgh. OC 1 May 1834.   [Cont'd]

HOWELL, John - Cont'd
  Griffith of Sophiasburgh, m. Elizabeth Lazier, 6 Sept 1806. O.C. 28
    April 1807.
  Richard of Sophiasburgh, b. about 1781; d. March 1, 1814. O.C. 28
    April 1807.
  Jacob of Sophiasburgh, m. Catharine Fox, 8 March 1812. OC 22 May 1820
  Catharine, m. Daniel Williams of Sophiasburgh. OC 25 June 1823.
  Nancy Jane. O.C. 23 Nov 1837.
  James R. of Tyendinaga, Thurlow. OC 7 March 1833; OC 1 June 1837.
  Hector of Sophiasburgh. OC 4 Feb 1836.
  Elizabeth. OC 15 March 1832.
  Lorrain, m. George Wilson of Sophiasburgh. OC 7 June 1826.

HOWELL, Mathew.
  William of Murray. O.C. 23 June 1824.

HOWEY, Robert of Gainsborough.
  Daniel of Crowland. OC 19 Aug 1806.
  Elizabeth, m. Joseph McCollum of Gainsborough. OC 11 Dec 1810.
  Cornelius of Gainsborough. OC 17 March 1812.
  Isaac J. of Wainfleet (Clinton). OC 12 Dec 1821. OC 28 June 1832.
  Samuel of Bayham. OC 18 Jan 1828.
  Robert of Gainsborough. OC 14 April 1836.
  Stephen of Bertie. OC 5 July 1826. OC 25 Nov 1842.

HUFF, Henry.
  Catherine, m. John Woolman of Niagara. OC 21 Feb 1807.
  Mary, m. Jacob Doren of Matilda. OC 13 March 1807.
  Elizabeth, m. Conrad Shaver. OC 22 June 1797.

HUFF, John of Haldimand Co.
  Abraham of Haldimand Co. OC 19 April 1808.
  Catherine, m. Oliver Burnham of Haldimand Co. OC 11 April 1809.
  John of Cayuga. OC 30 Nov 1837.
  Elizabeth, m. (1) ---- Connor; m. (2) John Norton of Haldimand Co. O.C.
    6 November 1829.

HUFF, Paul of Adolphustown.
  Elizabeth. O.C. 17 March 1807.
  William Moore of Adolphustown. OC 16 Feb 1810.
  James, b. Fishkill, Dutchess Co., 27 Jan 1774; m. Amy Garrison, on
    2 Jan 1796. Land Board Certificate, 13/6 Thurlow.
  Solomon.
  Charles of Adolphustown, m. Elizabeth Russell, 26 Aug 1803.

HUFF, Solomon of Adolphustown.
  Sarah, m. Jacob Dulmage of Adolphustown OC 23 March 1802.
  Catherine, m. Abraham Maybee.   [Cont'd]

HUFF, Solomon - Cont'd
Elizabeth, m. William Wright of Adolphustown. OC 13 July 1802.
Jane, m. Henry Hoover of Adolphustown. OC 13 July 1802.
William.
Richard of Adolphustown, m. Sophia Snider, 17 Sept 1806.
Mary, m. Henry Vandusen of Adolphustown, 27 Jan 1807.
Peter of Adolphustown, m. Ann Heald, 3 Sept 1812.
Solomon.

HUFFMAN, Christopher of Glanford, Sgt., N.J. Vols. Heir & Devisee
Commission, July, 1811.
Henry of Glanford. O.C. 20 June 1806.
Jacob of Glanford (Trafalgar). OC 30 Sept 1806.
Ann, m. Elisha Bingham of Glanford. OC 26 Jan 1820.
Paul of Glanford. OC 27 Aug 1840.
Godfrey of Glanford.
Elizabeth, m. ---- Choate of Glanford.

HUFFMAN, Jacob of Bertie Loyal Rangers. Died 22 March 1837 aged
about 78.
Abigail, m. Michael Beach of Bertie. OC 28 Apr 1812; 10 Dec 1818.
Rebecca, m. Winslow Hayward of Humberstone. OC 18 March 1818.
Ann. OC 13 Jan 1819.
Jacob of Malahide. O.C. 3 Jan 1833.
Margaret. OC 3 Nov 1836.
Catherine, m. ---- Johnson of Bertie. OC 3 Nov 1836.
Mary. OC 28 Oct 1835.
William of Bertie. OC 4 April 1833.
Elizabeth, m. David Adams of Malahide. OC 18 July 1833.

HUFFMAN, Nicholas of Bertie. Loyal Rangers.
Elizabeth, m. Michael Beach of Humberstone. OC 10 Apr 1805.
Mary, m. Henry Neher of Bertie. OC 15 May 1805.
Peggy (Margaret, 8 July 1796), m. George Ecker (Acre) of Clinton.
OC 8 Oct 1796. OC 26 Nov 1840.

HUFFNAIL, Andrew of Fredericksburgh.
Jacob of Fredericksburgh. OC 3 Nov 1836.

HUFFNAIL, Jopts (Jobest) of Adolphustown. Soldier, Col. Peters' Co., Loy-
al Rangers. Born 1724 in Albany Co.; d. March, 1785.
Barbara, m. ---- Mabee. OC 24 Feb 1801.
Catherine. O.C. 31 May 1803.
Mary, m. Henry Davis of Adolphustown. OC 30 Aug 1797.
Andrew of Fredericksburgh, m. Sarah; d. 30 Aug 1841, aged 70.

HUGHES, James of Marysburgh.
Joseph of Marysburgh O.C. 6 March 1821.   [Cont'd]

HUGHES, James - Cont'd
  Benjamin of Marysburgh. OC 19 May 1829.
  James of Marysburgh. OC 19 May 1829.

HUGHSON, Joshua
  Tamar, m. ---- Corbin of Niagara. OC 28 Aug 1818.

HUGHSON, Nathaniel of Barton, m. Rebecca, who died at Hamilton, 12 Aug
  1853, aet. 89 yrs.
  Tamar, m. Angus McFee. South Dorchester Tp. OC 16 Apr 1811.
  George of Barton. OC 16 Apr 1811.
  Robert L. of Barton. OC 27 Jan 1816.
  James of Barton, b. 1797; d. 29 June 1849. OC 13 Dec 1820.
  Elizabeth, m. Daniel McFee of Bertie. OC 7 Jan 1824.
  Hannah. OC 5 Nov 1828.
  Nathaniel of Barton. OC 2 March 1825.

HULBERT, Moses of Augusta.
  Deborah, m. Daniel Nettleton of Augusta. OC 18 June 1800.
  Desire, m. Thomas Brown of Marlborough. OC 23 June 1801, 30 May 1835
  Lyman of Augusta. OC 8 Oct 1808.
  Homan of Augusta. OC 22 Oct 1817.

HUMPHREY, James of Edwardsburgh. Soldier, Loyal Rangers.
  James Jr. OC 23 June 1801.
  Nancy, m. John Bice of Edwardsburgh. OC 26 Feb 1805.
  Margaret. OC 26 Feb 1805.
  Samuel of Edwardsburgh. OC 7 Aug 1811.
  Elizabeth, m. Bazaliel Thrasher of Edwardsburgh. OC 16 March 1825.

HUNSINGER, John of Louth.
  Margaret. OC 20 May 1817.
  Nancy. O.C. 20 May 1817.
  John of Louth. OC 22 May 1820.
  Peter of Grantham. OC 26 Nov 1823.
  Mary, m. John Mills of Yarmouth. OC 14 May 1840.
  Wait of Grantham. OC 3 Nov 1836.

HUNT, Edward of Humberstone.
  David of Pelham. OC 10 March 1819.
  Nancy. OC 20 Feb 1840.
  Mary, Aaron Stringer of Woodhouse. OC 27 Aug 1840.
  Thomas of Gainsborough. OC 7 Aug 1834.
  Lewis of Pelham. OC 7 Aug 1834.

HUNTER, David of Edwardsburgh, m. Leah McIlmoyle.
  Sarah, m. Jabez Andrews of Yonge. OC 15 March 1803.
  Marvin of Yonge. OC 15 March 1803.   [Cont'd]

HUNTER, David - Cont'd
    Socrates of Yonge. OC 2 Dec 1806.
    Jane, m. Robert McCarger of South Gower. OC 17 Feb 1816.
    Samuel of Edwardsburgh, bapt. 7 March 1792. OC 13 Feb 1816.
    David of South Gower. OC 11 Dec 1822. OC 20 May 1829.
    Nelson of Oxford-on-Rideau. OC 21 Oct 1837.
    Francis of South Gower. OC 27 June 1836.
    Elizabeth. OC 29 Sept 1836.
    Jonathan of Yonge. OC 28 Oct 1835.
    John of Oxford (South Gower). OC 22 Dec 1832. OC 27 June 1833.
    Peter of Oxford. OC 28 Feb 1833.
    James of South Gower. OC 11 Oct 1832.
    Mary, m. Lewis Kilborn of South Gower. OC 3 May 1826.

HUNTER, James of Barton.
    Walter of Barton. OC 26 March 1811.
    James of Barton. OC 26 March 1811.
    Jane, m. John Snider of Barton. OC 29 Dec 1819.
    Margaret, m. Frederick Snider of Trafalgar. OC 29 Dec 1819.
    Mary. OC 21 Feb 1821.

HURD, Anner of Augusta, widow of Phineas Hurd. OC 5 March 1811.
    Asahel of Marlborough. OC 5 March 1810.
    Molly, m. Elijah Bottom of Augusta. OC 20 Feb 1810.
    Isaac of Augusta. OC 13 Nov 1818.
    Andrew of Augusta, m. Margaret Mitchell. OC 14 July 1819.
    Jabez of Augusta. OC 24 Jan 1821.

HUTCHINSON, Asa of Yonge.
    Mary, m. Cornelius Losee of Matilda. OC 13 March 1807.
    Jesse of Yonge. OC 10 May 1812.
    Anna, m. Daniel Day of Yonge. OC 19 May 1812.

HUYCK, John of Adolphustown, m. Sarah; committed suicide in summer of
    1807.
    Jane, bapt. 7 Feb 1791; Samuel Dorland of Adolphustown. OC 17 Feb 1807.
    John of Adolphustown, m. Jemima Clapp. OC 26 Jan 1808.
    Burger of Adolphustown, m. Phoebe Clapp. OC 23 Feb 1809.
    Ruth, m. Lawrence Lewis of Adolphustown. OC 16 Feb 1811.
    Edward of Adolphustown, m. Elizabeth German. OC 7 Feb 1821.

HUYCK, Peter of Ameliasburgh.
    Ann, m. Peter Waldron of Ameliasburgh. OC 30 May 1834.
    Cornelius P. of Ameliasburgh. OC 30 May 1834.
    Henry P. of Ameliasburgh OC 30 May 1834.
    Catharine, m. ---- Shuler of Ameliasburgh. OC 5 June 1834.
    Joseph P. of Thurlow. OC 24 March 1835.

JACKSON, Henry of Edwardsburgh, m. Sarah Clott.
  Rachel, m. Ezekiel Spicer of Edwardsburgh. OC 31 May 1803.
  Sarah, bapt. 12 Feb 1789; m. Francis LaGrow of Edwardsburgh. OC 27
    November 1834.
  Anna J., m. Oliver D. Shaver of Edwardsburgh. OC 3 Dec 1835.
  Mary, m. Luther Elliott of Kingston. O.C. 4 July 1833.
  Jane, m. Alexander Markel of Mountain. OC 27 Feb 1834.
  Henry of Edwardsburgh. OC 24 March 1835.

JACKSON, James of Ernestown. Pvt., Loyal Rangers.
  Nancy, m. John Howard Jr. of Amherst Island 2 Oct 1788. Land Board
    Certificate, 9/6 Pittsburgh.
  Catharine, m. ---- George. Land Board Certificate, 16/8 Loughborough.

JACKSON, James of Ernestown, Augusta and Mountain.
  Elisha of Mountain. O.C. 1 April 1840.
  Levina, m. William Campbell of Portland. OC 21 May 1840.
  Diadema, m. Cornelius Mills of Loughborough. OC 21 May 1840.
  John of Mountain. OC 24 Sept 1840.
  James of Mountain. OC 28 Jan 1841.
  Thomas of Mountain. OC 9 March 1837.
  Elizabeth, m. John Richardson of Mountain. OC 9 Mar 1837; 29 June 1837.
  George of Mountain. OC 9 March 1837.
  Samuel of Portland. OC 2 May 1836.
  Erastus of Loughborough. OC 4 Dec 1834.
  Phineas of Portland. OC 4 Dec 1834.

JACKSON, Jethro of Richmond.
  Felica, m. Solomon Tyler of Richmond 13 Feb 1800. OC 15 Dec 1807.
  Joseph of Richmond. OC 8 Feb 1808.
  Nancy, m. William Prindle of Fredericksburgh. OC 20 Aug 1808.
  Jethro of Ernestown, b. 11 Aug 1786. OC 7 Feb 1809.
  Jonathan C. of Richmond. OC 25 Feb 1812.
  Fanny, m. John Pencil Jr. of Fredericksburgh. OC 20 May 1817.
  Loraine, m. Joseph Card of Richmond. OC 26 July 1820.

JACKSON, Peter of Augusta.
  Margaret, m. Nathaniel W. Allan of Portland. OC 15 May 1835.
  Arilla, m. Sylvanus Deo of Portland. OC 15 May 1835.
  William of Portland. OC 15 May 1835.
  Maria, m. William Randolph of Portland. OC 15 May 1835.
  Elijah of Portland. OC 4 Feb 1836.
  Jacob of Portland. OC 11 Feb 1836.

JACKSON, Thomas of Ernestown and Leeds.
  Margaret, m. ---- Fairfield of Town of Bath. OC 17 Nov 1836.
  Mark of Pittsburgh. OC 4 Dec 1834.
  Vincent of Pittsburgh. OC 5 Jan 1835.

JACOCKS, David of Osnabruck.
    Mary, m. ---- Philips. OC 8 July 1801.
    Elizabeth, m. ---- Bush of Osnabruck. OC 10 June 1800.
    Nancy, m. William Millross of Osnabruck. OC 25 Feb 1806.
    Margaret, m. Asahel Geralds of Osnabruck. OC 25 Feb 1806.
    David of Osnabruck. OC 23 Nov 1816.
    Hannah, m. ---- Cutler. OC 20 May 1817.
    William of Osnabruck. OC 20 May 1817.
    Diana, m. John McQuarie of Cornwall. OC 18 March 1818.

JARVIS, William of Niagara and York.
    Eliza, m. William B. Robinson of Whitchurch. OC 3 Dec 1828.

JESSUP, Edward Sr. of Augusta. Major, Loyal Rangers. Born 1736. Died at
    Prescott, Feb., 1816.
    Edward of Augusta, U. E. OC 8 Oct 1796.
    Abigail, m. James Walker, surgeon, in 1781. OC 8 Oct 1796.

JESSUP, Edward Jr. of Augusta. Lt., Loyal Rangers. Born 1766; m. Sus-
    annah, dau of Capt. Simeon Covill; d. at Prescott, 1815.
    Eliza, m. Ormond Jones of Brockville 4 Oct 1834. OC 10 Aug 1837.
    Henry Joseph of Augusta. OC 1 Dec 1836.
    Ann Maria, m. Edwin Church of Augusta. OC 4 Sept 1834.
    Hamilton Dibble of Augusta, m. Sophia Matilda Trudeau. OC 5 March 1835
    James of Elizabethtown. OC 5 March 1835.
    Edward of Augusta. OC 12 Feb 1831.
    George C. of Augusta. OC 7 May 1828.

JESSUP, Joseph of Elizabethtown. Will dated 6 Dec 1821, filed 25 Mar 1822.
    Hannah, m. John McIntosh of Elizabethtown; d. 17 Jan 1852. OC 19 May
        1812.
    a natural dau of Mary, later wife of Abraham Boulton of Elizabethtown.
    Issue of John and Hannah McIntosh:
        James, d. unm.
        Joseph Jessup of Yonge, m. Jane Ann.
        John of Yonge, m. Janet.
        Elizabeth, m. Ninian Bates of Yonge 21 Feb 1837.
        Mary Ann, m. Robert Young of Vienna, Bayham Twp.

JOHN, Capt., alias Deserontyon, Mohawk Chief.
    Peter of Grand River. OC 20 May 1817.
    Margaret, m. Joseph Brant Jr. of Tyendinaga; d. 3 Aug 1852, aged 75.
        OC 29 June 1837.

JOHNS, Solomon of Elizabethtown.
    Solomon of Town of Niagara. OC 1 July 1818.

JOHNSON, Brant of Haldimand Co. Lt., Indian Dept. Died on Grand River in
  Haldimand Co., 28 March 1818. [He and his family were at Niagara in 1783
  The Ontario Register, 1: 210]
  Mary, m. John J. Lefferty of Chippawa 17 Aug 1800; d. 22 May 1850, ae
    73. OC 8 Oct 1796.
  Sarah, m. ---- Ruggles of Mohawk Village. OC 8 Oct 1796.
  Elizabeth, m. Ralfe Clench of Niagara; d. 15 Aug 1850, aged 77. OC 21
    July 1796.
  Jemima, m. Alexander Stewart of Niagara 7 Dec 1796. Died 1841. OC 8
    October 1796.

JOHNSON, Elizabeth, widow of Capt. John Johnson, Indian Dept. [See The
  Ontario Register, 1: 211]
  Elizabeth, m. Lt. Daniel Servos of Niagara. OC 17 April 1807.

JOHNSON, George of Matilda.
  Mary. OC 3 March 1809. Matilda.
  George of Matilda. OC 20 May 1817.

JOHNSON, Col. Guy
  Ann. OC 21 July 1797.
  Mary, m. Capt. Colin Campbell in 1783.
  Julia. Heir and Devisee Commission, 21 July 1823.

JOHNSON, John of Stamford.
  William of Stamford. OC 23 June 1836.
  Elizabeth, m. Hugh Wilson of Thorold. OC 2 Oct 1829.
  Mehetable, m. Henry C. Green. OC 1 Sept 1831.
  John of Thorold. OC 17 Feb 1825.

JOHNSON, Jonas.
  Job of Pelham. OC 2 Dec 1806.
  Sarah, m. Richard McAlpine of Pelham. OC 2 Dec 1806.
  Elizabeth, m. ---- Nunn of Pelham. OC 4 Feb 1807.
  Mary, m. Robert Simmerman of Clinton. OC 28 April 1812.
  Hannah, m. Francis Pettay of Gainsborough. OC 6 Aug 1816.

JOHNSON, Lawrence.
  William of Yonge Street. OC 8 Sept 1801.

JOHNSON, Rulif of Bertie and Grand River, m. Elizabeth [Sipes].
  Agnes, m. Charles McCartney of Beverly. OC 6 Aug 1816.
  Joachim of Grand River, bapt. 12 Apr 1793. OC 31 May 1820.
  William of Grand River. OC 26 July 1820.
  see also Johnston, Ralph.

JOHNSON, William of Soulanges. Lt. Natural son of Sir John Johnson. Lieut.
Batt. R.C.V. & Can. Voltigeurs. Married Margaret Clark. Died at the
Cascades in 1836, aged 66.
Edward Simon, b. 21 Oct 1803.
Gordon Warren, b. about 1812.
William Louis Villiers, b. about 1821.
Clarissa Ann, b. about 1804.
Amelia Maria, b. about 1820, m. Samuel I. B. Anderson of Cornwall.
William Henry, b. 21 Oct 1803. d. y. ?

JOHNSTON, Adam.
Margaret, m. John Dixon of Cornwall. OC 30 June 1801.
Jane, m. Daniel Whyatt of Cornwall. OC 11 March 1807.

JOHNSTON, Andrew of Ernestown.
Andrew T. of Fredericksburgh. OC 21 May 1834.

JOHNSTON, Daniel of Ernestown.
William of Ernestown. OC 31 May 1838. Jr.
Andrew T. of Ernestown. OC 3 Feb 1834.
James of Ernestown. OC 10 March 1834.
Isabella, m. George Young of Ernestown. OC 10 March 1834.
Catharine, m. Joseph Chatterton of Camden East. OC 10 March 1834.
Alatha, m. John Cook of Camden East. OC 10 March 1834.
Hannah, m. Moses Foster of Fredericksburgh. OC 10 March 1834.
David of Ernestown. OC 10 March 1834.
Sarah, m. Christopher Lemon of Ernestown. OC 10 March 1834.
Mary, m. James Foster of Ernestown. OC 1 May 1834.
Ruth, m. Jacob McLaughlin of Camden East. OC 1 May 1834.
Elizabeth, m. Peter Fralick of Fredericksburgh. OC 7 Aug 1834.
Lois. OC 5 Feb 1835.

JOHNSTON, James of Cornwall, Lot 16/3. Married Isabella Pescod who
died 11 June 1853, aged 84. He died 31 Aug 1839, aged 84.
John of Cornwall. OC 4 July 1815.
William of Cornwall. OC 4 July 1815.
Mary, bapt. 15 Dec 1793. OC 4 July 1815.
Jennet, bapt. 7 March 1796; m. James Gould of Charlottenburgh; died
7 January 1844, aged 48. OC 7 Feb 1821.
Adam of Cornwall, b. 28 Jan 1798; m. Catharine Storing. OC 4 July 1833.
Margaret, m. James Calvert of Cornwall. OC 4 July 1833.
George of Cornwall. OC 11 July 1833.
Robert of Cornwall. OC 11 July 1833.
Nancy, m. Alexander Mitchell of Hawkesbury. OC 22 Dec 1832.

JOHNSTON, James of Ernestown.
Hannah, m. Sheldon Hawley of Ernestown 16 Feb 1789. OC 27 Oct 1801.
William of Ernestown. OC 13 Sept 1803.   [Cont'd]

JOHNSTON, James - Cont'd
  Mary, m. William Juel of Ernestown 28 Nov 1805. OC 2 March 1807.
  John of Ernestown, m. Rachel Caton, 11 Nov 1805. OC 16 Feb 1811.
  James of Ernestown (Hamilton). OC 25 Feb 1812. OC 2 May 1836.
  Margaret, m. James Dean of Hope. OC 1 Nov 1838.
  Robert of Murray. OC 5 Sept 1839.
  Henry of Hope. OC 16 Feb 1837.
  Samuel of Murray. OC 27 April 1837.
  Jemima. OC 11 Feb 1836. Murray.
  Nancy, m. Henry Simmons of Murray. OC 11 Feb 1836.
  Elizabeth, m. Cornelius Van Atter of Hope. OC 2 May 1836.
  Andrew of Ernestown. OC 3 Feb 1834.
  Jacob of Ernestown. OC 31 May 1830.
  Nathan of Ernestown. OC 3 Jan 1827.

JOHNSTON, John. Capt., Indian Dept. Died 1786.
  William.

JOHNSTON, Ralph of Grand River. [See also Johnson, Rulif]
  Hannah, m. John Petrie of Grand River. OC 7 Nov 1839.
  Joseph of Grand River. OC 28 Feb 1833.

JOHNSTON, William of Ernestown. Capt. Six Nations. Indian Dept.
  step-dau. Ann McKay, m. Matthew Clark of Ernestown. Land Board
    Certificate, 11/9 Thurlow.
  step-son, Samuel McKay of Ernestown, m. Amarilla Hawley.

JONES, Daniel of Brockville.
  Sarah, bapt. 8 May 1785; m. Lewis Charlaud of Montreal. OC 4 July 1815.
  David of Brockville. OC 4 July 1815.
  Daniel of Brockville. OC 4 July 1815.
  Pamelia. OC 28 Sept 1820.
  Ann, m. Henry Corse of Dist. of Montreal. OC 28 Sept 1820.
  Charlotte, m. Philo Hawley of Brantford. OC 18 May 1837.

JONES, Ebenezer of Saltfleet.
  Catharine, m. Peter Springstead of Brantford. OC 18 May 1837.
  Augustus of Saltfleet. OC 12 Aug 1833.
  Rachel, m. Daniel McCrimmon of Saltfleet. OC 12 Aug 1833.
  Joseph of Saltfleet. OC 7 Oct 1826.
  Jacob of Malahide. OC 13 July 1841.
  Ebenezer of Malahide. OC 29 June 1843.
  Jonas of Malahide. OC 11 Aug 1847.

JONES, Ephraim of Augusta, m. Charlotte Coursol, March, 1779.
  Charlotte, b. 16 March 1786; m. Livius P. Sherwood of Elizabethtown;
    d. 16 Jan 1875. OC 26 Feb 1805.   [Cont'd]

JONES, Ephraim - Cont'd
  Sophia, b. 21 Feb 1785; m. John Stuart of Elizabethtown 21 Jan 1803;
    OC 4 June 1805.
  Charles of Elizabethtown, b. 28 Feb 1781; m. Mary Stuart, 8 June 1807;
    d. 21 Aug 1840. OC 9 July 1802.
  Lucy, b. 31 Dec 1787; m. Elnathan Hubbell of Elizabethtown. OC 5 Jan
    1808.
  William of Bastard, b. 6 May 1782; m. Amelia Macdonell; d. Brockville
    17 Nov 1831. OC 19 Feb 1817.
  Jonas of Brockville, b. 19 May 1791; m. Mary Elizabeth Ford; d. 8 July
    1848. OC 19 Feb 1817.
  Alpheus of Augusta, b. 28 Dec 1794; m. Frances Jones, 26 June 1820;
    d. 21 Dec 1863. OC 18 March 1818.
  Eliza, b. 27 July 1797; m. Henry John Boulton of Town of York 29 April
    1818; d. 21 May 1868. OC 10 June 1818.

JONES, James of Grantham. Soldier, Butler's Rangers. [He and his family
  were at Niagara in 1783. The Ontario Register. 1: 209]
  Elizabeth. OC 21 Oct 1800.
  Andrew of Beverly. OC 10 May 1797.
  Sarah, m. John Mann of Beverly. OC 14 Oct 1801.
  Ann. OC 31 May 1803. Grantham. 18 & 19/BF King.
  Mary, m. William Hodgkinson of Grantham. O.C. 23 Feb 1808.
  Leah. OC 20 May 1817. m. Tice?

JONES, John of Augusta. Capt. Married Catherine, who died 1804. He died
  1802. His will dated 13 Oct 1802. Heir & Devisee Commission 12 July 1826.
  John of Augusta. OC 15 March 1803.
  Ann. OC 15 March 1803.
  Deborah. OC 26 Feb 1805.
  David Dunham of Augusta. OC 21 Feb 1811.
  Harriet, m. Jacob Van Armam of Ernestown. OC 12 Nov 1811.
  Catherine, m. Gideon Van Arnam of Augusta. OC 19 May 1812.
  Thomas of Augusta. OC 11 July 1798.
  Augustus of Augusta. Died October, 1809.
  Sarah. OC 11 July 1798.

JONES, Solomon of Augusta, m. Mary Tunnicliffe.
  Ann, m. Rufus C. Henderson of Augusta. OC 27 Feb 1806.
  Jonathan of Augusta. OC 12 Nov 1811.
  Dunham of Augusta, m. Lucy Hurd. OC 28 Sept 1820.
  William Tunnicliff of Prescott. OC 30 May 1834.

JUDSON, Silas.
  Lyman of Yonge. OC 23 Sept 1800.
  Ann, m. Jonah Brown of Elizabethtown. OC 12 June 1798.

JULIEN, John of Howard.
    Margaret, m. Levi L. Clark of Howard. OC 28 Oct 1833.
    Martha. OC 28 Oct 1833. Dorchester.
    Ruth, m. Abraham Kilburn of Dorchester. OC 8 Jan 1835.

K

KARR, Norris of Darlington.
    John of Darlington. OC 20 June 1806.
    William of Whitby. OC 19 Feb 1823.
    Rachel, m. Enoch Davis of Whitby. OC 4 Oct 1826.

KEEFER, George, m. Catharine Lampman. OC 4 April 1797.
    Mary, m. ---- Lundy. OC 18 Aug 1801.

KEELER, James of Augusta.
    Elizabeth. OC 20 Feb 1810.
    Daniel of Augusta, m. Lizette de Lorimer. OC 9 Oct 1810.
    Jane. OC 11 Nov 1815.
    James Hamilton of Augusta. OC 22 Oct 1817.
    Mary A. OC 20 Oct 1819.
    William of Augusta. OC 4 Feb 1824.
    George of Augusta, m. Amanda Gile, 13 June 1819. OC 17 Oct 1828.
    Samuel of Augusta. OC 10 Sept 1849.

KELLER, Frederick of Kingston and Fredericksburgh, m. (1) Hannah ----.
  m. (2) Elizabeth Peters, 10 Aug 1791.
    Jacob of Kingston. OC 16 Nov 1807.
    Frederick of Fredericksburgh, m. Lenah. OC 25 May 1808.
    William of Fredericksburgh, bapt. 13 Nov 1787. OC 16 Feb 1810.
    John of Kingston, bapt. 8 June 1788. OC 25 Feb 1812.
    Samuel of Fredericksburgh, bapt. 1 Jan 1790; m. Rosanna Warner, on
        3 March 1807. OC 17 March 1812.
    Joseph of Fredericksburgh, bapt. 18 Dec 1792. OC 18 March 1818.
    Christopher of Fredericksburgh. OC 18 March 1818.
    Laney, bapt. 30 May 1798; m. Christopher Young of Fredericksburgh, on
        6 Feb 1814. OC 18 March 1818.
    David of Fredericksburgh, bapt. 15 Oct 1800. OC 28 May 1823.
    Julia Ann, m. ---- Dibble of Fredericksburgh. OC 16 Feb 1837.
    Henry of Fredericksburgh, m. Charlotte Scriver, 30 October 1832. OC
        21 March 1833.
    Hannah, m. ---- Sparrell of Fredericksburgh. OC 28 March 1833.
    Michael of Fredericksburgh, bapt. 4 March 1810; m. Margaret Scriver,
        on 4 Dec 1832. OC 13 June 1833.
    Elizabeth, bapt. 24 Nov 1802; m. Richard Kiser of Fredericksburgh, on
        17 Feb 1819. OC 19 Feb 1828.
    Mary, buried 4 Jan 1795.   [Cont'd]

KELLER, Frederick - Cont'd
  Catharine, m. Geo. Clapper of Fredericksburgh. OC 5 Feb 1835.
  Peter of Fredericksburgh. OC 1 Aug 1827.
  Mary, m. Isaac Asselstine of Fredericksburgh 20 March 1820. OC 22
    June 1825.

KELLER, Frederick.
  Mary, m. ---- Place of Madoc. OC 26 May 1843.
  John of Thurlow. OC 26 May 1843.
  Asa of Madoc. OC 26 May 1843.
  Jane. OC 2 Aug 1844.
  Phoebe Ann. OC 19 March 1842.

KELLER, John of Fredericksburgh, m. Lydia, dau Isaac Larraway Sr., U.E.
  Daughter Peggy bapt. 5 June 1805.
  Elizabeth, bapt. 29 Dec 1787; m. Aaron Lake of Ernestown. OC 17 Feb
    1807.
  Isaac of Fredericksburgh, m. Sally Haggard. OC 16 Feb 1810.
  Mary, bapt. 2 Oct 1791; m. Abraham Wood of Ernestown. OC 16 Feb 1810.
  Jane, bapt. 4 March 1798; m. Martin Clement of Fredericksburgh. OC
    26 March 1817.
  John of Fredericksburgh, bapt. 15 Sept 1793. OC 20 May 1817.
  Catharine, bapt. 13 Dec 1795; m. Christian Thompson of Fredericksburgh
    OC 13 June 1818.
  Hannah, m. Christian Koughnet of Fredericksburgh. OC 6 Feb 1822.
    OC 7 March 1827.
  Lydia, bapt. 29 Aug 1802; m. Benjamin Randell of Loughborough. OC 6
    January 1827.
  William of Loughborough, bapt. 11 May 1800. OC 2 June 1831.
  Peter, bapt. 25 Feb 1808.
  Layna, bapt. 18 April 1810; m. Benjamin Loyd of Fredericksburgh. OC
    7 March 1827.
  Margaret, m. ---- Koughnet of Fredericksburgh. OC 20 Feb 1830.
  Mary Ann, b. 7 June 1812; m. Peter Keller of Kingston. OC 2 June 1831.
  John, b. 22 Feb 1802.

KELLER, William of Fredericksburgh.
  Daniel of Fredericksburgh. OC 5 Nov 1835.

KELLY, Martin of Edwardsburgh.
  John of Montague. OC 26 July 1838.
  Margaret, m. ---- Everts of Montague. OC 26 July 1838.
  Martin of Montague. OC 26 July 1838.

KELSAY, James of Yonge.
  Mary, m. ---- Phillips of Yonge. OC 30 Sept 1800.
  Elizabeth, m. James Livingston of Yonge. OC 11 Feb 1799.
  John of Yonge. OC 15 Aug 1833.   [Cont'd]

KELSAY, James - Cont'd
  Eunice, m. Andrew Teed of Yonge. OC 15 Aug 1833.

KEMP, James of Fredericksburgh, m. (1) Phoebe Van Siclen, 26 Dec 1790,
  who was buried 3 Jan 1798. m. (2) Jane Anderson, 19 Aug 1799, who was
  buried 8 Sept 1799. He was buried 23 March 1803.
  Ann, bapt. 30 Oct 1791; m. Peter Fykes of Fredericksburgh. OC 17 Feb
    1807.
  John J. of Fredericksburgh, bapt. 27 Dec 1795. OC 13 June 1818.
  Phoebe, bapt. 7 Jan 1798; m. Cornelius A. Huyck of Ameliasburgh. OC
    8 March 1820.
  Emilia, m. Thomas Pruime of Whitchurch. OC 18 Feb 1824.
  Elizabeth, bapt. 13 Oct 1793.
  James C. of Ameliasburgh. OC 14 Dec 1827.

KEMP, Joseph of Ameliasburgh, m. Catharine.
  James of Ameliasburgh, bapt. 3 March 1793. OC 13 Feb 1816.
  John of Ameliasburgh, bapt. 30 Nov 1788. OC 1 July 1818.
  Anne, bapt. 10 Nov 1799; m. Jacob Stickles of Ameliasburgh. OC 4 Aug
    1836.
  Jacob, bapt. 15 May 1791.
  Philip, bapt. 31 May 1795; buried 31 Aug 1800.

KENDRICK, Duke William of York, m. Susannah. OC 27 March 1829.
  Andrew. OC 7 July 1836.
  Josiah. OC 7 July 1836.
  William of City of Toronto. OC 1 Dec 1836.
  Ann Eliza, m. James McFarlane of City of Toronto. OC 1 Dec 1836.
  Frances, m. George Playter of Gwillimbury West. OC 1 Dec 1836.
  Charlotte A., m. H.T. Gillet of Niagara. OC 1850 or 1851.

KENNEDY, Alexander of Charlottenburgh, Lot 11/3, m. Christina McDonell.
  John. OC 10 March 1801.
  Mary, m. Alexander McDonell of Lancaster 29 Aug 1809. OC 5 Apr 1810.
  Donald of Charlottenburgh. OC 17 March 1812.
  Jennet, m. Angus McDonell of Charlottenburgh in 1808. OC 17 Mar 1812.
  Anne, m. Donald McDonell of Charlottenburgh 23 Jan 1810. OC 11 Nov 1815
  Angus of Charlottenburgh. OC 23 Nov 1816.
  Alexander of Charlottenburgh, m. Flora McDonell, 1808. OC 26 Mar 1817.

KETCHESON, William of Sidney, b. 7 July 1759. See Christian Guardian,
  April 23, 1902.
  William of Sidney, m. Nancy. OC 8 Feb 1808.
  John of Sidney, b. 11 Nov 1788; d. 1 Oct 1873. OC 16 Feb 1810.
  Thomas of Sidney. OC 13 Feb 1816.
  Benjamin of Sidney. OC 13 Feb 1816.
  Elijah of Sidney. OC 20 May 1817.
  James of Sidney. OC 16 June 1819.   [Cont'd]

KETCHESON, William - Cont'd
    Sarah, m. Thomas Caton of Ernestown. OC 27 Feb 1818.
    Deborah, m. Saylor Reed of Thurlow. OC 10 Aug 1837.
    Phoebe. OC 5 June 1834. Huntingdon.

KETTLE, Jeremiah of Bertie. [Butler's Rangers. He and his family were at
    Niagara in 1783. The Ontario Register, 1: 202]
    Jeremiah. OC 7 May 1835.
    Hiram of Dumfries. OC 28 June 1832.

KILBORN, Benjamin of Elizabethtown.
    Samuel of Bastard. OC 24 Nov 1832.

KILLEN, Daniel. 11/1 Sidney. m. Anastasia.
    Catharine, d. 2 Jan 1847; m. (1) William Parsells of N. Y. City; m. (2)
        Alexander Vass.
    Anastasia, m. Edward Smith Parsells of N. Y. City.

KILLMAN, Jacob of Stamford.
    Catherine, m. William Weishuhn of Willoughby. OC 15 May 1805.
    Philip of Stamford. OC 17 June 1806.
    Robert of Stamford. OC 7 Nov 1809.
    Christina, m. George Garner of Stamford. OC 22 March 1797.
    Adam of Stamford. OC 24 Dec 1823.
    William of Stamford. OC 8 Feb 1827.
    Jacob. Land Board Certificate, 14 & 15/6 Pelham.

KIMMERLY, Andrew of Richmond, m. Susanna.
    John of Richmond. OC 16 Feb 1820.
    David of Richmond, b. 9 April 1793. OC 26 March 1817.
    Garret of Richmond. m. Catharine. OC 20 May 1817.
    Henry of Richmond, m. Margaret. OC 20 May 1817.
    Staats of Richmond. OC 20 May 1817.
    Jacob of Richmond, b. 9 April 1793. OC 20 May 1817.
    Andrew of Richmond. OC 2 April 1823.
    Peter of Richmond. OC 12 Sept 1833.
    George of Richmond. OC 27 Sept 1833.
    Adam of Tyendinaga, b. 20 Dec 1804. OC 27 Sept 1833.
    Sarah, m. Luke Bowen of Richmond. OC 4 Sept 1834.
    Edward of Richmond. OC 28 Feb 1835.
    Mary, b. 18 Apr 1816; m. John Roblin of Richmond. OC 28 Feb 1835.
    Catharine, m. Gilbert Solmes of Sophiasburgh. OC 22 June 1825.
    William of Richmond. OC 28 Apr 1825.

KING, Constant of Edwardsburgh, m. Sarah Endring, March, 1784 at
    Montreal.
    Isaac of Augusta. OC 24 April 1810.
    Stephen of Edwardsburgh. OC 4 Nov 1818.   [Cont'd]

KING, Constant - Cont'd
 Jacob of Edwardsburgh. OC 20 Oct 1819.
 John, bapt. 27 May 1793.
 William, bapt. 27 May 1793.
 Ann, m. Thomas Collins of Barton. OC 18 May 1837.
 Hannah, m. Solomon Whitney of Edwardsburgh. OC 2 May 1833.
 Elizabeth, m. Peter Moore of Edwardsburgh. OC 6 Dec 1837.

KINTNER, George of Osnabruck.
 Elizabeth, m. ---- Huff. OC 8 July 1801.
 Eleanor, m. John Hoople of Osnabruck. OC 5 Jan 1798.
 Mary, m. Joseph Latross of Osnabruck. OC 25 Feb 1806.
 Sarah. OC 25 Feb 1806.
 Barbara, m. William Runnalls of Williamsburgh. OC 25 Feb 1806.
 Mathias of Matilda. OC 7 March 1807.
 Hannah, m. Jacob Shove [i.e., Shaver ?] of Matilda. OC 7 Aug 1811.
 John of Matilda. OC 20 May 1817.
 Frederick of Matilda. OC 20 May 1817.

KNAPP, Benjamin of Colchester. [Served in Butler's Rangers. He and his
 family were at Niagara in 1783. The Ontario Register, 1: 208]
 Elizabeth, m. Cornelius Quick of Colchester. OC 20 Feb 1810.
 Catharine, m. Henry Starks of Colchester. OC 20 Feb 1810.
 Ann, m. Jacob Halsted of Colchester. OC 20 Feb 1810.
 Rachel, m. John Davies of Colchester. OC 16 Feb 1811.
 Daniel of Colchester. OC 19 May 1812. OC 11 Jan 1834.
 Benjamin of Chatham, m. Agnes Messmore. OC 12 Feb 1831.

KNAPP, Joseph of Montague, m. Elizabeth, dau Daniel Nettleton, U.E.; d.
 27 May 1836, aged 93 yrs. 15 Children.
 William of Augusta, m. Nancy Hamblin. OC 23 June 1801.
 Amos of Augusta, b. 1776; m. Rachel Van Camp; d. at Augusta, 5 June
 1853, aet. 77. OC 18 June 1800.
 Elizabeth, m. Eliphalet Wyatt of Augusta. OC 26 Feb 1805.
 Abraham of Montague, m. Mary Van Camp; d. at Prescott 13 Dec 1867 in
 83rd year. OC 17 March 1808.
 Joseph of Montague. OC 26 June 1810.
 Mary, m. Edward McCrea of Montague. OC 4 July 1815.
 Daniel of Montague, b. 26 June 1796; d. 20 May 1864. OC 10 Dec 1818.
 Amy. OC 1 May 1834.
 Reuben Acle of Montague, m. Elizabeth Ketchum, 25 Jan 1838. OC 3 Jan
 1833.
 Sybil, m. Isaac Merrick of Augusta. OC 19 June 1832.
 Nancy, m. Obadiah Thompkins of Montague. OC 1 March 1832.
 Sarah. OC 4 Feb 1830.
 Barnabas of Montague. OC 12 Nov 1827.

KNIGHT, Charles of Williamsburgh.
  Mary, m. Frederick Kintner of Matilda. OC 4 April 1839.
  Elizabeth, m. William Shannon of Matilda. OC 4 April 1837.
  William of Matilda. OC 31 Oct 1839.
  Charles of Matilda. OC 4 Jan 1840.
  Hannah, m. Joseph Rutherford of Williamsburgh. OC 29 June 1837.

KNIGHT, James of Cornwall. See OC 5 March 1828.
  Mary Ann. OC 5 Feb 1835. Charlottenburgh.
  Susannah, b. 6 Nov 1800; m. Francis Gardiner.
  Mary Ann, m. Baptiste Charbonneau.
  Margaret, m. Pierre Courtis.
  James Peter.
  Agnes, m. Alanson Clawson.

KNIGHT, Mahlon of Kingston.
  Cornelius of Kingston. OC 16 Nov 1797.
  Isaac of Kingston. OC 16 Nov 1797.
  John of Kingston, m. Mary Knapp, 22 Feb 1809. OC 16 Nov 1807.
  Mary, m. John Knapp of Kingston 15 July 1807. OC 23 Feb 1808.
  Peter of Kingston. OC 23 Feb 1808.

KOP, Philip. Soldier, R. R. N. Y.
  Catherine, m. Thomas Munro of Charlottenburgh. OC 9 March 1803.

KOUGHNET, William of Fredericksburgh.
  Peter of Fredericksburgh. OC 20 Feb 1809.
  Christian of Fredericksburgh. OC 25 Feb 1812.
  Mary. OC 4 Nov 1818.
  John of Loughborough. OC 1 Dec 1819. See OC 1 Aug 1827.
  Margaret, m. William Hayes of Fredericksburgh. OC 7 March 1827.
  William of Fredericksburgh. OC 2 April 1828.

L

LAKE, Christopher of Ernestown.
  Sarah, m. James Ward of Ernestown. OC 13 July 1802.
  John of Ernestown. OC 6 Dec 1803.
  Hannah, m. Francis Teeple of Ernestown. OC 6 Dec 1803.
  Henrietta, m. George Wood of Ernestown. OC 9 March 1809.
  Mary, m. Peter Freel of Loughborough. OC 16 Feb 1810.
  Aaron of Loughborough, m. Eliza Kellar, 1806.
  Henrietta, m. Henry Wood of Loughborough. OC 27 Feb 1818.
  Elizabeth, m. Daniel Walker of Murray (Ernestown). OC November, 1797
    OC 24 March 1835.

LAKE, James of Ernestown. Soldier, Col. Peters Corps.
  Jane, m. Benjamin Lake of Ernestown. OC 17 Feb 1807.
  James of Ernestown, m. Elizabeth Storms, 18 Mar 1813. OC 23 May 1809
  Margaret, m. James Hicks of Ernestown. OC 16 Feb 1810.
  Mary, m. Nathan Fellows of Ernestown 6 Aug 1812. OC 27 Feb 1818.
  Elizabeth, m. Calvin W. Millar of Ernestown. OC 11 July 1833.
  Sarah, m. ---- Althouse of Ernestown. OC 11 July 1833.
  step-son, Dennis, son of Nathaniel Lukes. Petition 13 July 1802.

LAKE, John Sr. of Ernestown.
  Ann, m. Benjamin Hicks of Ernestown. OC 25 Feb 1806.
  Benjamin of Ernestown. OC 30 Jan 1808.
  Mary, m. James Parrott of Ernestown. OC 13 Nov 1818.

LAKE, Nicholas of Ernestown and Sidney.
  Mary, m. Samuel Reed of Thurlow. OC 17 Feb 1807.
  Sarah, m. Solomon Reed of Thurlow. OC 28 Feb 1807.
  Hannah, m. John Hagerman of Sidney. OC 25 Sept 1804.
  Richard of Sidney. OC 17 Oct 1809. See OC 10 Jan 1843.
  John of Sidney. OC 26 March 1811.
  Letty, m. John Sine of Sidney. OC 28 April 1812.
  James of Sidney. OC 20 May 1818.

LAKE, Thomas of Wolford. Soldier, Loyal Rangers. Married Mychell.
  John of Wolford. OC 28 Jan 1804.
  Sarah, m. William Robinson of Wolford. O.C. 28 Jan 1804.
  Abrahm of Wolford. OC 28 Sept 1820. OC 14 Aug 1804.
  James of Wolford. OC 14 Aug 1804.
  Jane, m. James Wiltse of Yonge. OC 14 Feb 1798.
  Henrietta, m. David Hardy of Wolford. OC 31 May 1808.
  Garrett of Montague. OC 24 April 1810.
  Nicholas of Montague. OC 24 March 1835.

LAMB, Isaac of Elizabethtown.
  Rebecca, m. Thomas Wheelaughan of Elizabethtown. OC 20 May 1817.
  Mary, m. ---- Seeley. 15/9 Oxford.
  Jesse, m. Hannah Wing.

LAMBERT, Cornelius of Niagara. [Cpl., Butler's Rangers. He was at
  Niagara in 1783. The Ontario Register, 1: 198]
  Anna, m. ---- Overholt of Clinton. OC 7 Oct 1800.
  Julia, m. James Covenhoven of Niagara 6 Apr 1802. OC 6 Dec 1803.
  Fanny, m. Reuben Lambert of Niagara. OC 30 July 1806.
  Robert of Niagara. OC 3 May 1820.
  Arthur of Niagara. OC 12 June 1822.
  Pamilla, m. Christopher Overholt of Clinton. OC 16 Feb 1837.
  Lewis of Grantham. OC 3 Oct 1833. OC 4 May 1836.

LAMPMAN, Frederick of Stamford.
    Stephen of Stamford. OC 10 May 1838.
    Catherine, m. William Seburn of Thorold. OC 28 May 1840.
    Hannah. OC 28 Oct 1835.
    Anne Margaret, m. William Johnston of Toronto 13 Oct 1831. OC 28
        October 1835.
    Philip of Stamford. OC 28 Oct 1835.
    Henry of Stamford. OC 28 Oct 1835.
    Elizabeth, m. Matthew Thomas of Thorold 1 Oct 1829. OC 17 Feb 1825.
    George of Stamford. OC 17 Feb 1825.
    Frederick of Stamford. OC 17 Feb 1825.
    Peter of Stamford, m. Catherine Cole, 23 May 1832. OC 6 Nov 1829.
    William of Stamford. OC 6 Nov 1829.

LAMPMAN, Frederick Sr. of Stamford, m. Katharine. Died 1789?
    Abraham.
    Peter of Niagara, U. E.
    Frederick of Stamford, U. E.
    Mathias.
    Hannah.
    Leana.

LAMPMAN, Peter of Niagara, buried 28 Dec 1834, aged 86.
    Frederick of Niagara. OC 11 Nov 1806.
    Adam of Thorold. OC 9 Dec 1815.
    Peter of Niagara, m. Agnes Ann? OC 17 Feb 1816.
    John of Grantham, m. Mary Secord. OC 25 Feb 1818.
    Mary M. , m. Adam Stull of Niagara (Esquesing, 1825). OC 2 June 1819.
    Elizabeth, m. Abraham Secord of Niagara 27 May 1818. OC 16 June 1819.
    Ann, m. Thomas McBride of Thorold 24 April 1823. OC 1 Sept 1824.

LAMSON, William of Edwardsburgh. Ensign, Loyal Rangers, Capt. Fraser's
  Co. Appointed 22 June 1782.
    William of Edwardsburgh. OC 4 July 1833.
    Thomas of Edwardsburgh. OC 4 July 1833.
    Jonathan Jones of Edwardsburgh. OC 6 Dec 1832.
    Mary Keziah. OC 6 Dec 1832.
    Sarah, m. John Papineau of Edwardsburgh. OC 6 Dec 1832.

LAMSON, John of Edwardsburgh.
    Deborah, m. Jacob Van Camp of Edwardsburgh. OC 18 June 1799.
    William of Edwardsburgh. OC 30 June 1798.
    John of Edwardsburgh. OC 5 March 1811.
    Sarah. OC 13 Feb 1816.
    Esther. OC 13 Feb 1816.
    James of Edwardsburgh. OC 30 June 1798.

LAND, Abel of Barton, m. Elizabeth.
    William of Barton. OC 12 Sept 1806.
    Abel of Barton, b. Nova Scotia, 1787; d. Hamilton, 7 Aug 1848, aged 61.
       OC 3 March 1809.
    John of Barton. OC 27 Jan 1816.
    Elizabeth, bapt. 12 March 1809; m. Martin Osborne of Barton 17 Feb 1831
       OC 2 May 1833.
    Phoebe, m. Wm McIntyre of Ancaster. OC 2 Jan 1834.
    Rebecca, bapt. 12 March 1809; m. William Mann Smith of Glanford, 10
       Feb 1825. OC 2 Jan 1834.
    Abigail, m. Josiah Fowler of Barton 20 Nov 1834. OC 2 Feb 1832.
    Mary, m. John Sherman of Barton 26 Jan 1832. OC 6 Dec 1832. (John
       Sherman, s. Wm & Calista, b. 25 Mar., 1810).

LAND, Robert of Barton.
    Abigail, m. Isaiah McCarter of Nelson. OC 17 May 1820.
    Phoebe, m. Braithwaite Leeming of Barton. OC 14 May 1823.
    Rebecca. OC 17 Oct 1828.
    Hannah, m. Thomas H. Smith of Waterloo. OC 18 Feb 1843.
    Elizabeth, m. James Alderson of Waterloo. OC 18 Feb 1843.
    John of Barton. OC 18 Feb 1843.

LANDERS, Jabez of Yonge, m. Hannah, who d. 1849. He d. 1830, aged 84.
    Elizabeth, m. John Davison of Yonge. OC 28 Oct 1835.
    Margaret, m. Ashael Hayes of Yonge. OC 28 Oct 1835.
    Sarah, m. Derrick Hogaboom of Yonge. OC 28 Oct 1835.
    John of Yonge. OC 28 Oct 1835.
    Nathan of Yonge. OC 28 Oct 1835.
    Jabez of Yonge. OC 28 Oct 1835.
    Hezekiah Mills of Yonge, m. Rachel Woods, 5 Mar 1835. OC 28 Oct 1835.
    Ebenezer of South Crosby. OC 11 Feb 1836.
    Mary, m. Samuel Whitney. Born Yonge Twp., 15 May 1793.

LANDON, Asa of Augusta and Elizabethtown.
    Solomon of Elizabethtown. OC 17 April 1822.
    Elizabeth. OC 2 July 1840.
    Wellington of Yonge, m. Melissa Burritt. OC 26 March 1836.
    Nelson of Elizabethtown. OC 2 May 1833.
    Maria, m. Stephen Coolidge of Elizabethtown. OC 4 July 1833.
    Elisha of Elizabethtown. OC 27 Feb 1834.
    Harriet, m. Joseph Falkner of Augusta. OC 3 Jan 1827.

LANDON, Asa Sr.
    Hannah, m. ---- Clawson. OC 13 March 1807.

LANDON, Heman of Augusta.
    Rebecca. OC 22 Sept 1812.
    John of Augusta. OC 2 April 1816. s. Henry?   [Cont'd]

LANDON, Heman - Cont'd
 William of Augusta. OC 3 June 1817.
 Heman of Augusta. OC 28 May 1817.
 Asa of Augusta. OC 2 June 1819.
 Thomas of Augusta. OC 6 Oct 1831.
 Guy of Augusta. OC 2 March 1825.

LANDON, Samuel of Augusta.
 Electa, m. Daniel Burritt of Augusta. OC 24 Sept 1799.
 Pamella, m. ---- Collins of Augusta.
 Reuben of Augusta. OC 25 July 1798.
 Sarah, m. Abel Wright of Elmsley. OC 5 Feb 1835.

LANG, John.
 Elizabeth, m. John Cline of Cornwall. OC 5 Jan 1798.

LAPP, Jeremiah of Kingston and Ernestown.
 Elizabeth, m. Nathan Williams of Hamilton. OC 23 Feb 1808, 5 Feb 1835.
 Rachel, m. James Williams of Hamilton. OC 26 March 1811.
 Jeremiah of Hamilton, m. Sarah Perry, 14 April 1814. OC 12 August
  1818. OC 20 April 1816 ?
 Samuel of Hamilton, m. Katharine Keller, 4 Apr 1813. OC 12 Aug 1818.
 Anthony of Thurlow. OC 26 Feb 1819.
 Richard of Hamilton. OC 2 Oct 1822.

LA ROQUE, Francois of Ernestown.
 Mary Ann, m. Armstrong Williams of Ernestown. OC 12 July 1798.
 Pierre of Ernestown, m. Betsy Marcles, 1 Feb 1796.
 Francois of St. Hyachinthe, District of Montreal. OC 12 July 1798, 19
  January 1836.

LARROWAY, Abraham of Louth.
 Adam of Louth. OC 14 Dec 1816.
 Sophia, m. Thomas McClaskey of Blenheim. OC 20 July 1837.

LARROWAY, Harmonus of Fredericksburgh and Grantham.
 Hannah, m. Boyle Travers of Grantham 12 Dec 1816. OC 23 June 1819.
 Charlotte, m. Joseph Vanderlip of Grantham. OC 7 Aug 1822.
 Jane, m. John Decow Jr. of Thorold. OC 4 Jan 1840.
 Peter H. of Sandwich. OC 18 Feb 1843.

LARROWAY, Isaac Sr. of Fredericksburgh. 2nd Batt., K. R. R. N. Y. md.
 Hannah. OC 24 Nov 1807.
 Lydia, m. John Keller of Fredericksburgh. OC 8 July 1797.
 Mary, m. Archibald Nicholson of Camden East. OC 8 July 1797.
 Isaac.
 Abraham of Fredericksburgh. m. Katharine Dies, 6 July 1790.

LARRAWAY, Jonas of Louth. [A Jonas Larraway served in Butler's Rangers
He and his family were at Niagara in 1783. The Ontario Register, 1: 198]
Mary, m. Lambert Acre of Grantham. OC 8 Oct 1796.
Jane, m. John Dennis of Thorold. OC 10 March 1804.
Dorothy, m. Harman Truax of Reach. OC 24 Sept 1840.

LARRAWAY, Peter of Fredericksburgh. m. Elizabeth Smith.
John Smith of Fredericksburgh, bapt. 11 Jan 1795. OC 26 Nov 1823.
Eleanor, b. 11 Oct 1800; m. Hugh Stephenson of Hallowell. OC 7 May 1828
Jane, bapt. 8 July 1792; m. Abraham Fry of Frederksbg. OC 19 July 1826.
Hannah, m. James Murray of Fredericksburgh 25 March 1822. OC 1850
    or 1851.
Elizabeth, b. 16 Aug 1804.

LA RUE, Henry of Yonge.
Mary. OC 4 June 1805.
Rebecca, m. Nathaniel Powers of Yonge. OC 16 Aug 1810.
Henry of Yonge. OC 24 Dec 1811.
Criness of Yonge. OC 19 May 1812.
Rachel, m. Horatio Bradshaw of Elizabethtown. O.C. 28 July 1836.

LA RUE, William of Yonge.
Eleanor, m. George Kerr of Yonge. OC 17 Jan 1839.
Phoebe, m. Edward Cassidy of Yonge. OC 7 Aug 1834.
Sarah. OC 7 Aug 1834.

LAUGHLIN, Alexander of Ernestown and Sidney.
Mary, m. John Lake of Loughborough. OC 27 Feb 1818.
John of Ernestown. OC 27 Feb 1818.
James of Ernestown, m. Elizabeth Davey. OC 5 Nov 1818.
Jacob of Camden East. OC 8 March 1820.
Colin of Madoc. OC 4 Sept 1834.
Duncan of Madoc. OC 4 Sept 1834.
Ronald of Rawdon. OC 4 Sept 1834.

LAWRENCE, George of Niagara. Died 1848. [Served in Butler's Rangers,
and was at Niagara in 1783. The Ontario Register, 1: 199]
William of Niagara. OC 19 Aug 1806.
John of Niagara. OC 20 Aug 1811.
Peter of Thorold. OC 20 May 1817.
Elizabeth, m. John Emmett of Grantham. OC 20 May 1817.
George of Niagara. OC 20 May 1817.
Benjamin of Niagara. OC 6 March 1822.
James of Niagara. OC 2 July 1829.

LAWRENCE, John of Niagara.
Francis of Niagara. OC 20 May 1817.

LAWRENCE, John of Augusta and Edwardsburgh, m. Margaret Switzer.
    Elizabeth, m. Robert Bickham of Wolford. OC 7 July 1802.
    Rebecca, m. David Breakenridge Jr. of Augusta. OC 7 July 1802.
    Agnes, bapt. 13 Feb 1789; m. Samuel Dulmage of Edwardsburgh. OC 28
      May 1811.
    John of Edwardsburgh. OC 13 June 1818.

LAWRENCE, Richard of York, Woodhouse, Southwold, Harwich.
    Margaret, m. Robert Johnston of Town of York 14 Dec 1813. OC 29 April
      1818.
    John of Darlington, blacksmith. OC 13 April 1819.
    Elizabeth, m. Elisha Tarbox of Markham. OC 15 Oct 1819.
    Mary Ann, m. Thomas Johnston of Town of York 10 Aug 1819. OC 19 Apr
      1820.
    Haddash. OC 28 Oct 1835. Trafalgar.
    Jane, m. Mathias Teetzel of Trafalgar. OC 4 July 1833.
    Rebecca, m. James Hamilton of Toronto. OC 7 March 1833.
    Richard of Trafalgar. OC 5 May 1831.

LAWSON, John J. of Ameliasburgh.
    John of Murray. OC 14 July 1819.
    Catherine, m. Henry S. Allard of Murray. OC 16 Feb 1830.
    Sarah, m. Job Young of Ameliasburgh. OC 1 Nov 1826.
    Phoebe, m. Aaron Pierson of Ameliasburgh. OC 22 June 1825.

LEAHY, William of Augusta.
    Onner, m. Duncan Grant of River Rideau (Marlborough). OC 30 Sept 1800.
    John. OC 26 May 1801.
    Robert. OC 26 May 1801.
    Elizabeth, m. John Trumbell of Elizabethtown. OC 26 May 1801.
    Phoebe, m. Daniel Sabens of Matilda. OC 19 April 1816.
    Gideon of Kitley. OC 8 Sept 1836.

LEECH, Catharine of Yonge.
    dau Catharine Munro, m. Thomas Proctor of Yonge. OC 5 March 1808.
    son Daniel Munro of Yonge. OC 23 Feb 1809.
    dau Sarah Ward, m. Cruth Paterson of Yonge. OC 23 Feb 1809.
    son Timothy Munro of Yonge. OC 24 Dec 1811.
    dau Freelove Golden, m. Walter Adams of Yonge. OC 25 Feb 1818.
    son John Munro of Yonge. OC 15 May 1835.

LEMON, John of Lancaster, m. Rachel McDonell.
    John of Lancaster, bapt. 27 March 1791. OC 7 May 1828.
    Richard of Lancaster. OC 7 May 1828.
    Jane, bapt. 29 March 1788; m. John McDonell of Lancaster. OC 6 Aug 1816.

LEMON, Joseph of Crowland.
    Mary, m. Joseph Ruth of Crowland. OC 22 May 1820.

LEWIS, Barent of Adolphustown.
   John B. of Adolphustown. OC 1 April 1840.
   Dorothy, m. ---- Hermanee of Adolphustown. OC 4 Feb 1836.
   Sarah N., m. George German of Adolphustown. OC 22 Feb 1834.

LEWIS, William.
   Thomas of Grantham. OC 7 May 1811.

LEWIS, William of Camden East, m. Elizabeth Babcock.
   Elizabeth, m. Joseph Pope of Adolphustown. OC 22 Feb 1810.
   Sarah, m. John Woheath of Camden East. OC 16 Feb 1810.
   William of Camden East. OC 16 Feb 1810.
   Samuel of Camden East. OC 16 Feb 1811.
   Kezia, m. Samuel Milligan of Camden East. OC 4 Nov 1818.
   Mary, m. Philip Snider of Camden East. OC 1 Nov 1820.
   Thaddeus of Camden East. OC 12 June 1834.
   Benjamin of Camden East. OC 2 Sept 1830.
   Rachel, m. John Pomeroy of Camden East. OC 24 Jan 1828.

LICKERS, Henry.
   Joseph of Grand River. OC 19 April 1820.

LIGHTHEART, Daniel of Adolphustown, Ernestown, and Darlington.
   Mary, m. Abel Conat Jr. of Darlington. OC 16 March 1802.
   Daniel of Darlington. OC 3 June 1817.
   Francis of Darlington. OC 2 Feb 1819.
   Isaac of Toronto. OC 10 March 1819.
   Jacob of Toronto. OC 14 May 1823.
   Elizabeth, m. Clariman Herriman. OC 12 Jan 1837.
   William of Toronto. OC 3 April 1834.

LINDSAY, James of Fredericksburgh and Thurlow, m.(1) Losina, dau of
   Simeon and Sarah Wright; m.(2) Hannah, dau of Everhart Wager, U.E.
   John of Fredericksburgh, bapt. 9 Feb 1789. OC 16 Feb 1811.
   Margaret, bapt. 7 June 1791; m. William Rogers of Fredericksburgh,
      22 March 1808. OC 25 Feb 1812.
   James of Fredericksburgh, bapt. 9 July 1797; OC 2 Apr 1823; 18 Mar 1818.
   Elizabeth, bapt. 10 July 1793; m. Andrew Huffman of Ernestown. OC 13
      June 1818.
   Lany, m. James McGrath of Thurlow. OC 16 June 1819.
   Jane, m. James Rogers of Marysburgh. OC 24 Feb 1820.
   Catharine, bapt. 29 Jan 1795; m. Gideon Rogers of Thurlow 29 March
      1814. OC 6 March 1821.
   William of Ameliasburgh. OC 8 Dec 1835.
   Ralph B. of Sidney. OC 4 Dec 1834.
   Ephraim of Thurlow. OC 3 May 1826.
   Thomas of Thurlow. OC 3 May 1826.   [Cont'd]

LINDSAY, James - Cont'd
Sarah, m. Henry Sinclair of Thurlow. OC 3 May 1826.

LINDSEY, John of Ernestown.
Lucius of Madoc. OC 27 Nov 1834.
Edison of Huntingdon. OC 4 Dec 1834.

LINK, John of Cornwall.
Mathias of Cornwall. OC 16 Feb 1811.
John of Cornwall. OC 16 Feb 1811.
Michael of Cornwall. OC 26 March 1817.
Noah Dickinson of Town of Prescott. OC 5 Feb 1835.
Catharine Eve, m. Daniel Myers of Matilda. OC 24 March 1835.
Mary Magdalen, m. Cyrus Teal of Matilda. OC 24 March 1835.
Elizabeth. OC 24 March 1835.
Jacob John of Prescott. OC 24 March 1835.
William of Cornwall. OC 6 Feb 1828.

LINK, Mathias of Osnabruck.
Catharine, m. John Waldroff of Osnabruck. OC 13 March 1807.
Lany, m. Jacob Smith Jr. of Ernestown. OC 5 June 1810.

LIPPINCOTT, Richard.
dau Esther Borden, m. George Taylor Denison of York 18 December 1806. OC 19 April 1808.

LITTLE, John of Sandwich.
Margaret, m. William Forsyth of Town of Sandwich. OC 13 June 1818.
James W. of Sandwich. OC 12 July 1820.
William of Sandwich. OC 6 April 1837.
Eliza, m. Nicholas Lyttle of Colchester. OC 7 March 1827.

LIVINGSTON, Daniel of Kitley.
William of Bastard. OC 14 Feb 1798.
John of Kitley. OC 11 Feb 1836. OC 7 July 1836.

LIVINGSTON, John.
Mary, m. Benjamin McIntosh of Charlottenburgh. OC 5 Jan 1798.

LOBDELL, Daniel of Kingston.
Elizabeth. OC 16 May 1818.
Frances, m. George Kenter of Kingston. OC 17 Dec 1836.
Jane, m. Andrew P. Shorts of Richmond. OC 2 Jan 1834.
Daniel of Loughborough. OC 10 Jan 1833.
Charlotte, m. Solomon Huff of Adolphustown. OC 5 Jan 1827.
Joseph of Ernestown. OC 22 June 1825.

LOCKWOOD, Benjamin of Glanford, m. Keziah Springer dau of David and
Margaret (Oliver) Springer. He died 1857, aged 86 y. 5 m. 8 d. His wife
died 28 March 1860, aged 83 y. 5 m. 4 d.
Sarah, m. James Fisher of Glanford. OC 28 July 1819.
Margaret, m. Jesse Bennett of Westminster 19 Oct 1826. OC 28 July 1820
Angeline, m. Anthony Stilts of Barton 4 Apr 1819. OC 26 July 1820.
Daniel of Carradoc, m. Hester Bateman 24 Nov 1828. OC 6 Dec 1832.
Keziah, m. James Nash of Carradoc 20 Nov 1832. OC 25 July 1833.
Henrietta, b. Feb., 1806; m. William B. Sampson of Mersea (Mosa), 25
    July 1825; d. 5 March 1862. OC 7 Aug 1834; OC 18 Feb 1843. Note:
    Henrietta B. Lockwood m. Wm B. Samson, 25 July 1825.
Mary, m. Archibald Miller of Delaware, 1831; d. 13 Oct 1887. OC 8
    December 1832.
Martha, m. Jonathan Miller of Ekfrid. OC 8 Dec 1832.
David of Carradoc. OC 8 Dec 1832.
Henry of Carradoc. OC 8 Dec 1832.

LOCKWOOD, Josiah.
Sarah, m. John Wagstaff of Town of Niagara. OC 10 March 1804.
James of York, tinsmith, m. Margaret Owen, 13 May 1810. OC 2 Jan 1811

LONDON, Batholemew of Pelham. Died February, 1801. See Moore, OC 12
May 1801. See Robertson's Landmarks, v. 6, p. 280.
Mehitabel, m. Andrew Whitsell of Pelham. OC 20 May 1817.
Richard of Saltfleet. OC 16 Feb 1837.
Hannah, m. John Cowell of Binbrook.
Catharine, m. John Richtenburgh of Saltfleet.
Jane, m. John McDavid of Saltfleet. OC 19 Jan 1833.

LORIMER, Francois.
Chevalier of Edwardsburgh. OC 23 Dec 1800.

LOSEE, Cornelius of Matilda.
Lavina, m. John Adam Friermouth Jr. of Lansdowne. OC 23 June 1836.
Elizabeth, m. William Robison of Bastard. OC 23 June 1836.
Mary, m. Charles W. Kendall of Lansdowne. OC 23 June 1836.

LOSEE, Joshua of Matilda.
James of Matilda. OC 20 March 1807.
Charity, m. William Soules of Matilda. OC 26 Jan 1808.
Elizabeth, m. Oliver Everts of Augusta. OC 22 Sept 1812.

LOTT, John Sr. of Thurlow and Sidney.
Peter. OC 30 Aug 1797. OC 27 Nov 1834.
Elizabeth, m. Gottlieb Mikel of Ameliasburgh. OC 6 July 1798.
Battis of Sidney. OC 28 July 1801.
Margaret, m. John McMullin of Sidney. OC 25 Oct 1803.
John of Sidney. OC 27 November 1834.   [Cont'd]

LOTT, John - Cont'd
Catharine, m. Charles Rogge of Town of Kingston. OC 18 March 1818.
Catharine, spinster of Thurlow. OC 17 March 1836.

LOTTRIDGE, Robert.
William of Saltfleet. OC 21 April 1798.
Elizabeth, m. William Wier of Grand River. OC 9 March 1837.
George of Saltfleet.
John of Saltfleet.
Robert of Saltfleet.

LOUCKS, Abraham of Fredericksburgh, m. Anne Kemp.
Catharine, m. Garrett Kimmerly of Richmond. OC 25 Feb 1809.
George of Fredericksburgh. OC 18 May 1833.
Hannah, m. James Van Alstine of Fredericksburgh. OC 18 May 1833.
Jacob of Fredericksburgh, bapt. 26 Nov 1792. OC 1 Aug 1827.
Elizabeth, bapt. 2 Nov 1794; m. Joseph Prevost of Hallowell. OC 16 Mar
    1825.
John, bapt. 11 Dec 1796.
Abraham K. of Fredericksburgh, bapt. 3 June 1807. OC 31 May 1830.
Charles of Fredericksburgh, bapt. 2 Sept 1810. OC 7 March 1833.
Abraham, b. 28 April 1800.
Peggy, b. 3 Apr 1805; m. ---- Warner of Fredericksburgh. OC 2 Jan 1829.
Isaac of Fredericksburgh. OC 7 March 1833.

LOUCKS, George of Fredericksburgh, m. Sarah Lyons, 26 Nov 1792.
Thomas L. of Camden East. OC 15 March 1838.
Mary, bapt. 29 Sept 1799; m. Frederick Conway of Camden 18 April 1821.
    OC 8 May 1833.
Francis of Camden, bapt. 17 Feb 1811. OC 8 May 1833.
Esther, bapt. 14 July 1805; m. George Clark of Camden. OC 8 May 1833.
Jacob of Sheffield, bapt. 7 Aug 1808. OC 18 May 1833.
John, bapt. 16 Nov 1794.
Susanna, bapt. 11 Dec 1796; m. John Shorts of Sophiasburgh. OC 19 July
    1826.
Catharine, b. 21 March 1802; m. ---- Conway of Sheffield. OC 12 June
    1834.

LOUCKS, Jacob of Osnabruck.
Elizabeth, m. Michael Empey of Osnabruck. OC 4 July 1815.
Jacob of Osnabruck. OC 18 March 1818.
Mary, m. James Barnhart. OC 9 Feb 1832.

LOUCKS, Joseph of Osnabruck and Williamsburgh.
Peter J. of Osnabruck. OC 19 April 1816.
Mary, m. Barney Reed of Augusta. OC 20 May 1817.
Henry of Williamsburgh. OC 3 June 1817.
John of Williamsburgh. OC 13 Nov 1818.   [Cont'd]

LOUCKS, Joseph - Cont'd
  Jacob of Williamsburgh. OC 6 Nov 1834.
  Nancy, m. William Dafoe of Williamsburgh. OC 2 Feb 1825.
  Joseph J. of Williamsburgh. OC 2 Feb 1825.

LOUCKS, Nicholas of Matilda.
  Margaret, m. Richard F. Powers of York. OC 21 July 1801.
  Abraham of Fredericksburgh. Oldest son.

LOUCKS, Richard.
  Nancy, m. John Crysler of Williamsburgh. OC 25 Feb 1806.
  Catharine, m. Nicholas Ault of Osnabruck. OC 25 Feb 1806.
  Adam of Osnabruck. OC 20 March 1807.

LOW, John of Sophiasburgh, m. Susan.
  Peter of Sophiasburgh. OC 25 Feb 1812.
  Phoebe, m. Comfort Wood of Hallowell. OC 25 Feb 1812.
  John of Sophiasburgh. OC 28 April 1812.
  Mehitable, m. ---- Brayley of Kingston. OC 31 Oct 1821.
  Susan. (Idiot) OC 11 Oct 1830.

LOYD, Daniel of Fredericksburgh, m. Dorothy.
  Thomas of Fredericksburgh, bapt. 5 Feb 1792. OC 20 Feb 1809.
  Edward of Fredericksburgh, bapt. 9 Jan 1791. OC 25 Feb 1812.
  Elizabeth, bapt. 6 March 1796; m. John Sills of Fredericksburgh. OC 13
      June 1818.
  John D. of Fredericksburgh, bapt. 5 Feb 1792. OC 2 April 1823.
  Daniel of Fredericksburgh, bapt. 13 May 1798. OC 18 Feb 1824.
  Adam of Thurlow, bapt. 12 Apr 1801; m. Isabella Clark. OC 16 Feb 1837.
  Catharine, bapt. 1 Jan 1794.
  Layna, buried 22 Jan 1795.

LOYD, George Henry of Fredericksburgh, m. Catharine Young, 5 Aug 1792.
  Elmida Margaret, m. Henry Ruttan of Sophiasburgh. OC 7 Feb 1839.
  Jacob of Fredericksburgh. OC 18 June 1840.
  Laney, m. Amos Caverly of Sidney. OC 6 Aug 1840.
  Benjamin of Thurlow, bapt. 17 March 1799. OC 21 May 1834.
  John Caleb of Fredericksburgh, bapt. 19 March 1809. OC 18 Feb 1834.
  George of Fredericksburgh, bapt. 3 July 1803. OC 18 Feb 1834.
  Richard of Fredericksburgh, bapt. 8 Feb 1797. OC 18 Feb 1834.
  Elizabeth, bapt. 20 Jan 1811; m. William Van Koughnet of Fredericks-
      burgh. OC 18 Feb 1834.
  Nelson of Fredericksburgh, bapt. 25 April 1813. OC 3 April 1834.
  Stephen of Thurlow, bapt. 22 Feb 1807. OC 30 May 1834.
  Edward of Fredericksburgh, bapt. 3 May 1795(?) OC 21 May 1834.
  Henry, bapt. 27 Oct 1793; buried 12 Feb 1794.
  Elsie, m. ---- Hazzard of Madoc. OC 27 Nov 1834.
  Mary, m. John Keller of Fredericksburgh. OC 8 Jan 1835.

LOYD, Richard of Fredericksburgh, m. Mary Maybee, 3 June 1791.
  Elizabeth, bapt. 1 Jan 1794; m. John Scriver of Fredericksburgh, 3 Feb
    1810. OC 6 Feb 1822. See OC 8 Dec 1840.

LOYST, Andrew of Fredericksburgh.
  Catherine C., m. Alexander Stalker of Sheffield. OC 22 Sept 1836.
  Jane, m. Conrad Dafoe of Sidney. OC 28 Oct 1835.
  Margaret, m. ---- Peterson of Ameliasburgh. OC 5 Nov 1835.
  Eleanor. OC 26 May 1836.
  Deborah, m. Francis Gangon of Richmond. OC 19 Dec 1833.
  Elizabeth, m. William McKim of Sheffield. OC 19 Dec 1833.
  Andrew of Richmond. OC 19 Dec 1833.
  Isaiah of Sheffield. OC 19 Dec 1833.
  Joseph of Sheffield. OC 19 Dec 1833.
  Nancy, bapt. 11 Dec 1792; m. Henry Paddleford of Sheffield. O.C. 19
    Dec 1833.
  Mary, m. ---- Batty of Haldimand Twp. OC 1 Feb 1826.

LOYST, Henry of Fredericksburgh.
  Abraham of Fredericksburgh. OC 14 June 1838.
  John of Fredericksburgh. OC 18 Oct 1838.
  Henry of Fredericksburgh. OC 6 Aug 1840.
  Eleanor, m. Philip Garrison of Fredericksburgh. OC 27 Feb 1834.
  Deborah. OC 27 Feb 1834.
  William, bapt. 2 June 1791.
  Elizabeth, m. John Garrison of Richmond. OC 27 Nov 1834.
  Peter of Fredericksburgh. OC 22 June 1825.

LUCAS, Amos of Fredericksburgh.
  Mary, m. Simeon King of Fredericksburgh. O.C. 16 Feb 1811.
  George. Bapt. Fredericksburgh 13 Nov 1787.
  Daniel. See OC 24 April 1833.
  Susanna, m. Johann Georg Schmitt, later called John George Smith.

LUTES, Sampson of Niagara.
  George of Delaware. OC 8 Oct 1805.
  Sarah, m. Richard Harris of Grantham. OC 10 May 1797.

LYMBURNER, John of Caistor.
  Levina, m. Merrit Johnson of Caistor. OC 29 Aug 1839.
  Margaret, m. Conrad Dennis of Thorold. OC 20 July 1837.
  Almira, m. Stephen Swick of Caistor. OC 20 July 1837.
  Catharine, m. David Smith of Caistor. OC 20 July 1837.
  James of Caistor. OC 20 July 1837.
  John of Caistor. OC 20 July 1837.
  Jonathan of Caistor. OC 20 July 1837.

LYMBURNER, Margaret of Caistor.
  William of Etobicoke. OC 29 May 1807.   [Cont'd]

LYMBURNER, Margaret - Cont'd
    Robert of Etobicoke. OC 29 May 1807.
    Nancy, m(1) Andrew Clark of York. OC 18 June 1807. m(2) -- McPherson.
    James of York. OC 13 Oct 1807.
    Alexander of York. OC 13 Oct 1807.
    Mathew of Caistor. OC 30 Oct 1810. m. ---- Young.
    John of Caistor.

LYMBURNER, Mathew of Niagara; m. a dau of Jacob Young, Sgt., Rogers'
Rangers.
    William of Ancaster. OC 28 July 1836.
    Robert of Caistor. OC 4 Feb 1836.
    Caroline, m. Henry Fonger of Ancaster. OC 3 April 1834.
    Hiram of Caistor. OC 6 Aug 1829.
    Christopher of Canborough. OC 7 July 1831.
    Sarah, m. George Johnson of Ancaster. OC 7 July 1831.
    Michael of Caistor. OC 7 July 1831.
    Jacob of Caistor. OC 7 July 1831.
    Mathew of Vaughan. OC 6 Aug 1828.

Mc

McARTHUR, Archibald of Charlottenburgh.
    Arthur of Charlottenburgh. OC 28 July 1836.
    Peter of Charlottenburgh. OC 28 July 1836.
    Donald of Charlottenburgh. OC 11 Aug 1836.

McARTHUR, Donald of Charlottenburgh.
    Catharine, m. ---- Grant of Charlottenburgh. OC 21 Sept 1800.
    Peter of Charlottenburgh. OC 6 Oct 1819.

McARTHUR, John of Thurlow. Soldier, Loyal Rangers.
    Charles of Murray. OC 23 June 1801.

McARTHUR, Peter of Charlottenburgh.
    Elizabeth. OC 23 June 1836.
    Elspy. OC 18 Aug 1836.
    Catharine, m. John McArthur of Charlottenburgh. OC 28 Oct 1835.
    Mary, m. Robert McNaughton of Kenyon. OC 8 Dec 1835.
    John of Charlottenburgh. OC 14 April 1836.
    Christian, m. John Baker of Town of Kingston. OC 8 Jan 1835.

MACAULAY, Robert of Town of Kingston, m. Ann dau of John Kirby Sr. and
sister of the Hon. John Kirby. She d. at Kingston 20 Jan 1850 aged 80 yrs.
    Hon. John of Town of Kingston; m. Helen McPherson, 23 Oct 1833; died
        at Kingston 10 Aug 1857 in 65th yr. OC 16 May 1818.
    Robert of Kingston. OC 28 June 1820.   [Cont'd]

MACAULAY, Robert - Cont'd
Rev. William of Hamilton, m. Anne Catharine Geddes. m. (2) Charlotte
Sarah, 2nd dau of Capt. Henry Le Vesconte, R. N. , of Seymour, 4 Jan
1853. O. C. 1 Oct 1823.

McBEAN, Donald of Charlottenburgh.
Nancy. Land Board Certificate, 12/2 Kenyon.

McBEAN, Gilles of Cornwall.
Benjamin of Cornwall. OC 20 May 1817.
Gilles of Cornwall. OC 20 May 1817.
Emelia. OC 18 Aug 1819.
Ann, m. Richard Anderson of Cornwall. OC 18 Aug 1819.
Catharine, m. Gabriel G. Worden of Town of Cornwall. OC 25 July 1833.

McCAFFREY, John.
Mary, m. ---- De Groote. OC 11 July 1799.

McCALL, Donald of Charlotteville.
Elizabeth, m. ---- Fairchild of Charlotteville. OC 11 Nov 1800.
Catharine, m. James Munro of Charlotteville. OC 8 July 1801.
James of Charlotteville. OC 18 Feb 1806.
Mary, m. Ephraim Cole Mitchell of Charlotteville. OC 23 Jan 1811.
Hugh of Charlotteville. OC 19 Feb 1817.

McCLELLAN, William of Stamford.
John of Stamford. OC 13 July 1796.
William of Stamford. OC 16 April 1811.
Jane, m. William Howard. OC 7 Aug 1811.

McCOLLUM, James of Gainsborough, m. (1) Sarah Campbell. m. (2) Eunice
French. See O. H. S. v. 6, p. 86.
Daniel of Gainsborough. OC 7 Nov 1809.
Peter of Grimsby, m. Mary Campbell. OC 7 Nov 1809.
Sally, m. Isaac Carroll of Glanford. OC 16 Aug 1810.
Joseph of Gainsborough. OC 11 Dec 1810.
John of Gainsborough, b. 30 Jan 1773; m. Sarah Sternberg. OC 16 Apr 1811.
Elizabeth, m. William Land of Nelson. OC 3 June 1817.
Mary, m. Christopher Row of Flamborough West. OC 20 May 1817.
Margaret, m. Robert Donaldson of Niagara. O. C 29 June 1838.
Rachel, m. Alexander Campbell of Esquesing. OC 4 May 1836.
Stephen of Trafalgar. OC 7 Aug 1828.

McCOOL, Archibald, m. Margaret.
Margaret, m. ---- Walker of Townsend. OC 1 Sept 1801.
Mary, m. (1) ---- Daugherty. m (2) John Wells of Townsend. OC 24 Feb
1801.
Martha, m. John McCall of Charlotteville. OC 1 Sept 1801.

McCORMICK, Alexander of Colchester.
   William of Colchester, m. Mary Cornwall. OC 30 June 1819.
   Elizabeth. OC 30 June 1819.
   Mary, m. John Farriss of Colchester. OC 21 Feb 1821.
   Mathew of Colchester. OC 21 Feb 1821.
   Alexander of Colchester. OC 21 Feb 1821.
   John of Colchester. OC 21 Feb 1821.
   Ann, m. ---- Stockwell of Colchester. OC 21 Feb 1821.

McCREADY, David of Elizabethtown. He was born 10 Feb 1752; resided most
   of early life in town of Whitehorn, Wigtonshire, Scotland; came to America
   in 1774 and settled in town of Half Moon, Saratoga Co., N.Y.; came to
   Elizabethtown in 1795. He died at Brockville on 11 Feb 1819. His wife,
   Katharine Donnan was born 15 April 1741, d. 21 June 1829 at Brockville.
   David of Elizabethtown, b. at Half Moon, N.Y. 25 Oct 1780; m. Mary
      Clow. OC 20 May 1817.
   Margaret, b. Half Moon, N.Y., 5 June 1783; m. Nehemiah Seaman of
      Elizabethtown. OC 20 May 1817.
   Anthony of Elizabethtown, b. Half Moon, N.Y., 25 Jan 1778; m. Rachel
      Buell; d. 18 Feb 1853. OC 31 July 1817.
   Jane, b. Whitehorn, Scotland, 19 July 1773.
   John of Elizabethtown, b. Half Moon, N.Y., 6 June 1775; m. Anne Grant.
      OC 3 July 1798.

McCRIMMON, Donald of Marysburgh (Binbrook, 1831)
   John of Marysburgh. OC 16 Aug 1810.
   Catharine, m. Oliver Crouse of Marysburgh. OC 25 Feb 1812.
   Elizabeth, m. Augustus Miller of Town of Kingston. OC 23 Nov 1816.
   John of Hallowell. OC 13 Nov 1818.
   Duncan of Hallowell. OC 14 July 1819.
   Nancy, m. Samuel Ryckman of Town of Hamilton. OC 3 Nov 1831.
   Archibald of Binbrook. OC 7 Jan 1830.
   Daniel of Hallowell. OC 23 Feb 1830.
   William of Hallowell. OC 3 April 1830.
   Peter of Marysburgh. OC 14 Sept 1825.

McCUE, William of Yonge.
   Mahala, m. Elijah Weller of Yonge. OC 5 March 1811. OC 21 Mar 1844.
   John of Yonge. OC 14 Dec 1816.
   Abraham of Yonge. OC 19 Sept 1839.
   Peter of Yonge. OC 8 Dec 1835.
   Mary. OC 5 Sept 1833.
   Catharine, m. Jarry Pattison of Yonge. OC 5 Sept 1833.
   Charlotte, m. ---- Dowsley. OC 7 Aug 1828.
   William of Port Hope. OC 6 Sept 1826.

MACDONALD, Adam of Edwardsburgh.
   Jacob of Edwardsburgh. OC 2 May 1833.

MACDONALD, Adam - Cont'd
Mary, m. James Duncan of Edwardsburgh. OC 2 May 1833.
Catharine, m. Samuel McDonell. OC 8 May 1833.
James of Edwardsburgh. OC 9 May 1834.
Philip of Edwardsburgh. OC 9 May 1834.
Fanny, m. Benjamin Duperont of Edwardsburgh. OC 7 Feb 1833.
Daniel of Edwardsburgh. OC 10 Dec 1832.
Adam of Edwardsburgh. OC 8 Dec 1832.
Elizabeth, m. Benjamin Buchanan. OC 8 Dec 1832.
John of Edwardsburgh. OC 8 Dec 1832.

McDONALD, Allan of Gainsborough. Sgt., Butler's Rangers. Surveyor. OC
14 June 1794. OC 8 March 1808. M. Ann, dau George Fields, U.E.
Alexander of Gainsborough. OC 19 April 1808.
Hannah, m. John Lipicombe of Howard. OC 12 July 1808.

McDONALD, Donald of Ernestown.
Roderick of Murray. OC 27 Aug 1840.

McDONALD, Duncan of W. half 12/4 Charlottenburgh. OC 31 May 1830.
Angus of Moore. OC 1 July 1830.
Donald of Charlottenburgh. OC 1 July 1830.

McDONALD, Randall of Newark.
Catharine, m. Nathan J. Fowler of Haldimand County. OC 8 July 1806.

McDONALD, Roderick of Cornwall.
John. OC 13 Jan 1832.
Barbara. OC 13 Jan 1832.
Donald. OC 13 Jan 1832.
Mary. OC 13 Jan 1832.

McDONELL, Alexander (Aberchalder) Capt. 1st Batt., R.R.N.Y.
Helen, m. Richard N. Wilkinson of Cornwall, 10 May 1792. OC 11 July
1796.
John, b. 1758, Inverness-shire, Scotland. Capt., Butler's Rangers. OC
17 August 1795.
Hugh. Lt., 1st Batt., K.R.R.N.Y.
Chichester. Lt., Butler's Rangers.
Janet, m. Alexander (Greenfield) McDonell of Glengarry 6 Feb 1769; died
23 January 1788 aged 36.
Isabel, m. Capt. Andrew Ross, 31st Reg't, about 1779.

McDONELL, Alexander (Bane) of Charlottenburgh.
Jenet. OC 14 Nov 1821.
Allan Bane of Charlottenburgh. OC 14 Nov 1821.
John of Charlottenburgh. OC 14 Nov 1821.
Ranald of Charlottenburgh. OC 14 Nov 1821.

McDONELL, Alexander (Ben Beg) of 23/9 Charlottenburgh.
Alexander of Charlottenburgh. OC 13 Nov 1818.
Eleanor, m. Ewen Kennedy of Charlottenburgh. OC 13 Nov 1818.
Angus of Charlottenburgh. OC 13 Nov 1818.

McDONELL, Alexander (Black) of W. half 12/1 Charlottenburgh. K.R.R.N.Y.
Gillis of Charlottenburgh. OC 28 April 1815.
Mary. OC 28 April 1815.
Ranald of Charlottenburgh. OC 23 Nov 1816.
John of Charlottenburgh. OC 23 July 1823.
Alexander of Charlottenburgh. OC 31 Oct 1809.

McDONELL, Alexander (Deaf), E. half 10 south side Middle Branch, River
aux Raisins, Cornwall. Died prior to November 1815.
John of Cornwall. OC 14 Jan 1812.
Angus of Cornwall. OC 14 Jan 1812.
Allan of Cornwall. OC 11 Nov 1815.
Christy, m. Duncan Scott of Cornwall. OC 11 Nov 1815.
Alexander of Cornwall. OC 23 Nov 1816.
Mary, m. John McPherson of Charlottenburgh. OC 23 Nov 1816.
Catharine. OC 23 Nov 1816.

McDONELL, Alexander (King's Son) of Cornwall.
Alexander of Cornwall. OC 2 Feb 1819.
Catharine, m. Archibald McDonell of Cornwall, Ass't Adj. Gen. of Militia.
OC 7 Feb 1821.
Janet, m. (1) Alexander McMillan of Cornwall. OC 7 Feb 1821. m. (2)
Duncan McDonell of St. Andrews, Cornwall, lumber merchant.

McDONELL, Alexander (Roy). E. half 12/Front, Charlottenburgh. In Nov.,
1785, family consisted of himself and wife.
Jennet, m. Duncan McDougall of Lancaster. OC 7 Aug 1811.
John of Charlottenburgh. OC 28 April 1815.
Margaret. OC 28 April 1815.
Mary. OC 23 Nov 1816.
Allen of Charlottenburgh. OC 25 Feb 1818.
Donald of Charlottenburgh. OC 12 July 1820.
James of Charlottenburgh. OC 23 July 1823.
Hugh of Charlottenburgh. Land Board Certificate, 13/6 Lochiel.

McDONELL, Alexander (McIain) of Charlottenburgh.
Ann. OC 3 March 1809.
Catharine, m. Angus McDonell of Charlottenburgh. OC 3 March 1809.

McDONELL, Alexander of Black River. (McRail). K.R.R.N.Y.
Duncan of Charlottenburgh. OC 25 June 1807.
Margaret. OC 25 June 1807.

McDONELL, Alexander of E. half 9/1 Charlottenburgh. OC 7 Dec 1802. In November 1785, family consisted of himself, wife and 1 child.
  Elizabeth. OC 6 Aug 1816.
  Amelia, m. Alexander McGillis of Charlottenburgh. OC 6 Aug 1816.
  Marjery, m. John McDonell of Charlottenburgh. OC 23 July 1823.
  Angus of Charlottenburgh. OC 28 July 1836.
  Nelly, m. Thomas Murphy of Charlottenburgh. OC 29 Sept 1824.

McDONELL, Alexander (Simcoe) of Charlottenburgh.
  Alexander of Charlottenburgh. OC 11 Jan 1834.
  Catharine. OC 11 Jan 1834.
  Mary, m. Lewis McDonnell of Charlottenburgh. OC 27 Feb 1834.

McDONELL, Alexander of 45/Front, south side River aux Raisins Lancaster.
  Eleanor, m. ---- McLellan of Lancaster. OC 10 March 1801.

McDONELL, Alexander of East half 45, north branch River aux Raisins, Charlottenburgh.
  Hugh of Charlottenburgh. OC 25 Feb 1812.

McDONELL, Alexander of Charlottenburgh. Corp'l, Queen's Rangers.
  Jennet. OC 6 Aug 1816.
  John of Charlottenburgh. OC 23 Nov 1816.

McDONELL, Allan (Collachie), Capt. 84th Regt. Died at Quebec in 1792, aet. 80.
  Catharine, b. about 1771; m. Miles McDonell of Scothouse, Feb., 1798; d. August, 1799. OC 13 July 1796.
  Alexander of York, Lt., Butler's Rangers; b. Inverness, Scotland, 1762; d. 18 March 1842. OC 16 Oct 1792.
  Angus of Yorktown, First Clerk, Leg. Assembly; d. October, 1804.
  James, Ensign, 84th Regt. & Capt. 43 Regt. Died prior to March, 1807.
  Henrietta, m. ---- MacLean, Surgeon in Army.

McDONELL, Allan (Lundy) of Elizabethtown and Charlottenburgh. Commissary at Oswegatchie.
  Helen, m. James Mackenzie of Three Rivers, L.C. OC 13 Nov 1822.

McDONNELL, Allan of Kingston, m. Helen.
  Isabella, m. Donald McDonell of Town of Kingston. OC 9 May 1797.
  Mary, m. John Frederick Dame of Niagara (Three Rivers). OC 16 May 1797.
  Helen, m. Donald Kennedy of Glengarry County. OC 16 May 1797.
  Henrietta, m. Alexander Fisher of Adolphustown. OC 16 May 1797.

McDONELL, Allan of Matilda (Leek), Capt. Lt. 1st Batt., K.R.R.N.Y.; b. 1744; m. Margery; d. 1829. Brother to Rev. Roderick, Capt. Arch'd, 1st K.R.R.N.Y.; Lt. Ranald 2nd K.R.R.N.Y. [Cont'd]

McDONELL, Allan of Matilda - Cont'd
  Catharine, m. Simon Fraser (explorer). OC 25 Feb 1812.
  Mary, m. Richard Duncan Fraser of Edwardsburgh. OC 25 Feb 1812.
  James of Matilda, b. 1795; m. Amelia, widow of Wm Jones, 1835; died
      31 Aug 1847. OC 5 Oct 1818.
  John of Matilda, 1788 - 1833. Capt. Inc. Militia. Hon. OC 28 April 1815.
  Jane, m. Alexander Grant of Longueuil. OC 26 March 1817.
  Isabella, m. Angus McDonell of Lochiel. OC 26 Jan 1837.

McDONELL, Allan of E. half 17/2 Charlottenburgh.
  Alexander of Charlottenburgh. OC 23 June 1837.

McDONELL, Allen (Gray) of Charlottenburgh.
  Archibald of Charlottenburgh. OC 4 Feb 1819.

McDONELL, Allen of Charlottenburgh.
  Nancy, m. Alexander McDonell. OC 16 April 1799.

McDONELL, Andrew of Edwardsburgh.
  Almira. OC 28 Oct 1833.
  Anne, m. Abner Nettleton of Edwardsburgh. OC 28 Oct 1833.

McDONELL, Angus (Og) of W. half 18/5 (4 or 5), south side Middle Branch,
  River Aux Raisins, Cornwall. Soldier, 84th Regt.
  Mary. OC 4 July 1815.
  Alexander of Cornwall. OC 4 July 1815.
  Isabella. OC 11 Nov 1815.
  Margaret, m. John McDougall of Cornwall. OC 19 Feb 1817.
  Mary. OC 5 Nov 1818.
  Catharine. OC 5 Nov 1818.
  Isabella. OC 5 Nov 1818.
  Angus of Cornwall. OC 5 Feb 1823.
  John Roy of Cornwall. OC 5 Feb 1823.
  Nancy, m. Duncan McDonell of Cornwall. OC 2 Feb 1825.

McDONELL, Angus of W. half 14/5, south side Middle Branch, River aux
  Raisins, Cornwall. 84th Regt.
  Lauchlin of Cornwall. OC 15 March 1803.
  Catharine. OC 4 July 1815.
  Angus of Cornwall. OC 17 Feb 1816.
  John of Cornwall. OC 3 Dec 1835.
  Mary, m. Donald McDonell of Cornwall. OC 5 Jan 1798.

McDONELL, Angus. Capt., K.R.R.N.Y. See petition of Isabella McNabb,
  26 May 1801.

McDONELL, Lt. Archibald of Marysburgh.
  Niece, Isabella McDonell, 35/4 Marysburgh. Land Board Certificate.

McDONELL, Archibald (Leek) of Osnabruck. 1 & 2/1 Osnabruck. Capt. R. R.
N. Y., 1st Batt. Land in Hawkesbury, see OC 1 July 1797. Married Anne.
Died prior to February 1816.
  James Fraser of Cornwall. OC 28 Feb 1809.
  John of Cornwall, 8/13 Manvers. OC 17 Feb 1816.
  Isabella, m. ---- Walker. OC 19 April 1816.
  Ann, m. Hon. Alexander Fraserfield Fraser of Charlottenburgh. Died in
    1861. OC 28 July 1819.
  Mary, m. Lt. Donald AE. McDonell of Cornwall, H. P. 98th Regt., 4
    March 1819; d. 28 July 1882, Scothouse. OC 21 Feb 1821.
  Harriet, m. Duncan Greenfield McDonell of Charlottenburgh. OC 18 Sept
    1822.
  Helen. OC 18 Aug 1824.

McDONELL, Lt. Chichester, m. Flora McMillan.
  Anne, bapt. 20 July 1788.

McDONELL, Christian of Haldimand County, m. Susannah. Killed at Chippa-
wa, 1812-14.
  Susannah, m. James Logan of Haldimand Co. OC 12 July 1820.
  Elizabeth, m. John Farr of Cayuga. OC 4 Jan 1840.
  James of Dunn. OC 20 Feb 1840.
  John of Haldimand Co. OC 1 Aug 1827.

McDONELL, Daniel of Augusta.
  Rachel, m. James Hayes of Fredericksburgh. OC 28 Oct 1835.
  Clarissa. OC 28 Oct 1835.
  James of Ernestown. OC 26 May 1836.

McDONELL, Donald of Town of Kingston, m. Isabella dau Allan McDonell,
U. E., of Kingston.
  Mary, m. Peter Parry of Ernestown, 25 June 1805. OC 27 Feb 1806.
  Alexander of Hamilton. OC 24 Dec 1817.
  Isabella. OC 18 March 1818. Adolphustown.
  Elizabeth, m. John Baptiste Prynia of Marysburgh. OC 1 May 1834.

McDONELL, Donald of 1/9 Charlottenburgh.
  Ann, m. John McDonell of 7/8 Charlottenburgh. OC 16 June 1807.

McDONELL, Donald (Ban).
  Ronald of Wolfe Island. OC 22 May 1832.

McDONELL, Donald of 19/5 Charlottenburgh.
  Allan of Charlottenburgh. OC 20 May 1817.

McDONELL, Donald of W. half 2/2 Charlottenburgh.
  Mary. OC 6 Aug 1816.
  John of Charlottenburgh. OC 23 Nov 1816.   [Cont'd]

McDONELL, Donald - Cont'd
Catharine, m. Richard O'Keefe of Charlottenburgh. OC 26 Feb 1818.
Margaret, m. Donald McQueen of Charlottenburgh. OC 7 Jan 1824.

McDONELL, Donald of Charlottenburgh. Corp., 1st Batt., K. R. R. N. Y.
Elizabeth. OC 26 March 1817.
Alexander of Charlottenburgh. OC 20 May 1817.
Hugh of Charlottenburgh. OC 20 May 1817.
John of Charlottenburgh. OC 20 May 1817.
Ann, m. (1) Alexander McLeod. m. (2) John Fallon. OC 17 Oct 1828.

McDONELL, Donald of 12/5 Cornwall.
Duncan of Cornwall. OC 5 March 1828.

McDONELL, Donald of W. half 12/ , south side Middle Branch, River aux
Raisins, Cornwall.
Alexander of Cornwall, innkeeper. OC 7 Feb 1821. OC 25 Jan 1831.

McDONELL, Donald, 19/2 s. b. River aux Raisins, Charlottenburgh.
Mary. OC 10 March 1801.

McDONELL, Donald of W. half 22/4, south side River aux Raisins, Cornwall.
James of Cornwall. OC 4 July 1815.
John of Cornwall. OC 4 July 1815.
Sarah. OC 4 July 1815.
Alexander of Cornwall. OC 25 Feb 1818.
Angus of Cornwall. OC 16 June 1819.
Margaret, m. John McDonell of Lancaster. OC 2 Feb 1825.

McDONELL, Donald of 4/5 Cornwall. Soldier, 84th Regt.
Elizabeth, m. Alexander McDonell of Charlottenburgh. OC 6 Aug 1816.
Ann, m. Donald McDonell of Cornwall. OC 6 Aug 1816.
Sarah. OC 6 Aug 1816.
Mary, m. Alexander Scott of Cornwall. OC 6 Aug 1816.

McDONELL, Donald of E. half 1/ , south side River aux Raisins, Char-
lottenburgh.
John of Kenyon. OC 6 Aug 1816.
Angus of Charlottenburgh. OC 6 Aug 1816.
Duncan of Kenyon. OC 6 Aug 1816. 6/13 Manvers.

McDONELL, Donald of 4/ , south side Middle Branch River aux Raisins,
Cornwall. Corp., 84th Regt.
Ranald of Cornwall. OC 23 Nov 1816.

McDONELL, Donald of 4/ , south side River aux Raisins, Cornwall. Served
84th Regt.
Duncan of Cornwall. OC 23 Nov 1816.

McDONELL, Duncan of 17/5 south side Middle Branch River aux Raisins, Cornwall. Soldier, 84th Regt.
    Caty, m. Roswell Cook of Edwardsburgh. OC 25 Feb 1812. OC 13 Feb 1816
    Jane. OC 11 Nov 1815.
    Stephen of Cornwall. OC 3 Dec 1828.
    John of Cornwall. OC 4 July 1815.

McDONELL, Duncan of W. half 19 south side River aux Raisins, Cornwall.
    Angus. Land Board Certificate, 13/6 Lochiel.

McDONELL, Duncan (Glass) of N. half 6/ , south side River aux Raisins, Cornwall.
    Ranald of Cornwall. OC 25 Jan 1831.

McDONELL, Farquhar.
    Margaret, m. ---- Morgan. OC 30 June 1801.

McDONELL, Finnan of 24/6 Lancaster, formerly of Charlottenburgh. Sgt., 84th Regt. Md. Anne dau William Cameron of Charlottenburgh. See O.C. 4 September 1834.
    Ann, m. John MacKinnon of Lancaster. OC 7 Aug 1811.
    Mary. OC 2 March 1816.
    Isabella, m. John McDougall of Charlottenburgh. OC 6 Aug 1816.
    Donald of Lancaster. OC 3 June 1817.
    Mary, m. Donald McDonell of Lancaster. OC 24 Feb 1820.
    Catharine, m. Allan Williams of Lochiel. OC 12 Feb 1831.
    Malcolm of Lancaster. OC 16 Aug 1831.

McDONELL, Hugh. Soldier, K.R.R.N.Y., Capt. John McKenzie's Co.
    John of Charlottenburgh. OC 4 July 1798.

McDONELL, Hugh, of E. half 51/ , River aux Raisins, Charlottenburgh.
    Catharine, m. Donald McPherson of Charlottenburgh. OC 28 April 1815.
    William of Charlottenburgh. OC 19 Feb 1817.

McDONNELL, Hugh of Charlottenburgh.
    Donald of Charlottenburgh. OC 5 March 1828.
    Margaret. OC 5 March 1828.

McDONELL, Hugh of Lot C/4 Roxborough. Soldier, K.R.R.N.Y.
    Mary, m. Alexander Chisholm of Cornwall. OC 24 March 1819.

McDONELL, Hugh. Pvt., R.R.N.Y., Capt. Alex. McDonnell's Co.
    John of Charlottenburgh. OC 29 May 1807. 21/1 Cambridge.

McDONELL, James of Town of Kingston. Capt. RRNY. Went to Montreal.
    Allan of Town of Kingston. OC 23 Nov 1816.
    Angus of Town of Bath. OC 26 May 1836.

McDONELL, Capt. John of Cornwall (Scothouse), Spanish John. Capt., 1st
Batt., K. R. R. N. Y. Born 1727 or 28; m. Catherine dau Donald Macdonell,
Heir of Scothouse, who was killed at the Battle of Culloden; settled on Lot
19, n. s. Water Street, Town of Cornwall; 12 Children; d. 15 April 1810.
 John of Point Fortune, b. 30 Nov 1768; m. Magdeleine Poitras; d. 17 Apr
  1850. OC 11 June 1798.
 William Johnson of Boston, Mass., b. 17 March 1775; m. Lucy Waters;
  d. 3 Jan 1848. OC 11 June 1798.
 Miles of Cornwall, U. E. Ensign 1st K. R. R. N. Y. Died 28 June 1828.
 Penelope, m. John Beikie of Cornwall. OC 5 Jan 1798.
 Mary, m. Archibald McDonell of Lancaster. See OC 7 April 1812.
 Donald (Lieut.) killed in Revolutionary War. (Butler's Rangers).

McDONELL, John (Aberchalder), Capt. Butler's Rangers. Lt. Col., Militia.
First Speaker U. C. Also served 2nd Batt. R. C. Vols. Md. Helen, dau of
Henry Yates of New York.
 Alexander of Town of Cornwall, m. Helen Wilkinson. OC 12 Dec 1821.

McDONELL, John of E. half 11/ , south side Middle Branch River aux Rai-
sins, Cornwall. Capt.
 Alexander of Cornwall. OC 27 March 1813.
 Archibald of Cornwall. OC 11 Nov 1815.

McDONELL, John of 17/ , (W. half 16/5), south side Middle Branch, River
aux Raisins, Cornwall.
 Catharine, m. George Shakel of Cornwall 10 Nov 1794 (Montreal). See
  OC 3 Dec 1835. OC 18 March 1818.
 Margaret. OC 5 Jan 1798.

McDONELL, John of Wainfleet.
 Catharine, m. ---- Farr of Wainfleet. OC 9 March 1803.
 William of Gainsborough. OC 25 Nov 1818.
 Peter of Wainfleet. OC 5 April 1825.

McDONELL, John of E. half 14/3 south side River aux Raisins, Charlottenbg.
 Angus of Charlottenburgh. OC 23 Nov 1816. OC 5 July 1830.
 Donald of Charlottenburgh. OC 23 Nov 1816. 14/13 ?

McDONELL, John of E. half 9/2 south side River aux Raisins, Charlottenbg.
 Janet. OC 4 July 1815.

McDONELL, John of Edwardsburgh. Soldier, K. R. R. N. Y.
 Catharine, m. ---- Bryant. OC 23 June 1801.
 Flora. OC 26 Feb 1805.
 Mary. OC 22 Feb 1805. Williamsburgh.
 Jennett, m. Nathaniel Leonard of New Johnstown. OC 23 Feb 1809.
 Phoebe, m. Conrad Burns of Edwardsburgh. OC 13 Feb 1816.
 Andrew of Edwardsburgh. OC 15 June 1797, 4 July 1833.   [Cont'd]

McDONELL, John - Cont'd
  Elizabeth, m. John Shepherd of Edwardsburgh. OC 13 Feb 1816.
  Martha, m. Thomas Main Jr. of Edwardsburgh. OC 15 June 1797.
  John of Town of Kingston. OC 4 Dec 1834.
  Daniel of Edwardsburgh. OC 15 June 1797.

McDONELL, John of Lot 11/5 Cornwall.
  Margaret, m. Ranald McDonell of Cornwall. OC 6 Aug 1816.
  Donald of Cornwall. OC 21 Feb 1821.

McDONELL, John of 10/5 Cornwall.
  Ronald of Cornwall. OC 2 Dec 1840.

McDONELL, John (Black). E. half 12/3 s. s. River aux Raisins, Charlottenb.
  Flora. OC 20 Nov 1809.
  Catharine. OC 4 July 1815.
  Donald of Charlottenburgh. OC 23 Nov 1816.
  Angus of Charlottenburgh. OC 23 Nov 1816.
  Elizabeth. OC 26 March 1817. See OC 17 March 1834.
  Duncan of Charlottenburgh. OC 8 March 1830.
  John of Charlottenburgh. OC 9 March 1830.
  Donald of Charlottenburgh. OC 9 March 1830.

McDONELL, John (Roy). 20/4 south side Middle Branch, River aux Raisins,
  Cornwall.
  Mary. OC 21 July 1812.
  Sarah, m. John McDonald of Charlottenburgh. OC 21 July 1812.
  Archibald of Cornwall. OC 8 May 1818.
  Catharine. OC 8 May 1818.
  Ranald of Cornwall. OC 5 April 1825.

McDONELL, John (Ardnabie) of Charlottenburgh.
  Allan of Charlottenburgh. OC 14 Nov 1821.
  Isabella. OC 14 Nov 1821.
  Ann. OC 14 Nov 1821.
  Alexander of Charlottenburgh. OC 14 Nov 1821.
  John of Lancaster. OC 8 March 1830.

McDONELL, John (Roy), of Charlottenburgh.
  Mary, m. Malcolm McDonell of Lancaster. OC 4 Sept 1834.
  Ann. OC 4 Sept 1834.
  Catharine. OC 4 Sept 1834.
  Angus Roy of Charlottenburgh. OC 4 Sept 1834.
  John of Charlottenburgh. OC 4 Sept 1834.
  Roderick of Charlottenburgh. OC 4 Sept 1834.
  Ranold of Charlottenburgh. OC 27 Nov 1834.
  Flora, m. Alexander McLaughlin of Charlottenburgh. OC 28 Oct 1835.

McDONELL, John (Ban). W. half 9/2 s.s. River aux Raisins, Charlottenburgh. William of Charlottenburgh. OC 25 Feb 1818.

McDONELL, John. 14/4 Charlottenburgh.
Finnan of Charlottenburgh. OC 15 March 1803.

McDONELL, John of Charlottenburgh.
Donald of Charlottenburgh, b. 1767. Land Board Certificate, 32/5 Lancaster. See Heir & Devisee Commission 8 June 1809.
Angus of Charlottenburgh. Land Board Certificate, 33/5 Lancaster.

McDONELL, Miles of Scothouse, Cornwall. Ensign, 1st Batt., K.R.R.N.Y. Born 1767. His wife, Isabella Macdonell, died 31 Aug 1794. Served R.C. Vols. Married in York Town by Rev. Edmund Burke in February, 1798, Miss Catharine McDonnell, dau of Allan McDonell (Collachie). She died in Kingston and was buried there 8 Aug 1799. In Champlain Society's v. 23, 1937, p.126, Mrs. Miles McDonell is mentioned as the dau of Capt. McDonald of Morar, Inverness.
    Amelia, m. (1) William Jones of Augusta. OC 11 Aug 1812. m. (2) James McDonell of Matilda, 1835.
    Donald Aeneas of Cornwall, m. Mary Macdonell, 4 March 1819; d. 11 March 1879. OC 22 May 1820.
    Alexander Coll of Cornwall. Lt. 104th Regt. Drowned 1812(?) O.C. 21 February 1821.
    Catharine, m. Lt. Joseph Frobisher, Glengarry Light Infantry, 1809. O.C. 21 February 1821.
    Isabella, m. Alexander McDonell of Charlottenburgh. OC 8 March 1830.

McDONELL, Peter of Grand River.
    Hiram of Charlottenburgh. OC 17 Sept 1823.
    Elizabeth, m. William Moore of Charlotteville. OC 19 Aug 1833.

McDONELL, Ranald of Cornwall (Leek). Ensign 2d Batt. R.R.N.Y. Married Margery or Marcella Robertson. See OC 4 Nov 1800.
    Elizabeth, m. Donald McDonell of Cornwall (Lt.Col., Glengarry Militia), 5 April 1813. He was the son of Alex. (Greenfield). OC 17 Feb 1816.
    Catharine, m. Dr. Ambrose Blacklock of Charlottenburgh, 15 May 1816. OC 17 February 1816.
    Jane, m. Hamilton Walker of Prescott; d. Prescott 5 May 1847, aged 50. OC 6 August 1816.

McDONELL, Ranald of W. half 11/5 Cornwall. 84th Regt.
    Isabella, m. ---- Kennedy. OC 16 June 1819.
    Ann, m. ---- McDiarmid. OC 16 March 1837.

McDONELL, Ranald (King's Son) of Cornwall.
    Allan of Cornwall. OC 7 Feb 1821.

McDONELL, Ranald of Charlottenburgh. Pensioner. Died prior to March 1803.
John of Charlottenburgh. OC 9 March 1803.

McDONELL, Randy of Yonge. OC 7 March 1829.
Esther, m. John F. June of Yonge. OC 15 May 1835.
Mary, m. Freeman Hillard of Yonge. OC 28 Oct 1835.
Randy. OC 15 March 1832.
Daniel of Yonge. OC 7 May 1829.
James of Yonge. OC 7 May 1829.
Samuel of Lansdowne. OC 7 May 1829.

McDONELL, Roderick of Charlottenburgh. Soldier, R. R. N. Y.
James of Charlottenburgh. OC 4 July 1807.
Mary. Land Board Certificate. 11/8 Lancaster.

McDONELL, Roderick of 6/8 Cornwall.
Catharine, m. Edward Roach. OC 25 January 1831.

McDOUGALL, John of Lancaster, Lot 33/Front. He was born in Scotland;
came to America in 1773; m. Catharine Grant, dau Alexander Grant, 1784.
Duncan of Lancaster, b. 28 Jan 1786. OC 29 May 1807.
Donald of Lancaster, bapt. 5 June 1791. OC 20 Nov 1810.
Isabella, bapt. 12 June 1791. OC 13 Oct 1812.
Alexander of Lancaster, bapt. 24 Feb 1794. OC 23 Nov 1816.
John of Lancaster, bapt. 19 March 1797. OC 5 Nov 1818.
Roderick of Lancaster. OC 18 Sept 1822.
William of Lancaster. OC 23 June 1824.

McDOUGALL, John of York.
Mary, m. Joseph Harrison of York 24 April 1802. OC 21 Feb 1807.
Ann, m. John Jaffray of York 27 July 1804. OC 28 Feb 1807.
Dorothy, m. Jarrus Ashley of York 29 Dec 1807. OC 23 May 1809.
John of York, m. Mary Porter, 31 May 1816. OC 22 Jan 1811.
Sarah, m. Leonard Ashley of Vaughan 7 Feb 1814. OC 17 Feb 1816.
Hannah, m. John Holmes of York 25 Jan 1819. OC 21 April 1819.
Daniel of York, m. Hannah Matthews; d. 1870. OC 21 April 1819. See
    Beers' "Co. of York", p. 10.
Helen. OC 2 July 1829.

MacDOUGALL, Peter of Ernestown.
Catherine. OC 19 Dec 1806. Ernestown.
Isabella, m. Samuel Williams of Ernestown 15 Mar 1807. OC 19 Dec 1806.
John of Ernestown. OC 17 Aug 1808.
Rhoda. OC 27 Feb 1818.
Hannah, m. Justus Bartels. OC 17 Nov 1797.

McEATHRON, Daniel of Elizabethtown, m. Mary dau Sgt. John Beach, U. E.
Stephen of Elizabethtown. OC 30 April 1823.   [Cont'd]

McEATHRON, Daniel - Cont'd
  John Reid of Elizabethtown, bapt. 5 June 1796. OC 13 June 1818.
  Nancy, bapt. 5 June 1796; m. (1) Nathan Clerk of Elizabethtown. OC 14
    July 1819. m. (2) ---- Baxter.
  Peter of Elizabethtown. OC 28 June 1832.
  Alexander of Elizabethtown. OC 28 April 1825.

McEWEN, David of Cornwall.
  Mary, m. Barney Cain of Charlottenburgh. OC 6 Aug 1816.

McGAW, Patrick of Clinton, b. in Ireland about 1745, a weaver by trade.
  Elizabeth, m. James Ross of Clinton.
  Catherine, m. Alexander Collins of Wainfleet. OC 9 July 1802.
  John of Clinton. OC 4 Feb 1807.
  Eleanor, m. Lewis Buckner of Clinton. OC 23 May 1809.
  Mary, m. Martin Buckner of Clinton. OC 23 May 1809.
  Hannah, m. George Parker of Clinton. OC 27 Jan 1816.
  Jane. OC 27 Jan 1816.
  Charles of Middleton. OC 23 June 1821.
  William of Walpole. OC 18 May 1819.
  Hugh of Clinton. OC 8 March 1820.
  Alexander of Clinton. OC 12 June 1822.
  Patrick of Clinton. OC 12 June 1822.

McGILLIES, Donald of E. half 3/1 south side Fiver aux Raisins.
  Ann, m. John Hay of Charlottenburgh. OC 6 Aug 1816.

McGILLIES, Donald of 3/2 Charlottenburgh.
  Catherine, m. Archibald McDougall of Charlottenburgh. OC 25 Oct 1803.

McGILLIES, Donald Jr. of E. half 3/ , South Branch, River aux Raisins,
  Charlottenburgh.
  Duncan of Charlottenburgh. OC 28 April 1815.
  Alexander of Charlottenburgh. OC 28 Nov 1809.
  Gilles of Charlottenburgh. OC 21 March 1821.
  John of Charlottenburgh. OC 24 Dec 1823.
  Angus of Cornwall. OC 6 Feb 1828.
  Ann, m. John Hay. OC 6 Aug 1816.

McGILLIS, Donald Sr. of Charlottenburgh.
  Mary. OC 7 Feb 1833.
  Donald of Charlottenburgh. OC 7 Feb 1833.

McGILLIES, John of Charlottenburgh. Lt., N.Y. Highland Vols.
  Mary. OC 26 March 1811. Charlottenburgh.
  Catharine. OC 28 April 1815.
  Donald of Charlottenburgh. OC 28 April 1815.
  Isabella. OC 28 April 1815.   [Cont'd]

McGILLIES, John - Cont'd
  Ann. OC 28 July 1819.

McGINN or McGINNIS, George of Ernestown and Amherst Island.
  Timothy of Amherst Island. OC 29 March 1803.
  Catharine. OC 25 Feb 1818.
  William of Amherst Island. OC 25 Feb 1818.
  George of Amherst. OC 25 Feb 1818.
  Mary Ann, m. Thomas Hopper of Amherst Island. OC 28 Feb 1829.
  Sarah Ann, m. Joseph Stapley of Amherst Island. OC 7 May 1829.
  dau, m. William Eadus of Gananoque.

McGLOGHLON, William of Cornwall. His wife, Margaret Gillespie, died 29
  July 1844, aged 93.
  Robert of Cornwall. OC 5 Jan 1798.
  David of Cornwall. OC 5 Jan 1798.
  William of Cornwall. OC 19 Dec 1806.
  John of Cornwall, bapt. 3 July 1788. OC 25 Feb 1818, OC 13 June 1818,
    OC 6 August 1818.
  George, bapt. 19 May 1793.

McGREGOR, Daniel of Cornwall.
  Nancy, m. Joseph Stafford of Moore. OC 27 Aug 1840.

McGREGOR, Donald of Elizabethtown.
  Mary, m. William Anderson of Dawn. OC 1 Dec 1836.

McGREGOR, Hugh of Charlottenburgh.
  Duncan of Charlottenburgh. OC 28 April 1807.
  Jane. OC 16 Nov 1807.
  Mary, m. William Urquhart of Charlottenburgh 21 Aug 1810. OC 16 April
    1811.
  Christiana. OC 7 Feb 1821.
  Catharine. OC 6 March 1821.

McGREGOR, James of Cornwall and Charlottenburgh. Sgt., Col. Guy Johns-
  ton's Forresters. Married Catharine McDonald, 14 Feb 1786.
  Eleanor, bapt. 23 May 1791. OC 23 May 1809.
  Donald of Charlottenburgh, bapt. 23 May 1791. OC 2 March 1816.
  Catharine, bapt. 20 Apr 1794. OC 2 March 1816.
  Angus of Charlottenburgh, bapt. 26 Feb 1792. OC 19 Feb 1817.
  Margaret, bapt. 20 March 1796. OC 25 Feb 1818.
  Ann, b. 18 Jan 1809; m. Alexander Cattanach of Lochiel. OC 19 Sept 1839.
  Isabella, b. 20 Jan 1811; m. Duncan McTavish of Lochiel. OC 24 Nov 1836
  Duncan of Charlottenburgh. OC 16 Feb 1837.
  Alexander of Charlottenburgh, b. 21 Dec 1802. OC 8 Dec 1835.
  Archibald John of Charlottenburgh, b. 14 March 1805. OC 2 Oct 1829.
  Peter, b. 18 Jan 1809. Died young.   [Cont'd]

McGREGOR, James - Cont'd
  John, b. 24 May 1798.
  James, b. 29 Sept 1807. Died young.

McGREGOR, John of Charlottenburgh. R. R. N. Y.
  Elizabeth. OC 6 Dec 1803.
  Nancy, m. Robert Shannon of Charlottenburgh. OC 6 Dec 1803.
  John of Charlottenburgh. OC 5 Nov 1818.
  Donald of Charlottenburgh. OC 2 Oct 1822.
  William of Charlottenburgh. OC 2 Oct 1822.

McGREGOR, Peter of Charlottenburgh. K. R. R. N. Y.
  Espey, m. ---- Ross of Mountain. OC 16 April 1799.
  Catharine. OC 5 Jan 1798.

McGRUER, Alexander of Charlottenburgh.
  Mary. OC 24 Feb 1820.
  Margaret. OC 24 Feb 1820.
  John of Charlottenburgh. OC 24 Dec 1823.
  Alexander of Charlottenburgh. OC 11 Oct 1838.
  Duncan of Charlottenburgh. OC 6 Feb 1841.
  Angus of Charlottenburgh. OC 16 Feb 1837.
  Catharine, m. John Dingwall of Charlottenburgh. OC 27 Feb 1834.
  William of Town of Kingston. OC 8 Jan 1835.
  Ewen of Charlottenburgh. OC 19 Nov 1831.
  Malcolm of Charlottenburgh. OC 8 March 1830.

McGRUER, John of Charlottenburgh. K. R. R. N. Y.
  Mary, m. ---- McIntyre. Land Board Certificate, 16/1 Lochiel.

McGUIN, Daniel of Kingston. Capt.
  Ann, m. Isaiah Van Order of Kingston. OC 16 Nov 1797. OC 29 June 1837.
  Anthony of Kingston. OC 16 Nov 1797.

McGUIRE, Patrick of Cornwall.
  Alexander of Cornwall. OC 13 June 1809.
  Daniel of Cornwall. OC 18 Aug 1810.
  Dorothy. OC 11 Nov 1815.
  Angus of Cornwall. OC 4 Feb 1818.
  Mary, m. William Emery of Cornwall. OC 1 June 1837.
  Catharine. OC 2 Feb 1825.
  John of Cornwall. OC 17 Feb 1825.
  Hugh of Cornwall. OC 22 July 1824.

McILMOYLE, John of Edwardsburgh, m. Mary Dysart; d. 22 Sept 1796.
  Mary, m. ---- Brown of Wolford. Land Board Certificate, 7/6 Bastard.
  Thomas of Edwardsburgh, U. E.

McILMOYLE, Thomas of Edwardsburgh, son of John McIlmoyle and Mary Dysart; m. Sarah Falkner, 27 Sept 1793; d. 1 March 1850, aged 89.
   James Dysart of Edwardsburgh, m. Clarissa McFarland. OC 13 Feb 1816.
   Eleanor, b. 4 June 1798; d. 27 May 1860 at Ottawa. OC 15 June 1820.
   Mary, bapt. 8 June 1796; m. Philemon Pennock of Edwardsburgh 22 Sept 1822; d. 28 Oct 1889 at Ottawa. OC 28 Nov 1821.
   John of Edwardsburgh. OC 7 July 1831.

McINTOSH, Alexander of Edwardsburgh.
   John of York, carpenter. OC 18 June 1799.
   Daniel of Town of Johnstown. OC 12 Nov 1811.

McINTOSH, Benjamin of Charlottenburgh.
   Flora. OC 28 April 1815.

McINTOSH, Daniel.
   William. OC 3 March 1801.

McINTOSH, John of Cornwall.
   Catherine, m. Elkana Daniels of Cornwall. OC 6 Aug 1840.

McINTOSH, John of 14/5 south side middle branch River aux Raisins Cornwall
   Ann, m. John Cameron Jr. of Cornwall. OC 15 Nov 1808.
   Mary. OC 15 Nov 1808. Cornwall.
   Peggy. OC 15 Nov 1808. Cornwall.
   Eleanor, m. Duncan McLellan of Charlottenburgh. OC 11 Nov 1815.
   Christy. OC 11 November 1815.

McINTYRE, Daniel of Grimsby.
   Jemima. OC 18 Nov 1800.
   Mary, m. ---- Willcocks of Grimsby. OC 18 Nov 1800.
   Daniel of Grimsby. OC 5 Aug 1807.
   James of Grimsby, b. New Jersey about 1769.

McINTYRE, Donald of Charlottenburgh.
   Nelly. OC 5 March 1828. OC 22 Dec 1832.
   Allan of Charlottenburgh. OC 22 Dec 1832.
   Catharine. OC 5 March 1828. OC 22 Dec 1832.
   Flora. OC 5 March 1828. OC 22 Dec 1832.
   Donald of Charlottenburgh. OC 22 Dec 1832. See OC 5 March 1828.
   Mary, m. Arthur Harkens of Town of Cornwall. OC 5 March 1828. OC 15 December 1832.
   Angus of Charlottenburgh. OC 2 May 1827.

McINTYRE, Donald of E. Half 15/3 south side River aux Raisins Charlottenbg
   Christy. OC 16 Feb 1811. Charlottenburgh.
   Nancy. OC 6 Aug 1816.
   John of Charlottenburgh. OC 23 Nov 1816.

McINTYRE, Duncan Sr.
Margaret, m. ---- McMartin of Charlottenburgh. OC 27 July 1802.

McINTYRE, Duncan of Lot 10 south side River aux Raisins, Charlottenburgh.
Mary. OC 11 June 1823.
Duncan of Charlottenburgh. OC 11 June 1823.

McINTYRE, Duncan Jr. of Charlottenburgh. Sgt., 1st Batt. K.R.R.N.Y.
Margaret, m. James Urquhart of Charlottenburgh. OC 7 Feb 1821.

McINTYRE, Jesse of Wolford.
Cloe, m. William Brown of Montague (Wolford).
Charlotte, m. Samuel Rose Jr. of Montague.
Martha, m. ---- Boyd. OC 23 June 1801.

McINTYRE, John of Charlottenburgh. K.R.R.N.Y.
Mary, m. ---- McGruer. Land Board Certificate, 16/1 Lochiel.

McINTYRE, John of Cornwall, innkeeper of Coteau du Lac, m. Sophia Mur-
chison (?)
Esther, bapt. 18 Feb 1790; m. Daniel McArthur of Montreal. OC 19 April
1816.
Margaret, m. James Stevenson of Cornwall. OC 19 April 1816.
Mary, m. James Gillis of Coteau du Lac. OC 19 April 1816.
Pencilled note by Reid: dau Alice b. 11 July 1803.

McINTYRE, John of Lot 41 north side River aux Raisins, Charlottenburgh.
Eleanor. OC 28 April 1815.
Allan of Charlottenburgh. OC 5 March 1823.
Janet. OC 5 March 1823.
Mary. OC 26 Dec 1834.
Joseph of Charlottenburgh. OC 26 Dec 1834.
John of Lancaster. OC 28 Feb 1835.

McINTYRE, John of Williamsburgh.
Robert of Cornwall. OC 4 July 1815.

McKAY, Angus.
Mary, m. ---- Chisholm. OC 3 March 1801.
Christy. OC 3 March 1801.
Christian, m. Hugh McKay of Charlottenburgh. OC 5 Jan 1798.

McKAY, Donald.
Catharine. OC 9 July 1802.

McKAY, Hugh of Charlottenburgh.
William of Charlottenburgh. Land Board Certificate, 8/3 Charlottenburgh.

McKAY, John of Cornwall.
  Catharine, m. (1) Archibald Grant; m. (2) Donald McMillan of Town of
    York. OC 25 Sept 1804.
  Margaret. OC 26 March 1817.
  Heppekiah, m. Donald McMillan of Cornwall. OC 20 May 1817.
  Eleanor, m. John McPhie of Lancaster. OC 18 March 1818.
  James of Cornwall. OC 5 Nov 1818.
  Angus of Charlottenburgh. OC 27 June 1833.
  Harriet, m. William Glassford of Cornwall. OC 27 Feb 1834.
  Alexander of Cornwall. OC 6 Dec 1832.
  John of Osnabruck. OC 20 Oct 1832.
  Ann. OC 6 Sept 1832. Charlottenburgh.

McKAY, William of Charlottenburgh.
  Elizabeth. OC 8 Dec 1835.
  Catharine. OC 8 Dec 1835.
  Anne, m. John McKenzie of Charlottenburgh. OC 2 May 1827.
  Christy. OC 3 Dec 1828.
  Mary. OC 3 Dec 1828.

McKAY, William Jr. of Charlottenburgh.
  Hugh of Charlottenburgh. OC 20 Oct 1832.

McKENZIE, Colin.
  Duncan of Portland. OC 28 June 1797.
  William of Amherst Island, m. Sarah Howard, 19 Sept 1803. OC 20 June
    1797.
  Caroline. OC 5 Sept 1833. Ernestown.
  Mary. OC 7 May 1828. Ernestown.
  Sarah A. OC 7 May 1828. Ernestown.
  Thomas of Ernestown. OC 5 Feb 1829.

McKENZIE, Duncan of Charlottenburgh, m. Isabel McKay of Charlottenburgh
1 April 1785.
  Catharine, bapt. 12 June 1791; m. Donald McLauren Jr. of Charlotten-
    burgh 22 March 1808. OC 3 March 1809.
  John of Charlottenburgh, bapt. 10 March 1790; schoolmaster. OC 18 June
    1811.
  William of Charlottenburgh, bapt. 18 May 1794. OC 11 Nov 1815.
  Donald of Charlottenburgh, bapt. 3 June 1796. OC 31 July 1817.
  Margaret, b. 28 Dec 1798; m. John McLennan of Charlottenburgh. OC 28
    July 1819.
  Janet, b. 23 Oct 1810. OC 1 Aug 1833.
  Anne, b. 23 April 1801.
  Christian (dau) b. 28 Nov 1805.
  Alexander, b. 24 May 1808.
  Isabella. OC 3 December 1828.

McKENZIE, Kenneth. Lt., K.R.R.N.Y.
Alexander of London, England. OC 8 Oct 1796. (Sir Alexander McKenzie, formerly partner in North West Co.)

McKIE, John of Point au Bodet. Sgt., K.R.R.N.Y.
Alexander of Lancaster. OC 15 Aug 1809.
James of Lancaster. OC 23 Nov 1816.
Mary, m. John Curry Jr. of Lancaster 23 March 1813. OC 23 Nov 1816.
Joseph of Lancaster. OC 23 Nov 1816.
John P. of Lancaster. OC 23 Nov 1816.
Elizabeth, m. William McDonell of Lancaster. OC 23 Nov 1816.
Peter of Lancaster. OC 11 Jan 1834.
William of Lancaster. OC 7 Aug 1834.
Catharine, m. John McIntyre of Lancaster. OC 7 Aug 1834.
Sarah, m. William Curry of Lancaster. OC 3 Jan 1833.
Anne, m. John Williams of Lancaster. OC 2 July 1829.

McKIM, James of Ernestown.
Nancy, b. at Sorel, 1781; m. John Grange of Richmond 10 Feb 1799; died 6 Sept 1852. OC 25 June 1800.
John of Ernestown, m. Lydia Switzer, 26 March 1812. OC 16 Nov 1807.
Mary, m. Archibald Caton of Ernestown 28 June 1810. OC 16 Feb 1811.
Eleanor, m. Ira Beeman of Richmond. OC 12 Nov 1811. OC 11 Nov 1815.
Sarah, m. William Rose of Ernestown (Richmond), 5 March 1805. OC 27 Feb 1812. OC 26 Jan 1837.
James of Ernestown. OC 20 June 1797.
Thomas of Richmond. OC 19 Feb 1828.

McKINNEY, Amos of Niagara and Fredericksburgh.
James of Niagara. OC 11 Dec 1806.
Eleanor, m. Marlow Reilly of Niagara. OC 26 Jan 1808.
John of Niagara. OC 26 Jan 1808.
Amos of Niagara. OC 26 Jan 1808.
Samuel Sherwood of Haldimand Twp. OC 23 Nov 1816.
Doyle of Bayham. OC 19 Feb 1817.
Elijah of Bayham, m. Catharine Hawn, 20 June 1820. (Note: Elijah Froom McKenny bapt. 8 March 1792 son of Amos McK & Jemima Sherwood of Fredericksburgh, 1792).
David of Augusta. OC 10 Dec 1818.

McLAREN, Hugh of W. half C/ River aux Raisins, Charlottenburgh.
Angus of Charlottenburgh. OC 5 March 1808.
Jennet. OC 22 Feb 1810.
Christy. OC 28 April 1815.
Catharine. OC 28 April 1815. OC 20 July 1837.
Catharine, m. John Miller of Charlottenburgh. OC 23 Nov 1816.
Malcolm of Charlottenburgh, blacksmith. OC 16 March 1825.

McLAREN, Hugh Ewen of Charlottenburgh.
Donald of Charlottenburgh. OC 3 Sept 1829.
Anne. OC 3 Sept 1829.

McLAREN, Peter. Lt. Jessup's Corps. Married Mary ----; she md. (2)
Samuel Wright of Elizabethtown. "md. Montreal, Mch 1784."
Archibald of Elizabethtown. OC 13 Nov 1797.
Nancy (Anna), m. Samuel Purdy of Elizabethtown. OC 17 Nov 1797.
Mary (Mercy ?), m. Sylvester Wright of Elizabethtown. Heir & Devisee
Commission, 21 July 1823. OC 17 Nov 1797.

McLAUGHLIN, Alexander of Charlottenburgh, W. half 9/Front.
Catharine. OC 15 March 1806.
Flora, m. Donald McKinnon of Charlottenburgh. OC 25 June 1807.
Malcolm of Charlottenburgh. OC 3 March 1809.
William of Charlottenburgh. OC 7 Aug 1811.
Amelia. OC 23 Nov 1816.
Lauchlin of Charlottenburgh. OC 2 Feb 1819.

McLAUGHLIN, James of Louth.
Elizabeth, m. George Campbell of Binbrook 3 Sept 1799. OC 11 July 1799.
James of Louth. OC 3 Nov 1807.
John of Louth. OC 9 Dec 1815.
Sarah, m. William Smith of Louth. OC 8 Sept 1819.
Jeremiah of Louth. OC 7 Oct 1826.

McLAUGHLIN, James of Gwillimbury West.
Margaret, m. John Foreman of Grantham. OC 1 Nov 1826.
James of Gwillimbury West. OC 8 Feb 1827.
Christina, m. William Love of Gwillimbury West. OC 8 Feb 1827.

McLAUGHLIN, James.
Mary, m. John Boice Jr. of Niagara 23 Oct 1797. OC 6 June 1799.
Ann, m. Joseph Haines of Niagara. OC 24 Nov 1801.

McLAUGHLIN, John Sr. of Town of Kingston, m. Elizabeth. See 8/7 Hamilton.
John of Kingston. OC 8 July 1797.
Elizabeth, m. Henry Cassady of Kingston. OC 31 Oct 1809.
Margaret, m. Joseph Franklin of Pittsburgh. OC 31 Oct 1809.
Mary, m. Nathaniel Lines of Town of Kingston 23 Nov 1808. OC 26 Sept
1809.
William of Kingston.

McLAUGHLIN, John Jr. of Kingston and Pittsburgh. See 8/7 Hamilton.
John of Pittsburgh, d. 27 Jan 1843. OC 18 April 1843.
Mary, m. Henry Hovert of Adolphustown. OC 18 April 1843.

McLEAN, Alexander of Elizabethtown. See Ont. Hist. Soc. v. 6, pp. 92-94.
He md. Anne Lang who d. 1805. He d. 1810. See Home and Foreign Record
of the Canada Presbyterian Church, December 1861, p. 40.
  Henry of Elizabethtown. OC 23 Nov 1797.
  John of Elizabethtown, b. 9 Oct 1775; d. 17 July 1861. OC 13 Nov 1797.

McLEAN, Donald.
  Margaret, m. Daniel Edson of Charlottenburgh 12 March 1805. O. C. 25
    June 1807.
  Mary, m. Alexander Ross of Lancaster. OC 5 Jan 1798.
  Allan of Charlottenburgh. OC 15 Nov 1808.
  Donald of Charlottenburgh. OC 25 July 1809.
  William of Charlottenburgh. Land Board Certificate, 5/2 Kenyon.

McLEAN, Duncan of Augusta, m. Dorothia. She d. at Augusta 20 Feb 1850,
aged 92.
  Robert of Augusta, m. Rebecca Deforest; d. 15 Jan 1816. OC 3 July 1798.
  William of Augusta. OC 26 March 1817.
  Ann, m. Duncan Thompson of Pittsburgh. OC 16 June 1819.
  Mary, m. John Wright of Augusta. OC 28 Oct 1835.
  Ruth, m. Samuel Brown of Augusta. OC 3 March 1836.
  Hannah. OC 7 May 1828.
  Dorothy, m. John Gates of Pittsburgh. OC 28 Nov 1826.
  Duncan of Augusta. OC 23 Dec 1825.
  Solomon of Augusta. OC 23 Dec 1825.

McLEAN, John of Elizabethtown and Pittsburgh, m. Mary White.
  Samuel of Pittsburgh, bapt. 11 Nov 1790, aged 7 yrs. OC 2 Dec 1806.
  Catherine, bapt. 11 Nov 1790, aged 8 yrs; m. Jonathan Milk of Elizabeth-
    town. OC 2 Dec 1806.
  Betsey, bapt. 11 March 1792; m. William Wilday of Augusta. OC 11 Dec
    1810.
  Sarah, bapt. 11 Nov 1790, aged 1 yr 3 ms; m. George Bryant of Pitts-
    burgh. OC 23 June 1819.
  John, bapt. 11 Nov 1790, aged 5 yrs.
  William Gibson of Pittsburgh, bapt. 11 March 1792. OC 28 Nov 1826.
  Robert of Pittsburgh, b. 13 Jan 1798. OC 28 Nov 1826.
  Alexander C. of Pittsburgh. OC 28 Nov 1826.

McLEAN, Murdock of Charlottenburgh. Sgt. K. R. R. N. Y. Md. Catharine.
  John of Charlottenburgh, bapt. 11 Feb 1786. OC 25 June 1807.
  Donald of Charlottenburgh. OC 13 Oct 1807.
  Alexander of Charlottenburgh. OC 28 April 1815.
  William of Town of Kingston. OC 18 July 1816.
  Barbara, bapt. 1 July 1797. OC 5 Nov 1818.
  James G. of Charlottenburgh. OC 13 Jan 1819.
  Margaret, m. Donald Cameron of North Gower. OC 6 Sept 1832.

McLEAN, William of Charlottenburgh.
    William. Land Board Certificate. 5/2 Kenyon. [But see Donald McLean]

McLELLAN, John of Cornwall and Charlottenburgh.
    dau Mary Jr. OC 25 Feb 1818.

McLELLAN, John of Lancaster (Charlottenburgh ?)
    Mary, m. James Drummond of Charlottenburgh. OC 9 July 1802.
    Duncan of Charlottenburgh. OC 9 July 1802.
    Catherine, m. John McDonald of Charlottenburgh. OC 30 July 1811.
    Margaret, m. Donald McDonald of Charlottenburgh. OC 7 Aug 1811.
    Janet. OC 12 Nov 1811.

McLENNAN, Kenneth of Charlottenburgh.
    William of Charlottenburgh. OC 14 June 1839.
    Jane, m. David Smith of Kenyon. OC 7 Aug 1834.
    Murdoch of Charlottenburgh. OC 4 Sept 1834.
    Annabel. OC 2 May 1827.
    John of Charlottenburgh. OC 7 May 1828.
    Robert of Charlottenburgh. OC 7 May 1828.

McLEOD, Isabella of Cornwall, widow of Malcolm McLeod, 17/11 Lancaster
OC 22 June 1809.
    Thomas of Cornwall. OC 19 June 1809.

McLEOD, William of Charlottenburgh.
    Catharine. OC 15 March 1806.
    William of Charlottenburgh. OC 19 Dec 1806.
    Jane. OC 25 June 1807.
    Janet. OC 16 Feb 1811.
    Eleanor, m. ---- Stuart. Land Board Certificate, 1/5 Osnabruck.

McMARTIN, John of Charlottenburgh. W. half 23/ . Md. Helen Cameron.
    Mary, m. Duncan Grant of Charlottenburgh 17 Dec 1799. OC 14 July 1801.
    Daniel of Charlottenburgh. OC 19 Dec 1806.
    Ann. OC 22 Feb 1810.
    Janet. OC 26 March 1817.
    Duncan of Charlottenburgh. OC 26 March 1817.
    John of Charlottenburgh. OC 26 March 1817.
    Malcolm of Charlottenburgh. OC 14 May 1823.
    Alexander of Charlottenburgh, b. 1 Apr 1799. OC 14 May 1823.
    James of Charlottenburgh, b. 27 March 1806. OC 1 Nov 1832.
    Finlay of Charlottenburgh. OC 2 Dec 1824.

McMARTIN, Malcolm of Charlottenburgh. Lt., 1st Batt. K.R.R.N.Y. He
married Margaret McIntyre.
    Duncan of Charlottenburgh, m. Barbara Robertson. OC 27 July 1802.
    Malcolm of Charlottenburgh. OC 2 March 1816.   [Cont'd]

McMARTIN, Malcolm - Cont'd
  Margaret, m. Alexander McGruer of Charlottenburgh 7 July 1795. O.C.
    5 Jan 1798.
  Jennett, bapt. 12 June 1791; m. John McMartin of Charlottenburgh 30 Apr
    1807. OC 17 June 1806.
  Peter of Charlottenburgh, m. Mary Sinclair. OC 28 Feb 1807.
  Alexander of Charlottenburgh, bapt. 12 June 1791. OC 20 Nov 1809.
  Eleanor. OC 2 March 1816.
  Martin of Charlottenburgh. OC 7 Feb 1821.
  (Peter McMartin m. 2. Catharine Ross, 20 Dec 1808).

McMASTERS, James of Adolphustown and Sidney, m. Mary.
  Nancy, bapt. 12 Jan 1789; m. Ira Belknap of Sidney. OC 28 Nov 1809.
  Catharine, bapt. 31 Dec 1787; m. George Finkle of Sidney. OC 28 Nov 1809
  James of Sidney, bapt. 21 Feb 1791. OC 13 Feb 1816.
  Jacob, bapt. 25 Jan 1796.
  John, bapt. 19 March 1798.
  Elizabeth, bapt. 24 June 1800.

McMASTERS, John.
  Hannah, m. Solomon Marshall of Sidney. OC 16 Feb 1811.

McMICHAEL, Edward of Walsingham.
  Hannah, m. William Backhouse of Walsingham. OC 7 Aug 1811. OC 26
    March 1817.
  Juliana, m. Anthony Fick. See OC 9 July 1827. OC 13th & 16th Feb 1816.
  James of Walsingham. OC 16 (13th ?) Feb 1816.
  Eliza, m. ---- Delong of Walsingham. OC 18 July 1816.
  William of Norwich. OC 9 Feb 1820.
  Hugh A. B. of Walsingham. OC 19 March 1840.
  Eleanor, m. Henry Ellis of Oakland. OC 15 March 1832.

McMICKING, Peter of Stamford.
  John of Stamford. OC 10 Nov 1801.
  Gilbert of Stamford. OC 16 April 1811.
  Catharine, m. William McClellan of Stamford. OC 16 April 1811.
  Agnes, m. John Robertson of Stamford. OC 25 Feb 1818.
  dau, m. David Bastido. OC 7 Oct 1796.

McMICKING, Thomas of Stamford.
  Sarah, m. William Johnston of Crowland. OC 13 April 1819.
  Eleanor. OC 13 April 1819.
  Thomas of Stamford. OC 13 April 1819.
  Jane. OC 29 May 1822.
  Mary. OC 30 April 1823.
  James of Stamford. OC 15 May 1835.
  William of Stamford. OC 5 July 1826.

McMILLAN, Donald of Cornwall. Lot 20, south side Middle Branch.
   Nancy, m. Lauchlin McDonell of Cornwall. OC 13 Oct 1807.
   Flora, m. Alexander McDonell of Cornwall. OC 18 March 1818.
   Sarah, m. John McMillan of Cornwall. OC 2 Feb 1819.
   Donald of Cornwall. OC 4 April 1833.
   Mary, m. Angus McDonald of Cornwall. OC 28 Nov 1826. OC 18 July 1833.

McMILLAN, Isabella of 1/5 Marlborough, widow of Dougall McMillan, RRNY.
   Christiana, m. John McGillies of Charlottenburgh. OC 19 Feb 1817.
   Mary, m. Alexander Campbell of Charlottenburgh. OC 10 Sept 1817.

McMULLEN, Daniel of Fredericksburgh, m. Catharine.
   Catharine. OC 23 Feb 1808. Fredericksburgh.
   Mary, m. Joshua Cadman of Fredericksburgh. OC 13 June 1809. (Dau.
      Mary, bapt. 28 Dec 1789, "MacMillan")
   Nancy, m. William Huff of Fredericksburgh. OC 26 March 1817.
   Elizabeth, bapt. 18 March 1792; m. ---- Fulford of Pittsburgh. OC 12
      July 1820.
   Valentine of Hallowell. OC 3 Jan 1827.
   Ann, m. Samuel Wood of Sophiasburgh. OC 3 Jan 1827.
   George of Pittsburgh. OC 7 May 1828.
   Daniel, bapt. 18 May 1788 (O. H. S. v. 1 p. 31); buried 4 Sept 1788.

McNABB, John of Niagara.
   Eliza, m. Archibald McDonell of Cornwall. OC 11 Nov 1815.
   John of Grantham. OC 31 Oct 1821.
   Helen, m. ---- McDougall. OC 31 Oct 1821.
   Alexander of Grantham. OC 31 Oct 1821.
   Mary. OC 10 July 1822. Cornwall.
   James Duncan of Grantham. OC 12 May 1824.

McNAIRN, John of Cornwall, m. Elizabeth Kerr.
   Agnes, m. John Forsyth of Cornwall. OC 6 Dec 1803. See Com. July 1826
   Elizabeth, m. Robert Colquhoun of Charlottenburgh. OC 16 Feb 1811.
   John of Cornwall. OC 16 Feb 1811.
   Hannah. OC 16 Feb 1811.
   William of Cornwall, bapt. 16 May 1790. OC 7 Aug 1811.
   Margaret, m. John Bailey of Cornwall. OC 25 Feb 1812.
   Alexander of Cornwall, bapt. 4 March 1792. OC 17 Feb 1816.

McNAUGHTON, Donald. E. half H/Front Charlottenburgh. m. Mary McDon-
ell. Died in Charlottenburgh, April, 1841.
   Elizabeth, d. unm. OC 6 Aug 1816.
   Robert of Charlottenburgh. OC 23 Nov 1816.
   John of Charlottenburgh, d. unm. Dec, 1888. P. L. S. OC 26 March 1817.
   Mary, m. James McDonell of Charlottenburgh 7 Oct 1811. OC 26 August
      1818.
   Catharine, m. Alexander McDonell of Cornwall. OC 17 Sept 1823. [Cont'd]

McNAUGHTON, Donald - Cont'd
Alexander of Charlottenburgh, d. 1876. OC 7 March 1827.
Margaret, m. John Chisholm. OC 7 March 1827.
Duncan of Charlottenburgh, d. in War of 1812, unm.

McNAUGHTON, John of Charlottenburgh.
Mary, bapt. 16 Sept 1787; m. ---- Ferguson of Charlottenburgh. OC 25
October 1803.
John of Charlottenburgh. OC 29 May 1807.

McNEIL, Archibald of Elizabethtown, m. Elizabeth Adams.
Christy, bapt. 9 March 1792. OC 25 Feb 1809. Town of Johnstown.
Martha, bapt. 9 March 1792; m. John Allen of Elizabethtown. OC 22 Oct
1817.
Elizabeth, bapt. 9 March 1792; m. Humphrey Barden of Edwardsburgh.
OC 4 Nov 1818.
William of Edwardsburgh, bapt. 9 March 1792. OC 6 Dec 1832.
James of Edwardsburgh. OC 6 Dec 1832.

McNEIL, William of Edwardsburgh, m. Jane Quail.
John of Augusta, bapt. 7 March 1792. OC 3 March 1809.
Christy, bapt. 22 May 1793; m. Thomas Rowling of Edwardsburgh. OC
16 February 1811.
William of Edwardsburgh, bapt. 3 June 1796. OC 2 March 1816.
Henry of Augusta, bapt. 7 March 1792. OC 22 Oct 1817.
Charles, bapt. 12 Feb 1789.
Charles of Edwardsburgh, bapt. 3 June 1796. OC 1 May 1834.
Hugh, b. 30 March 1798.
William Q. of Augusta. OC 7 Feb 1833.

McNISH, James of Elizabethtown.
Chloe. OC 14 April 1836.

McNISH, Joseph of Elizabethtown, m. Hannah.
Susanna, m. ---- Wright of Elizabethtown. OC 23 Sept 1800.
Anne, m. Henry McLean of Elizabethtown. OC 10 April 1805.
Hannah, m. Archibald McLean of Elizabethtown. OC 10 Apr 1805.
Sarah, m. ---- Reynolds. OC 10 April 1805.
John of Elizabethtown. OC 14 June 1811.
William of Elizabethtown. OC 14 June 1811.
Joseph of Elizabethtown, m. Olive. OC 29 Dec 1819.
Mary, m. William May of Yonge 9 Feb 1818. OC 7 March 1833.
Elizabeth, m. Joseph Wright of Elizabethtown. OC 7 March 1833.
Samuel.

McNUTT, James.
Gerrard of Fredericksburgh. OC 2 July 1799.
Sarah, m. ---- Peterson. OC 20 Nov 1798.   [Cont'd]

McNUTT, James - Cont'd
   Catherine, m. ---- Williams. OC 20 Nov 1798.
   James of Fredericksburgh. OC 30 Aug 1797.

McPHERSON, Alexander of Charlottenburgh. KRRNY. m. Catharine McKay.
   Angus of Charlottenburgh. OC 29 May 1807.
   Mary. OC 25 June 1807.
   Catharine, m. John Johnson Sutherland of Lancaster 26 January 1809.
      OC 16 April 1811.
   Duncan (?) bapt. 14 June 1789.
   Flora, m. ---- Grant. Land Board Certificate. 26/1 Lochiel.

McPHERSON, John of Ernestown.
   Christiana, m. ---- Penny of Thurlow. OC 7 Feb 1821.
   Malcolm of Thurlow. OC 28 Nov 1826.

McPHERSON, Murdock of Charlottenburgh, E. half 1/ . His wife Anne, 1786
   son Daniel bapt. 11 Feb 1786. m. (2)? Catherine Macdonnell.
   Donald of Charlottenburgh. OC 29 May 1807.
   Ann, m. Allan Kennedy of Charlottenburgh 8 Nov 1808. OC 22 Feb 1810.
   Mary. OC 16 Feb 1811.
   John of Charlottenburgh, bapt. 17 Apr 1791. OC 28 April 1815.

McPHERSON, Peter of Ernestown.
   Duncan of Ernestown. OC 16 Feb 1810.
   Margery. OC 27 Feb 1818.
   Peter of Ernestown. OC 27 Feb 1818.
   Mary. OC 27 Feb 1818.
   Elizabeth. OC 24 Nov 1836.
   Angus of Camden East. OC 10 March 1834.

McPHIE, Alexander.
   Catharine, m. Donald McDonell of Charlottenburgh. OC 3 April 1810.

McPHIE, Allan of Cornwall and Lancaster and Lochiel.
   Hugh of Cornwall. OC 3 April 1810.
   Jennet, m. Charles McKinnon of Lancaster. OC 3 June 1817.
   Daniel of Lancaster. OC 18 March 1818.
   Duncan of Lochiel. OC 23 June 1836.
   Margaret. OC 13 June 1836. Lochiel.
   Mary, m. Alexander Cameron of Kenyon. OC 26 Dec 1834.
   Ann, m. John McDonell of Wolfe Island. OC 8 June 1832.
   Catharine, m. Donald MacDonald, act'g Sgt. 79th Regt. OC 8 June 1832.
   Margery, m. Peter Lafleur of Wolfe Island. OC 8 June 1832.

McTAGGART, James of Fredericksburgh & Sophiasburgh, m. Anne.
   Samuel of Fredericksburgh. OC 8 July 1797.
   John of Sophiasburgh. OC 26 March 1817.   [Cont'd]

McTAGGART, James - Cont'd
Mary, m. George Parliament of Sophiasburgh 20 Oct 1807. OC 26 Jan 1808
James of Sophiasburgh, m. Phoebe Way, Feb., 1810. OC 16 Feb 1811.
Martha, bapt. 2 Oct 1791; m. Jacob Hand (?) of Hallowell 20 July 1813.
    OC 26 March 1817.
William of Sophiasburgh. OC 16 June 1819.
Robert of Sophiasburgh. OC 3 Nov 1831.
David of Sophiasburgh. OC 7 May 1828.

McVEY, John.
Catherine, m. ---- Stotts. OC 5 Nov 1799.
Mary, m. ---- Statts. OC 5 Nov 1799.
Daniel of Elizabethtown. OC 24 March 1819.

McWILLIAMS, John of Osnabruck.
Elizabeth, m. ---- Paupts. OC 10 June 1800.
David of Osnabruck. OC 17 March 1807.
John of Cornwall. OC 7 Aug 1810.
James of Osnabruck. OC 11 Nov 1815.
Nancy, m. Henry Winter of Osnabruck. OC 20 May 1817.
Robert of Cornwall. OC 13 June 1818.

M

MABEE, Lavinia, widow of Frederick Mabee. m. (2) William B. Hilton,
  formerly Sgt. King's American Dragoons.
Sarah, m. Silas Montross of Charlotteville. OC 23 March 1799.
Mary, m. David Secord of Charlotteville. OC 23 March 1799.
Anne, m. John Stone of Charlotteville. OC 17 March 1797.

MABEE, Lewis of Willoughby.
Dorothy, m. ---- Burger of Fort Erie. OC 29 Oct 1800.
Marice (Mary), m. John Palmer of Willoughby (Bertie). OC 27 Feb 1812,
    OC 20 May 1817.

MAIN, Thomas of Edwardsburgh.
Jenny, m. ---- Crawford. OC 23 June 1801.
Matthew. OC 23 June 1801.
James of Edwardsburgh. OC 5 March 1811.
Jane. OC 27 Sept 1833.
Henrietta. OC 17 March 1834.

MALCOLM, Finlay of Burford. He was b. about 1750 in north of Scotland.
Jennet, m. ---- Steinhoff of Woodhouse. OC 18 Aug 1801.
Sarah, m. Charles Eddy of Burford. OC 30 July 1806.
Duncan of Burford. OC 17 Sept 1823.   [Cont'd]

MALCOLM, Finlay - Cont'd
  Tryphena, m. Abraham Chapman of Burford. OC 30 July 1806.
  Margaret, m. Mathias Woodley of Burford. OC 19 April 1816.
  Hugh of Burford, m. Eliza; d. 1828. OC 17 Sept 1823.
  Finlay of Burford. OC 11 April 1797.
  John of Townsend. OC 11 April 1797.
  Peter of Burford. OC 4 Feb 1830.
  George of Oakland. OC 28 Oct 1835.
  Catharine, m. Justus Smith of Oakland. OC 4 April 1833.
  Eliakim of Oakland, D. P. S. OC 4 April 1833.
  James of Oakland, d. there in 1858 aet. 60 yrs. OC 4 April 1833.
  Charles of Oakland. OC 28 Feb 1829.
  Jennett, m. (2) Frederick Smith of Townsend. OC 15 May 1835.

MALLORY, Enoch of Yonge.
  Isaac of Yonge. OC 23 Nov 1816.
  Joseph of Yonge. OC 23 Nov 1816.
  Huldah, m. Isaiah Wood of Yonge. OC 13 June 1818.
  Jeremiah of Yonge. OC 3 Feb 1834.

MALLORY, Jeremiah of Yonge.
  Thomas of Yonge. OC 13 Oct 1836.
  Lorinda. OC 3 Feb 1834.
  Catharine. OC 3 Feb 1834.
  Mercy. OC 3 Feb 1834.
  Henry of Yonge. OC 19 Nov 1831.
  David 2nd of Yonge. OC 19 Nov 1831.
  Elisah of Yonge. OC 19 Nov 1831.
  Huldah, m. Thomas P. Kinion. OC 19 Nov 1831.

MANHART, David of Elizabethtown.
  Elizabeth, m. ---- Seeley of Elizabethtown. OC 23 Sept 1800.
  George of Elizabethtown. OC 13 Nov 1818.
  Margaret, m. William Hamblin of Elizabethtown. OC 13 Nov 1818.
  Henry of Elizabethtown. OC 4 April 1821.
  William of Elizabethtown. OC 25 July 1798.

MARACLE, Frederick of Niagara. wife Rebecca.
  Sarah, m. William Staats of Niagara. OC 28 Oct 1806.
  Elizabeth, m. James Bunting of Niagara. OC 6 Dec 1808.
  Mary. OC 12 Nov 1811.
  Benjamin of Niagara. OC 12 Nov 1811.
  Solomon of Niagara, bapt. 18 Feb 1793. OC 27 Feb 1818.
  Abraham of Niagara. OC 13 April 1819.
  Rebecca, m. John Clement of Niagara. OC 31 May 1820.
  Margaret, m. John Colby of Niagara. OC 15 May 1822.
  Catharine, m. Adam Clement of Zorra. OC 1 Aug 1833.
  Henry of Niagara. OC 19 Dec 1833.   [Cont'd]

MARACLE, Frederick - Cont'd
  Delilah, m. Alexander Rogers of Niagara 3 Apr 1828. OC 28 Feb 1835.
  Frederick of Niagara. OC 28 Feb 1835.

MARACLE, Jacob of Osnabruck.
  Jane, m. Donald McDonell of Ernestown. OC 16 Feb 1799; OC 1 Dec 1836.

MARACLE, John of Louth, m. Margaret.
  Sarah, m. Joseph Pettit of Willoughby. OC 16 Feb 1810.
  Clarinda, m. Moses Gilmore of Grantham. OC 20 May 1817.
  John Murray of Nelson, bapt. 8 Oct 1796. OC 21 Apr 1819.
  Abraham of Flamborough. OC 3 May 1820.
  Benjamin of Flamborough. OC 3 May 1820.
  Mary, m. William Petrie of Grand River. OC 17 May 1820.

MARCELLIS, John of Williamsburgh.
  Catherine, m. George Cook of Williamsburgh. OC 26 Feb 1805.
  Nancy. OC 25 Feb 1806.
  John of Williamsburgh. OC 17 March 1807.
  Thomas of Williamsburgh. OC 23 Feb 1808.
  Garret of Williamsburgh. OC 25 Feb 1812.
  Peter of Williamsburgh, bapt. 8 Jan 1791. OC 25 Feb 1812.
  Mary, m. John P. Empey of Osnabruck. OC 4 July 1815.

MARCELLIS, Peter of Clinton.
  Hannah, bapt. 2 Feb 1793. OC 16 July 1816.
  John of Clinton. OC 16 July 1816.
  Stephen of Clinton. OC 16 July 1816.
  Mary, m. Philander Hopkins of Clinton. OC 25 Feb 1819.
  Peter of Clinton. OC 14 Nov 1821.
  Margaret, m. John Lawrence of Clinton. OC 2 April 1823.
  Elizabeth, m. John Singer of Clinton. OC 8 Oct 1840.
  Phoebe, m. George Anger of Bertie. OC 3 Oct 1833.
  George of Clinton. OC 21 Feb 1832.

MARCELLUS, Sevares of Williamsburgh.
  Catherine, m. ---- Crowder. OC 10 June 1800.
  Mary, m. Adam Cassellman of Osnabruck. OC 26 Feb 1806.
  Elizabeth, m. Christian Walliser of Matilda. OC 5 March 1808.
  Lany. OC 27 March 1813. Williamsburgh.
  Catherine. OC 19 April 1816. Williamsburgh.
  Frederick of Williamsburgh. OC 19 April 1816.

MARKLAND, Thomas of Town of Kingston, m. Catharine, dau of Hanyost
  and Mary Herchmer. He d. 31 Jan 1840, aged 84 yrs.
  George Herchmer of Town of Kingston. OC 28 Feb 1818.

MARLETT, John of Edwardsburgh, m. Margaret; died 1846.
Anna Eliza, m. John Larby of Edwardsburgh. OC 12 June 1834.
Nelson of Edwardsburgh. OC 12 June 1834.
Susannah. OC 28 Feb 1851.
Nancy. OC 28 Oct 1850.
Huldah. OC 28 Feb 1851.
Marcus of Edwardsburgh. OC 28 Feb 1851.

MARSH, Abraham of Cornwall, m. Catharine French.
Sarah, m. Adam Dixon of Cornwall. OC 16 Feb 1811.
Clara. OC 16 Feb 1811.
Elizabeth, bapt. 4 March 1792; m. Robert McIntyre of Cornwall. OC 25
February 1812.
John of Cornwall. OC 25 Feb 1812.
Mary Ann, bapt. 12 Oct 1794. OC 17 Feb 1816.
Catherine, b. 28 Apr 1805; m. William G. Barnhart of Cornwall. OC 3
November 1836.
Marilla, m. John Telford of Cornwall. OC 28 Feb 1835.
Abraham of Cornwall, b. 28 Dec 1801. OC 2 Feb 1832.

MARSH, Joseph of Fredericksburgh. Soldier, King's Rangers. See O.C. 24
Jan 1828. He was buried 11 Feb 1788. m. Susannah. His widow md. (2)
James Parks, U.E., 14 June 1789.
Ann, bapt. 31 Dec 1787; m. Richard Woodcock of Fredericksburgh on 1
March 1801. OC 10 May 1803.
Lavinia, bapt. 10 March 1788; m. Abraham Woodcock Jr. of Fredericks-
burgh. OC 17 March 1807.
Benjamin of Fredericksburgh, bapt. 31 Dec 1787. OC 16 Feb 1810.
Robert of Marysburgh. OC 2 Oct 1834.
John of Sophiasburgh. OC 2 Oct 1834.
Mary. OC 14 Oct 1834. Marysburgh.

MARSH, Mathias of Sidney.
Edmund of Sidney. OC 3 June 1817.
William of Ameliasburgh. OC 3 June 1817.
Lucy, m. Stephen Young of Murray. OC 6 Feb 1822.
Charles of Sidney. OC 30 Nov 1837.
James of Sidney. OC 14 June 1839.
Almira. OC 26 Nov 1840.
Eliza Ann. OC 26 Nov 1840.
Charlotte. OC 26 Nov 1840.
Abraham of Ameliasburgh. OC 12 Feb 1831.
Henry of Sidney. OC 12 Feb 1831.
Samuel of Sidney. OC 12 Feb 1831.
Sarah, m. William Page of Ameliasburgh. OC 12 Feb 1831.
Clarry, m. Samuel Gilbert of Sidney. OC 12 Feb 1831.
Esther, m. Reuben White of Sidney. OC 12 Feb 1831.
Archibald. See OC 28 June 1796. [Cont'd]

MARSH, Mathias - Cont'd
  Mary. OC 25 Nov 1842.

MARSH, William Sr.
  Hannah, m. Asa Weller of Carrying Place. OC 28 June 1796.
  Mathias of Sidney, U. E.
  William Samuel of Hope. OC 22 June 1797.
  Samuel William of Hope, m. Jane Ostrum. OC 8 Oct 1796.
  Benjamin of Hope. OC 8 Oct 1796.
  Mary, m. Leonard Soper of Hope. OC 26 June 1797.

MARSH, William of St. John's.
  Charlotte, m. Jesse Southwick of Ameliasburgh. OC 5 Feb 1829.

MARSH, William.
  Johnson of Hope. OC 20 Feb 1840.
  Elizabeth, m. Jonathan Sexton of Hope. OC 4 May 1836.

MARTIN, Peter of Niagara. Butler's Rangers.
  George of Niagara. OC 16 June 1819.
  Jane, m. Richard Collins of Hope; d. 11 March 1828. OC 8 Feb 1827.

MARTIN, William.
  Phoebe, m. ---- Spicer of Augusta. OC 18 June 1800.
  Catherine, m. ---- Nicklinson. OC 21 April 1801.
  Sarah, m. ---- Hodgkins. OC 10 June 1800.

MATLOCK, Caleb of Pelham.
  Benjamin of Pelham. OC 5 June 1810.
  Rachel, m. ---- Bowman of Pelham. OC 8 Sept 1836.

MATTHEWS, James of Woodhouse.
  Anna, m. Daniel Hazen Jr. of Woodhouse. OC 19 Dec 1806.
  Sarah. OC 18 June 1811.
  Philip of Woodhouse. OC 23 Nov 1816.
  John of Woodhouse. OC 23 Nov 1816.
  Amy, m. Gregory Warwick of Malahide. OC 1 July 1819.
  Samuel William. OC 9 Feb 1832.
  James Freeman. OC 9 Feb 1832.
  George. OC 9 Feb 1832.
  Ninian Holmes. OC 9 Feb 1832.
  Amy, m. Jacob C. Boughner. OC 9 Feb 1832.

MATTHEWS, Jonathan of Grantham.
  Isaac of Pelham. OC 7 Aug 1810.
  Martha. OC 14 Dec 1816.
  Abraham of Windham. OC 19 Feb 1823.
  Peter of Malahide. OC 23 May 1833.   [Cont'd]

MATTHEWS, Jonathan - Cont'd
Thomas of Malahide, fanning mill maker. OC 19 Dec 1833.
Eve, m. James Butler of Malahide. OC 19 June 1832.
Lucy, m. Joshua Nelson of Caistor. OC 6 Sept 1826.

MATTICE, Adam of Osnabruck. Drummer, Butler's Rangers.
Sophia, m. Frederick Winter of Osnabruck. OC 20 May 1817.
Nancy. OC 20 May 1817.
Adam of Cornwall. OC 18 March 1818.
Abraham of Cornwall. OC 30 June 1819.
Priscilla. OC 28 Oct 1835. OC 3 Nov 1835.
Sarah. OC 2 Feb 1825.
Elizabeth. OC 2 Feb 1825.
John of Osnabruck. OC 2 Feb 1825.

MATTICE, John of Cornwall.
Leana, m. John Baker of Elizabethtown. OC 7 April 1807.
Margaret, m. William Raymond of Cornwall. OC 8 Feb 1808.
Sophia, m. Solomon Raymond of Cornwall. OC 5 March 1810.
Catharine. OC 5 March 1810.
George of Cornwall. OC 5 March 1810.
John of Cornwall. OC 18 March 1818.
Sarah, m. Le Grand Clark of Cornwall. OC 4 Feb 1824.
Michael of Cornwall. OC 4 Feb 1824.
William of York. OC 4 Feb 1824.

MATTICE, Nicholas of Elizabethtown and Bastard.
Isaac. OC 26 May 1801.
John of Bastard. OC 4 July 1809.
David of Bastard. OC 23 Nov 1816. OC 26 March 1817.
Mary Ann, m. Benjamin Shamway of Bastard. OC 13 June 1818.
Elizabeth, m. John Brass of Bastard. OC 10 Dec 1818.
Jane. OC 5 Oct 1837.
Caspar of Bastard. OC 8 Nov 1838.
Amelia, m. William P. Bates of Bastard 4 June 1832. OC 28 Oct 1835.
Abigail, m. Cyrus Eaton of Pittsburgh. OC 1 Aug 1833.

MATTICE, William of Osnabruck & Etobicoke. Soldier, Butler's Rangers.
Nicholas of Osnabruck. OC 3 April 1810.
Margaret, m. James Jackson of Etobicoke. OC 26 March 1817.
Mary, m. Adam Brown of Niagara, 25 June 1812. OC 25 Feb 1818.
William of Etobicoke. OC 12 July 1820.
John of Etobicoke, m. Rebecca Smith, 12 Nov 1821. OC 1 May 1822.
Jacob of Etobicoke. OC 8 Feb 1827.
Sally, m. John McVean of Toronto Gore 26 Sept 1826. OC 8 Feb 1827.
Solomon of Etobicoke, m. Jean Stuart, 3 Aug 1823. OC 22 July 1824. He
    m. (2) Jane Howden of Etobicoke, 25 Oct 1832.

MAY, William. Butler's Rangers.
    John of Caistor. OC 17 Aug 1795.
    Nancy. OC 4 April 1797.
    Catharine, m. Nicholas Smith of Pelham. OC 3 Aug 1795.
    Peter of Caistor, b. 20 May 1765 near Albany, N.Y.; m. Eve Clendenning;
        d. 7 June 1827. OC 17 Aug 1795.

MAYBEE, Abraham of Adolphustown, m. Anne.
    Jane, m. Dr. Samuel Neilson of Adolphustown 10 Nvo 1800. OC 25 Nov
        1800.
    Elizabeth, bapt. 24 Feb 1788; m. Noxon Harris of Adolphustown. OC 6
        January 1806.
    Abraham of Murray. OC 30 Aug 1797. OC 6 Aug 1840.
    Peter of Hallowell. OC 31 July 1797.
    Isaac, bapt. 10 July 1791.
    Robert McDowall of Adolphustown. OC 4 Sept 1834.

MAYBEE, John of Ernestown (Willoughby ?)
    John. OC 14 April 1801.
    Abraham of Ameliasburgh. OC 16 June 1819.
    Mary, m. David Rice of Thorold. OC 4 Jan 1840.
    Daniel of Marysburgh. OC 4 Feb 1835.
    Mary, m. Daniel Masters of Ameliasburgh. OC 28 Feb 1835.
    Henry of Ameliasburgh. OC 5 April 1825.
    Nancy, m. John Beam. OC 7 May 1842.

MEDDAUGH, James of Stamford.
    Ann, m. John Brooks of Queenston. OC 20 May 1817.
    John of Niagara. OC 30 June 1819.
    Joseph of Niagara. OC 12 June 1822.
    Deborah, m. Richard Clements of Niagara 10 Mar 1830. OC 24 Nov 1836.
    Benjamin of Niagara. OC 11 Feb 1836.
    Eliza. OC 2 May 1836. Niagara.
    Frances (dau). O.C. 23 Nov 1825. Niagara.

MEDDAUGH, James of Niagara.
    John of Niagara, m. Rebecca Fields. OC 8 Nov 1832.
    Hannah, m. Reuben Goodman of Grantham. OC 8 Nov 1832.

MEDDAUCH, John of Matilda, Sr.
    Catherine, m. William Stanford of Matilda. OC 18 June 1799; 26 Jan 1808.
    Polly [Mary], m. [Andrew] Sipes of Matilda, U.E. OC 27 June 1800.
    [John, md. Mary ----. A Bible record of their family is in TOR 1: 252]

MEDDOUGH, Martin of Osnabruck and Trafalgar.
    Mary, m. John Munro of Matilda. OC 3 March 1809.
    Elizabeth, m. Isaac King of Augusta. OC 24 April 1810.
    Margaret, m. William Osburn of Augusta. OC 24 April 1810.   [Cont'd]

MEDDOUGH, Martin - Cont'd
George of Flamborough East. OC 19 April 1816.
Martin of Flamborough East. OC 19 April 1816.
Phoebe, m. Thomas Henton of Trafalgar. OC 5 Oct 1818.
Eleanor, m. Stephen Belknap of Trafalgar. OC 30 Dec 1819.
Jacob of Trafalgar. OC 14 Nov 1821.
James of Trafalgar. OC 30 Oct 1822.
Sarah, m. James Sherburne of Trafalgar. OC 26 Oct 1825.
Jane, m. Richard Waggoner of Trafalgar. OC 22 July 1824.

MEDDAUGH, Stephen of Flamborough East, Nelson and Pickering.
Mary, m. Elias Rambough of Nelson. OC 16 Aug 1810.
Elizabeth, m. John McMullan of Saltfleet. OC 16 April 1811.
Stephen of Niagara. OC 3 June 1817.
Robert of Uxbridge. OC 8 Dec 1835.
Jacob of Barton. OC 11 July 1833.
Nelly, m. Richard Carroll of Oxford-on-Thames. OC 28 Oct 1833.
Catharine, m. James Depew of Barton. OC 5 April 1832.
Anne, m. Edward Mudge of Dumfries. OC 6 Nov 1829.
John of Pickering. OC 2 Feb 1825.
Margaret, m. Peter Thibado of York. OC 2 Feb 1825.

MEREDITH, Charles of Grimsby. North Carolina Regt. Born in Pennsyvania
about 1761.
John of Grimsby. OC 16 Dec 1815.
Richard of Grimsby. OC 3 Nov 1819.
Mary, m. Lewis Felker of Gainsborough. OC 17 April 1822.
Ann, m. Francis Headley of Grimsby. OC 24 Dec 1823.
Jesse of Grimsby. OC 24 Dec 1823.
Abraham of Grimsby. OC 27 June 1833.
Elizabeth, m. Myron Gould Durkee of Grimsby. OC 6 Dec 1832.
William of Grimsby. OC 4 Feb 1830.
Deborah, m. Seelye Walker of Grimsby. OC 10 May 1831.
Bethia, m. William Taylor of Grimsby. OC 5 Nov 1831.

MERKLEY, Frederick of Williamsburgh.
Elizabeth. OC 4 July 1815.
Catharine. OC 4 July 1815.
Mary. OC 4 July 1815.
Frederick of Matilda. OC 20 Feb 1840.
Michael F. of Williamsburgh. OC 25 July 1833.
John F. of Williamsburgh. OC 25 July 1833.
Rebecca, m. George Hummell of Winchester. OC 19 Aug 1833.

MERKLE, Henry of Williamsburgh.
Mary. OC 16 Feb 1811. Williamsburgh.
George of Williamsburgh. OC 25 Feb 1812.
Christopher of Williamsburgh. OC 25 Feb 1812.

MERKLEY, Henry of Williamsburgh.
Nancy, m. John J. Empey of Osnabruck. OC 18 March 1818.
Henry of Matilda. OC 11 Feb 1836.
Lany. OC 16 June 1834.
Sophrenus of Williamsburgh. OC 16 June 1834.
Sarah. OC 16 June 1834.
Jacob H. of Williamsburgh. OC 4 Sept 1834.
Catharine, m. John Deeks of Williamsburgh. OC 5 Feb 1835.
Elizabeth, m. John G. Crysler of Williamsburgh. OC 26 Oct 1825.

MERKLEY, Jacob of Williamsburgh.
John A. of Williamsburgh. OC 19 April 1816.

MERKLEY, Michael of Williamsburgh.
Elizabeth. OC 20 May 1817.
Jacob of Williamsburgh. OC 3 June 1817.
Mary, m. Suffrenus Casselman of Williamsburgh. OC 16 April 1818.
Catharine, m. Jacob Garlough of Williamsburgh. OC 18 March 1818.
Michael of Williamsburgh. OC 22 Jan 1823.
Nancy. OC 22 Jan 1823.
Christeen, m. Jacob Ross of Osnabruck. OC 10 Jan 1832.
Lany, m. Henry Barkley of Williamsburgh. OC 1 Aug 1833.
John M. of Williamsburgh. OC 5 Feb 1835.
George M. of Williamsburgh. OC 5 Feb 1835.
Margaret, m. Henry Bell of Williamsburgh. OC 5 Feb 1835.
Eleanor, m. Christian Casselman of Williamsburgh. OC 5 Feb 1835.

MERRITT, Thomas of Town of Niagara and Grantham, m. Mary Hamilton in
Charleston, S.C., 27 July 1781; He was born 28 Oct 1759; d. 12 May 1842;
His wife died 21 March 1843.
William Hamilton of Grantham, b. Bedford, N.Y., 3 July 1793; m. Cath-
arine Prendergast, 13 March 1815; d. 5 July 1862. OC 17 Feb 1816.
Ann Maria, b. 1797, bapt. 1 Oct 1797; m. Charles Ingersoll of Oxford-on
Thames, 5 Sept 1816; d. 20 Nov 1850, aged 53. OC 30 Oct 1822.
Susan, b. 1801; bapt. 28 Jan 1802; m. Elias Smith Adams of St. Cathar-
ines, 14 Oct 1823. OC 30 Oct 1822.
Caroline, b. 1791; m. James Gordon of Stamford, 2 Aug 1810. Drowned
Feb., 1824 at Queenston. OC 5 Feb 1823.
Amy, b. 1782. Died young.
Phoebe, b. 1784. Died young.

MEYERS, George W. of Sidney.
Tobias W. of Sidney. OC 6 Feb 1822.
Peter W. of Marysburgh. OC 6 Feb 1822.
Mary, m. James Vandevoort of Marysburgh. OC 6 Feb 1822.
Elley, m. George Westfall of Sidney. OC 6 Feb 1822.
Nancy W., m. John S. Meyers of Sidney. OC 1 May 1834.
John W. of Sidney. OC 20 July 1825; OC 1 May 1834.   [Cont'd]

MEYERS, George W.
Margaret, m. Peter Vanalstine of Sidney. OC 5 June 1834.

MEYERS, John Walden of Sidney. Capt.
Mary W., m. John Bleecker of Sidney. OC 13 Nov 1797. OC 8 Oct 1796.
Jacob W. of Thurlow. OC 7 Feb 1833.
Catharine W., m. John Bleecker of Sidney 7 Oct 1788. Land Board Certif-
icate, 8/2 Sidney.
Leonard W. of Sidney, m. Margaret Ackerman, 14 Apr 1793. OC 13 Nov
1797.
Ann W., m. ---- Gilbert. OC 13 Nov 1797.
Tobias W. of Sidney.
George W. of Sidney, m. Allida Van Alstine, 5 May 1789.

MIDDAUGH. See Meddaugh, etc.

MILLARD, Daniel of Townsend.
Peter of Townsend. OC 30 Oct 1810.
Squire of Woodhouse. OC 16 Feb 1811.
Daniel of Townsend. OC 16 Jan 1816.
Jason of Dumfries. OC 26 July 1820.
Jesse of Oakland. OC 5 March 1828.
John of Stamford. OC 2 July 1828.
Sarah, m. Elias Baker of Oakland. OC 28 Nov 1826.
Martin of Windham. OC 22 July 1824.

MILLARD, Thomas of Stamford.
Noah. m. Elsa Buckner. OC 12 July 1796.
Mary, m. Wareham Johnson of Stamford. OC 9 Feb 1820.

MILLER, Andrew of Bertie.
Peter of Bertie. OC 17 June 1819.
John of Yarmouth. OC 15 Aug 1821.
Andrew of Bertie. OC 9 Jan 1822.
Edward of Bertie. OC 2 April 1835.
Melinda, m. William Baxter of Bertie. OC 28 Oct 1835.
Jacob of Bertie. OC 10 Oct 1834.
Eliza Elizabeth. OC 28 March 1835.
Benjamin of Bertie. OC 5 July 1826.

MILLER, Andrew of Ernestown.
John of Ernestown. OC 29 Jan 1808.
Jacob of Ernestown. OC 25 Feb 1809.
Samuel of Ernestown, m. Amanda Hawley. OC 11 April 1833.
Peter of Ernestown. OC 3 Oct 1833.
Ann, m. Frederick Keller of Ernestown. OC 23 Nov 1825.

MILLER, Cornelius. Soldier, King's Rangers. Died s.p. His brother, John Miller, U.E., of Hallowell. Heir & Devisee Commission July 1829 no. 20.

MILLER, Garrett of Ernestown.
   Peter of Loughborough. OC 16 Nov 1797.
   Agnes. OC 16 Nov 1797.
   Elizabeth. OC 16 Feb 1811.
   Garrett of Ernestown, b. 18 Nov 1786; m. Nancy Foster (b. 1796- d. 1870)
      in 1821; d. 28 Dec 1863. OC 5 March 1811.
   William of Ernestown, b. 25 Nov 1783; m.(1) Hannah McKim; m.(2) Mrs.
      Jane Bell; d. 20 Oct 1863. OC 5 March 1811.
   Michael of Fredericksburgh. OC 25 Feb 1812. OC 18 March 1818.
   John of Ernestown, b. 19 Dec 1790; d. 15 Jan 1864. OC 3 Nov 1836.

MILLER, George.   (All O.C.'s below in 1850 or 1851).
   Sebastian of Ernestown.
   Ann, m. ---- Hartman of Ernestown.
   Alpheus of Ernestown.
   Jacob of Ernestown.
   William G. of Ernestown.
   Dorothy, m. ---- Baker of Camden.
   Juliana.
   Catherine.

MILLER, Jacob of Ernestown. Adjt.
   George of Ernestown. Notarial Record 3 Dec 1840.
   Mary, m. Zachariah Snyder of Ernestown. Land Board Certificate, 6/3
      Camden.

MILLER, John of Sophiasburgh and Hallowell.
   Nancy, m. Hugh Read of Hallowell. OC 23 Nov 1837.
   Mary, m. Daniel Hicks of Marysburgh. OC 15 March 1838.
   John Brock of Hallowell. OC 29 March 1838. OC 1850 or 51.
   Richard of Hallowell. OC 21 June 1838.
   William Case of Hallowell. OC 29 June 1838.
   Mahalla C. OC 18 July 1839.
   Margaret, m. Duncan McCrimmon of Hallowell. OC 27 April 1837.
   Jacob of Hallowell. OC 29 June 1837.
   Dorcas Y., m. Isaac Hare of Hallowell. OC 27 July 1837.
   Hannah, m. ---- Frederum of Fredericksburgh. OC 1850 or 1851.
   Elizabeth, m. ---- Baker of Ernestown. OC 1850 or 1851.

MILLER, Jonathan of Murray and Fredericksburgh.
   Luke C. of Ameliasburgh. OC 4 Dec 1834.
   Justus of Ameliasburgh. OC 4 Dec 1834.

MILLER, Peter. Sgt., Butler's Rangers.
   Thomas. OC 20 March 1797.   [Cont'd]

MILLER, Peter - Cont'd
Lanah, m. Peter Serviss of Matilda. OC 9 July 1802.

MILLER, Samuel of Fredericksburgh.
Phoebe. OC 6 Aug 1840.
Elizabeth, m. Charles Maze of Thurlow. OC 27 Oct 1836.
John C. of Camden East. OC 27 Oct 1836.
Samuel of Huntingdon. OC 27 Oct 1836.
Nancy, m. John M. Rambough of Fredericksburgh. OC 27 Oct 1836.
Patience, m. Abraham G. Dafoe of Huntingdon. OC 27 Oct 1836.
Catharine, m. John Spencer of Fredericksburgh. OC 1 June 1837.

MILLER, Stephen of Cornwall, m. Hannah French.
Lewis of Cornwall. OC 25 Aug 1838.
Elizabeth, bapt. 3 May 1796; m. Oliver Nimmock of Cornwall. OC 11 Oct
1838.
Stephen of Cornwall. OC 24 Nov 1836.
Jeremiah French of Cornwall, bapt. 21 Sept 1800. OC 16 Feb 1837.
Cornelius of Cornwall. OC 3 Dec 1835.
Amarilla, b. 7 June 1798; m. Alexander McCorquadale of Cornwall. OC
2 July 1829.
Calvin of Cornwall. OC 23 Feb 1830.
Elijah, bapt. 1 March 1795.

MILLER, Thomas of Niagara (St. Davids).
Mary, m. Luther Dunn of Niagara (St. Davids), 10 Dec 1828. OC 28 Oct
1835.
Peota (dau.) OC 7 March 1827. Stamford.
Ruth, m. Richard Coleman of Toronto. OC 18 Feb 1843.

MILLER, Zebedec.
Mary, m. ---- Trickey of Lansdowne. OC 18 Aug 1801.

MILLROSS, Andrew.
John. OC 10 June 1800.
Ann, m. John P. Helmer of Cornwall. OC 5 Jan 1798.
William of Osnabruck. OC 17 March 1807.

MILLROY, John of Cornwall, m. Margaret Kirkland who d. 24 Feb 1836 ae 69.
William of Cornwall. OC 31 Oct 1809.
Catharine, bapt. 15 Sept 1793; m. John Johnston of Cornwall; d. 7 April
1858 ae 65. OC 4 July 1815.
John of Cornwall, d. 7 Dec 1872 ae 82. OC 4 July 1815.
Ann, bapt. 23 Aug 1795. OC 18 March 1818.
James. OC 3 April 1828.

MILLS, John of Clinton.
Joseph of Grimsby. OC 27 June 1800.   [Cont'd]

MILLS, John - Cont'd
  Phoebe, m. ---- Adair of Clinton. OC 27 June 1800.
  Mary, m. ---- Null of Grimsby. OC 1 Sept 1801.
  Rachel, m. Robert Graham. OC 1 Sept 1801.
  Hannah, m. Lewis Beam of York. OC 20 Oct 1801. OC 17 April 1804.
  Sarah, m. ---- Boils of Markham. OC 4 May 1804.
  John of Grimsby. OC 3 June 1817.

MILTON, Thomas of Pittsburgh.
  Margaret Ann, m. Thomas Brown of Kingston. OC 15 Oct 1823.

MINAKER, John.
  Ludowick of Marysburgh. OC 30 Aug 1797.

MITCHELL, George of Cornwall and Charlottenburgh, m. Margaret McEwan.
  Hervey. OC 3 July 1798.
  Thomas of Charlottenburgh, bapt. 22 March 1795. OC 3 June 1817.
  Mary Eleanor, bapt. 1 Apr 1798; m. Thomas Dixon of Cornwall. OC 5 Nov
    1818.
  George C. of Yonge. OC 13 Nov 1818.
  Sarah, bapt. 21 Oct 1792.
  David of Bertie. OC 4 April 1833.

MITCHELL, John of Cornwall.
  Sarah, m. Stillman Rogers of Cornwall. OC 17 Feb 1816.

MITTS, Henry of Fredericksburgh and Thurlow.
  Abraham of Portland. OC 7 Aug 1834.
  Elizabeth. OC 7 Aug 1834.
  Reuben of Loughborough. OC 7 Aug 1834.
  David of Loughborough. OC 7 Aug 1834.

MITTS, John of Fredericksburgh.
  Susannah, bapt. 18 Dec 1792; m. George Behn of Fredericksburgh on 12
    June 1810. OC 16 Feb 1811.
  Jacob of Fredericksburgh, bapt. 10 Dec 1790. OC 2 March 1816.
  James B. of Fredericksburgh, bapt. 29 Jan 1795. OC 2 March 1816.
  Marian, m. Cornelius Alcombrack of Fredericksburgh 10 Jan 1816. OC
    6 August 1816.
  Jane, m. Edward Loyd of Fredericksburgh 18 Oct 1818. OC 2 May 1833.
  William B. of Fredericksburgh, bapt. 2 Nov 1808. OC 27 June 1833.
  Henry of Fredericksburgh, bapt. 12 July 1797. OC 3 April 1834.
  Margaret, m. Henry Alcombrack of Fredericksburgh. OC 22 July 1824.

MOKE, Philip of Osnabruck.
  Polly, m. John Fetterly of Osnabruck. OC 17 March 1807.
  Margaret. OC 3 March 1809.
  Simon of Osnabruck. OC 5 Nov 1818.

MOLLOY, James of Montreal.
James of Montreal. OC 18 Aug 1821.
Alice. OC 18 Aug 1821.

MONGER, Charles
Joseph of Colchester. OC 29 March 1808. OC 29 Sept 1824.

MONGER, William of Colchester.
Sarah, m. Ezekiel Boring Colchester. OC 19 May 1812.
Susannah, m. Joseph Quick of Colchester. OC 6 March 1822; 28 Oct 1835.

MONRO, John of Walsingham. Lt., N.J. Vols. He was born about 1761. See
2 & 3/9 Grimsby.
Charlotte, m. Paul Dusten of Walsingham. OC 23 Dec 1815.
Harriet Ann, m. William Galesby of Walsingham 19 Nov 1816. OC 23 Dec
1815.
Mary, m. Jeremiah Green of Townsend. OC 23 Dec 1815.
Amelia Sophia. OC 23 Dec 1815.
Eliza, m. Justus Munro of Middleton. OC 7 Mar 1828. OC 11 Mar 1828.
Naomi Opak, m. Henry R. Beamer of Windham. OC 5 Feb 1835.

MONTGOMERY, Archibald, m. Susannah dau Jesse & Ruth (Kennicot) Purdy.
Mary, m. Henry Brown of Elizabethtown. OC 5 March 1808.
Betsey Ann, m. Christian Holmes of Elizabethtown. OC 7 Aug 1811.
Jesse of Edwardsburgh. OC 28 Feb 1833.
Archibald of Edwardsburgh. OC 28 Feb 1833.

MONTROSS, Peter of Charlotteville.
Fanny, m. Thomas Price of Charlotteville. OC 5 Jan 1802.
Margaret, m. Lawrence Johnson of Charlotteville. OC 16 Feb 1802.
Anderson of Charlotteville. OC 16 Feb 1802.
Levy of Charlotteville. OC 16 Feb 1802.
Simon of Charlotteville. OC 15 April 1806.
Amy, m. Andrew McClish of Charlotteville. OC 3 Dec 1807.
Hannah, m. William Drake of Ancaster. OC 27 Nov 1815.
Peter of Charlotteville. OC 27 Jan 1816.
Silas of Charlotteville. OC 27 July 1797.

MOODY, Walter of York and Kingston.
Catharine, m. Robt Duff 30 April 1816. OC 4 April 1797.
James of Kingston, m. Jane Dawson. OC 4 April 1797.
William of York. OC 4 April 1797.
Walter of York. OC 4 April 1797.
Sarah, m. Abraham Mattice. OC 4 April 1797. See Robertson's Land-
marks, v. 6, p. 261, re Abr. Mattice.

MOORE, Dudley.
Roger. OC 20 June 1799.   [Cont'd]

MOORE, Dudley - Cont'd
  Rebecca. OC 24 Sept 1799.
  Dudley. OC 28 June 1799.

MOORE, Hosea of Yonge.
  Martha, m. George Bradley of Haldimand. OC 2 May 1836.
  Amos of Haldimand. OC 2 May 1836.
  James. OC 9 May 1836.
  (Martha, m. ---- Williams ?)

MOORE, Jeremiah of Pelham.
  Elizabeth, m. John Taylor Jr. of Pelham. OC 23 Feb 1809.
  Jeremiah of Pelham. OC 23 Feb 1809.
  Andrew of Pelham. OC 21 March 1809.
  Ann, m. Benjamin Hill of Thorold. OC 7 Nov 1809.
  James of Pelham. OC 25 Feb 1812.
  Mary, m. John Cohoe of Pelham. OC 2 March 1816.
  John of Pelham. OC 19 Feb 1817.
  Jacob, m. Rachel. OC 19 Feb 1817.

MOORE, Solomon of Louth and Bayham.
  Solomon of Bayham. OC 13 Nov 1822.
  Rebecca, m. Doyle McKenney of Malahide. OC 17 Sept 1823.
  Alexander of Bayham. OC 6 Aug 1840.
  Ann Isabel. OC 6 Aug 1840.
  George of Malahide. OC 16 Feb 1837.
  Mary Jane. OC 4 April 1833.
  Francis of Malahide. OC 2 Feb 1832.
  John Augustus of Burford. OC 30 March 1847.
  David of Windham. OC 30 March 1847.

MOORE, Sylvester of Edwardsburgh.
  Sarah, m. Hugh McKinloss of Kingston. OC 18 May 1833.
  Sylvester of Edwardsburgh. OC 25 Jan 1834.
  Peter of Edwardsburgh. OC 28 Feb 1833.
  William of Edwardsburgh. OC 28 Feb 1833.

MOORE, William.
  Nancy, m. Stephen Smith of Elizabethtown. OC 21 Sept 1837.

MORDEN, Daniel of Flamborough West. Pvt., K.R.R.N.Y.
  Jane, m. Samson Howell of Flamborough West. OC 16 Jan 1816.
  Ann, m. Moses Morden Jr. of Flamborough West. OC 2 April 1816. OC
    14 Aug 1846.
  Mary, m. John Davis of Flamborough West. OC 19 Feb 1817.
  Sarah, m. John White of Flamborough East. OC 27 Feb 1834.
  John of Flamborough West. OC 8 March 1830.
  Daniel of Flamborough West. OC 26 Oct 1825.   [Cont'd]

MORDEN, Daniel - Cont'd
  Sophia, m. James Murphy of Flamborough West. OC 1 July 1830.
  Ralph of Ancaster. OC 18 April 1843.

MORDEN, James of Sophiasburgh. Pvt., K. R. R. N. Y. Married Margaret
  Parliament, 27 Dec 1792; died October, 1840.
  Joseph James of Sophiasburgh. OC 25 Feb 1818.
  Isaac of Sophiasburgh. OC 22 Aug 1821.
  Richard J. of Sophiasburgh, b. 6 Dec 1801. OC 15 Oct 1823.
  George of Ameliasburgh. OC 15 Oct 1823.
  James of Sophiasburgh, b. 22 Jan 1798. OC 4 Feb 1824.
  John P. of Town of Belleville, b. 27 June 1806. OC 11 June 1840.
  Benjamin of Sophiasburgh. OC 27 June 1836.
  Andrew of Sophiasburgh. OC 1 Dec 1836.
  Lorrain, b. 7 Jan 1804. OC 8 June 1825.
  Margaret, b. 22 June 1812.

MORDEN, John of Flamborough West and Westminster, b. 21 Jan 1768, in
  Pennsylvania, son of Ralph and Ann Morden; d. Westminster 21 Jan 1832.
  dau., m. John Davis of Flamborough W. (? But see under Daniel Morden).
    OC 19 Feb 1817.
  William Sutton of London. OC 8 Nov 1832.
  Moses of London. OC 8 Nov 1832.
  James of London, b. 25 Oct 1800; m. Elizabeth Magarvin, 20 Feb 1821;
    d. 2 Nov 1851. OC 8 Nov 1832.
  Ralph of London. OC 8 Nov 1832.
  John of London, b. 25 Oct 1800; m. Mary A. Parkinson; d. 1855. OC 8
    November 1832.
  David of London. OC 17 March 1836.
  Micajah of London, m. Elizabeth Richards, 17 Feb 1825. OC 17 Mar 1836.
  Daniel of Westminster, d. 21 June 1860. OC 27 June 1835.
  Nancy, m. John Routledge of Westminster 29 March 1827; d. 5 Dec 1834.
    OC 27 June 1833.
  Eleanor, m. Rev. J. K. Williston, 16 Aug 1837. OC 28 Oct 1833.

MORDEN, John of Ameliasburgh, m. Eve dau Jacob Bowman, U. E.
  Richard S. of Ameliasburgh. OC 19 March 1840.
  Jacob of Sophiasburgh, d. 17 Apr 1841 ae 27 ys 9 ds. OC 27 Oct 1836.
  Joseph W. of Cramahe. OC 9 June 1836.
  Lorraine, b. 6 March 1802; m. James R. Snider of Ameliasburgh. OC 3
    May 1832.
  John Howell of Ameliasburgh, b. 18 Sept 1804. OC 22 Dec 1842.
  Lucretia Julia Ann b. 3 March 1810, m. Elias Clarke of Sophiasburgh on
    15 Sept 1831. OC 19 April 1847.
  James C. of Sophiasburgh. OC 28 Feb 1833.

MORDEN, Joseph, m. Laurania Howell; she m. (2) Matthew Forrest of RRNY
  Richard of Sophiasburgh. OC 1 July 1799.   [Cont'd]

MORDEN, Joseph - Cont'd
Catharine, m. ---- Lang of Haldimand Co. OC 28 March 1797.
Joseph of Sophiasburgh, d. in Feb 1836 without issue. OC 7 July 1798.
Lucretia, m. ---- Plummer of Kingston. OC 17 Nov 1797.

MORDEN, Ralph, m. Ann.
John of Flamborough West, U.E.
Ralph of Flamborough West. OC 8 July 1794.
James of Flamborough West. OC 8 July 1794.
Ann, m. Asahel Davis of Nelson. OC 8 July 1794.
Elizabeth, m. John Chrysler of Niagara. OC 8 July 1794.
Eleanor, m. Gilbert Field of Niagara.

MORDEN, Richard of Sophiasburgh, m. Anne Williams of Ernestown, 28 Dec 1790.
Joseph R. of Sophiasburgh. OC 13 Feb 1816.
John R. of Sophiasburgh. OC 13 Feb 1816.
Richard R. of Sophiasburgh, b. 27 Aug 1797. OC 16 June 1819.
Robert R. of Sophiasburgh, b. 4 Nov 1801. OC 29 May 1822.
William of Tyendinaga. OC 27 Aug 1840.
Sarah Lucretia, b. 29 July 1802. OC 7 May 1828.
Margaret, m. Peter Sanders of Sophiasburgh. OC 7 May 1828.
Daniel of Sophiasburgh. OC 2 Sept 1830.
James R. of Sophiasburgh. OC 22 June 1825.

MORRISON, David of Cornwall and Town of Niagara. OC 12 June 1798. See OC 8 March 1828.
Mary, m. Nathan Gookin of Town of Niagara. OC 6 Oct 1836. OC 27 July 1837.
Hannah, m. ---- Clarke of Niagara. OC 20 Oct 1836.
Betsy, m. ---- Towle of Niagara. OC 20 Oct 1836.
John of Niagara. OC 20 Oct 1836.

MORISON, Thomas of Charlottenburgh.
Catharine, m. Alexander Kennedy of Niagara. OC 6 May 1830.

MORRISON, William.
William of Edwardsburgh. OC 31 May 1803.

MOSHER, Lewis of Lansdowne, m. Mary dau John Freeman. See OC 26 Aug 1835.
Phoebe, m. Frederick Bush of Town of Kingston OC 4 July 1807.
Elizabeth, m. Henry Treaky of Yonge. OC 30 Oct 1810.
Sarah, m. Ashel Keys of Lansdowne. OC 11 Nov 1815.
Mary, m. John MacDonald of Yonge. OC 12 Nov 1817.
Fanny, m. Peter La Rue of Leeds. OC 19 Sept 1821.
John of Kingston, mariner, m. Caroline F. Munro, 20 Nov 1828. OC 17 1823.   [Cont'd]

MOSHER, Lewis - Cont'd
Thomas of Whitchurch. OC 9 March 1837.
Lewis of Wolfe Island. OC 28 Oct 1835.
Nicholas of Wolfe Island. OC 8 Dec 1835.
Reuben of Wolfe Island. OC 7 Oct 1830.

MOSHER, Nicholas of Augusta and Hope, m. Sarah dau Weston Allen, U.E.,
of Augusta.
Delilah, m. William Lee of Ernestown. OC 19 Dec 1806.
Margaret, m. Francis Hamblin of Augusta. OC 25 Feb 1812; 13 June 1818.
Ruth, m. Thomas Gage of Hope. OC 17 Feb 1816.
Mary. OC 17 Feb 1816.
Sarah, m. John Gilbert of Lansdowne. OC 5 March 1823.
Lucy, m. ---- Guffin of Thurlow. OC 27 Nov 1834.

MOSS, John of Malahide.
Maiden, m. Peter Newkirk of Walsingham. OC 6 Nov 1834.
Ann, m. Andrew Steinhoff of Woodhouse. OC 5 Feb 1835.

MOSS, Samuel of Osnabruck. Sgt., K.R.R.N.Y.
Martha. OC 13 March 1807.
Samuel of Osnabruck. OC 27 March 1813.
Thomas of Osnabruck. OC 4 July 1815.
Mary. OC 3 June 1817.
Peter of Osnabruck. OC 18 March 1818.
Joseph E. of Osnabruck. OC 17 Feb 1825.

MOSURE, John of Kingston.
William of Kingston. OC 21 Sept 1837.
Joseph of Kingston. OC 3 Feb 1834.
James of Kingston. OC 3 Feb 1834.
Mary, m. John Sheriff of Kingston. OC 3 Jan 1833.

MOTT, Edmund of Elizabethtown. Born 8 Aug 1767 in Dutchess Co., N.Y.
md. Amy, dau of Gershom Wing, U.E.
Diana, m. ---- Wright of Elizabethtown. OC 1850 or 1851.
Samuel W. of Elizabethtown. OC 1850 or 1851.

MOTT, Henry of Elizabethtown.
Reuben of Elizabethtown. OC 11 Dec 1810.
Clement of Elizabethtown. OC 1 Sept 1812.
Margaret, m. Samuel Raymond of Elizabethtown, 8 Dec 1814. OC 2 June
1819.
Braddock of Elizabethtown. OC 28 May 1823.
Sabrina, m. William Avery of Yonge 19 Jan 1818. OC 28 May 1823.
Samuel of Elizabethtown. OC 11 June 1823.
Nathaniel of Elizabethtown. OC 6 Jan 1831. OC 28 Nov 1839.

MOTT, Reuben of Elizabethtown.
  Elizabeth, m. Elkanah Billings Jr. of Elizabethtown. OC 4 June 1805.
  Margaret, m. Reuben Burritt of Elizabethtown. OC 5 Jan 1808.
  Lois, m. James Stephens of Elizabethtown. OC 26 Jan 1808.
  Stephen of Elizabethtown. OC 11 June 1823.
  Wellington W. of Elizabethtown. OC 15 Nov 1838.
  Elijah of Elizabethtown. OC 27 June 1839.
  Esther. OC 24 April 1835.
  Silas of Elizabethtown. OC 24 April 1835.
  Hiram of Elizabethtown. OC 27 Nov 1834.
  Henry of Elizabethtown. OC 6 Sept 1832.
  Francis. OC 24 Oct 1831.
  Peter of Elizabethtown. OC 6 Jan 1831.
  Jonathan of Elizabethtown. OC 11 May 1825.
  Joannah. OC 18 April 1843.

MOUNT, Moses, m. Jane dau of Charles Burtch, U. E.
  Roswell of Delaware, b. 1797; d. at York 19 Jan 1834. OC 27 November
    1822. M. L. A. for Middlesex.

MUCHMORE, Jonathan of "The Cedars", m. Mary Livingston. See Sir John
  Johnson's Petition. OC 30 Oct 1828.
  John of Charlottenburgh, bapt. 19 Aug 1784; m. Mary Westley, 1 Decem-
    ber 1808. OC 17 March 1804.
  Mary, bapt. 15 July 1786; m. Josephus Brown of Charlottenburgh 19 June
    1809. OC 25 June 1807.
  Elizabeth, bapt. 27 Dec 1782; m. Daniel Brown of Charlottenburgh, on
    19 June 1804. OC 25 June 1807.

MUCKLE, John.
  Eleanor, m. John Walker of Ancaster. OC 6 July 1802.
  James of Townsend. OC 2 Jan 1805.
  Margaret, m. Robert Henry of Townsend. OC 16 Aug 1810.
  John of Townsend. OC 3 July 1796.
  dau., m. John Hewett. OC 11 May 1797.

MULLOY, Thomas of Lancaster, Vaughan and Albion.
  John of Vaughan. OC 19 April 1820.
  Barnabas of Whitby. OC 19 April 1820.
  Hannah, m. Samuel Stanley of Vaughan 2 June 1820. OC 19 April 1820.
  Hugh of Vaughan, m. Mary Quinn, 23 March 1825. OC 19 April 1820.
  Catharine, m. James Young of Scarborough. OC 19 April 1820.
  Mary, m. Aaron Munshaw of Markham 22 Jan 1822. OC 13 June 1821.
  Elizabeth, m. Peter Vanderburgh Jr. of Markham 12 Sept 1822. OC 16
    October 1822.
  Margaret, m. John W. Brown of York. OC 5 May 1831.
  Laney, m. Martin Luther of Albion. OC 24 Sept 1824.

MUNRO, Daniel of Yonge.
   Timothy of Markham, m. Hulda Purdy, 10 Sept 1824. She died 1828. He
      died 1892. He m. (2) Elizabeth Button, 30 April 1829.
   Randy of Markham. OC 18 May 1837.
   George of Markham. OC 20 July 1837.
   Mary, m. ---- Lovekin of Clarke. OC 27 July 1837.
   Henry of Clarke. OC 27 July 1837.

MUNRO, Hugh of Edwardsburgh. Lieut., Loyal Rangers.
   Hugh of Edwardsburgh. OC 27 June 1800.
      Col. Hugh Munro d. in Edwardsburgh 4 Dec 1855, aged 90 years.

MUNRO, Hugh of Charlottenburgh. KRRNY. Married Catherine Campbell.
   Finlay of Charlottenburgh. OC 19 April 1808.
   Elizabeth, m. John McLeod of Lancaster 28 Dec 1809. OC 7 Aug 1811.
   Margaret, m. Duncan McGregor of Charlottenburgh 14 March 1811. OC
      7 Aug 1811.
   Murdock of Charlottenburgh, bapt. 12 June 1791. OC 25 Feb 1818.
   Nancy, m. ---- Ross. Land Board Certificate, 32/2 Lochiel.

MUNRO, John of Yonge, m. Hannah Alley.
   Samuel of Yonge (York), called "2nd". OC 16 June 1818. OC 1 Dec 1836.
   John, bapt. 27 May 1793.
   Alfred A. of Yonge. OC 28 July 1836.
   James of Toronto Tnp. OC 4 July 1833.
   Simon of Yonge. OC 2 April 1829.
   Hannah, m. William Judd of Yonge. OC 2 April 1829.
   Aseneth. OC 24 Nov 1832.
   Polly L., m. Henry Polly of Yonge 1 Jan 1824. OC 11 Aug 1829.

MUNRO, Hon. John of Matilda. Capt., KRRNY.
   John of Matilda. OC 28 June 1797.
   William Johnson of Matilda. OC 28 June 1797.
   Christeen, m. Philip Mount, surgeon, 29 Aug 1786. OC 28 June 1797.
   Henry of Montreal, surgeon. OC 28 June 1797.
   Cornelia, m. Allan Patterson of Matilda in Feb., 1784. OC 28 June 1797.
   Charlotte, m. ---- Delothiniere of Vaudreuil. OC 28 June 1797.
   Cornelius, m. Frances Delisle.

MUNRO, Robert Sr.
   James of Charlotteville. OC 25 July 1796.

MUNRO, Samuel of Yonge and York.
   Catharine, m. David S. Dean of Flamborough West. OC 21 April 1819.
   Elizabeth, m. Jonathan Dean of Flamborough West 4 Oct 1818. OC 21
      April 1819.
   Malcolm of Ernestown. OC 8 Sept 1836.
   Bradford A. of Camden East. OC 8 Sept 1836.   [Cont'd]

MUNRO, Samuel - Cont'd
   Charles W. of York. OC 11 July 1833.
   Peter of York. OC 5 May 1831.
   Justinia, m. Thomas Proctor of Toronto 16 Dec 1834. OC 28 Feb 1835.
   Samuel Reid of Chinguacousy. OC 17 Oct 1828.
   Esther. OC 12 May 1824. Yonge.
   Margaret. OC 12 May 1824. Yonge.

MUNRO, Thomas of /1 south side River aux Raisins, Charlottenburgh. He
   m. Catherine Ross.
   Philip of Williamsburgh. OC 23 Nov 1816.
   Andrew of Charlottenburgh, bapt. 23 March 1794. OC 23 Nov 1816.
   Donald of Charlottenburgh, bapt. 12 June 1791. OC 19 Feb 1817.
   Anne, bapt. 30 March 1796; m. Donald McArthur of Charlottenburgh. OC
      5 November 1818.
   William of Charlottenburgh. OC 30 Oct 1822.
   John of Charlottenburgh. OC 11 July 1833.
   Janet, m. Finlay Munro of Charlottenburgh. OC 29 Sept 1824.

MUNSALL, Moses.
   Benjamin Ruggles of Yonge. OC 7 Nov 1797.
   Mary, m. Jonathan Mills Church of Elizabethtown 11 May 1797; d. 3 Dec
      1812. OC 8 Feb 1808.
   Sarah, m. Peter Howard of Elizabethtown; d. 14 March 1831, aged 55.
      OC 8 Oct 1796.

MURCHISON, Duncan of Lancaster.
   Janet, m. Charles Rose of Charlottenburgh 14 Jan 1792. OC 4 July 1798.

MURCHISON, John Jr. of East half 22/1 Charlottenburgh.
   Alexander of Charlottenburgh. OC 16 July 1816.
   Barbara. OC 16 July 1816.
   Catherine. OC 8 Sept 1819.
   Kenneth of Charlottenburgh. OC 8 Sept 1819. (2nd K'th s. of John)
   Kenneth K. of Charlottenburgh. OC 8 Sept 1819.

MURCHISON, John.
   Sophia, m. ---- McIntire. OC 11 July 1799.
   Marjory, m. ---- Grant. OC 3 March 1801.
   Murdock. OC 3 March 1801.
   John of Town of York, m. Frances Hunt, 30 May 1808. OC 29 May 1807.

MURCHISON, John Jr.
   Kenneth of Charlottenburgh. OC 17 Aug 1808.

MURDOFF, George of Fredericksburgh. Sgt., KRRNY.
   George of Fredericksburgh.
   Thomas of Fredericksburgh.   [Cont'd]

MURDOFF, George - Cont'd
Nancy, m. Eppaphras Goodsell of Fredericksburgh 22 Nov 1800. OC 28
February 1799.
John of Fredericksburgh. OC 8 July 1801. OC 28 Feb 1835.
? Catharine, m. John McCall of Murray. OC 28 Oct 1835.
Lucy, m. James Russell. Land Board Certificate, 1/5 Storrington.

MYERS, John of Elizabethtown.
Nancy, m. Simon Clow of Elizabethtown. OC 28 Oct 1835.
Lydia, m. Samuel Randolph of Elizabethtown 18 Feb 1818. OC 12 Nov 1827.
Hannah, m. James Patrick of Elizabethtown. OC 28 Feb 1833; 6 Nov 1834.
Olive, m. William Daily of Elizabethtown. OC 8 Dec 1826; 28 Feb 1833.
Almena, m. John Elliott of Elizabethtown. OC 22 Dec 1832.
Lydia, m. (2) George Cole of Elizabethtown.

MYERS, Michael.
Christian of Cornwall. OC 11 July 1799.
Godfrey of Cornwall, m. Augusta Campbell, 21 Jan 1799. OC 11 July 1799
Mary M. , m. John Hahn of Cornwall, 1 Nov 1796. OC 30 June 1801.
Bastien of Cornwall. OC 17 March 1807.

N

NAPPING, John of Kingston.
David of Sidney. OC 27 April 1837.

NAUGHTON, Andrew.
Martha, b. 27 Feb 1762; m. William Buell of Elizabethtown 10 March
1782; d. 7 Dec 1823. OC 23 Sept 1800.
Melinda, m. Gardner Green of Hawkesbury. OC 17 March 1807.

NEAR (NEHER), John of Fredericksburgh.
Hannah, m. ---- Dingman of Fredericksburgh. OC 18 April 1839.
Elizabeth, m. John S. Clapper of Camden East. OC 21 May 1840.
Charles of Fredericksburgh. OC 1 Aug 1827.
Christian of Richmond. OC 5 Nov 1828.

NEILL, George of Charlotteville.
Mary, m. Elijah Hazen of Walsingham. OC 6 Feb 1819.
Desire, m. Adam Prockunier of Charlotteville. OC 6 Feb 1819.
Esther, m. John B. Hutchison. OC 14 April 1825.

NELLIS, Capt. Henry Wm. of Grand River. His widow Priscilla, OC 13 Oct
1796.
John of Haldimand Co., m. Mary Young. OC 23 June 1801.   [Cont'd]

NELLIS, Capt. Henry Wm. - Cont'd
Anne, m. Charles Anderson of Grimsby, innkeeper; d. May, 1811. OC 5
July 1796.
Abraham of Grimsby, m. Catharine Ball, 2 May 1797; d. July, 1839 in
64th year. OC 8 October 1796.
William of Grand River, m. Margaret Ball, 16 July 1799. OC 8 Oct 1796.
Warner of Walpole, m. Elizabeth Young. OC 7 July 1796.
Robert of Grimsby, m. Elizabeth. OC 26 June 1795.

NELLES, Robert of Grimsby, m. Elizabeth. [md. (1) Elizabeth, dau of John
Moore whose wife was a sister of Andrew Pettit. md. (2) Maria Jane Wadd-
ell. See Chadwick's Ontarian Families, v. 2, p. 155]
Henry of Grimsby, bapt. 2 Feb 1793; m. Sarah Fanning [dau John Fanning,
M. L. A. , of Chippawa, by his wife Sarah dau of Benjamin Willson, UE.
See The Ontario Register, 1: 93-94] OC 2 April 1816.
Margaret, m. Edward Pilkington of Niagara. OC 31 July 1817.
William Robt. of Grimsby, m. ---- O'Reilly. OC 15 May 1822.
Frances Matilda, m. James Ruthven; d. 15 Feb 1880. OC 18 Oct 1838.
Jane Clara, m. Robert Brown; d. 4 April 1890. OC 18 Oct 1838.
Charles of Grimsby, m. Elizabeth Millard; d. 23 Aug 1886. OC 23 Nov
1840.
Elizabeth, bapt. 4 May 1804; m. Rev. B. B. Stevens, 4 Sept 1820; d. 9 Dec
1880. OC 2 July 1829.
Guy Moore of Grimsby, bapt. 6 March 1811. OC 6 Dec 1832. (George M.)
Mary Ann, bapt. 7 Sept 1808; m. (1) George Richardson. m. (2) Dennis
Woolverton. OC 5 Feb 1831.
Abraham of Grand River, bapt. 2 June 1806; m. (1) Hannah Macklem; m.
(2) Sarah Macklem; d. 23 Dec 1884. OC 27 March 1829.
Emelia, m. Rev. James Lyon Alexander of Binbrook. OC 9 Aug 1848.
Robert, d. 2 Nov 1812, aet. 14.
Robert Waddell, b. 25 Sept 1825; d. 23 Oct 1825.
Sarah Maria, b. May, 1821; d. 2 June 1827.

NELLIS, Abraham, Grimsby, 1796, son of Capt. W. Henry Nellis (Old U. E.
List). Abraham, b. 4 Dec 1775; d. 7 July 1839; Member Leg. C., 1830;
J. P. ; Capt. 1st Riding Regt. Lincoln, 1797; Capt. 2nd West Riding, 1803;
Capt. 4th Lincoln (Flank Co.); Major, 10 Oct 1814; Prisoner of War, Nov.,
1813; paroled 22 Dec 1813; Lt. Col. 2nd Gore, 6 March 1820. His wife,
Catharine, b. 16 Sept 1777; d. 23 Dec 1829; dau of Jacob Ball Sr. , Twenty
Mile Creek; m. at Niagara, 2 May 1797.
Henry William, m. Ann Eliza dau Hon. Samuel Smith, York Tnp.
Margaret, m. William Ferris, M. D.
Maria Elizabeth, m. Rev. Wm. Sampson.
Helen Priscilla, m. Thomas Racey.
Catharine Matilda, m. Elijah Nelles.

NELLIS, William of Niagara, m. Margaret.
Abraham of Townsend. OC 25 Jan 1831.   [Cont'd]

NELLIS, William - Cont'd
  Nancy, b. 18 May 1792; m. Moses Barber of Townsend 7 July 1811; d. 27
    February 1873. OC 20 May 1817.
  John Adolphus of Grimsby, bapt. 20 July 1812. OC 6 Dec 1832.
  Catharine Elizabeth, bapt. 15 March 1809. OC 5 Feb 1831.
  Peter Ball of Grimsby, bapt. 25 Jan 1807. OC 27 March 1829.
  Margaret Maria, bapt. 22 March 1814.

NETTLETON, Amos
  Daniel. OC 24 Sept 1799.
  Sarah, m. ---- Lane of Augusta. OC 23 Sept 1800.
  Timothy. OC 23 June 1801.
  Elizabeth, m. Joseph Knapp. Land Board Certificate.

NETTLETON, Daniel.
  Barnabas. OC 24 Sept 1799.
  Mary. OC 24 Sept 1799.
  Sarah, m. Ziba Marcus Phillips of Wolford. OC 16 June 1807; 4 July 1815.
  Elizabeth, m. Joseph Knapp Sr. of Montague, Land Board Certificate,
    11/Broken Front, Escott.

NEVILLE, Edward of Colchester.
  George of Gosfield. OC 30 June 1819.
  Robert of Chatham. OC 2 Oct 1834.
  Francis (son). OC 9 Feb 1832.
  Edward of Gosfield. OC 2 Feb 1832.

NEWBERRY, William. Sgt., Butler's Rangers.
  Margaret. OC 2 March 1811. Crowland.
  Elizabeth, m. ---- Stringer of Willoughby. OC 16 May 1797.

NEWKIRK, James.
  Mary, m. John Muir of Grantham. OC 24 Oct 1831.

NEWKIRK, Samuel of Raleigh. His wife m. (2) Edward Watson of River
Thames.
  James of Raleigh. OC 20 Feb 1810.
  Elizabeth, m. Daniel Dolson of Raleigh. OC 20 Feb 1820.
  (Two children all issue).

NICHOLSON, Alexander of Thurlow, m. Sarah Hough dau of Barnabas Hough
U. E. From Daily Globe, Dec 21, 1852: Died at the residence of Wm Van-
dervoort in Sydney, on 12th inst., Sarah, relict of the late Alex. Nicholson
of Thurlow, aged 85 years.
  Robert of Fredericksburgh, m. Magdalene Bartley. OC 8 Feb 1808.
  Agnes, m. Patrick Morgan of Thurlow. OC 16 Feb 1810.
  Eunice, bapt. 10 July 1791. OC 20 Jan 1816.
  Barnabas of Thurlow. OC 18 March 1818.   [Cont'd]

NICHOLSON, Alexander - Cont'd
   Elizabeth, m. ---- Bartley of Sidney. OC 22 Feb 1834.
   John James McNabb of Thurlow. OC 3 April 1834.
   Hannah, m. Thomas T. Fralick of Sidney. OC 3 April 1834.
   Sterling H. of Thurlow. OC 2 Oct 1834.
   Abigail, b. 11 Apr 1807; m. William Vandervoort of Sidney 18 Apr 1826;
      d. 14 Oct 1873. OC 15 Dec 1832.
   Mary, m. John Brower, Brown ?, of Thurlow 6 Feb 1822. OC 22 July 1824
   Alexander of Thurlow. OC 22 July 1824.
   David of Thurlow, bapt. 23 June 1801. OC 22 July 1824.
   Samuel of Thurlow. OC 10 Jan 1833.
   Margaret, b. 27 Aug 1810.

NICHOLSON, Robert of Wolford; b. about 1747; m. Cynthia.
   Rachel, m. Michael Welch of Wolford. OC 27 Sept 1833.
   Harrison W. of Thurlow. OC 2 Oct 1834.
   Morgan of Huntingdon. OC 4 Dec 1834.
   Robert of Wolford. OC 1 July 1830.
   Phoebe, m. John Leahy of Wolford. OC 8 June 1832.

NOBLE, Solomon of Cornwall.
   Dorothy, m. Samuel Noble of Cornwall. OC 23 June 1836.

NOODLE, Adam of Williamsburgh. [Nudale on U. E. List]
   Dorothy, m. Peter Baker of Williamsburgh. OC 5 March 1810.
   Elizabeth, m. John Weager of Williamsburgh. OC 16 Feb 1811.
   Margaret. OC 30 July 1811.
   Adam of Williamsburgh, m. Mary M. Weager. OC 13 Nov 1818.
   Nancy, m. Abraham Cook of Williamsburgh. OC 27 June 1833.
   Thomas of Williamsburgh. OC 3 April 1834.

NORTH, Thomas.
   Elizabeth, m. William Kennedy of Grimsby. OC 25 July 1797.
   Mary, m. ---- O'Neal of Queenston. OC 24 March 1797.
   Ann, m. Benjamin Rawzell [Roszel] of Gainsborough. OC 4 Feb 1841.

O

O'CONNELLY, James of Louth.
   Joseph of Louth. OC 11 July 1833.
   Thomas of Louth. OC 11 July 1833.

OLIVER, Aaron of Richmond, m. Weltheyen Bennett.
    Charles K. of Richmond. OC 14 Oct 1842.
    Frederick A. of Richmond. OC 14 Oct 1842.
    Aaron of Camden, b. 26 April 1816. OC 14 Oct 1842.
    Elizabeth, bapt. 19 March 1798; m. ---- Sager of Richmond. OC 14 Oct
        1842.
    Catharine, b. 22 November 1805.

OLIVER, Cornelius of Richmond, m. (1) Mary. m. (2) Mary Woodcock, on 5
    July 1802.
    Peter of Fredericksburgh, bapt. 28 April 1811. OC 14 Oct 1842.
    Cornelius of Hungerford, bapt. 4 Nov 1807. OC 14 Oct 1842.
    Nicholas of Tyendinaga, bapt. 8 Nov 1803. OC 14 Oct 1842.
    Andrew of Cramahe, b. 31 Jan 1816. OC 14 Oct 1842.
    Mary, m. Jacob Cronk of Sophiasburgh. OC 14 Oct 1842.
    Jacob of Fredericksburgh. OC 14 Oct 1842.
    John of Tyendinaga, bapt. 14 June 1808. OC 14 Oct 1842.
    Frederick of Richmond, bapt. 24 Nov 1790. OC 14 Oct 1842.
    Catharine, m. James Philips of Fredericksburgh 3 Sept 1816. OC 14 Oct
        1842.
    Hannah Barbara, bapt. 7 Jan 1793; m. David B. Pringle of Sheffield 21
        July 1815. OC 14 Oct 1842.
    Ann, m. Jacob Dingman of Fredericksburgh. OC 22 Dec 1842.
    Elizabeth, m. Richard A. Woodcock of Thurlow. OC 22 Dec 1842.
    Hannah, bapt. 17 Sept 1809. OC 14 Oct 1842.
    Elsie, bapt. 21 Feb 1813.

OLIVER, Frederick.
    Elizabeth, m. Adam Sager of Richmond. See OC 9 March 1837.

O'NEAL, James of Ernestown. Lieut., Loyal Rangers. Widow Elizabeth. OC
    20 July 1797. Died 1784.
    Margaret, m. ---- Johnson. OC 20 July 1797. OC 26 Feb 1798.
    Richard. OC 2 Nov 1797.
    Alice, m. Thomas Cook Jr. of Town of Kingston 11 Sept 1803. OC 25 Feb
        1806.
    Mary, m. Moses Rogers, 26 Oct 1803. OC 26 Feb 1798. OC 2 June 1798.

ORSER, Arthur of Kingston.
    Mary. OC 19 Nov 1798.
    Isaac of Kingston. OC 26 March 1817.
    Joseph of Kingston. OC 17 March 1812.
    Gilbert of Kingston. OC 20 May 1817.
    Elizabeth, m. Abel B. Harrison of Kingston 15 Jan 1811; d. 15 Feb 1844.
        OC 18 March 1818.
    Horace of Kingston. OC 1 April 1840.
    Peter of Kingston. OC 3 Oct 1833.
    John of Kingston. OC 19 Dec 1833. OC 30 May 1834.   [Cont'd]

ORSER, Arthur - Cont'd
　　Phoebe, m. George Buck Jr. of Kingston. OC 3 Oct 1833.
　　William of Kingston. OC 30 May 1834.
　　Daniel of Kingston. OC 30 May 1834.

ORSER, Gilbert of Hallowell, m. Sarah.
　　Phoebe, m. John Goldsmith of Hallowell 19 June 1819. OC 22 May 1820.
　　Samuel of Hallowell, bapt. 23 Feb 1790. OC 22 Aug 1821.
　　Mary, m. Frederick French of Hallowell. OC 17 Oct 1821.
　　Elijah of Hallowell, m. Rachel Brown, 1 Jan 1816. OC 31 Oct 1821.
　　Abraham of Hallowell. OC 6 March 1822.
　　Jesse of Hallowell. OC 6 March 1822.
　　David of Hallowell. OC 14 Sept 1825.
　　Martha, m. Hezekiah Bettys of Cramahe. OC 16 Nov 1837.
　　Elizabeth, m. Vincent Ferguson of Hallowell. OC 30 May 1834.
　　Hannah, m. John Southard of Hallowell. OC 12 June 1834.
　　William of Hallowell. OC 27 Nov 1834.
　　Joseph of Hallowell. OC 28 Feb 1835.
　　Gilbert of Hallowell. OC 6 Oct 1831.
　　Ann, m. Isaac Ferguson of Hallowell. OC 6 Oct 1831.
　　Enoch of Hillier. OC 7 May 1828.

ORSER, Isaac of Kingston.
　　Ann, m. Nelson Williams of Loughborough. OC 16 June 1819.
　　Rebecca, m. John Lambert of Wolfe Island. OC 28 Oct 1835.
　　Gabriel of Wolfe Island. OC 28 Oct 1835.
　　Solomon of Reach. OC 19 May 1836.
　　Jeremiah of Wolfe Island. OC 30 May 1834.
　　Rhoda, m. Joel Tuttle Billings of Wolfe Island. OC 6 Nov 1834.
　　Nancy, m. Michael Turcott of Wolfe Island. OC 18 Feb 1843.

ORSER, Joseph, m. Ann.
　　John. In U.S.
　　Arthur of Kingston, U.E.
　　Isaac of Kingston, U.E.
　　Solomon of Kingston, U.E.
　　Gilbert of Hallowell, U.E.
　　Gabriel.
　　Rachel, m. John Warner of Kingston. Land Board Certif. 11/3 Kingston.

ORSER, Solomon of Kingston.
　　Hannah, m. William Hadley of Wolfe Island, 5 Feb 1811. OC 22 July 1818.
　　John of Grape Island. OC 5 Sept 1833.
　　Solomon of Kingston. OC 2 Sept 1830.

OSBURN, James of Markham, m. Sarah Smith. Died 1842. p. 552 York Biog.
　　Record.
　　Benjamin of Markham. OC 27 August 1840.　　　　　　　　[Cont'd]

OSBURN, James - Cont'd
  Rebecca, m. William Anderson of Markham. OC 28 July 1819.
  Sarah, m. Jonathan Tomlinson of Markham. OC 28 July 1819.
  Joseph of Markham. OC 19 Dec 1833.
  Elizabeth, m. Michael Hartney of Markham. OC 6 Dec 1832.
  James of Markham. OC 30 July 1811.

OSTERHOUT, William of Louth.
  Henry of Louth. OC 22 March 1820.
  Mary. OC 22 May 1820.
  Margaret. OC 4 Feb 1841.
  Azubah, m. Murdock Davis of Loughborough. OC 11 Aug 1836.
  George of Louth. OC 27 June 1833.
  Walter of Louth. OC 18 July 1833.
  Jane, m. Amos Bradshaw Thomas of Grantham. OC 2 Jan 1834.
  Eliza, m. John Smith of Louth. OC 17 Oct 1828.
  Jemima, m. Mark Reaveley of Louth. OC 17 Oct 1828.
  John of Louth. OC 2 Dec 1824.

OSTRUM, Ruliph. Died 17 Feb 1818.
  Daniel of Sidney. OC 31 Oct 1809.
  Sarah, m. Roswell Leavens of Thurlow. OC 7 Aug 1810.
  Abigail, m. David Purdy of Ernestown. OC 7 Aug 1810.
  Diana, m. Abel Gilbert of Sidney. OC 16 Feb 1811.
  Martha, m. John McIntosh of Thurlow. OC 7 May 1811.
  Jane, m. Samuel Wm. Marsh of Hope. OC 26 March 1817.
  Anthony of Sidney. OC 26 June 1797.
  Martha, m. (2) Donald McLellan of Thurlow.

OTTO, Gottlieb of Osnabruck.
  Peter of Osnabruck. OC 7 Aug 1811.
  Gottlieb of Osnabruck. OC 7 Aug 1811.
  Hannah. OC 19 April 1816.
  John of Osnabruck. OC 30 June 1819.

OUTHOUSE, Nicholas of Charlotteville.
  Hannah, m. John Caldwell of Lincoln Co. OC 31 March 1797.
  Sarah, m. Josiah Gilbert of Charlotteville (of Norwich). OC 8 July 1806;
      OC 5 October 1818.
  Deborah, m. D. Snyder of Charlotteville. OC 16 Aug 1810.
  Jane, m. Allen Andrews of Charlotteville. OC 20 Nov 1810.
  Anne, m. James Smith of Niagara. OC 17 March 1797.
  Anna, m. Isaac Lowell of Charlotteville. OC 7 April 1797.

OVERHOLT, Abraham of Thorold.
  Mary, m. James Rogers of Niagara. OC 27 Feb 1806.
  Abraham of Thorold. OC 26 Sept 1809.
  John of Thorold. OC 26 Sept 1809.   [Cont'd]

OVERHOLT, Abraham - Cont'd
   Elizabeth, m. Richard Phillips of Burford. OC 16 Jan 1816.
   Anne. OC 18 March 1818.
   William of Thorold. OC 5 Feb 1823.
   Martin of Pelham. OC 27 Aug 1840.
   Catharine, m. John Nicholas Bellinger of Pelham. OC 1 Sept 1831. OC 5
      January 1832.
   Isaac of Pelham. OC 1 Dec 1824.

OVERHOLT, Staats.
   Elizabeth, m. Jacob Fisher of Clinton. OC 19 Aug 1800.
   Susannah, m. ---- Singer.
   Mary, m. Henry Rott of Clinton. OC 25 May 1802.
   Christopher of Clinton. OC 23 June 1803.
   Isaac of Clinton. OC 3 July 1797.
   Jacob of Clinton. OC 11 April 1797.

P

PAGE, Joseph. Soldier, Butler's Rangers.
   Anne. OC 11 July 1799.

PALMER, Caleb of Marysburgh.
   Louisa Lucretia. OC 2 Oct 1834.
   Anson B. of Marysburgh. OC 2 Oct 1834.

PALMER, David of Grimsby.
   Elizabeth, m. ---- Skinner of Stamford. OC 18 Aug 1801.
   Hannah, b. New Jersey 15 March 1777; m. Alexander Brown of Thorold,
      1793; d. 23 August 1845. OC 21 July 1800.
   Daniel of Grimsby. OC 22 Feb 1834.
   Martha, m. Jonathan Bell of Howard. OC 22 Feb 1834.
   David of Clinton. OC 27 Feb 1834.
   Mary, m. Job Robins of Pelham. OC 27 Feb 1834.

PALMER, David of Thurlow & Sophiasburgh(?). Corp'l, King's Rangers.
   David of Thurlow. OC 16 Feb 1799.
   Samuel of Thurlow. OC 11 Feb 1806.
   James of Thurlow. OC 27 Nov 1815.
   Elizabeth, m. Abraham Bowen of Richmond. OC 18 March 1818.
   Thomas of Sidney. OC 26 Nov 1823.
   Patty, m. ---- Bowen of Thurlow. OC 17 March 1836.
   Daniel of Thurlow, m. Lois Bradshaw, 2 June 1806. OC 17 March 1836.
   Jacob of Thurlow. OC 21 March 1833.
   Hazelton of Marysburgh. OC 4 Dec 1834.
   John of Thurlow. OC 28 Feb 1833.   [Cont'd]

PALMER, David - Cont'd
Phoebe, m. Benjamin Simkins of Thurlow. OC 15 Dec 1832.
Caleb of Thurlow. OC 13 Nov 1797.

PAPTS, Adam of Osnabruck.
Mary, m. John Fetterly of Osnabruck. OC 5 Jan 1798.
Elizabeth, m. Gottlieb Otto Sr. of Osnabruck. OC 5 Jan 1798; 26 Jan 1808.
Frederick of Osnabruck, m. Mary Wardle. OC 5 Jan 1798.
Catharine, m. Jacob Sheets of Osnabruck. OC 5 Jan 1798.

PAPTS, Rudolph of Osnabruck and Etobicoke.
Catharine. OC 25 Feb 1809.
Jacob of Osnabruck. OC 16 Feb 1811.
Christiana, m. Joseph B. Abbot of Town of York 14 Nov 1811. OC 27
    March 1813.
Mary, m. Daniel Sairs of York 18 Feb 1822. OC 3 June 1817.
Ann, m. Amos Willcox of Toronto, 11 Nov 1818. OC 22 July 1818. OC 1
    August 1818.
Daniel of York. OC 3 Sept 1840.
John of York. OC 19 Dec 1833.
Adam of York. OC 1 May 1834.
William of York. OC 3 Dec 1828.
Richard of York. OC 1 Feb 1826.
Christina, m. (2) Elijah Dexter, 6 Jan 1819.

PARISH, Ezekiel of Yonge, m. Mary. See OC 3 Aug 1802.
Chloe, m. ---- Stevens of Bastard. OC 1 Sept 1801.
Eliada (son) of Yonge. OC 27 July 1804.
William of Yonge. Land Board Certificate, 10/8 Yonge.

PARK, James of Stamford.
James of Stamford. OC 31 July 1817.
Janet, m. Anselm Foster of Niagara. OC 19 May 1819.
Elizabeth, m. John McMillan of Niagara. OC 19 May 1819.
Hagar, m. John Davids of Town of Niagara. OC 7 July 1831.

PARKER, John of Wainfleet.
Mary, m. ---- Rees of Wainfleet. OC 11 July 1799.
Ann. OC 20 Feb 1810.
Elizabeth, m. Jesse Page of Wainfleet. OC 20 Feb 1810.
John of Wainfleet. OC 9 June 1812.
George of Wainfleet. OC 9 June 1812.
Susannah, m. Jarvis Thayer of Dunwich. OC 27 Jan 1816.
William of Gainsborough. OC 27 Jan 1816.

PARKS, Cyrenus of Fredericksburgh, m. Elizabeth.
Elizabeth, m. Peter McCabe of Fredericksburgh. OC 28 April 1807.
Archibald of Fredericksburgh. OC 16 Feb 1810.   [Cont'd]

PARKS, Cyrenus - Cont'd
  Clarinda, bapt. 27 Dec 1790. OC 13 Feb 1816.
  James of Fredericksburgh, bapt. 30 June 1796. OC 18 March 1818.
  Joseph of Thurlow, m. Sarah. See OC 12 June 1834. OC 8 July 1801.
  Daniel of Hamilton, bapt. 2 Feb 1801. OC 22 Apr 1831; 28 Oct 1835.
  John Cyrenus of Sheffield, bapt. 23 Jan 1792. OC 24 Jan 1828.
  Cyrenus, bapt. 6 Jan 1794.
  Elias of Fredericksburgh, bapt. 4 Feb 1799. OC 7 March 1827.
  Charlotte, bapt. 31 Jan 1803; m. ---- Huffman of Camden East. OC 12
    October 1841.
  Hannah, bapt. 28 Jan 1805; m. ---- Forshee of Richmond. OC 2 Oct 1834.
  David of Fredericksburgh, bapt. 16 Nov 1807. OC 21 March 1831.
  Susanna, bapt. 25 June 1810; m. ---- Watson of Richmond. OC 2 Oct 1834.
  Milo of Fredericksburgh, bapt. 18 Jan 1813. OC 12 June 1834.

PARKS, James of Fredericksburgh, m. (2) Susannah, widow of Joseph Marsh
  on 14 June 1789.
  Eunice, m. ---- Osborn of Elizabethtown. OC 23 Sept 1800.
  Nathaniel of Fredericksburgh, bapt. 4 March 1793. OC 13 Feb 1816. OC
    2 April 1823.
  Peter of Fredericksburgh, bapt. 12 Jan 1795. OC 2 April 1823.
  Cornelius, bapt. 24 June 1800. OC 2 April 1823.
  Hannah, m. Amos Osburn of Town of Ira, Oswego Co., N.Y. Not. Rec.
    9 November 1837.
  Mary, bapt. 23 Sept 1805; m. ---- Huffman of Fredericksburgh. OC 10
    March 1834.
  Sarah. OC 10 March 1834.
  William of Richmond, bapt. 29 Nov 1791. OC 30 May 1834.
  Rachel, bapt. 6 Sept 1796.
  Nathan, bapt. 30 May 1798.
  Elizabeth, bapt. 24 May 1802; m. Belyat Outwater of Fredericksburgh.
    OC 27 Nov 1834.
  Reuben of Fredericksburgh, bapt. 25 Jan 1808. OC 3 Jan 1833.

PARKS, Nathan of Cornwall.
  Mary, bapt. 21 June 1795; m. John Storen of Williamsburgh. OC 9 July
    1802.
  Sarah, m. Alexander Cameron of Cornwall.
  Abigail.
  Robert.
  Nathan of Cornwall. OC 1 June 1798.
  Eleanor, bapt. 30 July 1797.

PARKS, Nathaniel of Fredericksburgh, m. Rebecca.
  Jason of Fredericksburgh. OC 10 March 1834.
  Sila (dau.), bapt. 6 June 1803. OC 10 March 1834.
  Cyrenus of Fredericksburgh, bapt. 12 April 1802. OC 2 April 1823.
  Elizabeth, bapt. 7 October 1805.

PARKS, Robert of Cornwall.
    Mary, m. John Johnston of Cornwall. OC 4 July 1815.
    Lucretia. OC 4 July 1815.

PARSONS, Thomas of Raleigh.
    Thomas of Raleigh. OC 18 Feb 1824.
    Elizabeth, m. ---- Traxler of Chatham. OC 24 Nov 1836.
    Edward of Raleigh. OC 1 Aug 1833.
    Mary, m. John Sterling of Dover. OC 3 April 1834.
    Ann, m. Hector McDougall of Sombra. OC 23 Feb 1830.
    Ruth Catharine, m. ---- Girardin. OC 2 June 1831.

PARLOW, John of Matilda.
    John of Matilda. OC 28 Oct 1835.
    Sophia. OC 19 Dec 1833.
    Adeline. OC 19 Dec 1833.
    James of Matilda. OC 19 Dec 1833.
    Mary, m. Nicholas Browse of Matilda. OC 2 Jan 1834.
    Nancy, m. Jacob Brouse of Matilda. OC 2 Jan 1834.
    Grace. OC 2 Jan 1834.
    Margaret. OC 28 March 1835.

PARLOW, Lawrence.
    Grace, m. Paul Glasford of Matilda. OC 5 June 1810.

PARNELL, Abraham of Augusta and South Gower.
    Mary Ann, m. John Sellick of Oxford-on-Rideau. OC 13 Nov 1818.

PATTERSON, Daniel of Yonge.
    William of Yonge. OC 23 Sept 1800.
    Amy, m. Lemuel Mallory of Yonge. OC 16 April 1840.
    Rachel, m. ---- Seaman of Yonge. OC 16 April 1840.
    Cruth of Lansdowne. OC 22 Oct 1840.
    Grace. OC 17 Dec 1840.
    Johanna, m. ---- Young of Ernestown. OC 17 Dec 1840.

PAWLING, Benjamin of Grantham.
    Eleanor, m. Samuel Wood of Grantham. OC 5 March 1810.
    Henry of Grantham. OC 20 May 1817.
    Benjamin M. of Grantham. OC 18 Oct 1820.
    Jesse of Middleton. OC 24 March 1835. OC 22 Sept 1836.
    William Youngs of Crowland. OC 27 Oct 1834.

PAWLING, Jesse of Grantham.
    Ann, m. George Augustus Ball of Grantham. OC 8 Feb 1808.
    Henry of Grantham. OC 23 Feb 1808.
    Nathan of Grantham. OC 9 Aug 1820.
    John White of Grantham. OC 10 Jan 1821.

PECK, James of Ameliasburgh. Sr. or Jr. ?
  Samuel of Sophiasburgh, m. Judith Parliament. OC 5 July 1798. OC 26
    March 1817.
  James Jr. of Ameliasburgh. OC 5 July 1798. OC 6 Oct 1831.
  Cornelius of Sophiasburgh, m. Tinte Harris. OC 5 July 1798.
  Welmpy, m. Joseph Carle of Cramahe. OC 17 March 1812.
  Margaret, m. Reynard Brickman of Ameliasburgh. OC 20 Jan 1816.
  Sarah, m. George Boulter of Ameliasburgh. OC 19 Feb 1823.
  Rachel, m. John McTaggart of Sophiasburgh. OC 19 Feb 1823.
  Cornelia, m. Eliakim Mickle of Loughborough. OC 11 Aug 1836.
  Catharine, m. Charles Robert Bonter of Murray. OC 5 Feb 1835.
  John of Ameliasburgh. OC 21 March 1831.

PECK, James.
  Elizabeth, m. Andrew Barton of Sophiasburgh. OC 28 Feb 1829.
  Rachel, m. Joseph Allison of Sophiasburgh. OC 3 May 1826.
  Mary, m. John Wees of Ameliasburgh. OC 17 March 1824.

PEEBLES, Charles of Edwardsburgh, m. Margaret Finney.
  Margaret, m. James Sly of Edwardsburgh. OC 28 Feb 1833.
  John of Edwardsburgh. OC 6 Dec 1832.
  Charles of Edwardsburgh. OC 6 Dec 1832.
  Archibald of Edwardsburgh. OC 6 Dec 1832.
  Alexander of Edwardsburgh. OC 6 Dec 1832.
  Peter, bapt. 25 July 1800, aged 7 years.

PENCIL, John of Fredericksburgh.
  John of Fredericksburgh. OC 20 May 1817.

PENNOCK, Samuel of Elizabethtown.
  Albela (son). OC 26 May 1801.
  Rhoda, m. Daniel Root of Yonge. OC 30 June 1812.

PERCY, John of Ernestown.
  Rebecca, m. James Richardson of Camden East. OC 15 Nov 1808.
  Ann, m. Peter Forshee of Fredericksburgh. OC 15 Nov 1808.
  John of Ernestown. OC 25 Feb 1812.
  Michael of Camden East. OC 26 March 1817.

PERRY, James of Ernestown.
  James of Dawn. OC 11 Jan 1834.

PERRY, John of Fredericksburgh.
  Mary, m. Peter Cramer of Osnabruck. OC 23 Feb 1808.
  William of Ernestown. OC 16 June 1819. OC 4 Sept 1834.
  John of Ernestown. OC 15 March 1838.
  Julia Ann. OC 8 Aug 1839.
  Peter of Ernestown. OC 27 August 1840.   [Cont'd]

PERRY, John - Cont'd
Daniel of Loughborough. OC 28 Oct 1835.
Elizabeth, m. Andrew Peters of Ernestown. OC 28 Oct 1835.
Oscar of Elizabethtown. OC 26 May 1836.
Guisbert Rogers of Elizabethtown. OC 26 May 1836.
Stephen of Adolphustown. OC 14 March 1826.
Elley (dau.) OC 14 March 1826.

PERRY, Robert of Ernestown.
Daniel of Ernestown. OC 5 July 1800.
Hannah, m. Boyen Elsworth of Ernestown 21 Nov 1797. OC 19 Nov 1798.
David of Ernestown, m. Elizabeth Ward, 18 Oct 1802. OC 8 March 1803.
Ebenezer of Richmond, m. Apphia Randolph, 25 Nov 1806. Of Freder-
    icksburgh, OC 16 Feb 1810.
Mary, m. William Hawley, 1 May 1810. OC 16 Feb 1811.
Peter of Ernestown, b. 1793; m. Mary Ham; d. Saratoga, N.Y., 24 Aug
    1851. OC 7 April 1819.
Patience, m. Daniel Pomeroy of Ernestown 1 Oct 1793. Land Board Cer-
    tificate, 9/4 Pittsburgh.
Robert of Ernestown, m. Esther Aylesworth, 24 Oct 1793.

PERRY (PARRY), William Sr. of Ernestown. Pvt., Loyal Rangers. See OC
25 June 1807.
John of Fredericksburgh. OC 12 July 1798.
Esther, m. John Peters of Ernestown, Feb., 1809. OC 16 Feb 1811.
Peter of Portland. OC 25 Feb 1812.

PESCOD, John of Cornwall.
Isabella, m. James Johnston of Cornwall. OC 25 March 1806.

PETERS, Thomas of Edwardsburgh.
Jane, m. ---- Campbell of Edwardsburgh. OC 18 June 1800.
Mary, m. Eliakim Whitney of Town of New Johnstown. OC 31 May 1803.
Philip of York. OC 4 Feb 1812.
Rachel. OC 20 May 1817.
Frances, m. William Fish of Niagara. OC 1 Dec 1819.
Stephen of Edwardsburgh. OC 24 March 1835.

PETERSON, Abraham of Fredericksburgh, m. Mary.
Catharine, m. ---- Fitchett of Fredericksburgh. OC 17 March 1804.
Sophia, b. 14 Oct 1789; m. (1) William Black of Hallowell; m. (2) ----
    Williams. Died 24 Jan 1863. OC 17 March 1812.
Anne, m. Henry Loyst of Fredericksburgh. OC 28 Nov 1839.

PETERSON, Christian (Christopher) of Fredericksburgh.
Hannah, m. John Cronkhite of Fredericksburgh. OC 26 Jan 1808.
Elizabeth, m. William Howell of Fredericksburgh. OC 6 April 1839.
David of Fredericksburgh. OC 17 Sept 1840.   [Cont'd]

PETERSON, Christian (Christopher) - Cont'd
    Jacob C. of Fredericksburgh (Markham). OC 28 Oct 1835. OC 25 Aug 1836.
    Margaret. OC 18 May 1837.
    Ellen, m. Aaron Presler of Camden East. OC 12 June 1834.
    Eve, m. James Clark of Adolphustown. OC 15 Dec 1832.
    Sarah. OC 1 July 1830.
    James of Fredericksburgh. OC 6 Jan 1827.
    Cornelia, m. Jacob Oliver of Fredericksburgh. OC 6 Jan 1827.
    Christopher of Fredericksburgh. OC 19 July 1826.
    Mary, m. William Windover of Fredericksburgh. OC 1 Nov 1826.
    Paul of Fredericksburgh. OC 6 Jan 1827.
    Nicholas C. of Fredericksburgh. OC 8 Feb 1827.

PETERSON, Conrad of Elizabethtown. Died there 24 Aug 1845 in his 93d yr.
    William of Elizabethtown. OC 8 Sept 1836.
    Lucy, m. George Scott of Elizabethtown. OC 7 Aug 1834.
    James of Elizabethtown. OC 7 Aug 1834.
    Samuel of Elizabethtown. OC 21 March 1831.
    Elizabeth. OC 7 Aug 1824.
    Sarah. OC 7 Aug 1824.

PETERSON, Nicholas of Adolphustown.
    Nicholas of Adolphustown. OC 30 Jan 1808.
    John of Adolphustown. OC 23 Feb 1808.
    David of Adolphustown. OC 23 Feb 1808.
    Jacob of Adolphustown. OC 23 Feb 1810.
    Mary. OC 6 Aug 1816.
    Samuel of Fredericksburgh (Adolphustown). OC 26 March 1817. OC 3 Apr
        1819.
    Paul of Adolphustown. OC 17 March 1812.
    Elizabeth, m. Barnabas Brennan of Adolphustown. OC 6 March 1821.
    Lenah. OC 4 April 1839.
    James of Ameliasburgh. OC 4 Feb 1830.
    William of Adolphustown. OC 2 April 1828.
    Robert of Adolphustown. OC 6 Jan 1827.
    Leah. OC 6 Jan 1827.

PETERSON, Paul of Adolphustown and Fredericksburgh.
    David of Fredericksburgh. OC 18 March 1808.
    John of Fredericksburgh. OC 25 July 1809.
    Hannah, m. Jacob Finkle of Sidney 29 Oct 1809. OC 28 Nov 1809.
    Elizabeth, bapt. 21 Sept 1791; m. John Frederick Jr. of Fredericksburgh
        6 June 1811. OC 17 Feb 1816.
    Leah, m. ---- Anderson. OC 6 Aug 1816; 18 March 1818; 10 Jan 1843.
    Keziah. OC 6 Aug 1816.
    Lucretia. OC 18 March 1818.

PETREY (PETRIE), Joseph. [See The Ontario Register, v. 1, pp. 29, 206]
  Cordelia, m. John Reilly of Stamford. OC 17 March 1804.
  Mary, m. Jacob Killman Jr. of Stamford. OC 10 Nov 1801.
  Elizabeth, m. Paul Averill Jr. of Haldimand Co. OC 16 Feb 1811.
  Hannah, m. Joel Munro of Haldimand Co. OC 16 Feb 1811.
  Catharine, m. Stephen S. Poor of Haldimand Co. OC 16 Feb 1811.
  John of Grand River. OC 23 Nov 1816.
  Joseph of Grand River (Ancaster). OC 26 March 1817. OC 5 Jan 1832.
  Philip of Stamford. OC 26 March 1817.
  Abraham of Grand River. OC 20 May 1817.
  William of Grand River. OC 12 Jan 1820.
  Margaret, m. Jonathan Vermilyea of Grand River. OC 8 March 1820.
  Walter of Saltfleet. OC 7 Jan 1830.

PETTAY, Marjery of Gainsborough.
  Andrew of Gainsborough. OC 27 May 1794.
  William.
  Francis (son).
  Daniel.

PETTINGILL, Samuel of Kingston.
  William of Hillier. OC 3 Oct 1833.
  Catharine. OC 3 Oct 1833. Hillier.
  Harriett, m. ---- Stevenson of Hillier. OC 3 Oct 1833.
  Hannah, m. Adam Garrett of Hillier. OC 1 May 1834.
  Maria, m. John Osterhout of Hallowell. OC 1 May 1834.
  Martha Ann. OC 19 June 1834.
  Allen of Hillier. OC 18 July 1834.
  Samuel of Hallowell. OC 18 July 1834.
  Martin of Hillier. OC 18 July 1834.
  Arnot (son) of Hillier. OC 5 Jan 1835.
  Joseph of Hillier. OC 5 Jan 1835.

PETTIT, Daniel of Hallowell.
  Mary, m. ---- Ferguson. OC 23 June 1801.
  Prudence, m. Michael Cryderman of Marysburgh 7 April 1805. OC 23
    Februrary 1809.
  James of Hallowell. OC 25 June 1823.
  Daniel of Hallowell. OC 25 June 1823.
  Phoebe.   OC 4 Sept 1834.
  Elizabeth. OC 1 July 1830.
  William of Hallowell. OC 3 Jan 1827.
  Silvanus of Hallowell. OC 6 Jan 1827.

PETTIT, John of Grimsby. He died at Grimsby 9 June 1851 in 91st year. He
  had a brother, Andrew.
  Jonathan of Saltfleet. OC 2 Feb 1825.
  Ashman of Saltfleet. OC 2 Feb 1825.   [Cont'd]

PETTIT, John - Cont'd
　　Mary, m. Mathias Barber of Saltfleet. OC 2 Feb 1825.
　　John C. of Grimsby. OC 5 April 1825.

PETTIT, Nathaniel of Grimsby and Ancaster.
　　Mary, m. Peter Gordon of Ancaster. OC 22 April 1800.
　　Rachel, m. Lawrence Laurason of Grimsby. OC 12 May 1797. See Rachel
　　　　Williams in U.E. List.

PEW, Samuel of Stamford.
　　Robert of Stamford. OC 7 Nov 1809.
　　Hannah, m. Abraham Lampman. OC 8 Oct 1796.
　　Catharine, m. John Johnston of Thorold. OC 16 March 1825.

PHILLIPS, Elisha of Fredericksburgh, m. Elizabeth.
　　Ann, m. Jacob Dafoe of Fredericksburgh. OC 21 Oct 1806.
　　William of Fredericksburgh, bapt. 19 Oct 1788. OC 16 Feb 1810.
　　James of Fredericksburgh, bapt. 15 Sept 1793. OC 26 March 1817.
　　John of Fredericksburgh, bapt. 17 April 1791. OC 26 March 1817.
　　Asahel of Thurlow, bapt. 10 Dec 1797; m. Catharine Rickley. OC 30 May
　　　　1834.
　　George of Fredericksburgh, bapt. 18 Nov 1804. OC 8 Nov 1832.
　　Flora, bapt. 20 March 1809.
　　Elizabeth, bapt. 29 Sept 1811. OC 7 Aug 1834.

PHILLIPS, Jacob of Etobicoke.
　　Eli of Etobicoke. OC 6 Sept 1838.
　　Betsy, m. Henry Arnold of York. OC 2 March 1837.
　　Peggy (Margaret), m. Jonas Crisner (James Christner) of Etobicoke 2 Oct
　　　　1817. OC 9 March 1837.
　　Ann, m. John Fansleigh of York. OC 9 March 1837.
　　Jacob of York. OC 9 March 1837.
　　John of Etobicoke. OC 9 March 1837.
　　Levi of York. OC 9 March 1837.
　　Simeon of Etobicoke. OC 18 May 1837.
　　David of Etobicoke. OC 18 May 1837.

PHILLIPS, John.
　　Elizabeth, m. Nadab Eastman of Cornwall. OC 10 June 1800.
　　Jane, m. ---- Dennis. OC 30 Aug 1797.

PHILLIPS, Michael of Ernestown.
　　Affa (dau.) OC 22 Sept 1836.
　　Raymond of Wolford. OC 22 Sept 1836.

PHILLIPS, Nicholas Sr. Butler's Rangers. [At Niagara, 1783. TOR 1: 205]
　　Jacob of York. OC 28 June 1797.

PHILLIPS, Peter of Fredericksburgh, m. Margaret.
  John of Richmond, bapt. 26 Jan 1789. OC 10 Feb 1810.
  Peter of Fredericksburgh, bapt. 23 Jan 1792. OC 26 March 1817.
  Christopher of Camden East, b. 27 March 1814. OC 15 March 1838.
  Abraham of Cramahe, bapt. 16 Feb 1801. OC 13 April 1837.
  Ranselaer of Fredericksburgh. OC 2 May 1826.
  Albert of Fredericksburgh, bapt. 8 Jan 1809. OC 2 May 1836.
  James of Portland. OC 18 May 1833.
  Robert Gilbert of Fredericksburgh, b. 20 March 1805. OC 3 Oct 1833.
  Margaret, bapt. 23 Jan 1797. OC 3 Oct 1833.
  Mary, bapt. 8 Jan 1798.
  Sarah, bapt. 23 Feb 1807; m. James Peterson of Tyendinaga. OC 6 Nov
    1829.

PHILLIPS, William of Osnabruck.
  Jane. OC 25 Feb 1806. Osnabruck.
  Mary, m. Godfrey Warner of Osnabruck. OC 5 March 1808.
  William of Osnabruck. OC 7 Aug 1811.
  Elizabeth, m. Conrad Warner of Osnabruck. OC 15 March 1838.

PHILLIPS, Ziba Marcus of Augusta.
  Sarah Ann, Reuben Landon of Augusta. OC 25 Feb 1809.
  Jehiel H. of Augusta. OC 11 Nov 1815.
  Ziba Marcus of Augusta. OC 11 Nov 1815.
  Elizabeth D. , m. John Landon of Augusta. OC 28 Sept 1820.
  Marcia, m. William Van Arnam of Augusta. OC 4 Feb 1824.

PICKARD, Benjamin of Niagara. From "News of the Week" August 14, 1857:
  Died near Paris, Ont., aged 101, Benjamin Pickard, formerly of Niagara
  Tnp., and of Butler's Rangers (drummer).
  Frederick of Niagara, bapt. 5 Apr 1794. OC 13 Apr 1819.
  Hannah, m. Robert Saunderson of Niagara. OC 5 May 1819.
  Nicholas Wm. of Niagara, bapt. 4 May 1799. OC 31 May 1820.
  Joseph of Niagara. OC 18 July 1833.
  Courtland of Niagara. OC 28 April 1832.
  Benjamin of Grantham. OC 7 July 1831.
  James of Niagara. OC 5 Dec 1827.

PICKARD, James of Niagara.
  James of Niagara. OC 20 May 1817.
  Archibald of Niagara. OC 20 May 1817.
  William of Niagara. OC 13 Nov 1822.
  Elijah of Grantham. OC 27 Apr 1832.
  John of Niagara. OC 4 April 1827.

PICKARD, William of Niagara.
  Benjamin of Niagara. OC 2 May 1840.

PICKARD, William Sr. of Four Mile Creek.
    Mary, m. John Rowe of Stamford; d. 1797. OC 25 Apr 1797.
    Elizabeth, m. William Osterhout of Louth. OC 8 Oct 1796.
    Rebecca, m. Frederick Maracle of Niagara. OC 26 Feb 1797.
    Margaret, m. Jacob Dederick Sr. of Grantham. OC 7 April 1797.

PICKEL, John.
    Susannah. OC 25 Feb 1806.
    Nancy, m. John Black of Ameliasburgh. OC 25 Feb 1806.
    Henry of Fredericksburgh. OC 30 Jan 1808.
    Catharine, m. George Schriver of Fredericksburgh 3 March 1789. Land
       Board Certificate, 22/3 Camden.
    John Jr.

PILLAR, Michael of Williamsburgh.
    John of Williamsburgh. OC 19 Dec 1833.

PINE, Amos.
    Catharine, m. Samuel Way of Sophiasburgh. OC 18 Nov 1797.

PITMAN, Russell of Fredericksburgh and Thurlow, m. Diannah.
    Mary, m. William Anderson of Fredericksburgh. OC 11 Feb 1806.
    Susannah, m. John Latta of Thurlow 17 Nov 1800. OC 8 Feb 1808.
    Martha, m. John Carter of Thurlow. OC 17 March 1812.
    Martin of Thurlow. OC 4 Nov 1818.
    Thomas of Thurlow. OC 4 Nov 1818.

PLACE, William Simmons of Osnabruck and Townsend.
    Martha, m. David J. Read of Cornwall. OC 18 March 1808.
    Ann, m. John Shafer of Osnabruck. OC 17 Feb 1816.
    William of Townsend. OC 4 July 1833.
    Esther, m. William Winter of Townsend. OC 28 Oct 1833.
    Samuel of Osnabruck. OC 3 April 1834.

PLANT, Peter of Toronto.
    Jacob of Town of Brockville. OC 17 Dec 1840.
    Nicholas of Brockville. OC 17 Dec 1840.
    Adam of Elizabethtown. OC 12 Oct 1841.
    Christian of Elizabethtown. OC 12 Oct 1841.
    Michael of Elizabethtown. OC 1850 or 1851.
    Peter of Elizabethtown. OC 1850 or 1851.
    Magdalen, m. Peter Hanson of Elizabethtown. OC 1850 or 1851.

PLANTZ, John of Montreal.
    William of Kingston. OC 29 June 1843.

PLATTO, Christian.
    Caty, m. ---- Wychoff of Woodhouse. Land Board Certif, 2 & 3/2 Pelham.

PLATTO, Peter of Bertie, m. Gertrude, dau of Cornelius Bowen, U. E.
Christian of Bertie. OC 26 Nov 1823.
Christiana, m. Christopher Woolever of Bertie. OC 21 Sept 1837.
Elizabeth, m. ---- Edsal of Bertie. OC 8 Sept 1836.
Cornelius of Bertie. OC 24 March 1835.
Catharine, bapt. 12 April 1793; m. John Edsal of Bertie. OC 25 May 1825.
Jane, m. Benjamin Laur of Bertie. OC 19 Feb 1831.

PLAYTER, George of York, m. Elizabeth. See OC 28 Oct 1806. See Upper
Canada Gazette, 22 Nov 1832, for advertisement re sale of his property.
Sarah, m. David McGregor Rogers of Haldimand 6 Jan 1802. OC 18 Nov
1800.
Mary, m. Thomas Ward of Cramahe 30 Jan 1803; d. Port Hope 20 Feb
1847 in 65th yr. OC 31 May 1803.
Elizabeth, m. (1) Thomas Parry of York. OC 27 Aug 1805. m. (2) David
McG. Rogers of Haldimand; d. 18 Apr 1825 aet. 55 yrs.
Hannah. OC 9 July 1806.
Watson of York (Whitchurch), cabinetmaker, m. Priscilla. OC 10 May 1808.
George of York (Newmarket). OC 3 April 1810.
Eli of York, m. Sophia Beeman, 27 Nov 1806.
James of York, m. Hannah Miles, 24 Dec 1798
John of York, m. Sarah. From Mackenzie's Weekly Message, Aug 18,
1853: On the 14th inst., Jno. Playter Sr., on the Don, aet. 83.

POST, Frederick of Fredericksburgh.
Mary, m. John Bowen of Richmond. OC 2 July 1799.
Jane, m. John Percy of Camden East, 1813. OC 26 March 1817.
Raynard of Hallowell. OC 29 Dec 1819.
Jacob of Fredericksburgh. OC 17 Sept 1823.
Isaac of Fredericksburgh. OC 18 Aug 1824.

POTTER, Philip.
Rachel, m. Christopher Markle of Williamsburgh. OC 28 Feb 1798.

POTTER, William of Cornwall.
Elizabeth, m. Joseph Brownell of Cornwall. OC 4 April 1816.

POTTIER, John of Augusta.
Salome. OC 20 Sept 1838.
Rebecca, m. John Plumsteel of Elizabethtown. OC 28 Oct 1835.
Nelson of Elizabethtown. OC 17 March 1834.
Elizabeth. OC 3 July 1834.

POUND, Daniel of Bertie.
William of Bertie. OC 15 Nov 1808.
Sarah, m. Jeremiah Moore Jr. of Pelham. OC 15 Nov 1808.
David of Bertie. OC 2 March 1816.
John of Bertie. OC 2 March 1816.   [Cont'd]

POUND, Daniel - Cont'd
  Elijah of Malahide. OC 13 Feb 1816.
  Elizabeth, m. Jacob Zavitz of Bertie & Lobo. OC 2 Sept 1818.
  Rachel. OC 2 Sept 1818.
  Daniel of Bertie. OC 13 Nov 1822.
  Mercy Shreeves. OC 20 March 1822.
  Benjamin F. of Bertie. OC 6 Nov 1829.

POWELL, Abraham of Windham, b. State of New York, 1763; m. on Long
  Island River, St. John, N. B. , in 1784 to Ruth Wood; d. 1849.
  Polly, m. Daniel Walker of Woodhouse. OC 25 Feb 1809.
  Jacob of Charlotteville. OC 12 Oct 1810.
  William of Windham. OC 11 Nov 1815.
  Caleb of Windham. OC 19 April 1816.
  Israel Wood of Townsend, b. 1801; m. Melinda Boss; d. at Port Dover,
      1857. OC 23 June 1824.
  Phoebe, m. George Sovereign of Windham. OC 3 May 1826.

POWELL, John. Capt., Indian Dept.
  William of Bertie. OC 8 Oct 1808.
  Mary, m. John Maxwell of Bertie. OC 26 March 1817.

POWLEY, Jacob of Kingston.
  Elizabeth, m. William Albertson of Town of Kingston. OC 16 Nov 1797.
  Hannah, m. John Dingman of Kingston. OC 17 June 1806.
  William of Kingston. OC 16 Nov 1807.
  Francis of Kingston. OC 16 Nov 1807.
  James of Kingston. OC 16 Feb 1810.
  Jacob of Ernestown. OC 16 Feb 1810.
  Rebecca, m. Zachariah David of Kingston, 3 May 1814. OC 20 May 1817.
  Mary, m. Ira Darling of Loughborough. OC 10 Aug 1837.

PRENTICE, Daniel of Charlottenburgh, m. Mary Hamilton.
  Isabella, bapt. 14 Feb 1786; m. Ezra Adams of Charlottenburgh 1 Feb
      1798. OC 10 March 1801.
  Lewis of Charlottenburgh, m. Catharine McDonell, 25 June 1805. OC 31
      October 1809.
  John of Charlottenburgh. OC 7 August 1811.
  Ann, m. Nicholas Barnhart of Town of Cornwall. OC 11 Jan 1834.

PRENTICE, Richard.
  Daniel of Nepean. OC 1850 or 1851.
  Lydia, m. George Routliffe of Hull. OC 1850 or 1851.
  Deborah, m. David Moore of Hull. OC 1850 or 1851.

PRICE, Christian of Louth.
  Elizabeth, m. Jacob Culp of Clinton. OC 19 May 1819.
  David of Louth. OC 19 May 1819.   [Cont'd]

PRICE, Christian - Cont'd
Christian of Louth. OC 19 May 1819.
Peter of Louth. OC 19 May 1819.
Abraham of Louth. OC 17 March 1836.
Catharine. OC 19 Dec 1833.
Jacob of Louth. OC 19 Feb 1831.
John of Louth. OC 19 Feb 1831.
Mary, m. John McCarthy of Louth. OC 19 Feb 1831.
Nancy, m. John Haines of Grantham. OC 19 Feb 1831.

PRINDLE, Doctor of Fredericksburgh.
Lanah, m. Richard Prindle of Fredericksburgh. OC 21 Oct 1806.
Deborah, m. Elijah Kellogg of Fredericksburgh. OC 19 Aug 1833.
Daniel of Fredericksburgh. OC 4 Feb 1830.
Abraham of Fredericksburgh. OC 8 March 1826.

PRINDLE, Joel of Fredericksburgh.
Mary. OC 28 Feb 1799.
Francis S. (son) of Ernestown. OC 8 Feb 1808.
Joel of Townsend. OC 11 June 1840.
Lois, m. John Dafoe of Fredericksburgh.

PRINDLE, Joseph of Richmond.
John of Richmond. OC 16 Nov 1807.
Richard of Richmond. OC 16 Nov 1807.
Simeon of Richmond. OC 16 Nov 1807.
William of Richmond. OC 23 Feb 1808.
Joseph of Richmond. OC 16 Feb 1810.
Lois, m. John Windover of Richmond 18 Sept 1810. OC 25 Feb 1812.
David B. of Richmond. OC 26 Feb 1818.

PRINDLE, Timothy of Fredericksburgh.
Huldah, m. William Harrison Jr. of Marysburgh. OC 5 July 1798.
Timothy of Marysburgh. OC 9 July 1802.
Elisabeth. OC 25 June 1805. Fredericksburgh.
Esther, m. William Van Fradenburgh of Sophiasburgh. OC 21 Jan 1806.
Solomon H. of Rawdon. OC 1 Aug 1833.
Sarah. OC 1 Aug 1833. Marysburgh.
Drury (son) of Rawdon. OC 4 Dec 1834.
Joseph. Land Board Certificate, 35/4 Camden.

PRINDLE, William of Fredericksburgh.
Andrew of Fredericksburgh. OC 25 May 1808.
Jemima. OC 20 Aug 1808.
Hannah, m. Augustus Shorts of Fredericksburgh. OC 20 Aug 1808.
Eunice. OC 20 Aug 1808.
William of Fredericksburgh. OC 20 Aug 1808.
Lois, m. John Sanders of Town of Niagara. OC 25 Feb 1812.

PROCTOR, Joseph.
    Esther, m. Randy McDonell of Yonge. OC 8 Oct 1808.
    Thomas of Yonge. OC 29 Feb 1812.

PROSSOR, Richard of Cornwall. Soldier, KRRNY. Married Esther. She m.
    (2) ---- Place. He died May, 1795.
    Jesse of Osnabruck. OC 24 July 1822.
    Richard. Not. Rec. 5 Nov 1835.

PRUNNER, Peter Sr.
    Elizabeth, m. John Boice of Matilda. OC 17 March 1807.
    William of Osnabruck. OC 11 June 1840.
    Julia Ann. OC 28 Oct 1833. Williamsburgh.
    Polly. OC 28 Oct 1833. Williamsburgh.
    Adam of Williamsburgh. OC 2 Feb 1825.
    Nancy. OC 2 Feb 1825.
    Catharine. OC 2 Feb 1825.
    Elizabeth, m. David Fratts of Williamsburgh. OC 17 Feb 1825.
    John of Williamsburgh. OC 2 March 1825.

PRUYN, Herman of Fredericksburgh.
    Samuel of Thurlow. OC 4 Sept 1834.
    David of Sidney. OC 4 Sept 1834.
    Robert of Sidney. OC 29 Sept 1834.
    Hugh of Sidney. OC 2 Oct 1834.
    Absalom of Sophiasburgh. OC 2 Oct 1834.
    Mary, m. Stephen Fairfield of Ernestown 11 March 1799. OC 23 May 1798.

PRUYN, Mathew of Ernestown and Marysburgh. Heir & Devisee Commission
    July, 1831. m. Mary dau of Simon DeForest, U.E., 5 April 1790.
    Harmon of Ernestown. OC 5 March 1808.
    William Thatford of Ernestown, m. Mary Church, 3 April 1807. OC 25
        February 1809.
    Jane G., m. Samuel Byrns of Marysburgh. OC 6 March 1822.
    Rebecca. OC 1 May 1834.
    Mathew of Marysburgh. OC 7 Aug 1834.
    Sarah, m. John Stevens of Sophiasburgh. OC 2 July 1828.
    Catharine, m. Thomas Ellison Williamson of Marysburgh. OC 14 Sep 1825
    Martha, m. (1) ---- Wright; m. (2) John Byrns of Marysburgh. OC 18 Apr
        1843.
    Jane, m. (1) ---- Griffiths.
    Simon Ebenezer of Marysburgh. OC 14 Sept 1825.

PURBUS, John of Flamborough West.
    Eleanor, m. Peter Hanes of Flamborough West. OC 14 June 1811.
    Elizabeth, m. Miller Lawrison of Flamborough West. OC 26 March 1817.
    Jane, m. Andrew Van Every of Flamborough West. OC 18 March 1818.

PURDY, David of Ernestown, m. Abigail dau of Ruliph Ostrum, U. E.
   Gilbert of Ernestown. OC 16 Feb 1810.
   Ruliph of Ernestown. OC 20 Nov 1810.
   Elizabeth. OC 26 March 1817.
   Samuel D. of Ernestown. OC 12 July 1820.
   Micajah D. of Ernestown. OC 12 July 1820.
   Mary, m. John Abbott of Kingston. OC 12 July 1820.
   John of Sidney. OC 1 Dec 1836.
   Jacob of Ernestown. OC 1 Dec 1836.
   Joseph of Ernestown. OC 5 Feb 1835.

PURDY, Gilbert Sr. Guides and Pioneers. Married Mary. Lived at New
  Burgh, Ulster Co., N.Y. Died 1778.
   David of Ernestown, U. E.
   Gilbert of Kingston. OC 7 June 1800.
   Micajah of Kingston.
   Samuel.
   Mercy, m. John Everitt of Kingston. OC 3 March 1809.
   Rhoda.
   Mary.
   Charlotte, m. Nicholas Herchmer of Kingston. OC 17 Nov 1797.

PURDY, Gilbert Jr. of Kingston. He was b. January, 1762, son of Gilbert Sr.
  who was killed in the Revolutionary War, 1778. (See 13/2 Sidney).
   William James of Kingston. OC 3 Oct 1833.
   Gilbert of Kingston. OC 6 Aug 1829.
   Micajah of Kingston. OC 6 Aug 1829.
   Susannah, m. John Moore of Loughborough. OC 6 Aug 1829.
   Charlotte, m. Davis McCay of Kingston. OC 6 Aug 1829.
   Hosea of Kingston. OC 29 Aug 1810.
   Samuel of Kingston. OC 26 March 1817.
   Jesse of Kingston. OC 20 May 1817.
   Martha. OC 10 June 1818.
   David of Kingston. OC 12 Sept 1833.
   Mary, m. Joseph R. Caverley of Kingston 4 Jan 1809. OC 7 Aug 1810.

PURDY, Jesse of Elizabethtown, m. Ruth Kennicot.
   William of Yonge, b. 12 Aug 1769; m. Elizabeth Brundage; d. at Bath, 22
     January 1847. OC 17 March 1808.
   Thomas of Elizabethtown. OC 29 Sept 1819.
   Susannah, m. Archibald Montgomery of Elizabethtown.
   Hannah.

PUTMAN, Effron (Ephraim) of Cornwall. m. Miriam.
   Nancy, b. 3 Oct 1788; m. Aaron Brown Jr. of Cornwall. OC 25 Feb 1806.
   Robert of Cornwall, b. 3 July 1790. OC 16 Feb 1811.
   Sarah, b. 15 July 1792. OC 11 Nov 1815.
   Daniel of Cornwall. OC 5 Feb 1823.   [Cont'd]

PUTMAN, Effron - Cont'd
Maria, b. 29 Aug 1799; m. John H. Davies of Wolford. OC 13 June 1818.
Catharine, b. 30 Sept 1794.
Lucretia, b. 19 Feb 1797.

PUTMAN, Henry of Bertie, m. Hannah dau of Jacob Anguish, U.E.
Elizabeth. OC 25 Feb 1809.
Mary, m. ---- Fish. OC 25 Feb 1809.
John of Bertie. OC 26 Sept 1809.
Hannah. OC 20 May 1817.
Henry of Bertie. OC 9 May 1821.
Jacob of Bertie. OC 18 Feb 1824.
Jane, m. William Griffin of Thorold. OC 13 June 1836.

Q

QUANT, Jacob of Howard and Mosa.
Henry of Howard. OC 5 March 1823.
Jacob of Mosa. OC 23 July 1823.

R

RAMBOUGH, Amos of Osnabruck, m. Elizabeth.
William of Osnabruck. OC 17 March 1807.
John of Osnabruck. OC 23 Feb 1809.
Catharine, bapt. 13 July 1788; m. Henry Weager of Williamsburgh. OC 16 February 1810.
Margaret, bapt. 13 Feb 1791; m. Peter Helmer of Osnabruck. OC 16 Feb 1811.
David of Osnabruck. OC 14 Nov 1818.
Jacob of Osnabruck. OC 14 Nov 1818.

RAMBOUGH, Jacob.
Elizabeth, m. Jacob Empey of Cornwall, U.E.; d. 15 May 1814, aged 47. OC 5 Jan 1798.

RAMBOUGH, John of Osnabruck.
Mary, m. Jacob W. Empey of Osnabruck. OC 16 Feb 1811; 23 Nov 1816.
Elizabeth. OC 19 Apr 1816.
Jacob J. of Osnabruck. OC 22 Sept 1836.

RAMBOUGH, William of Fredericksburgh.
Jacob of Fredericksburgh. OC 19 April 1816.
Mary Barbara, bapt. 30 May 1790. OC 19 April 1816.
Margaret, bapt. 25 Dec 1791; m. William Sills of Fredericksburgh. OC 13 June 1818.   [Cont'd]

RAMBOUGH, William - Cont'd
 Christiana, m. Jacob Bush of Fredericksburgh. OC 27 June 1833.
 Electa, m. ---- Scriver of Fredericksburgh. OC 4 July 1833.
 Nicholas of Camden, m. Sarah Barnhart. OC 19 Aug 1833.
 John M. of Fredericksburgh. OC 5 Sept 1833.
 Temperance, m. ---- DeGroff of Fredericksburgh. OC 5 Feb 1835.
 Elizabeth, m. George Sills of Fredericksburgh. OC 15 Dec 1832.
 William N. of Fredericksburgh. OC 10 Dec 1832.

RAMSAY, Henry of Willoughby.
 Nancy, m. William Currant Jr. of Crowland. OC 16 Feb 1811.
 Elizabeth. OC 8 Sept 1819.
 James of Willoughby. OC 9 April 1820.

RANDOLPH, Benjamin of Yonge.
 Moses of Yonge. OC 26 May 1801.
 Suspended for proof from U. E. List, 12 Jan 1824, being only a settler.

RANKIN, James of Kingston and Hallowell, m. Phoebe Brown.
 Thomas of Hallowell. OC 12 June 1832.
 William of Hallowell. OC 6 Aug 1829.
 James of Hallowell, b. 13 March 1799; m. Elizabeth Johnson, 26 March
  1822. OC 19 July 1826.
 Phoebe, m. Varnum Burlingham of Hallowell. OC 5 May 1826.
 Catharine, b. 8 Sept 1801; m. James Potter Spencer of Hallowell 18 March
  1820. OC 5 May 1826.
 Mary Ann, m. Henry Dyer of Hallowell. OC 22 June 1825.

RANSIER, William of Kingston and Loughborough. He died at Loughborough
 19 September 1834, aged 74 years.
 George of Loughborough. OC 9 June 1836.
 Catharine, m. Seth Lyons of Kingston. OC 8 Nov 1832.
 Rachel, m. Joseph Ransier of Kingston 1 Jan 1818. OC 22 June 1825.
 William of Loughborough. OC 14 Sept 1825.

READ, William of Yonge and Kitley.
 Samuel of Kitley. OC 18 March 1818.
 John of Kitley. OC 18 March 1818.
 David of Kitley. OC 18 March 1818.
 Isabel, m. Solomon Soper of Kitley. OC 18 March 1818.
 Agnes, m. Elias McCollum of Kitley 13 Dec 1826. OC 14 July 1819.
 Margaret, m. Samuel Gray of Kitley. OC 23 June 1823.
 Elizabeth, m. William Magee of Kitley. OC 23 June 1823.
 Sarah. OC 9 Nov 1837.
 Jenett, m. ---- Hewett of Yonge. OC 23 Sept 1800.
 Mary, m. Peter Smith of Yonge. OC 28 Aug 1810.

REDDICK, Adam.
  Christopher of Williamsburgh. OC 1850 or 1851.
  George of Williamsburgh. OC 1850 or 1851.
  Elizabeth, m. ---- Merkley of Williamsburgh. OC 1850 or 1851.
  Sophia, m. ---- Bedstead of Williamsburgh. OC 1850 or 1851.

REDDICK, Christopher of Williamsburgh.
  Sarah, m. Alexander Bechsted of Williamsburgh. OC 9 July 1802.
  Mary, m. ---- Hanes of Williamsburgh. OC 28 Feb 1798.
  Adam of Williamsburgh, U.E.

REDDICK, John of Osnabruck, m. Peggy, dau of John Cadman Sr., U.E.
  Mary. OC 13 March 1807. Osnabruck.
  Hannah. OC 5 Jan 1808. Osnabruck.
  Catharine. OC 19 April 1816. Osnabruck.
  Deliah. OC 19 April 1816. Osnabruck.
  Adam of Osnabruck. OC 20 May 1817.

REDDICK, Philip of Ameliasburgh.
  Thomas of Ameliasburgh. OC 18 March 1818.
  Philip of Ameliasburgh. OC 4 Nov 1818.
  George of Ameliasburgh. OC 4 Nov 1818.
  David of Ameliasburgh. OC 4 Nov 1818.
  Polly, m. Perez Cooper of Cramahe. OC 28 Sept 1820.
  Margaret, m.(1) Isaac B. Glover of Ameliasburgh. OC 4 Feb 1824. m.(2)
      ---- Loveless.
  Ann, m. Abel Hubbell of Cramahe. OC 22 Oct 1840.
  Abigail, m. ---- McConnel of Thurlow. OC 4 Feb 1836.
  Nathan of Ameliasburgh. OC 2 Sept 1830.
  Sylvester of Ameliasburgh. OC 7 April 1824.
  John of Ameliasburgh. OC 28 April 1825.

REDDIN, Francis of Ernestown, m. Elizabeth, dau of Simon Snider, U.E.
  John of Ernestown. OC 26 March 1817.
  Simon of Ernestown. OC 20 May 1817.
  Rebecca, m. William Caton of Ernestown. OC 27 Feb 1818.
  Catharine. OC 27 Feb 1818.
  Clarissa, m. William Storms of Ernestown. OC 18 May 1833.
  Mary, m. ---- Timmerman of Ernestown. OC 27 June 1833.
  Elizabeth, m. Jeremiah Storms of Ernestown. OC 30 May 1834.
  George of Ernestown. OC 6 Oct 1831.
  Jacob of Ernestown. OC 31 May 1830.
  Stephen of Ernestown. OC 1 July 1830.
  Abraham of Kingston. OC 1 July 1830.

REDMOND, Nicholas of Matilda.
  Robert of Matilda, m. Lucy Chatterson. OC 20 May 1817.
  Gabriel of Wolford. OC 12 June 1834.   [Cont'd]

REDMOND, Nicholas - Cont'd
Mark of Matilda, m. Elizabeth Ault. OC 26 Nov 1831.
Lucretia, m. Richard Boulton of Matilda. OC 26 Nov 1831.

REED, Moses.
Sarah, m. ---- Burritt of Augusta. OC 30 Sept 1800.

REED, William of Thurlow.
Nancy, m. Elias Huffman of Richmond; d. 1841. OC 24 March 1835.

REID, George of Grantham.
Elizabeth, m. John Robertson of Grantham 30 March 1802. OC 9 March
    1803.
George of Grantham. OC 12 Nov 1811.
Cornelius of Grantham. OC 12 Nov 1811.
Mary. OC 18 March 1818.

REID, William of Grantham, m. Catharine Bessey.
Margaret, m. John R. Phenix of Grantham 26 June 1805. OC 17 June 1806.
Catharine, m. Peter Young of Grantham. OC 2 June 1819.
Robert of Grantham. OC 3 Nov 1819.
Elizabeth, m. Solomon Secord of Grantham. OC 22 May 1820.
John of Grantham. OC 2 May 1840.
George W. of Louth. OC 4 Dec 1834.
William of Grantham. OC 2 Oct 1829.
Mary. OC 13 May 1824.

REILLY, John of Stamford. [See The Ontario Register, 1: 204]
Mary, m. James Davidson of Stamford. OC 8 July 1806.
Daniel of Stamford. OC 17 June 1806.
Margaret. OC 30 Sept 1806.
Ann. OC 31 Oct 1809. Grantham. 24/1 Scott.
John of Stamford. OC 19 May 1801. OC 29 June 1820.
Catharine, m. Thomas Mercer of York. OC 14 Oct 1818.
Walter of Stamford. OC 16 June 1819.
Hannah, m. Frederick Near of Pelham. OC 3 Nov 1819.
Elizabeth, m. Adam Killman of Stamford. OC 31 May 1820.
James of Pelham. OC 2 May 1821.
William of Stamford. OC 8 Jan 1823.
Cordelia, m. John Smith of Erin. OC 27 Aug 1840.
Fanny. OC 19 Dec 1833.

REYNOLDS, Benjamin of Etobicoke. Soldier, KRRNY. Married at York, 16
December 1823, Benjamin Reynolds, widower, and Dolly Lormes, widcw,
both of Etobicoke.
Benjamin of Etobicoke, m. Eunice Peck, 20 Nov 1811. OC 30 Dec 1815.
Margaret, m. James Finch of Etobicoke 17 March 1808. OC 17 Mar 1812.
Sarah, m. Angus McDonald of Malden. OC 8 Oct 1808.   [Cont'd]

REYNOLDS, Benjamin - Cont'd
   Mary, m. David W. Homan of Etobicoke 22 July 1819. OC 19 Apr 1820.

REYNOLDS, Caleb of Barton, Trafalgar and Delaware.
   David of Barton. OC 18 March 1818.
   James of Barton. OC 5 May 1819.
   William of Barton, b. Barton 5 Apr 1793; m. Sarah Bostwick Bates born
      Harpersfield, N.Y., 19 Feb 1797, and d. 15 April 1836; d. Wellington
      Square, 16 Sept 1860. OC 5 May 1819.
   Sarah, m. William Tisdale of Trafalgar. OC 25 Aug 1819.
   Thomas of Barton. OC 5 Oct 1820.
   Benjamin of Barton. OC 2 Oct 1822.
   Alexander of Barton. OC 17 Dec 1836.
   George of Nelson. OC 17 Dec 1836.
   Charlotte, m. James Chep of Ancaster. OC 2 May 1833.
   Charles of Barton. OC 6 May 1830.
   Margaret, m. William English of Flamborough West. OC 23 June 1824.

REYNOLDS, Thomas. Commissary.
   Thomas of Malden. OC 27 May 1794.
   Ebenezer of Malden. OC 27 May 1794.
   Margaret. OC 27 May 1794.
   Robert of Malden. OC 27 May 1794.
   Catharine. OC 27 May 1794.

RICHARDS, Christopher of Clinton, born about 1745 in "the Jersies."
   Sarah, m. John Futrill of Niagara. OC 2 Jan 1811.
   Mary. OC 8 Sept 1819.
   John of Clinton. OC 8 Sept 1819.
   Arthur Grey of Clinton. OC 4 April 1833.
   Charles of Trafalgar. OC 9 Feb 1830.

RICHARDS, John of Hallowell (?). Lieut., Indian Dept.
   John of Amherst Island, m. Jane Howard, 26 Jan 1795. OC 17 Nov 1797;
      OC 23 Feb 1808.
   Jemima, m. Oliver Church Sr. of Fredericksburgh. OC 14 March 1809.
   Daniel. OC 17 Nov 1797.
   Owen of Hallowell, m. Dianah Spencer, 31 Dec 1789. OC 17 Nov 1797.
   Margaret, m. Hazelton Spencer, U.E. OC 29 Aug 1797; 18 Nov 1797.

RICHARDS, Owen of Hallowell, m. Diana Spencer, 31 Dec 1789.
   John of Hallowell, bapt. 6 March 1791. OC 25 Feb 1818.
   Eleanor, m. ---- Lane. OC 25 Feb 1818.
   Polly. OC 27 Feb 1818.
   Benjamin of Hallowell. OC 19 April 1820.
   Hazelton of Hallowell. OC 2 March 1825.

RICHARDSON, Asa of Fredericksburgh. Pvt., Loyal Rangers.
James of Camden East. OC 8 Feb 1808.
Thomas of Fredericksburgh. Land Board Certificate, 22/3 Richmond.

RICHARDSON, Thomas of Fredericksburgh.
Charlotte, m. Thomas Howard of Hallowell 14 Feb 1797. O.C. 8 March
1804. Only child. Heir & Devisee Commission, July 1831.

RICHARDSON, Thomas of Fredericksburgh.
Asa of Fredericksburgh, called Sr. OC 27 Feb 1834.
John of Marmora. OC 2 June 1836.
Rachel. OC 2 June 1836.
Samuel of Marmora. OC 17 Dec 1837.
Lucinda, m. ---- German of Belleville. OC 18 June 1840.
Laura, m. John McCann of Marmora. OC 16 April 1840.
Joshua of Sidney. OC 28 Nov 1839.
Lizette, m. James Williams of Sidney. OC 17 Oct 1839.
Susan, m. Truman Griswold of Sidney. OC 17 Oct 1839.
Mary, m. John Louis of Sophiasburgh. OC 14 June 1838.

RICKLEY, Andrew of Fredericksburgh. Sgt., King's Rangers. Md. Mary
Dafoe(?)
Mary, bapt. 31 Dec 1787; m. Lawrence Sharp of Fredericksburgh, 19 Nov
1804. OC 21 Oct 1806.
Elizabeth, bapt. 12 Jan 1789; m. William Phillips of Fredericksburgh, 21
Nov 1809. OC 16 Feb 1810.
Rosannah, m. Joseph Outwater, 21 Dec 1819. OC 19 April 1820.
George of Fredericksburgh, bapt. 30 June 1795. OC 19 April 1820.
John of Fredericksburgh, bapt. 2 June 1791; OC 19 April 1820.
Andrew of Fredericksburgh, bapt. 1 Sept 1793. OC 5 Feb 1829.
Jacob of Fredericksburgh, bapt. 3 Oct 1797. OC 28 March 1833.
Catharine, bapt. 24 May 1803; m. Asahel Phillips of Thurlow. OC 30 May
1834.
Elisha of Fredericksburgh. OC 5 Nov 1828.

RIDNOR, Henry Sr. of Ameliasburgh. Henry Rednor b. about 1768. Died at
Rednorsville, 18 May 1852.
Sophia, m. John Cole of Ameliasburgh. OC 26 Jan 1808.
Margaret, m. James Johnson of Ameliasburgh. OC 3 March 1809.
Mary, m. Henry Herman of Ameliasburgh. OC 25 Feb 1809.
John of Ameliasburgh. OC 23 Dec 1815.
Peter of Ameliasburgh. OC 20 Jan 1816. Jr.
Elizabeth. OC 17 Nov 1840. See OC 28 Feb 1835.

RISELAY, Christian of Bertie. [Butler's Rangers. Married Catharine Sipes.
For an account of their family see The Ontario Register, v. 4]
Hannah, m. Peter Young of Barton. OC 30 Sept 1806.
Rebecca, m. William Powell of Bertie. OC 23 Nov 1816.   [Cont'd]

RISELAY, Christian - Cont'd
Edmund of Bertie, m. Elizabeth Sophia [Meyer]. OC 9 Jan 1822.
John of Bertie. OC 8 Sept 1836.
Sophia, m. Jacob Miller of Bertie 20 Nov 1823. OC 28 Oct 1835.
Charlotte. OC 2 May 1833.
Barbara, m. Henry Bowen of Bertie. OC 28 Oct 1833.
Mary, m. Jacob Willson of Bertie. OC 23 June 1824.

ROBBINS, William of Charlottenburgh and North Crosby. m. Frances Emery.
Elizabeth. OC 16 Aug 1810.
Robert Emery of Bastard, bapt. 24 July 1791. OC 11 May 1825.
Mary, bapt. 27 Feb 1794; m. ---- Brower of Charlottenburgh. OC 1 April 1840.
Frances, m. John Grant of Montague. OC 5 Nov 1835.
Henry of Bastard. OC 11 July 1833.
Jane, m. Ralph Hodgson of North Crosby. OC 11 May 1825.
John of North Crosby. OC 11 May 1825.
William of Elizabethtown. OC 11 May 1825.

ROBERTSON, Daniel of Cornwall.
Barbara, m. ---- McMartin of Charlottenburgh. OC 27 July 1802.
Jennet, m. John Miller of Cornwall. OC 24 Feb 1820.

ROBERTSON, Joseph of Edwardsburgh.
Polly, m. ---- Watson of New Johnstown. OC 30 Sept 1800.

ROBERTSON, William of Edwardsburgh.
Joseph of Percy. OC 31 Jan 1839.
Henry of Percy. OC 31 Jan 1839.
Esther, m. James Prentice of Murray. OC 7 Feb 1839.
James of Seymour. OC 6 Aug 1840.
Susannah, m. David Fairman of Seymour. OC 6 Aug 1840.
Mary, m. John Clute of Seymour. OC 6 Aug 1840.
Sarah. OC 6 Aug 1840.
Margaret, m. Peter Dingman of Cramahe. OC 6 Aug 1840.
Lois, m. Thomas Varty of Murray. OC 6 Aug 1840.

ROBINS, James of Town of Kingston. (Ernestown). Lt., Loyal Rangers. Md.
Margaret, dau of Richard O'Neil of Albany Co., 28 Aug 1769.
Alice, m. Joseph Forsyth of Town of Kingston. OC 23 Nov 1802.
Sarah, m. Patrick Campbell of Town of Kingston 1 Sept 1804. OC 16 June 1807.
Richard of Ernestown, m. Mary Raymond, 16 Oct 1798. OC 8 July 1801.
James of Town of Kingston, bapt. 3 May 1789. OC 20 Feb 1810.
Alexander of Town of Kingston. OC 11 Nov 1815.
Henry of Town of Kingston, bapt. 16 Apr 1792. OC 11 Nov 1815.
William of Town of Kingston, m. Mary Crawford(?) OC 17 Nov 1797.

ROBINSON, Christopher of Town of Kingston and Town of York. His widow, Esther, md. Elisha Beman, 5 Sept 1802.

    Sarah Anne, m. D'Arcy Boulton Jr. of Town of York 13 Jan 1808. OC 29 March 1808.

    Mary, m. Stephen Heward of York, 27 Nov 1806. OC 28 April 1812.

    John Beverley of Town of York, b. 26 July 1791; m. Emma Walker, 1817; d. in Toronto 31 Jan 1863. OC 15 March 1815.

    Peter of Whitchurch, d. 8 July 1838 aged 53. OC 16 Jan 1816.

    William Benjamin of Whitchurch, m. Eliza Jarvis, 5 May 1822. OC 3 Dec 1828.

ROBINSON, Joseph.

    Margaret, m. ---- Buckner of Crowland. OC 16 May 1797.

ROBLIN, John.

    Maria, m. George H. Detlor of Napanee. OC 22 Dec 1842.

    Nancy, m. Thomas Flagler of Hillier. OC 22 Dec 1842.

    Philip J. of Ameliasburgh. OC 22 Dec 1842. m. Jane Casey.

    William M. of Fredericksburgh, m. Catharine Detlor. OC 22 Dec 1842.

    John of Richmond, m. Mary Kimmerly. OC 22 Dec 1842.

ROBLIN, Owen.

    Mary, m. ---- Orser. OC 19 Nov 1798.

    Rebecca, m. John Wood of Sophiasburgh 27 Oct 1793. OC 20 June 1797.

ROBLIN, Philip of Adolphustown.

    Mary, m. Marvill Garrison of Fredericksburgh. OC 8 June 1798.

    Elizabeth, m. Benjamin Clapp of Fredericksburgh 6 Apr 1803. OC 21 Jan 1806.

    Ann, m. William Ketcheson of Sidney. OC 17 Feb 1807.

    Fanny, m. Peter Ruttan of Adolphustown 7 July 1807. OC 16 Feb 1808.

    Levi of Sophiasburgh. OC 13 Feb 1816.

    David of Sidney. OC 4 Sept 1822.

    Owen of Ameliasburgh. OC 18 Jan 1834.

    Elizabeth, m. Joseph Foster of Camden East. OC 18 July 1834.

    Caleb of Sophiasburgh. OC 18 July 1834.

    John P. of Sophiasburgh. OC 7 May 1828.

    Keziah, m. George Drewry of Sophiasburgh 20 Nov 1820. OC 7 May 1828.

ROCH, John. Indian Dept.

    Mary, m. Francis Tessie of Cornwall. OC 10 Dec 1818.

ROGERS, Col. James of Fredericksburgh; his wife was the dau of Rev David McGregor of Londonderry, N. H. He died in Fredericksburgh on September 1790, aged 63 years.

    James.

    David McGregor of Haldimand, b. 23 Nov 1772; d. 13 July 1824.

    Margaret, m. Aaron Greeley.   [Cont'd]

ROGERS, Col. James - Cont'd
    Mary, m. John Armstrong of Sophiasburgh; buried 3 Dec 1793.
    Mary Ann, m. Col. John Peters of Sophiasburgh, 18 Feb 1790.

ROGERS, William of Ernestown. Pvt., Loyal Rangers.
    Amy, m. Martin Hawley of Ernestown. Land Board Certif., 27/5 Sidney.
    Catharine, m. David Wees of Ernestown. OC 28 June 1797.
    Armstrong of Ernestown. OC 25 Aug 1801.
    Joseph of Murray, m. Nancy Wees. OC 5 Dec 1827.
    John of Murray, m. Jerany Wees. OC 1 May 1834.
    Ephraim of Rawdon. OC 4 Sept 1834.
    Jededdiah of Hungerford. OC 4 Sept 1834.
    Rufus of Rawdon. OC 4 Sept 1834.
    Patience. OC 8 Sept 1836.
    Martitia, m. Latham Corbin of Leeds. OC 8 Sept 1836.

RORISON, Basil of Elizabethtown, m. Sarah.
    Sarah, m. Samuel Thomas of Augusta. OC 20 Feb 1810.
    James Murray of Elizabethtown (Kingston), m. Elizabeth Sherwood on 22
        March 1818. OC 22 Sept 1812.
    Jane, m. George Manhart of Elizabethtown. OC 26 March 1817.
    Robert of Pittsburgh. OC 27 Jan 1819.
    Mary, m. Oliver Eaton of Leeds. OC 28 June 1819.
    Clinton of Elizabethtown. OC 18 Aug 1836.
    Hugh U. of Elizabethtown. OC 12 Nov 1827.
    Basil of Pittsburgh. OC 30 Sept 1824.
    Agnes S., m. John Grant of Elizabethtown, 10 July 1828. OC 6 Oct 1831.

ROSE, Aaron of Edwardsburgh.
    Silas of Edwardsburgh. OC 14 June 1839.
    Aaron of Amherst Island. OC 13 June 1833.

ROSE, Alexander of Williamsburgh, b. in Schoharie Co., 1769, and d. 1835.
    Lydia. OC 18 March 1818.
    Samuel of Williamsburgh. OC 18 March 1818.
    James of Williamsburgh. OC 27 Aug 1840.
    Sybil, m. William Nash of Matilda. OC 11 Feb 1836.
    Harriet. OC 18 Feb 1836.
    Barnabas of Matilda. OC 3 March 1836.
    Elizabeth, m. Thomas Fulton of Williamsburgh. OC 11 April 1833.
    Jesse W. of Williamsburgh. OC 1 Aug 1833.
    Charles of Williamsburgh. OC 5 Feb 1835.
    William of Williamsburgh. OC 7 Feb 1833.
    Isaac N. of Williamsburgh, b. 14 July 1811; d. 12 Sept 1874. OC 7 Feb 1833.
    Huldah.
    Hugh.
    Robert.

ROSE, Alexander of Charlottenburgh.
  Mary, m. Kenneth McPherson of Lancaster. OC 6 Aug 1840.
  Isabella, m. Alexander McDougall of Lancaster. OC 6 Aug 1840.

ROSE, Charles of West half 8/1 Lancaster, Front Charlottenburgh. KRRNY.
  Married Janet, dau of Duncan Murchison, U. E., of Lancaster.
  Margery, bapt. 19 March 1793; m. Alexander McIntosh of Lancaster. OC
    28 April 1815.
  Margaret, m. Alexander McDonald of Lancaster. OC 6 Aug 1816.
  Anne, m. John McIntosh of Lancaster. OC 3 Jan 1833.
  Janet. OC 23 July 1823.

ROSE, Daniel of Ernestown, m. Eleanor, dau Alex. Campbell. See OC 17
  August 1795.
  William of Ernestown. OC 16 Feb 1811.
  Phoebe. OC 25 Feb 1812.
  Archibald of Ernestown. OC 25 Feb 1812.
  Jane. OC 25 Feb 1812.
  Mathias of Ernestown. OC 16 July 1816.
  Mary. OC 20 May 1817.

ROSE, Daniel of Niagara.
  James of Niagara. OC 31 Oct 1821.
  Alexander of Niagara. OC 28 Nov 1821.
  Lewis of Niagara. OC 28 Nov 1821.
  Jane. OC 28 Nov 1821.
  Margaret, m. ---- Thompson of Stamford. OC 1 May 1834.
  Peter of Trafalgar. OC 4 Sept 1834.

ROSE, Donald.
  William of Niagara. OC 9 July 1806.
  Nancy, m. William McKerlie of Stamford. OC 17 June 1806.

ROSE, Ezekiel of Edwardsburgh & Montague.
  Charles of Montague. OC 13 June 1818.
  Marintha, m. John Davis of Montague. OC 11 Oct 1838.
  Alvin of Montague. OC 9 March 1837.
  Laura, m. James H. Kerr of Montague. OC 28 Oct 1835.
  Omar of Montague. OC 7 Aug 1834.
  Mary, m. George Perry of Montague. OC 7 Feb 1833.
  Cloe, m. Asa Clothier of Oxford. OC 6 Sept 1832.
  Liddy, m. Christopher Wilson of Montague. OC 28 June 1832.
  John of Montague. OC 28 June 1832.

ROSE, Mathias Jr.
  Daniel of Ernestown. OC 16 Nov 1807.
  Robert of Ernestown. OC 16 Nov 1807.
  Jane, m. Isaac Reed of Thurlow. OC 16 Feb 1810.

ROSE, Mathias of Ernestown. Pvt., Loyal Rangers.
  Sarah, m. Edward McCafferty of Ernestown 25 Sept 1800. OC 25 Nov 1800.
  Patience, m. ---- Switzer of Marysburgh. OC 19 Nov 1798.
  Joseph of Ernestown. OC 3 Oct 1833. Son of Mathias Jr.?
  Step-son, John Burley. Land Board Certificate, 38/3 Camden.

ROSE, Moses of Montague.
  William of Montague. OC 15 March 1838.
  Levi of Montague. OC 27 Aug 1840.
  Samuel of Town of Niagara. OC 3 Sept 1840.
  Silas of Montague. OC 9 Feb 1830.
  David of Montague. OC 9 Feb 1830.
  Chloe. OC 9 Feb 1830.

ROSE, Samuel Sr., m. Chloe Canfield.
  Samuel of Wolford, m. Charlotte McIntyre.
  Chloe, bapt. 3 June 1796; m. David Froom of Edwardsburgh. OC 7 July
    1802.
  Susannah, bapt. 28 May 1793; m. William Morrison of Edwardsburgh. OC
    8 February 1808.
  Arza (son) of Montague. OC 18 March 1808. Bapt. 3 June 1796.
  Aaron of Edwardsburgh. OC 20 Aug 1808.
  John of Edwardsburgh. OC 19 April 1816.
  Rachel, bapt. 28 May 1793; m. Samuel Adams of Edwardsburgh. Not. Rec.
    26 Feb '05. OC 22 July 1818.
  Sarah.
  Charlotte. OC 20 Oct 1832. (dau. Sam Jr.?)
  Moses of Montague, U.E.
  David.
  Ezekiel of Montague, U.E.
  Jacob (?)

ROSE, William of Charlottenburgh.
  Jenny, m. ---- Murchison. OC 11 July 1799.
  Jennet, m. Duncan Bethune of Charlottenburgh. OC 6 Aug 1816.

ROSENBARGER, Jacob of Williamsburgh.
  Jacob of Williamsburgh. OC 5 March 1810.
  Elizabeth, m. Henry Hanes of Williamsburgh. OC 27 March 1813.
  Catharine, m. Capt. John Monro of Matilda. OC 3 Feb 1816; OC 3 Feb
    1834; OC 28 February 1842.
  Lany. OC 19 April 1816.
  Mary. OC 19 April 1816.
  Susannah. OC 19 April 1816.
  Dorothy, m. Jacob Merkley of Williamsburgh. OC 2 Sept 1818.
  Albertis of Williamsburgh. OC 2 May 1833.
  John of Williamsburgh. OC 1 Aug 1833.
  Dorothy, m. Jonathan Nichols of Oxford. OC 1 May 1834.

ROSS, Alexander of Charlottenburgh, 33/1 north side River aux Raisins.
Catharine, m. Alexander Bromley of Charlottenburgh. OC 7 Feb 1821.
Elizabeth, m. Walter Ross of Zorra. OC 26 Dec 1834.
Hugh of Charlottenburgh, d. Palmerston, Ont., 21 Jan 1892. OC 19 Feb
1831.
Colin of Charlottenburgh. OC 22 July 1824.
Janet, m. William Craig of Charlottenburgh. OC 10 Dec 1823.

ROSS, Alexander of Lancaster.
Alexander of Lancaster. OC 24 Nov 1836.
Allan of Lancaster. OC 24 Nov 1836.

ROSS, Donald.
Ann, m. William Martin of Charlottenburgh. OC 5 Jan 1798.

ROSS, Donald of W. Half 53/ north br. River aux Raisins, Charlottenburgh.
Isabella, m. Donald Cameron of Charlottenburgh. OC 25 Feb 1818.
David of Charlottenburgh. OC 25 Feb 1818.

ROSS, Donald of Charlottenburgh. KRRNY.
Nancy, m. ---- McKay. Land Board Certificate, 19/5 Lochiel.

ROSS, Donald of Charlottenburgh.
Duncan of Charlottenburgh. OC 10 Dec 1823.

ROSS, Jacob of Osnabruck, m. Christianne Merkley at Montreal, May, 1784.
She died at Aultsville, 15 Jan 1856, aged 98 yrs.
Michael of Osnabruck, d. there in June, 1878 aged 89. OC 16 Feb 1811.
Margaret, m. Nicholas Ault of Osnabruck. OC 19 April 1816.
Catharine, m. Jacob Hollister of Osnabruck. OC 8 Feb 1827.
Elizabeth, m. Adam W. Loucks of Osnabruck. OC 1 May 1834.

ROSS, John of Lancaster and Charlottenburgh.
Isabella, m. Alexander Mowat of Charlottenburgh 20 Sept 1808. OC 3
March 1809.
Ann, m. James Pierson of Charlottenburgh 21 Sept 1809. OC 3 Apr 1810.
Christy, m. Finlay Monro of Charlottenburgh 3 Nov 1808. OC 2 Apr 1816.
Thomas of Charlottenburgh. OC 26 March 1817.
Elizabeth, m. Donald Fisher of Charlottenburgh. OC 30 Oct 1822.
William of Roxborough. OC 5 March 1828.

ROSS, Philip of Charlottenburgh and Montreal.
Jennett, m. Malcolm Murray of Charlottenburgh. OC 19 April 1808.
John of Niagara. OC 4 March 1819.
Catharine. OC 14 May 1823.

ROSS, Thomas (Bain) of Lancaster. Lot 29.
Christy (dau.) OC 24 August 1802.   [Cont'd]

ROSS, Thomas (Bain) - Cont'd
    Thomas of Lancaster. OC 24 Aug 1802.

ROSS, Thomas (Ben) of Charlottenburgh.
    Hugh of Charlottenburgh. OC 9 July 1802.

ROSS, Thomas (Taylor). K. R. R. N. Y.
    Alexander of Charlottenburgh. OC 5 Jan 1798.

ROSS, Zenas of Fredericksburgh. Pvt., King's Rangers. Married Rachel,
    dau Simeon and Sarah Wright. From Rutland, Vt.
    Rachel, m. Michael Dafoe of Fredericksburgh. OC 20 Nov 1798.
    Dorcas, m. John Bush of Fredericksburgh 21 Feb 1803. OC 26 Jan 1808.
    Margaret, bapt. 30 June 1795; m. Solomon Wright of Hope. OC 20 Nov 1810.
    Leonard of Fredericksburgh, b. 9 Oct 1789; m. Sophia Jane Davis, 29 Oct
        1811; d. 12 March 1867. OC 16 Feb 1811.
    Wait of Fredericksburgh. OC 12 July 1797.
    William of Fredericksburgh. OC 12 July 1797.

ROUSEHORN, John of Kingston.
    Sarah Ann, m. Henry Christopher Searle of Town of Kingston. OC 21 Sept
        1837.
    Hannah. OC 11 Feb 1836.
    Christopher of Kingston. OC 30 May 1834.
    Caroline, m. Robert Brass of Storrington. OC 10 June 1846.
    Aaron Bryce Andrew. OC 27 May 1848.

ROWE, Frederick of Rainham.
    William of Rainham. OC 15 Dec 1821.
    Dennis of Rainham. OC 15 Dec 1821.
    Frederick of Walpole. OC 14 April 1836.
    Catharine. OC 3 April 1834.

ROWE, John of Stamford. Sgt., Butler's Rangers. [See TOR 1:198,200,201]
    m.(1) Leah Smith, b. Jan., 1768, d. 5 Sept 1793. m.(2) Mary Pickard. He
    was killed at the battle of Chippawa, 5 July 1814.
    Elizabeth, m. Robert Campbell of Grantham. OC 5 May 1819.
    George of Stamford, m. Elizabeth Ludlow. OC 21 Feb 1821.
    A child, d. 1793. See 216 Vol. 6, Robertson's Landmarks.

ROYS, Evan Sr.
    Loyreneah, m. Elias Williams of Vaughan, 2 Jan 1798. OC 6 June 1799.
    Sarah. OC 14 June 1798. Cornwall.
    Sybil, m. Jesse Wright of Williamsburgh. OC 28 March 1797.

ROYS, Evan Jr. of Cornwall.
    John of Cornwall. OC 17 Feb 1816.
    Hannah. OC 18 March 1818.   [Cont'd]

ROYS, Evan Jr. - Cont'd
　　Sybil. OC 16 April 1818.
　　Mary, m. Charles Latrace of Cornwall. OC 28 Oct 1835.
　　Catharine. OC 28 Oct 1835.

RUDERBACH, John of Edwardsburgh.
　　Hannah, m. Henry Anderson of Edwardsburgh. OC 15 June 1797.

RUNIONS, Henry of Cornwall, m. Hannah Barnhart.
　　William of Osnabruck, bapt. 16 May 1790. OC 16 Feb 1811.
　　Peter of Cornwall, bapt. 15 Jan 1797. OC 13 June 1818.
　　George of Osnabruck, bapt. 11 Dec 1791. OC 21 May 1834.
　　Jane. OC 26 March 1836.
　　Phillip of Osnabruck, b. 25 Dec 1809. OC 19 Dec 1833.
　　Samuel of Cornwall, b. 8 Dec 1800. OC 19 Dec 1833.
　　Catharine, b. 12 April 1807; m. Charles McCummond of Cornwall. OC 2
　　　　January 1834.
　　Hannah, b. 1 June 1805; m. Christopher Gallinger of Cornwall. OC 22
　　　　December 1832.
　　Henry of Cornwall. OC 20 Oct 1832.
　　John, b. 8 Feb 1803.

RUPERT, Jacob of Osnabruck.
　　Barbara, m. ---- Ulto [Otto ?] of Osnabruck. OC 27 Sept 1838.

RUPORT, Peter of Osnabruck.
　　Adam P. of Osnabruck. OC 26 Jan 1837.
　　Henry of Osnabruck. OC 2 May 1833.
　　Peter of Osnabruck. OC 2 May 1833.
　　Catharine, m. Henry Cole of Osnabruck. OC 7 Dec 1830. OC 27 Sept 1833.
　　Mary, m. Thomas Porter of Darlington. OC 27 Sept 1833.
　　Conrad of Osnabruck. OC 18 Jan 1828.
　　Elizabeth. OC 2 April 1828.

RUSH, Andrew of Ernestown and Camden East, m. Elizabeth Cook 1 Mar 1790
　　Samantha, bapt. 29 June 1791; m. Hammell Madden of Ernestown. OC 6
　　　　February 1823.
　　Sarah, bapt. 22 Jan 1799; m. John Sansburn of Camden E. OC 4 Feb 1836.
　　Andrew of Camden East, bapt. 9 Feb 1796. OC 4 Feb 1836.
　　Elizabeth, bapt. 22 Jan 1793; m. David Johnston of Ernestown 17 Apr 1821
　　　　OC 4 July 1833.

RUSH, Martin of Ameliasburgh.
　　Elizabeth, m. Conrad Frederick of Ameliasburgh. OC 14 Feb 1798.
　　James of Ameliasburgh. OC 20 May 1817. Jr. ?
　　Martin of Ameliasburgh. OC 4 April 1821. Jr. ?
　　Catharine, m. Asa Blanchard of Ameliasburgh. OC 2 Sept 1830. OC 11
　　　　June 1840.

RUSH, Martin Jr. of Ameliasburgh.
   John of Ameliasburgh. OC 6 Jan 1816.

RUTTAN, Peter of Adolphustown. Capt., N.J. Vols. From "News of the
   Week" Dec 15, 1859 and from McKenzie's Message Dec 10, 1859: Died at
   Brougham on 1st Dec., Mary Mathews dau of Capt. Ruttan who fought on
   the British side in the War of the American Revolution, and mother of
   Peter Mathews who was executed in 1837; aged 90 yrs.
      Peter of Adolphustown, m. Jemima Sloot, 5 Dec 1790. OC 16 Nov 1797.
      Joseph of Adolphustown, m. Alley Canniff, 3 June 1805. OC 16 Feb 1810.

RUTTAN, Peter of Adolphustown. Sr. or Jr. ?
   John of Adolphustown. OC 6 April 1839.
   David of Fredericksburgh. OC 11 April 1833.

RUTTAN, William of Adolphustown. Lieut., N.J. Vols. Md. Margaret Steel.
   Peter William of Adolphustown, m. Fanny Roblin, 7 July 1807. OC 22
      February 1808. From "Daily Leader" May 7, 1861: Col. Peter W.
      Ruttan, eldest son, d. Northport, Sophiasburgh, 28 Apr 1861 in 74th yr.
   Daniel of Adolphustown, m. Rhoda Haight, 16 Jan 1812. OC 25 Feb 1812.
   Elizabeth, m. (1) Hugh C. Thomson of Town of Kingston. m. (2) Rev. Dr.
      Adam Townley. OC 20 Aug 1817.
   Abraham W. of Adolphustown. OC 28 Nov 1821.
   Mathew of Haldimand. OC 25 June 1823.
   Jacob of Adolphustown. OC 24 March 1835.
   Charles Stuart of Hamilton. OC 7 Dec 1830.
   Henry of Haldimand, m. Mary Jones, 26 May 1816. OC 15 March 1815.

RUTTER, George (John George) of Adolphustown, m. Elizabeth. He died in
   Adolphustown 21 Sept 1848, aged 98 yrs.
   Michael of Adolphustown. OC 8 Feb 1808.
   Mary, bapt. 7 March 1791. OC 25 Feb 1812.
   John of Adolphustown, bapt. 7 March 1791. Hatter. OC 31 July 1817.
   Alexander of Adolphustown, bapt. 27 Feb 1794. OC 31 July 1817.
   Allida, bapt. 14 Feb 1793. OC 29 Dec 1819.
   Elizabeth, m. William N. Fletcher of Adolphustown. OC 2 Apr 1835.
   George of Adolphustown. OC 18 May 1833.
   Peter of Adolphustown. OC 7 Aug 1834.
   Amelia, m. Samuel Wood of Sophiasburgh. OC 5 Feb 1835.
   Catharine, m. Richard Cole of Murray. OC 5 Feb 1835.
   Lavinia, m. Benjamin Ryckman of Adolphustown 11 July 1821. OC 28 Sept
      1825; OC 2 Sept 1830.

RYCKMAN, Edward of Sophiasburgh and Flamborough West. He moved to
   Hamilton in 1812, and to Flamborough W. in 1816. He was born about 1763
   and died July 27, 1846, aged 83.
   Elizabeth, m. Jacob Markle of Flamborough W. OC 23 July 1823.
   Abraham of Flamborough W. OC 21 March 1833.   [Cont'd]

RYCKMAN, Edward - Cont'd
Catharine, m. Solomon Washburn of Flamborough W. OC 7 Aug 1822.
Susannah, m. John Simcoe Green of Flamborough W. OC 7 Aug 1822.
John W. of Flamborough W., b. Sophiasburgh, 9 Nov 1805; d. 4 July 1852.
OC 23 July 1823.

RYCKMAN, John of Barton. Lt., Indian Dept. m. Elizabeth. OC 12 Jan 1798.
Mary, m. Benjamin Springer of Block 2. (Lt. John) OC 24 April 1810.
Eunice, m. Hugh Buckborough of Ancaster. (Lt. John) OC 17 March 1812.
Samuel of Barton. OC 23 Nov 1816. (John d. prior to 28 July 1820). From
Can. News, March 12, 1868: Died Feb 18, at Hamilton, Rachel, relict
of the late Samuel Ryckman, aet. 81 yrs.
Albert of Haldimand Co. (London Tnp.) OC 28 July 1820.
Nancy, m. Phineas Allen of Tecumseth. ? OC 12 Nov 1840.
Susan, m. Isaac Kerr of Ancaster. Flam. W. ? OC 3 Nov 1836.
John J. of Town of Hamilton. OC 11 July 1833.
Cornelius of Yarmouth. OC 5 Feb 1835.
Samuel J. OC 3 Nov 1831.

RYCKMAN, John of Adolphustown and Sophiasburgh, m. Susannah Brown
(Bruyn), 12 June 1760; of Hackensack, N.J. See OC 30 Aug 1797.
Tobias of Sophiasburgh, U.E.
Mary. Died young.
Edward of Sophiasburgh, U.E.
John of Sophiasburgh.
Catharine. Died young.
Abraham of Loughborough. OC 26 April 1811.
Susannah, m. John Lowe of Sophiasburgh.

RYCKMAN, Tobias of Sophiasburgh.
James of Ernestown. OC 16 Feb 1811.
Elizabeth, m. Enoch Solomon of Hallowell 22 July 1807. OC 12 Nov 1811.
Edward of Sophiasburgh. OC 25 Feb 1812.
Samuel C. of Sophiasburgh. OC 31 July 1817.
John of Sophiasburgh. OC 31 July 1817.
Susannah, m. Adam Shuvelt of Ameliasburgh. OC 3 April 1834.
Benjamin of Sophiasburgh. OC 17 March 1824.
Daniel of Sophiasburgh. OC 17 March 1824.

RYERSE, Samuel of Woodhouse.
Elizabeth, m. Garrison Liger of Woodhouse. OC 1 June 1802.
Samuel of Woodhouse. OC 23 April 1805.
Amelia, m. John Harris, R.N., of Woodhouse. OC 2 March 1816.
George J. of Woodhouse. OC 4 April 1816.
Edward P. of Woodhouse. OC 17 March 1824.

RYERSON, Joseph of Charlotteville, b. 28 Feb 1761, son of Lukos Ryerson;
m. Sophia Mehetable Stickney.   [Cont'd]

RYERSON, Joseph - Cont'd
   Hetty, m. John Williams of Charlotteville; d. 17 March 1832. OC 23 Dec
      1806.
   Polly. OC 23 Dec 1806.
   Elizabeth, m. James Mitchell of Charlotteville; d. 18 April 1835, aged 40.
      OC 4 July 1815.
   Samuel of Charlotteville. OC 27 Nov 1815.
   Joseph Wm. of Charlotteville. OC 2 Sept 1818.
   John of Charlotteville. OC 15 Aug 1821.
   Edwy of Town of Hamilton. OC 9 June 1836.
   Egerton of Charlotteville. OC 19 July 1826.

S

SAGER, Adam of Richmond.
   Susannah. OC 16 Feb 1811.
   Mary, m. ---- Sanderson of Richmond. OC 22 Feb 1834.
   Frederick A. of Richmond. OC 22 Feb 1834.
   Staats A. of Richmond. OC 1 May 1834.
   Sally, m. Amos Schermerhorn of Richmond. OC 5 July 1830.

SAGER, Frederick of Niagara and Richmond. [Butler's Rangers. He and his
   family were at Niagara in 1783. See The Ontario Register, 1:200]
   Staats F. of Richmond. OC 28 Feb 1804.
   Mary, m. Carr Draper of Richmond 12 July 1815. OC 25 July 1809.
   Susannah, Amos Richardson of Fredericksburgh, 9 March 1802.
   Henry of Flamborough East. OC 9 June 1812.
   Frederick of Ameliasburgh. OC 27 Jan 1816.
   Peter of Bertie. OC 4 Sept 1822.
   Catharine, m. Essery Kibby. OC 11 Nov 1852.

SAGER, John.
   Christina, m. Andrew Rancier. OC 29 July 1795.

SAUNDERS, William.
   Elizabeth. OC 18 June 1799.

SAVER, John of Matilda.
   Hannah. OC 9 July 1802.
   Esther. OC 9 July 1802.
   Elizabeth. OC 9 July 1802.
   John of Matilda. OC 19 April 1816.
   Mary. OC 19 April 1816.
   Margaret, m. Levi Shaver of Matilda. OC 23 June 1828.
   Mary, m. Chris. Keeler of Matilda. OC 16 Feb 1810.
   Jacob. OC 18 June 1799.   [Cont'd]

SAVER, John - Cont'd
Catharine. OC 16 Feb 1810. Matilda. [She is said to have married Capt.
George Drummond. Carter's "Story of Dundas" p.441]

SCHAFFER, Nicholas of Osnabruck. Corp'l, Butler's Rangers.
Getty, m. Geo. Carman of Matilda. OC 16 June 1807.
Eve, m. Philip W. Empey of Osnabruck. OC 12 Feb 1811; 19 April 1816.
Catharine. OC 25 Feb 1812.
John of Osnabruck. OC 25 Feb 1812.
Henry of Osnabruck. OC 19 April 1816.
Jacob of Osnabruck. OC 19 April 1816.
Martinas of Osnabruck. OC 19 April 1816.

SCHERMERHORN, William of Fredericksburgh.
Mary, m. William Williams of Sophiasburgh. OC 12 July 1797.
Jenny, m. William Richardson of Fredericksburgh 16 Apr 1801. OC 9
March 1803.
Lany, m. Thomas Lyons of Sophiasburgh. OC 21 Feb 1807.

SCHNEIDER, Conrad Sr. of Williamsburgh.
Andrew of Williamsburgh.
Conrad of Williamsburgh. OC 19 April 1816.

SCHRAM, Frederick of Louth. Soldier, Butler's Rangers. m. Angelica.
Catharine, m. John Paterson of Louth. OC 5 March 1808.
Frederick Augustus of Louth, bapt. 13 July 1792. OC 20 May 1817.
Magdalen. OC 20 May 1817.
Sarah, m. Frederick Kievil of Flamborough West. OC 1 April 1840.
Eliza, m. Abraham Markle of Flamborough West. OC 5 Feb 1831.
Elsa, m. William Cole of Louth. OC 28 March 1797.
Garrett of Louth. OC 21 Aug 1797.

SCHRAM, Jeremiah of Pelham and Westminster, m. ---- Fralick.
Catharine, m. (1) Hugh Thompson of Pelham. OC 14 Jan 1812. m. (2)
Thomas Poole.
Benjamin of Westminster. OC 27 Jan 1816.
William of Westminster. OC 6 March 1822.
Mary. OC 9 Aug 1820.
Elizabeth, m. Calvin Burtch of Westminster. OC 7 Feb 1821.
Nelson Brock of Westminster. OC 31 Oct 1839.
Ann, m. John Kiles of Westminster. OC 31 Oct 1839.
Peter of Westminster. OC 28 March 1833.
Jane, m. James Uptergrove of Westminster. OC 11 July 1833.
Charlotte, m. James McNamus of Westminster 4 Sept 1824. OC 10 March
1834.
John, bapt. 19 Aug 1792.
Sarah, m. James Beattie of Westminster, 8 Jan 1827. OC 23 July 1832.

SCHRAM, John of Grantham.
    Jacob of Pelham. OC 8 Feb 1808.
    Henry of Grantham. OC 23 Feb 1808.
    Elizabeth, m. Resiah Force of Louth. OC 6 Dec 1808.
    Eleanor, m. Martin Boyer of Grantham. OC 24 April 1810.
    Christeen, m. John Soper of Grantham. OC 27 March 1813; 30 June 1819.
    William of Louth. OC 27 Feb 1818.
    Margaret. OC 18 March 1818.
    Catharine, m. John Smith of Gainsborough. OC 17 Nov 1819.
    John of Niagara. OC 28 Sept 1820. OC 26 Nov 1823.
    George of Townsend. OC 3 April 1822.
    Elizabeth, m. ---- Haven of Erin. OC 3 Sept 1840.
    Hannah, m. Alexander McQueen of Pelham. OC 5 July 1832.

SCHRAM, John of Pelham.
    Jeremiah of Gainsborough. OC 3 Nov 1831.
    Margaret. OC 5 Jan 1832.

SCHRAM, Valentine of Louth.
    Peter of Louth. OC 20 May 1817.
    Mary, m. Albanus Haines of Louth. OC 20 May 1817.
    Catharine. OC 20 May 1817.
    William of Niagara. OC 29 April 1818.
    George Adam of Louth. OC 19 May 1819.

SCHWARDFEGER, John Augustine.
    Dorothy, m. Joseph Tillabough of Williamsburgh. OC 26 Feb 1806.
    John Augustine of Williamsburgh. OC 17 March 1807.

SCOTT, Francis of Augusta.
    Helchey, m. Calvin Whitney of Augusta. OC 27 Aug 1840.

SCOTT, John of Augusta.
    William of Augusta. OC 5 Nov 1799. OC 14 July 1819.
    John of Augusta. OC 6 Dec 1832.
    Margaret, m. Orrin Sherwood of Augusta. OC 3 May 1832.
    David of Augusta. Not. Rec., 11 Dec 1810. m. Henrietta.

SCRATCH, Leonard of Gosfield. Soldier, Butler's Rangers. He died 1830.
    Isabella, m. Wyndel Wigle of Gosfield. OC 30 Jan 1808.
    Susannah, m. John Wigle of Gosfield. OC 30 Jan 1808.
    Catharine, m. George Friend of Gosfield. OC 30 Jan 1808.
    Peter of Gosfield. OC 9 March 1809. OC 15 Nov 1820.
    Henry of Gosfield. OC 3 May 1832.
    John of Gosfield. OC 27 April 1832.

SCRIVER, George of Fredericksburgh, m. Catharine Pickle, 3 March 1789,
    dau of John Pickle Sr. of Fredericksburgh.   [Cont'd]

SCRIVER, George - Cont'd
John of Fredericksburgh, bapt. 24 Feb 1790; m. Elizabeth Loyd, 3 Feb 1810. OC 25 Feb 1812.
George of Fredericksburgh. OC 20 Aug 1817.
Walter C. of Fredericksburgh. OC 16 Feb 1837.
Lavina, b. 24 Feb 1810; m. Simon Ashley of Fredericksburgh 8 March 1831. OC 11 April 1833.
Margaret, b. 26 March 1812; m. Michael Keller of Fredericksburgh 4 Dec 1832. OC 13 June 1833.
Rachel, b. 8 Jan 1808; m. ---- James of Fredericksburgh. OC 19 Aug 1833
Mary, bapt. 29 Jan 1795; m. John B. Snider of Camden East. OC 2 Jan 1833.
Rosanna, bapt. 23 Sept 1791; buried 2 Oct 1791.
Susanna, b. 9 Dec 1800; m. David Boice of Loughborough 11 March 1819. OC 2 July 1829.
Reuben of Fredericksburgh, b. 10 Jan 1806. OC 6 Nov 1829.
Caroline, m. Apollus B. Hill, 24 Sept 1833. OC 6 Nov 1829.
Jacob of Fredericksburgh, b. 10 Oct 1802. OC 1 Aug 1827.
Nancy, bapt. 3 Oct 1798. OC 1 Aug 1827.
Elizabeth, bapt. 26 Sept 1796.

SEAGER, Jacob.
Lydia. OC 23 Feb 1808. Barton.

SEALEY, Joseph of Augusta.
Mary, m. Joseph Faulkiner of Elizabethtown, Oct., 1792. OC 5 Nov 1799.
Kezia, m. Shubel Seelye of Elizabethtown. OC 9 July 1802.
Charlotte, m. Oliver Sweet of Augusta. OC 17 March 1836.

SECORD, Daniel of Grand River.
Daniel of Grand River. OC 19 Aug 1806.
Margaret, m. Robert Ennis of Grand River. Block 2. OC 11 Oct 1810.
John of Grand River. OC 4 Feb 1830.

SECORD, David of Niagara. St. Davids. Born 2 Aug 1759 son of James and Madelaine (Badeau) Secord. m. (1) ---- Millard. m. (2) Catharine Smith, D.U.E. m. (3) Polly Dunn, nee Page. Died 9 Aug 1844.
Sarah of St. Davids. OC 2 March 1811. m. ---- Cummings.
David of Niagara. OC 27 Nov 1815. OC 23 May 1851.
James of Village of Queenston, m. Mary Fralick. 26 March 1817.
Stephen of Niagara. OC 2 June 1819.
Elizabeth. OC 15 Oct 1840, m. ---- Armstrong.
Mary, m. William H. Woodruff of St. Davids 16 Nov 1841. OC 15 Oct 1840
Ryall of Niagara. OC 2 May 1836.
Robert of Niagara. OC 3 April 1834.
Philip of Niagara. OC 23 Sept 1831.
George of York, hatter. OC 6 Aug 1829.
Elijah of Niagara. OC 10 June 1846.   [Cont'd]

SECORD, David - Cont'd
   John of Niagara. OC 16 March 1825.
   Solomon of Chinguacousy. OC 3 May 1826.

SECORD, James of Niagara. Lt., Indian Dept. Died at Niagara, 1784.
   James of Niagara, b. 7 July 1773; m. Laura Ingersoll; d. 22 Feb 1841.
   David of Niagara. OC 3 Aug 1795.
   Solomon of Louth, U. E.

SECORD, John Sr. of Niagara.
   Catharine, m. Elias Smith of Niagara. OC 23 April 1799.
   Sarah, m. Isaac Swayze of Niagara. OC 8 Oct 1796.

SECORD, John Jr. of Niagara.
   Daniel of Niagara. OC 9 March 1803.
   John of Niagara, m. Janet Crooks. OC 23 Feb 1808.
   Mary, m. John Lampman of Grantham. OC 25 Feb 1818.
   Abraham Wartman of Niagara, b. 3 Apr 1795; m. Elizabeth Lampman, 27
      May 1818; d. 4 May 1852. OC 25 Feb 1818.
   Elijah of Ancaster, m. Mary R. Rosseaux. OC 26 March 1811.
   Cortlandt of Niagara, m. Sarah Winterbottom. OC 1815 or 16.

SECORD, John of Burford.
   Asa of Oakland. OC 13 Dec 1826. (?)
   Deborah, m. John Ellis of Burford. OC 27 Nov 1822.
   Mary, m. John Doyle of Burford. OC 2 March 1816.
   James of Burford. OC 26 Jan 1820.

SECORD, Peter Sr. He died at Talbot Road on April, 1818, aged nearly 103.
   Fanny, m. John Braley of Crowland. OC 25 April 1797.
   Margery, m. Daniel Millard of Charlotteville. OC 27 Nov 1804.
   Elizabeth, m. Colin McKenzie of Charlotteville. OC 9 March 1803.
   Lucretia, m. ---- Bailey. OC 12 July 1796.
   Sarah, m. George Snively of Crowland. OC 2 Jan 1834.
   Anna, m. Alexander Logan of Moulton. OC 16 March 1830.
   Lucy, m. Francis Goring of Niagara. Land Board Certif. 3/1 Gainsboro.
   Anna, m(2) Mathew Stanfield.

SECORD, Silas of Charlotteville.
   Moses of Charlotteville. OC 24 Feb 1808.
   Silas of Charlotteville. OC 28 May 1811.
   Jane, m. William Henderson of Woodhouse. OC 14 Jan 1812.
   Lucretia, m. Joseph Andrus of Walsingham. OC 20 May 1817.
   Mary, m. Thomas Neville of Bayham. OC 21 Feb 1821.
   John of Charlotteville. OC 4 Jan 1840.
   Maiden, m. John Beers. OC 13 June 1809.
   Peter of Charlotteville. OC 2 March 1825.

SECORD, Solomon of Louth. Lieut., Butler's Rangers. d. 22 Jan 1799 ae 43.
Clementine, m. George Reid Jr. of Grantham, 23 Aug 1804. OC 17 June
1806.
Ann, m. Elias Smith Jr. of Niagara, 4 Nov 1802. OC 9 March 1811.
James of Louth. OC 9 March 1811.
Magdalena, m. Peter Hare Jr. of Clinton. OC 9 March 1816.
Harriet, bapt. 17 Oct 1792; m. David Cole of Louth. OC 3 May 1820.
Edwin of Grantham. OC 22 May 1820.
William Bowman of Trafalgar. OC 4 Jan 1840.
George of Louth. OC 12 May 1824.

SECORD, Stephen of Niagara, son of James and Madelaine (Badeau) Secord,
b. 20 Aug 1757; m. Ann De Forest dau of Simon De Forest, U.E., in Feb.,
1784; d. 31 March 1808. His wife b. July, 1767, d. 10 October 1841.
Mary, b. 20 Feb 1785; m. Richard Robison of Town of Kingston, 17 Feb
1803; d. 30 Dec 1865. OC 26 Feb 1805.
James of Niagara, b. 19 Apr 1787; d. unmd. 3 Jan 1832. OC 13 June 1809.
David of Richmond, b. 19 July 1790; m. Ann Carscallen; d. 27 July 1846.
OC 2 March 1816.
William Edwin of Niagara, b. 26 March 1797; m. Frances Holden; d. 5
January 1881. OC 30 June 1819.
Elizabeth, b. 7 March 1793; d. unmd. 22 Aug 1814.
Magdalene. OC 28 Feb 1833.
Samuel of Niagara. OC 7 Aug 1829.
Julia Ann, m. William Stull of Esquesing. OC 17 Nov 1830.
Richard of Chinguacousy. OC 3 May 1826.

SEE, Hermanus of Ernestown, m. Rachel Stover.
Blonden, m. Frederick York of Ernestown 23 June 1812. OC 20 May 1817.
Hannah, m. Jacob Stover of Ernestown. OC 27 June 1833.
Joseph of Sheffield, b. 29 March 1812; m. Eliza Davy. OC 4 July 1833.
Catharine, m. John Irish of Sheffield. OC 19 Dec 1833.
Hester, m. William Burley of Ernestown 14 Agu 1816. OC 19 June 1834.
Rachel, m. Robert Richardson of Ernestown. OC 27 Nov 1834.
Martin of Ernestown. OC 5 Feb 1835.
Elizabeth, m. Solomon Barrager of Sheffield. OC 28 Feb 1835.

SEELYE, Augustus.
Ruth, m. ---- Judson of Elizabethtown. OC 29 July 1800.
Margaret, m. (1) ---- Wickwire. OC 13 April 1799. m. (2) Benjamin
Salts of Elizabethtown.
Jane, m. Frederick(?) Elliott of Elizabethtown. OC 20 Oct 1801.
Sarah, m. Hassard Willcox of Loughborough. OC 16 Feb 1811.
Joseph of Elizabethtown. OC 14 Jan 1812.

SEELYE, Justus of Elizabethtown. Drummer, Loyal Rangers.
Orilla, m. John G. Borden of Elizabethtown. OC 24 April 1810.
John of Elizabethtown. OC 22 Oct 1817.   [Cont'd]

SEELYE, Justus - Cont'd
   Guy of Elizabethtown. OC 21 Feb 1821.
   Peter of Augusta. OC 26 June 1822.
   Olive, m. Edmund G. Rawson of Elizabethtown. OC 6 Nov 1834.
   Betsey, m. Enos Beach Jr. OC 24 Oct 1831.
   Charlotte, m. Matthew Bebe of Leeds. OC 31 May 1830.

SELLICK, Dayle of Edwardsburgh, m. Mary Boyd.
   Mary. OC 2 March 1816.
   Sarah, m. William McLaughlin of Edwardsburgh. OC 2 March 1816.
   John of Oxford-on-Rideau, bapt. 11 March 1792; m. Mary Ann Parnell.
      OC 22 Oct 1817.
   Ira, of Edwardsburgh, b. 8 Aug 1797. OC 18 Oct 1820.
   James of Edwardsburgh. OC 30 Aug 1838.
   Rosannah, m. Emery Whitney of Edwardsburgh. OC 5 Sept 1833.
   Joseph of Edwardsburgh. OC 28 Oct 1833.
   Daily of Oxford. OC 28 Feb 1833.
   Thomas of Edwardsburgh. OC 7 Aug 1829.

SENCEBAUGH, Christian of Haldimand Co. Wainfleet.
   Jacob of Haldimand Co. OC 19 Apr 1808.
   Mary. OC 29 Aug 1810.
   Nancy, m. William Parker of Gainsborough. OC 27 Jan 1816.
   Jane, m. Edmund Hodges of Caistor. OC 9 March 1816.
   William of Wainfleet. OC 26 Nov 1823.
   Catharine, m. John McCollum of Lewiston, N.Y. Not. Rec. 3 Oct 1839,
      and 2 Dec 1840.
   Elmira, m. Joel Dills of Gainsborough. OC 15 May 1835.
   Mary Ann. OC 28 March 1835.
   Christian of Wainfleet. OC 28 March 1835.
   Henry of Wainfleet. OC 28 March 1835.
   Susannah, m. Duncan Davidson of Wainfleet. OC 12 May 1824.
   Elizabeth, m. David Merritt of Wainfleet. OC 17 March 1824.
   John of Wainfleet. OC 17 March 1824.

SENN, Joseph of Bertie and Grand River. Sgt., Butler's Rangers.
   Joseph of Grand River. OC 14 April 1824.
   Catharine, m. Frederick Windecker of Grand River. OC 11 May 1825.

SERVIS, John of Osnabruck.
   Elizabeth, m. Josiah Baldwin of Osnabruck. OC 23 June 1821.
   Jacob of Osnabruck. OC 23 June 1821.

SERVIS, Philip.
   Ellen, m. ---- Waldorf of Nepean. OC 1850 or 1851.
   Agnes, m. ---- Green of Bytown. OC 1850 or 1851.
   Hannah, m. ---- Eastman of North Gower. OC 1850 or 1851.
   Jemima, m. ---- Carrigan of Nepean. OC 1850 or 1851.   [Cont'd]

SERVIS, Philip - Cont'd
  Margaret, m. ---- Rupert of Osnabruck. OC 1850 or 1851.

SERVOS, Christopher of Osnabruck.
  Ann, m. Peter Cain. OC 26 Jan 1797.
  Sarah, m. George Brownell of Cornwall. OC 24 March 1829.
  John T. of Osnabruck. OC 17 Feb 1825.

SERVOS, Daniel of Niagara.
  John Dease of Niagara. OC 17 Feb 1807.
  William Street of Niagara. OC 20 Feb 1811.
  Daniel K. of Niagara. OC 6 Aug 1816.
  Catharine. OC 26 Jan 1797.
  Magdalene, m. John Whittemore of Niagara; d. at Niagara 3 May 1854.
    OC 26 Jan 1797.

SERVOS, Jacob of Gainsborough. Lieut.
  Rebecca. OC 4 Feb 1836.
  Mary. OC 4 Feb 1836.
  Catharine, m. ---- North of Gainsborough. OC 19 May 1836.
  William of Gainsborough. OC 7 Aug 1834.
  Elizabeth. OC 17 Aug 1842.
  Caroline. OC 17 Aug 1842.
  Abraham of Gainsborough. OC 28 April 1825.
  Robert of Gainsborough. OC 28 April 1825.
  Clarissa. OC 28 April 1825.
  Jacob of Gainsborough. OC 28 April 1835.

SERVOS, John of Matilda.
  Elizabeth. OC 25 Feb 1812.
  Sarah. OC 1 Aug 1833.
  Nancy, m. John Waring of Williamsburgh. OC 1 Aug 1833.
  Diana, m. Elijah Tuttle of Matilda. OC 1 Nov 1833.

SERVOS (SERVISS), Mary.
  Polly, m. James Seeley of Matilda. OC 8 Feb 1808.
  Katharine, m. Adam Knough of Matilda. OC 23 Feb 1808.
  Philip of Matilda. OC 14 March 1809.
  Lany, m. Henry Fisher of Matilda. OC 7 Aug 1811.

SERVOS (SERVISS), Peter of Osnabruck. Soldier, 2d Batt., R.R.N.Y. OC
  24 March 1807.
  John of Osnabruck. OC 20 March 1807.
  Thomas of Osnabruck. OC 20 March 1807.
  Peter of Osnabruck. OC 20 March 1807.
  Philip of Osnabruck. OC 20 March 1807.
  Lanah, m. John Empey Jr. of Osnabruck. OC 20 March 1807.
  Elizabeth. OC 26 Jan 1808.   [Cont'd]

SERVOS (SERVISS), Peter - Cont'd
  Margaret, m. William Runnions of Osnabruck. OC 7 Aug 1811.

SERVOS, Philip of Matilda.
  John of Haldimand. OC 18 June 1799.
  Jacob of Matilda. OC 22 June 1797.
  Mary, m. ---- Shaver of Matilda. OC 22 June 1797.
  Catharine, m. Adam Canuffe of Matilda. OC 22 June 1797.

SHANNON, David of Beverly, b. in Penna. about 1755.
  Mary, m. Jacob Surerus of Flamborough West. OC 14 June 1811.
  William of Flamborough West. OC 6 Jan 1816.
  Jane, m. William Rogers of Beverly. OC 16 Jan 1816.
  Elizabeth. OC 29 Dec 1837.
  Henry of Beverly. OC 15 May 1835.
  Sarah, m. Benjamin Copeland of Ancaster. OC 28 Oct 1835.
  David of Beverly. OC 27 June 1833.
  Margaret, m. Richard Macdonald of Flamborough West. OC 12 Apr 1832.
  Anna, m. William Kelly of Beverly. OC 1 March 1832.
  Lemuel of Dumfries. OC 10 Dec 1841.

SHARP, Cornelius of Adolphustown.
  Canniff of Madoc. OC 2 Oct 1834.
  Huldah. OC 4 Dec 1834. Madoc.

SHARP, Guysbart of Ernestown.
  Tiney (dau.). OC 5 July 1800.
  Cynthia, m. Samuel Casey of Adolphustown 21 Nov 1808. OC 25 Feb 1809.
  Betsey, m. Titus Simons of Ernestown 5 Feb 1811. OC 25 Feb 1812.
  Catharine, m. John Bell of Ernestown. OC 11 March 1812.
  Allida, m. Ellice Kirby of Ernestown, 20 Jan 1820. OC 4 Jan 1840.
  John G. of Ernestown. OC 8 March 1806.

SHARP, John of Edwardsburgh.
  Peter of Elizabethtown. OC 27 Aug 1840.
  Jane. OC 28 Oct 1835.
  Michael of Edwardsburgh. OC 3 March 1836.
  Philip of Edwardsburgh. OC 3 March 1836.

SHARP, John of Ernestown.
  Hannah, m. Henry Lasher of Ernestown. OC 19 April 1816.
  Allada, m. William Miller of Ernestown 20 Sept 1818. OC 19 Apr 1816.
  Lucas of Ernestown. OC 27 Feb 1818.

SHAVER, Adam of Ernestown.
  Lavinia, m. Milo Haight of Ernestown. OC 16 Feb 1837.

SHAVER, Adam of Matilda.
George A. of Matilda. OC 25 July 1833.
Caroline, m. Richard H. Ellison of Matilda. OC 25 July 1833.
Samuel of Matilda. OC 22 Dec 1832.
Samuel N. of Matilda. OC 10 Dec 1832.
Henry A. of Matilda. OC 6 Dec 1832.

SHAVER, Adam N. of Matilda.
Catharina, m. Philip Empey of Osnabruck. OC 26 Jan 1808.
John A. of Matilda. OC 9 March 1809.
Margaret, m. Nicholas Wert of Osnabruck. OC 17 Oct 1809; 3 Oct 1833.
Diana, m. John A. Bockus of Osnabruck. OC 2 Jan 1834.
Rachel, m. Conrad Weart of Osnabruck. OC 17 Jan 1829.
Levi of Matilda. OC 5 Feb 1829.

SHAVER, Adam P. of Matilda.
Margaret, m. Nicholas Weart of Matilda (?). OC 4 April 1816. [See above]
Margaret. OC 27 April 1816.
Mary. OC 27 April 1816.
Elizabeth, m. Josiah Loverin of Elizabethtown. OC 13 June 1818.
Lavina, m. ---- Ellison of Matilda. OC 28 Feb 1833.
Catharine, m. Luke Bowen of Matilda. OC 8 Nov 1832.

SHAVER, Conrad. All O.C.'s for his family are 1850 or 1851.
Julia, m. Simon Ault of Matilda.
Fanny, m. Frederick Brouse of Matilda.
Eliza. OC 1850 or 1851.
Mary, m. Nicholas Freese of Matilda.
Nancy, m. William Flanders of Matilda.

SHAVER, Frederick of Osnabruck. Died April or May 1818. See OC 28 Feb
1835. OC 26 April 1838.
John F. of Osnabruck. Died about 1862. OC 4 April 1839.
Nicholas of Osnabruck. OC 4 April 1839.
Peter of Osnabruck. OC 4 April 1839.
Hannah, m. Adam Ruport of Osnabruck. OC 4 April 1839.
Mary Elizabeth, m. Jacob Price of Osnabruck. OC 4 April 1839.
Sarah, m. Gottlieb Otto of Osnabruck. OC 4 April 1839.
Eve, m. Barnabas Hollister of Osnabruck. OC 27 June 1839.

SHAVER, Jacob of Matilda.
Elijah J. of Oxford. OC 26 Sept 1839.
William J. of Mountain. OC 7 May 1840.
Nicholas T. of South Gower. OC 7 May 1840.

SHAVER, John N. of Matilda. He d. there 17 Sept 1838, aged 81 years.
Margaret, m. Philip Servos of Matilda. OC 19 April 1816.
Nicholas of Matilda. OC 19 April 1816.   [Cont'd]

SHAVER, John N. - Cont'd
  John of Matilda. OC 15 Dec 1821.
  James of Matilda. OC 15 Dec 1821.
  Mary, m. Henry Manhart of Elizabethtown(?) OC 3 Oct 1833.
  George of Matilda. OC 12 June 1834(?)

SHAVER, John P. of Matilda.
  John J. of Osnabruck. OC 30 June 1819.
  David of Osnabruck. OC 4 Feb 1830.
  Christeen m. Andrew Summers of Osnabruck. OC 17 Feb 1825.
  Edward of Matilda. OC 17 Feb 1816.
  James P. of Osnabruck. OC 28 Sept 1825.

SHAVER, John Sr.
  Hannah, m. Peter W. Jackson of Edwardsburgh. OC 9 July 1802.

SHAVER, John.
  Barbara, m. ---- Carman. OC 18 June 1799.

SHAVER, Philip.
  Margaret, m. ---- Snider. OC 18 June 1799.
  Conrad of Matilda. OC 5 July 1800.

SHAW, Aeneas of York.   m. (1) Ann, dau of Richard Gosline
  of Newton, N.Y. Died 1 Jan 1806. m. (2) Margaret Hickman England dau of
  Capt. Poole H. England, 47th Reg't, 11 Oct 1809. His widow m. Rev. Wm.
  Leeming at Stamford 13 Jan 1823. He died 15 Feb 1815.
    Anne, bapt. 16 June 1799; m. (1) Joseph Scott, R.N., of York, 1 Nov 1816
      OC 9 Jan 1822. m. (2) John S. Baldwin of York, 27 Feb 1822. OC 5 Sep
      1833. OC 28 April 1836.
    Isabella, b. 23 Aug 1787; m. John Powell of Niagara 8 Aug 1808; d. Tor-
      onto, 5 Aug 1850, aged 65.
    Charlotte Stuart, b. 12 May 1802; m. Rev. Ephraim Evans of Stamford,
      27 June 1832; d. 16 Nov 1872. OC 5 June 1833. OC 12 May 1836.
    Mary, b. 14 Aug 1804; m. James J. Ralston of Niagara 16 June 1828;
      OC 12 August 1833.
    Ann, b. 3 July 1794.
    Sophia, b. 31 May 1792, Nashwaak River, N.B. Died unmd. 1 Dec 1870
      at Yorkville, Ont.
    Charles, b. 10 July 1786.
    Aeneas, b. 25 May 1789.
    Richard, b. 16 July 1790.
    George. OC 21 August 1795.

SHAW (SHOFF), Michael of Townsend. Butler's Rangers. Married Freelove
  dau of Jabez Culver. OC 21 July 1796. OC 24 Jan 1797.
    Dennis of Townsend, m. ----Loder. OC 12 Oct 1810.
    Jacob of Townsend, m. Mary Carpenter. OC 26 July 1820.   [Cont'd]

SHAW (SHOFF), Michael - Cont'd
　　Anna, m. Peter Martin of Burford. OC 6 March 1821.
　　Michael of Townsend, m. Elizabeth Baldwin; d. 2 May 1842. OC 23 Dec
　　　　1815.
　　Selinda, m. Job Slaught of Townsend. OC 22 Aug 1821.
　　Vincent of Townsend, m. Elizabeth Martin. OC 28 Nov 1839.
　　Dorothy, m. Adam Book of Ancaster. OC 5 Feb 1831.

SHAW, William of Fredericksburgh, m. Jane.
　　Alexander. OC 2 July 1799.
　　James of Fredericksburgh. OC 6 Dec 1808.
　　Jane, m. Daniel McPherson of Fredericksburgh. OC 25 Feb 1818.
　　Jacob of Fredericksburgh, bapt. 29 Jan 1795. OC 25 Feb 1818.
　　Margaret, bapt. 12 Oct 1790. OC 25 Feb 1818.
　　Nancy, bapt. 1 Jan 1793.
　　Elizabeth, buried 2 May 1783.

SHEEHAN, Walter Butler of Town of Niagara, m. Elizabeth P., dau of Capt.
　Andrews of the "Ontario". He died 16 July 1806, aged 42.
　　Walter Butler of Niagara. OC 12 Nov 1811.
　　Ann Isabell, bapt. 26 Aug 1792. OC 15 March 1815.
　　William James of Grand River, bapt. 1 Jan 1794. OC 9 Dec 1815.
　　Henry Ford of Woodhouse. OC 8 Sept 1819.
　　Eliza, bapt. 26 Aug 1792.
　　James M. of Haldimand Co. OC 4 Feb 1830.
　　George Hill of Haldimand Co. OC 22 June 1825.

SHEETS, George of Cornwall.
　　Mary Ann, m. James T. Green of Belleville. OC 3 Nov 1836.
　　George of Cornwall. OC 27 May 1833.
　　Maria, m. George McEwan of Cornwall. OC 14 Oct 1834.

SHEETS, Jacob of Osnabruck.
　　Abraham of Osnabruck. OC 3 March 1836.
　　David of Osnabruck. OC 2 May 1833.
　　William of Osnabruck. OC 2 May 1833.
　　Magdalen, m. William Cochran of Osnabruck. OC 19 Aug 1833.
　　Margaret, m. John Dafoe of Osnabruck. OC 4 Sept 1834.
　　Catharine, m. John Waldorf of Osnabruck. OC 23 Feb 1830.
　　Sally, m. George Waldroff of Osnabruck. OC 12 Oct 1841.
　　Jacob of Osnabruck. OC 12 Oct 1841.

SHEETS, William of Cornwall, m. Dorothy, dau of Frederick Goos.
　　George of Cornwall. OC 9 Oct 1810.
　　Frederick of Cornwall. OC 16 July 1816.
　　Jacob of Cornwall. OC 30 June 1819. Bapt. 16 May 1790.
　　John of Cornwall. OC 30 June 1819.
　　Mary, m. David Stores of Cornwall. OC 29 Sept 1836.　　　　　　[Cont'd]

SHEETS, William - Cont'd
  Guy of Cornwall. OC 6 April 1837.
  William of Cornwall. OC 29 Sept 1836.
  Joseph of Cornwall. OC 27 April 1837.
  Asa of Cornwall. OC 16 March 1825.

SHELL, John.
  Catharine, m. ---- Markle of Matilda. OC 17 March 1804.
  Mary, m. John Haverly of Williamsburgh. OC 22 Feb 1810.
  Ann, m. George Ross of Cornwall. OC 20 Oct 1832.

SHERMAN, Simeon.
  Margaret, m. Edmund Long of Longueuil. OC 17 March 1807.
  William of Hawkesbury. OC 24 March 1807.
  Jonathan of Hawkesbury. OC 24 March 1807.
  Susannah, m. Joseph P. Cass of Longueuil. OC 17 March 1807.
  Hannah, m. Benjamin Eastman Sr. of Cornwall.

SHERRARD, William of Thurlow. Loyal American Regt.
  James W. of Sidney. OC 17 March 1807.
  Elizabeth, m. John Lake of Thurlow. OC 20 March 1807.
  Eunice, m. William Searls of Sidney. OC 20 March 1811.
  Nathaniel of Thurlow. OC 17 March 1812.
  William of Sidney. OC 14 June 1797.

SHERWOOD, Abel of Wainfleet.
  Levy of Wainfleet. OC 8 Oct 1808.
  Ann. OC 15 Aug 1809.
  Catharine, m. John Smith of Pelham. OC 18 June 1811.
  John of Pelham. OC 24 Feb 1820.
  Phoebe, m. James Smith of Townsend. OC 22 Dec 1842.

SHERWOOD, Justus of Augusta. Capt., Loyal Rangers. Married Sarah
  Bottum, who died at Montreal on 19 Aug 1818. He died at Three Rivers
  in summer of 1798 on his way with his rafts to Quebec.
    Diana, m. Samuel Smades of Augusta. OC 3 July 1799.
    Sarah, bapt. 13 Feb 1789, m. Andrew McCollum of Augusta. OC 27 Feb
      1806.
    Harriet, bapt. 13 Feb 1789; m. Dr. Benjamin Trask of Montreal. OC 16
      February 1811.
    Sophia, m. Jonathan Jones; d. 4 Oct 1813, aged 22.
    Livius Peters. M. P. P.
    Samuel. M. P. P.

SHERWOOD, Reuben of Elizabethtown. Married 2ndly Persis.
  Clarissa, b. 1800; m. George Richard Ferguson of Elizabethtown. OC 25
    June 1823.
  Eliza, b. 1809. OC 2 May 1836.   [Cont'd]

SHERWOOD, Reuben - Cont'd
 Emily, b. 1802; m. ---- Dingman. OC 8 June 1825.
 Minerva Ann, b. 7 April 1818; m. William McDonald of Montreal.
 Edwin Reuben of Bastard, b. 1820. OC 14 June 1851.

SHERWOOD, Thomas of Elizabethtown, m. Annah dau Samuel Brownson Sr.,
 U.E.
 James of Elizabethtown. OC 25 March 1806. From "Montreal Witness"
  Sept 10, 1856: James Sherwood, d. 1856; b. Elizabethtown, Septem-
  ber, 1784. First white child born there.
 Seth of Elizabethtown. d. 1816. OC 30 June 1812.
 Lois, m. Bemslee Buell of Elizabethtown; d. at Gates, N.Y., 19 June
  1849. OC 13 Nov 1797.
 Adiel of Brockville. OC 30 June 1797.
 Reuben of Elizabethtown, U.E.

SHIBLEY, Jacob of Portland and Ernestown.
 Emily, m. ---- Day of Portland. OC 9 March 1837.
 Jane. OC 9 March 1837.
 John of Portland. OC 9 March 1837.

SHIBLEY, John of Ernestown.
 Jane, b. Ernestown, 7 July 1786; m. Conrad Huffman of Ernestown 5 Feb
  1804; d. 10 May 1865. OC 25 Feb 1806.
 Margaret. OC 17 Feb 1807.
 Elizabeth. OC 20 Feb 1809.
 John of Ernestown. OC 16 Feb 1810. See OC 18 July 1834.
 Mary, m. George Rouse of Ernestown 31 July 1810. OC 16 Feb 1811.
 Nancy, m. David Goldsmith of Hallowell. OC 26 March 1817.
 Tiney (son). OC 20 May 1817.
 Cynthia. OC 27 Feb 1818.
 Henry of Ernestown, m. Charlotte Day. OC 27 Feb 1818.
 Hannah, m. John C. Vosburg of Ernestown. OC Nov, 1797; 26 May 1836.
 David of Ernestown. OC 27 June 1833.
 Jacob of Ernestown. OC 20 June 1797. M.P.P.

SHIPMAN, Daniel.
 David. OC 13 Nov 1797.

SHIPPEY, Zebulon of Howard. He died in 1821. See OC 1 July 1830.
 John of Howard. OC 28 Nov 1826.
 Lydia, m. Frederick Lampman of Grimsby 31 Nov 1806. OC 19 Feb 1831.
 Thomas of Raleigh. OC 26 July 1836.
 Zebulon of Chatham. OC 22 Dec 1837.
 Rozanna, m. John Parker of Howard. OC 28 Oct 1835.

SHOEMAN, William.
 Baltus. OC 18 Nov 1797.

SHOREY, David of Ernestown.
    Miles of Fredericksburgh. OC 2 April 1835.
    Rufus of Ernestown. OC 2 Jan 1833.
    Elisha of Ernestown. OC 6 Jan 1827.

SHORTS, Augustus of Fredericksburgh.
    Mary. OC 31 Dec 1840.
    Samuel D. of Richmond. OC 17 Dec 1836.
    Elizabeth, m. Thos G. Hughes of Richmond. OC 28 Oct 1835.
    Andrew P. of Richmond. OC 28 Oct 1835.
    William of Fredericksburgh. OC 4 Feb 1836.
    Philip of Hallowell. OC 4 Feb 1836.
    Hannah. OC 18 Feb 1836.

SHORTS, John.
    Mary, m. Casper Vandusen of Adolphustown. Land Board Certificate,
      23/5 Thurlow.

SHOWERS, Michael. [Butler's Rangers. In 1774 he resided in what is now
    Bradford County, Pa. He died in Wentworth Co., Ont., in 1796]
    Catharine, m. Charles Stewart of Barton. OC 15 May 1805.
    Daniel of Barton. OC 8 Feb 1808.
    Mary, m. William Lottridge of Saltfleet. OC 17 March 1804.
    Sarah, m. David Van Every of Flamborough West. OC 17 Aug 1795.
    Lena, m. Charles Depue of Barton. OC 17 Aug 1795.
    Hannah, b. 30 Sept 1769; m. John Aikman of Ancaster 13 Aug 1787; died
      1863. OC 17 March 1797.
    Ann, m. ---- Smith of Glanford. OC 1 Sept 1797.

SILLS, Conrad of Fredericksburgh, m. Sarah.
    Elizabeth, bapt. 13 Feb 1791; m. George Dafoe of Fredericksburgh, 30
      Sept 1806. OC 5 March 1810.
    Mary, bapt. 6 Sept 1796; m. Joshua Cadman of Fredericksburgh. OC 13
      June 1818.
    Layner, bapt. 30 March 1800; m. Peter Simmon of Fredericksburgh, 22
      September 1815. OC 13 June 1818.
    Rachel, bapt. 14 May 1797; m. Joseph Williams of Ernestown. OC 16
      June 1818.
    Hannah, m. John Dafoe of Fredericksburgh 30 Jan 1810. OC 19 Apr 1820.
    Sarah, bapt. 20 Oct 1805; m. ---- Green of Fredericksburgh. OC 13 June
      1833.
    Conrad of Fredericksburgh, bapt. 24 June 1810. OC 13 June 1833.
    Robert of Fredericksburgh, bapt. 17 July 1803. OC 2 Sept 1830.
    Christeena, bapt. 8 Aug 1807; m. ---- Phillips of Fredericksburgh. OC
      8 Nov 1832.
    Joseph, buried 24 Feb 1794.

SILLS, George of Fredericksburgh.
  George B. of Fredericksburgh. OC 3 Sept 1840.
  Elisha of Fredericksburgh. OC 11 Feb 1836.
  John of Fredericksburgh. OC 4 April 1833.
  John A. of Fredericksburgh. OC 13 June 1833.
  William of Fredericksburgh. OC 19 Dec 1833.
  James of Fredericksburgh. OC 3 Apr 1834.
  Flora Helen, m. Joseph Johnson of Hallowell. OC 28 April 1832.

SILLS, John of Fredericksburgh, m. Isabel Bell, 23 Feb 1794. His widow
married Martin Hough of Fredericksburgh 12 Oct 1801. He was buried 21
November 1800.
  William B. of Fredericksburgh, bapt. 23 Sept 1794. OC 13 June 1833.
  Peter, bapt. 26 June 1796. OC 5 Sept 1833.
  Mary Ann, bapt. 14 Sept 1800; m. Samuel Barnhart of Fredericksburgh,
    28 Sept 1819. OC 5 Sept 1833.
  George of Fredericksburgh, bapt. 19 Aug 1798; m. Elizabeth Rambough,
    1 May 1819. OC 15 Dec 1832.

SILLS, Lawrence of Fredericksburgh, m. Monykey Scouten on 30 Apr 1792.
  Margaret, bapt. 11 June 1793; m. William Huff of Loughborough. OC 4
    August 1836.
  Conrad of Loughborough, bapt. 14 May 1797. OC 18 May 1833.
  Sarah, m. ---- Beckwith of Rawdon. OC 1 May 1834.
  John of Loughborough, bapt. 31 May 1795. OC 30 May 1834.
  Rachel E., m. Samuel Hullett of Loughborough. OC 5 March 1835.
  Mary Ann, m. Peter Denyes of Thurlow. OC 28 March 1835.

SILMESER, Martin.
  Elizabeth, m. ---- Crysler. OC 18 June 1799.

SILMESER, Nicholas of Williamsburgh, Cornwall, m. Margaret Eamer.
  Elizabeth, m. ---- Crawford. OC 10 June 1800.
  Philip of Cornwall. OC 5 Oct 1818. OC 21 Feb 1821.
  Nicholas of Cornwall. OC 5 Oct 1818.
  Henry of Cornwall. OC 16 June 1819.
  Christopher of Cornwall. OC 21 Feb 1821.
  John of Cornwall, bapt. 29 Oct 1797.

SILVERTHORN, Thomas of Stamford.
  John of Stamford. OC 21 March 1809. "the Elder"
  Polly, m. Robert Brooks of Stamford. OC 20 Nov 1809.
  Nancy, m. William Lundy of Stamford. OC 20 Nov 1809.
  Winnifred, m. Jonas Howey of Stamford. OC 16 Aug 1810.
  George of Stamford. OC 27 Jan 1816.

SIMMERMAN, Mathias of Clinton.
  Philip of Clinton. OC 20 Nov 1810.   [Cont'd]

SIMMERMAN, Mathias - Cont'd
   Adam of Clinton. OC 20 Nov 1810.
   Mathias of Clinton. OC 3 April 1819.
   Joseph of Clinton. OC 5 May 1819.
   John of Clinton. OC 8 Aug 1821.
   Margaret. OC 4 April 1833.
   William of Clinton. OC 11 April 1833.
   Charity, m. ---- Triller of Nelson. OC 7 Feb 1833.
   Mary, m. James R. Henry of Clinton. OC 7 Feb 1833.
   Jeremiah of Clinton. OC 7 Feb 1833.

SIMMON, William of Osnabruck.
   Marinda, m. Elijah Lennox of Matilda. OC 19 April 1816.

SIMMONS, Henry. Lt., Loyal Rangers.
   John of Ernestown.
   Catharine, m. Francis Pruyn of Ernestown. OC 8 July 1797.

SIMMONS, Henry of Sidney. Pvt., Loyal Rangers.
   Moses of Ernestown. OC 16 Nov 1807.
   Daniel of Ernestown. OC 5 March 1810.
   Christeen. OC 25 Feb 1812.
   Nicholas of Ernestown. OC 25 Feb 1812.
   Christeen, m. James Hennessy of Ameliasburgh. Land Board Certificate, 33/5 Sidney.
   Anne, m. Timothy Porter of Sidney, 11 March 1788. Land Board Certificate, 85/3 Ameliasburgh.

SIMMONS, John.
   Elizabeth, m. Callahan McCarthy of Ernestown. OC 7 Aug 1810.
   Gregory of Pittsburgh. OC 27 Nov 1834.

SIMMONS, Moses of Ernestown, m. Margaret Allen.
   Margaret, m. Peter Davy of Ernestown. OC 10 Dec 1818.
   Elizabeth, m. John O'Neil of Ernestown. OC 5 Feb 1823.
   Nelson of Westminster. OC 4 July 1833. (Samuel Neilson b. 4 Mar 1812)
   Timothy of Westminster, b. 13 Oct 1801. OC 3 Apr 1834.
   Francis of Ernestown, b. 9 Feb 1806. OC 12 Feb 1831.
   Hannah, m. Richard Patrick of Westminster. OC 4 Sept 1834.
   William H. of Ernestown. OC 12 Feb 1831.
   Catharine, m. Michael Davy of Ernestown. OC 12 Feb 1831.

SIMMONS, Nicholas of Sidney, m. Sarah Hannah
   Margaret, m. Arva Rose of Sidney(?) OC 20 Jan 1816.
   Catharine Hannah, b. 14 July 1810. OC 19 Dec 1833.
   Mary, m. Samuel Ward of Ernestown. OC 19 Dec 1833.
   Margaret, b. 12 Jan 1808; m. George Amey of Loughborough. OC 30 May
     1834.   [Cont'd]

SIMMONS, Nicholas - Cont'd
Henry of Ernestown, b. 29 April 1801. OC 30 May 1834.
Harmonus of Sidney. Land Board Certificate, 3/8 Thurlow.

SIMON, John of Charlottenburgh.
Jane, m. John McDonell of Charlottenburgh. OC 6 Aug 1816.

SIMONS, Caleb of Elizabethtown (Seaman)
Elizabeth, m. ---- Shipman. OC 30 July 1799.
Stephen of West Gwillimbury. OC 2 July 1840.
James of Elizabethtown. OC 27 Aug 1840.
Sarah, m. William Manhart of Elizabethtown. OC 8 Oct 1840.
Smith of Yonge. OC 22 Oct 1840.

SIMONS, Titus of Kingston, York & Flamborough, m. Jerusha Kingsley. She
died February, 1798. He d. at Flamborough, 1824. See Ont. Hist. Soc. v. 23
p. 470.
Jerusha, m. John Detlor of York. OC 8 July 1801.
Mary, m. Simon McNabb of York. OC 7 Sept 1802.
Elizabeth, b. Montreal 20 Aug 1781; m. Dr. Seth Meachem of Thurlow, 12
March 1807; d. Belleville, 22 Aug 1846. OC 23 June 1803.
Sophia Augusta, m. (1) John Carpenter, m. (2) Wm Brown. OC 16 Aug 1804.
John Kingsley of Thurlow, m. Margaret Fraser; d. Flamborough West 27
May 1832. OC 21 March 1809.
Lucinda, m. John Cummings of Flamborough West. OC 27 Nov 1815.
Walter W. of Flamborough West, m. Elizabeth McKay. OC 14 May 1816.
Amelia, m. John Laurason of Beverly. OC 2 April 1816.
Titus Geer of Flamborough West, b. 30 Jan 1765; m. Elizabeth Green; d.
20 August 1829 at Flamborough West. m. (2) Hannah Coon, widow of
Samuel Van Every.

SIMS, Joseph of Bertie.
Elizabeth, m. Boswell Delier of Haldimand Co. OC 17 Dec 1837.
Mark of Haldimand Co. OC 27 Aug 1833.
George of Bertie. OC 8 March 1826.

SINGLETON, George of Thurlow. Capt., KRRNY. He was buried 23 Sept
1789. OC 10 June 1797.
John of Thurlow, m. Margaret Canniff, 3 Feb 1811. OC 16 Feb 1810. Only
heir.

SIPES, Andrew of Matilda, b. 1764; m. Mary Middaugh. [Butler's Rangers.
For a Bible record of their family, see The Ontario Register, 1: 250-252]
Sarah, m. Julius Grant of Niagara. OC 17 March 1808.
Cornelia, m. Samuel Robertson of Matilda. OC 18 March 1818.
Diana, m. David Robertson of Matilda. OC 18 March 1818.
Mary, m. John C. Tillabough of Williamsburgh. OC 18 March 1818.
Jacob of Matilda. OC 18 March 1818.   [Cont'd]

SIPES, Andrew - Cont'd
    Hannah, m. Hugh Rose of Matilda. OC 12 Jan 1837.
    George of Matilda. OC 11 May 1837.
    Eve, m. Samuel Rose. OC 8 Dec 1835.
    Charlotte, m. James Smyth of Matilda. OC 18 Feb 1836.
    Elizabeth, m. William Munro of Winchester. OC 18 Feb 1836.
    Catharine, m. Alexander Rose of Matilda. OC 26 March 1836.
    Peter of Matilda. OC 27 June 1833.
    Andrew of Matilda. OC 7 Feb 1833.

SIPES, Hannah. [She came into Niagara in 1778 being then the widow of Jacob
Sipes. They resided in what is now Bradford Co., Pa. She m. (2) about 1780
Edward Stooks. Two of her sons served in Butler's Rangers]
    Sarah, m. George Windecker of Camden W. OC 22 July 1797.
    Elizabeth, m. [Ralph] Johnson of Bertie. Land Board Certificate, 4/6 &
        6/7, Bertie.
    Eve, m. Peter Wintemute of Bertie. OC 8 Dec 1808.
    Catharine, m. Christian Riselay [of Bertie]. OC 17 March 1797.

SIPES, Jacob of Beverly. [Butler's Rangers. m. Catharine dau of Frederick
Williams, U.E.]
    Juliana, m. James McCartney of Beverly. OC 23 Nov 1816.
    Jacob of Glanford, bapt. 12 Apr 1793; m. Priscilla Young. OC 20 May 1818
    Hannah, m. Aaron Cornell of Waterloo. OC 3 Apr 1819. [In Beverly, 1852]
    Jonas of Beverly. OC 22 May 1820. [b. 11 Oct 1793, d. s. p. 5 May 1825]
    Mary, m. Enoch Cornell of Beverly. OC 13 June 1821.
    Rebecca, m. David Mulholland of Beverly. OC 11 July 1833.
    Andrew of Beverly. OC 26 Dec 1834.
    John of Beverly. OC 19 Jan 1833.
    Catharine, m. Bemsley Davis of Beverly. OC 9 Feb 1828.

SIPES, Jacob.
    Margaret, m. John McCarty of Bertie. OC 23 Feb 1808.

SIPES, Jonas of Bertie and later Markham. [m. Rachel dau of Henry Bush]
    Sarah, m. Francis Smith of Markham 23 Jan 1811. OC 20 May 1817.
    Hannah, m. Frederick Keopke of Markham. OC 22 July 1818.
    James of Crowland. OC 19 Aug 1833. [m. 3 March 1823 at Stamford,
        Pamela Fearo. They res in Blenheim, Oxford Co., 1851/61]

SKINNER, Benjamin of Stamford. See Heir & Devisee Com., July, 1836.
    Salome, m. William Coam of Stamford. OC 6 Feb 1828.
    Sarah, m. Nathaniel Beckon of Pelham. OC 2 Feb 1826.
    Martha. OC 2 Feb 1825.

SKINNER, Haggai of Stamford.
    Huldah, m. Shubal Park of Wainfleet. OC 7 Aug 1810.
    Lydia, m. Stephen Peer of Stamford. OC 16 Apr 1809.   [Cont'd]

SKINNER, Haggai - Cont'd
  Alice. OC 16 April 1809.
  Rachel, m. Frederick Smith of Pelham. OC 14 Jan 1812.
  Haggai of Stamford. OC 20 May 1817. OC 26 Jan 1837.
  Joel of Stamford. OC 20 May 1817.

SKINNER, Timothy of Stamford.
  Patience, m. Henry Baker of Ernestown. OC 20 May 1817.

SLACK, Joseph of Bastard, b. 16 Apr 1760; m. Margaret Phillips (b. 9 July
  1761) in 1782. She was a dau of Philip Phillips and Mary (Jenkins) Saunders
  widow of Ebenezer Saunders. Mary Slack, b. 9 July 1782. Wm Slack, b. 4
  August 1784.
  Mary, m. Benoni Wiltse Jr. of Yonge. OC 30 July 1799.

SLAGHT, James of Niagara.
  Hannah, m. Lawrence Jennings of Pelham. OC 19 Dec 1809.
  Amy, m. Nathan Fields of Harwich. OC 22 Feb 1810.
  Rebecca, m. Barnabas McIntee of Louth. OC 19 Nov 1816.
  Sarah, m. Colin McCollum of Wainfleet. OC 18 March 1818.
  Susannah, m. Jeremiah Tuttle of Bertie. OC 7 Aug 1834.

SLIGHTER, John.
  Mary, m. Lawrence Moore of Pelham. OC 14 June 1811; 21 March 1844.

SLINGERLAND, Anthony.
  Elizabeth, m. (1) Daniel Robison. Heir & Devisee Com. 13 July 1841(?)
    m. (2) John Van Eynen of Niagara.
  Magdalen, m. Joseph Lovett of Grimsby. OC 13 July 1841.
  Clarissa, m. Moses Merritt of Saltfleet. OC 13 July 1841.
  Anthony of Caistor. OC 13 July 1841.
  David of Saltfleet. OC 13 July 1841.
  Mary, m. William Wylie of Gainsborough. OC 13 July 1841.
  Francis (son) of Burford. OC 10 Dec 1841.
  Garrett of Walpole. OC 13 July 1841.
  John of Erin. OC 22 Dec 1842.

SLINGERLAND, Garrett of Niagara.
  Walter James, bapt. 23 July 1818. OC 23 May 1839.
  Henry Rosa of Norwich, bapt. 30 Sept 1813. OC 5 Nov 1835; 14 May 1840.
  Clarissa, m. ---- Bellinger of Niagara. OC 28 Oct 1835.
  Anthony of Niagara, bapt. 25 Sept 1803. OC 20 Oct 1832.
  Maria Bridget, bapt. 28 Sept 1806; m. John Slocum of Niagara. OC 6 Aug
    1829.
  Laura, bapt. 5 April 1801.

SLINGERLAND, Richard of Clinton, m. Elizabeth.
  John of Clinton. OC 22 May 1820.   [Cont'd]

SLINGERLAND, Richard - Cont'd
   Mary, bapt. 24 Apr 1803; m. James Wheeler of Charlotteville. OC 28 June
      1820.
   Peggy, bapt. 15 July 1792.
   Emanuel, bapt. 14 Sept 1800.
   Harman of Grantham. OC 28 April 1825.

SLOOT, Michael of Adolphustown and Albion. He served, from October 1779,
   as a Lieut. in Capt. James Smith's Co. of Refugee Volunteers under Lt. Col
   A. Cuyler. Lived at Mount Sinai, N. Y.
   Jemima, m. Peter Ruttan of Adolphustown 5 Dec 1790. OC 16 Nov 1797.

SMADES, Joel of Hope, formerly of Wolford, m. Helen Barton.
   Elsie, bapt. 27 May 1793. OC 17 Feb 1816.
   Charity, m. Moses Wood of Hope. OC 17 Feb 1816.
   Rachel, m. James Hall of Hallowell. OC 17 Oct 1828.
   William of Huntley. OC 6 Sept 1847.
   Benjamin of Yonge. OC 10 Dec 1832.

SMITH, Comfort of Fredericksburgh.
   Sally, m. John Clapp of Fredericksburgh, bapt. 29 May 1792. OC 23 Feb
      1809.
   Elizabeth, m. David Foot of Fredericksburgh. OC 25 Feb 1809.
   Eleazer N. of Huntingdon. OC 4 Sept 1834.
   Tyrus of Huntingdon. OC 4 Sept 1834.
   Catharine. OC 2 Oct 1834.
   Richard of Hungerford. OC 14 Oct 1834.

SMITH, Dennis of Edwardsburgh, m. Martha Tuttle.
   Mary, m. William Miller of Kingston, bapt. 3 June 1796. OC 23 June 1837
   Russell, b. 12 May 1798.

SMITH, Elias of Hope, m. Catharine. Ten children.
   Catharine, m. James Sculthorpe of Hope. OC 6 June 1799.
   Sarah, m. John Shuter of Hope. OC 25 Oct 1803.
   Mary, m. Robert C. Wilkins of Ameliasburgh. OC 22 Feb 1808.
   John David of Hope. OC 19 April 1808.
   Eliza, m. Joseph B. Walton of Sophiasburgh. OC 16 Feb 1811.
   Elias of Hope, m. Elizabeth Harris; d. at Port Hope 8 May 1825, aet. 50.
      OC 3 July 1797.
   Susannah, m. ---- Potter.
   Peter, b. Halifax, N. S. , 25 Sept 1773; d. Jamaica, W. I. , 1798.
   David of New York City.
   Hetty, m. David Bedford (?)

SMITH, Elias of Niagara, m. Catharine dau of John Secord Sr. , U. E.
   Phoebe, m. George Adams of Niagara, tanner, 7 Dec 1794. OC 25 Ap 1797.
   Mary, m. James Durham of Niagara. OC 7 Apr 1797.   [Cont'd]

SMITH, Elias - Cont'd
Ann, m. George Turney of Niagara 20 Dec 1801. OC 9 July 1802.
Elizabeth, m. Duncan Clow of Niagara 7 Oct 1802. OC 9 March 1803.
Elias of Niagara. OC 19 Aug 1806.
John of Niagara. OC 11 Feb 1807.
William Lewis of Niagara. OC 9 March 1811.
Sarah, m. John B. Clement of Niagara. OC 8 Sept 1819.

SMITH, Frederick. Butler's Rangers. [He and his family were at Niagara in
in 1783. The Ontario Register, v.1, p. 200]
Margaret, m. John Maracle of Louth. OC 17 August 1795.
Leah, m. John Rowe of Stamford, d. 1793.
Mary, m. Robert Campbell of Grantham.

SMITH, George of Elizabethtown.
Wellington of Sidney. OC 19 March 1840.
Ann, m. ---- Harris. OC 19 March 1840.
Rachel, m. ---- Tuttle of Madoc. OC 19 March 1840.
Dr. Martin Luther of Sidney. OC 1 April 1840.
Philip of Sidney. OC 1 April 1840.
Samuel of Sidney. OC 1 April 1840.
Amos of Sidney. OC 3 Sept 1840.
Hiram of Sidney. OC 3 Sept 1840.
James W. of Fredericksburgh. OC 31 Dec 1840.
Robert H. of Fredericksburgh. OC 31 Dec 1840.

SMITH, Hart of Crowland and Windham.
John of Crowland. OC 9 March 1809.
Catharine, m. John Doan of Charlotteville. OC 28 May 1811.
Elizabeth. OC 7 April 1812.
Aaron of Windham. OC 7 April 1812.
Benjamin of Southwold. OC 4 Oct 1826.

SMITH, Henry of Louth, m. Catharine. [Butler's Rangers. He and his wife
were at Niagara in 1783. The Ontario Register, 1:198]
Mary. OC 16 June 1819.
Rachel. OC 16 June 1819.
Daniel of Louth. OC 16 June 1819.
Benjamin of Louth, bapt. 2 Feb 1793. OC 16 June 1819.
George Nelson of Louth. OC 27 June 1833.
Amy. OC 2 July 1829.
Jesse of Louth. OC 2 Dec 1824.

SMITH, Henry of Marysburgh.
Frederica, m. ---- Meyers of Marysburgh. OC 5 July 1798.

SMITH, Jacob Sr. of Glanford. Pvt., New Jersey Vols. Born 9 Sept 1739;
m. Elizabeth Lewis who was born 13 Oct 1741. [Cont'd]

SMITH, Jacob - Cont'd
Ann, m. James McClary of Glanford. OC 30 Sept 1806.
Lewis of Glanford. OC 3 July 1797.
Edmond.
Jacob of Glanford. OC 3 July 1797.
Elizabeth, m. Christopher Beamer of Louth. OC 27 Feb 1806.
David.
Godfrey.
Amos.
Mary, m. Francis Hartwell of Glanford. OC 8 March 1813.
Charlotte, m. Jonathan Wright of Oxford. OC 10 March 1804.
George Frederick of Glanford, m. Elizabeth. OC 6 Aug 1816.
Amelia. OC 28 May 1811.
Christiana.
Martha, m. Bela Hibbard of Glanford. OC 8 March 1813.

SMITH, Jacob Sr. of Fredericksburgh.
Barbara, m. Jacob Fretz of Fredericksburgh. OC 20 Nov 1798.
Nicholas of Fredericksburgh. OC 20 May 1817.
Jacob of Fredericksburgh. OC 4 Nov 1818. OC 1 Aug 1827.
Margaret, m. Mathew German of Fredericksburgh 13 Sept 1813; died at
    Adolphustown 11 Jan 1831 aged 37. OC 7 Feb 1821.
Elizabeth, m. Conrad Johnson of Fredericksburgh 23 March 1817. OC 7
    February 1821.
Catharine, m. Joel Johnson of Hallowell. OC 17 March 1836.
George J. of Fredericksburgh. OC 8 Aug 1833.
Annah, m. ---- Baker of Fredericksburgh. OC 27 Aug 1833.
Rebecca, m. ---- Edgar of Fredericksburgh. OC 27 Aug 1833.

SMITH, James of Charlottenburgh, m. Margaret Grant.
Ann. OC 29 May 1807. Charlottenburgh.
William of Charlottenburgh. OC 20 Nov 1809.
Janet, bapt. 14 Nov 1790; m. Alexander McIntyre of Charlottenburgh.
    OC 7 August 1811.
Elizabeth, bapt. 23 Dec 1793; m. Hugh McPhie of Charlottenburgh. OC 23
    November 1816.
Alexander of Charlottenburgh. OC 23 Nov 1816.
Elizabeth, bapt. 15 March 1795. (Isabel) OC 23 Nov 1816.
John of Charlottenburgh. OC 23 Nov 1816.
Duncan of Charlottenburgh, bapt. 21 April 1797. OC 5 Nov 1818; OC 5 Feb
    1823.
Margaret. OC 10 Jan 1833.
James of Charlottenburgh. OC 3 July 1828.
Catharine, m. Lytle Glasford of Charlottenburgh. OC 1 Sept 1824.

SMITH, James of Pelham and Toronto. A native of Pennsylvania, b. about
    1763. Came to Upper Canada 1794, settled on Lots 18 & 19, Con 9, Pelham
    Name inserted on U. E. List by OC 24 December 1811.   [Cont'd]

SMITH, James - Cont'd
  Phoebe, m. John Chambers of Pelham. OC 2 March 1816.
  Mary, m. Daniel Pettay of Toronto. OC 20 May 1817.
  John of Toronto. OC 20 May 1817.
  James of Pelham. OC 4 April 1821.
  Elizabeth, m. Henry Johnson of Gainsborough. OC 19 March 1823.
  Peter of Toronto. OC 5 May 1831.
  George of Toronto. OC 27 June 1833.
  Ann, m. Isaac Chambers of Stamford. OC 27 June 1833.
  Hannah, m. Miel Dean of Toronto. OC 27 June 1833.

SMITH, John of Augusta, m. Irene Reid, 1789. (Pencilled note on back of
  card: Sarah Spicer, 1792; John bapt. 11 Mar 1792; Mary, ditto; Dennis,
  bapt. 27 May 1793. Iren Reid: Irene, bapt. 11 March 1792; Lilly Isabel,
  bapt. 1 June 1796.)
  Rebecca, bapt. 12 Feb 1789; m. Amos Deming of Augusta. OC 25 March
    1806.
  Mary, m. Aaron Brooks of Augusta. OC 12 Nov 1811.
  John of Augusta. OC 14 Jan 1812. Of Wolford, OC 28 Oct 1835.
  James of Augusta. OC 26 June 1822.
  Benjamin of Augusta. OC 7 Jan 1824.
  Daniel of Elizabethtown. OC 12 Sept 1833. OC 14 April 1836.
  Susannah, m. John Dunn. OC 28 Oct 1833.
  Joseph of Augusta. OC 30 May 1834.

SMITH, John of Fredericksburgh and Augusta.
  Randall of Thurlow. OC 27 Nov 1834.

SMITH, John Sr. of Cornwall.
  Mary, m. Jacob Waggoner Jr. of Cornwall. OC 5 Jan 1798.
  George of Cornwall. OC 25 Feb 1812.
  Catharine, m. James O'Bryan of Waterloo. OC 19 April 1820.

SMITH, John Sr. of Ancaster and the Grand River. Of "the Jersies".
  Anna. OC 6 July 1802.
  Lydia, m. James Macklem of Stamford. OC 6 July 1802.
  Eleanor, m. John Thomas of Grand River, 2 Apr 1791. OC 13 July 1796.
  Hannah. OC 13 July 1796.
  Elizabeth. OC 13 July 1796.
  William Kennedy of Grand River, b. 1764; d. at Brantford, 1848, aged 83.
    OC 17 March 1797.
  John.
  Joseph of Grand River.

SMITH, John of Richmond.
  Caleb of Richmond. OC 24 April 1835.
  John of Richmond. OC 24 April 1835.
  Mathias of Richmond. OC 24 April 1835.   [Cont'd]

SMITH, John of Richmond - Cont'd
    Peter of Richmond. OC 24 April 1835.
    Elizabeth, m. ---- Stafford of Tyendinaga. OC 24 April 1835.
    Margaret, m. Ralph P. Abbott of Tyendinaga. OC 7 Jan 1836.
    Mary, m. ---- MacDonald of Richmond. OC 6 Nov 1834.
    Rebecca, m. Henry Schermerhorn of Richmond. OC 1 April 1840.

SMITH, Michael of Fredericksburgh.
    Barbara, m. Daniel McLean Schouten of Ernestown. OC 17 Feb 1807.
    George of Fredericksburgh. OC 30 June 1812.
    Jacob A. of Fredericksburgh. OC 7 Feb 1821.
    Angus of Pittsburgh. OC 4 Sept 1834.
    Archibald of Pittsburgh. OC 4 Sept 1834.

SMITH, Nicholas of Pelham.
    Robert of Pelham. OC 5 May 1819.
    William of Pelham. OC 22 May 1820.
    Frederick of Thorold. OC 22 May 1820.
    James of Pelham. OC 22 May 1820.
    Magdalen, m. John Bessey of Grantham. OC 17 Oct 1821.
    John of Louth. OC 18 July 1833.
    Parmelia, m. Jacob Hainer of Grantham. OC 19 Dec 1833.
    Catharine Ann. OC 2 Jan 1834.
    Peter of Nissouri. OC 25 Jan 1834.
    Mary, m. William Adams of Louth. OC 19 Jan 1833.
    Lavinia, m. William E. Parnall of Grantham. OC 6 Sept 1832.
    Rachel, m. Elijah Gleason of Pelham. OC 17 Dec 1831.
    Henry of Pelham. OC 2 July 1829.
    Margaret, m. Solomon Bonaparte Rose of Grantham. OC 2 Sept 1830.

SMITH, Peter of Kingston Town, m. Ann. She d. at Toronto 12 Apr 1846 ae 73.
    David John, bapt. 21 Aug 1796; d. 5 Dec 1848. Of Town of Kingston. OC 20
        May 1818.
    Margaret F., bapt. 25 March 1798; m. George B. Willis, Lieut. 6th Batt.
        R. A. OC 20 May 1816.
    Jennet, bapt. 29 June 1800; m. Donald Bethune of Cobourg; d. Toronto, 13
        March 1877, aet. 76. OC 29 April 1835.
    Ann, bapt. 13 April 1802; buried 9 April 1803.
    Ann, bapt. 30 Sept 1804; died 14 May 1825.
    William, bapt. 23 Nov 1806.
    Mary Graham, bapt. 14 Jan 1810; m. Henry Sherwood of City of Toronto;
        d. Ottawa, 15 Aug 1886 aged 77. OC 6 Aug 1840.
    Christian, m. Wm. Longworth Dames of Kingston. OC 18 Feb 1843.

SMITH, Peter Jr. of Charlottenburgh. Soldier, K. R. R. N. Y.
    Ann, m. John McDonell of Charlottenburgh 17 May 1808. OC 23 May 1809.
    Janet. OC 16 Feb 1811. Charlottenburgh.
    John of Charlottenburgh. OC 25 Feb 1818.   [Cont'd]

SMITH, Peter Jr. - Cont'd
Isabella. OC 5 April 1820.

SMITH, Peter Sr. of Charlottenburgh. 84th Regt.
Isabella. OC 28 April 1815.
John of Charlottenburgh. OC 19 Feb 1817.
Mary. OC 19 Feb 1817.
Alexander of Charlottenburgh. OC 4 Feb 1824.

SMITH, Peter of W. Half 37, north side River aux Raisins, Charlottenburgh.
David of Charlottenburgh. OC 14 May 1823.

SMITH, Peter of West half 5/ south side River aux Raisins, Charlottenburgh.
William of Charlottenburgh. OC 19 Feb 1817. Jr.

SMITH, Philip of Fredericksburgh.
Mathias of Fredericksburgh. OC 8 Feb 1808.
Margaret, m. Amos Scott of Fredericksburgh 6 Jan 1812. OC 25 Feb 1812
Catharine, m. William Edgar of Fredericksburgh. OC 4 Nov 1818.
Mary. OC 2 July 1828.

SMITH, Richard of Osnabruck.
James of Osnabruck. OC 18 March 1818.
John of Osnabruck. OC 17 Feb 1825.

SMITH, Richard of Sidney.
Rhoda. OC 2 April 1823.
Hiffabold (dau.), m. ---- Martin of Tyendinaga. OC 6 Aug 1840.
Richard of Sidney. OC 1 June 1837.
Elizabeth. OC 3 March 1836. Thurlow.
Sarah, m. Peter Frederick of Sidney. OC 3 April 1834.
Samuel of Sidney. OC 1 May 1834.
Bethany, m. ---- Simmons of Sidney. OC 1 May 1834.
Nicholas of Clarke. OC 21 Feb 1833.
Mary, m. Uriah Place of Sidney. OC 23 June 1824.

SMITH, Robert of Elizabethtown.
Increase of Elizabethtown. OC 6 March 1809.
James of Tar Island. OC 28 August 1818.

SMITH, Hon. Samuel of Etobicoke, son of James Smith; m. 21 Oct 1799,
Jane Isabella (Mary?) dau of Dr. Joseph Clarke. She was b. 8 Feb 1779,
d. 20 Sept 1826. He d. 20 Oct 1826.
Samuel Bois of City of Toronto, d. July, 1882. OC 1 Dec 1836.
Margaret Leah, m. James McDonnell of City of Toronto, 19 Dec 1835; d.
22 Nov 1892. OC 1 Dec 1836.
Isabella. OC 8 May 1828.
Charlotte Augusta. OC 19 March 1842.   [Cont'd]

SMITH, Hon. Samuel - Cont'd
  Harriet Louisa, m. William Henry Lee, Clerk, Exec. Council, 1 Sept 1842; d. October, 1893. OC 12 Jan 1837.
  Ann, b. 20 July 1801; m. Henry W. Nelles of Grimsby 11 Feb 1829. OC 8 May 1828.
  Mary Ellen, m. Frederick K. Augustus Ball of Grimsby 29 July 1847; OC 19 March 1842.
  Emma Lucretia. OC 8 May 1832. OC 28 Sept 1832.
  Catharine, bapt. 26 April 1807; d. at Hamilton, 24 Dec 1851, unm. OC 8 May 1832. OC 28 Sept 1832.
  James A. of St. Catharines. OC 14 Oct 1842.
  Elvira, bapt. 1818.

SMITH, Samuel of Kingston.
  Amy, m. ---- Lapp of Kingston. OC 16 Nov 1797.
  Annah, m. Eleazer Youmans of Camden E. OC 25 Feb 1812.

SMITH, Thomas.
  Charles Arthur of Sandwich. OC 7 March 1807.

SMYTH, John of Augusta and Elizabethtown.
  Daniel of Augusta. OC 11 Nov 1815.
  John of Elizabethtown. OC 11 Nov 1815.
  Sarah, m. David Everts of Augusta. OC 13 June 1818.
  Elizabeth, m. William Short of Yonge. OC 13 June 1818.
  Irena, m. William Everts of Elizabethtown. OC 14 July 1819.

SMYTH, Patrick of Kingston, d. at William Henry, Lower Canada.
  Charles of Kingston, m. Margaret. OC 18 Aug 1810.
  Mary, m. Peter Grant of Kingston. OC 18 Aug 1810.
  Eliza Montague. OC 18 Aug 1810.
  Catharine, m. Henry Murney of Kingston, 5 Jan 1803; d. 6 Feb 1851 aged 73 years. OC 18 Aug 1810.
  William Bayard of Kingston, d. there 26 July 1843, aged 49 years. OC 16 June 1819.
  Patrick of Town of Kingston, m. Ann Stuart, 16 June 1806.

SMYTH, Thomas of Elizabethtown.
  Rosamond, m. Thomas Sparham Jr. of Town of Kingston. OC 28 Apr 1807
  Lavinia. OC 20 April 1837. Wolford.
  Terence of Wolford (South Crosby). OC 2 June 1831. OC 20 July 1837.
  Mary, m. John Purvis of Yonge. OC 24 April 1835.
  Marilla, m. ---- Easton of Yonge. OC 3 April 1835.
  Rachel. OC 2 Oct 1834.
  Henry George of Elizabethtown. OC 7 April 1831.
  Maria. OC 7 April 1831.
  Cordelia. OC 7 April 1831.

SNETSINGER, Mathias of Cornwall. R. R. N. Y. m. Christiana Astin at Montreal, July, 1785.
Christiana, m. Henry Cane of Cornwall. OC 17 March 1812.
Catharine. OC 17 March 1812.
Mathias of Cornwall. OC 17 March 1812.
George of Cornwall. OC 23 Nov 1816.
Frederick of Cornwall. OC 23 Nov 1816.
Ann, m. ---- Putman of Cornwall. OC 28 March 1833.
Christian of Cornwall. OC 27 May 1833.

SNIDER, Abraham of Ernestown, m. Rachel dau of Jonas Amey, U. E.
John of Ernestown. OC 16 Feb 1811.
Rachel, m. John Abrahams of Ernestown. OC 26 March 1817.
Jonas of Ernestown. OC 16 Dec 1818.
Eve. OC 22 March 1820.
Mary, m. Nicholas Amey of Ernestown. OC 19 Sept 1839.
Martin of Ernestown. OC 30 May 1835.
Hannah, b. 10 March 1810; m. Edward Hagerman of Thurlow. OC 24
    March 1835.
Clarissa. OC 10 Jan 1833.
Rebecca, b. 8 Jan 1813; m. ---- Stover of Ernestown. OC 3 Jan 1833.
Sarah, m. ---- Asselstine of Ernestown. OC 28 April 1832.
Abraham of Ernestown. OC 14 Nov 1831.
Simon of Ernestown. OC 7 April 1824.
Susannah, b. 24 March 1808.

SNIDER, Conrod.
John of Williamsburgh. OC 18 June 1799. OC 9 July 1801(?)

SNIDER, John of Ernestown (Schneider). See OC 9 April 1831. OC 7 July 1831.
m. Elizabeth, dau of Nicholas Amey, U. E.
Isaac of Ernestown (lunatic) OC 22 Feb 1810.
Nicholas of Ernestown, m. Susannah Fryrmouth, 28 Apr 1817. OC 25 Feb
    1812.
Abraham of Ernestown. OC 26 March 1817.
Simon of Ernestown. OC 27 Feb 1818.
Sarah, m. Zebe Babcock of Ernestown, 18 Oct 1818. OC 27 Feb 1818; OC
    4 Sept 1834.
John of Ernestown. OC 5 Feb 1823.
Edward of Ernestown. OC 25 Aug 1838.
George of Ernestown. OC 16 April 1840. OC 21 March 1833.
William of Ernestown. OC 11 Feb 1836.
Peter of Ernestown. OC 11 July 1833.
Susannah, b. 24 March 1808; m. David Hartman of Ernestown. OC 25 Jan
    1834.
Mary, m. Daniel Wood of Loughborough. OC 30 May 1834.
Rebecca, b. 6 August 1810; m. George Hartman of Camden East. OC 5
    February 1835.

SNIDER, John.
  Peter of Augusta. OC 25 Nov 1800.
  Hannah, m. Elijah Carley of Augusta. OC 22 Dec 1797.

SNIDER, Marcus of Ernestown, m. Elizabeth.
  Sarah, m. Samuel Taylor of Thurlow. OC 17 May 1820.
  Susannah, bapt. 8 May 1791; m. John Brown of Malahide. OC 28 Feb 1829.
  Dorcas, m. Joseph Peters of Ernestown. OC 28 Oct 1835.
  Elizabeth, m. Samuel Harris of Ernestown.

SNIDER, Simon of Ernestown. Pvt., Loyal Rangers.
  Philip of Ernestown. OC 31 May 1803.
  Elizabeth, m. Francis Reddin of Ernestown. Land Board Certificate,
    11/7 Camden.

SNIDER, William.
  William. OC 18 June 1799.

SNIDER, Zachariah of Ernestown.
  Jacob of Ernestown, m. Lydia Wright, 2 Feb 1819. OC 13 Nov 1818.
  Jeremiah of Ernestown. OC 5 Nov 1818.
  Jane. OC 26 Nov 1823.
  Mary, m. John Caton of Ernestown 19 April 1814. OC 10 March 1834. OC
    3 November 1836.
  Rachel. OC 21 March 1833.
  Zachariah of Ernestown. OC 27 June 1833.
  Elizabeth, m. James Parrott of Ernestown 23 May 1816. OC 11 July 1833.

SNOOK, Martin of Kingston.
  Catharine, m. John Grass of Kingston 19 March 1799; d. 18 Feb 1846 in
    70th year. OC 16 Feb 1811.
  Tunis of Kingston, m. Catharine Wartman, 31 July 1812. OC 16 Feb 1811.
  Ambrose of Kingston. OC 16 Feb 1811.
  Elizabeth. OC 16 Feb 1811.
  Dorothy, m. Frederick Buck of Kingston. OC 26 March 1817.
  George of Kingston. OC 26 March 1817.
  Cornelia, m. Conrad Staker of Kingston. OC 7 March 1810.

SNYDER, Adam of Cornwall. Soldier, R. R. N. Y.
  Catharine, m. Joseph Southworth of Williamsburgh. OC 26 Feb 1806.
  Hannah. OC 26 Feb 1806. Williamsburgh.
  Margaret. OC 5 March 1810. Williamsburgh.
  Adam of Williamsburgh. OC 12 Dec 1821.
  Lany, m. John Lister of Finch. OC 4 Sept 1834.

SNYDER, Isaac of Ernestown.
  Mary, m. Stephen Montgomery of Ernestown 8 Sept 1816. OC 5 Feb 1823.
  John of Ernestown. OC 5 Feb 1823.   [Cont'd]

SNYDER, Isaac - Cont'd
Elizabeth, m. Ezekiel Burley of Clarke. OC 9 Nov 1837.
Catharine, m. Benjamin Van Luven of Camden East. OC 16 June 1834.
David of Ernestown. OC 18 July 1834.

SNYDER, Jacob of Lancaster.
Dorothy, m. George Cline of Lancaster. OC 10 June 1800.
Catharine, m. Jeremiah Snyder of Lancaster. OC 5 Jan 1798.
Jacob of Lancaster. OC 9 July 1802.
Elizabeth, m. John Curry of Lancaster. OC 13 March 1807.
Mary, m. George Curry of Lancaster. OC 22 Feb 1810.
Susanna, m. John Young of Lancaster. OC 9 March 1802.

SNYDER, Jeremiah of Lancaster, m. Catharine dau of Jacob Snyder of Lan-
caster.
Catharine, m. David Amey of Ernestown 11 Feb 1807. OC 26 Jan 1808.
Mary, m. John See of Lancaster. OC 3 March 1809.
John of Lancaster, bapt. 14 Jan 1790. OC 12 Oct 1810.
Elizabeth, bapt. 28 Aug 1791; m. James Williams of Lancaster, 16 Jan
1810. OC 7 Aug 1811.
David of Lancaster, bapt. 5 Jan 1794. OC 21 June 1819.
Susannah, m. William Fleming of Lancaster. OC 2 Oct 1822.
Simeon of Lancaster, bapt. 16 April 1796. OC 3 Dec 1828.
Maria, m. John Kennedy of Lancaster. OC 12 June 1834.
Eleanor. OC 2 Oct 1834.
Jacob of Lancaster. OC 3 Dec 1828.
Israel of Lancaster. OC 1 Dec 1824.
Jeremiah of Lancaster. OC 2 Dec 1824.
Elizabeth, m. William McKee of Lancaster. OC 7 May 1842.

SNYDER, John of Lancaster.
Leaney, m. ---- See of Lancaster. OC 5 Jan 1798.
Hannah, m. James Young Sr. of Lancaster. OC 14 March 1809.
John of South Gower. OC 17 Oct 1828.

SNYDER, William Jr., m. Anne Bigford.
Elizabeth, m. ---- Ault. OC 1 Dec 1831.
David, bapt. 12 March 1792.

SNYDER, William Sr. of Edwardsburgh, m. Ruth Crandall.
Margaret, m. Joel Adams of Edwardsburgh. OC 16 June 1807.
Solomon of Edwardsburgh. OC 13 Oct 1807.
William (adult ?) bapt. 12 March 1792.
David of Edwardsburgh. OC 3 March 1836.
Betsey, m. ---- Ault. See OC 28 March 1833.
Mary Ann, m. Gideon Adams of Edwardsburgh. OC 27 June 1833.

SOPER, John.
  Sarah, m. Christopher Van Sicklen of Grantham. OC 7 Nov 1797.
  Phoebe, m. William Price, 24 Oct 1793. OC 7 July 1796.

SOPER, Samuel. Soldier, Butler's Rangers. (Heir & Devisee Commission,
  18 July 1825) He died about 1785. His wife Bathsheba m. (2) James Willson
  of Grantham. She died in 1818 or 1819.
  John of Grantham (Clarke). OC 13 July 1796.
  Phoebe, m. William Price of Grantham. OC 21 Oct 1795. OC 1 Sept 1804.

SOULES, Daniel of Vaughan.
  Hannah, m. Barnet Vanderburgh of Vaughan 18 July 1811. OC 9 June 1812.
  David of Vaughan, m. Mrs. Elizabeth Elson, 23 Aug 1810. OC 27 Nov 1815.
  Thomas of Gwillimbury East. OC 16 Jan 1816.
  William of Gwillimbury East, m. Hannah Graham, 22 Jan 1815. OC 16
      January 1816.
  Elizabeth, m. Samuel Lount of Whitchurch. OC 28 July 1819.
  James of Vaughan. OC 28 July 1819.
  John. OC 1 Aug 1833.
  George of Vaughan. OC 7 March 1833.
  Peter of Vaughan. OC 3 Dec 1829.
  Sarah, m. James Williams, 1823. OC 3 Dec 1829.

SPENCER, Andrew of Sophiasburgh.
  Edy, m. David Willcocks of Thurlow. OC 11 June 1823.
  Daniel of Ameliasburgh. OC 9 March 1837.
  Freeman of Sidney. OC 2 Oct 1834.
  Asa of Ameliasburgh. OC 8 Feb 1827.
  Deborah. OC 8 Feb 1827.
  Enos of Sophiasburgh. OC 1 Nov 1826.

SPENCER, Benjamin.
  Lt. Hazelton, U.E., m. Margaret Richards.
  Abel of Vermont.
  Barnabas.
  Augustus of Sophiasburgh, m. Sarah Conger, 1 Nov 1789.
  John of Hamilton, Sheriff. OC 1 Sept 1797. OC 24 March 1819.
  Sarah.
  Dianah, m. Owen Richards of Hallowell 31 Dec 1789. Land Board Certifi-
      cate, 2/3 S.E. side East Lake, Hallowell.

SPENCER, Benjamin of Sophiasburgh. See W. half 18/4 Richmond. Soldier,
  King's Rangers.
  Caroline. OC 4 Sept 1834.
  Mary. OC 4 Sept 1834.
  Sarah. OC 4 Sept 1834.
  Robinson of Madoc. OC 2 Oct 1834.
  Draper of Rawdon. OC 2 Oct 1834.

SPENCER, Hazelton of Fredericksburgh, m. Margaret, dau of Lieut. John
Richards, U. E. OC 29 Aug 1797; OC 18 Nov 1797. He was buried 7 Feb 1813.
Benjamin Conger of Fredericksburgh, bapt. 5 Apr 1789; d. Brighton, 14
Oct 1850, aged 62. OC 16 Feb 1810.
John of Yonge, Surgeon, bapt. 2 Oct 1791. OC 17 Feb 1816.
William Taylor of Fredericksburgh, bapt. 27 Aug 1797. OC 15 Dec 1832.
Hazleton, bapt. 25 April 1802.
Margaret, bapt. 23 March 1800; m. ---- Conger of Hallowell. OC 11 July
1833.
Juliana, bapt. 20 May 1804; m. William Sloan of Fredericksburgh. OC 10
March 1834.
Daniel B. A., bapt. 15 June 1806.
Cecelia, bapt. 29 Sept 1811. OC 10 March 1834.
Augustus of Cramahe. OC 28 Oct 1835.
Richard of Cramahe. OC 2 May 1836.

SPENCER, Henry of Richmond. His mother, Patience Spencer, U. E. See 31
& 32/10 Clarke. OC 25 July 1797. 3191 Com.
Rufus of Richmond. OC 12 March 1849.
Isaac of Richmond. OC 12 March 1849.
James of Richmond. OC 12 March 1849.
William of Fredericksburgh. OC 12 March 1849.

SPENCER, Robert of Stamford.
Abigail, m. John Fralick of Stamford. OC 18 March 1818.

SPICER, Ezekiel.
Elijah of Elizabethtown. OC 7 Dec 1802.
Jabez of Augusta. OC 7 Dec 1802.
Susannah, m. John Bostwick of Augusta. OC 31 May 1803.
Catharine, m. Stephen Todd Beach of Elizabethtown. OC 29 March 1803.

SPORBECK, Jacob of Niagara, m. Margaret Cockell. She m. Alexander
Allen, 6 June 1793.
Jacob of Niagara. OC 28 February 1807.
John of Beverly. OC 28 February 1807.
Elizabeth, m. George Upper of Niagara. OC 15 June 1820.

SPRINGER, David, m. Margaret Oliver. David never came to Canada; he
was killed in the colonies. His widow did come to Canada.
Daniel of Barton. OC 29 July 1797.
Benjamin of Grand River, m. Mary Ryckman. OC 24 May 1794.
Richard of Barton, U. E., m. Sarah Boyce.
Rachel, m. Caleb Reynolds of Barton. OC 24 May 1794.
Henrietta, m. Richard Beasley of Barton. OC 24 May 1794.
Mary (called Lucy). OC 24 May 1794.
Keziah, b. Oct., 1776; m. Benjamin Lockwood of Glanford; d. 28 March
1860. OC 14 June 1798. [Cont'd]

SPRINGER, David - Cont'd
Martha, m. John Treanor of Barton. OC 24 May 1794.

SPRINGER, Richard of Barton.
Margaret, m. Nathaniel Crowell of Barton; d. 24 Feb 1876.
Hannah, m. James Ferris of Niagara. OC 26 March 1817.
Sarah, m. Day Knight of Barton. OC 13 Dec 1820.
Elizabeth, m. John Depew of Barton. OC 2 May 1821.
Mary, bapt. 21 Sept 1792; m. Alexander Aikman of Ancaster. OC 2 May
1821.
David R. of Barton, d. at Burlington 26 Aug 1888 ae 76. OC 2 May 1821.
Lucinda, m. David Everitt of Flamborough West. OC 25 Jan 1834.
Richard of Glanford. OC 25 Jan 1834.
Oliver T. of Barton. OC 6 Nov 1834.

SPRINGSTEEN, Daniel of Gainsborough.
Rebecca, m. ---- Horton of Gainsborough. OC 2 Feb 1832.

SPRINGSTEEN, Gasper of Gainsborough.
Nancy, m. William Furlow of Gainsborough. OC 10 Jan 1821.
Elizabeth, m. John Creighton. OC 10 Jan 1821.
John of Gainsborough. OC 10 Jan 1821.
Mary, m. David Gee of Niagara. OC 7 Feb 1821.
Allan of Gainsborough. OC 4 Sept 1822.
Jane, m. William Gee of Gainsborough. OC 10 April 1834.
Robert of Gainsborough. OC 10 April 1834.
Gilbert of Gainsborough. OC 14 Oct 1834.
Joseph of Gainsborough. OC 28 Feb 1835.

SPRINGSTEEN, Staats of Stamford. Soldier, Butler's Rangers.

SPURGIN, William of Charlotteville.
Samuel of Charlotteville. OC 26 March 1817.
Sally, m. Joseph Anderson of Charlotteville. OC 6 Feb 1828.

STAATS, Sylvester. [Sgt., Butler's Rangers. He and his wife Frany were at
Niagara in 1783. The Ontario Register, 1: 198]
William of Niagara [born 1783]. OC 16 June 1808.

STACEY, John.
Elizabeth, m. Thomas Smith of Charlotteville. OC 5 Jan 1802.

STALKER, Elizabeth of Kingston, widow of Nathan. See OC 16 June 1807.
Margaret, m. George Harper of Kingston. OC 17 Nov 1797.
Conrad of Kingston, m. Cornelia Snook. OC 13 Nov 1797.
Henry of Kingston, m. Sarah Emons. OC 13 Nov 1797.

STARR, George of Hawkesbury.
Hiram of Hawkesbury. OC 29 March 1808.

STATA, Henry of Williamsburgh.
Elizabeth, m. Jacob Markley of Williamsburgh. OC 25 Feb 1806.
Roxanna. OC 13 March 1807.
Henry of Williamsburgh. OC 7 Aug 1811.
Nancy, m. John Shaver of Williamsburgh. OC 19 April 1816.
Philip of Williamsburgh. OC 19 April 1816.
Bastion of Williamsburgh. OC 28 Feb 1798.
Mary, m. Philip Barkley of Williamsburgh. OC 28 Feb 1798.

STATA, Martin of Matilda.
Jacob of Thurlow. OC 4 Sept 1834.

STATA, Philip of Osnabruck.
Elizabeth, m. Hugh McCracken of Osnabruck; d. 1869. OC 19 Apr 1816.
Catharine, m. George Smith of Cornwall. OC 19 April 1816.
Andrew of Osnabruck. OC 18 March 1818.
Rebecca, m. Adam Campbell of Osnabruck. OC 8 Feb 1827.

STEEL, Mathew of Sophiasburgh, m. Elizabeth dau of Matthew Benson, U. E.
Mary, m. John Rattan of Adolphustown. OC 14 March 1809.
Jane, m. Stephen Bourdett of Sophiasburgh. OC 3 March 1809.
Margaret, m. Jacob Hoover of Adolphustown. OC 16 Feb 1811.
Abraham of Sophiasburgh. OC 1 May 1822.
Elizabeth, m. David Bourdett of Sophiasburgh. OC 29 May 1822.
John of Hallowell. OC 7 May 1828.
Rachel. OC 19 July 1826.

STEEL, William of Humberstone, b. about 1744 in Ireland, weaver by trade.
Ann, m. Daniel Bearss of Humberstone. OC 20 May 1817.
David of Humberstone. OC 20 May 1817.
Solomon of Humberstone. OC 14 Nov 1818.
Jonathan of Humberstone. OC 13 April 1819.
Mary, m. Joseph Rice of Stamford. OC 16 June 1819.
Samuel of Humberstone. OC 17 Sept 1823.
William of Humberstone. OC 7 July 1831.

STEPHENSON, Francis of Louth. Capt., Queen's Rangers. m. Eleanor; d.
April, 1807.
Simcoe of Louth, m. Catharine Hainer, 19 May 1808. OC 6 Dec 1798.
Louisa. OC 6 Dec 1798.
Eleanor, m. Solomon Moore of Louth. OC 6 Dec 1798.
Harriet, m. David Hainer of Grantham. OC 6 Dec 1798.
Sarah, m. William D. Powell Jr. of Louth 25 July 1801; d. 1834, aet 54.
OC 6 Dec 1798.
Francis Hay of Louth. OC 6 Dec 1798.   [Cont'd]

STEPHENSON, Francis - Cont'd
David Townsend of Louth. OC 6 Dec 1798.
George Beckwith.
John Augustus of Etobicoke, b. 10 Oct 1783; m. Mary Coon; d. 7 Feb 1853.
    OC 6 Dec 1798.

STEVENS, Aaron of Niagara.
Adam of Niagara. OC 25 Feb 1812.
John of Trafalgar, m. Catharine; d. 1814. OC 9 June 1812.
Nicholas of Niagara. OC 9 Dec 1815.
Joseph of Niagara, bapt. 25 Aug 1799. OC 16 June 1819.
William of Niagara. OC 9 Feb 1820.
Margaret. OC 15 June 1820.
Catharine. OC 15 June 1820.
Samuel Thompson of Niagara, bapt. 19 April 1801. OC 2 Oct 1822.
Mary Ann, m. Walter Butler of Niagara. OC 1 May 1834.
Alexander of Clinton, bapt. 22 May 1811. OC 1 May 1834.
Daniel of Niagara. OC 25 Jan 1831.

STEVENS, Abel Sr. of Bastard.
Eunice, m. Carey Haskins of South Crosby. OC 22 June 1793.
David B. of Bastard. See OC 7 March 1829.
Elihu of Bastard. OC 22 June 1793.
Sarah. OC 22 June 1793.
Marian. OC 22 June 1793.

STEVENS, John of Stamford.
Mary, m. Jacob Cochenour of Flamborough West. OC 23 Nov 1816.
Elizabeth, b. 1764; m. (1) Frederick Dochstader. m(2) William Van Every
    of Niagara. d. 1857. OC August, 1796.

STEVENS, Roger of Marlborough. Ensign.
Sarah. OC 23 June 1801.
Christopher Babity of Marlborough. OC 25 Feb 1812.
Guy Carleton of Augusta. Not. Rec. 4 July 1836. OC 28 Oct 1835.
Mary, m. Solomon Story of Elizabethtown. OC 13 Nov 1797.
Moses of Bastard. OC 14 Feb 1798.
Martha, m. ---- Burritt. Land Board Certificate, 12/1 Gloucester.

STEVENS, James of Hope.
Nancy, m. Charles Goheen of Hamilton. OC 26 March 1817.
Simeon of Hope. OC 26 March 1817.
Hannah, m. Samuel Marvin of Hope. OC 20 May 1817.
Jemima, m. John Vorse of Hope. OC 20 May 1817.
David of Hope. OC 17 Aug 1820.
John of Hope. OC 29 May 1822.
Anne, m. Joseph Demorest of Darlington. OC 25 June 1823.
Hiram B. of Hamilton. OC 1 Aug 1833.

STEWART, Alexander of Niagara, m. Jemima Johnson, dau of Lt. Brant
Johnson, U. E. , 7 Dec 1796. Buried 3 Feb 1813.
   Alexander of Town of York, bapt. 17 Dec 1797; m. Mary Anderson, 20 July
      1821. OC 14 Oct 1818.
   Elizabeth Clench. OC 20 Feb 1840.
   Mary, bapt. 14 Dec 1803; m. John Claus of Town of Niagara, 4 Jan 1825.
      OC 3 Nov 1836.
   Brant Johnson, bapt. 28 Apr 1811; OC 14 Feb 1832.
   William, bapt. 27 Oct 1799.
   Margaret, bapt. 8 March 1801. OC 28 Feb 1829.

STEWART, George of Barton.
   George of Barton. OC 24 Nov 1801.
   Charles of Barton, m. Catharine Showers. OC 15 May 1805.
   Mary, m. Richard Cockrell of Ancaster. OC 27 June 1806.
   John of Barton. OC 16 April 1811.
   Susannah. OC 16 April 1811.
   Rachel, m. William Weed Waterbury of Saltfleet. OC 13 Feb 1816; OC 2
      May 1833.
   David of Nelson. OC 18 March 1818.
   James of Barton. OC 29 April 1819.
   William of Barton. OC 18 May 1819.
   Elizabeth. OC 6 July 1825.

STEWART, James of Gosfield and Niagara.
   Charles of Gosfield. OC 17 Feb 1816.
   Susannah, m. John Johnson of Rainham. OC 15 March 1838.

STEWART, Thomas.
   Ann, m. Cornelius Duggan of Burford. OC 4 April 1797.

STILES, Selah of Norwich, m. Amy. OC 8 July 1797.
   Selah of Norwich. OC 21 July 1831.
   Peter of Norwich. OC 18 July 1833.
   Levina, m. Simeon Post of Norwich. OC 7 April 1824.

STINE, John. Sgt., N. J. Vols.
   Catharine, m. ---- Lemon of Woodhouse. OC 12 July 1796.

STOCKWELL, John of Colchester.
   James of Colchester, b. 1783 in Michigan; d. at Mersea, 13 Oct 1852. OC
      28 April 1807.
   Elizabeth, m. John Brown of Town of Sandwich. OC 16 Nov 1807.
   Sarah, m. Joseph Mireau of Dover. OC 17 May 1820.
   Anne, m. Isaac Dolson of Dover. OC 21 May 1840.
   Lucinda, m. Joel Doty of Colchester. OC 22 Oct 1840.
   John of Malden. OC 8 Sept 1836.
   Mary, m. ---- Little of Colchester. OC 4 Feb 1836.   [Cont'd]

STOCKWELL, John - Cont'd
  Alexander of Colchester. OC 4 April 1833.
  Charles of Colchester. OC 1 Aug 1833.
  Hannah, m. David Clarke of Colchester. OC 4 Feb 1830.

STONE, Joel of Leeds, m. (1) Leah Moore, 23 March 1780 at New York; m(2)
  Abigail, widow of ---- Dayton. Died at Gananoque on 20 Nov 1833.
  William M. of Leeds. OC 27 Jan 1807.
  Mary, m. Charles McDonald of Leeds, 5 March 1811.

STONE, John of Charlotteville.
  Melvin of Charlotteville. OC 22 July 1824.
  Theodosia, m. James Dease. OC 3 Oct 1839.
  Helen, m. Samuel Greenlee of Dereham. OC 30 March 1837.
  Elizabeth. OC 30 May 1835.
  Rebecca. OC 30 May 1835.
  William of Charlotteville. OC 25 Jan 1834.
  Joseph of Charlotteville. OC 12 June 1834.
  Joan, m. Joseph Parke of Woodhouse. OC 8 Dec 1832.
  Mary Anne, m. Abijah Tucker of Charlotteville. OC 5 May 1831.

STONEBURNER, Jacob of Cornwall.
  Ann. OC 16 June 1808. Cornwall.
  Leonard of Cornwall, m. Elizabeth Cadman. OC 26 Sept 1809.
  Mary, m. Philip Helmer of Cornwall. OC 20 Nov 1809.
  John of Cornwall. OC 26 March 1817.
  Jacob of Cornwall. OC 20 May 1817.

STONER, John of Scarborough. [Butler's Rangers. He and his family were at
  Niagara in 1783. The Ontario Register, 1: 198]
  Henry of Scarborough. OC 21 June 1808.
  Elizabeth, m. John Dubey of Scarborough. OC 16 Jan 1816.
  Margaret, m. John Kilner of Scarborough 25 May 1815. OC 16 Jan 1816.
  Hannah, m. John Ellis of Scarborough 30 Dec 1816. OC 16 Jan 1816.
  Peter of Scarborough, m. Polly Secor, 29 July 1816. OC 27 Jan 1816.
  Mary, m. Charles Terwilliger of Whitby. OC 23 Nov 1816.
  John of Scarborough. OC 18 Feb 1836.
  Abraham of Scarborough. OC 18 Nov 1830.

STONER, Peter of Pickering and Niagara. Soldier, Butler's Rangers.
  Hannah, m. Thomas Conat of Darlington. OC 27 June 1808.
  Abraham of Pickering. OC 4 May 1816.
  Elizabeth, m. James McIntee of Louth. OC 3 June 1817.
  Anna Maria, m. Joseph Merrill of Pickering. OC 13 March 1819.

STOOKS, Edward of Matilda and Vaughan. Pvt., K. R. R. N. Y. His wife was
  formerly Mrs. Hannah Sipes [q.v.] Matilda 7/6; 23 & S. half 3/5.
  Richard of Vaughan. OC 29 July 1806.   [Cont'd]

STOOKS, Edward - Cont'd
   John C. OC 26 June 1797.

STORING, George of Fredericksburgh (Williamsburgh), m. Hannah, dau. of
Henry Timberlake.
   Dorothy, m. Samuel Arnold of York. OC 20 June 1806.
   John of Sidney. OC 10 Aug 1837.
   Jacob of Fredericksburgh. OC 4 Feb 1836.
   George of Richmond, b. Sept., 1800. OC 28 Feb 1835. OC 4 Feb 1836.
   Catharine, m. James Garrison of Thurlow. OC 3 March 1836.
   Lawrence of Fredericksburgh. OC 24 March 1835.
   Henry, b. 17 Dec 1804.

STORING, John of Matilda.
   Catharine, m. Adam Johnston of Cornwall. OC 4 July 1833.

STORMS, Gilbert.
   Sarah, m. Jacob Stover of Ernestown. OC 25 Feb 1806.
   Gilbert of Ernestown. OC 16 Nov 1807.
   David of Ernestown. OC 5 March 1810.
   Henry of Ernestown. Land Board Certificate, 25/5 Ernestown.

STORMS, Jeremiah of Marysburgh, m. Mary dau of Elisha Crane of Marys-
burgh. See OC 30 Aug 1797. Jeremiah Storms and Mrs. Mary Lloyd were
married 19 February 1792.
   Henry of Niagara. OC 18 Oct 1838.
   Elisha of Marysburgh. OC 18 Oct 1838.
   Gilbert of Marysburgh. OC 1 Nov 1838.
   Jemima, m. James Harrison of Marysburgh. OC 1 Nov 1838.
   Rachel, m. John Turner of Marysburgh. OC 1 Nov 1838.
   William of Camden East. OC 15 Aug 1839.
   Eleanor, m. David Snider of Camden East. OC 15 Aug 1839.
   Jeremiah of Ernestown. OC 20 Feb 1840.

STOVER, Martin of Ernestown.
   Elizabeth, m. John Laughlin of Ernestown. OC 25 Feb 1806.
   Martin of Ernestown, m. Hannah Laughlin. OC 29 Jan 1808.
   John of Ernestown. Land Board Certificate, 18/7 Ernestown.
   Rachel, m. Herman See of Ernestown. OC 17 Nov 1797.

STRADER (STRADA), Henry. See Heir & Devisee Com. 244 - 1840.
   Elizabeth, m. Andrew Beard (Baird) of Williamsburgh (Elizabethtown,
      1840) OC 31 May 1803.
   Susannah, m. Isaac Putney of Matilda. OC 31 May 1803.
   Nancy, m. Obadiah Putney of Matilda (Town of Lisbon, N.Y., 1840) OC
      25 February 1806.
   Mathalane, m. John Van Camp.
   Mary, m. David Soper of Matilda. OC 6 Sept 1832.

STRADER, John of Matilda.
   Jacob of Matilda. OC 25 Feb 1809.
   Hannah, m. Andrew Barriger of Matilda, Sr. OC 17 Feb 1816.
   Mary, m. John Barriger of Matilda, Sr. OC 17 Feb 1816.
   Elizabeth, m. Peter CrowBergher of Matilda. OC 2 March 1816.
   Henry of Matilda. OC 20 May 1817.
   John of Matilda, b. 15 June 1787; d. June, 1888. OC 20 May 1817.
   Dorothy, m. Duncan McArthur of Matilda. OC 11 April 1833.
   Catharine, m. Jacob Barkley of Matilda. OC 6 Dec 1832.
   William of Matilda. OC 1 July 1830.
   Sophia, m. William Shaver of Matilda. OC 5 March 1828.

STRADER, Simon.
   Sophia, m. William Clow of Elizabethtown; d. 25 Nov 1851 in 86th yr. OC
      8 November 1797.

STREET, Samuel
   Mary, m. ---- Usher; d. 26 Feb 1828. OC 21 July 1796.

STREET, Samuel of Augusta and Wolford, m. Phoebe VanCamp.
   John of Wolford, bapt. 11 March 1792. OC 20 Feb 1810.
   Mary. OC 20 Feb 1810.
   Elizabeth, m. William Holladay of Wolford. OC 16 Feb 1811.
   Timothy of Augusta, bapt. 11 March 1792. OC 2 March 1816.
   Peter of Wolford. OC 18 March 1818.

STRICKER, Sampson of Hallowell, m. Ursula, dau of Joseph and Mercy
   (Carpenter) Clapp.
   Mercy. OC 13 June 1805.
   Sarah, m. Stephen Palen of Hallowell. OC 21 Oct 1806.
   Sarah, m. John Link of Fredericksburgh. OC 25 Feb 1818; 18 July 1834.
   Joseph of Hallowell. OC 12 Dec 1821.
   Ruth, m. Joseph Palmer of Ameliasburgh. OC 6 March 1822.
   Rhoda, m. ---- Clapp of Marysburgh. OC 1 May 1834.
   Jarvis C. of Hallowell. OC 19 July 1826.
   James of Hallowell. OC 19 July 1826.
   John C. of Hallowell. OC 19 July 1826.

STUART, George of Osnabruck. Indian Dept. Md. Barbara Ferguson. OC
   17 January 1829.
   Electa. OC 27 Feb 1834.
   Susan, m. Henry Hodgin of Osnabruck. OC 3 April 1834.
   William of Osnabruck. OC 3 April 1834.
   Gilbert of Osnabruck, b. 3 Dec 1803. OC 3 April 1834.
   John of Osnabruck. OC 3 April 1834.
   James of Osnabruck. OC 3 April 1834.
   Christy, m. Samuel Moss of Osnabruck. OC 3 April 1834.
   Barbara, bapt. 25 May 1794.

STUART, Rev. John of Town of Kingston.
  Charles of Kingston, b. 31 March 1782; m. Mary Ross, 18 May 1805;
    buried 26 Dec 1816. OC 2 June 1798.
  James of City of Quebec, m. Elizabeth Roberts, 14 March 1818. OC 2
    June 1798.
  Mary, m. Charles Jones of Elizabethtown 8 June 1807; d. 25 Oct 1812.
    OC 2 June 1798.
  Ann, bapt. 25 June 1790; m. Patrick Smyth of Town of Kingston, 16 June
    1806. OC 2 June 1798.
  Jane, bapt. 28 Oct 1784; d. unmd. 15 March 1815. OC 2 June 1798.
  John of Kingston, b. 23 Aug 1777. OC 2 June 1798.
  George O'Kill of Kingston, b. 29 June 1776; m. Ann Ellice Robison, 24
    September 1816. d. 5 Oct 1862. OC 10 Nov 1797.
  Andrew of Kingston (Quebec); d. Feb., 1840. OC 2 June 1798.

STULL, Latham of Grantham and Esquesing, m. Ann Catharine Hatt. From
  "Canadian News" Nov 11, 1857: Died on 10th Oct 1857 at Esquesing, Mrs.
  Ann Catharine Hatt Stull, widow of the late Latham Stull, aged 89 yrs.
  Jacob of Grantham, m. Margaret Young. OC 20 Aug 1811.
  William of Grantham, m. Julia Ann Secord, 31 Jan 1830. OC 20 Aug 1811.
  Adam of Grantham, b. 6 June 1793; m. Mary M. Lampman; d. 9 Aug 1859.
    OC 14 December 1816.
  Hannah, m. Samuel Kennedy. OC 14 December 1816.
  George of Grantham, m. Jane Chrysler. OC 2 June 1819.
  John of Grantham, m. Maria Traver, 23 Dec 1824. OC 4 March 1824.

SUMMERS, Andrew of Charlottenburgh.
  Elizabeth, m. John Cameron of Charlottenburgh, 23 Dec 1800. OC 16 Dec
    1800.
  Christian, m. Christopher Empey of Cornwall. OC 5 Jan 1798.
  Andrew of Charlottenburgh. OC 19 Dec 1806.
  Catharine, m. Benjamin Doyle of Blenheim. OC 4 Apr 1797; 20 Aug 1808.

SUMMERS, Jacob of W. half 11/1 Charlottenburgh, m. Anne Cameron.
  Catharine, bapt. 20 Apr 1790; m. John Clark of Charlottenburgh, 4 Oct
    1808. OC 31 Oct 1809.
  John of Charlottenburgh, bapt. 25 Dec 1791. OC 28 April 1815.
  Andrew of Charlottenburgh, bapt. 28 Feb 1794. OC 23 Nov 1816.
  Elizabeth, bapt. 16 Nov 1795; m. James Cameron of Charlottenburgh. OC
    26 March 1817.
  James of Charlottenburgh. OC 21 June 1819.
  Nancy, m. Thomas Ross of Lancaster. OC 28 Sept 1820.
  Alexander of Charlottenburgh. OC 23 July 1823.
  Margaret, m. Alexander Fraser of Charlottenburgh. OC 10 March 1834.
  Daniel of Charlottenburgh. OC 6 Dec 1832.
  David of Charlottenburgh. OC 6 Sept 1832.
  Christeen, m. Laughlin McLauchlin of Charlottenburgh. OC 1 Nov 1826.

SUTHERLAND, George of Lancaster.
  Donald of Lancaster. OC 14 May 1823.
  Mary. OC 14 May 1823.
  Roderick of Charlottenburgh. OC 25 Feb 1836.
  John of Lancaster. OC 19 Dec 1833.
  Isabella, m. Thomas Munro of Charlottenburgh. OC 4 Sept 1834.

SUTHERLAND, Walter of Lancaster, Lt. KRRNY, m. Anne Campbell.
  Maria Ann, m. Hector McKay of Lancaster 4 Aug 1801. OC 17 Nov 1801.
  John Johnson of Lancaster, bapt. 2 Oct 1785, m. Catharine McPherson,
      26 Jan 1809; d. 16 March 1817.
  Barbara, bapt. 21 Feb 1791; m. Walter Alexander Gunn of Lancaster 5
      April 1808.
  Isabella, bapt. 8 Jan 1792, m. John Gunn of Amherstburgh. OC 2 June
      1808. See OC 11 Feb 1806.
  Anne, bapt. 12 May 1793.
  Catharine, bapt. 6 Sept 1795.

SWARTS, Henry of Thorold and Blenheim.
  George of Thorold. OC 25 Aug 1819.
  Anna, m. John Vrooman of Thorold. OC 8 Sept 1819.
  Philip of Thorold. OC 22 May 1820.
  William of Blenheim. OC 28 Sept 1820.
  Mary Catharine. OC 11 Oct 1838.
  Peter of Westminster. OC 3 April 1834.
  James of Blenheim. OC 6 Dec 1832.
  Maria. OC 24 Dec 1831. Blenheim.
  John of Thorold. OC 5 Dec 1827.

SWAYZE, Caleb.
  Susanna, m. Anthony Sharp of Ancaster. OC 20 Aug 1811.
  Lydia, m. David Horton of Pelham, Sr. OC 20 May 1817.

SWAYZE, Isaac of Niagara, m. (1) Sarah Secord, dau of John Sr., U. E. She
  was buried 18 Dec 1804. m. (2) Mrs. Lena (Eleanor) Ferris 18 Sept 1806.
  Benjamin of Niagara. OC 15 May 1805.
  Catharine, b. 13 March 1793; m. Gilbert McMicking of Stamford. OC 16
      April 1811.
  Mary, m. James Willson of Niagara. OC 16 June 1819.
  Ellen, bapt. 26 Jan 1817; m. John Scott of Niagara 15 Jan 1828. OC 4 Dec
      1834.
  William Dixon of Niagara, bapt. 26 Jan 1817; m. MaryDurham, 3 March
      1830. OC 4 Dec 1834.
  Maria, bapt. 26 Jan 1817. OC 4 Dec 1834.
  Francis Gore of Niagara, bapt. 17 March 1807; m. Frances Cowell, 4 Feb
      1829. OC 8 May 1828.

SWEET, Oliver of Augusta, m. Charlotte dau of Joseph Sealey, U. E.
   Mercy, m. Nathaniel Mann of Brockville. OC 17 March 1836.
   Lucinda, m. Benjamin Robinson of Brockville. OC 17 March 1836.
   Darius T. of Elizabethtown. OC 17 March 1836.
   Timothy of Elizabethtown. OC 17 March 1836.
   Mary, m. Arunah St. John of Elizabethtown. OC 17 March 1836.

SWITZER, Philip of Marysburgh.
   Peter of Marysburgh. OC 8 Feb 1808.
   John of Marysburgh. OC 8 Feb 1808.
   Christopher of Marysburgh. OC 31 May 1820.
   Samuel G. of Camden East. OC 9 May 1834.
   David of Camden East. OC 9 May 1834.
   Sarah Ann Maria, m. Ernest Drader of Camden East. OC 3 July 1834.
   Daniel Rose of Camden East. OC 2 Oct 1834.
   Jane, m. Amos Card of Camden East. OC 5 Feb 1835.
   Mathias of Marysburgh. OC 19 June 1832.
   Norris (son) of Camden East. OC 8 Feb 1827.

T

TAYLOR, Christine, wife of Robert Taylor. m. (2) William Harrison. Died
   1796. OC 30 Aug 1797. OC 20 March 1822.
   Mary. OC 13 Nov 1797. Hamilton Tnp.
   Ann.
   Robert.
   Christine. OC 13 Nov 1797.
   Nelly. OC 13 Nov 1797.

TAYLOR, John of Ernestown. Sgt. , 34th Regt.
   Elizabeth, m. ---- Proudfoot. 25/3 Storrington. Land Board Certificate.

TAYLOR, John of Thurlow.
   Mary Ann C. OC 27 Aug 1840.
   Margaret, m. ---- Harris of Sidney. OC 5 June 1834.
   John of Thurlow. OC 26 Feb 1828.
   William Johnston of Thurlow. OC 13 July 1841.

TAYLOR, William of Kingston.
   Margaret, m. Peter Holmes of Thurlow. OC 25 Feb 1809.
   Eleanor, m. John Wilson of Town of Kingston. OC 17 March 1812.
   William of Thurlow. OC 20 May 1817.
   Mary, m. ---- Mountain of Kingston. OC 20 July 1837.

TEEPLE, Peter of Oxford-on-Thames.
   William of Oxford-on-Thames. OC 14 Jan 1812.   [Cont'd]

TEEPLE, Peter - Cont'd
  Lavinia, m. ---- Burdick of Oxford-on-Thames. OC 17 July 1805.
  Edward of Oxford-on-Thames. OC 30 Dec 1815.
  Susannah, m. Archibald Burtch of Oxford-on-Thames. OC 16 Jan 1816.
  Frederick of Oxford-on-Thames. OC 23 Nov 1816.
  Luke of Charlotteville. OC 20 May 1817.
  Stephen H. of Oxford-on-Thames. OC 6 Feb 1822.
  Mary, m. Andrus Davis of Yarmouth. OC 5 March 1823.
  Phoebe, b. 16 April 1801; m. ---- Tisdale; d. Aylmer, Ont., 21 Oct 1870.
      OC 9 July 1823.
  Pellum of Oxford-on-Thames. OC 8 Dec 1832.
  Lemuel Covel of Oxford-on-Thames. OC 2 Feb 1832.
  Simon P. of Oxford-on-Thames. OC 7 Jan 1830.
  Oliver M. of Zorra. OC 25 Jan 1831.

TENBROOK, Peter of Niagara. Capt., Butler's Rangers. m. Anna, dau of
  Johan Jost Herkimer, and sister of Hanyost Herchmer, U. E., of Kingston.
  He was buried 26 Sept 1804. (Note. Mrs Priscilla Tenbroeck died in Gran-
  tham on 18 Sept 1849)
  Nicholas Herkimer of Town of Niagara. OC 4 Jan 1840.
  Catharine, m. George Forsyth, 25 July 1804. OC 17 March 1797.
  Nancy, m. Thomas Butler of Niagara. OC 17 March 1797.
  Major Jacob of Niagara, m. Priscilla Read, 9 July 1797. OC 17 Aug 1795.

TERRY, Parshall of York, m. Rhoda Skinner. Mrs Rhoda Terry m. (2) Wm.
  Cornell of Scarborough. See 8/1 Scarborough.
  Submission, m. Alexander Galloway of York. OC 4 March 1800.
  Mary, m. Joseph Lutz. OC 27 March 1800.
  Parshall of the Don Mills. OC 13 May 1800.
  Sarah Maria, twin, b. 22 Dec 1796, m. Edward Wm. Thompson of Mark-
      ham 23 March 1815. OC 4 July 1815.
  Deborah Augusta, twin, b. 22 Dec 1796; m. John Starkes Thomas of
      Markham. OC 13 March 1819.
  Timothy of Scarborough. OC 5 May 1819.
  William of Thorold, innkeeper. OC 8 Sept 1819. OC 23 June 1828.
  Agnes. OC 6 Feb 1822.
  Ann, b. 18 August 1802; m. Hiram Davis Lee of Westminster; d. 1874.
      OC 26 Jan 1837.
  Eliza, m. John Farquharson of Whitby. OC 3 Dec 1829.
  Amy, m. Isaac Cornell of Scarborough. OC 6 May 1830.
  Lydia, m. George Thomson of Scarborough 26 Feb 1823. OC 31 Jan 1826.

THATCHER, John of Saltfleet.
  Elizabeth, m. Robert Van Duzen of Saltfleet. OC 19 May 1812.
  Mary, m. Thomas Corner of Nelson. OC 5 May 1819.
  Edmund of Trafalgar. OC 29 Dec 1819.
  John of Saltfleet. OC 29 Dec 1819.
  William of Saltfleet. OC 29 Dec 1819.   [Cont'd]

THATCHER, John - Cont'd
   Emily, m. James Deen of Saltfleet. OC 19 Jan 1833.
   Nancy, m. David Underhill of Saltfleet. OC 3 May 1832.
   Enoch of Saltfleet. OC 2 Feb 1832.
   Amos of Saltfleet. OC 29 April 1824.

THOMAS, Jacob of Niagara.
   Benjamin of Pelham. OC 30 Sept 1806.
   Mary, m. James Buckley of Rainham. OC 14 July 1819.
   Bathsheba, m. John Howey of Gainsborough. OC 22 May 1820.
   Ann. OC 30 May 1821.
   Isaac of Pelham. OC 30 May 1821.
   Sarah, m. Christian Rayner of Pelham. OC 27 June 1833.
   Elizabeth, m. William Potts of Pelham. OC 27 June 1833.
   Jacob of Pelham. OC 25 July 1833.
   Phoebe, m. Peter Sloat of Pelham. OC 3 Nov 1831.
   John of Pelham. OC 1850 or 1851.

THOMAS, James. K. R. R. N. Y.
   Christina, m. Major Slater of Niagara, 25 Aug 1799.

THOMAS, Peter of Ernestown.
   William of Ernestown. OC 31 May 1803.
   Mary, m. Jacob Hartman of Ernestown. OC 13 March 1807.
   Elizabeth, m. Israel Amey of Ernestown. OC 17 March 1807.
   Dorothy, m. Archibald Carscallen of Ernestown, 18 Jan 1810. OC 16 Feb 1811.
   Robert of York. OC 31 May 1820.
   Peter of Ernestown, m. Ann Bernard, 16 Aug 1818. OC 7 May 1828.
   Hannah, m. David Daly of Ernestown 11 March 1819. OC 5 April 1825.

THOMPSON, Archibald of Scarborough (Kingston), m. Elizabeth McKay at Quebec, 1778.
   Janet, m. James Elliott of Scarborough 16 Sept 1802. OC 15 Jan 1803.
   Andrew of Scarborough, m. Sarah Smith, 8 March 1810. OC 13 Sept 1803.
   Mary, m. John Scarlett of York 5 July 1810. OC 12 March 1805.
   Elizabeth, m. Thomas Forfar of Flamborough East, 11 Aug 1806. OC 30 Sept 1806.
   Helen, bapt. 31 May 1789, m. James Fenwick of Markham, 29 Dec 1808. OC 20 Aug 1811.
   Edward William of Markham, m. Sarah M. Terry, 23 March 1815. OC 4 July 1815.
   Hugh Christopher of Town of Kingston, m. Elizabeth Ruttan. OC 11 Nov 1815.
   Alexander Stewart of Scarborough, bapt. 9 Oct 1796; m. Anne Pringle, 2 June 1818. OC 22 Oct 1817.
   Archibald John of Scarborough, m. Hannah Walton? OC 21 April 1819.
   George of Scarborough, m. Lydia Terry, 26 Feb 1823. OC 29 May 1822.

THOMPSON, George of Clinton.
  Nicholas Bayard of Clinton. OC 4 Feb 1807.
  Anna Maria. OC 17 Oct 1809.
  Guy C. of Clinton. OC 12 Jan 1820.
  Miranda. OC 31 May 1820.
  Sarah. OC 1 Oct 1823.
  William of Louth. OC 20 Nov 1823.
  John of Louth. OC 1 Feb 1826.

THOMPSON, Jacob.
  Jane, m. John Milton of Pittsburgh. OC 16 Nov 1797.
  Esther, m. Reuben Mott of Elizabethtown. OC 2 Sept 1818.

THOMPSON, Peter of Stamford. Soldier, Butler's Rangers.
  Mary, m. John Bunting of Stamford. OC 24 May 1805.
  Charlotte, m. Dugald Carmichael of Stamford. OC 8 Sept 1819.

THOMPSON, Samuel.
  Andrew of Niagara. OC 5 March 1810.

THOMPSON, William of Fredericksburgh.
  Andrew of Fredericksburgh. OC 6 Feb 1822.
  Christian (son) of Fredericksburgh. OC 6 Feb 1822.
  Samuel of Fredericksburgh. OC 6 Feb 1822.
  John of Fredericksburgh. OC 21 March 1834.
  William of Fredericksburgh. OC 19 Feb 1828.
  Alexander of Camden East. OC 1850 or 1851.
  Levi of Camden East. OC 1850 or 1851.

THOMSON, Archibald of Stamford. His wife died August, 1823.
  James of Stamford. OC 8 July 1806.
  Margaret Emery, m. James Thomson of Stamford. OC 17 Feb 1807.
  Benjamin of Stamford. OC 2 June 1819.
  Richard of Stamford. OC 2 June 1819.
  Nelly, m. ---- Murray of Stamford. OC 2 May 1836.
  Isabel, m. William Finlay of Stamford. OC 13 April 1825.

THROOP, Daniel.
  Abigail, m. ---- Baldwin. OC 3 July 1798.
  Olive, m. Ira Bishop of Wolford. OC 3 July 1798.
  Amy. OC 20 June 1799.
  Daniel. OC 22 July 1797.

TILLABOUGH, Christian Sr.
  Mary, m. Philip Frymire of Williamsburgh. OC 20 March 1807.
  Joseph of Williamsburgh, m. Dorothy Schwerdfeger. OC 26 Jan 1808.
  John of Matilda. OC 26 Jan 1808.
  David of Williamsburgh. OC 16 April 1818.   [Cont'd]

TILLABOUGH, Christian Sr. - Cont'd
Nicholas of Montague. OC 7 June 1831.

TILLABOUGH, Martin of Matilda.
John of Matilda. OC 8 Feb 1808.
Peter of Matilda. OC 8 Feb 1808.
Christian of Matilda, m. Catharine Van Camp. OC 7 Aug 1811.

TOMPKINS, Israel of Augusta and Wolford, m. Rebecca, dau of ---- Brown,
U. E. Land Board Certificate, 1 Apr 1794, 6/Front Escott.
George of Oxford-on-Rideau, d. 4 Jan 1813. OC 20 Feb 1808.
Obadiah of Oxford-on-Rideau, m. Nancy Knapp. OC 28 April 1812.
Nathan of Oxford-on-Rideau. OC 5 Nov 1818.
Jesse of Oxford-on-Rideau, m. Sylvia. OC 23 June 1836.
Asa of Augusta. OC 28 Oct 1835.
Samuel of Wolford. OC 24 Jan 1833.
Elisha of Wolford. OC 21 Feb 1832.
Israel.
Phebe.

TOPP, John of Malden.
Abraham of Barton. OC 21 Jan 1824.

TREANOR, John of Barton and Glanford.
David of Glanford. OC 21 April 1819.
Henrietta, m. Hiram Chase of Glanford. OC 26 Jan 1820.
John of Glanford. OC 23 Aug 1820.
Catharine, m. Peter McKee of Glanford. OC 4 Feb 1824.
Oliver of Glanford. OC 2 June 1831.
Mary, m. Levius Simpkins of Mount Pleasant. OC 2 June 1831.
Richard of Toronto. OC 12 Oct 1841.

TROMPOUR, John of Sophiasburgh.
Paul of Hallowell. OC 17 March 1804.
Catharine, m. James Orsburn of Sophiasburgh. OC 13 March 1807.
Tina, m. Robert Curlett of Sophiasburgh. OC 13 March 1807.
Deborah, m. Nehemiah Osburn of Sophiasburgh. OC 26 March 1817.
William of Hallowell. OC 1 Aug 1833.

TROMPOUR, Paul of Adolphustown. Cornet, Delancey's Horse. Died March,
1813.
Elizabeth, m. Thomas J. Dorland of Adolphustown. OC 28 Feb 1807.
Joseph of Adolphustown. OC 16 Nov 1807.
John P. of Adolphustown. OC 16 Nov 1807.
Christeen, m. James Cumming of Hallowell, 11 Oct 1807. OC 23 Feb 1808.
Deborah, m. Simeon Washburn of Hallowell, 11 Dec 1811. OC 25 Feb 1812.
Catharine, m. John McCuaig of Ameliasburgh; d. at Town of Hamilton, 16
January 1860. OC 9 December 1815.   [Cont'd]

TROMPOUR, Paul - Cont'd
  Charlotte, m. Charles Hayward of Hallowell. OC 28 Oct 1835.
  Christeen, m. (2) Rev. Thomas Morley of Hallowell.
  Sarah, m. John S. Heermans of Whitby and N. Y. City.

TURNER, Edward of Chatham. [His step-father was Jordan Avery; the family
  was at Niagara in 1783. The Ontario Register, 1: 213]
  Mary, m. James Huff of Mersea. OC 11 Nov 1815. OC 6 Sept 1820.
  Morris of Chatham. OC 11 Nov 1815.
  Hannah, m. Michael Salway of Colchester. OC 30 June 1819.
  Ann, m. David Sticklestell of Chatham. OC 2 Feb 1837.
  Sarah. OC 18 Feb 1834.
  Japheth of Howard. OC 18 Feb 1843.
  Ruth. OC 18 Feb 1843.
  Elizabeth, m. ---- Frider of Chatham. OC 1850 or 1851.

TUTTLE, Jonathan of Edwardsburgh.
  Abigail, m. ---- Hosier. OC 5 Nov 1799.
  Ruth, m. Daniel Fell of Augusta.
  John of Kingston. OC 13 Oct 1836.

TUTTLE, Solomon of Cornwall, m. Dolly Gallinger.
  Catharine, m. Martin Selimser of Cornwall. OC 27 Dec 1808.
  Olive, bapt. 22 June 1794; m. Robert Putnam of Cornwall. OC 26 March
    1817.
  Sarah, bapt. 16 Oct 1796.

TWOHEY, John. Soldier, K. R. R. N. Y. , m. Rachel.
  Mary. OC 22 Feb 1808.
  Eunice. OC 20 Feb 1808.
  John of Augusta, b. about 1775. OC 8 Oct 1808.
  Abraham of Augusta, b. about 1785. OC 8 Oct 1808.
  Sanford of Bastard. OC 20 May 1817.
  Susannah, m. James Mann of Bastard. OC 8 Oct 1830.

TYLER, Gerrard of Fredericksburgh.
  Samantha, m. Gilbert Harris of Fredericksburgh. OC 20 July 1797.
  Zalmon of Richmond. OC 25 May 1802.
  Hannah, m. Alexander Hanna of Sidney. OC 21 May 1840.

U

ULMAN, Francis of Williamsburgh.
  Elizabeth, m. Henry Frauts of Williamsburgh. OC 20 March 1807.
  Mary, m. William Empey of Osnabruck. OC 20 March 1807.
  John of Osnabruck. OC 7 Aug 1811.
  Agnes. OC 23 June 1836. Hawkesbury.   [Cont'd]

ULMAN, Francis - Cont'd
  Catharine, m. George Markley of Williamsburgh. OC 25 Feb 1812.
  Mary Magdalaine. OC 23 June 1836. Argenteuil, Lower Canada.
  Henry of Cornwall. OC 3 Dec 1835.
  Philip of Williamsburgh. OC 4 Sept 1834. OC 5 Feb 1835.

URQUHART, William of Charlottenburgh, m. Janet.
  Catharine, m. Peter Campbell of Charlottenburgh 18 March 1802. OC 9
    July 1802.
  William of Charlottenburgh, m. Mary McGregor, 21 Aug 1810. OC 19 Dec
    1806.
  Kenneth of Charlottenburgh. OC 25 Juen 1807.
  Margaret, m. Robert McLaren of Kenyon. OC 18 March 1808.
  Christy, bapt. 12 June 1791; m. Thomas Ross of Lancaster 2 Nov 1809.
    OC 22 Feb 1810.
  Isabella, bapt. 12 June 1791; m. Donald Anderson (?) of St. George. OC
    22 Feb 1810.
  John of Charlottenburgh, m. Christian McLennan. OC 27 March 1813.
  James of Charlottenburgh, bapt. 12 Feb 1792, m. Margaret McIntyre. OC
    23 November 1816.

UTMAN, Henry of Williamsburgh.
  Isaac of Williamsburgh. OC 29 Sept 1836.
  Lydia, m. William Stewart of Oxford. OC 9 March 1837.
  Mary, m. Christian Barkley of Williamsburgh. OC 21 March 1833.
  Elizabeth, m. John Baxter of Matilda. OC 27 May 1833.
  Christy. OC 24 March 1835.
  Catharine, m. John A. Merkley of Williamsburgh. OC 7 March 1833.
  Adam of Williamsburgh. OC 28 Feb 1833.
  Henry of Matilda. OC 10 Jan 1833.

V

VALLEAU, Peter of Adolphustown. He was b. May, 1751 in Bergen Co., N.J.
  m. (1) Jannetie (ne Lasireor, Lozier) widow of Andrew Zabriskie, of Bergen
  Co. m. (2) widow of his cousin, Charity Lozier. She died 1836.
  Mary, b. 10 Feb 1787; m. John Benson of Sophiasburgh 17 Nov 1801; died
    Sept. , 1855. OC 21 Jan 1806.
  Hildebrand of Adolphustown, b. 5 June 1775 in Bergen Co., N.J.; m. Eliz-
    Campbell, 25 Aug 1800; d. 13 Apr 1837. OC 12 June 1797.
  Cornelius of Adolphustown, b. 17 March 1777 in Bergen Co., N.J.; m.
    Anne Rowe, 1798; d. 1858. OC 12 June 1797.

VAN ALLEN, Jacob of Matilda.
  Jacob of Matilda. OC 17 March 1807.
  John of Matilda. OC 7 Aug 1811.
  Peter of Matilda. OC 19 April 1816.   [Cont'd]

VAN ALLEN, Jacob - Cont'd
  Henry of Matilda. OC 18 March 1818.
  Isaac of Matilda. OC 2 May 1833.
  Elizabeth, m. Conrad Casselman of Williamsburgh. OC 24 Nov 1832.
  Gilbert of Matilda. OC 6 Dec 1832.
  Dinah, m. John Hickey Jr. of Williamsburgh. OC 2 Feb 1825.

VAN ALSTINE, Hermanus. See OC 12 June 1834.
  Suffrenus of Niagara. OC 24 Jan 1797.

VAN ALSTINE, Isaac.
  Jane, m. Jonas Van Alstine of Richmond. OC 8 July 1797.

VAN ALSTINE, Jacob of Grantham.
  Catharine. OC 20 May 1817.
  Margaret. OC 30 June 1819.
  David of Grantham. OC 22 May 1820.
  John of Grantham. OC 15 Nov 1820.
  Sarah. OC 31 Jan 1826.

VAN ALSTINE, Lambert of Fredericksburgh.
  Duncan of Ernestown. OC 11 March 1819.
  Jacob of Haldimand. OC 11 March 1819.
  David of Fredericksburgh. OC 25 June 1840.
  Alexander. Not. Rec. 23 Feb 1837.
  Barnard of Kingston. OC 9 Nov 1835.
  Isaac of Kingston. OC 14 April 1836.
  John of Whitby. OC 28 Feb 1835.
  Lydia, m. Matthew McCay of Kingston. OC 6 Oct 1831.
  James of Fredericksburgh. OC 1 April 1830.
  Lambert of Fredericksburgh. OC 29 Sept 1824.

VAN ALSTINE, Lydia of Fredericksburgh.
  Isaac J. of Richmond. OC 9 March 1808.
  James of Richmond. OC 16 Feb 1810.

VAN ALSTINE, Peter of Adolphustown.
  Allada, m. George W. Meyers of Sidney 5 May 1789. Land Board Certifi-
    cate, 30/5 Sidney.
  Alexander of Adolphustown, m. Ursula Allen, 26 June 1798. OC 8 July
    1797.
  Cornelius of Adolphustown, m. Rachel Dunham, 29 Dec 1801. OC 30 Aug
    1797.

VAN ARNAM, Jacob of Sorel.
  John of Ernestown. OC 28 Aug 1810.
  Jacob of Ernestown. OC 12 Nov 1811.
  Richard of Augusta. OC 15 Aug 1833.

VAN CAMP, Jacob of Matilda and Augusta, m. Hannah.
  Catharine, b. May, 1774; m. Joshua Losee of Marlborough 3 March 1794;
      d. Oct 16, 1850. OC 26 March 1836. OC 22 June 1797.
  Jacob of Haldimand (Augusta). OC 18 June 1799.
  William of Augusta. OC 18 June 1799. OC 28 June 1820.
  Rachel, m. Amos Knapp of Augusta. OC 7 July 1802.
  Elizabeth, m. Benjamin Mosher of Marlborough. OC 17 March 1808.
  Mary, m. Abraham Knapp of Augusta. OC 11 Nov 1815.
  Elizabeth, m. Edward Van Arnam of Augusta. OC 11 Nov 1815.
  Tunis of Cornwall, tanner. OC 21 Feb 1821.
  John of Elizabethtown. OC 7 Sept 1840.

VAN CAMP, John of Matilda.
  Catharine, m. Christian Tillibough of Matilda. OC 7 April 1812.
  Mary, m. John Saver of Matilda. OC 19 April 1816.
  John of Matilda. OC 19 April 1816.
  Sarah, m. ---- Teal of Matilda. OC 5 Nov 1819.
  Rachel. OC 13 June 1836.
  Elijah of Matilda. OC 23 June 1828.

VAN CAMP, Peter. Died in 1783 at Montreal.
  Jacob of Matilda, U. E.
  Mary, m. John Boice of Matilda.
  Phoebe, m. Samuel Street of Wolford, March, 1784. OC 18 June 1800.
  Simon, in U. S.
  Thomas, in U. S.
  Hetty, m. William Leahy of Augusta.
  John of Matilda, U. E.

VANCLEFT, John.
  Jesse of Fredericksburgh. OC 3 March 1809.

VAN de BOGART, Francis of Fredericksburgh.
  Nicholas of Richmond. OC 25 Feb 1812.
  William of Richmond. OC 13 Feb 1816.
  Mary Ann. OC 13 Feb 1816.

VANDECAR, Rulof of Ernestown and Glanford, m. Sarah, dau of Silas and
Rachel Reynolds.
  Lanah, bapt. 8 July 1788, m. Jeremiah Conat of Darlington. OC 8 July
      1806.
  Elizabeth, bapt. 3 July 1789; m. Henry Smith of Glanford. OC 14 June 1811.
  Silas of Ameliasburgh. OC 2 March 1816.
  Benjamin of Glanford. OC 5 May 1819.
  Anna, m. George Rouse of Burford. OC 31 May 1820.
  John of Glanford. OC 26 Jan 1837.
  Nancy, m. ---- Arnold of Saltfleet. OC 24 Oct 1831.
  Solomon of Glanford. OC 18 Feb 1824.

VANDERBURGH, Garrett of Richmond, m. Barbara Campbell in Montreal,
February, 1784. He d. at Richmond 14 Apr 1835 in his 94th year.
  Elizabeth, m. John German of Richmond. OC 10 March 1834.
  Mary, m. ---- Oliver of Richmond. Land Board Certificate, 11/6 Rich-
    mond.

VANDERLIP, Frederick.
  Elizabeth, m. John Muirhead of Stamford. OC 8 Oct 1796; OC 24 March
    1797; OC 12 May 1808.

VANDERLIP, William of Niagara and Ancaster, m. Elizabeth.
  Ann, m. Seth Bradshaw of Town of Niagara. OC 20 Nov 1809.
  Jenny (Jane), m. Haggai Westbrook of Burford. OC 19 Apr 1816. OC 9
    May 1821.
  Edward of Ancaster. OC 6 Aug 1816.
  William of Ancaster. OC 4 Sept 1822.
  James of Ancaster. OC 24 Nov 1836.

VAN DUZEN, Casparus of Sophiasburgh, son of Robert Vandusen and Christina Ham (m. 1750), b. 19 Apr 1761; m. Hannah Mary dau of John W. Shorts
and Rosannah Monk, on 16 Feb 1796. Died 23 Dec 1838. His wife d. 26 Oct
1862 at Hilton, Ont.
  Robert of Sophiasburgh, b. 2 Apr 1799; m. (1) Elizabeth Roblin. m. (2)
    Mary Ann Brown; d. 25 May 1873. OC 2 Oct 1822.
  John of Sophiasburgh, b. 7 Dec 1787; m. (1) Mary Armstrong, 15 May 1810;
    m. (2) Patience Aldrich; d. 4 June 1856. OC 3 Jan 1827.
  a son, b. 22 Apr 1788; d. 24 Apr 1788.
  Catharine, b. 23 July 1789; m. John Johnson of Hallowell 30 Dec 1810; d.
    18 Apr 1836. OC 28 Nov 1826; OC 24 March 1835.
  Fanny, b. 5 Dec 1792.
  Mary, b. 15 Jan 1794; d. 9 Feb 1813, unmarried.
  Rosannah, b. 29 Jan 1797; m. John W. Terwilliger of Hallowell 4 Apr 1815;
    OC 7 May 1828.
  Amelia, b. 13 Jan 1802; m. James Lent, 12 Feb 1824; d. 10 Aug 1882. OC
    19 July 1826.
  Elizabeth, b. 16 Aug 1804; m. James Davis of Thurlow 12 June 1828. d. 6
    June 1833. OC 6 Oct 1831.
  Rachel, b. 13 Jan 1807; m. Lewis R. Snider of Sophiasburgh 21 Feb 1837;
    d. 13 Sept 1876. OC 24 March 1835.
  Charlotte Croel, b. 5 Nov 1810; m. Abram Huff, 16 June 1841; d. 27 April
    1857. OC 24 March 1835.
  Peter Jasper Monk of Sophiasburgh, b. 4 June 1815; m. Deborah Davis, 30
    Sept 1835; d. 30 Oct 1895 at Madison, Wis. OC 21 June 1838.

VANDUZEN, Conrad of Marysburgh, son of Robert Vandusen and Christina
Ham, b. 23 Apr 1751; m. (1) Hannah Coon of Dutchess Co., N.Y. in 1771.
(His wife b. 30 June 1753; d. 8 March 1791). He d. 23 Nov 1827. He m. (2)
Millicent (Ferguson) Hoover dau of Richard Ferguson, U.E., 31 July 1791.

VANDUZEN, Conrad - Cont'd

Catharine, b. 1774; m. David Brown of Adolphustown 2 Feb 1792; d. 31 Dec 1884. OC 25 Nov 1800.

Henry of Fredericksburgh, b. Jan 16, 1786; m. (1) Mary Huff, 27 Jan 1807 m. (2) Hannah Hortman, 6 Apr 1816; d. 28 July 1871. OC 8 Feb 1808.

Rachel, b. 14 Dec 1793; m. William Carson of Marysburgh; d. 14 March 1877. OC 16 Feb 1811.

Hannah, b. 12 Apr 1792; m. John Toby of Adolphustown 19 March 1810; d. 10 May 1850. OC 16 Feb 1811.

Susannah, bapt. 14 June 1789; m. John Dingman of Marysburgh 27 Jan 1812; OC 16 Feb 1811.

Phoebe, b. 26 Nov 1795; m. Thomas Carson of Marysburgh 11 June 1815; d. 12 Nov 1845. OC 18 March 1818.

Sarah, b. 26 May 1798; m. Jacob Roblin of Adolphustown 7 Aug 1816; d. 14 Dec 1883. OC 18 March 1818.

Daniel of Marysburgh, b. 29 Jan 1800; d. 16 July 1826. OC 8 March 1826.

Conrad of Adolphustown, b. 14 Dec 1801; d. 18 Aug 1878. OC 27 June 1833.

Arra Ham (son), b. 4 May 1804; d. 16 Oct 1890.

William, b. 8 Feb 1806; d. 8 Feb 1873.

Roswell of Sophiasburgh, b. 20 Aug 1808; d. 23 Apr 1892. OC 12 Sept 1833.

James Yeoman of Hallowell, b. 10 Aug 1810. OC 12 Sept 1833.

Jacob Richard, b. 26 May 1813.

VAN DUZEN, Joseph of Sophiasburgh.

Frances, m. Levi Bates of Hamilton. OC 11 Sept 1832.

VAN EVERY, Benjamin. Soldier, Butler's Rangers. His wife, Mary, m. (2) ---- Slingerland.

John Cox, bapt. 24 Sept 1792.

VAN EVERY, David of Flamborough West and Dumfries. Sgt., Butler's Rangers; m. Sarah Showers. [He and his family were at Niagara in 1783. The Ontario Register, 1:198]

David of Flamborough West. OC 13 April 1802.

Hannah, m. ---- Conner of Flamborough West. OC 6 Dec 1803.

Samuel of Ancaster. OC 6 Dec 1803.

John of Ancaster. OC 23 Nov 1816.

Michael of Flamborough West. OC 23 Nov 1816.

William of Dumfries. OC 27 June 1821.

Andrew of Dumfries. OC 5 March 1823.

Peter of Dumfries. OC 15 Nov 1820.

Charles of Flamborough West, b. 2 Sept 1797. OC 5 Nov 1823.

Mary. OC 2 Feb 1825.

Elizabeth, m. William Lennington of Dumfries. OC 15 May 1832.

VAN EVERY, McGregor, m. Mary; d. Sept., 1786 at Niagara. See OC 10 Dec 1832; OC 22 July 1797. [His household was at Niagara, 1783. TOR 1:198]

Phoebe, m. Henry Young of Ancaster. OC 8 July 1801.　　　　[Cont'd]

VAN EVERY, McGregor - Cont'd
Andrew of Flamborough West, m. Jane Purbus, 3 March 1794. OC 5 Feb 1807.
David of Flamborough West, m. Sarah Showers.
Henry.
Samuel of Flamborough West, m. Hannah Coon.
William of Niagara, b. 1769; m. Elizabeth, widow of Fred. Dochstader; d. 1832.

VAN EVERY, Samuel of Flamborough West. Soldier, Butler's Rangers. He m. Hannah Coon. She m. (2) Titus Geer Simons.
Peter of Flamborough West, bapt. 3 March 1794. OC 23 Nov 1816.
Elizabeth, m. Joseph Rymal of Ancaster 23 Feb 1819. OC 17 March 1824.
William B. of Barton. OC 6 July 1825.
Mary, m. George Rymal of Barton. OC 13 May 1824.

VAN EVERY, William of Niagara. Soldier, Butler's Rangers, m. Elizabeth Stevens. He d. 1832, aged 67. She d. 1857, aged 93.
Elizabeth, m. Peter Weaver of Niagara. OC 16 Aug 1810.
Mary, m. Peter Warner of Niagara. OC 18 June 1811.
John of Niagara. OC 25 Feb 1818.
Phoebe. OC 25 Feb 1818.
Rebecca, m. Christopher Williams of Westminster. OC 17 Feb 1831.
Peter of Stamford. OC 16 April 1840.
Joseph of Stamford. OC 1 Dec 1831.

VAN HORN, Cornelius of Adolphustown, b. about 1755 and d. April, 1815.
John of Sophiasburgh, bapt. 7 Feb 1791. OC 20 May 1817.
Peter of Adolphustown. OC 22 Oct 1817.
Margaret, m. Paul Clapp of Adolphustown. OC 8 March 1820.
Cornelius of Hillier. OC 2 July 1828.

VAN KLEEK, Simon of Hawkesbury.
Simon of Hawkesbury. OC 29 March 1808.

VAN KOUGHNET, John of Cornwall.
Ann, m. Solomon Y. Chesley of Cornwall. OC 27 Feb 1834.
Margaret. OC 27 Feb 1834.

VAN KOUGHNET, Michael of Cornwall. Sgt., R. R. N. Y.
John of Cornwall. OC 9 March 1803.
Polly. OC 2 March 1807.
Anne Eve, m. Richard T. Everitt of Cornwall. OC 16 Nov 1807.
Elizabeth, m. Richard McBean of Cornwall. OC 16 Feb 1811.
Margaret, m. Dr. Noah Dickenson. OC 16 Feb 1811.
Philip of Town of Cornwall, b. 2 Apr 1790; m. Harriet Sophia Scott, 1 Apr 1819; d. 7 May 1873. OC 18 March 1818.
Christian, m. Wm Cline of Cornwall; d. 1 Nov 1853 ae 56. OC 7 Feb 1833.

VAN KOUGHNET, William. See Koughnet.

VAN SICKLE, Isaac of Ancaster, m. Jane.
Delila, m. David Palmer of Ancaster. OC 22 March 1820.
Jane, m. James Lemon of Charlotteville. OC 30 April 1823.
Rachel, m. Mordecai Wilson of Ancaster. OC 9 March 1837.
Isaac of Ancaster. OC 11 April 1833.
John of Grimsby. OC 27 Sept 1833.
Priscilla, b. 25 Nov 1801; m. Sept., 1817, Daniel Buckner; d. 1 May 1833.
Anna, m. William Kitchen of Ancaster. OC 18 Aug 1824.
Sarah, m. Henry Weaver of Beverly. OC 23 June 1824.

VAN SKIVER, John of Adolphustown and Sophiasburgh.
Samuel of Adolphustown. OC 12 Dec 1821.
John of Sophiasburgh. OC 25 June 1823.
Anna. OC 22 July 1836.
Cornelius of Hallowell. OC 28 Oct 1835.
James of Sophiasburgh. OC 4 Feb 1836.
Deborah, m. ---- McTaggart of Sophiasburgh. OC 21 March 1833.
Jemima, m. Jacob Adams of Marysburgh. OC 21 March 1831.
Susan, m. Robert McTaggart of Sophiasburgh. OC 7 June 1826.
Mary, m. John McTaggart of Sidney 17 March 1819. OC 22 July 1824.

VENT, Adam of Ernestown.
Philip of Ernestown. OC 31 May 1803. OC 8 March 1828.
Catharine, m. John Poncet of Kingston. OC 17 March 1804.
Hannah, m. Henry Brezee of Ernestown. OC 23 Feb 1810.
John of Ernestown. OC 29 June 1838.
Elizabeth, m. David Huffman of Ernestown. OC 16 April 1840.

VINCENT, Elijah of Willoughby.
Abigail, m. John Ammerman of Willoughby 10 Apr 1809. OC 16 Feb 1811.
m. (2) Thomas Burns.
Thomas of Willoughby. OC 14 June 1839.
Lewis of Willoughby. OC 18 Jan 1828.
Mary, m. Daniel Shaneholts of Willoughby. OC 17 Feb 1825.

VOLLOCK, Isaac, m. Mary.
Sarah, m. Benoni Crumb of Louth. OC 17 March 1806.
Catharine, m. ---- Hainer of Grantham. OC 11 March 1797.

VOLLOCK, Storm of Canborough.
Catharine. OC 28 Oct 1835.
George of Canborough. OC 28 Oct 1835.
Isaac of Haldimand Co. OC 28 Nov 1826.
Peter of Haldimand Co. OC 28 Nov 1826.
Jacob of Haldimand Co. OC 28 Nov 1826.

VROOMAN, Adam of Niagara. [Sgt., Butler's Ranger; at Niagara in 1783 with
wife and child. The Ontario Register, 1: 200]
   Rachel, m. Solomon Skinner of Niagara 2 Oct 1800. OC 25 Aug 1801.
   Solomon of Niagara, m. Mary Brown, 19 March 1807. OC 19 Aug 1806.
   Arent Schuyler De Peyster of Niagara. OC 9 July 1811.
   Adam of Niagara. OC 4 July 1815.
   George of Niagara. OC 20 Aug 1817.
   James of Kingston. OC 19 May 1819.
   Elizabeth, m. John Field of Niagara. OC 16 June 1819.

W

WAGER, Everhart.
   Hannah, m. James Lindsey of Fredericksburgh. OC 25 July 1797.

WAGER, Thomas of Fredericksburgh.
   George of Fredericksburgh. OC 26 March 1817. OC 5 Oct 1818.
   William of Fredericksburgh. OC 13 June 1818.
   Thomas of Fredericksburgh, m. Mary Hoffman. OC 13 June 1818.
   James of Camden East. OC 1 June 1837.
   Susannah, m. Philip Wager of Camden East. OC 28 Oct 1835.
   Christian, m. Benjamin Marsh of Camden East 13 Nov 1820. OC 27 Aug
      1833.
   Elizabeth, m. Francis Powley of Kingston. OC 19 Dec 1833.
   Lorany, m. Peter Akey of Camden East 17 June 1822. OC 2 Jan 1834.
   David of Fredericksburgh. OC 22 Dec 1832.
   John of Fredericksburgh. OC 22 Dec 1832.
   Magdalene, m. ---- Hart of Fredericksburgh. OC Dec., 1832.
   Margaret, m. Peter Barnhart of Fredericksburgh. OC 1 Aug 1827.

WAGER, William of Fredericksburgh.
   Silla, m. Elias Jackson of Fredericksburgh. OC 16 May 1839.
   Elias of Fredericksburgh. OC 24 Oct 1839.
   Ephraim of Camden East. OC 27 Oct 1836.
   Henry M. of Fredericksburgh. OC 28 Oct 1836.
   Elizabeth, m. Samuel Miller Jr. of Fredericksburgh. OC 28 Feb 1835.
   Philip of Camden East. OC 28 March 1835.
   Thomas Carver of Camden East. OC 28 March 1835.
   James Joseph of Camden East. OC 28 March 1835.
   Peter of Fredericksburgh. OC 28 March 1835.
   Jacob of Fredericksburgh. OC 28 March 1835.
   Michael O'Bryan of Camden East. OC 28 March 1835.
   William of Camden East. OC 28 March 1835.

WAGGONER, George of Osnabruck.
   George of Osnabruck. OC 4 Sept 1834.

WAGGONER, Henry of Matilda.
  Rose Ann, m. John Trudel of Williamsburgh. OC 19 March 1836.

WAGGONER, Jacob Sr. of Cornwall. KRRNY. m. Hannah Waite.
  Mary, m. Elijah Hollister of Cornwall. OC 5 Jan 1798.
  Margaret, bapt. 11 Feb 1786; m. George Warner of Osnabruck. OC 13
    March 1807.
  Nancy. OC 5 March 1808.
  Catharine, bapt. 13 Feb 1791; m. James McWilliams of Osnabruck. OC
    11 Nov 1815.
  Jacob of Cornwall, m. Mary Smith.
  Henry of Cornwall, m. Mary Eastman.
  Solomon of Osnabruck. OC 5 Nov 1818.
  George of Osnabruck. OC 30 Nov 1837.
  Nancy, m. Varnum Polly of Cornwall. OC 2 Oct 1834.

WAGGONER, Jacob Jr. of Osnabruck.
  Catharine, m. Phillip J. Empey of Osnabruck. OC 29 June 1837.
  William of Osnabruck. OC 5 Nov 1835.
  Margaret. OC 5 Nov 1835.
  Mary, m. William Polly of Cornwall. OC 5 Nov 1835.

WAIT, Joseph of Matilda and Charlottenburgh and of Chambly, L. C. Soldier,
  K. R. R. N. Y.
  Margaret. OC 28 April 1815.
  Jane. OC 28 April 1815.
  Catharine. OC 6 Aug 1816.
  Ann, b. 19 Nov 1798; m. James Cheeld of Town of Kingston. OC 10 Aug 1837.
  Grace. OC 24 Apr 1835.
  John of Glengarry. OC 4 Sept 1834.
  Sarah, b. 28 April 1800, m. William Kelly of Town of Kingston. OC 5 Feb
    1835.

WALBRIDGE, Asa of Thurlow. Vol. Delancey's Regt. See OC 21 March 1809.

WALDROFF, Martin Sr., m. Leana.
  Margaret, m. Daniel Smith of Cornwall. OC 5 Jan 1798.
  Mary, m. Martin Link. OC 5 Jan 1798.
  Leana, m. Amos Rambough of Osnabruck. OC 22 Sept 1836.
  John, m. Catharine. d. May, 1832.
  Martin.
  Ann Eve, m. Simon Clark of Osnabruck. OC 5 March 1810; Montreal,
    Notarial Record 26 Jan 1808.

WALKER, Daniel Sr. of Ernestown. Pvt., Loyal Rangers.
  Mary, m. Bruin Hough of Kingston, 16 Dec 1790. Land Board Certificate,
    7/6 Storrington.
  Daniel of Ernestown.

WALKER, Daniel of Ernestown.
  Elizabeth. OC 28 Nov 1839.
  Joshua of Murray. OC 18 Nov 1835.
  John of Ernestown. OC 8 Aug 1833.
  Susannah, m. John Farewell of Loughborough. OC 18 July 1834.
  Christopher of Haldimand. OC 8 Jan 1835.

WALKER, Jacob.
  Jane, m. James O'Connelly of Louth. OC 5 May 1819.
  dau., m. Walter Clendenning of Gainsborough. OC 29 July 1795.

WALKER, Weeden of Ernestown.
  John of Ernestown. OC 7 May 1811. Malahide. OC 27 March 1829.
  Daniel of Ernestown. OC 25 Feb 1812.
  Hazelton of Ernestown. OC 17 March 1812.
  Catharine, m. Nathan Clark Rowe of Kingston 9 Apr 1821. OC 28 Sept 1820
  Weeden of Ernestown. OC 28 Oct 1835.
  Robison of Ernestown. OC 4 Feb 1830.
  Charles of Ernestown. OC 5 Feb 1829.
  Johnston of Ernestown. OC 5 Feb 1829.
  John of Ernestown. OC 27 March 1829.
  Mary. OC 22 June 1825.
  Sarah. OC 22 June 1825.

WALKER, William of Clinton.
  Thomas. OC 23 June 1801.
  Ann, m. John Henry of Clinton. OC 17 Oct 1809.
  Margaret, m. William McCool of Townsend. OC 7 Aug 1810.
  Sarah, m. Joseph McCool of Townsend. OC 14 March 1811.
  Philip of Clinton. OC 24 Nov 1824.

WALKER, William of Ernestown.
  Solomon of Ernestown. OC 14 March 1809.
  Mary, m. Edward Lee of Ernestown. OC 13 June 1809.
  Hannah. OC 13 June 1809.
  Esther, m. Sheldon Hawley of Ernestown 22 March 1818. OC 5 Feb 1823.
  Hudson of Ernestown. OC 19 Feb 1823.
  Sarah, m. Joel Smith of Ernestown. OC 11 June 1840.
  Lavina, m. John Raymond of Ernestown. OC 28 Oct 1835.

WALLISER, Anthony.
  Laney, m. Jacob Shaver of Matilda. OC 26 Feb 1806.

WALTER, Philip.
  Hannah, m. Peter Loucks of Williamsburgh. OC 25 Feb 1806.
  Mary, m. Jacob Ealigh of Osnabruck. OC 26 Feb 1806.
  Elizabeth, m. Nicholas Frymire of Williamsburgh. OC 13 March 1807.

WANNAMAKER, Peter of Ameliasburgh. Sgt., N.J. Vols.
Abigail, m. Zachariah Herrington of Ameliasburgh. OC 12 Nov 1811.
Phoebe, m. Amos Wait of Ameliasburgh. OC 14 Nov 1821.
James P. of Ameliasburgh. OC 27 June 1833.
Catharine, m. Israel Sweet of Ameliasburgh. OC 5 June 1834.

WARD, Ashel of Markham, Trafalgar and York.
Mary, m. (1) David Edmunds of York. OC 11 Aug 1812. m. (2) Joseph
Johnson.
Clarissa, m. John Lawrence of York. OC 11 Aug 1812.
Rhoda. OC 27 Aug 1840.
Kezia. OC 2 May 1833. (Saltfleet)
Cordelia, m. David Spreingstead of Saltfleet. OC 19 Jan 1833.
Phoebe, m. Casper Teneyck of Binbrook. OC 19 Jan 1833.
Lydia, m. John Springstead of Saltfleet. OC 24 Dec 1832.
Sarah, m. George Cain of Marmora. OC 25 May 1846.
Note: If Ashel was of Elizabethtown his wife was Jemima Comstock. Dau.
Sarah, bapt. 26 May 1793.

WARDELL, Michael of Gainsborough.
Hannah. OC 27 Feb 1818.
Elizabeth, m. George Field of Harwich. OC 29 Nov 1820.

WARDLE, Peter.
Mary, m. Frederick Papts of Osnabruck. OC 5 Jan 1798.

WARNER, Christian, b. Beaver Dams, Albany Co., N.Y., 7 Nov 1754; d. 21
March 1833.
Elizabeth, m. Adam Crysler of Thorold. OC 11 May 1797.
Mary, m. John Fox of Niagara. OC 17 June 1806.
Barbara, m. Samuel Jones of Grantham. OC 21 Feb 1807; 16 June 1808.
Margaret, m. Abraham Overholt of Pelham. OC 16 April 1811.
Michael of Niagara. OC 18 June 1811.
Peter of Niagara, m. Mary Van Every. OC 18 June 1811.
Matthew of Niagara. OC 13 April 1819.
Phoebe, m. Morris Wurts of Niagara. OC 6 March 1822.
Charity. OC 6 March 1822.
Sarah, m. Peter Marsh of Saltfleet. OC 7 March 1827.

WARNER, Levi of Fredericksburgh.
Rosanna, m. ---- Falloon of Fredericksburgh. OC 9 March 1837.

WARNER, Michael of Osnabruck.
Coonrad of Cornwall. OC 5 Jan 1798.
George of Cornwall. OC 5 Jan 1798.
Catharine, m. John Campbell of Osnabruck. OC 13 March 1807.
Adam of Osnabruck. OC 16 July 1816.
John of Osnabruck. OC 16 July 1816.   [Cont'd]

WARNER, Michael - Cont'd
  Margaret, m. George Gallinger of Osnabruck. OC 5 Jan 1798; 21 Dec 1840.
  Michael of Osnabruck. OC 7 Aug 1834.

WART, George of Williamsburgh.
  Mary Catharine, m. Edward Michael Kotzeback of Williamsburgh. OC 26
    March 1840.
  Julian (dau.) OC 28 Oct 1835.
  Frederick of Williamsburgh. OC 3 March 1836.
  George of Williamsburgh. OC 4 July 1833.
  Christian of Williamsburgh. OC 4 July 1833.
  Dorothy, m. Hiram Hays of Williamsburgh. OC 2 May 1827.

WARTMAN, Abraham of Kingston. Died 1787.
  Barnabas of Kingston. OC 17 Nov 1797.
  Peter of Kingston, U. E.
  John.

WARTMAN, Peter of Kingston, m. Eve Grass dau of Capt. Michael Grass of
  Kingston. She d. 16 May 1858. He d. 1824.
  Margaret, bapt. 13 July 1788; m. Alexander Wright of Kingston. OC 23
    February 1808.
  Catharine, bapt. 10 Feb 1793; m. Joseph P. Caverly of Kingston 31 July
    1812. OC 28 April 1815.
  Mary, m. Peter Coon of Kingston. OC 28 April 1815.
  Elizabeth, bapt. 9 Nov 1794; m. Joseph Merritt of Kingston 16 Sept 1811;
    d. 4 April 1874. OC 2 March 1816.
  John, bapt. 23 Oct 1796.
  Peter of Kingston. OC 5 Sept 1833.
  Daniel of Kingston. OC 4 Dec 1834.
  Henry of Kingston. OC 28 March 1835.
  Sarah, m. Calvin W. Day of Kingston

WASHBURN, Ebenezer of Hallowell, m. (1) Sarah De Forest. m. (2) Hannah,
  widow of John McBride of York, 24 Jan 1803.
  Hannah, m. Rev. Robert McDowall of Ernestown. OC 9 July 1802.
  Mary, m. Eliphalet Adams of Hallowell 15 Jan 1805. OC 26 Feb 1806.
  Hon. Simeon of Hallowell, m. Deborah Trumpour, 11 Dec 1811. OC 8 Feb
    1808.
  William of Hallowell. OC 16 Feb 1811.
  Daniel of Town of Kingston, bapt. 28 Oct 1892; m. Mary McLean dau of
    Hon. Allan McLean, June, 1814. OC 4 July 1815; 18 Feb 1843.
  Simon Ebenezer of York, bapt. 18 Oct 1795; m. Margaret Fitzgibbon, 12
    April 1821; d. 29 Sept 1837 aged 44. OC 16 Feb 1816.
  Abigail, bapt. 14 Apr 1799; m. John Medcalf of Hallowell 8 Jan 1814. OC
    26 March 1817.
  Sarah, b. 7 Apr 1802; m. Mathew Patterson of Hallowell. OC 16 Apr 1823.
  Sarah, bapt. 6 March 1791; buried 18 Oct 1791.

WATSON, Major of Augusta.
John of Augusta. OC 21 Jan 1841.

WEAGER, Jacob of Williamsburgh, son of Everhart Weager (Wager). m. at
Montreal, Oct., 1784, Mary, dau of Lt. Henry Hare, U. E.
John of Williamsburgh. OC 16 Feb 1810.
Henry of Williamsburgh. OC 16 Feb 1811.
Elizabeth, m. John Van Allen of Williamsburgh. OC 4 July 1815.
Frederica, m. Michael Cook Jr. of Williamsburgh. OC 13 Nov 1818.
Mary Magdalen, m. Adam Noodle Jr. of Williamsburgh. OC 13 Nov 1818.
Nancy. OC 5 Nov 1818.
Maria, m. Isaac Van Allan of Matilda. OC 16 June 1834.
Jacob of Williamsburgh. OC 7 March 1833.
Margaret, m. William Casselman of Williamsburgh. OC 24 Nov 1832.

WEART, Andrew of Osnabruck.
Mary. OC 13 March 1807.
John of Osnabruck. OC 16 Feb 1811.
Rachel, m. Peter Van Allen of Matilda. OC 12 June 1834.

WEART, Conradt of Osnabruck.
Catharine, m. Freeborn Brayton of Elizabethtown. OC 22 Feb 1810.
Christeen. OC 13 Oct 1836. Thurlow.
Dorothy. OC 13 Oct 1836. Thurlow.
John C. of Osnabruck. OC 3 Apr 1834.
George of Osnabruck. OC 29 Sept 1824.
Peter of Osnabruck. OC 29 Sept 1824.

WEATHERHEAD, Samuel of Augusta, m. Magdalen dau of Abial Haskins, UE.
Margaret, bapt. 13 Feb 1789; m. Richard Arnold of Augusta; d. 10 May
1835. OC 13 March 1807.
John of Augusta, b. 1790; d. Brockville 24 Aug 1860. OC 19 May 1812; OC
15 Dec 1821.
James of Augusta, b. 8 Sept 1797. OC 28 Sept 1820.
Alexander of Elmsley. OC 18 July 1834.
William of Crosby. OC 18 July 1834.
Eleanor, m. Terrence Smyth of South Crosby. OC 5 Feb 1835.

WEAVER, Francis of Grantham, m. Elizabeth Alcombrack.
Peter of Grantham, m. Elizabeth Van Every. OC 6 Dec 1808.
Jeremiah of Grantham. OC 13 Feb 1816.
John of Grantham. OC 30 June 1819.
Catharine, m. Josiah Hunnewell of Stamford. OC 9 Feb 1820; 4 May 1836.
Baltus of Grantham. OC 17 May 1820.
Maria, m. Samuel Condon of Niagara. OC 5 Feb 1835; 24 Nov 1836.
Jacob of Grantham. OC 2 Feb 1832.
Elizabeth, m. Samuel Secord of Niagara. OC 6 May 1830.
Adam of Grantham. OC 6 May 1830.   [Cont'd]

WEAVER, Francis - Cont'd
   Hannah, m. Jacob Flanders. OC 7 May 1828.

WEAVER, John.
   Elizabeth, m. Jacob Anderson of Williamsburgh. OC 13 March 1807.

WEAVER, Peter.
   Jacob of Williamsburgh. OC 22 Dec 1842.
   John of Williamsburgh. OC 22 Dec 1842.
   Christy Ann, m. James Southworth of Williamsburgh. OC 22 Dec 1842.
   Simon of Williamsburgh. OC 22 Dec 1842.
   George of Williamsburgh. OC 22 Dec 1842.
   William of Williamsburgh. OC 22 Dec 1842.
   Frederick of Williamsburgh. OC 22 Dec 1842.
   Nancy, m. Christopher Hanes of Williamsburgh. OC 22 Dec 1842.
   Elizabeth, m. Henry Weager of Williamsburgh. OC 17 Aug 1842.

WEES, David.
   Ira of Ernestown. OC 22 Dec 1842.
   Ezra of Camden. OC 22 Dec 1842.
   David R. of Camden. OC 22 Dec 1842.
   Samuel of Richmond. OC 22 Dec 1842.
   Peter of Ernestown. OC 22 Dec 1842.
   Anne, m. James Williams of Camden. OC 22 Dec 1842.
   Margaret, m. William Close of Ernestown. OC 22 Dec 1842.
   Hannah, m. William Thompson of Camden. OC 22 Dec 1842.
   Mary, m. Arthur Yerex of Hallowell. OC 22 Dec 1842.

WEES, John of Ernestown. Pvt., 2d Batt. KRRNY. His widow Julian, OC 13
   November 1797.
   Catharine, m. ---- Sager. Land Board Certificate, 87/2 Ameliasburgh.
   David of Ernestown, m. Catharine Rogers, 16 July 1793. OC 26 June 1797.
   John of Ernestown, m. Jane Campbell, 7 Oct 1794. OC 22 June 1797.
   Francis of Ameliasburgh. OC 13 Nov 1797.
   Peter of Ernestown, m. Lana Banta. OC 31 May 1803.
   Nancy, m. Joseph Rogers of Murray. OC 22 Feb 1808.
   Jerany, m. John Rogers of Ernestown 17 Jan 1797. OC 22 Feb 1808.
   William of Ernestown, m. Mary Barnhart. OC 27 Oct 1801.
   Elizabeth. OC 14 March 1810.

WEES, John of Ameliasburgh.
   Julian (dau.) m. E. Harlow of Rawdon. OC 3 March 1836.
   Catharine, m. Francis McConnell of Rawdon. OC 3 March 1836.
   Olive, m. John Clark of Rawdon. OC 3 March 1836.
   Phoebe, m. Thomas Green of Rawdon. OC 3 March 1836.
   Margaret, m. Henry McMullen of Rawdon. OC 3 March 1836.
   William of Rawdon. OC 3 March 1836.
   Henry of Huntingdon. OC 14 March 1839.   [Cont'd]

WEES, John - Cont'd
Silas of Rawdon. OC 4 April 1839.

WELCH, Samuel, m. Mary.
Elizabeth. OC. 25 Feb 1806. Fredericksburgh.
John of Camden East. OC 30 Jan 1808.
Rachel, bapt. 12 Oct 1790; m. ---- Willoughby. See OC 6 Feb 1830. OC
16 Feb 1811.
David of Fredericksburgh, bapt. 25 Jan 1792. OC 22 June 1825.
Catharine, bapt. 13 Jan 1789.
Phoebe. OC 22 July 1824. OC 29 July 1844.

WELCH, Thomas of Charlotteville, m. Mary, dau of Thomas Mitchell of
Harford County, Maryland.
Francis Legh of Charlotteville, b. 12 March 1789, m. Elsie Fairchild,
1818; d. 14 Oct 1884. OC 3 April 1810.
Aquila Mitchell of Charlotteville. OC 19 Feb 1817.

WELLBANK, Thomas of Marysburgh.
John of Marysburgh. OC 2 Feb 1837.
David of Marysburgh. OC 28 Oct 1837.
Thomas of Marysburgh. OC 28 Oct 1837.
Margaret, m. Joseph Danbury of Marysburgh. OC 11 Feb 1836.
William of Marysburgh. OC 11 Feb 1836.

WEMPLE, Barnabas of Amherst Island, m. Catharine.
Catharine. OC 3 March 1809.
John of Amherst Island. OC 5 March 1810.
Mary, bapt. 12 June 1791; m. Duncan McDonald of Town of Kingston. OC
27 Feb 1818. OC 3 March 1831.
Margaret. OC 16 June 1819.
Michael of Amherst Island. OC 13 June 1833.
William of Amherst Island. OC 27 June 1833.
Rachel, bapt. 3 July 1803; m. ---- Howard of Amherst Island. OC 3
March 1831.

WERT, Andrew of Osnabruck.
John A. of Osnabruck.

WERT, John Jr. of Osnabruck.
Hannah, m. Jacob Eaman Jr. of Osnabruck. OC 18 March 1818.
Margaret, m. George Eaman of Osnabruck. OC 13 June 1818.
John J. of Osnabruck. OC 5 Nov 1818.
Dorothy. OC 5 Nov 1818.
Catharine, m. ---- Hill of Osnabruck. OC 2 May 1833.
Mary, m. John Morgan of Osnabruck. OC 1 July 1830.

WESTBROOK, Anthony of Grand River. [For a biographical detail concerning
   him, see The Ontario Register, v. 2, p. 7]
   Andrew of Delaware. OC 8 Oct 1796. The Traitor.
   Haggai of Burford, m. Jenney Vanderlip. OC 19 April 1816. (Oakland) OC
      9 May 1821.
   Elizabeth, m. (1) Benjamin Byecroft of Ancaster. OC 24 Feb 1801.
      m. (2) ---- Sage of Ancaster.
   Alexander of Oakland.
   Major John of Brantford, m. Elizabeth Gage.

WHEATON, John of Sandwich. Died at Town of Kingston 26 Feb 1814 ae 69.
   Margaret, m. John Science of Dover. OC 16 Apr 1811.
   Elizabeth, m. Thomas Thompson of Raleigh. OC 16 April 1811.
   Catharine, m. Israel Barrett of Raleigh. OC 16 April 1811.
   Rebecca. OC 7 Aug 1811.

WHEELER, Ephraim.
   Hepzibat, m. Caleb McWilliams of York. OC 23 June 1801.
   Peter of Niagara. OC 26 Oct 1802.

WHITE, Joseph.
   Lydia, m. ---- Livingston of Kitley. OC 23 Sept 1800.
   Sally, m. Darling Smith of Elizabethtown. OC 25 Feb 1809.
   John of Elizabethtown. OC 5 Sept 1833.

WHITE, Joseph Jr. Died in autumn of 1791.
   John of Elizabethtown.

WHITE, Joseph Sr.
   Abigail, m. Truman Stone of Elizabethtown. OC 5 Jan 1808.

WHITLEY, John of Elizabethtown.
   Mary, m. Benjamin Huntley of Bastard. OC 9 July 1811.
   Jenny, m. George Sheppard of Elizabethtown. OC 19 May 1812. OC 26
      March 1817.
   Phoebe, m. George Wright of Elizabethtown. OC 19 May 1812.
   Sally, m. Peter Seeley of Elizabethtown. OC 15 May 1835.
   Abigail, m. Joseph Jarvis of Elizabethtown. OC 18 May 1833.
   James of Elizabethtown. OC 17 March 1824.
   Samuel of Elizabethtown. OC 22 July 1824.

WHITNEY, Elijah.
   Elizabeth, m. ---- Downs of Elizabethtown. OC 23 Sept 1800.
   Clarinda, m. ---- Wooley of Elizabethtown. OC 11 Oct 1799.

WHITSELL, Andrew of Pelham.
   Elizabeth, m. Daniel Roy of Gainsborough. OC 5 March 1808.
   Andrew of Pelham. OC 3 April 1810.   [Cont'd]

WHITSELL, Andrew - Cont'd
David of Saltfleet. OC 9 Feb 1820.
Margaret, m. Joseph London of Saltfleet. OC 22 May 1820.
Aaron of Malahide. OC 8 March 1830.
Moses of Beverly. OC 21 Feb 1832.

WHITTLE, Richard of Colchester.
Thomas of Colchester. OC 23 Feb 1808.
John of Colchester. OC 23 Feb 1808.

WICKWIRE, Jonathan of Elizabethtown and Augusta.
Livius of Matilda. OC 28 Feb 1809.
Eunice. OC 5 March 1810. Matilda.
Elizabeth. OC 5 March 1810. Matilda.
Samuel of Matilda. OC 20 May 1817.
Jonathan of Matilda. OC 20 May 1817.
James of Matilda. OC 20 May 1817.

WICKWIRE, Livius of Elizabethtown, m. Margaret.
Jane, b. 6 June 1797; m. Gilbert Griffin of Yonge. OC 2 June 1819.
Mary, b. 6 Feb 1793. OC 2 June 1819.
Philip of Elizabethtown. OC 29 Dec 1819.
Livius, b. 20 March 1795.

WICKWIRE, Philip of St. Johns, L. C.
James of Augusta. OC 2 Dec 1806.
John of Augusta. OC 2 Dec 1806.

WILKINS, Robert.
Ann, m. Moses Carnahan of Adolphustown. OC 7 July 1796.
Sarah. OC 16 May 1797.
Robert Charles.

WILKINSON, Richard Norton of Cornwall. Lt., Indian Dept. m. (1) Amelia,
sister of Lt. Peter Everitt, KRRNY, 14 Dec 1773. m. (2) Helen (Eleanor),
dau of Alexander McDonell (Aberchalder), 10 May 1792. See 13/5 Haldimand.
Eliza, m. (1) Nathaniel Taylor Jr. of Town of Kingston 5 March 1798.
m. (2) Thomas Dickson of Queenston 17 Nov 1799. Died 5 Sept 1802.
Walter Butler of Town of Cornwall, m. Cecilia Bethune, 8 March 1803;
d. Sept., 1807. OC 31 May 1803.
Alexander of Cornwall, bapt. 2 Nov 1793. OC 21 Jan 1824.
Mary Johnston, bapt. 11 Nov 1795. See OC 21 Jan 1824.
Anne.
Helen, m. Alexander (Yates) McDonell of Cornwall. OC 1850.

WILLCOX, Elisha.
Asa of Colchester. OC 24 Nov 1807. OC 17 March 1824.

WILLCOX, Hassard. Capt. Delancey's Corps. Severely wounded at Battle of
Bennington and nine days later at New York. August, 1777.
    Sarah, m. Freeborn Watson of Ernestown. OC 16 Feb 1810.
    Hassard of Loughborough, m. Sarah Seelye. OC 16 Feb 1811.
    William of Ernestown. OC 22 July 1797.

WILLIAMS, Albert of Ernestown, m. Catharine.
    James of Camden East, bapt. 11 Feb 1788. OC 8 Feb 1808.
    Robert Lord of Camden East, bapt. 14 Nov 1789. OC 16 Feb 1810.
    Mary, bapt. 11 June 1793; m. William Airhart of Ernestown. OC 12 Nov
        1811.
    Jane, bapt. 3 Feb 1800; m. David Van Volkenburgh of Ernestown 5 Dec
        1814. OC 27 June 1821.
    Nancy, bapt. 9 July 1797; m. Landon Wurtz of Markham. OC 25 July 1821.
    Lucinda, bapt. 30 Sept 1810; m. ---- Hough of Ernestown. OC 5 Oct 1837.
    Grace, bapt. 4 Nov 1806; m. John McNutt of Camden E. OC 4 July 1833.
    George of Loughborough, bapt. 21 Dec 1791; m. Mary Freeman. OC 2 July
        1829.
    Elizabeth, bapt. 9 March 1795.
    Catharine, bapt. 13 March 1804; m. Jacob C. Peterson of Thurlow. OC 4
        August 1831.
    Sarah, bapt. 8 July 1810; m. Daniel Rose Switzer of Camden East. OC 28
        February 1835.
    Eleazer M., bapt. 30 Sept 1810.

WILLIAMS, David Sr. Loyal Rangers.
    David of Ernestown. OC 7 June 1800.
    Elias of Vaughan, m. Loyrennah (or Loyreah) Roys, 2 Jan 1798. OC 6
        June 1799.
    Cloe, m. ---- McDonell of Ernestown. OC 25 Aug 1801.
    Susanna, m. Joel Smith of Ernestown 4 Feb 1802. OC 23 March 1802.
    Sarah, m. John Gifford of Ernestown 8 April 1800. OC 31 May 1803.
    Mary, m. William Cotter of Ernestown 11 Dec 1788. Land Board Certifi-
        cate 5 May 1790.

WILLIAMS, Frederick of Niagara and Barton.
    Rebecca, stepdaughter ?, m. Alexander Markle of Flamborough East. OC
        13 July 1802.
    Mary, m. Thomas Smith of Flamborough West. OC 4 May 1802.
    [Catharine], m. Jacob Sipes [of Bertie and, later, Beverly] OC 18 Ap 1797.
    Phoebe, m. Hugh Reade of Barton. OC 2 May 1833.
    Mary, m. Jacob Meddaugh of Barton. OC 11 July 1833.
    George of Barton. OC 2 Oct 1834.
    Frederick of Barton. OC 19 Jan 1833.
    Jane. OC 2 Feb 1832.
    David of Barton. OC 5 Nov 1828.

WILLIAMS, John of Fredericksburgh.
    Sarah Ann, m. Daniel Ross of Ernestown. OC 24 March 1835.
    Jane. OC 24 March 1835.

WILLIAMS, John Sr. of Ernestown. (See below; one family or two?)
    Ann, m. Richard Morden of Sophiasburgh 28 Dec 1790. OC 21 June 1799.
    Joshua of Ernestown. OC 18 June 1800.
    Ruth, m. ---- Lent of Ernestown. OC 5 July 1800.
    Richard of Fredericksburgh. OC 16 Feb 1811.
    Margaret. OC 25 Feb 1812.
    Henry of Fredericksburgh. OC 14 Oct 1818.
    Daniel of Fredericksburgh. OC 15 March 1838.
    John of Fredericksburgh. OC 18 July 1839.
    Hannah, m. John Vanmear of Thurlow. OC 12 Nov 1840.
    Catharine. OC 4 Feb 1836.

WILLIAMS, John Sr. of Ernestown. Pvt., Loyal Rangers.
    James of Ernestown, m. Amy Perry 31 Dec 1789. Land Board Certificate, 8/5 Sidney.
    Joshua of Ernestown. OC 18 June 1800.
    John Jr., U.E., of Fredericksburgh.
    Catharine, m. ---- Ross. Land Board Certificate, 71/4 Ameliasburgh.
    Ann, m. Richard Morden of Sophiasburgh. OC 21 June 1799.
    Ruth, m. ---- Lent of Ernestown. OC 5 July 1800.
    Mary, m. ---- Rogers of Ernestown. OC 31 Aug 1801.

WILLIAMS, Moses of Lancaster, m. Sarah Curry. She m.(2) William Oney of Lancaster, 13 February 1813.
    Mary, m. John Dunn Jr. of Lancaster. OC 18 March 1808.
    James of Lancaster. OC 5 March 1810.
    Moses of Lancaster, bapt. 22 Feb 1790. OC 16 April 1811.
    John of Charlottenburgh, bapt. 19 Feb 1792. OC 23 Nov 1816.
    Walter of Lancaster, bapt. 21 Sept 1795. OC 23 Nov 1816.
    Ann Elizabeth, bapt. 12 Feb 1797; m. James Lennox of Kingston. OC 4 September 1834.
    Elsa, m. George Cline of Lancaster. OC 12 Nov 1827.
    William of Lancaster. OC 1 Feb 1826.
    Catharine. OC 2 Dec 1824.

WILLIAMS, Nathan.
    John Loveless of Yarmouth. OC 25 July 1821.

WILLIAMS, Samuel of Saltfleet.
    Joseph of Saltfleet. OC 20 May 1817.
    Elizabeth, m. Oliver Earls of Saltfleet. OC 3 June 1817.
    Samuel of Saltfleet. OC 3 March 1836.
    Phoebe, m. ---- Morrison of Saltfleet. OC 19 Jan 1833.
    Margaret. OC 3 May 1832.

WILLIAMS, Thomas of Raleigh.
  John of Raleigh. OC 20 Aug 1817.
  James of Raleigh. OC 2 May 1821.
  Maria, m. Francis Drake of Raleigh. OC 28 Oct 1835.
  Thomas of Harwich. OC 6 Nov 1829.
  Margaret, m. Mark Sterling of Tilbury. OC 1 April 1830.

WILLSON, Benjamin of Bertie. (33 & 37/4 Wainfleet). [For notes on his fami-
  ly, see The Ontario Register, 1:94]
  Ann [or Hannah] m. Mathias Haun Jr. of Bertie. OC 10 May 1797.
  Sarah, m. John Fanning of Chippawa, d. 19 Aug 1801. OC 25 Apr 1797.
  Crowell of Crowland, U. E. , d. Aug. , 1832 aged 70. [m. at Westfield,
    N. J. , Hannah, dau of Jacob Crane]
  [Capt. Gilman Willson of Dunwich, m. Hannah Sipes]
  [John of Bertie, m. Esther Haun dau of Mathias Haun Sr.]

WILLSON, Crowell of Willoughby. Buried in Crowland [Lyons Creek] 13 Aug
  1832 aged 70. Son of Benjamin Willson, U. E. See 6/16 Bertie.
  Margaret. OC 27 April 1811. [m. Simon Davis of Malahide]
  Ann, m. Jacob Cook of Crowland. OC 27 April 1811.
  Benjamin of Willoughby. OC 25 Feb 1812. [Removed to St. Thomas]
  Sarah, m. Isaac Ostrander of Malahide. OC 2 March 1816.
  Hannah, m. James McCredie of Malahide. OC 19 March 1823.
  John of Crowland. OC 26 June 1822; 18 August 1847. [Resided Howard]
  Stephen of Wainfleet. OC 24 Nov 1836. [m. Ann Priestman]
  Hiram of Crowland. OC 27 June 1833. [Later of Wainfleet]
  Crowell of Crowland. OC 22 July 1824. [m. Amy]
  Pamilla, m. John J. Rhodes of London. OC 28 Feb 1833.
  [Jacob of Wainfleet, b. 14 Apr 1796, d. 1825/26; m. Elizabeth Zest]
  [Eliza, dau of 2d mge, m. Hiram Powers of Malahide]
  [Charlotte, dau of 2d mge, m. Joseph Reavley of Port Robinson]

WILSON, Jacob of Charlotteville.
  Mary, m. John Smith of Townsend. OC 23 Feb 1809.
  Catharine, m. John Pettit of Windham. OC 16 Feb 1811.
  Philip of Windham. OC 16 Feb 1811.
  William of Charlotteville. OC 9 Nov 1825.
  Peter of Charlotteville. OC 17 Nov 1830.
  Charity, m. John McCall Jr. of Windham. OC 28 Oct 1835.

WILLSON, John Jr. of Lot 18, w. s. Yonge St. Son of John Willson of Mark-
  ham.
  John of York, m. Mary Cummer, 16 Jan 1809. OC 4 Dec 1806.
  Rebecca, m. David Smith of York 15 May 1804. OC 13 Jan 1807.
  Stillwell of York, m. Slatina Montgomery, 31 Dec 1816. OC 16 Dec 1815.
    [In 1861 they resided in Harwich; they are buried at Trinity Anglican
    Church Howard: Stillwill "born June 2, 1793 ae 69y 11m 21ds", Statira
    his wife d. Nov 20, 1887 ae 91 ys]

WILLSON, Irish John of Stamford.
  Thomas of Stamford, m. Abigail [Pettit]. OC 7 Oct 1796. See OC 25 Feb
    1797.
  Elizabeth, m. William Robison of Stamford, tanner. OC 9 July 1802.
  Andrew of Markham. OC 9 July 1802.
  Margaret, m. John McFarland of Niagara; d. Oct., 1809. Sketch of Mc-
    Farlan Family in "Empire", Sept 8, 1888. OC 31 May 1803.
  William of Stamford. OC 13 Sept 1803.
  James of Niagara. OC 1 Sept 1797.
  Robert of Stamford. OC 28 Sept 1820.
  McFarland of Woodhouse. OC 8 March 1826.
  Charles of Stamford. OC 8 Oct 1797.

WILLSON, John Sr. D. on 6 June 1804, Rebecca, wife of John Willson of
  Yonge St., in 63rd yr. of her age.
  William Ladner of Markham. OC 31 Jan 1809.
  John of Yonge St., U.E.

WILLSON, John of Thorold. Sgt., Butler's Rangers. [He and his family were
  at Niagara in 1783. The Ontario Register, 1: 199]
  Andrew of Thorold. OC 9 March 1803.
  Hugh of Thorold. OC 9 March 1803.
  Nancy, m. Aaron London of Toronto. OC 26 Jan 1820.
  Susannah, m. Peter Wolfe of Thorold. OC 16 May 1797.
  Margaret, m. ---- Smith of Crowland. OC 5 Jan 1798.

WILSON, Joseph of Windham.
  John of Crowland. OC 23 April 1805.
  Joseph of Windham. OC 16 Aug 1810.
  Mary, m. Mitchell Cairo of Windham. OC 26 March 1811. Named as
    Michael Carrow of Windham, OC 28 Oct 1835.
  Elizabeth, m. John Van Atter of Windham. OC 25 Feb 1812.
  Uzal of Windham. OC 27 March 1813.
  Sarah, m. Henry Cline of Middleton. OC 30 May 1835.
  James H. of Townsend. OC 28 Oct 1835.
  Joel of Windham. OC 3 April 1834.
  Andrew T. of Windham. OC 5 Feb 1835.

WILSON, Samuel of South Gower.
  James of South Gower. OC 28 Sept 1820.

WILTSE, Benoni Jr. of Yonge, m. Mary, dau of Joseph Slack, U.E. He was
  born 25 Dec 1777, son of Benoni Wiltse Sr., U.E.
  Charlotte, b. 2 Nov 1800, m. Abner Smith of Yonge, 1817; d. in Michigan
    25 July 1896. OC 2 June 1831.
  Lucy, b. 12 July 1802; m. Cornel Hunt of Yonge. OC 15 May 1832.
  Margaret, b. 12 Dec 1804; m. Henry Coleman of Elizabethtown; d. 5 April
    1863. OC 23 June 1824. m. 27 Jan 1821.   [Cont'd]

WILTSE, Benoni Jr. - Cont'd

    Sarah, b. 4 June 1806; m. Joseph Danby of Lansdown. OC 2 June 1831.

    Clarissa, m. Abner M. Case of Yonge. OC 2 June 1831.

    Joseph, 2nd of Yonge, b. 4 July 1811; m. Ann Blanchard. OC 19 June 1832.

    James Jr. of Yonge, b. 17 July 1813; m. Electa Wiltse. OC 2 June 1831.

    Benoni of Yonge, b. 9 Aug 1815; m. Mary Tetson. OC 16 May 1839.

    Experience   Speedy. OC 7 March 1833. m. Abr. Wing.

    Laura, m. Sidney Smith.

WILTSE, Benoni Sr. of Yonge. He was b. 2 July 1758 s. of Jeremiah Wiltse of Hopewell, Dutchess Co., N.Y. & his second wife, Mary Smith. He m. 22 May 1777, Rachel Marks (b. 1 Nov 1759, d. 15 Oct 1829). He d. 24 Aug 1824.

    Benoni of Yonge, b. 25 Dec 1777; m. Mary Slack   Land Board Certificate, 11/8 Yonge.

    Joseph of Yonge, b. 17 Apr 1782; m. Drusilla Howland, 13 Feb 1803. OC 15 March 1803.

    Susannah, b. 18 Apr 1782. OC 30 July 1799.

    Elizabeth, b. 4 Nov 1784; m. John Connolly of Yonge. OC 15 March 1803.

    James of Augusta, b. 6 Oct 1786; m. Christine Coleman; d. 1870. OC 30 June 1812.

    Rachel, b. 18 March 1789. OC 12 Nov 1811.

    Comfort Martin of Yonge, b. 28 Dec 1790; m. Hester Coleman; d. 1870. OC 30 June 1812.

    Mary, b. 28 Dec 1790; m. Daniel Brown of Yonge. OC 9 July 1811.

    Hannah, b. 10 Aug 1792; m. Samuel Kelsay of Yonge. OC 11 Nov 1815.

    Sarah, b. 19 Nov 1794; m. William Howland of Yonge. OC 30 June 1812.

    William, b. 29 Aug 1797; m. Sarah Phillips. OC 19 May 1819.

    Philip M. of Yonge, b. 30 Sept 1799; m. Rachel Dunham. OC 12 Dec 1821.

WILTSE, James of Yonge. Soldier, Loyal Rangers, m. Jane, dau of Thomas Lake, U.E. He was b. 10 March 1764, s. of Jeremiah Wiltse of Hopewell, Dutchess Co., N.Y., & his second wife, Mary Smith.

    Cornelius of Yonge, m. Susan Sixbee. OC 9 July 1811.

    Leonard of Yonge, m. Hannah Herrington. OC 18 March 1818.

    Henry of Yonge, m. Elizabeth Slack. OC 18 March 1818.

    Truman of Yonge, m. Eleanor Smith. OC 19 May 1819. OC 19 Oct 1837.

    Elizabeth, m. Eri Hayes of Elizabethtown 17 Dec 1829. OC 19 June 1832.

    Pamelia, m. Abner Case. OC 19 June 1832.

    Sarah, m. Joseph Bingham of Yonge. OC 6 Jan 1831.

    Samuel of Yonge, m. Rosana Baker, 20 Jan 1829. OC 11 May 1825.

    William of Yonge, m. Margaret Slack. OC 11 May 1825.

    Mercy, m. Daniel Derbyshire of Yonge. OC 11 May 1825.

    Mary, m. John Wiltse of Yonge. OC 28 April 1812.

WILTSE, John of Yonge. He was b. 31 March 1748, s. of Jeremiah Wiltse of Hopewell, Dutchess Co., N.Y., & his first wife, Mary Cornell. He m. (1) Anna, dau of David Cary, 1771. She d. 1788. m. (2) Mary Catharine Conley,

29 Nov 1789. She was born 11 Apr 1773, d. 3 July 1803. He d. 26 July 1801.
Ruth, b. 6 Apr 1772; m. Thomas How of Yonge. OC 22 Dec 1797.
Solomon, b. 27 Oct 1773; m. Elizabeth Dennis. OC 11 July 1798.
Cornelius, b. 17 Oct 1775; m. Patience Mott. OC 11 July 1798.
John, b. 1 Dec 1778; m. Susannah Wiltse.
Rhoda, b. 15 Oct 1780; m. James Brown. OC 30 July 1799.
Sarah, b. 9 June 1783; m. Oliver Brown of Elizabethtown; d. 20 Feb 1841.
  OC 9 July 1811.
Mary, b. 7 Sept 1785; m. Wing Walker of Augusta. OC 5 Jan 1808.
Anna, b. 11 Aug 1788; m. Lemuel Cornell of Kitley. OC 20 Oct 1836.
Elizabeth, b. 3 Oct 1790; m. Richard Jacqua of Yonge. OC 28 Aug 1810.
Catharine, b. 18 July 1792; m. Samuel Slack ?
Phoebe, b. 21 June 1794; m. Thomas How of Yonge. OC 20 May 1817.
Abigail, b. 20 Sept 1796.
Henry of Bastard, b. 7 Feb 1799; m. Hannah Knapp. OC 1 May 1834.
Matilda, b. 9 Oct 1801; m. John Robinson of Yonge. OC 11 May 1825.

WINDECKER, Henry. [Butler's Rangers. He and his family were at Niagara
in 1783. The Ontario Register, v.1, p.199]
  Mary, m. Frederick Anger Jr. of Bertie. OC 26 May 1796; 4 July 1796.
  Elizabeth, m. Daniel Young of Barton. OC 8 July 1796.
  Catharine, m. Peter Bower of Niagara. OC 5 March 1811.
  Barbara, m. J. Fleming of Aldborough. OC 9 Feb 1820.
  George of Camden W., m. Sarah Sipes. OC 11 May 1797.
  Margaret, m. John Kitson. Land Board Certificate.

WING, Gershom of Elizabethtown. He was b. 2 Dec 1744 in Dutchess Co.,
N.Y. s. of Jedediah Wing. His wife, Rebecca, dau of Daniel & Hannah
Chase; m. 12 Sept 1764.
  Hannah, m. Jesse Lamb of Elizabethtown; d. 5 Nov 1852. OC 29 July 1800.
  Ruth, m. ---- Closson. OC 26 May 1801.
  Amy, m. Edmund Mott of Elizabethtown. OC 13 Nov 1797.
  Elizabeth, m. Benjamin Yates of Yonge. OC 5 Feb 1807.
  Daniel of Yonge. OC 5 Feb 1807.
  Thirza, m. Isaac Booth of Elizabethtown. OC 21 March 1809.
  Deborah. OC 9 July 1811.
  Anna, m. Isaac Aikin of Yonge. OC 9 July 1811.
  Matthew.
  Jedediah.

WINTER, Henry.
  Elizabeth, m. Peter Ruport of Osnabruck. OC 13 March 1807.

WINTER, Peter of Osnabruck and Bertie, & Etobicoke & Nelson.
  Nicholas of Bertie, m. Sarah Winter 24 Aug 1819. OC 5 Oct 1818.
  Solomon of Etobicoke. OC 15 Oct 1819.
  Henry of Bertie. OC 22 Jan 1823.
  John of Dumfries. OC 14 May 1840.   [Cont'd]

WINTER, Peter - Cont'd
  Mary Ann, m. Jacob M. Crane of Yarmouth. OC 27 Sept 1838.
  George of Nelson. OC 24 Nov 1836.

WINTERMUTE, Abraham of Willoughby.
  William of Willoughby. OC 20 Feb 1840.
  Mary Catharine, m. Calvin Goodenough of Willoughby. OC 4 May 1836.
  Abraham of Willoughby. OC 4 July 1833.
  Anna, m. Ezra Bailey of Willoughby. OC 7 Aug 1834.

WINTERMUTE, Benjamin of Bertie, m. Hannah [dau of John Smith Sr.]
  Mary. OC 11 Nov 1815.
  Anna. OC 22 July 1818.
  John of Bertie. OC 14 Nov 1818.
  Philip of Bertie. OC 23 Nov 1816.
  Abraham of Bertie, bapt. 12 April 1793. OC 23 Nov 1816.
  Margaret, m. [Dr. Josiah] Trowbridge of Bertie. OC 6 Sept 1832.
  Eleanor, m. John Warren of Southwold. OC 6 Sept 1832.
  Julia. OC 6 Sept 1832. [m. Henry B. Warren]

WINTERMUTE, John of Humberstone. Butler's Rangers.
  Margaret. OC 21 Nov 1799.
  Mary, m. Moses Doan of Humberstone. OC 23 May 1809.
  Eve, m. Job Strawn of Humberstone. OC 25 Feb 1812.
  Catharine, m. Hiram Strawn of Yarmouth. OC 5 May 1831.
  [Elizabeth, m. ---- Dennis]
  [Hannah, m. ---- Weaver]
  [John of Humberstone]

WINTERMUTE, Peter of Bertie, m. Eve [Sipes]. Died 1 Dec 1838 ae 87.
  Hannah, m. Edmund Warren of Bertie. OC 23 Feb 1808.
  Jacob of Bertie. OC 8 Dec 1808.
  Philip of Bertie. OC 12 Feb 1811.
  James of Bertie, b. 17 March 1782; d. 25 June 1858. OC 12 Feb 1811.
  Elizabeth, m. Edmund Raymond of Bertie 23 Feb 1800. OC 12 Feb 1811.
  William of Bertie. OC 20 May 1817.
  Mary. OC 8 Sept 1819. [m. George David Nettle of Bertie]
  John of Bertie. OC 27 June 1833.
  Peter, bapt. 12 April 1793.
  Alexander of Bertie. OC 20 Oct 1832.
  Sarah. OC 23 June 1824. [m. William Anthony]

WINTERMUTE, Philip [d. 1779. For an account of his family see The Ontario
  Register, v.1, pp. 24-40]
  Elizabeth, m. Joseph Petrie of Haldimand County. OC 16 April 1811.

WOOD, Benjamin of Charlottenburgh, m. Agnes Benedict.
  Jennet, m. John Snyder of Lancaster. OC 3 March 1809.   [Cont'd]

WOOD, Benjamin - Cont'd
 Roger of Charlottenburgh, bapt. 31 Jan 1790. OC 7 Aug 1811.
 Mary, m. Duncan Ferguson of Cornwall 20 March 1815. OC 20 May 1817.
 David of Cornwall, carpenter. OC 4 Nov 1818.
 Hiram of Cornwall, bapt. 26 Sept 1795. OC 5 Feb 1823.
 Jonah of Cornwall, b. 20 May 1804. OC 28 Nov 1826.
 Sarah, m. David See of Lancaster. OC 24 Oct 1839.

WOOD, George of Cornwall, surgeon.
 Mary, m. Benjamin French of Cornwall. OC 23 Nov 1816.
 Guy C. of Town of Cornwall, m. Margaret Munro, 29 July 1822. OC 23
   November 1816.
 Ann, m. (1) Andrew McGill of Montreal 6 Oct 1803. m. (2) Rev. Dr. John
   Strachan of Town of York 9 May 1807. OC 19 Feb 1817.
 Frances, m. John Robert Small of Town of Cornwall. OC 10 June 1818;
   OC 31 March 1845.

WOOD, John of Cornwall and Osnabruck.
 William of Cornwall. OC 4 July 1815.
 Ann, m. Rudolph Papst of Osnabruck. OC 11 Oct 1838.
 Benjamin Paul of Cornwall. OC 11 Oct 1838.
 Robert of Cornwall. OC 19 Dec 1833.
 Sarah. OC 25 Jan 1831.
 John of Cornwall. OC 27 March 1829.
 Isabella, m. Peter Papst of Cornwall. OC 27 March 1829.

WOOD, Jonas Jr. of Williamsburgh and Uxbridge.
 Sarah, m. Hugh Conliff of Williamsburgh. OC 16 April 1818.
 Charity, m. Moses Mitchell of Williamsburgh. OC 18 March 1818.
 Jonas of Williamsburgh. OC 2 Sept 1818.
 Stephen of Cornwall. OC 16 June 1819.
 Samuel of Markham. OC 19 Dec 1833.
 Nathaniel of Markham. OC 2 Jan 1834.
 Rebecca, m. Martin Grant of Uxbridge. OC 24 Nov 1832.
 Moses of Hope. OC 31 March 1824.

WOOD, Jonas Sr.
 Nathan of York and Cornwall, d. Cornwall, 19 Feb 1869 aged 99. OC 8
   March 1803.
 William of Cornwall, U. E., d. Cornwall, 11 Aug 1850 ae 88.
 Stephen of Cornwall, d. 2 May 1860 ae 81.
 Benjamin of Charlottenburgh, U. E.
 John of Cornwall, U. E.
 Jonas Jr. of Williamsburgh and Uxbridge, U. E.
 Roger of Osnabruck, U. E.
 Sarah, m. (1) Robert Johnson of Cornwall. m. (2) Abel Butler of Charlot-
   tenburgh 27 Jan 1800. OC 24 Feb 1820.

WOOD, Nathan of Cornwall. See OC Martha Berder, 3 Feb 1847. Wm Wood,
20 Sept 1844.
    Adam J. of Cornwall. OC 15 March 1838.
    Stephen of Cornwall. OC 26 March 1840.
    Sarah, m. John Selimser of Cornwall. OC 11 Feb 1836.
    Elizabeth, m. Tunis Hart of Cornwall. OC 18 Feb 1836.
    Mary. OC 18 Feb 1836.
    Leonard of Cornwall. OC 17 March 1836.
    Benjamin of Cornwall. OC 2 May 1836.

WOOD, Roger of Osnabruck.
    Martha, m. ---- Markle of Osnabruck. OC 15 Feb 1838.
    William of Osnabruck. OC 22 Sept 1836.
    Sarah, m. Joseph Adams of Osnabruck. OC 22 Sept 1836.
    John R. of Osnabruck, b. 8 May 1808. OC 16 Feb 1837.
    Margaret, m. John T. Papst. OC 30 March 1837.

WOOD, Thomas of Elizabethtown.
    Lorana, m. Benjamin George of Elizabethtown. OC 28 July 1836.

WOOD, William of Cornwall, m. Sarah Dickson. (Note on back of card:
Hannah DeWitt, widow of Wm. Wood of Cornwall and sister of Jacob DeWitt,
M. P., Montreal, died at Montreal on 12 March 1857, aet. 80 ys 4 ms.)
    Sarah, bapt. 29 May 1796. OC 4 Nov 1818.
    Eleanor. OC 14 July 1819.
    Margaret. OC 14 July 1819.
    Elizabeth. OC 5 Feb 1823.
    Jonas, bapt. 8 Nov 1789.
    Mary Jane, bapt. 1 April 1792. OC 1 Nov 1832.
    Ann. OC 1 Nov 1832.
    John of Cornwall. OC 17 Feb 1825.

WOODCOCK, Abraham of Fredericksburgh.
    Allada, bapt. 29 May 1792(?), m. Peter Woodcock of Fredericksburgh.
        OC 16 Feb 1810.
    Mary, m. William Wood of Loughborough. OC 22 July 1836.
    David of Portland. OC 4 July 1833.
    Abraham of Portland. OC 19 Dec 1833.
    Christopher of Loughborough. OC 3 April 1834.
    Hannah. OC 3 April 1834.
    Jacob of Loughborough (Whitchurch Tp.), b. 1814, m. Jane Hyland; died
        1896. OC 3 April 1834.
    Elizabeth, m. James Park of Sheffield. OC 3 April 1834.
    John of Sheffield. OC 1 May 1834.
    Nicholas of Portland. OC 10 Jan 1833.
    Paul of Portland. OC 5 April 1832.

WOODLEY, George of Grantham and Burford, m. (1) Christina ----. m. (2)
Catharine Bowman, 12 Feb 1797.
Hannah, m. Jonas Olmstead of Burford. OC 21 Oct 1806.
Mary, m. Israel Olmstead of Townsend. OC 16 Jan 1816.
Mathias of Burford, bapt. 13 Jan 1794, m. Margaret Malcolm. OC 19 Apr
1816. See OC 10 Oct 1834.
John, bapt. 17 March 1795.
John of Burford, bapt. 10 April 1798. OC 23 Nov 1816.
George of Burford. OC 28 June 1820.
Elizabeth, m. Theron Averill of Grand River. OC 25 July 1821.
Anthony, bapt. 6 Sept 1801.
David of Oakland. OC 21 May 1840.

WOOLLEY, John.
Litey (dau.), m. ---- Freel of Yonge. OC 22 Dec 1801.

WOOLMAN, Francis.
Hannah, m. Lawson Warren of Williamsburgh. OC 2 May 1836.

WRAGG, John.
Anne, m. ---- Plate of Elizabethtown. OC 24 Feb 1801.

WRIGHT, Amos of Cornwall and Augusta.
Abraham of Markham. OC 29 Dec 1819.
William of Vaughan, m. (1) Susannah Munshaw, 22 Aug 1815. m. (2) Sophia
Cleveland of Gwillimbury, spinster, 22 May 1817. OC 15 Oct 1823.

WRIGHT, Asahel of Elizabethtown, b. 18 Aug 1754 at Mansfield, Conn., s.
of Ebenezer and Mercy (Leach) Wright, m. 1788 Eva dau Joseph Hayes (or
Haines?).
Joseph of Augusta, b. at Cornwall, 10 May 1789; m. (1) Elizabeth Bissell
in 1809. D. 1819. m. (2) Mrs. Elizabeth McNish, 20 Sept 1820; died 9
Nov 1876. OC 22 Oct 1817.
John of Augusta, b. 10 May 1790; m. Mrs. Mary McLean; d. March 1867.
OC 22 October 1817.
Abel of Augusta, b. 8 May 1791; m. Sarah Landon; d. near Perth, 1872.
OC 18 August 1819.
Elizabeth, b. 7 Dec 1792; m. Samuel Brown.
Asahel of Augusta, b. 27 May 1794; m. (1) Eleanor Carpenter 13 Feb 1802;
m. (2) Mrs. Elizabeth Hurd. OC 2 June 1819.
Amos of Augusta, b. 23 Dec 1797; m. Minerva Wing; d. 1875. OC 2 June 1819
Catharine, b. 6 Dec 1800; m. William Wood of Augusta. OC 16 June 1834.
Michael of Augusta, b. 1 Jan 1796; m. Susanna Wright, 3 Nov 1825. OC 16
June 1818.

WRIGHT, Asahel.
Mark of Elmsley, m. (1) Mary McNish, 14 July 1825. m. (2) Amy Holden,
7 Aug 1839. OC 24 October 1831.

WRIGHT, Ebenezer.
Rebecca, m. Henry Mace of Cornwall. OC 7 Dec 1802.

WRIGHT, Edward of Town of York.
Margaret, m. Michael Mealley of Town of York. OC 22 July 1818.
Jane, m. William Hill of Town of York 22 Dec 1816. OC 22 July 1818.
Edward of Town of York, m. Sophia Gilbert, 9 March 1817. OC 22 July 1818.
George of York. OC 16 April 1823.
Simcoe of Ernestown. OC 3 April 1834.
Elizabeth, m. Aaron Lick of Nelson. OC 11 May 1825.

WRIGHT, Gabriel.
Gabriel of Bayham. OC 13 July 1841.

WRIGHT, Jesse.
Clarecy, m. Jeremiah Tuttle of Matilda. OC 13 March 1807.

WRIGHT, Mary [widow] of Kingston, m. Abraham Peterson of Hallowell.
Hannah, m. Arthur Yeomans of Kingston. OC 27 Oct 1801.
Mary, m. Henry Bartley of Hallowell. OC 5 March 1808.
Samuel of Hallowell. OC 23 Feb 1809.

WRIGHT, Robert of Sidney.
Charity, m. Caleb Benedict of Thurlow. OC 16 Feb 1811.
Mary, m. (1) Joseph Sarles of Sidney. OC 13 Feb 1816. m. (2) James Brooks.
John of Sidney. OC 13 Feb 1816.
Eleanor, m. ---- Althouse of Sidney. OC 3 March 1836.
Thomas of Sidney. OC 27 June 1833.
Daniel of Thurlow. OC 7 June 1826.

WRIGHT, Samuel Sr. of Elizabethtown.
Samuel of Elizabethtown. OC 27 Dec 1808. OC 22 Sept 1812.
Timothy of Elizabethtown. OC 22 Jan 1811.
Sarah, m. Robert Davidson of Elizabethtown. OC 11 Dec 1810.
Lois, m. Samuel Heck of Augusta. OC 7 Nov 1797.

WRIGHT, Samuel.
Ruth, m. James Cameron of Ernestown. OC 8 Feb 1808.

WRIGHT, Wait of Fredericksburgh and Hope.
Daniel of Kingston. OC 12 Nov 1811.
Margaret, m. John Batter of Hope. OC 17 Feb 1816.
Wait of Hope. OC 17 Feb 1816.
Electa, m. Daniel Hudgins of Darlington. OC 28 July 1819.
Rachel, m. William Hudgins of Marysburgh. OC 26 July 1820.
John J. of Clarke. OC 19 Feb 1823.   [Cont'd]

WRIGHT, Wait - Cont'd
   Simeon of Darlington. OC 25 June 1823.
   Amos of Clarke. OC 2 May 1827.
   Joshua of Darlington. OC 1 Aug 1827.
   Smith of Darlington. OC 1 Aug 1827.
   James of Darlington. OC 12 Nov 1827.
   Hannah. OC 12 Nov 1827.
   Pamelia. OC 12 Nov 1827.

WRIGHT, William B. of Elizabethtown.
   Rosetta, m. Asa Closson of Augusta. OC 20 May 1817.
   Hester Slack. OC 18 March 1818. Yonge.
   Minerva, m. Charles Dudley of Elizabethtown. OC 5 Nov 1835.
   Charles W. of Elizabethtown. OC 26 Oct 1825.
   William Henry of Elizabethtown. OC 2 March 1825.

WRIGHT, William of Elizabethtown.
   Hannah, m. Joseph Slack of Elizabethtown. OC 13 June 1818.
   Israel H. of Yonge. OC 6 Sept 1832.

WRONG, John of Gainsborough.
   John of Gainsborough. OC 20 Nov 1810.
   Gilbert of Malahide. OC 16 May 1819.

WYCOFF, Peter of Niagara.
   Peter of Woodhouse. OC 23 Nov 1816.
   Margaret, m. Isaac Gilbert of Woodhouse. OC 20 May 1817.

Y

YATES, John.
   Maria, m. ---- Rose. OC 5 Nov 1799.
   Elizabeth, m. ---- Ferguson of Elizabethtown.
   Philip of Bathurst Dist. OC 28 Sept 1820.

YEOMANS, Arthur.
   Arthur of Marysburgh. OC 30 Aug 1797.
   James of Sidney. OC 31 May 1808.
   Jemima, m. William Yourex of Hallowell. OC 17 Nov 1797.

YOUNG, Abraham of Haldimand Co.
   Catharine, m. Henry Nelles of Grand River. OC 5 May 1819.
   Joseph of Woodhouse. OC 9 Aug 1820.
   Rachel, m. Henry Young of Barton. OC 21 March 1821.
   Henry of Grand River. OC 12 April 1838.
   Ezekiel of Grand River. OC 17 Nov 1836.
   Daniel of Grand River. OC 17 Nov 1836.   [Cont'd]

YOUNG, Abraham - Cont'd
  Warner of London. OC 3 Dec 1835.
  Abraham of Indian Lands. OC 11 Feb 1836.
  William of Barton. OC 19 Dec 1833.
  John of Flamborough West. OC 6 Dec 1832.

YOUNG, Daniel of Barton. Sgt., Butler's Rangers.
  Daniel of Barton. OC 8 July 1806.
  Catherine, m. James Wintermute of Bertie. OC 12 Feb 1811.
  Adam of Barton. OC 23 Nov 1816.
  Dorothy, m. Jacob Wintermute of Bertie. OC 8 Sept 1819.
  Henry of Barton. OC 22 May 1820.
  Priscilla, m. Jacob Sipes of Glanford. OC 17 Sept 1823.
  James of Barton. OC 24 March 1835.
  John of Barton. OC 28 June 1832.
  Elizabeth, m. Simon Bradt of Barton. OC 9 Nov 1825.
  Frederick of Ancaster. OC 11 May 1825.
  George of Ancaster. OC 11 May 1825.

YOUNG, Daniel of Hallowell, m. Dorcas, dau of David Conger, 2 March 1790
  Rachel, bapt. 26 Feb 1799; m. David Stinson of Hallowell, 29 March 1814.
    OC 13 Feb 1816.
  Guy H. of Hallowell, bapt. 6 Sept 1791; m. Susan Clark, 16 March 1817.
    OC 13 Feb 1816.
  David of Hallowell, bapt. 26 Feb 1794. OC 13 Feb 1816.
  William of Hallowell, bapt. 17 Feb 1796. OC 18 March 1818.
  Rosannah, m. William Emerson of Thurlow. OC 3 Dec 1835.
  Dorcas, m. James Williams of Hallowell. OC 1 Aug 1833.
  Daniel of Hallowell. OC 5 Sept 1833.
  John of Hallowell. OC 1 May 1834.
  Glorannah, m. C. Williams of Hallowell. OC 7 May 1828.

YOUNG, Henry of Fredericksburgh, m. Eleanor.
  Jacob of Fredericksburgh. OC 25 May 1808.
  Peter of Fredericksburgh. OC 20 Feb 1809.
  Christopher of Fredericksburgh, bapt. 12 Jan 1789. OC 16 Feb 1810.
  John of Hallowell. OC 20 May 1817.
  Gasper of Fredericksburgh. OC 12 July 1820.
  George of Ernestown. OC 19 Aug 1833.
  Andrew of Fredericksburgh. OC 28 Feb 1829.
  Tobias of Fredericksburgh. OC 20 July 1825.

YOUNG, Henry of Sophiasburgh and Hallowell. Lt., RRNY. OC 16 Oct 1822.
  Sarah, m. ---- Miller of Sophiasburgh. OC 20 June 1797.
  Hannah, m. ---- Cole of Adolphustown. OC 26 July 1820.
  Richard of Hallowell. OC 10 Aug 1837.
  Gloranna, m. James Osburn of Sophiasburgh. OC 23 Nov 1837.
  Catharine, m. ---- Dyer. OC 25 Aug 1836.   [Cont'd]

YOUNG, Henry - Cont'd
William of Niagara. OC 27 July 1837.

YOUNG, Henry of Ancaster and Grand River, m. Phoebe Van Every.
Mary, m. John Nellis of Haldimand Co. OC 20 Nov 1810.
Peter of Grand River, bapt. 6 March 1794. OC 27 Jan 1816.
David of Ancaster, blacksmith. OC 23 Nov 1816.
John H. of London. OC 2 April 1828.
William of Thorold. OC 3 Dec 1828.

YOUNG, Jacob. Sgt., Rogers' Rangers.
dau., m. Mathew Lymburner of Caistor. OC 18 April 1797.

YOUNG, James of Lancaster, m. Hannah Snyder.
John. OC 3 March 1801.
James. OC 3 March 1801.
Thomas of Lancaster. OC 24 Aug 1802.
Hannah, m. ---- Snyder of Lancaster 2 Sept 1806. OC 24 Aug 1801.
Jane, bapt. 25 June 1788; m. Ebenezer Blair of Lancaster. OC 20 Nov 1809.
Elizabeth, OC 17 March 1812. m. Henry Runnions of Cornwall. OC 19
December 1833.
David of Whitby, bapt. 3 Oct 1793. OC 18 March 1818.
Anthony of Scarborough. OC 29 April 1818.
William, bapt. 6 June 1790.

YOUNG, John of Grand River. Lt., Indian Dept.
John of Haldimand Co. OC 18 April 1797.
Elizabeth, m. Warner Nelles of Walpole. OC 7 July 1796.
Joseph of Grand River. OC 30 July 1806.
Catharine, m. William Facer of Grantham. OC 2 June 1819.
Ann, m. Cornelius Reid of Grantham. OC 2 June 1819.

YOUNG, John. Sgt., Butler's Rangers.
Mary, m. James Cudney of Niagara, 15 Nov 1807. OC 8 Feb 1808.

YOUNG, John Peter Jr., of Grantham and Louth.
Peter of Louth. OC 30 May 1821.
Jeremiah of Louth. OC 30 May 1821.
John of Louth. OC 3 Apr 1822.
Aaron of Nelson. OC 21 March 1833.
Mary, m. Alpheus Peer of Nelson. OC 2 May 1833.
Henry of Nassagewaya. OC 2 May 1827.
James of Nelson. OC 11 May 1825.

YOUNGS, Peter of Fredericksburgh and Marysburgh.
Ichabod of Thurlow. OC 4 Sept 1834.
Francis of Thurlow. OC 4 Sept 1834.
Oliver of Marysburgh. OC 4 Sept 1834.

YOUNG, Philip of Thorold and Middleton.
   David of Thorold. OC 30 June 1819.
   Peter of Thorold. OC 30 June 1819.
   Catharine of Grantham. OC 28 June 1820.
   John of Zorra. OC 7 Dec 1825.
   Philip of Thorold. OC 7 Dec 1825.
   Jeremiah of Ancaster, wheelwright. OC 16 June 1834.
   Jane, m. Gideon Inglis of Dumfries. OC 1 April 1840.
   Alexander of Bertie. OC 13 Jan 1831.
   William of Zorra. OC 3 Jan 1827.
   Dorothy, of Grantham. OC 29 Sept 1824.

YOUNG, Robert of Roxborough and Charlottenburgh, m. Flora McDonell.
   Elizabeth, of Charlottenburgh. OC 31 Oct 1809.
   Allan of Charlottenburgh, bapt. 28 Feb 1792. OC 23 Nov 1816.
   William of Charlottenburgh, bapt. 28 Nov 1793. OC 23 Nov 1816.
   George of Charlottenburgh, bapt. 20 Jan 1796. OC 20 May 1817.
   Christy. OC 29 Sept 1824.
   Robert of Charlottenburgh. OC 29 Sept 1824.

YOUNG, Stephen of Fredericksburgh, m. Anne.
   Daniel of Fredericksburgh, bapt. 1 Nov 1789. OC 25 July 1809.
   Richard of Fredericksburgh. OC 25 July 1809.
   John of Fredericksburgh, bapt. 24 July 1791. OC 22 Sept 1819.
   George of Grantham. OC 15 June 1820.
   Elizabeth, bapt. 16 Jan 1803; m. ---- Hart of Fredericksburgh. OC 18
      February 1824.
   Stephen of Fredericksburgh, bapt. 5 Apr 1801. OC 23 June 1836.
   David of Fredericksburgh, bapt. 15 Nov 1807. OC 4 April 1833.
   Peter S. of Fredericksburgh, bapt. 7 Apr 1805. OC 13 June 1833.
   William D. of Fredericksburgh, bapt. 25 June 1797.   OC 27 June 1833.
   Elijah of Fredericksburgh. OC 7 May 1828.

YOUNGLOVE, Ezekiel of Thorold.
   Margaret, m. John McIlwain of Thorold. OC 9 July 1802.
   Mary, m. John Bowman of Thorold. OC 9 March 1803.
   Dorcas, m. Jacob Bowman of Thorold. OC 10 March 1804.
   John of Thorold. OC 11 Dec 1810.
   David of Scarborough. OC 30 Nov 1815.

YOUREX, John of Kingston.
   William L. of Tyendinaga. OC 28 July 1836.
   Elijah of Kingston. OC 4 Aug 1836.
   Anna, m. ---- Brundage of Kingston. OC 2 Jan 1834.
   John of Kingston. OC 2 Jan 1834.
   Charity. OC 2 Jan 1834.
   Catharine, m. Samuel Merrill of Hallowell. OC 1 July 1830.

ZERON, Christopher. Pvt., 1st Batt., K.R.R.N.Y.
  Dorothy, m. Eli Moody of Osnabruck. OC 25 Feb 1806.
  John of Osnabruck. Land Board Certificate, 8/4 Osnabruck.
  David of Osnabruck. Land Board Certificate, 8/4 Osnabruck.

ZUFELT, Henry of Hallowell, m. Elizabeth Young.
  Sarah, m. James Ryckman of Ernestown. OC 16 Feb 1811.
  Eleanor, m. John Van Sickler of Ernestown. OC 16 Feb 1811.
  Hannah, m. Daniel Hull of Hallowell. OC 12 Nov 1811.
  Adam of Ameliasburgh. OC 20 Aug 1817.
  Mary, m. Edward Ryckman of Hallowell. OC 6 Sept 1820.
  Hannah, m. ---- Platt of Percy. OC 1 May 1834.
  Alpheus of Percy. OC 1 May 1834.
  Daniel of Percy. OC 1 May 1834.
  Catharine, m. Joseph Terwilliger of Hallowell. OC 16 June 1834.
  George of Percy. OC 4 Sept 1834.

ADDENDA

ALGER, Elisha of Cramahe.
  Christeen, m. Aaron Elsworth of Hamilton. OC 20 May 1817.
  Rhoda, m. Abraham Van Blarcom of Sophiasburgh. OC 14 Oct 1818.
  Irena, m. Peter Van Blarcom of Sophiasburgh. OC 25 Feb 1819.
  Peter of Cramahe. OC 22 Feb 1808.
  Sarah, m. Solomon Huff of Ameliasburgh. OC 17 Mar 1807, 18 Feb 1836.
  Lydia, m. James Mosher of Sophiasburgh. OC 17 March 1807.
  Eunice, m. John Post of Ameliasburgh. OC 8 June 1798.

BIRDSALL, Jeremiah of Cramahe.
  Catharine, m. William A. McDonald of Cramahe. OC 21 Sept 1837.
  Joshua of Percy. OC 18 May 1837.
  Andrew of Yonge. OC 3 July 1834.
  Diana, m. Reuben Palmer of Kitley. OC 3 July 1834.
  Benjamin A., of Yonge. OC 2 Oct 1834.

BLAKELEY, John of Hallowell and Haldimand.
  John of Haldimand. OC 8 Oct 1840.
  Elizabeth, m. ---- Ruscow of Cramahe. OC 20 July 1837.
  Rebecca, m. Nathaniel Mix of Asphodel. OC 28 Oct 1835.
  Asenath, m. Duncan McDonald. OC 1 Aug 1833.
  Samuel of Cramahe. OC 30 May 1834.
  Sophia. OC 30 May 1834.
  Esther, m. Paul Drew of Cornwall. OC 27 March 1829.

BLEECKER, John of Marysburgh, Sophiasburgh and Murray.
  m. Catharine W. Myers 7 Oct 1788.
  John R. of Murray. OC 28 July 1819; m. Elizabeth C. Richards 8 June 1812.
  Tobias of Thurlow. OC 24 July 1822.
  Henry of Sidney. OC 15 Oct 1840.
  Catherine. OC 12 Nov 1840.
  George of Sidney, bapt. 7 March 1791. OC 7 May 1828.
  Gilbert of Sidney. OC 7 May 1828.
  Jane, m. William Ripsom of Murray. OC 7 May 1828.

CAMPBELL, Oliver of Cramahe. OC 30 Aug 1797.
    John of Cramahe. OC 3 July 1797.
    Stephen of Cramahe. OC 3 July 1797.
    William of Cramahe. OC 3 July 1797.
    Cornelius of Cramahe. OC 18 Apr 1843.

CARLE, William of Cramahe.
    Mary, m. Joseph Snyder of Thurlow. OC 16 Feb 1811.
    Catherine, m. Asa Worden of Thurlow. OC 16 Feb 1811.
    Joseph of Cramahe. OC 2 March 1811.
    Hannah, m. Daniel Masters of Cramahe. OC 17 March 1812.
    Deborah, m. Robert Grace of Thurlow. OC 24 Feb 1820.

CHISHOLM, Alexander. Capt. Ont Archives Report (1904) pp. 345-6.
    James of Murray. OC 4 May 1836.
    Charles of Murray. OC 4 May 1836.
    Angus of Murray. OC 4 May 1836.

CROWDER, John of Cornwall, Osnabruck & Haldimand; m. Margaret Jacocks.
    John of Haldimand. OC 7 March 1822.
    Francis (son) of Haldimand. OC 19 Jan 1833; bapt. 24 Dec 1793.
    Isaac of Haldimand. OC 25 June 1840.
    Ruth. OC 8 Oct 1840.
    Rachel, m. John Kintner of Matilda. OC 3 Dec 1835.
    Nancy, m. William C. Bush of Haldimand. OC 19 Dec 1833.
    Eleanor, m. Joshua Walker of Haldimand. OC 19 Jan 1833.

CRYDERMAN, Michael of Marysburgh, Hallowell and Cramahe. See Ontario
    Archives Report (1904) p. 1110. m. Mary.
    Catharine, m. Caleb Elsworth Jr. of Hallowell. OC 26 Feb 1806.
    Jacob of Marysburgh. OC 16 Feb 1810. Bapt. 18 July 1788.
    Levina, m. Thomas Goheen of Hamilton. OC 14 Jan 1812.
    Elizabeth, m. Daniel Alger of Hallowell. OC 27 Feb 1812.
    Michael of Hallowell. OC 25 Feb 1818.
    Henry of Ameliasburgh. OC 4 Jan 1840.
    Daniel of Darlington. OC 3 Sept 1840.
    Annis, m. James Warner of Percy. OC 12 Nov 1840.
    Adna (son) of Cramahe. OC 12 Nov 1840.
    Almira. OC 12 Nov 1840.
    Mary Jane. OC 12 Nov 1840.
    Valentine of Cramahe. OC 1 May 1834.
    James P. of Cramahe. OC 1 May 1834.
    John of Cramahe. OC 1 May 1834.
    Joseph W. of Ameliasburgh. OC 8 Feb 1827.

FERGUSON, Jacob of Fredericksburgh and Hamilton.
    Joanna, m. ---- Burnham. OC 7 July 1801.
    Nancy, m. John Randall of Hamilton. OC 20 May 1817.   [Cont'd]

FERGUSON, Jacob - Cont'd
   Richard of Hamilton. OC 20 May 1817.
   Elethear, m. Isaac Secor Jr. of Scarborough. OC 2 June 1819.
   Sarah, m. Noadiah Sawyer of Scarborough. OC 26 Nov 1840.
   David. Land Board Certificate, 24/8 Thurlow.

GAFFIELD, Nathaniel A. of Marysburgh, Sophiasburgh and Cramahe. Sol-
   dier, Loyal Rangers. OC 1 July 1819. (Alias Amherst Ferrel).
   Sarah, m. Joel Halsted of Cramahe. OC 26 Feb 1805.
   Unis, m. John Mix of Cramahe. OC 26 Feb 1805.
   James of Cramahe. OC 17 Oct 1809. See OC 11 Sept 1844.
   Jonathan of Cramahe. OC 9 Dec 1815. Born 1787.
   Phoebe, m. Nathan Hubbell of Toronto. OC 14 July 1819.
   Oliver of Cramahe. OC 25 July 1833. m. Rhoda.

GOHEEN, Thomas of Hamilton.
   Charles of Hamilton. OC 17 Aug 1808.
   Thomas of Hamilton. OC 17 Aug 1808.
   Elizabeth. OC 6 Dec 1808.
   Samuel of Hamilton. OC 20 May 1808.
   Jesse of Hamilton. OC 24 Feb 1820.

GOSLEE, Mathew of Yonge and Cramahe. Died 1830. He md. 11 August 1782
   Ann Schuyler at Albany, N. Y. His wife d. 31 Apr 1850 aged 88 in the village
   of Colborne.
   James D. of Cramahe. OC 2 March 1816.

GRANT, John of Lot 30/10 n. s. River aux Raisins, Charlottenburgh.
   Duncan of Charlottenburgh. OC 30 Apr 1823.

GRANT, Lewis of Charlottenburgh.
   Ranald of 7th Concession, Lancaster. OC 4 Sept 1834.
   Alexander of Charlottenburgh. OC 4 Sept 1834.
   John of Charlottenburgh. OC 4 Sept 1834.
   James of Charlottenburgh. OC 4 Sept 1834.
   Angus of Charlottenburgh. OC 4 Sept 1834.
   Mary. OC 4 Sept 1834.
   Flora. OC 4 Sept 1834.
   Margaret. OC 4 Sept 1834.
   Janet. OC 4 Sept 1834.

HARRIS, Baltus of Hamilton.
   Joseph of Hamilton. OC 27 Jan 1816.
   Elizabeth. OC 27 Jan 1816.
   Getty, m. John Vanattoe of Hamilton. OC 16 Feb 1816.
   Tentey, m. James Taylor of Sophiasburgh. OC 26 March 1817.
   Catharine, m. John Smith of Hamilton. OC 20 May 1817.
   Anna, m. Roger B. Woolcutt of Hamilton. OC 3 June 1817.   [Cont'd]

HARRIS, Baltus - Cont'd
 Rachel, m. John Hannahs of Hamilton. OC 18 March 1818.
 Hannah, m. Henry Stoner of Hamilton. OC 18 Sept 1822.
 Gertrude, m. ---- Haskell. OC 1 Apr 1840.
 Alley, m. David Bedford of Hope. OC 5 Feb 1829.

IRISH, Peter of Haldimand and Cramahe.
 Mary Ann, m. Isaac Doolittle of Haldimand. OC 19 Feb 1817.
 Daniel of Etobicoke. OC 22 Apr 1819.
 Jedediah of Etobicoke. OC 24 March 1819.
 Sarah, m. Weedin Walker of Ernestown. OC 21 March 1821.
 Ransaeller of Kingston. OC 2 Oct 1834.
 Mahlon of Kingston. OC 2 Oct 1834.
 Abraham of Ernestown. Land Board Certificate. 26/5 Ernestown.

JARMAN (GERMAN ?), John of Cramahe.
 Catherine, m. Joel Whitcomb of Queenston. OC 11 June 1840.

LOUCKS, Henry of Fredericksburgh and Murray.
 Gabriel of Portland. OC 4 Sept 1834.
 Barnabas of Portland. OC 4 Sept 1834.
 Elizabeth. OC 2 Oct 1834. Portland.
 Margaret. OC 2 Oct 1834. Loughborough.

McARTHUR, Charles of Augusta and Murray.
 Mary Amy. OC 17 Feb 1807.
 Neil of Thurlow. OC 17 Feb 1807.
 John of Sidney. OC 25 Feb 1812.
 Martha, m. John Maybee of Thurlow. OC 11 Nov 1815.

McDOUGALL, John of Ernestown and Hamilton.
 Elizabeth, m. Henry Fisher of Hamilton. OC 24 Feb 1820.
 Allan of Hamilton. OC 24 Feb 1820.

McGRATH, Owen of Fredericksburgh and Hamilton. m. Catharine.
 Jean. OC 8 July 1797; m. Gershom Tucker of Ernestown.
 Rachel. OC 8 July 1797. m. William Robins of Ernestown. OC 3 April
   1819. 7/7 Huntingdon.
 Catherine, m. Joseph Watson of Elizabethtown. OC 7 Sept 1840. Bapt. 27
   December 1790.
 Owen of Moulton. OC 18 June 1840. Bapt. 9 Sept 1788.
 Samuel, bapt. 21 Jan 1793, buried 30 Aug 1794.

McILMOYLE, Hugh of Edwardsburgh and Hamilton.
 John of Hamilton. OC 10 May 1819.
 William of Hamilton. OC 18 Feb 1824.
 Hugh of Hamilton. OC 4 Aug 1831.
 Nancy, m. Orland Mowrey of Hamilton. OC 18 Aug 1824.

MUSTARD, John.
    Elizabeth, m. 28 Jan 1800 Wm Calder of Charlottenburgh. OC 3 Mar 1801.

NICKERSON, Elihud of Hamilton and Grantham.
    Nathaniel of Hamilton. OC 19 Apr 1808.
    John of Hamilton. OC 6 Dec 1808.
    Mary. OC 20 May 1817. m. ---- Hodgkinson.
    Elihud of Uxbridge. OC 31 July 1817.
    Enos of Grantham. OC 1 Nov 1820.
    Eunice. OC 17 Oct 1828.
    Catharine, m. 30 July 1827 Robert McKinney of Malahide. OC 12 Dec 1829.
    Levi of Grantham. OC 11 Feb 1836.
    David Vergan of Southwold. OC 28 March 1835.

OLIVER, John of Richmond and Murray. m. Rachel Kelly 13 March 1803.
    Samuel of Murray. OC 15 Aug 1839.
    Elizabeth, m. Elias Pickle of Murray. OC 3 Oct 1839.
    David of Richmond. OC 15 May 1835.
    Frederick of Richmond. OC 5 Sept 1833. Born 15 July 1804.
    Mary, m. ---- Dennis of Richmond. OC 22 Feb 1834.
    Catharine. OC 28 Feb 1835.
    Jane. OC 28 Feb 1835.
    Sanford of Camden East. OC 13 May 1842.
    Sally. OC 13 May 1842.
    Cornelius. born 8 May 1810.

PETERS, John of Cramahe. Ensign, Loyal Rangers.
    Mary Ann Barnet. OC 9 Dec 1815.
    John of Cramahe. OC 20 May 1817.
    David McGregor Rogers of Haldimand. OC 21 Sept 1837.
    Ann B. of Cramahe. OC 3 March 1836.

PORTER, Timothy.
    Elizabeth, m. ---- Rogers of Murray. OC 4 Apr 1839.
    Ruma (dau.). OC 4 Apr 1839.
    Christina, m. Peter Livingston of Murray. OC 11 Feb 1836.
    Sarah, m. Richard Parcels of Murray. OC 11 Feb 1836.

PURDY, Gilbert Jr. of Kingston and Haldimand. (How U.E. ?)
    Margaret, m. David Sprague Frost of Murray. OC 1 June 1837.
    Joseph of Haldimand. OC 10 Aug 1837.
    Jacob of Haldimand. OC 10 Aug 1837.
    Mary, m. John Sheeler of Haldimand. OC 27 Aug 1840.

PURDY, Joseph of Hamilton.
    Polly, m. John Eastman of Hamilton. OC 22 Feb 1808.
    Daniel of Hamilton. OC 22 Feb 1808.
    Nancy, m. John Vaughan of Hamilton. OC 22 Feb 1808.   [Cont'd]

PURDY, Joseph - Cont'd
  Benjamin of Hamilton, OC 22 Feb 1808; of Haldimand, OC 20 July 1837.
  Betsey, m. John McEvers of Hamilton. OC 23 Feb 1808. She d. 13 April
    1851 ae 78 yrs.
  Joseph of Hamilton. OC 1 Sept 1797.

SHERWOOD, Samuel of Thurlow and Murray.
  Samuel Harris of Murray. OC 3 Feb 1816.
  William of Murray. OC 6 Dec 1826.

SIMMONS, Daniel of Ernestown and Hamilton.
  Catherine, m. Peter Fisher of Grimsby. OC 1 Apr 1840.
  James of Grimsby. OC 2 May 1836.
  Elizabeth. OC 2 May 1836. (Idiot).
  Esther, m. ---- MacGuin of Kingston. OC 3 Apr 1834.
  Samantha. OC 2 Oct 1834. Sidney.
  Barnabas of Pittsburgh. OC 27 Nov 1834.
  Simeon of Saltfleet. OC 6 Aug 1829.
  Maria. OC 5 July 1830. Hamilton Tp.
  Hannah, m. David Harris of Hamilton Tp. OC 31 Jan 1826.
  Henry of Hamilton. OC 15 Oct 1824.
  John of Hamilton. OC 15 Oct 1824.

SIMPSON, Obadiah of Adolphustown and Cramahe. Born about 1765 in North
  Carolina. A ship-carpenter.
  Obadiah of Cramahe. OC 20 May 1817.
  Jeremiah of Cramahe. OC 20 May 1817.
  Deborah, m. Daniel Johnson of Murray. OC 14 June 1839.
  Benjamin of Hallowell. OC 8 May 1833.
  Luther Z. of Sophiasburgh. OC 2 Oct 1834.
  Eunice. OC 27 Nov 1834. Sophiasburgh.
  Aurelia (dau.) OC 4 Dec 1834. Sophiasburgh.
  Polly, m. Joseph Gibson of Murray. OC 19 July 1826.
  John of Cramahe. OC 17 June 1797.

SIMSON, William of Cramahe.
  Thomas of Cramahe. OC 25 Feb 1809.
  William of Cramahe. OC 3 March 1809.
  James of Cramahe. OC 17 Feb 1816.
  John of Cramahe. OC 13 Feb 1816.
  Obadiah of Cramahe. OC 13 June 1818.
  Jacob of Cramahe. OC 7 Feb 1821.
  Nancy, m. Phil Goddard of Cramahe. OC 17 Dec 1840.
  Priscilla, m. William Fuller of Ancaster. OC 3 Oct 1833.
  Keziah, m. Reuben Tompkins of Cramahe. OC 3 Feb 1834.
  Sarah, m. John Clark of Haldimand. OC 26 May 1843.

SMITH, Daniel of Fredericksburgh and Percy. Ont. Archives 1904 Report,
p. 1006.
  Ashman of Camden East. OC 4 Dec 1834.
  Sebastien of Camden East. OC 4 Dec 1834.

SMITH, William of Hamilton.
  Elizabeth, m. Humphrey Gifford of Hamilton. OC 20 May 1817.

SMITH, William of Sophiasburgh.
  Caroline, m. John Van Camp. OC 20 Feb 1840.

VANORDER, Mathew of Kingston.
  Margaret, m. William Howe of Kingston. OC 7 March 1807.
  Patty, m. Noel Pugsley of Bastard. OC 29 Sept 1836.
  Elizabeth, m. John Burnett of Kingston. OC 16 Nov 1797.

INDEX OF STRAY NAMES
AND OF THE ADDENDA

Reid's compilation is essentially in alphabetical order by family name. For example, the Stewart families are listed one after the other in the text. It seemed unnecessary, therefore, to include those names in the index. Listed in the entries, however, are the names of the spouses of many of the Stewarts. Thus, Charles Stewart married Catharine Showers, while Mary Stewart married Richard Cockrell. There is an index entry for Catharine Showers and also index entries for Richard Cockrell and for Mary (Stewart) Cockrell.

All names in the Addenda, however, have been indexed. It is only necessary, then, to look in two places, the main text and the index, to ascertain whether or not a particular name is mentioned.

AIKMAN - Cont'd
  Hannah (Showers) 288
  John 288
  Mary (Springer) 306
AINSLEY, Joannah 39
AIRHART, Mary (Williams) 338
  William 338
AKEY, Lorany 328
  Peter 328
ALBERTSON, William 254
  Elizabeth (Powley) 254
ALBRANT, Eliz. (Coons) 73
  Henry 73
  John 70
  Nancy (Collison) 70
ALCOMBRACK, Cornelius 226
  Elizabeth 333
  Henry 226
  Marian (Mitts) 226
  Margaret (Mitts) 226
ALDERSON, James 176
  Elizabeth (Land) 176
ALDRICH, Patience 324
ALDRIDGE, David 91
  Rachel (Dingman) 91
ALEXANDER, Jas Lyon 236
  Emelia (Nelles) 236
ALGER, Charles 21
  Christeen 355
  Daniel 356
  Elisha 355
  Elizabeth (Cryderman) 356
  Eunice 355
  Irena 355
  Lydia 355
  Peter 355
  Rhoda 355
  Sarah 355
  Sophia (Benson) 21
ALGIRE, Cath. (Frymire) 121
  Daniel 78
  Jacob 121
  Lydia (Cryderman) 78
ALGUIRE, Jacob 78
  Hannah (Cryderman) 78
ALLAIR, Ettiene 113
  Magdalen (Fralick) 113
ALLAN, Marg't (Jackson) 162
  Nathaniel W. 162
ALLARD, Henry S. 179
  Catherine (Lawson) 179
ALLEN, Alexander 68, 305
  Ann (Dougall) 93
  Eleanor (Davis) 84
  George 68
  John 212
  Jonathan 93
  Margaret 290
  Margaret (Cockell) 68, 305
  Martha (McNeil) 212

ALLEN - Cont'd
  Nancy (Ryckman) 273
  Phineas 273
  Sarah 231
  Sarah (Cole) 68
  Ursula 322
  Weston 231
  William 84
ALLEY, Hannah 233
ALLISON, Cyrus R. 153
  Eve (Hoover) 153
  Joseph 246
  Joseph B. 153
  Mary (Hoover) 153
  Rachel (Peck) 246
ALPORT, Eliz. (Bonesteel) 25
ALTHOUSE,
  Eleanor (Wright) 348
  Lucretia (Duzenberry) 96
  Sarah (Lake) 174
AMAN,
  Margaret (Countryman) 75
AMEY, Cath. (Snyder) 303
  David 5, 303
  Elizabeth 301
  Elizabeth (Baker) 13
  Elizabeth (Thomas) 317
  Eva 1
  George 290
  Hannah 29
  Israel 317
  Jonas 301
  Joseph 13
  Margaret (Simmons) 290
  Mary 10
  Mary (Baker) 13
  Mary (Davey) 83
  Mary (Snider) 301
  Nicholas 10, 301
  Peter 13
  Rachel (Snider) 301
AMMERMAN,
  Abigail (Vincent) 327
  John 327
ANDERSON,
  Amelia M. (Johnson) 165
  Ann (McBean) 187
  Anne (Nellis) 236
  Catharine 3
  Charles 236
  Donald 321
  Eleanor (Galbreath) 121
  Elizabeth (Weaver) 334
  Hannah (Adams) 2
  Hannah (Ruderbach) 271
  Henry 3, 271
  Isabella (Urquhart) 321
  Jacob 334
  Jane 170
  Jannett (Clark) 63

ANDERSON - Cont'd
  Jean (Herchmer) 147
  John 2, 121, 156
  Joseph 147, 306
  Leah (Peterson) 248
  Mary 309
  Mary (Dixon) 91
  Mary (Fykes) 121
  Mary (McGregor) 201
  Mary (Pitman) 252
  Mary Ann (Howard) 156
  Rebecca (Osburn) 241
  Richard 187
  Sally (Spurgin) 306
  Samuel I. B. 165
  William 91,121,201,241,252
ANDREWS, ---- Capt. 285
  Allen 241
  Eliza 99
  Elizabeth P. 285
  Jabez 160
  Jane (Outhouse) 241
  Sarah (Hunter) 160
ANDRUS, Joseph 278
  Lucretia (Secord) 278
ANGER, Augustus 39
  Christina 156
  Frederick Jr. 343
  Frederick Sr. 156
  George 216
  Henry 100
  Margaret (Elsworth) 100
  Mary (Windecker) 343
  Phoebe (Marcellis) 216
  Rosanna (Buck) 39
  Sarah (Elsworth) 100
  William 100
ANGUISH, Hannah 258
  Jacob 258
ANNABLE, Ann (Dixon) 91
  John Jr. 91
ANSLEY, Daniel 42
  Elizabeth (Dawson) 85
  Hannah (Burnett) 42
  Henry 85
  Ozias 39
ANTHONY, William 344
  Sarah (Wintermute) 344
APPLEBEE, Dorcus (Dixon) 91
  Margaret (Bessey) 22
ARMSTRONG, Adolphus 93
  Charity (Dopp) 93
  Elizabeth (Alguire) 4
  Elizabeth (Secord) 277
  Henry 15
  James 101
  John 4, 266
  Margaret (Barkley) 15
  Mary 324
  Mary (Emmett) 101

BARKLEY - Cont'd
  Jacob 11, 312
  John 123
  Lany (Merkley) 222
  Mary (Bouck) 26
  Mary (Stata) 307
  Mary (Utman) 321
  Nancy (Ault) 11
  Philip 307
BARNARD, Margaret 40
BARNET.
  see Peters, Mary Ann 359
BARNHART, Ann (Prentice) 254
  Catherine (Marsh) 217
  Hannah 271
  James 183
  Margaret (Wager) 328
  Mary 334
  Mary (Loucks) 183
  Mary Ann (Sills) 289
  Nicholas 254
  Peter 328
  Samuel 289
  Sarah 259
  William G. 217
BARNS, George 52
  Sarah (Cannon) 52
BARNUM, Barna 156
  John 61
  Mary (House) 156
  Nancy (Chrysdale) 61
BARRAGER, Eliz. (See) 279
  Solomon 279
BARRETT, Israel 336
  Catharine (Wheaton) 336
BARRIGER, Andrew 312
  Hannah (Strader) 312
  John 312
  Mary (Cole) 69
  Mary (Strader) 312
  Peter 69
BARRY, Eleanor (Cain) 46
BARTELS, Justus 199
  Hannah (MacDougall) 199
BARTLES, William 54
  Mary (Carscallen) 54
BARTLEY, Anne (Fisher) 111
  Elizabeth (Nicholson) 238
  Henry 348
  John M. (Dr.) 111
  Magdalene 237
  Mary (Wright) 348
BARTON, Andrew 246
  Eliza (Dixon) 91
  Elizabeth (Diamond) 90
  Elizabeth (Peck) 246
  George 91
  Helen 294
  Margaret (Bourdett) 27
  Peter 90

BARTON - Cont'd
  Samuel H. 27
BASSETT,
  Susannah (Hoople) 153
BASTIDO, David 210
BATEMAN, Hester 182
BATES,
  Amelia (Mattice) 219
  Elizabeth (McIntosh) 163
  Frances (VanDuzen) 325
  Levi 325
  Ninian 163
  Sarah Bostwick 262
  William P. 219
BATESON, John 2
  Mary Ann (Adams) 2
BATTER, Betsey (Bedford) 19
  Elias 19
  John 348
  Margaret (Wright) 348
BATTY, Mary (Loyst) 185
BAXTER, Daniel 27
  Elizabeth (Albrant) 3
  Elizabeth (Utman) 321
  John 321
  Margaret (Bender) 20
  Melinda (Miller) 223
  Nancy (McEathron) 200
  Rebecca (Bowen) 27
  William 3, 223
BAYMAN, James 132
  Jane (Gray) 132
BEACH, Abigail (Huffman) 159
  Betsey (Seelye) 280
  Catharine (Spicer) 305
  Elizabeth (Huffman) 159
  Enos Jr. 280
  John 108, 199
  Mary 199
  Mary (Ferro) 108
  Michael 159
  Stephen Todd 305
  Temantha 19
BEAM, Hannah (Mills) 226
  Jacob 39
  John 220
  Lewis 226
  Mary (Buckner) 39
  Nancy (Maybee) 220
BEAMER, Christopher 296
  Elizabeth (Smith) 296
  Henry R. 227
  Naomi Opak (Monro) 227
  Margaret (Fisher) 111
  Philip 111
BEARD, Andrew 311
  Elizabeth (Strader) 311
BEARSS, Ann (Steel) 307
  Daniel 307
BEASLEY, Richard 305

BEASLEY - Cont'd
  Henrietta (Springer) 305
BEATTIE, James 275
  Sarah (Schram) 275
BEBE, Charlotte (Seelye) 280
  Matthew 280
BECHSTED, Alexander 260
  Sarah (Reddick) 260
BECKETT, Eve (Bowman) 29
  Stephen 29
BECKON, Nathaniel 292
  Sarah (Skinner) 292
BECKWITH, Sarah (Sills) 289
BEDFORD, Alley (Harris) 358
  Betsy 18
  Catharine 16
  David 294, 358
  Hetty (Smith) 294
BEDSTEAD,
  Catharine (Casselman) 56
  Henry 138
  John V. 56
  Margaret (Hanes) 138
  Moses 11
  Parmelia (Ault) 11
  Sarah (Frymire) 121
  Sophia (Reddick) 260
  see also Bechsted.
BEEBE, Deborah (Hare) 139
  Joshua 139
  James C. 134
  Mary (Groomes) 134
  see also Bebe.
BEEMAN, Eleanor (McKim) 206
  Ira 206
  Sophia 253
  see also Beman.
BEEMER, Abraham 70
  Adam 29
  Eve (Bowman) 29
  George 94
  Hannah 28
  Jacob 94
  Rebecca (Doyle) 94
  Sarah (Doyle) 94
  Unice (Collver) 70
BEERS, John 278
  Maiden (Secord) 278
BEHN, George 226
  Susannah (Mitts) 226
BEIKIE, John 196
  Penelope (McDonell) 196
BELCHER, Ann (Green) 133
  John 133
BELKNAP,
  Eleanor (Meddough) 221
  Ira 210
  Nancy (McMasters) 210
  Stephen 221
BELL, Anne (Brisco) 34

BUCKNER - Cont'd
  Sarah (Forsyth) 112
BUELL, Bemslee 287
  Elizabeth (Bouck) 26
  Lois (Sherwood) 287
  Martha (Naughton) 235
  Rachel 188
  Samuel P. 26
  William 235
BUKER, Mary 119
  Melvin 119
BULLOCK, Richard 66
  Margaret (Clench) 66
BUNTING, Eliz. (Maracle) 215
  James 215
  John 318
  Mary (Thompson) 318
BURCH, Eleanor (Bender) 20
  John 20
BURDICK, Lavinia (Teeple) 316
BURGER, Dorothy (Mabee) 214
  James 76
  Ruth (Crawford) 76
BURHAM, Lyman 92
  Catharine (Docksteder) 92
BURK, Anne (Haggart) 135
  Hiram 135
BURKE, Edmund (Rev.) 198
BURKHOLDER, Michael 84
  Susan (Davis) 84
BURLEY, Eliz. (Snyder) 303
  Ezekiel 303
  Hester (See) 279
  John 268
  William 279
BURLINGHAM, Varnum 259
  Phoebe (Rankin) 259
BURN, Catherine 88
BURNETT,
  Elizabeth (Van Order) 361
  Hannah 9
  John 361
BURNHAM, Avery 7
  Catherine (Huff) 158
  Charles 67
  Eliza (Anger) 7
  Hannah (Harris) 140
  Joanna (Ferguson) 356
  John 140
  Margaret (Anger) 7
  Oliver 7, 158
  Thirza (Closson) 67
BURNS, Abigail (Vincent) 327
  Conrad 196
  Hannah (Fields) 109
  James 109
  Phoebe (McDonell) 196
  Thomas 327
  see also Byrns.
BURNSIDE, Betsey (Brouse) 35

BURRITT, Almira 26
  Charles 95
  Daniel 177
  Electa (Landon) 177
  Margaret (Mott) 232
  Martha (Dulmage) 95
  Martha (Stevens) 308
  Melissa 176
  Reuben 232
  Sarah (Reed) 261
BURSETT, Charles 91
  Leah (Dingman) 91
BURTCH, Archibald 316
  Calvin 275
  Charles 232
  Elizabeth (Schram) 275
  Jane 232
  Levi 32
  Nancy (Bradt) 32
  Susannah (Teeple) 316
BURTEL. see Bartles.
BURTON, Henry 4
  Margaret (Alguire) 4
BUSH,
  Christiana (Rambough) 259
  Dorcas (Ross) 270
  Elizabeth (Jacocks) 163
  Frederick 230
  Henry 292
  Jacob 259
  John 270
  Nancy (Crowder) 356
  Phoebe (Mosher) 230
  Rachel 292
  Rachel (Casselman) 57
  William C. 356
BUTLER, Abel 345
  Abigail (Dayton) 85
  Ann (Clement) 65
  Elizabeth (Coltman) 70
  Eve (Matthews) 219
  Frances E. 137
  Ira 27
  James 219
  Mary Ann (Bourdett) 27
  Mary Ann (Stevens) 308
  Nancy (Tenbrook) 316
  Sarah (Wood) 345
  Thomas 316
  Truelove 85
  Walter 308
  William 70
BUTTERFIELD,
  Josiah 63
  Sarah (Clark) 63
BUTTON, Elizabeth 233
BYAM, Joana (Buckner) 39
  John 39
BYECROFT, Benjamin 336
  Elizabeth (Westbrook) 336

BYRNS, Jane G. (Pruyn) 256
  John 256
  Martha (Pruyn) 256
  Samuel 256

C

CADMAN, Amy 151
  Elizabeth 310
  John Sr. 260
  Joshua 211, 288
  Mary (McMullen) 211
  Mary (Sills) 288
  Peggy 260
  Sylvia 133
  William 133
CAIN, Ann (Servos) 281
  Barney 200
  George 331
  Mary (McEwen) 200
  Michael 125
  Peter 281
  Sarah (Gilbert) 125
  Sarah (Ward) 331
CAIRO, Mitchell 341
CALDER, William 359
  Elizabeth (Mustard) 359
CALDWELL, Elizabeth 58
  Hannah (Outhouse) 241
  John 241
  Mishel (Boyce) 30
  William 30
CALLACHAN, Margaret 63
CALLENDER, Asa 140
  Catherine (Harris) 140
CALVERT, James 165
  Margaret (Johnston) 165
CAMERON, Alex. 44, 213, 244
  Ann (McIntosh) 203
  Anne 195, 313
  Archibald 61
  Catherine (Butler) 44
  Donald 208, 269
  Elizabeth (Summers) 313
  Flora 81
  Helen 209
  Isabella (Ross) 269
  James 313, 348
  Jane 107
  Janet 122
  John 313
  John Jr. 203
  Margaret (McLean) 208
  Mary 81
  Mary (Chisholm) 61 (2)
  Mary (McPhie) 213
  Ruth (Wright) 348
  Sarah (Parks) 244
  William 195

DAVIS - Cont'd
  Asahel 230
  Azubah (Osterhout) 241
  Bemsley 292
  Catharine (Elsworth) 100
  Catharine (Sipes) 292
  Christian (Bowen) 27
  Deborah 324
  Elizabeth (Banta) 15
  Elizabeth (VanDuzen) 324
  Enoch 168
  Henry 159
  Henry Jr. 49
  Isaac 15
  James 324
  John 100, 228, 229, 267
  Margaret (Cornell) 74
  Margaret (Willson) 340
  Marintha (Rose) 267
  Mary (Dougherty) 94
  Mary (Huffnail) 159
  Mary (Morden) 228
  Mary (Teeple) 316
  Murdock 241
  Rachel (Karr) 168
  Sarah (Campbell) 49
  Sarah (Clark) 64
  Simon 340
  Sophia Jane 270
  Thaddeus 64
  William 27
DAVISON, John 176
  Elizabeth (Landers) 176
DAVY,
  Catharine (Simmons) 290
  Elisabeth (Friermouth) 120
  Eliza 279
  Elizabeth (Clement) 65
  Margaret (Simmons) 290
  Michael 120, 290
  Peter 65, 290
DAWSEY, John H. 92
  Mary (Dolson) 92
DAWSON, Jane 227
DAY, Anna (Hutchinson) 161
  Calvin W. 332
  Charlotte 287
  Daniel 161
  Emily (Shibley) 287
  Lewis 149
  Mary (Hill) 149
  Sarah (Wartman) 332
DAYNARD, Andrew 107
  Charlotte (Ferguson) 107
  Eleanor (Ferguson) 107
  Elizabeth (Ferguson) 107
  John 107
  Peter 107
DAYTON, Abigail 310
  Abraham 119

DAYTON - Cont'd
  Hannah (Elliott) 99
  Nathan 99
  Rose (Freel) 119
DEACON, Margaret 87
DEAN, Cath. (Munro) 233
  David S. 233
  Elizabeth (Munro) 233
  Hannah (Smith) 297
  James 166
  Jonathan 233
  Marg't (Johnston) 166
  Miel 297
  Polly (Burtch) 43
  Silas 43
DEANS, James 125
  Margaret (German) 125
DEASE, James 310
  Sarah (Holmes) 152
  Theodosia (Stone) 310
DECEW, John 92
  Cath. (Docksteder) 92
DE COST, Elizabeth 43
DECOW, Jane (Larroway) 177
  John Jr. 177
DEDERICK, Anne (Foster)112
  Jacob Sr. 252
  Margaret (Pickard) 252
  Robert 112
DEEKS, Cath. (Merkley) 222
  John 222
DEEN, James 317
  Emily (Thatcher) 317
DEFIELD, Joseph 7
  Eliz. (Anderson) 7
DEFOREST, Abraham 29
  Ann 279
  Elizabeth (Bowman) 29
  Mary 256
  Rebecca 208
  Sarah 332
  Simon 256, 279
DEGROFF,
  Temperance (Rambough)259
DEGROOTE,
  Mary (McCaffrey) 187
DEGROTE, Mary (Caffrey) 45
  Peter 134
  Phoebe (Griffin) 134
DELIER, Boswell 291
  Elizabeth (Sims) 291
DELISLE, Frances 233
DELL, Peter 135
  Tryphena (Haggerty) 135
DELONG, Cath. (Dempsey) 87
  Eliza (McMichael) 210
  Simon 87
DELORIEZ, Judy (Hazell) 145
  John 145
DELORIMER, Lizette 168

DELOTHINIERE,
  Charlotte (Munro) 233
DEMILLE, Elizabeth 113
DEMING, Amos 297
  Elizabeth (Hoople) 152
  Henry 152
  Rebecca (Smith) 297
DEMOREST, Angelica (Bowen)28
  Anne (Stevens) 308
  Guilliame 27
  Hannah (Bourdett) 27
  James 28
  Joseph 308
DENISON, George Taylor 181
  Esther Borden (Lippincott)181
DENNIS, Aaron 36
  Adam 92
  Ann (Horton) 154
  Catharine (Brown) 36
  Conrad 185
  Elizabeth 343
  Elizabeth (Horton) 154
  Elizabeth (Wintermute) 344
  Jane (Larraway) 178
  Jane (Phillips) 250
  Joel 154
  John 154, 178
  Leah (Doan) 92
  Margaret (Lymburner) 185
  Mary (Oliver) 359
DENSBAUGH, Elizabeth 137
DENT, Susannah (Arnold) 10
DENYES, Peter 289
  Mary Ann (Sills) 289
DEO, Arilla (Jackson) 162
  Sylvanus 162
DE PEEL, Eve (Acre) 1
  Nicholas 1
DEPEW, Cath. (Meddaugh) 221
  Elizabeth (Springer) 306
  James 221
  John 306
DEPUE, Charles 288
  Lena (Showers) 288
DERBYSHIRE, Daniel 342
  Mercy (Wiltse) 342
DE RUSHE, Anne (Brants) 33
  Anthony 33
DESERONTI, Margaret 33
DESERONTYON. 163
DESHEA, Levi 141
  Margaret (Harson) 141
DETLOR, Catharine 265
  George H. 265
  Jerusha (Simons) 291
  John 291
  Maria (Roblin) 265
DEUEL, Eliza (Crysler) 79
  Lydia Jane (Burley) 41
  Seneca 79

HAVILAND, John Jr. 105
　Esther (Fairchild) 105
HAWES, Marg't (Casselman) 56
　Peter 56
HAWKINS, Phoebe 140
HAWKS, Selah 62
　Jerusha (Church) 62
HAWLEY, Amanda 223
　Amarilla 166
　Amy (Rogers) 266
　Azubah 30
　Charlotte (File) 110
　Charlotte (Jones) 166
　Elizabeth (Canniff) 51
　Esther (Walker) 330
　Hannah (Johnston) 165
　Henry 110
　Ichabod 105
　Martin 266
　Mary (Fairfield) 105
　Mary (Perry) 247
　Mary Ann 103
　Nabby 105
　Philo 166
　Ruth 34
　Sarah 103
　Sheldon 165, 330
　William 247
HAWN, Catharine 206
　Conrad 101
　Purlina (Empey) 101
　see also Hahn.
HAY, Ann (McGillies) 200
　John 200
HAYCOCK, Edward 44
　Mary (Butler) 44
HAYES, Ashael 176
　Elizabeth (Hill) 149
　Elizabeth (Wiltse) 342
　Eri 342
　Eva 347
　James 193
　Joseph 347
　Margaret (Koughnet) 173
　Margaret (Landers) 176
　Rachel (McDonell) 193
　Samuel 149
　William 173
HAYS, Dorothy (Wart) 332
　Hiram 332
HAYWARD, Charles 320
　Charlotte (Trompour) 320
　Rebecca (Huffman) 159
　Winslow 159
HAZELTON, Helche (Barton) 17
HAZEN, Anna (Matthews) 218
　Daniel Jr. 218
　Elijah 235
　Mary (Neill) 235
HAZZARD, Elsie (Loyd) 184

HEADLEY, Francis 221
　Ann (Meredith) 221
HEALD, Ann 159
HECK, Lois (Wright) 348
　Samuel 348
HEERMANS, John S. 320
　Sarah (Trompour) 320
HELMER, Ann (Millross) 225
　Catharine (Baker) 13
　Catherine (Alguire) 4
　Eleanor (Hardy) 138
　John 4, 13
　John P. 225
　Margaret (Rambough) 258
　Mary (Stoneburner) 310
　Nancy 80
　Peter 258
　Philip 310
　Thomas 138
HENDERSHOT, William 28
　Christeen (Bowman) 28
HENDERSON, Ann (Jones) 167
　David 108
　Elizabeth (Ferris) 108
　Jane (Secord) 278
　Mary (Brouse) 35
　Rufus C. 167
　William 278
HENN, Michael 146
　Sarah (Hendershot) 146
HENNESSY, James 290
　Christeen (Simmons) 290
HENRY, Ann (Walker) 330
　Christy (Bethune) 23
　Helen 150
　James R. 290
　Jesse 74
　John 330
　Margaret (Hare) 139
　Margaret (Muckle) 232
　Mary (Cosbey) 74
　Mary (Simmerman) 290
　R. 139
　Robert 23, 232
HENTON, Thomas 221
　Phoebe (Meddough) 221
HERCHMER, Catharine 216
　Charlotte (Purdy) 257
　Hanyost 216, 316
　Mary 216
　Nicholas 257
HERKIMER, Anna 316
　Johan Jost 316
HERMAN, Henry 263
　Mary (Ridnor) 263
HERMANEE,
　Dorothy (Lewis) 180
HERON, Harriet (Hill) 150
　Helen (Henry) 150
　Henry 147

HERON - Cont'd
　Richard 150
　Susannah (Henry) (Hill) 147
HERRIMAN, Clariman 180
　Elizabeth (Lightheart) 180
HERRINGTON,
　Abigail (Wannamaker) 331
　Hannah 342
　Zachariah 331
HESS, Wilhelmina 96
HESSE, Catherine (Bell) 20
HEWARD, Mary (Robinson) 265
　Stephen 265
HEWETT, ---- (Muckle) 232
　Jenett (Read) 259
　John 232
HEWITT, Eliz. (Gordon) 127
　George 127
　John B. 157
　Pamelia (Howard) 157
HIBBARD, Bela 296
　Charles 39
　Elizabeth (Buck) 39
　Elizabeth (Carr) 53
　Martha (Smith) 296
　Samuel 53
HICK, Sophia 95
HICKEY, Dinah (VanAllen) 322
　John 57, 322
　Margaret (Casselman) 57
　Sally 79
HICKS, Ann (Lake) 174
　Benjamin 174
　Daniel 224
　Dorcas (Burley) 41
　Elizabeth 155
　James 174
　Margaret (Lake) 174
　Mary (Miller) 224
HILL, Aaron 32
　Anne 151
　Ann (Moore) 228
　Apollus B. 277
　Archibald 91
　Benjamin 228
　Benoni 147
　Caroline (Scriver) 277
　Catharine (Wert) 335
　Christiana (Brant) 32
　Elizabeth (Adams) 2
　Eve (Dingman) 91
　Hannah 25
　Jane (Wright) 348
　Mary 85
　Polly (Closson) 67
　Reuben 2
　Susannah (Henry) 147
　Thomas 67
　William 348
HILLARD, Freeman 199

L

McCRIMMON - Cont'd
  Margaret (Miller) 224
  Rachel (Jones) 166
McCUAIG, John 319
  Catharine (Trompour) 319
McCUE, Cath. (Elliott) 100
McCUEN, William 6
  Lucy Ann (Anderson) 6
McCUIN, Sarah (Carr) 54
McCUMMOND, Charles 271
  Catharine (Runions) 271
McCURDY, Jonathan 114
  Mary (Franks) 114
McCUTCHEON, James 110
  Minerva (Finkle) 110
McDAVID, Jane (London) 182
  John 182
McDIARMID, Ann (McDonell)198
MacDONALD,
  Catharine (McPhie) 213
  Donald 213
  John 230
  Margaret (Shannon) 282
  Mary (Mosher) 230
  Mary (Smith) 298
  Richard 282
McDONALD,
  Alexander 267
  Allan 109
  Angus 55, 113, 211, 261
  Ann (Fields) 109
  Asenath (Blakeley) 355
  Catharine 201
  Catharine (Birdsall) 355
  Catherine (McLellan) 209
  Charles 310
  Donald 55, 209
  Duncan 335, 355
  Elizabeth (Cass) 55
  John 197, 209
  Margaret (Fox) 113
  Margaret (McLellan) 209
  Margaret (Rose) 267
  Mary (McMillan) 211
  Mary (Stone) 310
  Mary (Wemple) 335
  Minerva Ann (Sherwood) 287
  Nancy (Cass) 55
  Sarah (McDonell) 197
  Sarah (Reynolds) 261
  William 287
  William A. 355
MACDONELL, Amelia 167
  John 116
  Mary 116
McDONELL,
  Alexander 6, 49, 130, 132,
    134, 170, 211, 337
  Allan 111
  Angus 130, 170

McDONELL - Cont'd
  Ann (McPhie) 213
  Ann (Smith) 298
  Anne (Kennedy) 170
  Archibald 211
  Catharine 254
  Catharine (Grant) 130 (2)
  Catharine (MacDonald) 189
  Cath. (McNaughton) 211
  Catharine (McPhie) 213
  Charlotte (Gray) 132
  Christian 29
  Christina 170
  Cloe (Williams) 338
  Donald 53, 170, 213, 216
  Eliza (McNabb) 211
  Elizabeth (McKie) 206
  Esther (Proctor) 256
  Flora 170, 352
  Flora (McMillan) 211
  Harriet 134
  Helen 337
  Henrietta 111
  Isabella (Graham) 129
  James 211
  Jane (Lemon) 179
  Jane (Maracle) 216
  Jane (Simon) 291
  Janet 134
  Janet (Cameron) 49
  Jennet (Kennedy) 170
  John 16, 51, 79, 152, 179,
    213, 291, 298
  Katherine (Cameron) 49
  Lauchlin 211
  Louisa H. (Anderson) 6
  Magdaline 134
  Margaret (Carpenter) 53
  Margaret (Crysler) 79
  Mary 149, 211
  Mary (Barnhart) 16
  Mary (Grant) 130
  Mary (Kennedy) 170
  Mehetable (Holmes) 152
  Nancy (Grant) 130
  Nancy (McMillan) 211
  Peter 152
  Phoebe (Campbell) 51
  Rachel 179
  Randy 256
  Samuel 189
  Sarah (Holmes) 152
  Susannah (Bowman) 29
  William 206
MacDONNELL,
  Catherine 213
  James 299
  Marg't Leah (Smith) 299
McDOUGALL, Alex'r 267
  Allan 358

McDOUGALL - Cont'd
  Ann (Parsons) 245
  Archibald 200
  Catherine (McGillies) 200
  Duncan 190
  Elizabeth 358
  Hector 245
  Helen (McNabb) 211
  Isabella (McDonell) 195
  Isabella (Rose) 267
  Jennet (McDonell) 190
  John 192, 195, 358
  Margaret (McDonell) 192
McDOWALL, Robert (Rev.) 332
  Hannah (Washburn) 332
McEACHRON, Mary 45
McEATHRON, Daniel 18
  Mary (Beach) 18
McERLAIN, Michael 70
  Nelly (Collison) 70
McEVERS, Betsey (Purdy) 360
  John 360
McEWAN, George 285
  Margaret 226
  Maria (Sheets) 285
McEWEN, David Jr. 98
  Margaret 98
  Mary (Eastman) 98
McFARLAND, Clarissa 203
  John 341
  Margaret (Willson) 341
McFARLANE, James 170
  Ann Eliza (Kendrick) 170
McFEE, Angus 160
  Daniel 160
  Elizabeth (Hughson) 160
  Tamar (Hughson) 160
McGARVIN. see Magarvin.
McGILL, Andrew 345
  Ann (Wood) 345
McGILLIES, John 211
  Christiana (McMillan) 211
McGILLIS, Alexander 191
  Amelia (McDonell) 191
McGILLIVRAY, Malcolm 59
  Eleanor (Chisholm) 59
McGINNIS, Marg't (Howard) 156
  William 156
McGOWN, Catharine (Carr) 53
  Joseph 53
McGRATH, Catharine 358
  James 180
  Jean 358
  Lany (Lindsay) 180
  Owen 358
  Rachel 358
  Samuel 358
McGREGOR, David (Rev.) 265
  Duncan 233
  Gregor 108

M

ORSER - Cont'd
  Mary (Roblin) 265
  Phoebe 127
OSBORN, Eunice (Parks) 244
OSBORNE, Martin 176
  Phoebe (Land) 176
OSBURN, Amos 244
  Deborah (Trompour) 319
  Gloranna (Young) 350
  Hannah (Parks) 244
  James 350
  Marg't (Meddough) 220
  Nehemiah 319
  Rebecca 7
  William 220
  see also Orsburn.
OSTERHOUT,
  Elizabeth (Pickard) 252
  John 249
  Maria (Pettingill) 249
  William 252
OSTRANDER, Andrew 84
  Isaac 340
  Jane (Davis) 84
  Lydia (Davis) 84
  Peter 84
  Sarah (Willson) 340
OSTRUM, Abigail 257
  Daniel 61
  Isabel (Chrysdale) 61
  Jane 218
  Ruliph 257
OSWALD, Mathias 1
  Hannah (Acre) 1
OTTO, Eliz. (Papts) 243
  Gottlieb 283
  Gottlieb Sr. 243
  Sarah (Shaver) 283
  see also Ulto.
OUDENDYKE, Wm. 127
  Mary (Goldsmith) 127
OUTERKIRK,
  Catharine (Barkley) 15
  Henry 118
  Lenah (Fratts) 118
  Peter 15
OUTWATER, Belyat 244
  Belyatter 64
  Elizabeth (Parks) 244
  Harris 36
  Joseph 263
  Mary (Clark) 64
  Rosannah 263
  Sarah (Brown) 36
OVERFIELD, Manuel 105
  Sarah 62
  Sarah (Fairfield) 105
OVERHOLT, Abraham 331
  Anna (Lambert) 174
  Christopher 174

OVERHOLT - Cont'd
  John 147
  Margaret (Warner) 331
  Pamilla (Lambert) 174
  Sarah (Henn) 147
OWEN, Abner 39
  Elizabeth (Buckner) 39
  Margaret 182
OWENS, Benjamin 146
  Sarah (Hendershot) 146
OXHAM, William 155
  Susannah (Hough) 155

P

PADDLEFORD, Henry 185
  Nancy (Loyst) 185
PAGE, Eliz. (Parker) 243
  Jesse 243
  Polly (Dunn) 277
  Sarah (Haines) 136
  Sarah (Marsh) 217
  Susannah 75
  Thomas Otway 136
  William 217
PALEN, Stephen 312
  Sarah (Stricker) 312
PALMER, Catharine 140
  Daniel 31
  David 96, 327
  Delila (Van Sickle) 327
  Diana (Birdsall) 355
  Elizabeth (Dulyea) 96
  John 214
  Joseph 312
  Lois (Bradshaw) 31
  Lydia (Andrews) 7
  Mary (Mabee) 214
  Neil 7
  Reuben 355
  Ruth (Stricker) 312
PAPINEAU, John 175
  Sarah (Lamson) 175
PAPST, Ann (Wood) 345
  Isabella (Wood) 345
  Jacob 31
  John T. 346
  Margaret (Wood) 346
  Mary (Bradshaw) 31
  Peter 345
  Rudolph 345
PAPTS, Frederick 331
  Mary (Wardle) 331
PARCELS, Richard 359
  Sarah (Porter) 359
PARK, Eliz. (Woodcock) 346
  Huldah (Skinner) 292
  James 346
  Shubal 292

PARKE, Joan (Stone) 310
  Joseph 310
PARKER, Deborah (Cox) 75
  Elizabeth (Hoffman) 151
  George 200
  Hannah (McGaw) 200
  John 48, 287
  Margaret (Cameron) 48
  Nancy (Sencebaugh) 280
  Robert 151
  Rozanna 287
  William 75, 280
PARKINSON, Mary A. 229
PARKS, Elizabeth (Comer) 70
  James 217
  Susannah Marsh 217
PARLIAMENT, George 69, 214
  Jane 69
  Judith 246
  Margaret 229
  Mary (McTaggart) 214
PARNALL, Lavinia (Smith) 298
  William E. 298
PARNELL, Mary Ann 280
PARROTT, Elizabeth (Snider) 302
  James 174, 302
  Mary (Lake) 174
PARRY, Elizabeth (Playter) 253
  Mary (McDonell) 193
  Peter 193
  Thomas 253
PARSELLS, Anastasis (Killen) 171
  Catharine (Killen) 171
  Edward Smith 171
  William 171
  see also Parcels.
PATERSON, Cath. (Schram) 275
  Cruth 179
  John 275
  Sarah Ward 179
PATRICK, Hannah (Myers) 235
  Hannah (Simmons) 290
  James 235
  Richard 290
PATTERSON, Allan 233
  Catharine (Gilmore) 125
  Clarinda (Hainer) 136
  Cornelia (Munro) 233
  Daniel 34
  Eunice (French) 119
  Ira 119
  John 136
  Margaret (Brisbin) 34
  Margaret (Campbell) 51
  Mathew 332
  Nicholas 125
  Sarah (Washburn) 332
PATTISON, Cath. (McCue) 188
  Jarry 188
  Katherine (Buck) 38

T

TRYON, Ann (Fairchild) 104
TUCKER, Abijah 310
  Gershom 358
  Mary Anne (Stone) 310
  Jean (McGrath) 358
  Susannah (Fraser) 117
  William 117
TUNNICLIFFE, Mary 167
TURCOTT, Michael 240
  Nancy (Orser) 240
TURNBULL, John 103
  Charlotte (Everitt) 103
TURNER, John 311
  Rachel (Storms) 311
TURNEY, Ann (Smith) 295
  Eunice (Gould) 128
  George 295
  John 128
TURTLE, Mary (Carr) 54
  Newman 54
TUTTLE, Clarecy (Wright) 348
  Diana (Servos) 281
  Dolly (Gallinger) 123
  Elijah 281
  Jeremiah 293, 348
  Martha 294
  Rachel (Smith) 295
  Solomon 123
  Susannah (Slaght) 293
TYLER, Felica (Jackson) 162
  Solomon 162

U

ULMAN, Francis 118
  Catharine (Fratts) 118
ULTO, Barbara (Rupert) 271
UMPHREY, Alexander 24
  Esther (Black) 24
UNDERHILL, David 317
  Nancy (Thatcher) 317
UPPER,
  Elizabeth (Cockle) 68
  Elizabeth (Sporbeck) 305
  George 305
  John 68
UPTERGROVE,
  James 275
  Jane (Schram) 275
URQUHART,
  James 204
  Margaret (McIntyre) 204
  Mary (McGregor) 201
  William 201
USHER,
  Mary (Street) 312
UTMAN,
  Hannah (Crowder) 77
  Henry 77

V

VAIL, Mary (Davis) 84
  William 84
VALLEAU,
  Catharine (German) 124
  Mary 21
  William 124
VALLEY, Godfrey 56
  Olive (Cass) 56
VAN ALLAN, Dinah 148
VAN ALLEN,
  Elizabeth (Weager) 333
  Isaac 333
  John 333
  Maria (Weager) 333
  Peter 333
  Rachel (Weart) 333
VAN ALSTINE, Alex'r 4
  Allida 223
  Ann (Bell) 20
  Catharine 33
  Hannah (Loucks) 183
  James 183
  Lambert 20
  Margaret (Meyers) 223
  Peter 223
  Ursula (Allen) 4
  William 33
VAN ARNAM,
  Catherine (Jones) 167
  Edward 323
  Elizabeth (VanCamp) 323
  Gideon 167
  Harriet (Jones) 167
  Jacob 167
  Marcia (Phillips) 251
  William 251
VAN ATTER, Cornelius 166
  Elizabeth (Johnston) 166
  Elizabeth (Wilson) 341
  John 341
VAN ATTOE, John 357
  Getty (Harris) 357
VAN BLARCOM, Abraham 355
  Irena (Alger) 355
  Peter 355
  Rhoda (Alger) 355
VAN BUREN, Peter 5
  Elizabeth (Althouse) 5
VAN CAMP, Abigail (Coons) 73
  Caroline (Smith) 361
  Catharine 319
  Catharine (Brouse) 35
  Catherine (Carman) 35, 53
  Deborah (Lamson) 175
  Elijah 35
  Jacob 175

VAN CAMP - Cont'd
  John 35, 53, 73, 119, 311, 361
  Mary 172
  Mary (Frees) 119
  Mathalane (Strader) 311
  Phoebe 312
  Rachel 172
VANDERBURGH, Barnet 304
  Elizabeth 124
  Elizabeth (Fulton) 121
  Elizabeth (Mulloy) 232
  Hannah (Soules) 304
  Peter Jr. 232
  Richard 121
VANDERLIP,
  Charlotte (Larroway) 177
  Jenney 336
  Joseph 177
  Mary (File) 110
  Robert 110
VANDERVOORT,
  Abigail (Nicholson) 238
  William 237, 238
VANDEVOORT,
  Catharine (Hess) 147
  James 222
  Mary (Meyers) 222
  Samuel 147
VANDEWARKER, Jacob 63
  Margaret (Clark) 63
VAN DOREN, Ann Eliza 40
VAN DRESSER,
  Amelia (George) 124
VAN DUSEN, Casper 288
  Henry 159
  Mary 115
  Mary (Huff) 159
  Mary (Shorts) 288
VAN DUZEN, Conrad 108
  Elizabeth (Thatcher) 316
  Jacob 119
  Mary (French) 119
  Millicent (Ferguson) 108
  Robert 316
VAN DYCK, Arent 126
  Jozina (Goes) 126
VAN EVERY, Andrew 256
  David 288
  Elizabeth 333
  Elizabeth (Stevens) 308
  Hannah (Beasley) 19
  Hannah (Coon) 72, 291
  Jane (Purbus) 256
  Mary 331
  Phoebe 351
  Samuel 72, 291
  Sarah (Showers) 288
  William 308
  William B. 19
VAN EYNEN, John 293

WALKER - Cont'd
  Mary (Wiltse) 343
  Polly (Powell) 254
  Robinson 115
  Sarah (Irish) 358
  Seelye 221
  Summers 22
  Susan (Ball) 15
  Weedin 358
  Wing 343
WALLACE, Eliza (Arnold) 10
  William F. 10
WALLASER, Christiana (Fell)106
WALLIS, James 111
  Janet (Fisher) 111
WALLISER, Christian 216
  Elizabeth (Marcellus) 216
WALLISON, Nicholas 4
  Margaret (Alguire) 4
WALT, Amos. see Wait
WALTER,
  Magdalina (Carman) 53
  Martin 53
  Mary (Carman) 53
  Sally (Fraser) 115
  Simon 115
WALTERHOUSE, Joseph 39
  Margaret (Buck) 39
WALTON, Abial 91
  Eliza (Smith) 294
  Hannah 317
  Joseph B. 294
  Leah (Dingman) 91
WANNAMAKER,
  Ann (Dempsey) 87
  Mary (Babcock) 12
  William 87
WARD, Abigail (Adair) 1
  Ashel 1
  Catharine (Denyke) 88
  Charlotte (Fraser) 115
  Elizabeth 247
  Geo. 25
  Horace 115
  James 173
  John 88
  Margaret (Ball) 14
  Mary (Playter) 253
  Mary (Simmons) 290
  Samuel 290
  Sarah 179
  Sarah (Lake) 173
  Thomas 253
WARDLE, Mary 243
WARING, John 281
  Nancy (Servos) 281
WARLEY, Peter 146
  Margaret (Helmer) 146
WARNER, Ann 34
  Annis (Cryderman) 356

WARNER - Cont'd
  Conrad 251
  Elizabeth (Phillips) 251
  George 329
  Godfrey 251
  James 356
  John 240
  Margaret 122, 123
  Margaret (Waggoner) 329
  Mary (Phillips) 251
  Mary (VanEvery) 326
  Michael 122
  Peggy (Loucks) 183
  Peter 326
  Rachel (Orser) 240
  Rosanna 168
WARREN, Cath. (Agler) 3
  Edmund 344
  Eleanor (Wintermute) 344
  Elizabeth (Fraser) 115
  Hannah (Wintermute) 344
  Hannah (Woolman) 347
  Henry 3
  Henry B. 344
  James 115
  John 344
  Julia (Wintermute) 344
  Lawson 347
  Roby (Butler) 44
  Sheldon 44
WART, Conrad 110
  Elizabeth (Fike) 110
  Elizabeth (Hoople) 152
  Jane (Finney) 110
  John 110
  John J. 152
WARTMAN, Catharine 302
  Eve (Grass) 132
  Peter 132
WARWICK, Gregory 218
  Amy (Matthews) 218
WASHBURN,
  Catharine (Ryckman) 273
  Deborah (Trompour) 319
  Ebenezer 86
  Sarah (Deforest) 86
  Simeon 319
  Solomon 273
WATERBURY, Ann 98
  Rachel (Stewart) 309
  William Weed 309
WATERMAN, Phoebe 89
WATERS, Lucy 196
WATSON,
  Catherine (McGrath) 358
  Edward 237
  Freeborn 338
  Jane (Asselstine) 10
  John 4, 10, 134
  Joseph 358

WATSON - Cont'd
  Orpah (Griffin) 134
  Polly (Robertson) 264
  Rachel (Allen) 4
  Sarah (Willcox) 338
  Susanna (Parks) 244
WAY, Catharine (Pine) 252
  John 55
  Mary (Casey) 55
  Phoebe 214
  Reuben 87
  Samuel 252
  Sarah (Demill) 87
WEAGENT, Catharine (Cook) 72
  Samuel 72
WEAGER, Cath. (Rambough) 258
  Elizabeth (Noodle) 238
  Elizabeth (Weaver) 334
  Henry 258, 334
  Jacob 138
  John 238
  Mary (Hare) 138
  Mary M. 238
WEART, Catherine (Ault) 11
  Conrad 283
  John 11
  Rachel (Shaver) 283
WEATHERHEAD,
  Magdalene (Haskins) 142
  Margaret 10
  Samuel 142
WEAVER, Eliz. (VanEvery) 326
  Hannah (Wintermute) 344
  Henry 327
  Jacob 78
  John 56
  Margaret (Casselman) 56
  Margaret (Crumb) 78
  Peter 326
  Sarah (VanSickle) 327
WEEKS, Mary (Brooks) 35
  Stephen 35
WEES, Catharine (Rogers) 266
  David 266
  Jerany 266
  John 246
  Margaret (Babcock) 12
  Mary 154
  Mary (Peck) 246
  Nancy 266
  Phoebe (Babcock) 12
WEIR, William 86
  Hannah (Deforest) 86
WEISHUHN, William 171
  Catherine (Killman) 171
WELCH, Christian 25
  Michael 238
  Rachel (Nicholson) 238
WELLER, Asa 218
  Elijah 188

www.ingramcontent.com/pod-product-compliance
Lightning Source LLC
Chambersburg PA
CBHW050559270326
41926CB00012B/2112